ESSAYS ON PLUTARCH'S *LIVES*

ESSAYS ON
Plutarch's *Lives*

Edited by
Barbara Scardigli

CLARENDON PRESS · OXFORD
1995

Oxford University Press, Walton Street, Oxford OX2 6DP
Oxford New York
Athens Auckland Bangkok Bombay
Calcutta Cape Town Dar es Salaam Delhi
Florence Hong Kong Istanbul Karachi
Kuala Lumpur Madras Madrid Melbourne
Mexico City Nairobi Paris Singapore
Taipei Tokyo Toronto

and associated companies in
Berlin Ibadan

Oxford is a trade mark of Oxford University Press

Published in the United States
by Oxford University Press Inc, New York

© *Oxford University Press 1995*

British Library Cataloguing in Publication Data
Data available

Library of Congress Cataloguing in Publication Data
Essays on Plutarch's lives /edited by Barbara Scardigli.
Includes bibliographical references.
1. Plutarch. Lives. 2. Biography as a literary form. 3. Greece—
Biography—History and criticism. Rome—Biography—History and
criticism. I. Scardigli, Barbara.
PA4385.E87   1994   938'.007202—dc20   94-6880
ISBN 0-19-814076-2

1 3 5 7 9 10 8 6 4 2

Typeset by Datix International Limited, Bungay, Suffolk
Printed in Great Britain
on acid-free paper by
Bookcraft (Bath) Ltd., Midsomer Norton

ACKNOWLEDGEMENTS

My gratitude, together with that of the authors whose contributions are here reprinted, goes to Oxford University Press for publishing this volume. I am particularly grateful to C. B. R. Pelling, without whose generous help the clumsy English of my introduction would not have been transformed into an elegant prose, and to Juliane Kerkhecker for her translation of Wilamowitz, whose German style is notoriously complex. Some parts of my introduction are similar to the new introduction to volume vii of the Rizzoli editions (*Coriolanus–Alcibiades*), but they have been completely revised and expanded.

B.S.

The editor and the Press are grateful to the publishers of the following journals and books for permission to reprint.
  1. Translated from the *Reden und Vorträge*, ii (5) 1967 (1922), 247–79.
  2. Reprinted from *Greece and Rome*, 13 (1966), 139–54.
  3. Reprinted from *Journal of Roman Studies*, 56 (1966), 61–74.
  4. Reprinted from *Journal of Hellenic Studies*, 100 (1980), 127–41.
  5. Reprinted from *Greek, Roman and Byzantine Studies*, 16
  5. (1975), 77–85.
  6. Reprinted from *Hermes*, 109 (1981), 85–104.
  7. Reprinted from *Proceedings of the Cambridge Philological Association* (1966), 37–47.
  8. Reprinted from *Journal of Hellenic Studies*, 108 (1988), 83–93.
  9. Reprinted from *Journal of Hellenic Studies*, 100 (1990), 126–45.
  10. Reprinted from *Journal of Hellenic Studies*, 99 (1979), 74–96, with added postscript.
  11. Reprinted from *Past Perspectives: Studies in Greek and Roman Historical Writing* (Cambridge, 1986), 159–87.
  12. Reprinted from *Journal of Roman Studies*, 53 (1963), 21–8.

CONTENTS

Introduction   1
BARBARA SCARDIGLI

1. Plutarch as Biographer   47
U. VON WILAMOWITZ-MOELLENDORF

2. On Reading Plutarch's *Lives*   75
D. A. RUSSELL

3. Towards a Chronology of Plutarch's Works   95
C. P. JONES

4. Plutarch's Adaptation of his Source-Material   125
C. B. R. PELLING

5. Plutarch's Comparison of Pericles and Fabius Maximus   155
PHILIP A. STADTER

6. Plutarch's *Parallel Lives:* The Choice of Heroes   165
JOSEPH GEIGER

7. Plutarch, *Alcibiades* 1–16   191
D. A. RUSSELL

8. Tragedy and Epic in Plutarch's *Alexander*   209
J. M. MOSSMAN

9. Hellenic Culture and the Roman Heroes of Plutarch   229
S. C. R. SWAIN

10. Plutarch's Method of Work in the Roman *Lives* Postscript   265
C. B. R. PELLING

11. Plutarch and Roman Politics   319
C. B. R. PELLING

12. Plutarch's *Life* of Coriolanus   357
D. A. RUSSELL

Index of Sources   373

General Index   395

Introduction

BARBARA SCARDIGLI

I

This volume collects articles on the most important themes of Plutarch's Greek and Roman *Lives*. It includes contributions from 1963 to 1990 on Plutarch's life, milieu, and culture; on questions of programme, method, and composition; on the chronological order of composition and the cross-references from one *Life* to another; on the possibility that several biographies were edited simultaneously; on the methods Plutarch adopted to summarize his own reading and research; on the choice of subjects and of sources (Plutarch often shows very good judgement in both aspects); on his compositional techniques, which show with particular clarity procedures very common in ancient historical writing—adaptation, simplification, contamination, displacement, linking of unconnected events, addition, selective explanation of fact; and on the criteria for selecting the Greek and Roman pairs.

Fuller reflection is perhaps required on the traditions of historiography, and especially those of Graeco-Roman biography. That might help us to see more precisely how Plutarch followed pre-existent literary traditions as they had evolved through generations of writers, philosophers, and politicians; and a clearer notion of that heritage might in turn cast light on Plutarch's own contribution in bringing biography to the level which, to judge from the surviving evidence, represents the high point of the genre. The tracing of these influences is not straightforward, and we are not dealing with clear linear developments. But it may still be worthwhile to point to some of the more significant elements and stages.

II

It should immediately be said that traces of any sort of literary work may be found anywhere in either *Lives* or *Moralia*. It still seems that the *Lives* naturally show a preference for material that can crudely be defined as 'historical'.

Plutarch obviously knew the works of Homer and Hesiod,[1] and Homer probably inspired him in certain descriptions of epic scenes, especially battles. Probably he also knew the poems of Sappho, Alcaeus, and Archilochus, Solon's elegies, and the work of Ion of Chios: Solon's elegies mark the first Attic poetry which takes the form of a personal testimony,[2] and Ion's *Epidemiai* (his accounts of his travels) form the beginning of a memoir-literature: Ion offers concrete portraits of individuals of his day, giving details of physiognomy and of daily life.[3]

Plutarch was a critical writer, who often felt reservations about details he found in his sources. The fifth-century Stesimbrotus of Thasos was the earliest writer about whom he felt this sort of suspicion.[4] He wrote on the same figures as Plutarch, and Plutarch knew his work at first hand:[5] Stesimbrotus' book on Themistocles, Thucydides son of Melesias, and Pericles (Athenaeus 13. 589de) is cited and used in *Themistocles, Cimon,* and *Pericles*.[6] He was famous for his anti-Athenian sentiments[7] and defended only the

[1] See Ziegler (1952), 915; Momigliano (1971), 23; de Wet (1988), 15–21; Lamberton (1988).

[2] This is clear from some passages of the *Eunomia* and in the elegy *De Salaminia* (see, for instance, the edition of West (1972), ii. 120–2); cf. also Frazier (1988a), 299.

[3] Frost (1961), 18; Momigliano (1971), 30; Gentili–Cerri (1978), 15–17; Frost (1980), 16; Strasburger (1986), 5; Dover (1986); Stadter (1989), lxi–lxii; Meister (1988), 83; Meister (1989), 43–4; Blamire (1989), 5; Ampolo (1990), 215.

[4] Esp. concerning Pericles (*Cim.* 14. 3, 16. 1; *Per.* 13. 15–16; 36. 1 = *FGrHist* 107 FF 5–6, 8–11, with Jacoby's commentary); Stuart (1928), 44–6.

[5] Jacoby, *FGrHist* 107, Kommentar 344; Stadter (1989), lxii–lxiii.

[6] Dihle (1956), 46–7; Meinhardt (1957), 21; Gossage (1967), 51; Strasburger (1986), 2–3; Ferrarese (1975), 23–4; Frost (1980), 16; Fuscagni (1989), 59–66; Meister (1989), 43; Blamire (1989), 5–6.

[7] Perhaps for this reason Plutarch does not rely on him at all heavily: cf. Stadter (1989), 99. On other polemical currents concerning Pericles in the 5th cent. see e.g. Ferrarese (1975), 24–9.

pro-Spartan Cimon.[8] Other biographies too show traces of
a similar pamphlet-literature, both Greek (for example in
Demosthenes and *Demetrius*) and Roman (for example in
Caesar, *Cato minor*, and *Antony*). Plutarch knew its dangers:
only a little before composing the *Parallel Lives* he had
written his pamphlet 'On Herodotus' malevolence',[9] in
which he had criticized Herodotus for his unfair evaluation of
the merits of particular Greek states, particularly Boeotia.[10]
Herodotus is himself rich in biographical material: there
is the section on Cyrus (1. 107–35), for instance, which
includes the story of his youth, or that on Cambyses (3. 1–
66).[11] These may have inspired Plutarch in a general rather
than a specific way. He also makes specific use of Herodotus' work in the *Aristides*: he probably found little about
this hero in other authors.[12] *Aristides* offered Plutarch the
possibility of contrasting the 'Just One' (an image created
by Herodotus) with a Themistocles;[13] one might compare
the way in which Pelopidas, not a significant figure in
isolation,[14] established a useful foil for Epaminondas.
Aristophanes too provided much material for a biographer, and his comedies were familiar to Plutarch:[15] he
had probably read them years before,[16] and quoted them
later by heart for some excursuses on Pericles and Nicias

[8] Gomme (1945), i. 36; Dihle (1956), 49–50; Fuscagni (1989), 66.
[9] *De Herodoti malignitate.* Cf. Wilamowitz (1926), 271 (see below, p. 68); Theander (1951), 32; Russell (1973), 60–1. Mossman (1988), 93 (below, pp. 209–28)
discovers Herodotean elements in the *Alexander*.
[10] Wilamowitz (1926), 272, see below, p. 68; Russell (1973), 60.
[11] See Homeyer (1962), 76–9 and Vandiver (1990), 249–53, who think they
may have been inspired by Persian biographical sources. Cf. also Gallo (1974),
176 and Evans (1991), 41–88.
[12] Gomme (1945), 63, 71. Cf. Martin (1961); Calabi (1964), xiv–xv; Homeyer
(1963), 151; Frost (1980), 8–11.
[13] Frost (1961), 38–57; (1980), 72. On the biographical treatment of Themistocles in Herodotus, see Homeyer (1962), 81–3; Gossage (1967), 65; Valgiglio
(1987*b*), 1746.
[14] Wilamowitz (1926), 262 n. 1 (see below, p.60, n.22); in the *Pelopidas*: Georgiadou (1992*a*), 4226–8.
[15] See the *Comparationis Aristophanis et Menandri compendium*: Gomme
(1945), 79; Ziegler (1952), 872, 915; Frost (1961), 74–6; Momigliano (1971), 39;
Stadter (1989), lxiv. *Pace* Wilamowitz (1926), 269 (see below, p.66) one should
assume that Plutarch knew Aristophanes at first hand: cf. Samutkina (1984),
104–11; Frazier (1988*a*), 300–4.
[16] Pelling (1979), 74, see below, p. 266.

and their contemporaries[17]—though not without criticizing the poet's licentious excesses.[18]

Thucydides of course devotes little space to biographical particulars, though he knows and brings out the importance of individuals in politics and warfare. Thucydides is of central importance for the study of at least three of Plutarch's *Lives* (*Pericles*, *Nicias*, and *Alcibiades*),[19] though less for the information he offers than for the possibility of comparison which he provides.[20] After praising Thucydides as inimitable and pointing to his magnificent pathos, vividness, and diversity ($\pi\alpha\theta\eta\tau\iota\kappa\dot{\omega}\tau\alpha\tau\sigma\varsigma$, $\dot{\epsilon}\nu\alpha\rho\gamma\dot{\epsilon}\sigma\tau\alpha\tau\sigma\varsigma$, $\pi\sigma\iota\kappa\iota\lambda\dot{\omega}\tau\alpha\tau\sigma\varsigma$), Plutarch affirms his intention to collect material which was less familiar ($\tau\dot{\alpha}$ $\delta\iota\alpha\phi\epsilon\dot{\upsilon}\gamma\sigma\nu\tau\alpha$ $\tau\sigma\dot{\upsilon}\varsigma$ $\pi\sigma\lambda\lambda\sigma\dot{\upsilon}\varsigma$);[21] he will not follow the example of Timaeus,[22] who aspired to outdo Philistus and Thucydides. Though Plutarch admired Thucydides unreservedly, he could not find in him all the material which suited his ultimate intention of providing an indication of his subject's character and personality ($\kappa\alpha\tau\alpha\nu\dot{\sigma}\eta\sigma\iota\varsigma$ $\ddot{\eta}\theta\sigma\upsilon\varsigma$ $\kappa\alpha\dot{\iota}$ $\tau\rho\dot{\sigma}\pi\sigma\upsilon$). Thus he integrates Thucydides with other material.[23] That material is drawn partly from first-hand documents; partly from writers later than Thucydides, largely historians who (as the introduction to *Nicias* makes clear) followed a different direction, style, and method;[24] and partly from his own subtle personal reflections on the various individuals. Plutarch's knowledge and use of Thucydides and of a good number of alternative authors provide a particularly clear insight into his technique, and this confirms his tendency to seek out

[17] Cf. e.g. Schreiner (1976), 41–4; de Wet (1988), 13–14; Stadter (1989), lxiii–lxvi. Probably Plutarch also found some information in the short biographies dedicated to the personages cited in comedies, the so-called $\kappa\omega\mu\omega\delta\sigma\dot{\upsilon}\mu\epsilon\nu\sigma\iota$: see Steinhausen (1910), 71–2.

[18] Cf. e.g. *De liberis educ.* 14. 10 c; *Quomod. adul. ab amico intern.* 27. 6b/c.

[19] Westlake (1968), 23–42 on Pericles, 86–96 and 169–211 on Nicias, 212–60 on Alcibiades. Cf. Schuller (1991), 104.

[20] See Gomme (1945), 65–74; Ferrarese (1975), 26–7; Stadter (1990), 85; Nicolaidis (1988), 322–8; Alonso Núñez (1991), 4–5.

[21] For discussion of these $\pi\sigma\lambda\lambda\sigma\dot{\iota}$ (certainly Plutarch's public) cf. Citti (1983); Franco (1991), 125. Cf. also Wardman (1974), 155–7; Schneeweiss (1985), 149–51.

[22] See also the criticisms in *Dion* 36.

[23] See Pelling (1992), 11–17.

[24] Cf. Russell (1973), 116, who justly maintains that Plutarch had no intention of rivalling Thucydides. See also Wardman (1971), 258.

historical sources and to adapt them to his biographical aims.

On the other hand, he was also influenced by currents typical of the fourth century, which originated in the areas of philosophy and rhetoric. These, unlike Thucydides, focused more on personality than on individual actions. We can see this if we compare Plutarch's writings with the various dialogues which Plato devoted to the figure of Socrates:[25] these contain many biographical details.[26] Plutarch applies similar principles to delineate the figure of the teacher in the parts of his *Lives* which concern the formation and education of a hero,[27] and the Platonic influence is revealed also in the language of some biographies.[28] We should therefore assume that a considerable familiarity with Plato's philosophy and writings underlies Plutarch's writing in the *Lives*.

Plutarch was also influenced by those works of Xenophon[29] which are close to biography and autobiography, *Anabasis*,[30] *Cyropaedia*,[31] *Apology*, *Apomnemoneumata*, *Symposium*, *Oikonomikos*, some of these also devoted to Socrates;[32] and by the orator Isocrates, who influenced Xenophon's *Agesilaus* with his *Euagoras*, an encomium containing precise biographical references.[33] Xenophon's *Agesi-*

---

[25] Dihle (1956), 13–34; Deiger (1985), 19.

[26] Dihle (1956), 13–34; Meister (1989), 183. See also von Fritz (1972), 326–7.

[27] See Schneeweiss (1985), 157–9. Plutarch dedicated several works, now lost, to Plato and his school: see the *Lamprias catalogue*, Nos. 63, 64, 71, 134. On the influence of Platonic thinking on *Demetrius* cf. de Lacy (1952), 168–71; Valgiglio (1992), 4008; on *Cicero, Cato minor*, and *Brutus*, cf. Swain (1990a), 193.

[28] Cf. e.g. Mugelli (1986), 225–8; Ghilli (1988), 239–40; Guerrini (1990), 268. In general Plutarch's language has been very little studied (La Penna (1987), 306), but there are some essays in *ANRW* ii. 33. 6 (see below, p. 31).

[29] Theander (1951), 51; cf. also Homeyer (1962), 85.

[30] e.g. in *Anab.* 1. 9, containing a portrait of Cyrus, or in *Anab.* 2. 6, with its description of the Greek generals who died at the king's hands. Autobiographical traces can be found in the description of the return of the Ten Thousand, though they differ from our own conception of autobiography: that is indeed true of everything we know of pre-Hellenistic 'autobiographical' material. See Most (1989), 122–7.

[31] Defined by Cicero (*Brut.* 29. 112) as *vita et disciplina ... praeclara* (cf. *ad fam.* 9. 25. 1) and compared, as unsuited to Romans, with Aemilius Scaurus' *tres libri de vita ipsius acta* (see below). On Xenophon's *Cyropaedia* see Hirsch (1985), 67–71, Due (1989), esp. 117–35, and Tatum (1989), 180–5.

[32] See Meister (1989), 84; Ampolo (1990), 214.

[33] Cf. Leo (1881), 211; Dihle (1956), 27; Jenkinson (1967), 3; Bowersock (1984), xviii–xix; Gentili–Cerri (1978), 25; Krischer (1982), 59–63; Pelling (1990), 26–8; de Voto (1982), 16–20.

laus itself served Plutarch in his biography of the Spartan king[34] and in *Artaxerxes*,[35] but it is not the principal source of either: in the former work unfavourable material is presented about the hero,[36] which probably derives from contemporary sources; as for the latter, Xenophon in both *Cyropaedia* and *Anabasis* supports Cyrus against Artaxerxes II.[37] His contemporary, Ctesias of Cnidos,[38] presumably followed the same approach.[39] By contrast, Cleitarchus' father Deinon of Colophon[40] must have written an account favourable to Artaxerxes.

All things considered, it again emerges that Plutarch borrows more often from historiography than from other material. In the particular case of *Artaxerxes* it may even be the very abundance of material on life in the Persian court which inspired Plutarch to devote a work to this figure, who had few merits, rather than to his more interesting brother.[41]

Plutarch was familiar with Aristotle as well as Plato,[42] whether regarding philosophy, political constitutions,

---

[34] Flacelière (1973), 88–90; Hamilton (1992), 4213–18.

[35] Flacelière (1979), 8–10; Wardman (1974), 157–9; Orsi (1987a), xxx–xxxi; Franco (1991), 130–1.

[36] Flacelière (1973), 86–7; Hamilton (1992), 4202, 4218–21.

[37] See Orsi (1979/80), 114–17.

[38] König (1977), 102–6. On Ctesias cf. also Moggi (1987), 2085–6; Eck (1990), 421; Will (1991), 122–4. Although Ctesias with his tragic exposition shares some characteristics with Aristotle and his school, it is hard to suppose that there was any contact (Flach (1985), 51). Ctesias possibly influenced Duris: Marasco (1988), 48–51.

[39] Plutarch expresses strong reservations about Ctesias' fanciful representations and untrustworthy stories: Orsi (1979/80), 121 and (1987a), xxxii.

[40] Orsi (1979/80), 117 and (1987a), xxxiv–xxxv. In only a few barbarians (specifically Artaxerxes: *Art.* 1. 1, 2. 1, 4. 4–5, 30. 9) can we find that πρᾳότης, a virtue in which Greeks are superior to barbarians: see Nicolaidis (1986), 239–41.

[41] Wilamowitz (1926), 271, see below, p. 68.

[42] He knew the Ἀθηναίων Πολιτεία (see Ziegler (1952), 922; Stadter (1989), lxxiv), which contains biographical material on Solon; and the Λακεδαιμονίων Πολιτεία, which he used in the *Lives* of the Spartan legislators (Mazzarino (1966), ii. 2, 146, who emphasizes Plutarch's reaction to Aristotle's criticism of Lycurgus; see also Marasco (1978), 170–81, Schneeweiss (1979), 376–82). Other sources are quoted in Piccirilli (1980), 1759–63 and Podlecki–Duane (1992), 4101. Plutarch also draws from Aristotle in the *de mul. virt.* (Stadter (1965), 130–2), and mentions him expressly in the *Quaest. Rom.* (265d = fr. 609 Rose). Citations of Aristotle in other *Lives* (e.g. *Cam.* 22. 4, *Per.* 9. 2) are purely casual.

ethics, or biographical facts.[43] That can also be demonstrated concerning Theophrastus,[44] whose main interest for
Plutarch must have concerned the Aristotelian school; perhaps he also knew Theophrastus' lost rhetorical work 'On
history', περὶ ἱστορίας, quoted in the list of his works in
Diogenes Laertius (5. 47: cf. Cic. *Orat.* 12. 39).[45]

III

It is well known that Friedrich Leo[46] pointed to the Peripatos as the originator of two veins of biography. One, according to Leo, was an erudite-antiquarian vein, classified and
ordered according to topics and disregarding chronological
data: that type was generally preferred for artists and scholars. The other, he claimed, was an ethical-political vein,
with biographical narration in chronological order: this was
preferred for political men whose virtue was manifest in
their actions, since it was precisely these actions which were
considered to demonstrate their virtue.[47] This second current may have led to Nepos, with his biographies organized
chronologically; the first led, through the Alexandrian grammarians, to Suetonius and his thematic ordering.[48] Plutarch
occupies an intermediate position and represents a special
case, both because he discuses the difference between history and biography and because he knows and uses historical
writings.

Peripatetic authors wrote not only *Lives*, βίοι (a term
understood by the Peripatos both as 'forms of life' and as
single biographies)[49] but also '*On* Lives', περὶ βίων. It is

---

[43] On Aristotle's influence on the development of biography see also Stadter
(1965), 130–2, and von Fritz (1972), 326–7.

[44] Cf. Homeyer (1963), 150; Stadter (1989), lxxv. The *Lamprias catalogue*
includes (53) the work περὶ Θεοφράστου (πολιτικῶν) πρὸς τοὺς καιρούς, certainly
based on Theophrastus: Regenbogen (1940), 1517; Ziegler (1952), 922.

[45] See Wehrli (1947), 70.

[46] Leo (1881), 103, 120, 133–5, 179–80, 187, 315–23. Criticism in Gallo (1967),
152–4.

[47] Cf. Levi (1987), ii, 1733.

[48] See Polman (1974), 170–2; Jenkinson (1973), 709; Wallace-Hadrill (1983),
70–2.

[49] Homeyer (1963), 149; Gallo (1967), 157–9.

evidently impossible to form a precise idea of the degree to which Plutarch used these authors: their works survive in too fragmentary a state, and the testimonia afforded by Plutarch himself are too modest.

However, some parts of Plutarch's *Themistocles*, for example, may be traced to a Peripatetic author, who may be Phanias of Eresos,[50] cited five times in the *Life*: but Plutarch does not seem to have used him frequently even here, and hardly at all in *Solon* and *Aristides*.[51]

The idealization of Phocion[52] may have derived originally from two authors with similar Peripatetic positions: Phocion's collaborator Demetrius of Phaleron,[53] a friend of Theophrastus, who wrote an autobiographical work on his political activities; and Theophrastus' pupil the mimetic-tragic historian Duris of Samos,[54] author of ἱστορίαι, 'histories' (see below). Various passages in *Demetrius* and *Demosthenes* also recall those two authors, but for the first Plutarch seems also to have used threads of Macedonian and threads of Athenian historiography,[55] while for the second he drew on Demosthenes himself[56] and the Alexandrian Hermippus of Smyrna.[57]

The influence of the Peripatos is rather to be sought elsewhere, less in the derivation of factual material than in certain other elements which Plutarch assimilated: in some general principles useful for composition, for example, or in some programmatic declarations, or in the insertion of

[50] See Bodin (1917), 132–7; Stuart (1928), 132–3; Momigliano (1971), 78; Homeyer (1963), 151.

[51] Homeyer (1963), 148; Momigliano (1971), 77. For *Solon* one might think of Peripatetic material (Hermippus?) in addition to other influences: cf. Paladini (1956), 382; Piccirilli (1977), xxi–xxii.

[52] Homeyer (1963), 151; Gehrke (1976), 195–8; Bearzot (1985), 16–34, who describes the contradiction between Peripatetic and historiographical parties; Meister (1989), 187; Tritle (1988), 34–5, and (1992), 4267–70.

[53] On Demetrius of Phaleron: Homeyer (1963), 151; Wehrli (1968) IV, fr. 10; Mossé (1969), 162. On other sources, Bearzot (1984), 75–90.

[54] On Duris: Kebric (1977), 14–54; Brugnoli (1987a), 292; Marasco (1981b) 41–5; Walbank (1988), 257; Pédech (1989), 257–389; Burelli Bergese (1990), 50; Tritle (1992), 4281.

[55] Details in Flacelière (1977), 12–13; Marasco (1983), 43–54; Andrei (1989), 42–9.

[56] Cf. Leo (1881), 176; Flacelière (1976), 6–7; Homeyer (1963), 151.

[57] Flacelière (1976), 7–8.

anecdotes into a historical context, and so on. He must have
been influenced occasionally by the typology of the Peripatos, something which we know particularly from the work
of Theophrastus. That is visible in those cases where we
can see Plutarch's heroes influenced by stereotypes: Nicias
has something of the 'superstitious man', for instance, the
δεισιδαίμων;[58] Alcibiades shows traces of the 'flatterer', the
κόλαξ;[59] then there are the many Greeks and Romans who
are inspired by an ambiguous 'ambition', φιλοτιμία,[60] or are
equally ambiguously 'spirited', θυμοειδείς,[61] and go on to
accomplish great feats, useful to the community, or instead
cast their states into great hardship. One can be aware of
the influence of these types while acknowledging that Plutarch's figures are much more complex,[62] and not at all
stereotyped portraits without individual human traits.

The idea that a person's character may change is evident
in Theophrastus[63] and persists in, for instance, Polybius.[64]
Plutarch analyses changes of character in a more varied
manner. They may come from recognizable causes, from a
change of fortune,[65] or from a voluntary decision to abandon the path of virtue and duty. Sertorius (*Sert.* 10. 5–7)
changes in consequence of the adverse circumstances which

[58] Cf. Dihle (1956), 73; Pelling (1988b), 262; Canfora (1987), 83–6.
[59] Russell (1966b), 37 (= below, p. 192) and (1973), 96, 108, 124. So also
Cleopatra, mistress of κολάκεια in *Antony*: Pelling (1980), 138, see below, p. 149,
and (1988a), 35.
[60] On various interpretations of φιλοτιμία see Martin (1961), 331–4; Lavery
(1971), 133–4; Wardman (1974), 116–24; Pelling (1989), 212; Swain (1990b), 133
(= below, p. 242); see also Frazier (1988b), 119–26; Walsh (1992), 209; 218–21.
[61] Wardman (1955), 97, 102–7; Russell (1973), 106: '*Cimon* is a sermon on the
use of wealth, *Coriolanus* on anger, *Pyrrhus* on "always wanting more", *Antony* on
the danger of love, and so on'.
[62] Pelling (1988b), 262. See also Podlecki–Duane (1992), 4065–6 and De Blois
(1992), 4572.
[63] Fr. 146, ed. Wimmer, p. 449 (= Plut. *Per.* 38. 2). See Russell (1966a), 145–
7 (= below, pp. 83–6); 1973), 105–6; Stadter (1989), 343; Valgiglio (1992),
4009. In *Pericles* there has been an earlier μεταβολή as well, Pericles' change of
political style (between autocratic to democratic) and change of manner of life: cf.
Steidle (1951), 155; Breebart (1971), 262–4. The conception may perhaps originate
in a contemporary and hostile tradition, and is misapplied by Plutarch: so
Ferrarese (1975), 2–8.
[64] See 8. 5 (cf. Plut. *Arat.* 49–53) on Philip V (Leo (1881), 246–7, and Walbank
(1938), 55–64; Gill (1983), 478–81) or 9. 22–3 and 10. 6 on Hannibal.
[65] Timoleon and Aemilius provide cases of such reactions to χαλεπὴ τύχη: see
Swain (1989a), 314–16; 323–34. See also Swain (1989c), 286–92.

befall him:[66] therefore his change ($\mu\epsilon\tau\alpha\betao\lambda\eta$) is in a sense comprehensible.[67] In contrast, the nature ($\phi\upsilon\sigma\iota\varsigma$) of Marius never changed in Plutarch's view (*Sulla* 30. 6), being hard and cruel from the outset, whereas Sulla's wavered initially between good and bad and worsened gradually.[68] It is natural that this declaration about Marius' evil nature should be found in the *Sulla* rather than in his own *Life*: otherwise Marius would have found his place among the negative examples of the *Lives* (see below).

The famous declaration by Plutarch in *Alexander*[69]—that he aspires to compose biographies, not history—must also be traced back to principles proclaimed by the Peripatos: that is confirmed by Cornelius Nepos (*Pel.* 1. 1).[70] We might compare other programmatic statements, especially in Aristotle: for example, on the difference between the historian and the poet (*Poet.* 9. 2–3, 1450ª35–ᵇ11),[71] or between historiography referring to facts, which means political history, and rhetoric (*Rhet.* 1. 4. 11, 1360ª37–9).

Polybius' later distinction between his treatments of Philopoemen in the lost encomium and in the *Histories* is also close to this distinction between historiography and biography: he acknowledges that in a historical work the author cannot confine himself to facts and circumstances but must also discuss personality (10. 21. 4), but still draws a distinction between eulogy and history (10. 21. 8).

The principle of comparison is another feature which surely derives from the Peripatos. Antitheses are already visible in Aristotle's own examples,[72] and they later developed further, especially in the collections of *Bioi* of individu-

[66] Cf. Bergen (1962), esp. 89–94; Russell (1966a), 146; see below, p. 84, Gill (1983), 479; Swain (1989b), 67–8.

[67] Dihle (1956), 62. Shortly before his death Alexander becomes superstitious (*Alex.* 74–5), and thus changes his relationship with the men around him.

[68] The catalogue of his faults is present already in chs. 1–2. Cf. Gill (1983), 479; Stadter (1992), 43.

[69] *Alex.* 1. 2. In *Galba* (2. 3), written before the *Parallel Lives*, Plutarch already makes use of Peripatetic tradition: see Kesisoglou (1984), xv; Valgiglio (1987a), 57; Georgiadou (1988), 350–2.

[70] 'Vereor . . . ne non uitam eius enarrare sed historiam uidear scribere.'

[71] Cf. Zoepffel (1975), 12–17; Homeyer (1963), 152.

[72] Cf. Hillard (1987), 35, and the comparison between Aristides and Themistocles in Ἀθηναίων Πολιτεία 23 and *Rhet.* 1. 9, 1368ª18–19, where Aristotle views comparison as a typical element in eulogy.

als of a particular class—persons of philosophical or historical importance.[73] The comparative principle is taken over
by Plutarch and is seen in many ways in his biographies:[74]
for instance, in several places where he points to rivalry or
friendship between two protagonists,[75] as well as in the
praefationes[76] and the *synkriseis*.[77]

Plutarch goes beyond Peripatetic theory, for the Peripatos
could not yet conceive of comparison between a Greek and
a foreign figure: a barbarian could not have counted as an
equal partner.[78] Plutarch's contrasts owe their origin to
more practical requirements (see below), and are a typical
invention of Roman times. The parallels are more important
to him than the contrasts: they indeed reflect a basic feature
of his mentality. They regard not only the people and
their experiences, fortunes, or natures, their πάθη, τύχαι, or
φύσεις,[79] but also their circumstances, social background,
and even some aspects of style: that is clear, for example, in
the treatment of the death of Philopoemen (*Phil.* 20) and
that of Hannibal in *Flamininus*.[80]

The zeal of the Peripatetic collectors is reflected in collections of anecdotes, famous sayings, and proverbs and
maxims concerning political figures, artists, or scholars.
The style of these collections was probably similar to that

[73] Leo (1881), 150; Homeyer (1963), 150; Jenkinson (1973), 710.

[74] e.g. in the contrast between good and bad fortune and between lack of
military ability and military valour (see Homeyer (1963), 157; Deremetz (1990),
67). Russell (1966a: 150 = below, p. 89) demonstrates how Fabius Maximus is
compared with five other generals, three of whom (Flaminius, Minucius, and
Varro) meet disaster through imprudence, the fourth (Marcellus) proves a good
colleague, and the last (Scipio) outshines the hero himself. Cf. also Wardman
(1974), 27–8.

[75] e.g. the contrasts in enmity between Cimon and Pericles, between Marius
and Sulla, and in friendship between Epaminondas and Pelopidas and between
Brutus and Cassius.

[76] e.g. *Phoc.* 1–4, with its distinctions of fortune and misfortune and of
different sorts of virtue: cf. Homeyer (1963), 152; Geiger (1988), 252.

[77] A few comparisons had already been drawn between Greeks and Romans:
Scipio and Lycurgus (Pol. 10. 2. 8–13), Themistocles and Coriolanus (see below);
among Plutarch's own pairs, Alexander and Caesar had a precedent (Vell. 2. 41.
1–2) and so did Demosthenes and Cicero (*Dem.* 3.2). Cf. Jones (1971), 106 n. 18.
See also Bucher-Isler (1972), 76; Deremetz (1990), 57.

[78] Cf. Brugnoli (1987b), 61.

[79] Cf. e.g. Pérez Jiménez (1973), 101–4; Swain (1989a).

[80] See Pelling (1989), 212–13 and (1986a), 87.

whose traces we occasionally find in Aristotle's own writings, in for instance Ἀθηναίων Πολιτεία 16. 6, or in the sayings
of famous politicians and generals in the *Rhetoric*.[81] Such
sayings (ἀποφθέγματα), examples (παραδείγματα), wonders
(θαυμάσια), paradoxes (παράδοξα), and other sentences could
reveal human virtues and vices, and Aristotelian scholars
transferred these interests to works of a biographical character and to independent collections (all now lost). In these
the individual sentences and episodes became detached from
their original contexts.[82] In the *Lives* themselves, both
Greek and Roman, we can find traces of this genre, with
collections of instances skilfully integrated into the narrative
context in order to delineate ethical behaviour. For example,
we find an impressive number of sayings attributed to
Agesilaus, presumably drawn from an independent collection; less conspicuously, there are also a considerable
number of sayings and episodes in *Lives* such as *Phocion*
and *Cicero*.[83] At Rome we find the category of *exempla*,
collections fairly similar to those of Aristotle and the Peripatos which were used in the rhetorical schools for teaching
and entertainment: those are already attested in the time of
the Republic.[84]

It thus seems practically certain that Plutarch was directly
or indirectly influenced by Peripatetic models: but the
development of Peripatetic literary forms may be more
important than the identification of specific works, particularly biographies, which might have served as sources.

---

[81] Homeyer (1963), 147, with further bibliography; Gossage (1967), 59. Similar
collections can be found in other Peripatetic works: Gallo (1974), 182.

[82] Plutarch himself, or an author writing under his name, made similar collections which are extant: the *Apophthegmata regum et imperatorum*, the *Apophthegmata Laconica*, and the *Apophthegmata Lacaenarum* (cf. Fuhrmann (1988), 3–14).
The *Sayings of kings and Commanders* have a dedicatory preface to the emperor
Trajan in which Plutarch refers to Greek and Roman rulers, lawgivers, and
monarchs. For uncertainty on their authenticity see Weissenberger (1895), 56–68;
Ziegler (1952), 863–5; Pettine (1988), introd.

[83] For Agesilaus see *Apoph. reg.* 190f–191d, *Apoph. Lac.* 208b–215b. On the
sayings attributed to Phocion: Gehrke (1976), 121–38; Tritle (1988), 29–34, and
(1992), 4287–8; Cicero: Mugelli (1991), 296–9.

[84] Bibliography in Wehrli (1973), 197 n. 17.

IV

Fourth-century historiography generally moves away from
the Peripatos. (Duris, whose predilection for tragic style
may even go back to Aristotle, is an exception.)[85] This
applies in particular to two representatives of so-called
'rhetorical historiography', Theopompus of Chios and Ephorus of Cyme, and to two Sicilian fourth-century historians,
Philistus of Syracuse and Timaeus of Tauromenium. Philistus, the eyewitness of the period of Dionysius I and II, is
generally considered a friend of tyrannies; Timaeus, narrator of the stories of Greek Sicilian cities and author of
many geographical and ethnographical excursuses, is taken
to have been a personal enemy of the tyrant Agathocles.[86]
Both of them are used in Plutarch's two Sicilian *Lives*, *Dion*
and *Timoleon*.[87] Ephorus and Theopompus, whom Plutarch
also used for these[88] and other[89] biographies, have been
taken to be followers of Isocrates (Cic. *De orat.* 2. 57. 94; 3,
36; *Brut.* 204): however that may be, they certainly distinguished themselves for the application of rhetorical and
ethical considerations to the writing of history.[90] With
them also begins the practice of making historical compilations and summaries:[91] in other words, a method of working
that would become typical of all historical writing, including

[85] Flach (1985), 44; Meister (1989), 99–100 is more sceptical. Cf. also Zegers
(1959), 76–80.
[86] Cf. Flach (1985), 38; Pearson (1987), 191–259; Moggi (1987), 2089–90. On
Philistus see Zoepffel (1965), esp. 64–6, and (1993), 40–50; Meister (1989), 68–9;
Will (1991), 124; Sordi (1988), 160; Meissner (1993), 288–95. On Timaeus see
Brown (1958), 43–9; Meister (1967), 2–3, and (1989), 132–7; Sanders (1992), 209–
15; Meissner (1993), 299–300.
[87] Cf. *Tim.* 4. 6, *Dion* 24. 10. See Westlake (1938), 69–74; (1953/4), 294–300 =
(1969), 238–50; Fontana (1958), 6–8; Flacelière (1966), 5–10; Talbert (1974), 25;
Sordi (1983), 16–17; Shrimpton (1991), 88–9.
[88] Meister (1989), 92. Cf. Westlake (1969), 236–39; Talbert (1974), 36–7;
Sanders (1979/80), 78; Muccioli (1990), 168.
[89] Although Plutarch quotes Ephorus only in passing in *Them.*, *Cimon, Per.*,
Alc., Lys., and *Pelop.*, he must have known him very well. On the ample use of
Ephorus in *de mul. virt.* see Stadter (1965), 37–8, 59–68; 127–8.
[90] Flach (1985), 38–42; Bonamente (1973/4; 1979), 5; Flower (1986), 12–15;
Nickel (1991), 237.
[91] Momigliano (1981), 316. Theopompus wrote, for example, an epitome of
Herodotus (Meister (1989), 91). See also Pédech (1989), 40–1; Will (1991), 127

Plutarch. It is no coincidence that Ephorus is also the first author to have produced a universal history of the political and military events of Greece and of the peoples who came into conflict with the Greeks.[92] His successor here is, at least in some sense, Polybius (Pol. 5. 33. 2). But Theopompus' *Philippica* were also not too far removed from this: the primary axis of that work consisted in the treatment of the personality and deeds of Philip II, but only a small part of the work really concerned the Macedonian king, and it was basically a universal history.[93] Philip V later gave instructions that the work should be shortened to include only the parts which concerned Macedonia (T 31, in Phot. *Bibl.* No. 176, p. 121a, 35).

Ephorus was not a maker of personal inquiries and did not base his work on autopsy,[94] whereas Theopompus' section on his own times may be considered a first-hand account.[95] Their level was inferior to that of their predecessors and they were severely criticized by the Peripatos;[96] Plutarch too took them to task for their excessive rhetoric and their lack of a sense of reality.[97] Concerning Theopompus in particular he reveals a perplexity which is similar to that he shows towards Herodotus (see above).[98]

The *Philippica*, like the *Hellenica*,[99] also confirm the development of an interest in the individual in the fourth century:[100] so, a little later, do the accounts of Alexander the Great. With the advent of Philip and Alexander, then the growth of the monarchical Hellenistic states in the East,

[92] Momigliano (1981), 316; Alonso Núñez (1988), 176; Nickel (1991), 236. The account actually consists of juxtapositions of single events: Meister (1989), 88.

[93] Alonso Núñez (1988), 178–9; Meister (1989), 91; Flower (1986), 137–40.

[94] Pol. 12. 25–26. 1–6. Cf. Schepens (1977), 110–11; Meister (1989), 89; Will (1991), 126; Nickel (1991), 236–7.

[95] On Philip see Shrimpton (1977), 123–4; (1991), 41–42; on Theopompus' treatment of his private life, Goukowsky (1991), 138–4.

[96] Flach (1985), 42. See the polemic of Duris (*FGrHist* 76 F 1) against Ephorus and Theopompus with Wehrli (1947), 63–4.

[97] *Praec. ger. reip.* 803b.

[98] Cf. e.g. Theopompus' exaggerated presentation of Demosthenes' oration on the deaths at Chaeronea (*Demosth.* 21. 2 and also 13. 1), or *Ages.* 33. 1. In general, Russell (1973), 104; Wardman (1974), 173.

[99] See von Fritz (1972), 347; Moggi (1987), 2084; Will (1991), 130–2; Shrimpton (1991), 40–52.

[100] Pédech (1989), 65–206; Meister (1989), 91; Goukowsky (1991), 138–41.

historiography more and more approximates to true biography and the Greek world becomes acquainted with the
Roman world.[101]

Plutarch must have known at least some of the works
written about Alexander by several of his companions:[102]
some of these were historical narrations, composed for
instance by Ptolemy or Aristobulus some time after his
death on the basis of their personal memory—works which
were basically serious, despite an element of fantasy;[103]
others were composed during the expedition itself or immediately after it, for example those of Chares, Callisthenes,
Onesicritus, and Nearchus, and these often contained still
more fictitious and tendentious elements.[104] We cannot be
certain that Plutarch used the second group, who were
earlier than Ptolemy and Aristobulus; but the conclusion of
I. Rabe's dissertation[105] is fairly convincing, that Plutarch
knew most of these authors at first hand, and made his own
independent excerpts.

The author used most frequently in *Alexander* must have
been Cleitarchus son of Deinon (see above).[106] He too was
nearly contemporary with the events, but was not an eyewitness. He inaugurated the so-called 'Vulgate' (used by Diodorus, Curtius Rufus, and Justin),[107] and his predilection
for the sensational aspects of human behaviour and for
mirabilia foreshadows the new 'tragic' style of historiography seen in Duris and Phylarchus. Duris, as mentioned
above, had criticized Ephorus and Theopompus for the
lack of mimetic power ($\mu\acute{\iota}\mu\eta\sigma\iota\varsigma$) and of pleasure in their
accounts ($\mathring{\eta}\delta o\nu\mathring{\eta}$ $\mathring{\epsilon}\nu$ $\tau\mathring{\omega}$ $\phi\rho\acute{\alpha}\sigma\alpha\iota$) (*FGrHist* 76 F1 = Phot.
Bibl. No. 176, p. 121a, 41).

These writers strike a new note in historiography.[108]

[101] Momigliano (1981), 317; Barigazzi (1984), 270–86; Valgiglio (1992), 4048–50.
[102] Cf. Hamilton (1969), li.
[103] Goukowsky (1991), 145–9.
[104] Pédech (1977), 129–38 and (1984), esp. 407–13; Wirth (1988), 247–50;
Meister (1989), 108–13; Goukowsky (1991), 141. Callisthenes' *Hellenica* were surely
used by Plutarch in his Boeotian *Lives*, *Epaminondas* and *Pelopidas*: cf. Fuscagni
(1975).
[105] Rabe (1964).
[106] Hamilton (1969), li–lii, lvii–lix.
[107] Meister (1989), 119–23; Goukowsky (1991), 150–3.
[108] Geiger (1981), 91; Pédech (1989), 400–42.

They prefer the dramatic aspects and passions (πάθη) to the history of political events (πραγματικὴ ἱστορία) represented in this period by Hieronymus of Cardia[109] and Polybius,[110] in both cases at an extremely high level. Plutarch used the (lost) history of Hieronymus in *Eumenes, Demetrius,* and *Pyrrhus*,[111] and Polybius for the *Agis-Cleomenes* and *Philopoemen* among the Greek *Lives* and *Aemilius, Cato maior, Flamininus,* and the lost *Scipio* among the Roman (see below). But he borrowed a great deal from the historians of the 'tragic' style as well,[112] even though their material did not correspond to his optimistic temperament and his educational purposes.[113]

Plutarch knew other material too from the same period which might seem to approximate more closely to biography, for it delineated personality from a more highly focused point of view. The first such class was that of the memoir, often written by the protagonist himself: Pyrrhus and Aratus of Sicyon both offered examples.[114] The second was encomium, such as that written by Polybius on Philopoemen. Aratus composed his memoirs to defend himself and his political line towards Macedonia; Polybius too made use of them (2. 56. 1).[115] Polybius' *Philopoemen* seems to

[109] Jacoby (1913); Hornblower (1981), esp. 107–79; Alonso Núñez (1988), 181–2.

[110] For the use of Polybius see e.g. Theunissen (1935), 95–8, 241–3.

[111] See Leo (1881), 175; Westlake (1969), 313–28; Hornblower (1981), 68; Lévêque (1957), 22–6, 63–5; La Bua (1971), 1–21; Garoufalias (1979), 153.

[112] See e.g. on Duris: *Per.* 28. 3, *Demosth.* 21. 2, *Alc.* 32. 2. Cf. von Fritz (1972), 331; Strasburger (1966), 996–7; Mastrocinque (1983), 243–7; Tornea (1988), esp. 63–8; Walbank (1988), 259–60; Meister (1989), 96–9. On Phylarchus: *Them.* 32. 4 with Wardman (1974), 172; Frost (1980), 324. He is also criticized by Polybius (2. 56–63), in an exaggerated way: see e.g. Gabba (1957), 5–13; Meister (1975), 93–108, and (1989), 100–2; Flach (1985), 53. On Plutarch's own frequent inclusion of tragic elements cf. McCaslin (1989), 77–102. Pelling (1990), 24 n. 1, has a good comparison between Polybius' and Plutarch's criticism of Phylarchus.

[113] Wardman (1974), 173.

[114] Cf. Theunissen (1935), 4–6; Koster (1937), xv–xviii; Wehrli (1947), 59; Theander (1951), 53; Walbank (1957), i. 27; Altheim (1961), 91–5; Errington (1969), 228; Geiger (1981), 90; see below, p. 173; Marasco (1981a), 30; Orsi (1987a), x–xi, (1987b), 60, and (1991), 16–17; Meister (1988), 85–6, and (1989), 188; Vercruysse (1988), 22–3; Meissner (1993), 303–10.

[115] Pédech (1951), 82–101; Marasco (1981a), 34–6; Achleitner (1982), 499–500; Gentili–Cerri (1978), 26; Meister (1989), 155; Orsi (1990), 150–3.

have been an interesting example of Hellenistic encomium, after the manner of Xenophon and Isocrates.[116]

One must conclude that Plutarch's Greek *Lives* occupy a fluid and intermediate position in the history of biography. If anything, they approximate more closely to the work of a historian[117] than to the more straightforward biographical forms. However, in the variety of his own work he provides the most striking indication of the immense number of variations of biographical works, each single genre of which had its own tradition—encomium, autobiographical and biographical narrative, history-writing centring on one particular personage. It is hard to say whether before Plutarch there had already been so many fusions, combinations, and adaptations.

Scholars vary in their interpretations of some remarks of Cornelius Nepos (*Epam.* 4. 6, *Proem.* 1, 1), speaking of *complures scriptores* who produced volumes of lives *excellentium virorum*,[118] and Cicero (*De Orat.* 2. 341), mentioning *laudationes* honouring certain Greek political personages.[119] But these passages cannot take us far. More important are general questions about the likelihood of a rigid and narrow category of political biography, either concerning a specific category of persons or as a more universal genre.[120] It is also questionable whether any such rigid genre was appropriate to a man as broadminded as Plutarch, who drew on material of all sorts.

We know very little about Peripatetic or Hellenistic biography, but the genre must have treated not only writers, philosophers, and artists, but politicians too: why, after all, should they have been excluded? Here perhaps belong Theopompus' excursuses on the ten Athenian demagogues (*FGrHist* 115 F100), which probably consisted of short

---

[116] At the end of this encomiastic tradition we find the *Life of Augustus* by Nicolaus of Damascus (Wilamowitz (1926), 167–8, see below, pp. 64–5; Geiger (1985), 35), composed, unlike Polybius' *Philopoemen*, when Augustus was still alive (Delbianco–Scardigli (1983), 10–13).

[117] Dihle (1986), 19, speaks of 'gleitende Übergänge' between biography and encomium; see also García Valdes (1981), 320; La Penna (1987), 28.

[118] See Steidle (1951), 140, and against him, Geiger (1985), 34–44; but, criticizing Geiger, Moles (1989). According to Russell (1973), 107, Cornelius Nepos even adapted the form of his biographies to those of Hellenistic predecessors.

[119] Steidle (1951), 141; Wilkins (1892), 396.

[120] Moles (1989), 230, against Geiger.

biographies and political narration,[121] and some of the
biographies regarding Alexander.[122] It is also true that
citations in Athenaeus and Diogenes Laertius[123] do not
support Geiger's careful and precise, but over-restrictive,
argumentation which posits Cornelius Nepos alone as the
inventor of political biography. It is better to see Nepos'
innovation as 'bringing Greek-style biography to Rome'.[124]

V

In the Roman *Lives* we should again presume that Plutarch
used a variety of literary genres, although we should also
assume that he had some major difficulties in adapting his
material. It is indeed clear that for the Roman *Lives* he
could not only exploit works written in Greek, but also
drew information from materials in Latin. Most scholars
today feel that Plutarch's approach to Latin works may not
have been very different from the experience of a modern
scholar who reads works in both native and foreign languages.[125] Naturally, in the Roman *Lives* there are few
citations from the works of Latin poets or philosophers,
and equally few from collections of antiquarian information
or anything similar;[126] that contrasts with Plutarch's
familiar enormous baggage of Greek culture within the
Greek *Lives*. There are also many more references to material not clearly defined—'they say' (λέγουσι or φασί), 'it is
said' (λέγεται), 'it seems' (δοκεῖ), and so on.[127] On the other

---

[121] Dionysius of Halicarnassus (*ad Pomp.* 6. 4 = *FGrHist* 115 T 20a) maintains
that he set out βίους ἀνδρῶν καὶ πράξεις καὶ τέλη καὶ τύχας, but that he also looked for
the secret motivations behind actions, and he explored the πάθη τῆς ψυχῆς: see
Gentili–Cerri (1978), 8–9; Gabba (1982), 803; Pédech (1989), 183–91; Sacks
(1983), 80–3.

[122] Moles (1989), 232.

[123] See Leo (1881), 23–4, 120–4; Mejer (1978), 90–5 ('Biographies of philosophers').

[124] Moles (1989), 232.

[125] See Wilamowitz (1926), 258–9, see below, p. 57; Barrow (1976), 150–2;
Pelling (1988a), 6; Jones (1971), 76–7, 81–2 is more sceptical.

[126] See e.g. Wardman (1971), 259. On Plutarch's lack of interest in Romans as
philosophers see Swain (1990a); Steidle (1990), 169–70 n. 6; Desideri (1992b),
4562; De Blois (1992), 4571.

[127] Pauw (1980), 91–5; Hillard (1987), 28.

hand, he often explains Roman institutions and customs to his Greek readers, much more than he does the other way round. He knew of course what Polybius and Posidonius had written concerning Roman history, Roman politics, and Roman personages: both were the right authors to use for comparison between the Greek and Roman world[128] and for explanations of Roman politics and Roman life to a Greek audience.

At Rome, interest in the individual begins with Scipio Africanus and receives further stimulus in the age of the Gracchi.[129] Brief characterizations and above all idealizations of famous personalities had long been familiar to Romans through memoirs and encomia of living politicians,[130] or by speeches given as in Greece to honour them at their deaths.[131] Often these were preserved in private archives.[132] Yet it is unlikely that these documents (often falsified, as Cicero and Livy knew) constituted a model for Roman biography,[133] and equally improbable that Plutarch placed a high value on consulting them.

Instead, he knew works which were at least partly autobiographical, perhaps even those composed by Scipio Africanus and his relative Cornelius Nasica Corculum[134] and some of those composed in Latin by men who wished to

[128] Leo (1881), 150, 194. Polybius turns to the Greeks in 1. 3. 6–8 and he narrates how the Romans became lords over land and sea in the East; to the Romans in 6. 11. 3, where he hopes to find an audience that will understand his book on the Roman constitution, and at the end of his narrative he is convinced that all or most of the Romans would have been interested in his histories: see Flach (1985), 53. See also Walbank (1977), 156; and for Posidonius, Strasburger (1964/82), ii. 920.

[129] C. Gracchus wrote a *libellus* in his brother's defence (Plut. *C. Gr.* 8. 9, Cic. *De Div.* 2. 29. 62: cf. Sordi (1978), 299–301, esp. 325–30; Baldwin (1983), 67), and Plutarch may have consulted this at first hand. Perhaps he also read some of Gaius' speeches and some of Cornelia's letters (*C. Gr.* 13. 1, cf. Cic. Brut. 58.211); see Baldwin (1979), 101.

[130] Cic. *Brut.* 15. 62, *ornamenta et monumenta ad memoriam laudum domesticarum*. On orations mentioned by Cicero see Douglas (1966), 52. See also Cic. *Tusc.* 4. 2. 3 (from Cato, fr. 118P). Cf. Stuart (1928), 196–9.

[131] Liv. 8. 40. 4, *funebres laudes*. See Stuart (1928), 209–11; Baldwin (1983), 68–9; Lewis (1993), 658–9.

[132] Misch (1907), i. 131–2; cf. Bates (1983), 19–25; Jenkinson (1967), 2, and (1973), 705.

[133] Brugnoli (1987a), 295–6 n. 36. But Smith (1940) holds that they did.

[134] Meister (1989), 189, and (1988), 87. For Nasica see also Lehmann (1969), i. 400–12.

defend their conduct against accusations levelled against
them in the real world of politics, like Aemilius Scaurus
(cos. 115 BC), Rutilius Rufus (cos. 105 BC), Lutatius Catulus
(cos. 102 BC),[135] and Sulla.

From the viewpoint of literary genre this last group
probably shared some features with, for instance, the memoirs of Aratus, with their defence of political and military
activity; but they must have been simpler and closer to a
matter-of-fact report. Lutatius' and Rutilius' works might
have been consulted for Plutarch's *Marius* and *Sulla*; Sulla's
memoirs certainly provided the basis for the Plutarchian
biography,[136] and this is the explanation for many of the
positive aspects of Plutarch's account. Unlike his forerunners
and successors, Sulla seems to have loaded his memoirs
with sections of high dramatic intensity.[137]

In the second half of the first century BC we find the first
examples of Roman authors comparing Romans with
Greeks;[138] we know little about Varro and Atticus, whose
biographical works were probably unknown to Plutarch,[139]
but he certainly knew most of Cicero's works, some passages
of which could have inspired his own comparisons (for
instance the famous comparison of Themistocles and Coriolanus).[140] Indeed, the whole dialogue *Brutus* is permeated
by comparisons, between Greek orators (Demosthenes and
Hyperides, 138, 285, 290), between Roman ones (Antonius

---

[135] Details in Bates (1983), 121–48; 163–205; 206–18 and Lewis (1993), 660–9.
See also Flacelière (1971), 85; Flach (1985), 96.
[136] Brugnoli (1987*b*), 55. For a discussion of Sulla's memoirs see Scardigli
(1979), 89–91; Lewis (1991).
[137] Bates (1983), 206–13; Geiger (1985), 61; Ramage (1991), 93–5.
[138] Cf. Brugnoli (1987*a*), 299–301: Atticus published his genealogical mono-
graphs of illustrious families in 34 BC, and slightly earlier Varro had produced
fifteen books of brief portraits, full of topicality, of 700 persons (*Hebdomades uel
de imaginibus*): Gell. 3. 10. 17. See Riposati (1976), i. 77–8; Jones (1971), 106;
Baldwin (1979), 102, 113, and (1983), 67–9; 83–5; 93; Hillard (1987), 24. Somewhat later C. Iulius Hyginus published his *De vita rebusque inlustrium virorum*
(Gell. 1. 14. 1, 6. 1. 3): Hillard (1987), 24.
[139] He knew only the *De lingua latina*, as we can see from the passages
collected by Valgiglio (1976), ii. 571, which relate to the *Lives* of Romulus and
Numa and some passages in the *Moralia*.
[140] *Brut.* 41–3; cf. *Lael.* 42, *ad Att.* 9. 10. 3 and n. 141 (Gellius). See Alfonsi
(1950), 59–65; Russell (1973), 109; Noè (1979), 87; Geiger (1985), 91–2.

and Crassus, 138–44), and between Greeks and Romans.[141]

Cornelius Nepos is evidently of great importance to the genre of biography.[142] His roots are in the Peripatetic tradition,[143] but he was also influenced by the Alexandrians.[144] It seems that it was he who made the genre of *exempla* known to the Romans, and, although only a few fragments remain of his own *exempla*,[145] we can perhaps attribute to him the division between *exempla* of Greeks and Romans which we later find in Valerius Maximus.[146] His *Chronica* form another attempt to synchronize Greek and Roman historic events,[147] while the *De uiris illustribus* juxtaposes a book of biographies of illustrious non-Romans (Greeks and others) with a book of Romans (*Hann.* 13. 4). Only the book of three non-Roman *duces* has survived:[148] the book of kings, composed along the same lines, is entirely missing; the other books (also missing, apart from the *Atticus* and an excerpt of the *Cato*) concerned historians, philosophers, poets, and others, and included a comparison between Romans and Greeks.

Plutarch cites Nepos several times,[149] but less than one would expect; he uses him in only a few *Lives*,[150] and even there only marginally. A great many of the Roman *Lives* are based on historical works, which are often used for more than one biography, and it is sometimes possible to identify the material on which Plutarch is drawing. These authors are, for example, Livy, or perhaps older annalists, and

[141] For a precisely chronological comparison of Greeks and Romans who lived from the foundation of Rome to the beginning of the Second Punic War cf. Gell. 17. 21: e.g. Solon–Tarquinius Priscus; Peisistratus–Servius Tullius; Pythagoras–Tarquinius Superbus; Archilochus–Tullus Hostilius; Themistocles–Coriolanus (see above).
[142] Jenkinson (1967), 7, and (1973), 710–13. See also Geiger, below 181
[143] Jenkinson (1967), 7.
[144] Brugnoli (1987a), 299. On the biography of Atticus see now Millar (1988), 40–51, and Horsfall (1989), xv–xxi.
[145] Geiger (1985), 72–6.
[146] Geiger (1985), 74.
[147] Alfonsi (1942/3), 331; Geiger (1985), 69–72, and (1988), 248; Desideri (1992a), 4483–4.
[148] Gossage (1967), 60; Dionisotti (1982), 35–7; Horsfall (1989), xvii, 10–11.
[149] *Marc.* 30. 5, *Ti. Gr.* 21. 1, *Luc.* 43. 2. Cf. too *Comp. Pel. Marc.* 1. 5. Details in Geiger (1985), 117–20; see also Ramon (1994), 282–84.
[150] Sometimes there must have been a common source, for instance in *Alc.*: Russell (1973), 106–8.

Dionysius of Halicarnassus[151] and for the *Lives* of the regal period and for those of the third and second century (*Fabius, Marcellus, Cato the elder, Flamininus, Aemilius,* and *Scipio*): for this latter group Plutarch also uses Polybius,[152] and for some of them perhaps Cato himself.[153] For all of these Roman *Lives* the annalistic material is often integrated with items drawn from other types of historiographical work about which we know very little.

As for the late Republic, the *Histories* of Sallust are the basis for *Sertorius, Lucullus,* and to a certain extent *Pompey*.[154] Lost authors were also used: concrete and plausible proposals have been made concerning Asinius Pollio, whose histories began with the year 60 BC and were used, at first hand or in translation, by Appian, Cassius Dio, and Plutarch. According to Pelling,[155] Plutarch came to know Pollio's work only after writing *Lucullus* and *Cicero*: therefore Pollio must have provided the basic historical material, especially regarding internal politics, for *Crassus, Pompey, Caesar, Cato the younger, Brutus,* and *Antony,* all prepared simultaneously along with their Greek pairs. Perhaps it is to Pollio that we owe the images of a Pompey and Caesar analysed by Pelling a year later:[156] a Pompey continuously undecided and politically inert, and a Caesar always active, beginning as a champion of the people and marching on to tyranny.[157]

[151] In both of them we can find short biographical sketches, e.g. Dion. Hal. 5. 48 (Publicola), 7. 60–2 (Coriolanus), Liv. 1. 48–9 (Servius Tullius). Cf. Wardman (1974), 6.
[152] See above, p. 19; Theander (1951), 67–8; Errington (1969), 237. The traces of biographical style are insufficient to demonstrate biographical sources, as Smith (1940) thought.
[153] On the special position of Cato the elder cf. Hillard (1987), 30.
[154] See Olivieri Sangiacomo (1954), 230–46; Rizzo (1963), 25–30; Mora (1991), 172. We can say little about the relationship between Sallust and Posidonius, although the former certainly knew the latter's work: Malitz (1983), 57, is cautious.
[155] Pelling (1979), 76–80, 83–5, see below, pp. 270–7, 285–8. Steidle (1990) argues against Pelling that the figure of Caesar is already quite elaborate in *Cicero*, and he infers that Plutarch's initial plan included all the late Republican *Lives*: he is sceptical about Pelling's thesis that Plutarch's knowledge and familiarity with the late Republican period increased after *Cicero*. But it seems right to distinguish this *Life* from the six later ones.
[156] See Pelling (1980), 131–5 (= below, pp. 133–42), and La Penna (1987), 269–70, 283.
[157] Pelling (1986b), 159–60, 164–7, see below, pp. 319–21, 325–9; and now Steidle (1990), 172–86.

Plutarch must have become aware of the histories of
Pollio during the period in which he formulated his interest
in continuing his biographical studies (*Aem.* 1. 1, 1. 4).
Brutus must have been the first of the six biographies
which according to Pelling formed a group: probably it was
written immediately following *Aemilius*.[158]

Biographical material was also used to supplement the
Roman *Lives*. In particular, he must have supplemented
Pollio's account of the late Republic with many works
which may have been biographical, although we know only
titles of works or names of authors (often freedmen who
were emancipated by the figures they wrote about). Thus,
for instance, we know of a work by Cornelius Epicadas on
Sulla,[159] by Tiro on Cicero,[160] by L. Voltacilius Pitholaus
on Pompey,[161] and by C. Oppius on Caesar, Brutus, and
others.[162] We also know little about the memoirs of L.
Calpurnius Bibulus (*Brut.* 13. 2, 23. 2–4) and M. Valerius
Messala Corvinus,[163] the 'composition on the killing of
Caesar' (σύγγραμμα περὶ τῆς Καίσαρος ἀναιρέσεως) by Empylus of Rhodes,[164] and the work on the death of Brutus by
P. Volumnius (*Brut.* 48. 2, 51. 2). Since he cites them, it is
probable that Plutarch knew these works at first hand. He
must also have used first-hand material in *Cato the younger*,
especially but not only the work of Thrasea Paetus, who
borrowed from Cato's friend Munatius Rufus;[165] Plutarch
perhaps also knew Munatius himself.

In other cases we can sense the influence of biographical
material, sometimes over longer sections of a *Life*, without
being able to identify either a specific author or a clear-cut

[158] Cf. Jones (1966), 67 (= below, p. 109). See *Dion* 58. 10.
[159] Baldwin (1979), 101.
[160] Hillard (1987), 30, 37; Moles (1988), 29; Mora (1991), 183. See also Leo
(1881), 164–5.
[161] Suet. *de gramm. et rhet.* 27. 1 (Brugnoli (1963), 31). See Lewis (1966);
Treggiari (1969); Baldwin (1979), 101 and (1983), 67–9.
[162] Hillard (1987), 29; Pelling (1979), 85, see below, p. 289.
[163] On both: Hillard (1987), 33. On Messala: Valvo (1983), 1674–80; Mora
(1991), 191.
[164] Cf. Pelling (1979), 86–7, see below, pp. 290–4; Mora (1991), 191.
[165] Geiger (1979), 48–57; Pelling (1979), 85, see below, 289–90; Zecchini
(1980), 46–8; Hillard (1987), 30–1, 36. See also the comparison between Nepos
and Plutarch in Geiger (1988), 250–4.

attitude to a hero. This holds true for *Marius*, where, besides some material drawn from a mainly hostile source[166] and some from a second, neutral authority well versed in technical and military matters, we can also identify traces of a biography.[167]

There are also biographical and autobiographical passages in other genres, both literary and non-literary, which Plutarch seems to have known. For example, there was the poem of Licinius Archias, who accompanied Lucullus to the Orient (Cic. *Arch.* 9. 21, *ad Att.* 1. 16. 15),[168] the writings of Theophanes of Mytilene who participated personally in Pompey's campaign against Mithridates,[169] and the commentaries of Caesar (the *Bellum Civile* perhaps influenced the chapters on the battle of Pharsalus);[170] the history of Cassius Longinus would have had some bearing on Crassus' Parthian War, and that of Q. Dellius on Antony's[171] and there were also letters and speeches (especially those of Cicero and Brutus), pamphlets and invectives (such as Caesar's *Anticato*[172] and Cicero's *Philippics*)[173] or his *commentarii*—in Greek ὑπόμνημα—on his consulate.[174] We can also count on there being some oral information.[175]

---

[166] A source, indeed, of the highest quality, perhaps Posidonius: on his use by Plutarch in this *Life* see von Fritz (1943), 163–6 (200–3) and (1977), 183; Bringmann (1986), 55; Swain (1989c), 277.

[167] Cf. Scardigli (1977), esp. 219–20.

[168] Cf. Rizzo (1963), 31–7; Hillard (1987), 37–48; Scardigli (1989), 265.

[169] Cf. Gold (1985), where the influence of Theophanes as Pompey's adviser is perhaps exaggerated: Hillard (1987), 32.

[170] For the *Bellum Gallicum* cf. Zecchini (1978), 151–87; he thinks that Asinius Pollio was used by Plutarch, Appian, and Strabo; and Mora (1991), 177.

[171] On Cassius Longinus see Adcock (1966), 59; Flacelière (1972), 194; Garzetti (1987), 215. On Dellius: Pelling (1979), 88, and below, pp. 294–5; (1988a), 28; on both, Mora (1991), 174–5. On other contemporary sources in *Ant.* cf. De Wet (1990), 80–3.

[172] Details in Scardigli (1979), 137; Fehrle (1983), 15–18; Hillard (1987), 30–2; Mora (1991), 183.

[173] Russell (1973), 135; Pelling (1979), 89, and below, p. 296 (1980), 129–30 (= below, pp. 131–2), and (1988a), 27; Valgiglio (1982), 297; Moles (1988), 29–30; De Wet (1990), 83–4, even supposes that Plutarch knew Antony's reply as well.

[174] Cf. *Crass.* 13. 4, *Caes.* 8. 2, Cassius Dio 46. 21. 4, with Magnino (1963), xii–xiii; Lendle (1967), 95–7; Gelzer (1969), 117–18; Pelling (1985), 312–18.

[175] Cf. Theander (1951), 11–32; De Wet (1990), 81–2; cf. also Pelling (1990), 25.

VI

From this panorama emerges a range of different kinds of material used for the Roman *Lives*; its diversity is not inferior to that exploited for the Greek counterparts. Much of it comes from a vast array of historical works: the distinction he drew between biography and history therefore holds as good for the Roman as for the Greek *Lives*. The historical narratives served as a skeleton, and left him the freedom to integrate material from memoirs, encomia, letters, pamphlet-like writings, and biographies.[176] But even such additional material is often drawn from historical writings with a different tendency from that of his main narrative source. He offers a concrete programme which fits in well with the history of his own times, the reconciliation and essentially equivalent value of Greeks and Romans. In order to present this to a Roman public he naturally could not choose any protagonist other than political and military men, and he therefore had to use above all material from historical narratives.[177] Plutarch really made use of every possible source in order to render the historical account richer and more concrete, embellishing it with different and more personally focused items, attributing to the heroes (for instance in *Aristides*, *Coriolanus*, or *Publicola*) even merits which they probably lacked, and transferring to them deeds that really took place in different periods of history[178]—perhaps even the biographer's own day.[179]

It is precisely this dependence on historical material and on historiographical methods[180] which explains the frequency with which Plutarch, in the prefaces of the *Lives*,[181] feels the need to justify his choice of sources, or the methods

[176] Pelling (1979), 85–91, see below, pp. 285–300.

[177] Differently, Nicolaidis (1982–4), 93–114.

[178] See Affortunati in Affortunati–Scardigli (1992), 112–19 on the late Republican elements present in *Publ.*, derived by way of Valerius Antias and Dionysius of Halicarnassus.

[179] This is so in *Publ.* 8. 6; 15. 2; 19. 10; 23. 6. Another example is *Per.* 12–14: cf. Ameling (1985).

[180] Cf. Mazzarino (1966) ii. 2, 137–43.

[181] A list in Homeyer (1963), 156. Other themes, esp. ethical ones, are outlined by Stadter (1988).

he followed (for instance concerning the very concept of historical truth), or his digressions and supplements, and also to criticize his predecessors.

The impression he leaves of immediacy and originality substantially confirms the view adopted above: that Plutarch was more than a mere collector of secondary material, and that he was preoccupied with creating a work which was pleasant to read and at the same time instructive.[182]

The narrative technique in the *Lives of the Caesars* was also similar to that followed by historians;[183] but in the *Parallel Lives* the literary elaboration is more conspicuous, the psychological exploration is richer and more colourful, and the interpretations and personal opinions of the author himself are more frequent and more profound.

This progress is not only due to the greater skill and maturity which Plutarch developed as he went on writing; it also reflects, as Mazzarino (1966), ii. 2: 139 maintained, the different demands made on him by his own and by more distant times. His distinction between history and biography must be considered in these various perspectives.

---

[182] Plutarch in reality never respects the principle of presenting τὰ κυριώτατα καὶ κάλλιστα (*Tim*. 1. 1, *Per*. 1. 2) of his protagonist's actions: Leo (1881), 148, 158 (this goes back to Isocrates and his so-called scholars Ephorus and Theopompus: cf. Flach (1990), 156). Plutarch often inserted unfavourable information: for him this often implied a discussion or refutation of these data, and an effort to show heroes in a new light. Sometimes the contrary is also seen: in certain passages of some *Lives* the protagonists (for instance, Sulla, Marius, Coriolanus, Alcibiades) do not distinguish themselves very markedly from protagonists who explicitly formed a negative example (Demetrius and Antony). Russell (1966*a*), 143 (= below, p. 80) and others (see Mazzarino (1966), ii. 2 139) consider Coriolanus and Alcibiades the second deterrent pair. Recently Piccirilli (1990), 389–90, pointed out that 'the negative traits of Nicias do not depend so much on Plutarch's sources as on his personal conviction that Nicias represented a person who lacked initiative and the ability to grasp a crucial opportunity, etc., and was therefore not an example to imitate': see also Nicolaidis (1988), 319–20. In any case these heroes are prey to their own fragile nature, or are easily influenced for the worse by circumstances: Plutarch often recalls the reader's attention to this point and passes a pertinent comment. Demetrius and Antony probably constitute an exemplary case, since their amorality goes beyond the limits conceded by Plutarch himself to a great political or military leader. Even with heroes whom he greatly loved (Pericles, for example, among the Greeks, or the younger Cato or Brutus among the Romans), he introduces elements from unfavourable sources, though sometimes under the guise of refuting these very elements.

[183] Plutarch's *Lives* are considered closer to authors like Tacitus and Cassius Dio than to the other biographer of his day, Suetonius: cf. Dihle (1986), 37–8; Baldwin (1979), i. 115–17; Geiger (1985), 51; Mazzarino (1966), ii. 2, 139–40.

Mazzarino (ii. 2: 138) rightly points out that Plutarch is a 'historical researcher' and Gentili-Cerri (1978), 27, question the degree to which we can trust in over-rigid classifications of single literary genres.[184] Valgiglio[185] notes, in the course of a detailed inquiry into the terms *historia* and *bios*, that the terminology oscillated; Plutarch himself provides evidence of this. The two can have a narrow interdependence, or can be strongly opposed (p. 56), and *historia* can indicate either single works of (universal) history of the type composed by Ephorus and Polybius (see above), or a series of compositions (Theopompus) (p. 60); such works can reveal great deeds or small actions (*Alex.* 1. 2, *Nic.* 1. 2, *Cato min.* 24. 1), all of which are also manifest in maxims, jokes, decrees, votive inscriptions, and so on. This last type of evidence comes from literary genres which the pragmatic historian, writing about politics and warfare, may have avoided, preferring a more critical and austere vision of their narrative.[186] If we recall the distinction between *historia* and *bios*, we can see that Plutarch is making it clear that he is not a pragmatic historian of that sort, but rather a historian of ancient culture, and especially Greek culture: perhaps similar to Posidonius, but simpler, and also different.

VII

Most of the contributions reprinted in this volume have a literary or cultural orientation; this introduction seeks to place them in context through an analysis of the kind of materials which Plutarch used. Such questions—where Plutarch's material comes from, how he uses it, whether similar

[184] See also Russell (1963), esp. 27 (= below, pp. 357–72); Moles (1988), 35, 52; Pelling (1990), 29; Valgiglio (1992), 4051; and the opinion of Gallo on Mazzarino (1990), 12–14.

[185] Valgiglio (1987*a*), 50–60, and (1992), 4051. Cf. Wardman (1974), 10: 'But we should not forget that his stress on the differences between biography and history conceals the fact that there is a close relationship between his *Lives* and their sources in written history; which is other than the indebtedness of a secondary writer to his original, but not less important.'

[186] La Penna (1987), 283.

literary forms existed before him—are less arid than is
sometimes thought. It is precisely in the assessment of what
is *individual* to Plutarch—not only in the literary, philosophical, or moral fields but also from a historical viewpoint—
that his special qualities, style, and method, his superb
narrative technique and his psychological finesse fully
emerge.

Every scholar interested in any aspect of the ancient
world can find something of use somewhere in Plutarch:
therein lies the special attraction and unique importance of
his *œuvre*. The historian may find that some technical detail
is missing in a description of a military or political event,
but this will be compensated by the fullness of the biographical and psychological characterization of the hero: that hero
acts within the historical setting and influences it in a new
and precise direction. The result is a typically and distinctively Plutarchian creation.

Studies of these procedures which illustrate Plutarch's
outlook on morals, politics, and culture, and explain some
literary aspects of his methodology, are offered in this
volume by D. A. Russell. The article 'On Reading Plutarch's *Lives*' ends with a brief analysis of the *Lysander*
(1966a), and two other contributions are devoted to '*Alcibiades* 1–16' (1966b), which deals mainly with literary considerations, and to the 'Coriolanus' (1963), which brings out
Plutarch's suppressions and alterations by comparing them
to his only source, Dionysius of Halicarnassus.

Russell's interests and approach have been taken up with
even greater depth by C. B. R. Pelling and recently by S.
Swain. This volume reprints three articles by Pelling on the
techniques used in the Roman *Lives* and on the simultaneous preparation of *Crassus, Pompey, Caesar, Cato, Brutus,*
and *Antony*, inspired probably by Asinius Pollio (1979); on
the artistic and thematic devices used by Plutarch to adapt
material for these *Lives* (1980); and on Plutarch's distinct
interests in his analysis of Roman politics and his particular
emphasis on the *demos* in the later Roman *Lives* (1986b). Of
no less interest are Pelling's other works listed in the bibliography.

Swain's previous works had studied such aspects as Plutarch's conception of a Providence which determined the course of history (1989c), character changes influenced by environmental and social factors (1989b), and the pair *Aemilius–Timoleon* and their Tyche (1989a). In the essay reprinted in this volume he examines the benefits of Hellenic education and culture to individual Romans, and the effect of lack of education in characters such as Coriolanus and Marius.

Mossman turns to the tragic treatment of particular characters. In many *Lives* that implies a negative judgement, but in *Alexander* it serves to bring out the complexity of his personality.

Of the remaining contributions reprinted in this volume, Jones (1966) offers and discusses a chronological list of Plutarch's works, and dates the *Parallel Lives* and all the important essays to the period after the death of Domitian; Geiger (1981) offers a study of Nepos, Plutarch, and Hellenistic historiography, applying the results to *Aemilius* and *Timoleon*; Stadter (1975) writes on the shared 'mildness' (πρᾳότης) and contrasting qualities of Pericles and Fabius.

The dominance of literary and cultural interests is also visible in three further collections of essays, containing the contributions of scholars at international meetings on Plutarch which took place in Athens in 1987, in Oxford in 1989 and Siena in 1993.[187]

In the first[188] there are essays on the *Moralia* and the *Lives* treating a great variety of themes: for example, Plutarch's admiration for Athens, which is marked by his interest in the city's monuments, cults, myths, and institutions (Podlecki); his emphasis on the humanity of his characters, which is stronger than in historians like Thucydides (de Romilly); his tendency to exploit literary passages without considering the context (Frazier); his sophisticated narrative technique in *Cato minor*, brought out by a comparison

---

[187] This is also largely true of the national meetings which have taken place in Italy (e.g. 'Plutarco e le scienze', a cura di I Gallo, Atti IV Conv. Plutarcheo, Genova–Bocca di Magra (1991), Naples, 1993), Spain (e.g. 'Estudios sobre Plutarco: Obra y tradicions', Sympos. Espan. sobre Plutarco (Fuengirola, 1988), Malaga, 1990), and the USA (references in the review ΠΛΟΥΤΑΡΧΟΣ = Journ. Intern. Plut. Society), Logan.

[188] *Illiniois Classical Studies*, 13. 2 (1988), ed. M. Marcovich.

with Nepos (Geiger); the principal themes and literary
techniques of his proems (Stadter); his *Philopoemen* and
Flamininus (Swain); certain aspects of his characterization
(Pelling); his portrayal of Nicias and Crassus as examples to
be avoided (Nikolaidis); and the narration of factual events
in the *Otho* and the greater ethical emphasis in the *Galba*
(Georgiadou).

The second volume[189] contains seven papers on the
Lives delivered in the Oxford meeting, some devoted to
technical biographical aspects, others to historical problems.
The former group includes Mossman's paper on the importance of great heroes such as Achilles and Alexander in the
background of *Pyrrhus*; Brenk on the assimilation of Cleopatra to Isis and Antony to Osiris in various scenes of the
Antony, especially in that of their death; and Stadter on
Plutarch's comparison of Lysander and Sulla, two heroes
who appear to have nothing in common but whose connection lies in the paradoxical combination of common negative
and positive traits.

Of the articles on historical issues, Pelling's concerns the
relationship between Plutarch and Thucydides; Bosworth's
is on Plutarch's arbitrary treatment of material in *Eumenes*,
which he claims was created as a counterpart to *Sertorius*;
Garcia Moreno finds in Sertorius cynic-stoical concepts
and similarities with Heracles and Odysseus. Another contribution is on the subject of late Republican characteristics in
Publicola (Affortunati–Scardigli).

The same criteria have prevailed in the choice of recent
contributions on Plutarch in interdisciplinary volumes,
where Plutarch is included with other writers on classical
history, literature, and philosophy. One example was the
volume *Past Perspectives*, which included Pelling's article
on Plutarch's presentation of Roman politics (1986*b*, reprinted here); another was *Philosophia Togata*, which contains another article (1989) by Pelling, where the author
concentrated on the civilizing effect of Hellenic philosophical education in the Roman *Lives*.

[189] *Plutarch and the Historical Tradition*, ed. P. A. Stadter (London, 1992).
Essays of the third intern. conference at Siena (1993) will be published at Naples
(D'Auria), ed. I. Gallo in 1994.

Recent volumes of *Aufstieg und Niedergang der Römischen Welt*, ii. 33. 1 (1987) and ii. 33. 6 (1992), have also included material on Plutarch. A section of the first concerns Plutarch and Platonism in the Roman Empire,[190] while volume ii. 33. 6 is entirely devoted to Plutarch's *Lives* and *Moralia*. In this volume less attention is given to *Quellenforschung* as precisely defined[191] than to problems of narrative and stylistic technique,[192] to the language used by Plutarch,[193] to the structure and composition of the *Lives*,[194] to the moral and educational purpose,[195] or to artistic aspects.[196]

Valgiglio's contribution is a good synthesis of *Lives* and *Moralia*.[197] The studies in the volume on *synkrisis*, on internal comparisons and on parallelism[198] confirm the prevalent literary interest of modern scholars: it is notable that in the *synkriseis*, which essentially belong to the rhetorical tradition, Plutarch only seldom adds historical data which are not present in the *Lives* themselves.

This renewed interest in Plutarch is also confirmed by the numerous editions and translations, accompanied by commentaries of the highest level, which have appeared or are to appear in many countries. It is that interest which justifies the reprint of the contributions included in this volume.

[190] Cf. the contributions of Ch. Froiderfort, J. P. Hershbell, F. E. Brenk, U. Bianchi, and D. Tsekourakis.
[191] But see the essays of Hamilton and Tritle (1992) and those on autopsy and contemporary testimony of Desideri (1992a) and Buckler (1992).
[192] Frazier (1992) and Yaginuma (1992). See also Podelcki–Duane (1992).
[193] Frazier (1992), Brenk (1992), Yaginuma (1992) and Harrison (1992).
[194] Larmour (1992), Podlecki–Duane (1992), Valgiglio (1992), Ingenkamp (1992a).
[195] Valgiglio (1992), Ingenkamp (1992b).
[196] Georgiadou (1992b).
[197] Thus he concludes (1992: 4051): 'L'aspetto estrinseo è quello della storia-biografia, quello intrinseco è quello della morale'.
[198] Larmour (1992), Desideri (1992b), Georgiadou (1992a), Ingenkamp (1992a), Brenk (1992). Previous contributions on the subject include Stadter (1975) and (1988), Pelling (1986a), Frazier (1987), Swain (1988), Larmour (1988), and now also Stadter (1992).

REFERENCES

* Asterisks indicate contributions reprinted in this volume.

Achleitner, V. (1982): 'Polybios's Philopoimen-Biographie als Quelle des Livius', *Hermes*, 110: 499–502.

Adcock, F. E. (1966): *Marcus Crassus Millionaire* (Cambridge).

Affortunati, M., and Scardigli, B. (1992): 'Aspects of the Life of Publicola', in P. A. Stadter (ed.), *Plutarch and the Historical Tradition* (London), 109–31.

Alfonsi, L. (1942/3): 'Sulla cronica di Cornelio Nepote', *Rendic. Ist. Lomb.* 76: 331–40.

——(1950): 'Nepote fonte di Cicerone', *Rh. Mus.* 93: 59–65.

Alonso Núñez, M. J. (1988): 'The Emergence of Universal historiography from the 4th to the 2nd Centuries B.C.', in H. Verdin, G. Schepens, E. de Keyser (eds.), *Purposes of History: Studies in Greek Historiography from the Fourth to the Second Century* (Intern. Coll., Leuven; Louvain), 173–92.

——(ed.) (1991): *Geschichtsbild und Geschichtsdenken im Altertum* (Wege der Forschung, 631; Darmstadt), 1–7 (introd.).

Altheim, F. (1961): 'Pyrrhos' Hypomnemata', in *Untersuchungen zur Römischen Geschichte* (Frankfurt), 90–6.

Ameling, W. (1985): 'Plutarch, Perikles 12–14', *Hist.* 34: 47–63.

Ampolo, C. (1990): 'Inventare una biografia: Note sulle biografia greca ed i suoi precedenti alla luce di un nuovo documento epigrafico', *Quad. St.* 73: 213–24.

Andrei, O. (1989): *Plutarco: Demetrio* (Milan).

Baldwin, B. (1979): 'Biography at Rome', in C. Deroux (ed.), *Stud. in Lat. Lit. and Roman Hist.* (Brussels), i. 100–18.

——(1983): *Suetonius* (Amsterdam).

Barigazzi, A. (1984): 'Plutarco e il corso futuro della storia', *Prometheus*, 10: 264–86.

Barrow, R. H. (1976): *Plutarch and his Times* (London).

Bates, R. L. (1983): 'Memoirs and the Perception of History in the Roman Republic' (Diss., Pennsylvania).

Bearzot, C. (1984): 'Focione φίλος τοῦ βασιλέως: Il tema dell'amicizia con Alessandro nella tradizione biografica focioniana', in M. Sordi (ed.), *Alessandro Magno tra storia e mito* (Milan), 75–90.

——(1985): *Focione tra storia e trasfigurazione ideale* (Milan).

Bergen, K. (1962): *Charakterbilder bei Tacitus und Plutarch* (Cologne).

Blamire, A. (1989): *Plutarch: Life of Kimon* (Class. Handbook Bull. Suppl. 56; Inst. of Class. Stud., London).

Bodin, L. (1917): 'Histoire et biographie: Phanias d'Erèse', *REG* 30: 117–57.

Bonamente, G. (1973/4; pub. 1979): 'La storiografia di Teopompo tra classicità e ellenismo', *Ann. Ist. Ital. per gli Studi Storici*, 4: 1–86.

Bosworth, A. B. (1992): 'History and Artifice in Plutarch's *Eumenes*', in P. A. Stadter (ed.), *Plutarch and the Historical Tradition* (London).

Bowersock, G. W. (1984): *Xenophon: Scripta Minora* (Loeb vol. vii; London).

Breebaart, A. B. (1971): 'Plutarch and the Political Development of Pericles', *Mnem.* 4th ser. 24: 260–72.

Brenk, F. (1992a): 'Plutarch's Life *Markos Antonios*: A Literary and Cultural Study', in *ANRW* ii. 33. 6: 4347–915.

——(1992b): 'Antony–Osiris, Cleopatra–Isis: The end of Plutarch's *Antony*', in P. A. Stadter, *Plutarch and the Historical Tradition* (London, New York), 159–82.

Bringmann, K. (1986): 'Geschichte und Psychologie bei Poseidonius', in *Aspects de la Philos. Hellén., Entr. Fond. Hardt*, 32: 29–66.

Brown, T. S. (1958): *Timaeus of Tauromenium* (Berkeley, Los Angeles).

Brugnoli, G. (1963): *Suetonius: de grammaticis et rhetoribus* (Leipzig).

——(1987a): 'Biografi', *Dizionario Autori Greci e Latini*, i. 287–304.

——(1987b): 'La rappresentazione della storia nella tradizione biografica romana', *Dial. Arch. e Fil. Class. Univ. Genova*, 37–69.

Bucher-Isler, B. (1972): *Norm und Individualität in den Biographien Plutarchs* (Noctes Romanae, 13; Bern, Stuttgart).

Buckler, J. (1992), 'Plutarch and Autopsy', *ANRW* ii. 33. 6: 4788–830.

Burelli Bergese, L. (1990): 'L'ultimo Pirro', in *XV Misc. Greca e Rom.* (Rome), 44–121.

Calabi, I. (1964): *Plutarchi Vita Aristidis* (Florence).

Canfora, L. (1987): *Plutarco: Nicia* (Milan).

Citti, A. (1983): 'Plutarco Nic. 1.5', in *Scritti in om. a P. Treves* (Padua), 99–110.

De Blois, L. (1992), 'The Perception of Politics in Plutarch's Roman *Lives*', *ANRW* ii. 33. 6: 4568–615.

Delbianco, P., and Scardigli, B. (1983): *Nicolao di Damasco, Vita di Augusto* (Florence).

Deremetz, A. (1990): 'Plutarque: Histoire de l'origine et genèse du récit', *REG* 103: 54–78.

Desideri, P. (1992*a*): 'La formazione delle coppie nelle *Vite plutarchee*', *ANRW* ii. 33. 6: 4470–86.

——(1992*b*): 'I documenti di Plutarco', *ANRW* ii. 33. 6: 4536–67.

De Voto, J. G. (1982): 'Agesilaos II and the Politics of Sparta 404–377 B.C.' (Diss., Chicago).

De Wet, B. X. (1981): 'Aspects of Plutarch's Portrayal of Pompey', *Acta Cl.* 24: 119–32.

——(1988): 'Plutarch's Use of the Poets', *Acta Class.* 31: 13–25.

——(1990): 'Contemporary Sources in Plutarch's Life of Antony', *Hermes*, 118: 80–90.

Dihle, A. (1956): *Studien zur griechischen Biographie* (Göttingen).

——(1986): *Die Entstehung der historischen Biographie* (Sitz. Ber. Akad. Heidelberg, 3).

Dionisotti, A. C. (1982): 'Nepos and the Generals', *JRS* 72: 35–49.

Douglas, A. E. (1966): *M. Tulli Ciceronis Brutus* (Oxford).

Dover, K. J. (1986): 'Ion of Chios', in J. Boardman and C. E. Vafopoulou-Richardson (eds.), *Chios* (Oxford), 27–37.

Due, B. (1989): *The Cyropaedia: Xenophon's Aims and Methods* (Aarhus).

Eck, B. (1990): 'Sur la vie de Ctésias', *REG* 103: 409–33.

Errington, R. M. (1969): *Philopoemen* (Oxford).

Evans, J. A. S. (1991): *Herodotus: Explorer of the Past* (Princeton, NJ).

Fehrle, R. (1983): *Cato Uticensis* (Darmstadt).

Ferrarese, P. (1975), 'Caratteri della tradizione antipericlea nella "Vita di Pericle" di Plutarco', *Contr. Ist. St. Ant.* 3: 21–30.

Flacelière, R. (1966): *Vies IV (Timoléon–Paul Emile)* (Paris).

——(1971): *Vies VI (Pyrrhos–Marius)* (Paris).

——(1972): *Vies VII (Nicias–Crassus)* (Paris).

——(1973): *Vies VIII (Agésilas–Pompée)* (Paris).

——(1976): *Vies XII (Démosthène–Cicéron)* (Paris).

——(1977): *Vies XIII (Démetrios–Antoine)* (Paris).

——(1979): *Vies XV (Artaxerxès–Aratus)* (Paris).

Flach, D. (1985): *Einführung in die römische Geschichtsschreibung* (Darmstadt).

——(1990): 'Review of Dihle, Entstehung', *Anz. Altert.* 43: 155–9.

Flower, M. A. (1986): 'Theopompus of Chius' (Diss. Brown University).

Fontana, M. J. (1958): 'Fortuna di Timoleonte: Rassegna delle fonti letterarie', *Kokalos*, 4: 6–14.

Franco, C. (1991): 'Trittico plutarcheo', *Prometheus*, 17: 124–31.

Frazier, F. (1987): 'A propos de la composition des couples dans les *Vies parallèles* de Plutarque', *RPh.* 61: 65–75.

——(1988a): 'Remarques à propos de l'usage des citations en matière de chronologie dans les Vies', *Illinois Classical Studies*, 13/2: 297–309.

——(1988b): 'A propos de la "philotimia" dans les Vies: Quelques jalons dans l'histoire d'une notion', *RPh.* 63: 109–27.

——(1992): 'Contribution à l'étude de la composition des Vies de Plutarque: L'élaboration des grandes scènes', *ANRW* ii. 33. 6: 4487–535.

Fritz, K. von (1943): 'Sallust and the Attitude of the Roman Nobility at the Time of the Wars against Jugurtha', *TAPA* 74: 134–68; repr. and trans. into German in V. Pöschl (ed.), *Sallust* (Wege der Forschung, 94: Darmstadt), 155–205.

——(1972): 'Die Bedeutung des Aristoteles für die Geschichtsschreibung', *Entr. Fond. Hardt*, 4: 85–145; repr. in F. P. Hagen (ed.), *Ethik und Politik des Aristoteles* (Wege der Forschung, 208; Darmstadt), 313–67.

——(1977): 'Poseidonius als Historiker', in *Historiographia Antiqua* (in hon. of W. Peremans) (Louvain), 163–93.

Frost, F. J. (1961): 'The Scholarship of Plutarch' (Diss. Univ. of California).

——(1980): *Plutarch's Themistocles: A Historical Commentary* (Princeton, NJ).

Fuhrmann, F. (1988): *Plutarque, Œuvres morales*, ii. *Apophtegmes de rois et de généraux—apophtegmes laconiens* (Paris).

Fuscagni, S. (1975): 'Callistene di Olinto e la Vita di Pelopida di Plutarco', *Contr. Ist. St. Ant.* 3: 31–55.

——(1989): *Plutarco: Cimone* (Milan).

Gabba, E. (1957): *Studi su Filarco: Le biografie plutarchee di Agide e Cleomene* (Pavia).

——(1982): 'La "storia di Roma archaica" di Dionigi d'Alicarnasso', *ANRW* ii. 30. 1: 799–816.

Gallo, I. (1967): 'La "Vita di Euripide" di Satiro e gli studi sulla biografia antica', *Par. Pass.* 22: 134–60.

——(1974): 'L'origine e lo sviluppo della biografia greca', *Stud. Urb.* 18: 173–86.

——(1990): 'Problemi vecchi e nuovi della biografia greca', *Quad. Liceo Class. Stellammare di Stabia*, 13: 9–27.

Garcia Moreno, L. A. (1992): 'Paradoxography and Political

Ideals in Plutarch's *Life of Sertorius*', in P. Stadter (ed.), *Plutarch and the Historical Tradition* (London, New York), 132–58.

García Valdés, M. (1981): 'Aproximación a la Vida de Cimon de Plutarco', in *Unidad y Pluralidad en el mundo antiguo* (Madrid), 317–24.

Garoufalias, P. (1979): *Pyrrhus, King of Epirus* (London).

Garzetti, A. (1987): *Plutarco: Crasso* (Milan).

Gehrke, H. J. (1976): *Phokion: Studien zur Erfassung seiner historischen Gestalt* (Zetemata, 6; Munich).

Geiger, J. (1979): 'Munatius Rufus and Thrasea Paetus on Cato the Younger', *Athen.* 57: 47–72.

*——(1981): 'Plutarch's *Parallel Lives*: The Choice of Heroes', *Hermes*, 109: 85–104.

——(1985): *Cornelius Nepos and Ancient Political Biography* (Historia Einzelschrift, 47; Wiesbaden).

——(1988): 'Nepos and Plutarch: From Latin to Greek Political Biography', *Illinois Classical Studies*, 13. 2: 245–56.

Gelzer, M. (1969): *Cicero: Ein biographischer Versuch* (Wiesbaden).

Gentili, B., and Cerri, G. (1978): 'L'idea di biografia nel pensiero greco', *Quad. Urb.* 18: 7–27.

Georgiadou, A. (1988): 'The *Lives of the Caesars* and Plutarch's Other *Lives*', *Illinois Classical Studies*, 13. 2: 349–56.

——(1992*a*): 'Bias and Character-Portrayal in the Lives of Pelopidas and Marcellus', *ANRW* ii. 33. 6: 4222–57.

——(1992*b*): Portraiture in the Lives of Plutarch, *ANRW* ii. 33. 6: 4616–23.

Ghilli, L. (1988): 'Spunti platonici ed altri echi in Plutarco, Vita di Fabio Massimo', *Ann. Fac. Lett. Siena*, 9: 237–40.

Gill, C. J. (1983): 'Character Development in Plutarch and Tacitus', *CQ*, NS 33: 469–87.

Gold, B. K. (1985): 'Pompey and Theophanes of Mytilene', *AJP* 106: 312–27.

Gomme, A. W. (1945, 1971): *A Historical Commentary on Thucydides* (Oxford).

Gossage, A. J. (1967): 'Plutarch', in T. A. Dorey (ed.), *Latin Biography* (London), 45–77.

Goukowsky, P. (1991): 'Die Alexanderhistoriker', in M. J. Alonso Núñez (ed.), *Geschichtsbild und Geschichtsdenken im Altertum* (Wege der Forschung, 631; Darmstadt), 136–65.

Guerrini, R. (1990): *Plutarco: Fabio Massimo* (Milan).

Hamilton, D. (1992): 'Plutarch's Life of Agesilaos', *ANRW* ii. 33. 6: 4200–21.

Hamilton, J. R. (1969): *Plutarch, Alexander: A Commentary* (Oxford).

Harrison, W. M. (1992): The Critical Trends in Scholarship on the Non-Philosophical Works in Plutarch's Moralia', *ANRW* ii. 33. 6: 4646–81.

Hillard, T. W. (1987): 'Plutarch's Late-Republican *Lives*: Between the Lines', *Antichthon*, 21: 19–48.

Hirsch, S. W. (1985): '1001 Iranian Nights: History and Fiction in Xenophon's Cyropaedia', in *The Greek Historians and History (Papers pres. to A. E. Raubitschek)* (Stanford), 67–73.

Homeyer, H. (1962): 'Zu den Anfängen der griechischen Biographie', *Phil.* 106: 76–86.

——(1963): 'Beobachtungen zu den hellenistischen Quellen der Plutarchviten', *Klio*, 41: 145–57.

Hornblower, J. (1981): *Hieronymus of Cardia* (Oxford).

Horsfall, N. (1989): *Cornelius Nepos: A Selection Including the Lives of Cato and Atticus* (Oxford).

Ingenkamp, H. G. (1992*a*): 'Plutarchs Leben der Gracchen: Eine Analyse', *ANRW* ii. 33. 6: 4298–346.

——(1992*b*): 'Plutarch und die konservative Verhaltensnorm', *ANRW* ii. 33. 6: 4624–45.

Jacoby, F. (1913): 'Hieronymus', in *R-E* 13: 1540–60.

Jenkinson, E. M. (1967): 'Nepos—An Introduction to Latin Biography', in T. A. Dorey (ed.), *Latin Biography* (London), 1–15.

——(1973): 'Genus scripturae leve: Cornelius Nepos and the Early History of Biography at Rome', *ANRW* i. 3: 703–19.

*Jones, C. P. (1966): 'Towards a Chronology of Plutarch's Works', *JRS* 56: 61–74.

——(1971): *Plutarch and Rome* (Oxford).

Kebric, R. B. (1977): *In the Shadow of Macedon: Duris of Samos* (Historia Einzelschrift, 29; Wiesbaden).

Kesisoglou, A. (1984): Πλουτάρχου Γάλβας (Athens).

König, F. W. (1977): *Die Persika des Ktesias von Knidos* (Graz).

Koster, A. J. (1937): *Plutarchi Vita Arati* (Leiden).

Krischer, T. (1982): 'Die Stellung der Biographie in der griechischen Literatur', *Hermes*, 110: 51–64.

La Bua, V. (1971): 'Prosseno e gli ΥΠΟΜΝΗΜΑΤΑ ΠΥΡΡΟΥ', in *III Miscell. Greca e Romana*, 1–61.

Lacy, P. de (1952): 'Biography and Tragedy in Plutarch', *AJP* 73: 159–71.

Lamberton, R. (1988): 'Plutarch, Hesiod and the Mouseia of Thespiai', *Illinois Classical Studies*, 13. 2: 491–504.

La Penna, A. (1987): *Plutarco: Cesare* (Milan).

Larmour, D. H. J. (1988): 'Plutarch's Compositional Methods in the *Theseus* and *Romulus*', TAPA 118: 361–75.

——(1992): 'Making Parallels: *Synkrisis* and Plutarch's *Themistocles and Camillus*, *ANRW* ii. 33. 6: 4154–200.

Lavery, G. B. (1971): 'Cicero's philarchia and Marius', *G&R* 18: 133–42.

Lehmann, G. A. (1969): 'Die Endphase des Perseuskrieges im Augenzeugen bericht des P. Cornelius Nasica', *Festschr. F. Altheim* (Münster) i. 387–412.

Lendle, O. (1967): 'Ciceros ὑπόμνημα περὶ τῆς ὑπατείας', *Hermes*, 95: 90–109.

Leo, Fr. (1881, repr. 1965): *Die griechisch-römische Biographie nach ihrer literarischen Form* (Leipzig).

Lévêque, P. (1957): *Pyrrhus* (Paris).

Levi, M. A. (1987): 'Plutarco', in *Diz. Autori Greci e Latini*, 1727–34.

Lewis, R. G. (1966): 'Pompeius' Freedman Biographer: Suetonius, *de gramm. et rhet.* 27', *CR*, NS 16: 271–3.

——(1991): 'Sulla's Autobiography: Scope and Economy', *Athen.* 79: 509–19.

——(1993): 'Imperial Autobiography: Augustus to Hadrian', *ANRW* ii. 34. 1: 629–706.

McCaslin, D. E. (1989): 'Polybius, Phylarchus and the Mantineian Tragedy of 223 B.C.', *Archaiognosia* (Athens, Dept. of Class. Stud.), 4, 1985/6 (1989), 77–102.

Magnino, D. (1963): *Plutarchi Vita Ciceronis* (Florence).

Malitz, J. (1983): *Die Historien des Poseidonius* (Zetemata, 79; Munich).

Marasco, G. (1978): 'Aristotele come fonte di Plutarco nelle biografie di Agide e Cleomene', *Athen.* 56: 170–81.

——(1981*a*): *Commento alle biografie plutarchee di Agide e Cleomene*, i (Rome).

——(1981*b*): 'Introduzione alla biografia plutarchea di Demetrio, I–II', *Sileno*, 7: 35–70.

——(1983): 'Introduzione alla biografia plutarchea di Demetrio, III', *Sileno*, 9: 35–54.

——(1988): 'Ctesia, Dinone, Eraclide di Cuma e le origini della storiografia "tragica"', *SIFC* III. 6: 48–67.

Marshall, A. (1993), 'Atticus and the genealogies', Latomus 52: 307–15.

Martin, H. (1961): 'The Character of Plutarch's Themistocles', *TAPA* 92: 326–39.

Mastrocinque, A. (1983), 'La liberazione di Tebe (379 A.C.) e le origini della storiografia tragica', in *Omaggio a P. Treves* (Padua), 237–47.

Mazzarino, S. (1966, repr. 1968): *Il pensiero storico classico* (Bari), i–iii.

Meinhardt, E. (1957): *Perikles bei Plutarch* (Frankfurt).

Meissner, B. (1993): 'Historiker zwischen Polis und Königshof: Studien zur Stellung der Geschichtsschreiber in der griechischen Gesellschaft in spätklass. u. frühhellenist. Zeit', *Hypomnemata*, 99 (Göttingen).

Meister, K. (1967): *Die sizilische Geschichte bei Diodor von den Anfängen bis zum Tod des Agathokles* (Diss. Munich).

—— (1975): *Historische Kritik bei Polybios* (Wiesbaden).

—— (1988): 'Autobiographische Literatur und Memoiren (Hypomnemata)—*FGrHist* 227–238', in H. Verdin, G. Schepens, E. de Keyser (eds.), *Purposes of History: Studies in Greek Historiography from the Fourth to the Second Century* (Intern. Coll., Leuven; Louvain), 83–9.

—— (1989): *Die griechische Geschichtsschreibung* (Stuttgart, Berlin).

Mejer, J. (1978): *Diogenes Laertius and his Hellenistic Background* (Hermes Einzelschr. 40; Stuttgart).

Millar, F. (1988): 'Cornelius Nepos "Atticus" and the Roman Revolution', *G&R* 35: 40–55.

Misch, G. (1907): *Geschichte der Autobiographie*, i (Leipzig).

Moggi, M. (1987): 'Storiografi greci minori', in *Diz. Autori Greci e Latini*, iii. 2075–109.

Moles, J. L. (1988): *Plutarch: Cicero* (Warminster).

—— (1989): review of Geiger (1985), *CR* 39: 229–33.

Momigliano, A. X. (1971): *The Development of Greek Biography* (Harvard).

—— (1981): 'Die Geschichtsschreibung', in *Neues Handbuch der Literaturwissenschaft*, ii (Wiesbaden), 305–36.

Mora, F. (1991): 'L'immagine dell'uomo politico romano di tarda età repubblicana nelle *Vite* di Plutarco', *Contr. Ist. St. Ant.* 17: 169–94.

Mossé, F. (1969): *La Tyrannie dans la Grèce antique* (Paris).

*Mossman, J. M. (1988): 'Tragedy and Epic in Plutarch's *Alexander*', *JHS* 108: 83–93.

—— (1992): 'Plutarch, Pyrrhus, and Alexander', in P. A. Stadter (ed.), *Plutarch and the Historical Tradition* (London, New York), 90–108.

Most, G. W. (1989): 'The Stranger's Stratagem: Self-Disclosure and Self-Sufficiency in Greek Culture', *JHS* 109: 114–33.

Muccioli, F. (1990): 'Osservazioni sull' uso di Timonide nella "Vita di Dione" di Plutarco', *Anc. Soc.* 21: 167–88.

Mugelli, B. (1986): 'Ritratto di Fabio Massimo (Plut. Fab. 1. 5–7) e spunti platonici (Resp. 503c–d, 537d)', *Ann. Fac. Lett. Siena*, 7: 225–9.

——(1991): 'Gli apophthegmata di Plutarco: L'esempio della Vita di Cicerone', *Ann. Fac. Lett. Siena*, 12: 293–9.

Nickel, D. (1991): 'Isokrates und die Geschichtsschreibung des 4. Jahrhunderts v. Chr.', *Phil.* 135: 233–9.

Nicolaidis, A. G. (1982–4, pub. 1987): 'Purpose of Plutarch's Lives and the Various Theories about it', *Archaiognosia* (Athens, Dept. of Class. Stud.), 3: 93–114.

——(1986): 'Ἑλληνικὸς-βαρβαρικός: Plutarch and Greek and Barbarian Characteristics', *WS* 99: 229–44.

——(1988): 'Is Plutarch Fair to Nicias?', *Ill. Class. Stud.* 13. 2: 319–33.

Noè, E. (1979): 'Ricerche su Dionigi d'Alicarnasso: La prima stasis a Roma e l'episodio di Coriolano', in E. Gabba (ed.), *Ricerche di storiografia greca di età romana* (Pisa), 21–116.

Olivieri Sangiacomo, L. (1954): *Sallustio* (Florence).

Orsi, D. (1979/80): 'Tracce di tendenza anticirea (Plutarco, Vita di Artaserse, cap. 1–19)', *Sileno*, 5–6: 113–46.

——(1987a): *Le Vite di Arato e Artaserse* (Milan).

——(1987b): 'Citazioni dalle Memorie di Arato in Plutarco', *Gerion*, 5: 57–68.

——(1990): 'Il tema antitirannico nella "Vita di Arato" plutarchea', *Graz. Beitr.* 17: 147–62.

——(1991): *L'alleanza acheo-macedone: Studi su Polibio I* (Bari).

Paladini, M. L. (1956): 'La tradizione dei Sette Savi e la "Vita di Solone" di Plutarco', *REG* 49: 377–411.

Pauw, D. A. (1980): 'Impersonal Expressions and Unidentified Spokesmen in Greek and Roman Historiography and Biography', *Acta Class.* 23: 83–95.

Pearson, L. (1987): *The Greek Historians of the West* (Atlanta).

Pédech, P. (1951): 'Polybe et l'Éloge des Philopoemen', *REG* 64: 82–103; repr. and trans. into German in K. Stiewe and N. Holzberg (eds.), *Polybios* (*Wege der Forschung*, 347; Darmstadt 1982), 140–61.

——(1977): 'Les Historiens d'Alexandre', in *Historiographia antiqua* (in hon. of W. Peremans) (Louvain), 119–138.

——(1984): *Historiens compagnons d'Alexandre* (Paris).

——(1989): *Trois historiens méconnus: Théopompe, Duris, Phylarque* (Paris).

*Pelling, C. B. R. (1979): 'Plutarch's Method of Work in the Roman *Lives*', *JHS* 99: 74–96.

*——(1980): 'Plutarch's Adaptation of his Source-Material, *JHS* 100: 127–41.

——(1985): 'Plutarch and Catiline', *Hermes*, 113: 311–29.

——(1986a): 'Synkrisis in Plutarch's *Lives*', in *Miscellanea Plutarchea, Quad. Giorn. Fil. Ferr.* 8: 83–96.

*——(1986b): 'Plutarch and Roman Politics', in I. S. Moxon, J. Smart, A. Woodman (eds.), *Past Perspectives: Studies in Greek and Roman Historical Writing*, Conf. in Leeds, 6–8 Apr. 1983 (Cambridge), 159–87.

——(1988a): *Plutarch's Life of Antony* (Cambridge).

——(1988b): 'Aspects of Plutarch's Characterisation', *Illinois Classical Studies*, 13/2: 257–74.

——(1989): 'Plutarch: Roman Heroes and Greek Culture', in M. Griffin and J. Barnes (eds.), *Philosophia Togata* (Oxford), 199–232.

——(1990): 'Truth and Fiction in Plutarch's *Lives*', in D. A. Russell (ed.), *Antonine Literature* (Oxford), 19–52.

——(1992): 'Plutarch and Thucydides', in P. A. Stadter (ed.), *Plutarch and the Historical Tradition* (London), 10–40.

Pérez Jiménez, A. (1973): 'Actitudes del hombre de frente a la Tyche en las Vidas paralelas de Plutarco', *Bol. Inst. Helen.* 7: 101–10.

Pettine, E. (1988): *Plutarco: Detti di re e di condottieri (Regum et imperatorum apophthegmata)* Introd., trad. e note (Salerno).

Piccirilli, L. (1977): *Plutarco: La Vita di Solone* (Milan).

——(1980): 'Cronologia alle fonti delle *Vitae Lycurgi et Numae* di Plutarco', in *Studi in on. di E. Manni*, V (Roma), 175–64.

——(1990): 'Nicia in Filisto e in Timeo', *RFC* 118: 385–90.

Podlecki, A. J. (1988): 'Plutarch and Athens', *Illinois Classical Studies*, 13. 2: 231–43.

——and Duane, S. (1992): 'A Survey of Work on Plutarch's Greek Lives, 1951–1988', *ANRW* ii. 33. 6: 4053–127.

Polman, G. H. (1974): 'Chronological Biography and "Akme" in Plutarch', *CPh.* 70: 169–77.

Rabe, I. (1964): *Quellenkritische Untersuchungen zu Plutarchs Alexanderbiographie* (Hamburg).

Ramage, E. S. (1991): 'Sulla's Propaganda', *Klio*, 73: 93–121.

Ramon, V. (1994): 'El "Cato" de Cornelio Nepote y los origines de la biografia politica grecolatina'. *Quad. Stor.* 93: 279–86.

Regenbogen, O. (1940): 'Theophrastos', *R-E* Suppl. 7: 1354–562.

Riposati, B. (1976): 'M. Terenzio Varrone: L'uomo e lo scrittore', *Atti Congr. Studi Varron.* (Rieti, 1974), i. 59–89.

Rizzo, F. (1963): *Le fonti per la storia delle conquiste pompeiane della Siria* (Suppl. *Kokalos*; Palermo).

Romilly, J. De (1988): 'Rencontres avec Plutarque', *Illinois Classical Studies*, 13. 2: 219–29.

*Russell, D. A. (1963): 'Plutarch's *Life* of Coriolanus', *JRS* 53: 21–8.

*——(1966a): 'On Reading Plutarch's *Lives*', *G&R* 16: 139–54.

*——(1966b): 'Plutarch, *Alcibiades* 1–16', *PCPA* 12: 37–47.

——(1973): *Plutarch* (London).

Sacks, K. S. (1983): 'Historiography in the Rhetorical Works of Dionysius of Halicarnassus', *Athen.* 61: 65–87.

Samutkina, L. A. (1984): 'Plutarque sur la comédie ancienne' (Russ.), *Pytann. Klass. Fil. (Lvov)*, 30: 104–11.

Sanders, L. J. (1979/80): 'Dionysios I and the Validity of the Hostile Tradition', *Script. Isr.* 5: 64–84.

——(1992): 'What did Timaeus think of Dion?', *Herm.* 120: 205–215.

Sansone, D. (1989): *Plutarch: Lives of Aristides and Cato* (Warminster).

Scardigli, B. (1977): 'Echi di attegiamenti pro e contro Mario in Plutarco', *Crit. St.* 14: 185–253.

——(1979): *Die Römerbiographien Plutarchs* (Munich).

——(1989): *Plutarco: Lucullo* (Milan).

Schepens, G. (1977): 'Historiographical Problems in Ephorus', in *Historiographia antiqua* (in hon. of W. Peremans) (Louvain), 95–118.

Schneeweiss, G. (1979): 'History and Philosophy in Plutarch', *Arktouros. Hell. Stud. pres. to B. M. W. Knox* (Berlin, New York), 376–82.

——(1985): 'Gegenstand und Absicht in den Biographien Plutarchs', in W. Suerbaum (ed.), *Festschr. F. Eckermann* (Munich), 147–62.

Schreiner, J. H. (1976): 'Anti-Thucydidean Studies in the Pentecontaetia', *Symb. Osl.* 52: 19–38.

Schuller, W. (1991): 'Die griechische Geschichtsschreibung der klassischen Zeit', in M. J. Alonso Núñez (ed.), *Geschichtsbild und Geschichtsdenken im Altertum* (Wege der Forschung 631; Darmstadt), 90–112.

Shrimpton, G. (1977): 'Theopompus' Treatment of Philip in the *Philippica*', *Phoenix*, 31: 123–44.

——(1991): *Theopompus the Historian* (Quebec).

Smith, R. E. (1940): 'Plutarch's Biographical Sources in the Roman Lives', *CQ* 34: 1–10.

Sordi, M. (1978): 'La tradizione storiografica su Tiberio Sempronio Gracco e la propaganda contemporanea', in *VI Misc. Greca e Romana* 290–330.

—— (1983): *La Sicilia dal 368 al 237* (Rome).

—— (1988): 'Filisto e la propaganda dionisiana', in H. Verdin, G. Schepens, E. de Keyser (eds.), *Purposes of History: Studies in Greek Historiography from the Fourth to the Second Century* (Intern. Coll. Leuven; Louvain), 159–71.

—— (1989): 'Pelopida da Tegira a Leuttra', in H. Beister and J. Buckler (eds.), *BOIOTIKA: Vortr. z. 5. intern. Böotien-Kolloquium für S. Lauffer 1986* (Munich), 123–30.

Stadter, P. A. (1965): *Plutarch's Historical Methods: An Analysis of the Mulierum Virtutes* (Cambridge, Mass.).

*—— (1975): 'Plutarch's Comparison of Pericles and Fabius Maximus', *GRBS* 16: 77–85.

—— (1987): 'The Rhetoric of Plutarch's Pericles', *Anc. Soc.* 18: 251–69.

—— (1988): 'The Proems of Plutarch's *Lives*', *Illinois Classical Studies*, 13. 2: 275–95.

—— (1989): *A Commentary on Plutarch's Pericles* (Chapel Hill, NC, London).

—— (1990): *Plutarco: Pericle* (Milan).

—— (1992): 'Paradoxical Paradigms: Lysander and Sulla', in P. A. Stadter (ed.), *Plutarch and the Historical Tradition* (London), 41–55.

Steidle, W. (1951): *Sueton und die antike Biographie* (Zetemata, 1; Munich).

—— (1990): 'Zu Plutarchs Biographien des Cicero und Pompeius', *Graz. Beitr.* 17: 163–86.

Steinhausen, J. (1910): *ΚΩΜΩΙΔΟΥΜΕΝΟΙ: De grammaticorum veterum studiis ad homines in comedia attica irrisos pertinentibus* (Bonn).

Strasburger, H. (1965): 'Poseidonius über die Römerherrschaft' (German version from 'Poseidonius on problems of the Roman Empire' JRS 55, 1965), in *Studien zur alten Gesch.* ii (1982), 920–45.

—— (1966): 'Die Wesensbestimmung der Geschichte durch die antike Geschichtsschreibung', *Sitz. Ber. Wiss. Gesellsch. Frankfurt*, 1–85; repr. in *Studien zur alten Gesch.* ii (1982), 963–1016.

—— (1986): 'Zu den Anfängen der griechischen Memoirenkunst', in *Forma et Subtilitas* (Festschrift W. Schöne) (Berlin), 1–7.

44   *Barbara Scardigli*

Stuart, D. R. (1928): *Epochs of Greek and Roman Biography* (Berkeley).
Swain, S. (1988): 'Plutarch's Philopoemen and Flamininus', *Illinois Classical Stud.* 13. 2: 335–48.
Swain, S. [*1989a*]: 'Plutarch's Aemilius and Timoleon', *Hist.* 39: 314–34.
——(1989*b*): 'Character Change in Plutarch', *Phoenix*, 43: 62–8.
——(1989*c*): 'Plutarch: Chance, Providence, and History', *AJP* 110: 272–302.
——(1990*a*): 'Plutarch's Lives of Cicero, Cato, and Brutus', *Hermes*, 118: 192–203.
*——(1990*b*): 'Hellenic Culture and the Roman Heroes of Plutarch', *JHS* 110: 126–45.
Talbert, R. J. A. (1974): *Timoleon and the Revival of Greek Sicily, 344–316 B.C.* (Cambridge).
Tatum, J. (1989): *Xenophon's Imperial Fictions: On 'The Education of Cyrus'* (Princeton, NJ).
Theander, C. (1951): *Plutarch und die Geschichte* (Lund).
Theunissen, W. P. (1935): *Ploutarchos' Leven van Aratos* (Nijmegen).
Toneatto, L. (1985): 'Lotta politica e assetto sociale a Sparta dopo la caduta di Cleomene III', *Index*, 180–248.
Tornea, L. (1988): *Duride di Samos: La maschera scenica nella storiografia ellenistica* (Salerno).
Treggiari, S. (1969), 'Pompeius' Freedman Biographer Again', *CR*, NS 19: 261–6.
Tritle, L. A. (1988): *Phocion the Good* (London, New York, Sydney).
——(1992): 'Plutarch's Life of Phocion: An Analysis and Critical Report', *ANRW* ii. 33. 6: 4258–97.
Valgiglio, E. (1976): 'Varrone in Plutarco', *Atti Congr. Studi Varron.* (Rieti, 1974), ii. 471–95.
——(1982): 'Alcuni aspetti di Cicerone come fonte di Plutarco', in *Studi in onore di Aristide Colonna* (Perugia), 283–99.
——(1987*a*): 'ἱστορία e βίος in Plutarco', *Orpheus*, 8: 50–70.
——(1987*b*): 'Plutarco', in *Diz. Aut. Greci e Latini*, 1734–55.
——(1992): 'Dagli *Ethica* ai *Bioi*', *ANRW* ii. 33. 6: 3998–4051.
Valvo, A. (1983): 'M. Valerio Messala Corvino negli studi più recenti', *ANRW* ii. 30. 3 (Berlin), 1663–80.
Vandiver, E. (1990): *Heroes in Herodotus: An Interaction of Myth and History* (Studien z. klass. Phil. 56; Frankfurt, Bern).
Vercruysse, M. (1988): 'A la recherche du mensonge et de la vérité: La Fonction des passages méthodologiques chez Polybe',

in H. Verdin, G. Schepens, E. de Keyser (eds.), *Purposes of History: Studies in Greek Historiography from the Fourth to the Second Century* (Intern. Coll. Leuven; Louvain), 17–38.

Walbank, F. W. (1938): 'Philippos Tragodoumenos', *JHS* 58: 55–68; repr. and trans. into German in K. Stiewe and N. Holzberg (eds.), *Polybios* (Wege der Forschung 347; Darmstadt, 1982), 1–23.

—— (1957): *A Commentary on Polybius*, i (Oxford).

—— (1977): 'Polybius' Last Ten Books' in *Historiographia antiqua* (in hon. of W. Peremans) (Louvain), 139–62.

—— (1988): 'Profit or Amusement: Some Thoughts on the Motives of Hellenistic Historians', in H. Verdin, G. Schepens, E. de Keyser (eds.), *Purposes of History: Studies in Greek Historiography from the Fourth to the Second Century* (Intern. Coll. Leuven; Louvain), 253–66.

Wallace-Hadrill, A. (1983): *Suetonius* (London).

Walsh, J. J. (1992): 'Syzygy, Theme and History: A Study in Plutarch's *Philopoemen* and *Flamininus*', *Phil.* 136: 208–33.

Wardman, A. E. (1955), 'Plutarch and Alexander', *CQ*, NS 5: 96–107.

—— (1971), 'Plutarch's Methods in the *Lives*', *CQ*, NS 21: 254–61.

—— (1974): *Plutarch's Lives* (London).

Wehrli, F. (1947): 'Die Geschichtsschreibung im Lichte der antiken Theorie', in *Eumusia* (in hon. of E. Howald), 54–71.

—— (1973): 'Gnome, Anekdote, und Biographie', *Mus. Helv.* 30: 193–208.

—— (1968): 'Demetrios von Phaleron', in *Die Schule des Aristoteles*, iv (Basel, Stuttgart).

Weissenberger, B. (1895): *Die Sprache Plutarchs von Chaironea und die pseudoplutarchischen Schriften* (Würzburg).

West, M. L. (1972): *Iambi et elegi graeci* (Oxford), ii.

Westlake, H. D. (1938): 'The Sources of Plutarch's Timoleon', *CQ* 32: 65–74.

—— (1953/4): 'The Sicilian Books of Theopompus' *Philippica*', *Hist.* 2: 288–307.

—— (1968): *Individuals in Thucydides* (Cambridge).

—— (1969): *Essays on the Greek Historians and Greek History* (New York, Manchester).

*Wilamowitz-Moellendorf, U. von (1926): 'Plutarch als Biograph', in *Reden und Vorträge*, 2. 4 (Berlin), 247–79.

Wilkins, A. S. (1892, repr. 1962): *Ciceronis de oratore libri tres* (Oxford).

Will, W. (1991): 'Die griechische Geschichtsschreibung des 4.

Jahrhunderts', in M. J. Alonso Núñez (ed.), *Geschichtsbild und Geschichtsdenken im Altertum* (Wege der Forschung, 631; Darmstadt), 113–35.

Wirth, G. (1988): 'Nearch, Alexander und die Diadochen, Spekulationen über einen Zusammenhang', *Tyche*, 3: 241–59.

Yaginuma, S. (1992): 'Plutarch's Language and Style', *ANRW* ii. 33. 6: 4726–42.

Zecchini, G. (1978): *Cassio Dione e la guerra gallica di Cesare* (Milan).

——(1980): 'La morte di Catone e l'opposizione intellettuale a Cesare e Augusto', *Athen.* 58: 39–56.

Zegers, N. (1959): *Wesen und Ursprung der tragischen Geschichtsschreibung* (Diss. Cologne).

Ziegler, K. (1952): 'Plutarchos', *R-E* 21: 635–962; repr. as 'Plutarchos von Chaironea' (Stuttgart, 1964).

Zoepffel, R. (1965): *Untersuchungen zum Geschichtswerk des Philistos von Syrakus* (Frankfurt).

——(1975): 'Historia und Geschichte bei Aristoteles', *SB Heidelb. Akad. Phil.-hist. Kl.* 1–7.

——1993: 'Le fonti scritte su Dionigi I di Siracusa', in *La monetazione dell'eta dionigiana*, Atti VIII Conv. del centro intern. di studi di numismatica, Naples 1983, 39–63.

I

Plutarch as Biographer

U. VON WILAMOWITZ-MOELLENDORF

From the fourteenth to the eighteenth century Plutarch attracted more readers than any other Greek author,[1] and was therefore the most influential outside the circles of scholarship.[2] Of course he was read in translation: even before the introduction of printing, Latin translations of several biographies circulated in Italy; subsequently the Greek text was printed beside the translation, but many people will still only have read the Latin. But the most important step was the French translation by Amyot, later translated into other languages. It was only through this translation that Shakespeare was able to come to know the material for his Roman tragedies, and only through this that Frederick the Great could read Plutarch. At that time Plutarch was regarded not only as a biographer but even more as a popular moral philosopher:[3] that is how he was viewed, and praised, by the grateful Montaigne;[4] and

[1] Before the war I had already written a preface for a new translation of a selection of biographies. This preface was even printed, but the project was not completed. This essay will include material which was composed then, but everything has been completely reconsidered and rewritten.

[2] This has been shown in the greatest scholarly detail by R. Hirzel, *Plutarch* (1912). That is the merit of the book.

[3] Still, it is indicative that no other Plutarchian book was more often printed and read than that on the upbringing of children, which is not authentic and is a very minor piece of writing, despite containing some valuable traditional ideas. That shows that people were reading Plutarch as an educator. Readers who still think Plutarch capable of composing that text expose the level of their own understanding of Plutarch. With so prolific and wide-ranging a writer, it comes about that many people either allow themselves a general judgement based on only one side of his production, or believe him capable of anything, failing to sense the unity of his personality that so clearly impresses itself on all his writings, despite their number and range.

[4] 'Je me puys malaisément desfayre de Plutarque. Il est si universel et si plein, qu'à toutes occasions et quelque sujet extravagant que vous ayez prins, il s'ingère à votre besogne et vous tend une main libérale et inespuisable de richesses et d'enbellisements.'

Goethe's knowledge of Plutarch, whom he had read out to himself for many years up to his death, surely went beyond the biographies.[5] But the other half of the Plutarchian *œuvre* inevitably fell into oblivion, not only because the time produced completely new philosophical systems, but also because interest in antiquity finally found its way to Plato and Aristotle. At the same time the growth of historical criticism explored the deficiencies of Plutarch as a historian, and the brilliance of his own reputation faded along with that of many of his heroes. Already by that time he would only rarely find a reader like Goethe, and now he will never again find such an amateur. Such criticism was necessary, and it was inevitable that unfairly disparaging judgements should be expressed: superior minds, such as Niebuhr and Humboldt, were rarely heeded by the many. But scholarship finally heals the wounds which it has to inflict, and where there is gold, it only gains by the removal of dross. To form a just view of a man and his work, one first has to know what kind of man he was; but then one also has to know what he aimed for, and finally the conditions of his time—what sort of man he *could* be, what he could hope for, what he could achieve. This is what I want to consider briefly, but only in so far as it is necessary for Plutarch the biographer.

Plutarch came from an old-established family of the little municipal town Chaeronea in Boeotia. He remained loyal to his native town, and this is itself a very important characteristic of the man. There stood, and now stands re-erected, the monumental lion to commemorate the battle which made Philip of Macedon ruler of all Greece. Many battles were decided at this spot and in the region of nearby Orchomenus, shining in the splendour of its mythical past: the bloodiest were those between Sulla and the generals of Mithridates. In those days the region had been completely devastated, and then the civil wars had brought repeated miseries; Plutarch's family had suffered along with the rest. But under the protection of the Empire the industry and competence of Plutarch's grandfather and father had re-

---

[5] The beautiful poem 'Dauer im Wechsel' draws its Heraclitean ideas from Plutarch, *On the E at Delphi* 392e.

stored the family's prosperity. It seems that this was the
only local family which stood out for its education and was
widely respected. These were the youthful memories and
these the surroundings which formed the life and ideas of
Plutarch. His heart beats for ancient Hellas, for ancient
Boeotia and its glory, but the peace which the Roman
Empire secured made him acquiesce in the dependence on
Roman officials. He is a loyal subject, though he does not
foster any illusions about the loss of freedom. He demands
active participation in the self-administration of the Greek
community, even if one always has to be prepared for the
possibility that a short rescript of the proconsul might
frustrate all one's efforts.[6]

Boeotia offered no possibilities for higher education, and
so Plutarch's father, who himself had no such education
and was more concerned with good horses than with any
scholarly discipline, sent his sons to Athens. He may well
have been interested only in giving them the kind of education which was necessary for a position in the world, and in
particular for interacting with Roman officials. This education was rhetorical, the complete mastering of language for
speaking and writing, and whatever 'general education' was
necessary for those purposes. Here too Plutarch learnt everything that was needed: to judge from the few pieces of this
kind which we possess, he could even have been an orator.
But that was not enough to satisfy him. He entered the
Academy, the school of Philosophy, where among other
things a compulsory grounding in Mathematics would teach
one to think properly. Admittedly, he did not find eminent
teachers; but it was precisely for his teaching in Mathematics that he expresses his gratitude to the head of the school,
Ammonius (cf. *On the E at Delphi* 391e); and the most
important effect of this teaching was to introduce him to
other philosophical systems, particularly Plato's. Philosophy never relinquished its hold on him, and he never lost
contact with his school; and yet he did not want to become
a professor, though he could certainly have risen to become
head of the school. Of course he remained an Academic,

---

[6] *Precepts on public life* 824e: the work is full of similar admonitions.

but an open-minded one: in scientific matters he follows the Peripatetics, and, though he clearly dislikes Epicurus and is wholly put off by the blustering of the Cynics, he is still very close to the Stoa of Posidonius.

During Plutarch's years as a student fell Nero's visit to Greece—his plunderings of works of art, his fear as a matricide of the god of Delphi, but also the enormous comedy of the liberation of Greece. Still, this was taken seriously by the Greeks themselves, and they strongly disliked the Flavians when they put an end to this hoax; this dislike too is obvious in Plutarch's writings. Apart from lesser pieces, his literary production seems to fall into the period after Domitian's reign. That emperor's overthrow and *damnatio memoriae* was partly caused by the oppression of free speech and by the persecution of philosophers. What Tacitus in his *Agricola* says about Rome holds true for the Empire as a whole.

Plutarch's father may well have been very unhappy about the scientific and scholarly inclinations of his son. He tried to involve him in affairs, he sent him off to the proconsul at Corinth and then even to Rome, for a longer stay; and there was probably more than one such journey,[7] for he saw Ravenna and Bedriacum as part of the entourage of some Roman acquaintances (*Otho* 14. 2, *Mar.* 2. 1). It seems that his father already had some valuable connections in Rome, and himself gained the citizenship through Mestrius Florus, a close friend of Vespasian.[8] Plutarch held this name, but we know this only from an inscription (*SIG*³ 829a = E. M. Smallwood, *Documents Illustrating the Principates of Nerva, Trajan, and Hadrian* 487); he himself never mentions his citizenship, and nowhere in literature is he called anything but Plutarch. This is no mere chance. He remained a Greek, and he was proud to appear a Greek—precisely because he had so many connections with Romans, either inherited or acquired by himself, which he cultivated all his

[7] *Table talk* 727b makes a second visit very probable, and this is confirmed by the fact that many people made contact with him from philosophical interest (*Dem.* 2). Anyway, this will have happened under the Flavians.

[8] Plutarch very frequently mentions a Mestrius Florus who is a frequent visitor at his house and seems to live in Greece. This is hardly possible for the friend of Vespasian; perhaps it was a son.

life. Of course his stay at Rome was of crucial importance
for his knowledge of the world and the people, for his
political attitude, and his historical judgement. In contrast,
one would never have suspected that he had seen Alexandria
as well, but for the fact that he himself once says so (*Table
talk* 678c). For he has no clear idea of anything Egyptian,
and no hint of any interest in Alexandria, the Ptolemies,
and the scholars of the Mouseion.[9]

It is not likely that he undertook any extended travels
later in life, since he married early and settled down in his
home town. This marriage seems to have been very important to him; as an old man (when he was presumably
already a widower) he mentions in a dialogue, in words
spoken by his son, that the couple came together despite
the open enmity of their parents (*Erotikos* 749b). This
entire dialogue is written to support the case of nature
against the doctrine of the philosophers, which adhered to
traditional practice; the dialogue argues that Eros too can
lead to marriage and that this is right, that the wife too may
fall in love, and may even take the initiative in suggesting
marriage. It need not follow that Timoxena really behaved
in this way when she married Plutarch. Still, they married
for love and against the wishes of their parents, for immediately after the wedding they went on a pilgrimage to Eros at
Thespiae to give him thanks.

It was a very successful marriage with many children,
supported by a depth of mutual feeling. The husband
expresses this in his published writings, a step for which
there is hardly any parallel in antiquity. No one will fail to
be moved by the letter which he addressed to his wife when
she had written to him of the death of one of the small

---

[9] It is true that Plutarch is one of the most important sources for Egyptian
religion and theology, but all this is taken from Greek books: nothing suggests
autopsy. A collection of Alexandrian proverbs is extant under his name, but so
much is extant under his name, and only one who understands nothing about
Plutarch will be taken in. Once, at *Erotikos* 755e, someone tells a story which is
truly a traveller's tale; but that does not mean that it is Plutarch's own experience.
The story is such a good one that I tell it here. Two neighbours, apparently in
Alexandria, are quarrelling about a snake which is moving along the ground
between the two houses. Each claims it is the 'agathos daemon' of his house. This
reflects the contemporary superstition which also posited a 'good daemon' of
Alexandria in the form of a snake.

children, and when he was too far away to return for the
funeral (*Consolation to his wife* 608a–12a). Of course one
must remember that this is only formally a private letter.[10]
This marriage against the parents' wishes must have dis-
turbed the harmony of the family for a while, and Plutarch's
works suggest some degree of tension between him and his
father; his mother is not mentioned; only for his grandfather
can the deepest affection be found, and there are continuing
friendly contacts with his two brothers. The principal point
is that on his marriage he became firmly settled in his home
town, and abandoned any possibility of an important career
in the wider world.

That is how we should begin by imagining him, and
there is indeed something special about it. Here we have a
man, sitting in his little Boeotian village, who has neither a
title nor a profession. He is a Roman citizen and an honorary
citizen of Athens, but that does not mean much: many
people are both. But this man does not even want to
become a somebody. He is well-off, but not one of those
rich people who pay for popularity and honours. Yet in his
hospitable house one does not only meet Greeks from all
over the province of Achaea, but people also come from
distant places, even though Chaeronea is never on anyone's
way; and there come not merely many Romans who have
retired to Greece (including consulars), but also high officials who are passing through, even the great Governor
from Corinth. In such a case the entertainment becomes as
much a burden as an honour, as it was for ourselves in
former days, when the generals on manœuvre billeted at an
estate. Yet the visitors might miss their host, because he
may be on the way to inspect the cleaning of the streets of
the little town, for he never regards any municipal office as
too lowly for his person (cf. *Precepts on public life* 811b–c).
Why should these people come, except for the man and his
personality? And the only place they can find him is his

---

[10] If one could take Plutarch literally, then Timoxena was herself a writer; but
it is easy to see that he himself wrote the essay against luxurious clothing which he
attributes to his wife (*Guidance on married life* 145a, cf. *Lamprias catalogue*, No.
113). In the same way he makes his brother Lamprias a narrator and participant
in several of his dialogues; on the same reasoning, Lamprias would have to be
regarded as himself the author.

home. Of course he returned their visits; certainly he appears at sanctuaries for various feast days (though for example he never mentions Olympia), and without doubt he
visits Athens for the celebrations at the Academy, for he is
a member. And where else could he use a library? For it is
unthinkable that he owned all the books which he has read.

We shall follow his biography one stage further. Towards
the end of the nineties, he took over the post of one of the
two governing priests at Delphi, an office which the holder
retained for life. He held this post up to his death, which
has to be put in the early years of Hadrian's reign. There
was no need to move to Delphi; he could reach the place on
the direct route in a day's ride; but sometimes he will
certainly have needed to stay at the sanctuary for some days
to fulfil his duties. The place became his second home, and
most of his works, including the more important ones and
in particular the *Parallel Lives*, were written after he had
become a priest.

In his case, the acceptance of the post meant that as a
believer he was ready to undertake the service of the god.
In his works he discusses certain problems: why so many
oracles had altogether ceased to exist (*On the decline of
oracles* 409c–440b); why in Delphi the Pythia, a simple
peasant woman, climbed the tripod only once a month and
gave answers only to simple people enquiring about small
household matters (cf. *On the Pythian oracles* 408c–d and
Greek Questions 292f); and why those answers were given
in straightforward prose whereas in older times the god had
answered kings and states with speech that was often artificially obscure (*On the Pythian oracles* 394d–409c). When he
discusses such questions, it is quite clear that he is trying to
quell doubts and fears by which he was himself tormented.
And he first had to prove to himself that the actions and the
personal divinity of Apollo were compatible with his philosophy, and he had to rediscover the meaning behind the
strange ceremonies which were still practised. This was
probably a more difficult task for him than to explain the
Egyptian religion and cult to a friend from Delphi when
she became priestess of the Egyptian gods (Clea, in *On
Isis and Osiris*: cf. 351e, 352c); but he honestly convinced

himself after long examination of his own soul. How many others would have rested quite content, in a superficial way, with fulfilling decently the traditional tasks of a priest!

How he did more than decently fulfil his task, without giving up his integrity as man and as philosopher, cannot be discussed here; nor is it necessary for the understanding of the *Lives*. Nor did this exercise any disturbing influence on his practical ethics. He never ceased lashing out at the humbug in the temples of Serapis,[11] and persisted in ignoring the miracles of Asclepius.[12] On the other hand, Plutarch always believed in contacts between man and god via dreams; he also believed in omens and portents and in the occasional intervention by the divine powers, though he certainly accepted only a very few of the stories along these lines transmitted by his sources for the *Lives*. Nor is this the place to relate Plutarch to the intellectual life of his time: that would require consideration of his contemporaries Apollonius of Tyana, Nicomachus of Gerasa, Dio of Prusa, and the Phrygian Epictetus. Just one point, because it is such a characteristic fact: Plutarch did not take the slightest notice of any of these men.[13] If one compares them, one might find one or other of them more attractive, but one has to admit that Plutarch is the most Hellenic of them all: he is indeed still a Hellene to the bone, and as such he was still very influential when philosophy and religion later returned to the doctrines of the Orient: that is shown by the extensive spread of his ethical writings.

Much of Plutarch's work is indicative of his broad interests and his versatility; but what made his personality so attractive in real life, and still strikes us as attractive today, on the whole emerges only incidentally. Some rhetorical declamations, which (we may note) reveal a considerable knowledge of literature, probably belong to his youth. He

[11] *Pyth. or.* 407c. There was a temple close nearby at Tithorea, probably his wife's birthplace.

[12] This god too was worshipped close to Plutarch's home, at Elateia. Asclepius even entered Delphi, but was never a major figure there.

[13] It is typical that he allows Musonius to be mentioned only once by Romans, *On the restraint of anger* 453d; he also on one occasion himself criticizes his Stoic arrogance and uncouthness, *On debt* (830b)—itself an anecdote which he picked up at Rome.

even produced some grammatical work, on his countryman Hesiod. Grammarians and doctors are counted among his acquaintances, and their approach was so familiar to him that he has many similes drawn from medicine. But he held that people must themselves preserve their health by, in particular, a prudent way of life, and philosophy, in the practical sense in which he understood it, had to exert an influence on this type of self-education. His writings are based on this premiss. So far it is easy to agree, but one has to regret that there is not more real science in his time. Without this, his taste for offering explanations of peculiar natural phenomena, many of which would not have stood up to thorough investigation, sadly becomes no more than a very disappointing game. He also wrote strictly philosophical essays, which are quite valuable for us; but on the whole he does no more than transpose late Hellenistic polemical writing into his own style: that shows that in their original versions they had become unpalatable to the changed tastes. If one adds that he reworked a historical story (to be *The Banquet of the Seven Wise Men* (146b–164d)), and that he began work on the *Lives* quite early, then he can be seen to be mapping out a range of literary activity of a vastness which few have been able to match.

Yet the man's influence rests largely with his popular ethical works. Here in particular we can sense the light and the warmth of the educational influence which he exercised in life: the mild, genial, yet also serious doctrine about how male and female, old and young can and should organize their lives correctly and profitably. All this never stays on the abstract level, but is always tailored for the circumstances in which the Greeks of his time and region had to live. These circumstances are limited, but it is exactly this quality which makes much of what he says valuable for all times. That is the personal achievement and merit of his works: to strike the moderate tone which fits them to society and life as he saw it, and suits his own character, far removed as it was from any exaggeration. One has to add the language which is so elegant, but at the same time free from any preciously classicizing mannerisms, with its flow of long but well-balanced periods. Everywhere examples

from ancient times and quotations from the poets are inter-
spersed, and, and especially, similes and analogies: he
had such a taste for these that he was able to compose a
whole book about the duties of married life from similes
and analogies, a very special wedding present (*Advice on
married life* 138a–146a). But with all these merits one should
not forget that the philosophical ideas mainly derive from
Hellenistic philosophy, and that Plutarch is not and does
not want to be an original thinker. That is of course true for
all his writings.

One can see how his production came to be so extensive
and wide-ranging. He read all the time, read all sorts of
things, made excerpts, and also made sketches or elaborated
lines of thought, so that they could be at hand when he
wanted to use them. He himself mentions such notes; and
we have some writings which seem to have been published
from these papers after his death, in their unfinished state.
These are easily distinguished from the excerpts, of which
we also have several. Thus it is understandable that many
other inauthentic writings have been assigned to his authorship. Of the genuine works, only a part survives; and some
things are greatly to be missed.

What is transmitted as the so-called *Moralia* is about the
same length as the collection of *Parallel Lives*. These *Lives*
were written under Trajan, and probably even later; Plutarch still intended to continue them when death called him
away.[14] That became his main task, to compare Roman and
Greek politicians and generals in pairs. He expected readers
from both peoples, for he dedicated the work to his friend
Sosius Senecio, who was consul for the second time as late
as 107, but probably had moved to the Roman colony of
Patrae even before that, and later lived there continuously.
He married his daughter to the equally successful Roscius
Pompeius Falco.[15] Falco himself had as one of his many
names that of the Spartan tyrant Iulius Eurycles, indicating

[14] *Marius* 29. 12 promises a *Life* of Metellus Numidicus. But Plutarch may
well have abandoned this idea, as the man was not at all worthy of this honour. In
On the malice of Herodotus 866b he promises a treatment of Leonidas; it is not
plausible that he fulfilled that promise.
[15] *PIR*[1] iii. 66: 255.

that his mother came from that family. We can see how the two peoples were already mixing in this period, how Romans had contact on an equal basis, continuously or transiently, with prominent Greeks. In this group Plutarch is the most distinguished example on the Greek side; he has learnt enough Latin to be able to use Latin historical sources,[16] and has accumulated detailed knowledge about Roman cults and customs, and made this knowledge available to his fellow Greeks. In this way his *Lives* serve the new direction of government taken by Trajan,[17] which then intensified to such an extent under Hadrian as to prefer Greeks over Romans, quite in contrast to the style of the Flavian regime. Dio of Prusa serves a similar purpose, when he travels the cities of the East to advertise Trajan and his 'kingship'. But the different means employed by the two philosophers to achieve the same purpose are highly characteristic.

Plutarch combines his subjects into pairs: that makes the equality of the two peoples plain. But none of the emperors appears, nor any of the kings after Alexander (for Demetrius did not rule an empire). If he had included Augustus, this deified figure would have had to be paid the necessary reverence, and therefore any parallel would have become improper. There is no evidence that Plutarch professed or participated in the cult of the emperor, not even when he

---

[16] Even if Greek was very common in all educated circles in Rome, and indeed even among many of the lower classes in that city, Plutarch must have learned some 'colloquial Latin' when he travelled to Northern Italy and stayed in the city for a longer period. He admits that it was only later that he undertook proper study of the language, and also confesses that he never reached the level where he could judge questions of style. Still, at the time of writing *Galba* and *Otho* he is already using the same Latin source as Tacitus and Suetonius, and that indicates his level of competence at that stage. One may add that the *Life* of *Sertorius* was hardly possible without using the difficult Sallust. One naturally assumes that the Roman friends helped him, just as Cicero had excerpts made by the Greek friends living in his house. Plutarch was certainly not able to read speeches of the Gracchi; but one still has the impression that the numerous quotations are an addition of Plutarch's own, and were not found in his historical sources. Since he was on the look-out for such pieces of evidence (most important for the biographer), it is quite probable that he looked for help. In *Ti. Gr.* 15–16 the main points of a speech, the κεφάλαια, are given: that rather supports such a hypothesis. Single *bons mots* could of course also have been found in the historians.

[17] It also has political significance that Plotina tried to use her influence on Hadrian on behalf of the Epicurean school.

was a Delphic priest, though it is obvious that he shared in the prescribed rituals. All his subjects are men of action. That means that the Romans are supposed to learn that even in this respect the old Hellenes are on equal terms with them. This is all the more effective since it is nowhere explicitly stated nor even hinted at as the goal of the collection. What is explicit is only the exemplary status of the men. It is a procession of heroes, and it has always been understood as such. If single figures such as Alcibiades–Coriolanus and Demetrius–Antonius are of a questionable moral standard, then the author explicitly apologizes for their inclusion.

When one looks at the complete work one should never forget these tendencies, however strictly one's interest in reading a biography is limited to its historical information. The most misguided and unfair verdicts have been delivered when the following two facts have not been sufficiently taken into account: first, that Plutarch is not a historian and does not want to be one, but a biographer and philosopher; and, secondly, that the biographies are grouped in pairs and have to be read as such. It is very much to be regretted that the first pair is missing, and with it the preface and the dedication to Senecio; but the fact that Plutarch had selected Epaminondas and Africanus the younger is significant enough. The two noblest of men could be compared, and only this could have been the point of the comparison; Epaminondas was the noblest to the Boeotian; for Scipio, Polybius had provided this interpretation, and that Plutarch should have turned first to Polybius is utterly understandable, for Polybius was the first to try to reconcile the Greeks to Roman domination. Some parallels were already traditional, such as Alexander and Caesar—although one has only to glance at the lion's head of the divine youth on the one hand, and the face of Caesar on the other, furrowed by all passions, in order to see that these two men can only be compared as complementary opposites. Similarly Demosthenes and Cicero had been and could be compared only as orators, but that is exactly what Plutarch rejects. Therefore in quite a few cases the combination is motivated only by an external factor, such as the fact that both Lysander

and Sulla were conquerors of Athens. But some of the pairs
are rather happily linked, especially the two revolutionary
Spartan kings with the Gracchi[18] and Sertorius with
Eumenes.[19] Sometimes Plutarch discusses the similarities
at the beginning of a book, sometimes he adds a comparison
at the end.[20] These comparisons are superficial and never
satisfying, which is why we never object when Plutarch
decides, as he often does, to omit them. He himself must
have been aware of the difficulty that sometimes he had to
find a counterpart for a man who simply could not be left
out of the series, a constraint which may explain why such
dissimilarities as that of Solon–Publicola were acceptable.

One cannot deny that some of the *Lives* have so much
historical narrative that we miss the specifically biographical
quality. This is particularly true for the Romans of the
Ciceronian age. Here Plutarch seems to have had excerpts
from a splendid but unidentifiable historical source: for
there was no tradition to preserve intimate personal details
for Lucullus and Crassus, and in Caesar's case such information was available for Plutarch only in a very limited
degree;[21] very different is the situation for Cicero, where
the loyal Tiro preserved the details. Yet in this very case
Plutarch displays a very considerable skill, in disentangling
his hero from the web of contemporary history. And if as
historians we find some passages unclear, then this should
simply remind us not to expect a biographer to write in the

[18] Even if it is a good match, there still remain some differences. Agis was a
well-meaning boy who, pushed by others, quickly meets a pathetic death, whereas
Tiberius Gracchus became prominent by his prudent and well-prepared reform
plan which did not die with his sudden death. In this case Plutarch tries to play
down such contrasts.

[19] The similarity does not only consist in fabulous successes on a far-distant
battlefield (successes which anyway had to remain short-lived), nor simply in the
other factors which Plutarch himself adduces. There are other traits too, such as,
on the one side, the domination over the Agyraspides by the belief in communication with Alexander the god (*Eum.* 13) and, for Sertorius, communication with
the gods through the white hind (*Sert.* 11).

[20] It is only in modern editions that these final remarks are printed as separate
sections: that gave rise to the mistaken modern convictions that they have been
lost in cases where they are absent, or that they are spurious in cases where they
are present.

[21] It is highly characteristic of Plutarch that he suppresses the suspicions of an
erotic liaison between Nicomedes and Caesar, for he must have known about
these.

manner of an historian. It will not always be easy for a
biographer to find a satisfactory ending when death calls
his hero away, but his achievements still have some impact
on events: and in this precise respect Plutarch several times
shows a remarkable and admirable skill. In the *Life* of
Alexander the last item we hear about is the unworthiness
of his successor: the early downfall of his posthumous son
was still to come, and is missing now only because the text
is mutilated. This episode was added to leave the reader
with the final impression that the empire died along with
the unrivalled and peerless emperor. In the *Life* of Caesar,
however, we are told that after his death the great daemon
which had accompanied him all his life continued to haunt
all his murderers (*Caes.* 69. 2); and the book closes with
that apparition which Brutus had at Philippi. The empire
of Caesar continues. The Athenians have expelled Themistocles, the author of their power: but the book concludes in a
reconciliatory way with the cult of the tomb which he did
finally receive in his native town. Alcibiades, the cause of
Athens' ruin, dies somewhere far from home, lonely and
miserably, in uncertain circumstances: only a hetaera at-
tends him. All these endings could have been shaped quite
differently. Themistocles could have drunk ox-blood as a
repentant traitor, to avoid having to lead an army against
Athens; Alcibiades could have been idealized as the pupil
whom Socrates loved. It is well worth while to reflect on
the artist's ways, which seem to us so much more rewarding
than the reasoning of the comparisons.[22]

What is especially irritating for the historian is the complete neglect of chronology. It is not only that the biographer is indifferent towards it: he even admits that the
Herodotean story of Solon's meeting with Croesus is chronologically impossible, but it was too good to miss—and after
all there were in any case so many other chronological

[22] Very characteristic is the *Life* of Pelopidas. He owed his inclusion only to his
Boeotian origin, and does not really fit the company. Plutarch knew precious little
about his personality. Every sentence shows his effort to find out something about
him. And in the end he sees no other way out but to contrast the solemn funeral
with the miserable downfall of Alexander of Pherae and to interpret the mutilation
of the corpse as a just punishment. This is the kind of brutality which is very
frequently found in Hellenistic historians, but it is unworthy of Plutarch.

contradictions (*Solon* 27); we too are not likely to ignore this story, for the reflection of a person in poetry often shows much more about a great man's character than the naked facts. Still, to discern and to do justice to myth as such would require a type of historical criticism that Plutarch could not possibly possess. (Incidentally, even today too many people think that a story is not worth a thought if it is not 'true', i.e. if it did not happen.) However, Plutarch indeed felt quite awkward when he told the *Lives* of Theseus and Romulus in a pragmatic way (*Thes.* 1); but his failure to recognize the mythical parts is not even the worst problem in these *Lives*: it is worse still that he could not produce a proper *bios*, even though he tried especially hard at their ends. Here Plutarch was guided by different motives: with Romulus and Numa he wanted to give his fellow-Greeks an idea of the origins of Rome and her constitution; therefore he found himself in the position of having to look for Greek parallels; then in *Lycurgus* the life of the Spartan state serves a similar function to that played in *Solon* by the characterization of the constitution, which takes up so much space alongside the presentation of Solon's own biography. All this is far removed from what biography proper should be. And there are quite a number of similar cases in the great work, though this fact should not affect the final judgement on its literary genre. The genre is biography, and time and again Plutarch protests against any suggestion that he is writing history. A clear understanding of this contrast is essential not merely to judge his work, but also to enjoy it.

The life of a person is not simply a career: not what that person has lived through, but how that person has lived. Therefore the different forms of life were first distinguished, and indeed we still use the opposition between *vita activa* and *vita contemplativa*—an echo of Aristotelian ethics, anticipated by Plato. It was thus that the Peripatetics, followed by other philosophical schools, first wrote 'On ways of life'; if the lives of individuals were treated in such books, as they naturally were, then they served as representatives of specific ways of life. Aristoxenus, who was close to the Aristotelian school without quite being a member, was

the first to write *Lives* of individuals; but even there we can
still see that he takes Pythagoras as a model for a particular
way of life, whereas Socrates and Plato are characterized in
hostile tones. The result was that the events of a life were of
relatively little interest. A *bios* is fundamentally different
from the exhaustive compilation of information concerning
the great figures of the past, the sort of collection which
Chamaeleon, for instance, produced for the poets. That
kind of work was carried out extensively by the pupils of
Callimachus, but if for instance the writings of Hermippus
'On Law-givers', 'Pythagoras', and so on are called *bioi*,[23]
that can only be meant as a shorthand expression. To
regard these writings as a special kind of biography runs
completely counter to Greek theory and practice. It is quite
permissible to use the word *vitae* for those biographical
notes which the grammarians put in front of their editions
of the classical authors, and those which filter from the
same tradition of scholarship into late compendia such as
Hesychius Illustris; and the Latin word is very handy, for
'Description of a Life', or even 'Life' is too inflated a term
for these clusters of notes. This is not a *bios* in the Greek
sense, and does not pretend to be one.[24]

This is the point where we should glance at another
literary genre: the encomium, which Isocrates created for
prose to rival the lyric poems for individual persons. The
genre derives from the memorial speech delivered in honour
of a dead person, where the orator pays homage to the
deceased and tries to elevate him to an ideal. This means
that the deeds are conveniently neglected at the expense of
the character, although it is true that Xenophon transferred
whole passages from his historical writings to his *Agesilaus*.
And indeed we do get a picture, even if an idealized one, of
Agesilaus, though not of Evagoras. It is wrong to criticize
this, but in such a case historians, and others too, have to

[23] Quite explicit is the phrasing in the subscription to *P. Oxy.* 1367, for the
epitome of Hermippus by Heraclides Lembos.
[24] Even Dionysius of Halicarnassus, who sometimes refers to these biographical
compilations, has not forgotten what a *bios* really is; at the beginning of the *Life* of
Deinarchus he sets it alongside the χαρακτήρ, and at the beginning of the *Life* of
Isaeus he says: περὶ τοῦ βίου τἀνδρὸς οἷός τις ἦν. Very apt is the definition in the
Etym. Magn.: εἶδος ζωῆς.

be careful and to look out for complementary information. In later times much was written of this kind: Polybius for example began his literary career with an encomium on Philopoemen. A similar work on the younger Cato, written long after its subject's death, was used by Plutarch; the *Agricola* of Tacitus also belongs to this category. Speeches in honour of living people were a further addition to the genre, and we have many of these on the late Roman emperors. Such topics were always dealt with in the schools of rhetoric. But not only does one have to draw a distinction between the different genres; it is always a rare exception if an encomium can claim to include material of historical value, and similarly a biography always has an ethical interest.

Since biography treated an idealized or at least characteristic way of life, writers first attempted the *bioi* of intellectual leaders and teachers of a people, not of men of action. On the other hand, in the course of the extensive literary production of the Hellenistic age (which was much richer than we tend to assume), the most important facts about generals and politicians were also collected in concise so-called biographies. Such writings may have been very widely read, but they still had no claim to be regarded as scientific writings or even as *belles-lettres*. True, Cornelius Nepos' similar compilation finds a place in Latin literature[25]—but that merely demonstrates the disparity in level between Greek and Roman literature.

Even though we have so lamentably little from Hellenistic times, we can still grasp the conception of *bios* in those cases where there survive more than just a handful of quotations. From the third century we possess the elegant pieces by Antigonus of Carystus. His books 'On the *bios* of Zeno', 'Arcesilaus', etc. (that is the form of the title)

---

[25] In Nepos' case another literary genre also comes into consideration—the rhetorical encomium—for instance, in the cases of Thrasybulus and Epaminondas. The schematic arrangement is very clear. Nothing of that kind survives from Hellenistic times, but we know of its existence. On the inventory of a Rhodian library (in Maiuri, *Nuova silloge epigrafica di Rodi e Cos* (1925), 15), we find an Aspasia and an Alcibiades: how dominant the narrative element could become in such works is visible in the ἐγκώμιον Ἡρακλέους by Matris, found in Diodorus (1. 24. 4).

represented the philosophers in their individual characters, in their daily teaching and dealings. Even if they were occasionally involved in the important events of their day, these events remained always in the backgound of the account; there was really no point in tracing chronologically the career of a scholar, his regular and uniform life. Fixed dates are not given. Surprisingly different are some surviving pages of the *Life* of Euripides by Satyrus; they show us how an author from the Alexandrian circle cast the scholarly material in the elevated form of a dialogue. For the tragedians (we have the last part of this work) it was possible to establish a chronological basis for a life through the fixed dates supplied by the plays' performances; Satyrus does use this information from time to time, but on the whole his writing is completely different from what those dates would lead us to produce. In opposition to the general view, Satyrus presented Euripides as, for instance, a pious worshipper of the gods. Satyrus also wrote about King Philip and Alcibiades; the nature of these works is unknown, but they were certainly not historical biographies.

Towards the end of the Hellenistic tradition we have substantial remains of an *Autobiography* and of a *Bios of Augustus*[26] by Nicolaus of Damascus. The Peripatetic wants to present himself as someone who is in command of all the virtues which the ethics of his school demand in a virtuous man; as for the *Life* of Augustus, a historian may find it irritating, for there is little in the way of facts, and the few that are given are presented in such a tendentious and distorted manner that one becomes suspicious of the rich circumstantial detail. But all this simply makes clearer Nicolaus' interest in giving a character sketch. One cannot say how far his narrative extended in time: probably to the point when the princeps—whom this oriental writer regarded as a king—was the sole and exclusive ruler. After all, the book was written during Augustus' lifetime. To such a biographer, childhood events were also important:[27]

[26] The full title was περὶ βίου καὶ ἀγωγῆς Καίσαρος, which shows that an explanatory addition for βίος was already thought desirable.

[27] Some titles (collected by Jacoby, *Hist. fr.* IIc 261) may suggest that similar stories of educational development had already been collected for other leaders, particularly Alexander; but we know nothing of them.

this is the only such case which we know about, and of high importance if only for its singularity. Usually one finds miraculous tales and prophecies instead, and this was still the case with the Romans; Nicolaus avoids these.

Nicolaus was a Peripatetic. We often give the same description to the scholars at Alexandria who were interested in biography, and Aristoxenus is very close to the Peripatos. Thus this peculiar genre of literature has its roots in the Aristotelian view of history, and it finds an analogue in the biologically orientated study of nature, where one book of the *History of Animals* is devoted to the characters of the animals. We can understand how Plutarch the philosopher, who constantly had the *bios* of his own time in view and at the same time always looks back to the exemplary greatness of the past, became a writer of *bioi*. He had already completed two collections when he began work on his *Parallel Lives*. The one collection was devoted to famous compatriots, from Heracles the Theban to a mythicial Phocian hero Daiphantus,[28] who in his native land was still remembered in cultic rituals. This was a description of a life of heroic and death-defying courage, shown by a nation of simple peasants fighting with the apparently insuperable Thessalian nobility; this biography stood impressively alongside the solemn life of the poet Pindar and of Crates from Thebes, the peculiar Cynic who was still such a pastoral adviser to his Thebans that no door was closed to him. This series of biographies was very well received; we would certainly like to have it, and would willingly give in exchange the *Lives* of Otho and Galba, which are preserved by chance from the series of *Lives* of the emperors from Augustus to Vitellius. The choice of subjects implies that it

---

[28] Plutarch himself mentions this biography, in the book where he collected heroic deeds of women for his Delphic friend Clea (*On the virtues of women* 244b); this was written at the same time as he was composing his main work. Pausanias (10. 1) found a different version of the story in his Delphic source. It is odd that Plutarch differs from that; odd too that Pausanias has not here used Plutarch, for he uses his *Pindar* and his *Epaminondas*, and the emperor Julian uses his *Crates*. Perhaps the Messenian Aristomenes was also included in this series as a pendant to Daiphantus. His shield was in the temple of Trophonius in Lebadeia, where Pausanias was still able to see it (4. 16). As a hero he helped the Thebans at Leuctra (Paus. 4. 32): Pausanias claims to have heard of this at Thebes, but may well draw it from Plutarch's *Epaminondas*.

must have been written under the Flavians. These are little more than an excerpt from a recently published historical work; there is little of a *bios*, and there is no consistent attempt to produce one. He also wrote a *Life* of the elder Scipio; sadly, we know no more than that bare fact. It must have been before he started the *Parallel Lives*, for otherwise it is inexplicable that this great man should not have been included in the collection. So this may have been an experimental work, which in the end led on to the great enterprise.[29] The *Life* of Scipio itself remained neglected.[30]

Naturally Plutarch exploited a *bios* where one existed. This is what he did in the *Life* of Cato Uticensis, and probably also for the elder Cato, whose life is so clearly presented with so many little personal traits; hardly any subject of a biography is characterized in such a detailed way. But these were exceptions; there were no Plutarchian biographies before Plutarch, even though modern scholars have fabricated them from nothing. That judgement is not affected by the fact that Plutarch used the compilations of the grammatici, where they offered him in easily accessible form the relevant passages from Old Comedy and other recondite pieces of ancient evidence. He used such material to enrich, in particular, the lives of the ancient Athenians, Themistocles,[31] Cimon, Nicias, Pericles,[32] Demosthenes.[33] This source must have been a very welcome supplement to

[29] The *Life* of Aratus was written for an acquaintance who descended (or claimed to descend) from the great man. Such claims were often made, corresponding to the general reverence for the past. The book gives the impression that it was written while he was engaged on the *Parallel Lives*.

[30] Some anecdotes from it may have been incorporated in the *Apophthegmata of kings*.

[31] Plutarch uses for this biography a collection of apophthegmata whose core is very ancient; hence many items carry conviction.

[32] Among other items, Plutarch must owe to such sources the seemingly credible material on the political debates of Pericles and Thucydides: these debates may contain some particular factual points. They must ultimately derive from eyewitnesses, but it is hopeless to guess at their identities.

[33] It is very telling that Plutarch made such little use of the speeches. He became less and less inclined to any kind of rhetoric, and he had no contact with any orator. He very clearly stated that he strongly disliked the fictitious speeches in historians like Ephorus and Theopompus (cf. *Precepts on public life* 803b). He laid correspondingly greater value on the apophthegma.

the historians, who talked only about the men's deeds. But in most cases such help was not available; sometimes there existed only one historical report, which Plutarch had to transform into a biography. For *Coriolanus* we have this historical source, Dionysius of Halicarnassus; and in this case the biographer took small liberties and added minor details here and there. His use of Timaeus for the biography of Timoleon will be similar, and for similar reasons. But wherever he was able to do so, Plutarch tried to use several historians, so that at some points he could follow one as a main source, and at others switch from one authority to another for different passages. It was, however, beyond his capacities to assimilate his material into a smooth and composite whole, and the presentation may consequently lack unity, as for example in *Eumenes*, where the first and the later sections are not wholly harmonized.

Plutarch was very well read, although not to the same degree in every area. But certainly he had read much more than scholars are usually prepared to acknowledge: they are misled by the learned citations drawn from the grammarians, which encourage a suspicion that the rest of the knowledge he displays may similarly stem from secondary sources. Still, a critical and attentive investigation can easily separate weft from warp. The Roman biographies are no help in settling this dispute, and may even be misleading: for in this case it was not feasible to extend his reading very far, and he also seems to have felt a very understandable awe before the hundred volumes of Livy. We can, however, use the cross-references to trace how he uses the same big historiographical work for several biographies. The case is different with Alexander. All his life Plutarch had read extensively about Alexander, and that was now very useful to him, allowing him to modify the battle-narrative by inserting small personal details.[34] It is short-sighted to doubt whether he had really read the great works of the

---

[34] We also possess two declamations on Alexander, probably written in Plutarch's youth: that allows a comparison which yields useful insights not merely about the material itself, but also about the way in which Plutarch exploited it. A short essay on the τύχη of Rome derives from Plutarch's posthumous papers; it is unfinished, and is partly a combination of two variant versions.

Greek historians in the original rather than an anthology, and these suspicions seem now to have been set aside. The matter can easily be proven in the case of a minor work, a by-product of these studies, the *Life* of Artaxerxes II. This was not a character worthy of a biography, and certainly none had previously existed; moreover, Plutarch did not write a proper *bios* of the king. But he read the works of Ctesias: the *Lives* of (for instance) Alcibiades and Lysander may have suggested this reading to him, and the *Life* of Alexander itself certainly made it desirable for him to develop a closer acquaintance with Persian ways; he even had recourse to the more recherché writer Dinon, who like Ctesias knew and described the Persian world. Thus Plutarch produced a book which gives a fair picture of the βίος Περσῶν, the way of life of the barbarian court.

Plutarch not only had a very thorough knowledge himself of the history of the ancient world before he embarked on his great work; he also presupposes it in his readers, as is made clear from the historical examples he uses in his other works. Herodotus, Thucydides, and Xenophon were the relevant writers for the great days of Classical Greece, and it was sufficient simply to allude to them.[35] Plutarch was prejudiced against Herodotus, for in his writings he thought (not entirely unreasonably) that the Boeotians had received unfair treatment. About this he wrote a passionate work, or rather rewrote an older and very learned work, of whose origin and sources we have no knowledge; and our ignorance on this point is suggestive, hinting at the great mass of such materials which may have been available for Plutarch to exploit. We should therefore not be too surprised if *Quellen-forschung* is all too often unsuccessful. The stylistic form, his very personal style—these are entirely and totally Plutarch's own. It is only after penetrating beyond this that we can distinguish the different characters of the various narratives which he uses: strong contrasts are perceptible—the

[35] The predominant position enjoyed by these three authors is especially clear in the case of the rhetor Aristides, who apart from these three did not even read Ephorus and Theopompus, although he could have had no objections to their style. But he did use Plutarch.

shallow phraseology of the worst of the Roman annalists, as in *Publicola*; the rich and dense details of the *Lives* of the Romans of the Ciceronian age; the gripping scenes in *Demetrius* and *Cleomenes*, and also in *Antonius* (in this case Plutarch must have used an excellent account of the relationship with Cleopatra, one which is completely different in tone from what one can glimpse in the other Roman *Lives*). In this last example Plutarch devoted considerable attention to elaborating the biography, and added several digressions, especially the one about the misanthrope Timon, who serves as a foil to the unsettled activity of Antonius—all this for the educational purposes of historical study. That excursus also offered Shakespeare the material for a second tragedy, apart from *Antony and Cleopatra* itself. Such extended digressions are not very frequent, but everywhere one can see Plutarch trying to smooth away roughness, to tone down, to understand, in order to forgive. Plutarch has too much taste, and also too much sense of fairness, to bluster in the manner of Theopompus or Timaeus, or to award a mark to a hero at the end of his life or after some special deed, along the pattern established by Ephorus and approvingly followed by Polybius. On the whole, Plutarch's personality remains in the background, but where he is engaged with special passion one can feel the warmth of it, and appreciate it all the more. When, for instance, in *Pericles* Plutarch praises the unrivalled brilliance and unfading glory of the Athenian acropolis and its buildings (chs. 12–13, especially 13. 4–5), this strikes a very different note from the empty *naïveté* of Pausanias, as he tries to emulate Herodotus. Dio of Prusa alone stands comparison, with his appreciation of the sublimity of the Olympian Zeus (*or.* 12). And it is also undisputed that Plutarch's *Life* of Pericles, and not least his chapter on the buildings, introduced the familiar expression 'the Periclean age' for this fullest bloom of Greek civilization.

So there are plenty of aspects of this narrator and biographer which deserve praise; yet it is precisely in his role as biographer that he makes one feel so strongly the oppressive limits within which Hellenistic biography had to operate. First, Hellenistic biography always looks for the same person, unaware of the differences imposed by the period in which that person lived. How else could one explain the fact that there are *Lives* of Theseus and Lycurgus? The psychology is philosophical and abstract, whereas the understanding of history is in the end wholly pragmatic. The demand that man should always do what is morally good and just itself becomes an unjust supposition, if one fails to take into account the fact that in different times very different things are seen as morally good and just—or at least as permissible, when set against the morality of politics. This comes about because historical criticism is as yet undeveloped, and it is not yet possible to think in the categories of a different time and a different mentality. A second point has to be added. A character's internal development is insufficiently taken into account; nor, as a result, are the contrasting forces which war against one another in the soul; but only if one has a firm hold on those can one hope to reach a conception of the individual. On the other hand, one has to remember that the 'character', that is the 'stamp', is a term drawn from that same Aristotelian school which promoted the investigation of human *bios*. The stamp is supposed to be attached to each soul in perpetuity; once one knows the stamp, one also knows the character, the personality of a human being once and for all. From this conception stems the claim of a rigid unity of character in poetry, as Horace demands (*Ars poetica* 105–27); that unity whose lack Aristotle bewails even in the *peripeteia* of the *IA* (*Poetics* 1454ª31–3). Polybius applies the same criteria to the figures active in his history: if something does not fit the character, then the person has yielded to external duress or to the pressure exerted by another person. The very different verdicts passed on Alexander encouraged the attempt to present the hero as developing gradually into an evildoer; but the very poor results of that attempt can be seen in the tradition of novelistic historiography. This is one of Plutarch's positive features, that he does not try to label his characters with one description or another, but even so he does not even consider the possibility of tracing their development. Nicolaus (*Life of Augustus* 4) tells a story from the infancy of Augustus, but only to demonstrate that even as a child he was already true to his character.[36] In this case, this was an artistic stroke—but also a slap in the face of truth. So far there has been no biographer who has understood the internal development and self-education of this man.

We should go further; it is not enough simply to identify this failing in Hellenistic psychologists and historians. We have to determine their attitude towards individuality. For it is exactly the struggle to free themselves from the bounds which tie the individual which typified the Ionians, as they fought for and attained the intellectual freedom which they gained and we retain—the Ionians and all their philosophers, even if today this is arrestingly clear only in the works of Xenophanes and Heraclitus. The poets are similar, Archilochus and Alcaeus, and there is nothing more moving in Sappho than when she admits to her feelings. How sharply does Herodotus describe peoples and Ion individuals! The Attic tragedians develop only slowly to the stage where they create human individuals, though only exceptionally—yet the Ionian Homer had already reached that level. Old Comedy does not go beyond caricature, which also in the minor Hellenistic genres forms a counterweight to the idealizing and generalizing style—but basically this is only a further form of stereotypical representation. And even though Menander introduces complete persons, this nevertheless soon develops into yet another, new kind of typology. Hellenistic poetry achieves next to nothing in this respect. The fifth century still produces people who parade their own personality with that familiar Ionian recklessness. It is very telling that there are stories about Alcibiades as a boy. That does not last.

It is Pindar, more than any historical source, who makes us familiar with the attitude which was dominant on the Greek mainland and which saw itself in contrast with the nature of the Ionians. On the mainland the ethics of class

[36] Polybius, 10. 21, says that he included Philopoemen's infancy in the encomium which he wrote after his subject's death, but that this was not a suitable topic for a work of history. In the same way the anecdotes about the young Alcibiades are preserved from the speeches delivered for him and against him, published shortly after his death. Encomium existed before Isocrates, who merely gave it its fixed form.

remained powerful and influential. What the 'good man' has to do is firm and clear; much is required, but each one has to be what all others are or should be. Strict rules are valid for all, and anyone who wants to differ will be considered arrogant and hated even by the gods themselves. This attitude remains influential, even after the narrow aristocratic society is overthrown and the words *arete* and 'good man' acquired different meanings. The mainland is victorious over Ionia. The Greek word for 'complacent' early acquires the pejorative sense of stubborn insolence. And then in the fourth century BC two other influences become very powerful, those of the Socratics and of rhetoric. The ethics and political ideas of Plato are unsympathetic to the individual; the poet in him was able to create individual figures, even boys—but directed these talents towards the realm of the eternal forms. In the school of the Peripatos the expression 'character' is coined; Theophrastus makes observations in order to depict types. The Stoic school with its ideal man disappears into unattainable heights, and by condemning every sort of passion it destroys the mode of expression, if no more, of the individual. Cynicism abjures society; even if Diogenes was an original, those who wanted to live like him again became types. Rhetoric also claims to educate, that is for life, but precisely for that reason it teaches its pupils to submit to life and society, to conform; and as the education and the rhetoric it conveys are general, and therefore common property, anyone educated in this way will always act in the same manner—cultured, inoffensive, engaging. πιθανός, which basically means that which generates agreement, becomes a praising epithet for people; we may like to remember that it is often used of hetaerae. Anyone who had received a rhetorical education did not want to undergo any further development; he thought himself prepared for life. We know this type of finished education and its results all too well from our own society. In English culture this stems partly from the class morality of the English aristocracy and partly from the obligations of a Calvinist way of life; it therefore takes a particularly false and intolerable form with the Philistines, for whom both aristocracy and Calvinism are unattainable. The great English novelists never tire of holding a mirror in front of this

society. A Hellene with philosophical education may well
have asked himself the further question, whether he was
progressing towards virtue (Plutarch has an elegant essay
on the subject), but there is no hint that anyone would have
gone back to examine the decisive years of late childhood,
in his own case or that of anyone else.

With the Macedonians, a fresh new people arose: great
men of decision who did not know about philosophical
kalokagathia or about the old *sophrosune*. All were impressed
by this characteristic, and not only when they found it in
Alexander. What were the origins of this Other, this disturbing greatness? To this question people found only the old,
traditional answer: it was superhuman, divine. Did not the
old Spartiate call the perfect man divine, and did not the
Delphic god order the veneration of numerous dead humans
as heroes? Even if one did not accept the presence of the
god in the living man, one could still talk about his daemon
within. With their Hellenization the Macedonians lost their
individuality—which was to become manifest only once
again, in the last Cleopatra, *fatale monstrum*.

Things went differently for the Romans. Here too the
Greek way of life, culture, and rhetoric may well have been
weakening; but the Romans kept not merely their language,
but also their *virtus*, those manly characteristics which are
no abstract concept. Nothing shows this more clearly than
reading first Plutarch's Greek biographies and then that of
the elder Cato. This man with all his rude and brutal
characteristics is there for us in person; not even the contradictory traits are missing, which alone can make a person
true to life. A similar roundness is also hinted, if no more,
in the case of Gaius Gracchus. Then there were Romans
who wrote their own autobiographies, something that no
Greek would ever have done (for the memoirs of Aratus,
like the *Memorabilia* of Xenophon, are rather works of self-
defence). Then there is Lucilius, whose self-revelation
Horace regarded as characteristic of the man, and Horace
himself, whom we love precisely for the marvellous frank-
ness which allows us to see straight into his heart. And
Cicero: he reflects about his own development, or at least
its rhetorical aspects, and describes it in the *Brutus*. What
Greek would ever have been able to do that, let alone go on

to sketch the characteristics of the orators of his day? In the same way Tacitus needed to be a Roman to be able to create the psychological development of his Tiberius.

Tacitus and Plutarch, two contemporaries, two counterparts. The outstanding artist of the two will always retain his superior status, but even historical scholarship may deliver a different judgement on the two men: and anyway what scholarship seeks in Plutarch is only a part of what he has to offer. Behind this is the amiable citizen of Chaeronea who continues to invite us into his hospitable home, where he will tell us many and various things about men and gods, as he drinks local Boeotian wine, and finally will point to the lion, the loyal guardian over the earthly tomb of the old, immortal greatness of Greece.

One final remark. We know him only through himself. He is a singular phenomenon, and behaves in his own way. That has its significance. At this same time, when language returns to Atticism, when the oracles break their silence, when Hadrianic archaism spreads in art, then a change occurs in the soul of men. It is still a long way to the two Gregories, of Nazianxus and of Nyssa, to Libanius, and finally to St. Augustine—not forgetting the Proclus of Marinus and the Isidorus of Damascus. These names alone show that Christianity was not the only factor to stimulate the capacity to consider the personal aspects of others, and of oneself. The movement had begun earlier. The mouthings of the florid orators and the impersonality of the compilers and the commentators should not mislead us. One has to look deeper, but still a reader can feel the individuality of people like Aristides, Galen, Clemens, even if it is not yet fully investigated. Furthermore, the modest emperor Marcus tries to name everyone who he thinks contributed to his inner formation (*To himself* 1). It is hardly mistaken to interpret the lack of similar Hellenistic examples as an indication of the less developed sensitivity of Hellenistic Greeks—but here our tradition simply fails us. We possess so many writings of, and about, the people of imperial times, and we can see them as persons. In this field there remains much to be done, and to point this out was a main purpose of this sketch. In the meanwhile I have tried to develop this myself in the case of Aristides.

2

On Reading Plutarch's *Lives*

D. A. RUSSELL

> 'Who's this, thy son?
> A pretty youth! What is his name?
>   'Plutarchus, sir.'
> 'Plutarchus! how came that about?'
>   'That year, sir,
> That I begot him, I bought Plutarch's Lives
> And fell so in love with the book, as I call'd my son
> By his name, in hope he should be like him,
> And write the lives of our great men.'
>
>   Ben Jonson, *The Devil is an Ass* (1616).

This of course was Renaissance enthusiasm. The fame and influence which Plutarch enjoyed in the days of the rediscovery of antiquity could not survive the revolutions in historical and scholarly attitudes that marked the nineteenth century. Instead of being thought of as a mirror of antiquity and of human nature, he became a 'secondary authority', to be used where the 'primary sources' failed, himself to be quarried by the *Quellenforscher* and left a ruin. The present neglect of the *Lives* in education is a consequence of this. And yet it should be obvious that, for the very historical purposes for which the book is now chiefly studied, it is misleading and dangerous to use what is plainly one of the most sophisticated products of ancient historiography without constant regard to the plans and purposes of its author. Fortunately, a good deal has been written, especially in the last twenty years, to redress the balance.[1] The present

---

[1] e.g. A. W. Gomme, *A Historical Commentary on Thucydides*, i (Oxford, 1945), 54–84; A Dihle, *Studien zur griechischen Biographie* (Göttingen, 1956); H. Erbse, *Hermes*, 84 (1956), 398 ff. on σύγκρισις; H. Martin, *Greek, Roman and Byzantine Studies*, 3 (1960), 65–73; T. F. Carney, *JHS* 80 (1960), 24–31 on *Marius*; D. A. Russell, *JRS* 53 (1963), 21–8, see below, pp. 357–72, on *Coriolanus*. But of course F. Leo, *Die griechisch-römische Biographie* (Leipzig, 1901) led the way.

paper[2] is a further contribution in the same direction, an
attempt to describe some of Plutarch's moral attitudes and
literary procedures with no more reference than is necessary
to the problem of his 'sources'. I venture to hope also that
it may encourage the reading of Plutarch, whether wholly
in Greek or partly in translation. It would indeed be a pity
if grammatical prudery or historical purism were to deny
young scholars the deaths of Cleopatra and Cato or the
adventure-story of Aratus' recovery of Sicyon, on the
ground that one of the most accomplished of Greek prose-
writers is 'bad for prose' and one of the most evocative
reconstructors of the past an unsure guide to the chronology
of the Pentecontaetia.

I begin by saying something about Plutarch's outlook on
morals and politics. Then I shall make a few remarks on
the literary form of the *Lives*. Finally, to illustrate some of
the points made, I offer a short analysis of *Lysander*, in
many ways a 'typical' product.

I

Plutarch, as he tells us himself,[3] undertook the writing of
biography at the instigation of someone else, but persevered
with it as a labour of love. The *Parallel Lives* are the most
ambitious literary plan of a long and fertile career. They
constitute nearly a half of the extant *œuvre*. Neither their
absolute nor their relative chronology can be determined
with certainty, though there are certain fixed points.[4] They
are clearly a work of late maturity: if we date them under
Trajan we shall hardly go wrong. How they are related to

---

[2] Written, in its main part, in 1963, and read to the Oxford Classical Society
and the Southampton Branch of the Classical Association; I wish to express my
thanks to these societies, and to others who have read and criticized. The best
conspectus of Plutarchian studies is the article by K. Ziegler in P-W (originally
published in 1949); for English readers, J. P. Mahaffy, *The Silver Age of the
Greek World* (Chicago, 1906), 339–402, is still useful. See also E. R. Dodds,
Greece & Rome, ii (1933), 97–107.

[3] *Aemilius Paulus*, prooemium.

[4] C. Stolz, *Zur relativen Chronologie der Parallelbiographien Plutarchs* (Lund,
1929).

Plutarch's output of teaching and writing may conveniently be seen from another book of the same period: the πολιτικὰ παραγγέλματα addressed to Menemachus of Sardis.[5] This advice, offered to a well-to-do youth on his entry into the political life of a tempestuous city, is enriched by illustrations which clearly come from the researches needed for the *Lives.* It is wrong to go into politics on an emotional impulse, like C. Gracchus.[6] It is essential to show care in choosing and using friends, and not fall into the errors of Solon and Agesilaus.[7] Quarrels and enmities are inevitable; even Themistocles and Aristides could not avoid them.[8] It is important to know how to delegate authority, as Pericles did.[9] Wealth is of course useful but poverty need be no bar, as Lamachus' career shows.[10]

Now these examples are intended to support practical advice, relevant to the real situations of Greek city life under the Empire. Of course Plutarch is aware of the frustrations and dangers of the time, and knows perfectly well that the story of Marathon ought now to be confined to the rhetor's classroom:[11] 'Take your speech home with you', Sulla had said to the Athenian envoys who made an untimely allusion to the glories of their past.[12] But at the same time he believes that there are lessons to be learned from the Classical history of Greece which are still valuable in public life, at least for their moral effect (ἠθοποιεῖν καὶ σωφρονίζειν). He gives a few examples: the vote of amnesty after the rule of the Thirty; the fining of Phrynichus for his ill-timed play on the Capture of Miletus; the joy of the *demos* when Cassander restored Thebes; its horror at a massacre in Argos; the respect for individuals shown at the time of the Harpalus scandal, when the house of a newly married couple was exempted from search.[13] All these

---

[5] T. Renoirte, *Les Conseils politiques de Plutarque* (Louvain, 1951).
[6] 798c, cf. *C. Gracch.* 22.
[7] 807d, cf. *Solon* 15; *Ages.* 13.
[8] 809b.
[9] 812c, cf. *Per.* 7; 11; 13.
[10] 822a ff.; 822e.
[11] 814c.
[12] *Sulla* 13. 4: ἄπιτε ὦ μακάριοι τοὺς λόγους τούτους ἀναλαβόντες.
[13] 814b.

show how a citizen body ought to be made to behave. And
the lessons are as applicable to the Greek cities of the
Empire as to Classical Athens, for they concern qualities
whose value is independent of the scale of political power:
humanity and magnanimity, the essentials (to Plutarch as to
us) of civilized life. It might, I think, plausibly be argued
that one of the leading themes of the *Parallel Lives* was to
demonstrate to the Romans that the greatness of Greece
had been *political* greatness, and that Ἑλληνικὴ παιδεία was a
road *ad rem publicam bene gerendam*. We may think of
Plutarch as answering the petulant prejudices of a Juvenal
(3. 60 ff.), and pointing out that not all *Graeculi* were
tightrope walkers. In the declamation *de gloria Atheniensium*,[14] he directly advances the view that the greatness of
Athens was due to her statesmen and generals rather than
to her poets and littérateurs.

There is another side to the relationship between Plutarch's moral teaching and his biographies. One purpose of
the *Lives*, and an important one, was clearly to provide a
repertoire of *exempla* for public men of Plutarch's own
day—this hardly needs pointing out—and he was not thinking solely of municipal politicians: the *Lives* were addressed
to an influential consular, Q. Sosius Senecio,[15] and the rise
of wealthy and locally powerful Greeks to positions of
imperial importance was of course a feature of Flavian and
Trajanic times. But to think of the *Lives* as *primarily* a work
of contemporary reference would be not only surprising but
wrong. There is all too much justice in the impression,
which most readers form, that Plutarch is somehow looking
down the wrong end of a telescope, and seeing the glory of
Athens and the awe-inspiring vicissitudes of the Hellenistic
and Roman worlds from a standpoint of limited experience
and scholastic rhetoric and morals. There is an extreme
example of this in *Pyrrhus* 13. In 284 Pyrrhus was the most
powerful monarch in the Balkan peninsula. Fortune
changed and he suddenly lost Macedonia. A single blow cut
him down to the insignificance of a petty chieftain. This

[14] *Moralia* 345c–351b: perhaps only one side of a rhetorical debate, but it gives
the impression of putting forward a view really held.
[15] His literary interests are attested also by Pliny, *Epist.* i. 13.

reversal of fortune is one of the pivotal points of Plutarch's vivid and exciting narrative. His comment therefore is meant as emphatic. It comes as a surprise. 'Fortune', he says, 'gave Pyrrhus the opportunity to enjoy his present advantages quietly and live at peace. But to trouble nobody and not be troubled himself was, in his opinion, a sickening bore (ἄλυν τινὰ ναυτιώδη). Like Achilles, he could not endure leisure.' Even though Achilles deserves a special place in this Life as Pyrrhus' ancestor,[16] the prim comment surely reveals in the historian a disabling lack of sympathy with the tensions and problems of power.

Now it is of course true that the consequences for the *Lives* of Plutarch's moral and educational preoccupations are serious and manifold. However much his historical interest and understanding deepened, as I believe it did, as the work progressed and expanded, this side of things remained in the forefront. It is responsible for much of the selection of detail: since the ultimate judgement to be made is a moral one, those points must be selected which are particularly valuable πρὸς κατανόησιν ἠθῶν, and these may well be trivialities and not the big battles.[17] It is responsible too for the impression of timelessness about Plutarch's world, since the criteria of private morality and expediency do not change. Plutarch is indeed aware of some development in standards; it is unreasonable to expect civilized moderation of the primitive barbarian Coriolanus. But on the whole he presents a millennium of history almost unshaded by sense of social or moral change. From Theseus to Otho, the interaction between individual and society follows a similar pattern. In childhood, the hero reveals his true nature to the discerning; in later life, he exercises his inborn and acquired qualities against the temptations of success and the vicissitudes of fortune until the time comes for his moral score to be added up. Again, Plutarch's educational interests engender certain definite prejudices. He shows particular respect for professionally congenial heroes: men of action with a touch of the philosopher about

---

[16] I doubt if this excuse will serve: cf. *Camillus* 12. 4 and *Aristides* 7. 8 for Achilles as a heroic model in other contexts.

[17] See *Alexander* I—Plutarch's clearest statement of purpose and method.

them. Dion and M. Brutus, the two Academics, are obvious examples; but the same tendency appears in *Marcellus* and *Lucullus*, and doubtless it was prominent in *Epaminondas* and *Scipio*, the first pair to be written, unfortunately (and surprisingly) lost.[18] He is convinced too that aristocratic government is best; and this persuasion, common it is true to most ancient historians, is reinforced by his devotion to Plato. It becomes another influence tending to 'iron out' differences of place and time: the *demos* is always and everywhere a menace.[19] Finally, the moralizing purpose sometimes leads to actual distortion and positive idealization. Plutarch admits this in *Cimon* (2. 4–5): it is not an historian's business, he says, to be particularly enthusiastic about bringing faults to light; he ought rather to feel some shame for the inability of human nature to produce instances of unalloyed virtue. It is as a deliberate exception[20] that he writes the lives of Demetrius and Antony, who are prime examples of the fact that μεγάλαι κακίαι can come out of μεγάλαι φύσεις. 'I do not do this to give pleasure', he says, 'but some knowledge of evil makes a man a more eager spectator and imitator of the good.' Coriolanus and Alcibiades are apparently another pair of deterrent examples; but there are of course many Lives, especially those of Roman *principes* of the civil war, which contain criticism and warning as well as encomium and protreptic; no candid reader will come from studying *Marius* or *Sulla* with the belief that Plutarch's world was a simple black and white one of heroes and villains.

Indeed, the *naïveté* of the *Lives*, which is real enough, and of which it is so easy to give a damning picture, lies much more in their initial conception and basic plan than in the execution. It is not often that Plutarch descends into the shades of *le monde rhétorique*,[21] where Lucian, Aelian, Valerius Maximus, and the rest move and have their being. Of course he does so sometimes: in the passage of *Pyrrhus*

[18] For Epaminondas, see Nepos' Life and Plutarch's *Pelopidas* and *de genio Socratis*. As the great Theban hero, he held a special place in Plutarch's affections.

[19] e.g. *Theseus* 25; *Camillus* 36; *Timoleon* 37; *Marius* 28.

[20] *Demetrius* 1, again an important Preface: see Dihle, op. cit. 74 ff.

[21] Cf. J. Bompaire, *Lucien écrivain* (Paris, 1958), 161 ff.

we have examined, often in *Solon*,[22] where he was drawing on the old and long-elaborated tradition of the Seven Sages. But again and again he is saved by his tremendous range of reading and great seriousness. He writes for ἄνδρες πολιτικοί, and is himself πολιτικός—even if only in relation to the works department of the municipality of Chaeronea. Moreover, he has a keen awareness if not of historical change, at least of the greatness of the past. The attempt to reduce motives to the philosophically and morally familiar in no way destroys the magnificence of the background against which the heroes move, the greatness of the events in which they took part, or the grandeur of their struggle with destiny. Indeed, the power of the *exempla* depends on their associations. They were human, like you and me and Menemachus; but this only becomes interesting because they are also larger than life and inhabitants of a bigger and better world. Few writers (perhaps only Livy among the ancients, and in a much more limited way) display such zest as Plutarch for the colourfulness of history and the excitement of action and adventure. Few have greater ability to convey by deft selection the emotional effect of events and personalities. The upshot is that the *Lives* did not turn out just a collection of improving tales for children—as, given their genesis, they might well have been—but something recognizable as a great historical work.

II

Let us next look a little more closely at the philosophical bases of Plutarch's concept of character. 'The *Lives*', says Vincenzo Cilento in a recent essay,[23] 'are the daughters not of history but of philosophy—above all, of the *Nicomachean Ethics*.' It has indeed long been common knowledge[24] that Aristotelian ethical doctrines are the basis of Plutarch's views on character. A man's ἦθος displays itself in his πράξεις and in his management of πάθη, which have gone to

[22] e.g. 5; 6; 28.
[23] *Transposizioni dell'antico* (Milan, 1961), 108.
[24] See Leo, op. cit. 178 ff., Dihle, op. cit. 60 ff. Note esp. *EN* 1103[a]14 ff., on ἦθος and ἔθος; ibid. 23 ff. on the part played by 'nature' and 'maturity'.

form it. He is born with certain tendencies—this is his
φύσις—which education may develop, diminish, or conceal,
but not fundamentally change or eradicate. Acts παρὰ φύσιν
may occur; but they are rare, and need special explanation.[25]
By the time a man is grown up, his pattern of conduct is
normally well enough established for predictions to be
made about how he will behave in most circumstances.
Philosophers and teachers of rhetoric had a lot to say about
this, building for the most part on the foundation of Aristotle's *Ethics* and the second book of the *Rhetoric*. They
classified ἤθη in such a way that the behaviour of an individual, once his type was recognized, could be predicted,
and his characteristics turned to good account by those who
wished to impose their opinions upon him. The historian or
biographer has to perform this process, as it were, in reverse. Generally speaking, what is recorded by tradition of
a great man is his πράξεις, and—a subdivision—his public
λόγοι. These, together with any significant minutiae that
happen to be preserved, form the evidence from which his
ἦθος and φύσις must be inferred. Plutarch's normal procedure in writing a Life is to state his conclusions on this
point fairly early—usually in connection with the hero's
education—and then justify them by the ensuing narrative.
Marius (2) provides a good example. Marius' natural courage (he is φύσει ἀνδρώδης) received an education more suited
to military than to civil life. It therefore resulted in inability
to control anger, a failing which became very serious when
he achieved power. His contempt for Greek letters, too,
was part of the same story; had he been persuaded to
sacrifice to the Greek Muses and Graces, he would not
have marred his military and political reputation by so ugly
a tail-piece (ἀμορφοτάτην κορωνίδα).[26] In the event, his hasty
temper, untimely ambition, and insatiable greed brought
him to the shipwreck of a cruel and savage old age. Having

[25] Examples in *Aem. Paul.* 30; *Mar.* 28; *Lucull.* 6. 2.

[26] Here again is the theme of Greek humanity and civilization as the cure for
the potential barbarity of Rome. We should recall that the violence of Roman
armies, bitterly remembered from the Mithridatic and civil wars, erupted again in
AD 69, and remained a menace. Cf. *Galba* 1, where Plutarch uses a Platonic
thought to interpret the situation. Similar themes are common in the *Lives*: e.g.
Cam. 12; *Coriol.* 15; *Numa* 3; *Marcellus* 22.

given this diagnosis, Plutarch goes on to the story which will justify it: ταῦτα μὲν οὖν ἐπὶ τῶν πράξεων αὐτῶν θεωρείσθω.

This procedure suggests a radical difference between Plutarch's concept of character and that with which modern biographers usually operate. Biography in modern times has been much concerned with the development of character. Maturation and senescence make the subject not only behave differently but *be* different in some fairly fundamental ways. Responsibility not only brings out latent capacity but makes it grow and trains it in new shapes. Many important things about a man's life are not inevitable and were not laid down at the beginning. This answers to our common feelings, though the more a writer is influenced by the clinicial attitudes of psychiatry or by the study of heredity, the more nicely he will limit the capacity of voluntary effort and external circumstance to alter the given pattern. Ancient writers, and Plutarch is no exception, have a more deterministic attitude. 'The hero is there, all one piece', as Cilento says, and his evolution is not described. Nevertheless, the question of the interaction between natural qualities and circumstances is at the heart of all biography, and it is natural that Plutarch should have thought about it, and worth while reflecting on what he says. The question of 'changes' of character was, of course, not new; it was handled by Theophrastus[27] and we find it in Polybius.[28] Plutarch promises a discussion in *Sulla* 30. 5: 'Marius was a hard man from the outset, and became more so; he did not change his φύσις as a result of power. Not so Sulla; *his* first dealings with fortune had shown a moderate and civilized character . . . he gives us good ground for complaining that the effect of great power is to prevent character (τὰ ἤθη) remaining as it was, and to produce violence, vanity, and inhumanity. Whether this is a change (κίνησις καὶ μεταβολή) in φύσις as a result of fortune, or rather the revelation, under the stimulus of power, of evil already there, is a question for another work[29] to determine.' In

---

[27] Plu. *Per.* 38. 2.

[28] 9. 22–3 (Hannibal).

[29] The ἑτέρα πραγματεία is not extant, and no recorded title suggests a place where Plutarch may have handled the subject.

this passage, then, Plutarch admits the possibility of a
change in ἤθη, the acquired portion of character—normally
complete at maturity, but not given at birth; as to change of
φύσις, he leaves open the question whether this might really
occur or whether what happens is simply a progressive
revelation of latent characteristics.[30] Similarly, in *Sertorius*
10—a different case, corruption not by power but by disaster. Late in his life, Sertorius, who had previously been
humane and gentle, behaved with great cruelty to certain
hostages. One interpretation of this, says Plutarch, would
be to say that his real φύσις was at last revealed; it was not
truly ἤμερος, but necessity had caused its true quality to be
deliberately concealed by rational control. He does not
himself accept this account, on the ground that, while no
true, philosophically based ἀρετή can be changed into its
opposite by fortune, in other circumstances good general
intentions (προαιρέσεις) and natures (φύσεις) can sometimes
be perverted as a result of great and undeserved misfor-
tunes. What happens is that they 'change their ἤθος with
their luck'.[31] So with Sertorius: his harshness towards his
opponents came from exasperation at the unfavourable turn
of fortune which had overtaken him.

The μεταβολή which Pericles' character underwent is of a
somewhat different kind. Gomme[32] speaks of a 'radical
change in Pericles' methods of conducting public affairs,
amounting practically to a change in his character'. It is
worth looking more closely. Plutarch's problem here, as has
often been seen, was to explain how Pericles, whom he
admires and believes to have ruled ἀριστοκρατικῶς (9. 1), can
also have been the architect of democracy, which is by

---

[30] The second is of course the common ancient view. One thinks of Tacitus'
Tiberius, *Ann.* vi. 51: in his last degradation *suo tantum ingenio utebatur* (= τῇ
αὐτοῦ φύσει ἐχρῆτο). A recent producer of *Timon of Athens* (Stratford, 1965) felt (as
he reports on the programme) the need to satisfy himself that the generous Timon
and the misanthrope could really be the same person; he does so by supposing
that bankruptcy and ingratitude revealed Timon's true nature, and that his
behaviour in prosperity was simply acting a fantasy. This is to put a modern
psychological gloss on the orthodox ancient view.

[31] Τῷ δαίμονι συμμεταβαλεῖν τὸ ἤθος—an adaptation of Heraclitus' ἤθος ἀνθρώπῳ
δαίμων (fr. 119).

[32] Op. cit. 66.

definition a perverted πολιτεία. In 7, he describes how, when Aristides, Themistocles, and Cimon were safely out of the way, Pericles παρὰ τὴν αὑτοῦ φύσιν ἥκιστα δημοτικὴν οὖσαν joined the democratic side. In 9, not very consistently, this move is represented as an answer to Cimon's popularity: unable to afford to be generous with his private wealth, Pericles proceeded πρὸς τὴν τῶν δημοσίων διανομήν, to splash public property around. Finally (14. 2–15. 3) Thucydides was ostracized and Pericles' power was established without challenge. He was no longer the same man, nor amenable (χειροήθης) to the *demos* as he had been before. At last he had become a true doctor, not afraid of harsh remedies where they were needed. Now there is no question here of a change of original endowment; Pericles' final phase is in harmony with his first and with his φύσις. Nor was his assumption of a democratic ἦθος due to circumstances beyond his control; it was deliberate policy, means to an end. Parallels therefore are not Sertorius and Sulla but Marius (28) who became ὑγρὸς καὶ δημοτικὸς παρὰ τὴν αὑτοῦ φύσιν in his candidature for his sixth consulship, and the chameleon-like behaviour of Alcibiades, an athlete at Sparta and a drunkard in Thrace.[33] Such assumption of a part need mean little more than a superficial and conscious change in manners.

In short, Plutarch's conception of change or development in character is nothing original or out of the way in Greek thought. Ἦθος, which he associates, after Aristotle, with ἔθος, is confined on the whole to the overt and public elements of personality. It can certainly change, as a result of circumstances or by deliberate effort; as its essence is to be observable to the world, Plutarch does not distinguish between unconscious changes of personality and mere play-acting. The given or inherited part of personality (φύσις), on the other hand, is never clearly said to change, though the possibility at least of degeneration is left open.[34] Of positive

---

[33] *Alcibiades* 23; Alcibiades is here represented very much as the 'flatterer' (κόλαξ) of *de adulatore et amico*, 51d.

[34] It must be borne in mind that Plutarch is no more consistent in terminology than most ancient writers. The distinction between ἦθος and φύσις, which I here treat as fundamental, is sometimes blurred: *Dion* 8; *Demetrius* 2; *Numa* 3. 7; *Lysander* 2 compared with 23.

development of φύσις, radical amelioration through responsibility or conversion, there is no word. These are limitations, to modern feelings a missing dimension; they confine and impoverish his biographic art, but it would be amazing if he had been able to transcend them.

III

Much has been written about the development of biography before Plutarch;[35] comparatively little certainty has been achieved. The 'prehistory' of the genre, as it were, consists of the Socratic literature, fourth-century encomia like those by Isocrates and Xenophon, and biographical excursuses in history, as in Xenophon and Theopompus. Aristotle's school made a decisive impact. It was a consequence of Peripatetic scholarship that biographies of philosophers and literary men proliferated in Hellenistic times. It was, as we have seen, from the *Ethics* and *Rhetoric* that the categories of ἤθη used by the biographer were derived. But Hellenistic biography has foundered with few traces, sharing the fate of most Hellenistic prose; the Atticizing revival of the early Empire handed down to the last age of antiquity and hence to Byzantium a fair share of its own voluminous works and of the classical models it admired, but not the despised Hellenistics, against whom the revival was itself a reaction. So our knowledge of the genre, at least in Greek, is based almost wholly on Plutarch;[36] for all we know, the scale and scope of the Plutarchian βίος could be his own invention. The Roman Nepos, who does survive from the earlier period, works on a comparatively humble and naïve level: where he is not an encomiast, he is not much more than an excerptor of history.

   Plutarch is quite clear himself that *he* is not writing history: οὔτε γὰρ ἱστορίας γράφομεν ἀλλὰ βίους.[37] He has little

---

[35] See (besides Dihle and Leo, see above, n. 1) A. von Mess in *Rh. Mus.* 70 (1915), 337 ff.; (1916), 79 ff.; D. R. Stuart, *Epochs of Greek and Roman Biography* (Berkeley, Calif., 1928); A. S. Osley, in *Greece & Rome*, 15 (1946), 7–20.

[36] Roman biography is another story; see W. Steidle, *Sueton und die antike Biographie* (Munich, 1951).

[37] *Alexander* 1.

room for the larger elements of historical composition—
speeches, battles, geographical excursuses. He is not bound
to relate everything; he can epitomize at one point and
expand at another. He is not bound to chronology, but can
arrange his material in other ways if he likes.[38] He does not
have to assume the Olympian, half-poetical grandeur of
history, but can descend on occasion to trivialities or to the
informality of personal comment or philosophical argument.
But of course the βίος is usually based on history.[39] It is
rarely based on a single history. Plutarch had read very
widely, and remembered more than a modern scholar easily
thinks possible. Even when he has perforce to follow a
leading historian for his main narrative, he supplements it
from all manner of sources—philosophers, antiquarians,
commentaries on comedy, and so on. It is never easy to
find a passage of any length which clearly comes from one
'source', and in which the process of selection and epitomiz-
ing can be seen in detail. *Coriolanus* and *Nicias* probably
afford the best opportunities of comparing final product
with raw material, though other Lives present chances here
and there. Two types of modification seem to be specially
significant. One is the attribution of motives of an emotional
kind, where the historian deals rather in expediency and
rational calculation. This seems to occur a good deal in
Coriolanus;[40] we should remember that motivation is one of
the elements in ancient historical writing most likely to be
determined by literary considerations rather than by recorded fact. The other is the attribution of public or commu-
nal action to the hero's own initiative: Pelopidas becomes
unduly prominent at Leuctra, Aristides at Marathon, Sertorius with Cinna and Marius in 87.[41] This of course may
distort history more seriously, and it is not always easily

[38] One must always be on the watch for this. One example: *Alcib.* 15 looks like
straight narrative, but the events described in 15. 6 (walls of Patrae) took place
two years before the incidents at Argos described in 15. 3–5. The whole chapter is
in fact a treatment of a single aspect of Alcibiades' policy, not a narrative.
[39] Exceptions include *Timoleon* and *Philopoemen*, where earlier biographies
existed, and *Aratus*, whose own memoirs survived.
[40] *JRS*, loc. cit. above, n. 1.
[41] *Pelopidas* 15–17; *Aristides* 5; *Sertorius* 5. 5; add *Publicola* 21, with R.
Flacelière's comments (Budé edn. (Paris, 1961), 55).

detected. It is a natural consequence of the concentration on one figure, and it occurs most readily where the available material (as with Pelopidas) was small.

We must turn now from the content of the *Lives* to their actual form and arrangement: in terms of ancient rhetoric, from *inventio* to *dispositio*. And we see at once that, despite wide variations, there does seem to be a recognizable and rather complex favoured structure. It fits some types of career better than others: Alcibiades and Sulla better than Aristides and Numa. *Lysander*, which I discuss below, demonstrates it quite well. It would be an ideal fit for Sir Winston Churchill. We should have in fact nine divisions:

1. Ancestry.
2. Personality revealed in childhood anecdotes.
3. Campaigns as a boy (μειράκιον).
4. Entry into politics.
5. First main climax: Gallipoli.
6. In the wilderness in war and peace.
7. Second main climax: Dunkirk and the war.
8. Dramatic change of fortune in 1945.
9. Post-war governments, old age, death, funeral, children.

Add an elaborate Preface, a few digressions (on Blenheim, say, and the historical associations of the Hellespont) and a comparison with some other figure, and a very Plutarchian framework will emerge. Childhood and 'the wilderness' will be handled with many anecdotes; the main events of the two wars will be treated epitome-fashion, but there will be a good deal of vivid narrative, much of it drawn from the subject's own books. A hero who is ἱστορικός as well as πολιτικός will earn special praise for that.

It would be wrong to pursue a fancy too far, but I think this one is a convenient short cut, since it throws into relief most of the principles of arrangement which Plutarch usually strives for: his emphasis on education, where the ἦθος is formed and first seen; the pin-pointing of débuts, climaxes, and reverses of fortune which shape and make memorable the whole narrative; and the concern for variation between narrative and description.[42] But there is one point where the model fails conspicuously: it does not bring out the importance of comparison (σύγκρισις) at all levels of Plutarch's activity. This is an essential point to grasp.

The formal comparisons which are found at the end of most of the books of the *Parallel Lives* were at one time much admired. Less rhetorical ages find them uncongenial. The ingenuity seems wasted on trivial similarities and differences. These exercises, however, were in a sense the genesis of the whole enterprise. They come from the rhetor's classroom—they are akin to the debate in *de sollertia animalium* on whether land-animals or water-animals are the more intelligent. But just as the *Lives* transcend the limitations set by the notion of an historical figure as a moral *exemplum*, so they escape the constricting influence of these rhetorical set pieces.[43] Plutarch's real narrative genius and deep moral seriousness ensure this. Rarely, if ever, are the comparisons allowed to distort the picture given in the *Lives*. Anyway, they were always written afterwards.

Instead, the spirit of σύγκρισις reveals itself in other and more profitable ways. The character of a hero may be clarified by a succession of comparisons with others. Thus Fabius Maximus, the embodiment of strategic caution, is brought into contact successively with five less circumspect commanders. Three of these, Flaminius, Minucius, and Varro, suffer for their imprudence. With the fourth, Marcellus, Fabius forms an invincible combination: one is Rome's shield, the other her sword. Only when the fifth rival, Scipio, appears, does Fabius' caution become fruitless and negative; indeed (25. 3–4) it degenerates into malignant φιλοτιμία, which makes him want to put a spoke into Scipio's wheel just for the sake of doing so. Thus what we may call 'syncritical' technique is used throughout to throw the

---

[42] A. Weizsäcker, *Untersuchungen über Plutarchs biographische Technik* (Berlin, 1931), elaborated the concept of 'chronological' and 'eidological' elements in the *Lives*. The distinction is valuable, but the alternation between the two often takes place within very short passages, and it is over-simplification to think of the *Lives* as made up of alternating masses of these two types of writing.

[43] For σύγκρισις as an elementary rhetorical exercise (προγύμνασμα) see, e.g., Hermogenes, pp. 18 ff. Rabe; D. L. Clark, *Rhetoric in Greco-Roman Education* (New York, 1957), 198 f.

main character into relief and display both his virtues and his limitations. *Fabius* is the most elaborate example of this technique, but it is found also in *Pericles*—where the hero is contrasted successively with Cimon, Tolmides, and Thucydides—and in *Marius, Lysander, Antony*, and some other Lives.

Σύγκρισις is a key idea for the understanding of Plutarch's purposes and methods of arrangement. Nor is it fanciful to see in his style, with its innumerable comparisons and μέν ... δέ sentences, the same tendency at work in a more microscopic field. But that, as he would say himself, belongs to ἄλλη πραγματεία.

IV

Lysander is not one of the most brilliant Lives, but it provides convenient examples of many of the features to which I have tried to draw attention. It is a well-composed Life, based mostly on historians: Xenophon, Theopompus, and (to a less degree) Ephorus. It has been well studied from a 'source-criticism' point of view.[44]

Plutarch begins with a striking Preface, meant to seize the reader's attention. He corrects a popular fallacy current at Delphi: the statue at the door of the Treasury of the Acanthians represents, he tells us, not Brasidas but Lysander. Let us call this προοίμιον ἀπὸ οἰκείου, following a hint in Lucian[45] about historians' prefaces: they should aim, he says, at securing προσοχή and εὐμάθεια though they need make no special effort for εὔνοια; and προσοχή is secured if the topic broached is 'great', 'essential', 'familiar', or 'useful'. Plutarch chooses the familiar. Having thus ensnared his audience—and incidentally conveyed some information about Lysander's appearance—Plutarch proceeds (2) to his hero's family and upbringing. He is later going to make use of the judgement that Lysander was (*a*) ambitious, φιλότιμος, (*b*) sly and deceitful. At this stage, we are told

---

[44] R. Dippel, Diss. Giessen, 1898 (*Quae ratio intercedat inter Xenophontis historiam Graecam et Plutarchi vitas quaeritur*).
[45] *De conscribenda historia*, 53.

that his ambition was the result of the competitive spirit of
Spartan education: 'there is no great call to blame his φύσις
for it.' His submissiveness to authority and prudent εὐκολία
were, however, natural endowment. Though Plutarch does
not make the point, it is easy to see that these characteristics
could degenerate into the disingenuousness of his later
career. He was also, we are told, μελαγχολικός—i.e. impulsive and unstable;[46] Plutarch makes use of this later (28. 1),
where he associates the progress of the condition with
Lysander's worsening temper and growing cruelty. We are
also reminded of a peculiarity (ἴδιον) or paradox of his
career—namely that he imbued his country with φιλοπλουτία, while remaining uncorrupted and indeed penniless
himself. This also is taken up later (16–17).

The initial character-drawing is followed by the opening
of the narrative (3). This is in what may be called 'epitome
style'. A single long period leads from a general statement
that the war was dragging on and Alcibiades reviving Athenian sea-power to the decisive moment of Lysander's dis-
patch as admiral. Everything leads up to the last word of
the whole sentence: ἐκπέμπουσιν ἐπὶ τὴν τῆς θαλάττης ἡγεμονίαν Λύσανδρον. But before the detailed narrative begins, there
follows what is perhaps another appeal ἀπὸ τοῦ οἰκείου,
another move to 'make history live'. Lysander goes to
Ephesus and rescues it from the threat of being swamped
and barbarized by the influx of the surrounding Lydian
population; he is thus, adds Plutarch, responsible for the
present greatness of the city.

The narrative of Lysander's part in the last stages of the
war occupies cc. 4–15. It is too long to analyse here. Something has gone wrong with the chronology of the surrender
of Athens. There are distortions of a characteristic kind, in
which initiatives are given to Lysander which were not
really his. There is a prominent 'syncritical' theme (7)
in the contrast between the foxy Lysander and the bluff
Callicratidas.

The war over, there follows (16–17) the story of the
iniquities of Gylippus, followed by a disquisition of

---

[46] Cf. Aristot. *EN* 1150[b]25. Plutarch's authority for the fact is Aristotle: *Probl.*
953[a]20.

Plutarch's on the folly of the Spartan government in thinking that they might allow the public possession of coin
without fomenting private φιλαργυρία. All this too is 'syncritical': Lysander's personal incorruptibility is thrown into
relief by the contrast with Gylippus and the average Spartan.

Chapter 18 is devoted to the honours paid to Lysander.
This is the acme of his power and fame; the beginning of
the next chapter clearly marks a change. His φιλοτιμία (19.
1), always galling to his equals, was now aggravated by
arrogance induced by flattery, and he developed a tendency
to extremes both of kindness and cruelty. Nothing would
now satisfy his anger but the extermination of the offender.
This characterization leads naturally to the account of his
recall; but Plutarch surprisingly inserts at this point a long
digression on the σκυτάλη—an antiquarian curiosity already
mentioned in 14. This insertion should warn us not to
investigate his artistic motives too delicately. It is hard to
believe that he is simply following a source which *happened
to have* an antiquarian note here, and yet even more unconvincing to argue that he thought 19 rhetorically a better
place for such a pause in the action than the account of the
surrender of Athens. What we have before us is best
described as a misplaced footnote.

Outwitted by Pharnabazus, who he hoped might give
testimony in his favour but who in fact out-foxed him,
Lysander with difficulty obtains leave from the ephors to
go to Libya to the oracle of Ammon. He is not long away.
On his return he is sent to Athens to maintain the rule of
the Thirty, only to be snubbed by King Pausanias, though
the latter's policy was proved wrong by subsequent events.
There is more σύγκρισις here (21–2): Lysander the honest
patriot against the double-dealing king. And lest this should
seem paradoxical in view of Lysander's earlier reputation
for craftiness, his outspokenness to his opponents is demonstrated (22) by a series of anecdotes, quotations from his
λόγοι.

We then pass to a new and important topic and a new
σύγκρισις: his relations with Agesilaus. Lysander plays the
decisive part in the accession of the new king; but, once
established, Agesilaus proves something of a thorn in the

flesh. When the two first arrived in Asia, Lysander's fame eclipsed the king's, but Agesilaus soon countered and destroyed his rival's influence. Now Plutarch has left another account (*Agesilaus* 7–8) of this rivalry between these two φιλότιμοι φύσεις, and a comparison between the two narratives is instructive. One point is that, although both Lives admit Agesilaus to be somewhat to blame, the Life of Lysander makes this seem much worse by drawing attention to the obligation he owed in return for Lysander's help in putting him on the throne. Another is that the Life of Lysander makes the stages in the decline of its hero's influence rather more complicated. First, Agesilaus stops doing favours for his friends. Lysander then tells them to go straight to the king if they want anything. But they still keep up their personal contact with Lysander, and this testimony to his popularity irks Agesilaus even more than the original situation. The success of a rival is always more galling when deserved by his personal qualities than when it can be attributed to unavoidable circumstances. In *Agesilaus*, this evidence of pure φθόνος on the king's part is omitted; indeed (7), it is suggested that he was not φθονερός, but simply very φιλότιμος.

There remain two episodes. The first (24–6) is Lysander's plan for revolution and opening up the kingship to all Heraclids: here Plutarch has a long account from a philosophical source (25 end) of the oracles with which he backed his proposals. The second (27–9) comprises the Boeotian war and Lysander's death at Haliartus. Here Plutarch is again expansive, because another of his special interests, Boeotian antiquities, is touched, and there is a good deal of local detail about the Haliartus region.

The closing chapter (30) is, as often, quiet and factual. The *Lives* do not as a rule have perorations. Lysander died poor. Though his revolutionary ideas became known, he was none the less honoured after his death, and his daughter's suitors were punished for backing out of their marriages when they found how poor the family was.

Such is the Life of Lysander. It gives at least the outline of a psychological study of the hero. It marks the acme and failures of his career, and contrasts him with the clashing

94   *D. A. Russell*

personalities of Callicratidas, Gylippus, Pausanias, and Agesilaus. It is diversified by digressions and much local Boeotian and Delphian material. Indeed, one suspects it was
written at Delphi—or why should Plutarch say (29) that
Lysander's monument is 'by the side of the road as you
go *from* Delphi *to* Chaeronea'? In short, it is a microcosm
of the habits of thought and writing, the attitudes to the
past, and the range of interests which make Plutarchian
biography what it is.[47]

[47] A note on editions of the *Lives* may be useful. The Teubner by Ziegler and
others, now being revised, gives the standard critical text. The Loeb, while fairly
reliable in translation, gives little help in interpretation; the new Budé, by R.
Flacelière, which now extends to three volumes (12 *Lives*), is much more useful.
The old separate editions of *Themistocles, Nicias, Gracchi, Sulla, Demosthenes,
Pericles, Timoleon,* by H. A. Holden may still be of use in schools, but should be
used with caution. Of more recent editions may be mentioned *Aratus* and *Dion* by
W. H. Porter, *Caesar* by A. Garzetti, *Cicero* by D. Magnino, *Aristides* by Ida
Limentani, *Demetrius* by E. Manni (these Italian editions are all in Biblioteca di
Studi Superiori, La Nuova Italia).

3

Towards a Chronology of Plutarch's Works

C. P. JONES

The belief is widespread that the majority of Plutarch's works was written after the death of Domitian in 96, when the author was a comparatively old man. So far, however, the foundations for this belief have not been firmly laid. The latest study of Plutarchian chronology, that of Ziegler,[1] omits much, and new evidence is constantly accruing. The following study is an attempt to make use of all the material now available that bears on the dating of Plutarch's works. It cannot be definitive: there may be omissions, certain problems (such as that of Plutarch's marriage and the number of his children) appear insoluble, and new data, particularly new inscriptions, that affect the question are sure to turn up.

The study has five parts. In Part I the dating of two of the *moralia* is discussed separately, since the argument is complex and has not been advanced before. In Part II I have considered Plutarch's relations with Hadrian and the date of his death. Part III comprises a discussion of the chronology and the methods of publication of the *Parallel Lives*. This is a question at once insoluble in its entirety and yet indispensable for the present study. In Part IV I have reviewed the chronology of that fraction of Plutarch's works that can be dated securely (stylistic evidence has not been admitted). Finally in Part V some conclusions are drawn about the significance of these dates for Plutarch's career and development.

For their help in the preparation of this article I wish to thank most deeply Professors H. Bloch, G. W. Bowersock, and A. D. Momigliano.

[1] K. Ziegler, *RE* 21 (1951—also published separately, 1949), 708 ff. (henceforth cited as 'Ziegler').

I. THE DATES OF COMPOSITION OF THE *DE COHIBENDA*
IRA AND THE *DE TRANQUILLITATE ANIMI*

A hitherto neglected detail provides a valuable clue to the *terminus post* of the dialogue *de cohibenda ira*. The principal speaker, Fundanus, is generally agreed to be C. Minicius Fundanus, suffect consul in 107, and as proconsul of Asia in 122/3 the recipient of a famous rescript from Hadrian.[2] In the dialogue Plutarch makes Fundanus refer to the effects of his anger on 'my wife and little daughters' (τῇ γυναικὶ καὶ τοῖς θυγατρίοις, 455 F), and this serves to date the work. For in one of his letters Pliny refers to the death of Fundanus' younger daughter (*Ep.* 5, 16), and moreover mentions her age according to the manuscripts, *nondum annos* XIIII *impleverat*. This can be proved to be not quite correct, since by a lucky chance yet another text concerning this girl is extant. In 1881 her funerary urn was found in Rome, and its legend revealed that at her death she was not quite thirteen: *v(ixit) a(nnos) xii m(enses) xi d(ies) vii*.[3] Pliny's text must be emended accordingly, for it is unduly conservative to assume that he had mistaken the girl's age rather than that one of his scribes in the course of centuries added a single stroke before the following 'impleverat'.[4]

It is clear from Pliny that when his younger daughter died, Fundanus was a widower and left with only the other daughter.[5] These two daughters, then, are the θυγάτρια to which Plutarch refers, and the *terminus post* of his treatise is the birth of the younger daughter, about thirteen years before Pliny's letter was written. Since its date can be shown by comparison with others in the same book to be about 105 or 106,[6] the *terminus post* of Plutarch's dialogue must be 92–3.

In defining the *terminus ante* it is important to distinguish

---

[2] *PIR* M 433; Groag, *RE* 15: 1820 ff.
[3] *ILS* 1030.
[4] So G. P. Goold, *Phoenix*, 17 (1963), 144.
[5] Pliny, ib., 'sororem patrem adhortabatur'.
[6] Syme, *Tacitus* (1958), 661.

the dramatic date from the date of composition. The former must, of course, be between 92–3 and 105–6; a date early in this period is suggested by Plutarch's reference to Fundanus' wife as still living, and by his use of the diminutive θυγάτρια. To ascertain the date of composition is more difficult. The analogy of other of Plutarch's dialogues cannot be invoked: the *de cohibenda ira* is almost unique in that the main dialogue is not introduced by a first-person narrative (like Plato's *Republic*) or by a secondary dialogue (like the *Symposium*), but like the *Gorgias* consists of a single dialogue. In favour of assuming that the *de cohibenda ira* describes a situation which obtained at the time of writing, there is the consideration that Plutarch would hardly have portrayed Fundanus' wife and daughter as still alive when in reality both were dead. If this is so, the dramatic date, like the date of composition, will be not later than about 100; otherwise the work will have been written at any time between 93 and Plutarch's death.

Fundanus is mentioned in only one other work of Plutarch, the *de tranquillitate animi*. For this work a *terminus ante* has been proposed on the evidence of the words τοὺς Ῥωμαίων ὅρα βασιλεῖς, ὧν οὐδεὶς υἱῷ τὴν ἀρχὴν ἀπέλιπε (467 E). By Plutarch's day βασιλεύς had come to be widely used as the usual term for the emperor;[7] and since the first emperor to be succeeded by his son was Vespasian, whom Titus succeeded in 79, it has been held that this year is the *terminus ante* of Plutarch's work.[8]

Two linguistic arguments, however, can be adduced to prove that in this sentence Plutarch cannot have meant to refer to the emperors. First, βασιλεύς is not at all his usual term for 'emperor'. To refer to the title, on the one hand, he uses αὐτοκράτωρ: thus 'to proclaim Galba emperor' is αὐτοκράτορα Γάλβαν ἀναγορεῦσαι (*Galba* 2), and 'an embassy to the emperor', when no emperor in particular is meant, is πρεσβεία πρὸς αὐτοκράτορα (*praec. ger. reip.* 805 A). To refer

[7] A. Wifstrand, Δρᾶγμα *Nilsson* (1939), 529 ff.
[8] So J. P. Mahaffy, *Greek World under Roman Sway* (1890), 346 n. 1, followed by E. H. Alton, *CR* 32 (1918), 150; T. Renoirte, *Les 'Conseils Politiques' de Plutarque* (1951), 139. Against, W. C. Helmbold, edition of Plutarch's *Moralia*, Loeb Library, vol. vi (1939), 185 n. (e). The issue is ignored by Ziegler.

to specific emperors, however, he uses Καῖσαρ.⁹ In the very few places where he uses βασιλεύς of a Roman emperor, he does so in the sense of αὐτοκράτωρ, not of Καῖσαρ.¹⁰ If in the *de tranquillitate animi* he had wished to refer to the emperors, in the specific sense of 'all those who have so far been emperors', he would have used Καίσαρες, just as elsewhere he refers in this sense to the 'house of the Caesars' (ὁ Καισάρων οἶκος, *Galba* 3). Second, the simple υἱός in ordinary usage did not distinguish adoptive from natural sons: Plutarch himself refers to Augustus as the 'son' of Julius Caesar (*de fort. Rom.* 319 D). It follows that he cannot refer here to the emperors, since before Vespasian Augustus and Claudius had already been succeeded by their adoptive sons. By βασιλεῖς he means not the emperors of Rome but the seven kings, none of whom 'left his power to his son', either natural or adoptive.¹¹

Other arguments, so far overlooked by students of Plutarch, suggest for the *de tranquillitate animi* a date considerably later than 79. These arguments are powerful and convergent.

First, the evidence of prosopography. In this treatise Plutarch refers to Minicius Fundanus as ὁ κράτιστος (464 F), a term denoting the respect due to an eminent man. To be consul in 107 and proconsul of Asia in 122/3, Fundanus cannot have been born much, if at all, before 60; with this agrees the fact that his younger daughter was born in 92–3. 79 is far too early for Plutarch to speak of him so deferentially. It is more appropriate after his consulate in 107.

Second, a point of history. In a well-known passage of the same treatise, Plutarch censures those from Chios, Galatia, and Bithynia who are not satisfied with reputation and influence in their native cities, but 'complain that they do not wear patrician shoes; if they do, that they are not yet Roman praetors; if they are praetors, that they are not yet

⁹ Thus Tiberius: *de def. orac.* 419 D, *de exil.* 602 E, *an seni* 794 B; Gaius: *Galba* 9, 12; Claudius: ib. 12; Vespasian: *amat.* 770 C; Titus: *de tuenda san.* 124 C (but Τίτος ὁ αὐτοκράτωρ, 123 D); Trajan: *de primo frig.* 949 E. Καῖσαρ alone usually designates Augustus: thus *Rom.* 17. 3; *Per.* 1. 1; *Cic.* 49. 5 f.; *Marc.* 30. 10 f., *al.*
¹⁰ Thus *quaest. conviv.* 630 F, 632 F, 655 F. Cf., however, *de def. orac.* 419 E.
¹¹ Even if Plutarch thought with Livy (1. 46. 4) that Tarquinius Priscus was the father of Tarquinius Superbus, still Priscus did not 'leave his power' to Superbus, but was succeeded by Servius Tullius.

consuls; if they are consuls, that they were named last and not first' (470 c).[12] Though men from the Greek East had long since become Roman praetors,[13] the first of them to attain the consulate did so in 90, and the first *consul ordinarius* from the Orient held office precisely in 105.[14] The whole sentence presupposes a date not earlier than the reign of Trajan, who first admitted Easterners in large numbers to the Roman senate.[15]

The *de tranquillitate animi* and the *de cohibenda ira* are united both by affinity of subject and because in both of them, and nowhere else, Plutarch mentions Minicius Fundanus and his Greek friend Eros (*de cohib. ira* 453 c, *de tranqu. animi* 464 f). It has already been established that the *de cohibenda ira* was written after 92–3; and hence a final argument for the dating of the *de tranquillitate animi* to the same period. Both were written in the years which were demonstrably those of Plutarch's greatest literary activity.

The newly established date of the *de tranquillitate animi* has also a prosopographical consequence; the Paccius to whom it is addressed emerges as a person of Trajanic or early Hadrianic date. He was, it seems, a man of heavy responsibilities (468 c), of good connections (465 A), and with 'a forensic reputation second to none' (ib.). His name can therefore be added to the roster of orators contemporary with Pliny and Tacitus.[16] Though he can still not be identified with any known Paccius, the new date encourages speculation about the unique brick-stamp, dated 123, 'ex figlinis Pacciorum'.[17]

[12] On the use of πατρίκιοι for senatorial, not patrician shoes, see Mau, *RE* 3: 1340 f.

[13] Q. Pompeius Macer from Mitylene in 15 (*ILS* 9349); M. Plancius Varus from Perge in Pamphylia (S. Jameson, *JRS* 55 (1965), 54 ff.), and M. Antonius Flamma from Cyrene (*PIR*² A 831; cf. J. Reynolds, *JRS* 49 (1959), 97) under Nero; and, about the same time, L. Servenius Cornutus from Acmonia in Phrygia (*ILS* 8817). Cf. Syme, *Tacitus* (1958), 509 n. 4.

[14] C. Caristanius Fronto from Pisidian Antioch in 90 (*ILS* 9485: for the consulate, see N. Alfieri, *Athenaeum*, 26 (1948), 116); Ti. Julius Celsus Polemaeanus from Ephesus or Sardis in 92 (*ILS* 8971), and C. Antius A. Julius Quadratus from Pergamum in 94 (*ILS* 8819). Cf. Syme, op. cit. 510. Quadratus was *cos. II ord.* in 105.

[15] On Trajan's policy towards Eastern senators, see most recently M. Hammond, *JRS* 47 (1957), 79; Chr. Habicht, *Istamb. Mitt.* 9/10 (1959–60), 121 f.

[16] Syme, op. cit. 668 ff.

[17] Published by H. Bloch, to whom I owe this reference, *HSCP* 56–7 (1947), 75, No. 353.

II. PLUTARCH AND HADRIAN

That Plutarch survived to the reign of Hadrian is well attested by an inscription and by Eusebius: the inscription, probably set up soon after 117, shows that Plutarch was still priest at Delphi and epimelete of the Amphictyons, and according to Eusebius in 119 he was 'appointed in his old age by the emperor to be procurator of Hellas'.[18]

It is not at all impossible that Plutarch met and knew the emperor. Hadrian visited Greece three times,[19] and lavished an attention on Delphi that caused many statues to be erected in his honour and the Delphians to hail him as the restorer of the city.[20] Consequently, it is tempting to scan Plutarch's writings for references to him. But in vain: as will appear, there is no passage in which a clear reference to Hadrian can be discerned, and indeed no work of Plutarch that can safely be dated to his reign on any grounds. It appears rather that Plutarch died shortly after 117.

The principal passage in which a reference to the new emperor has been seen occurs in the dialogue de Pythiae oraculis (408 F ff.). The speaker, who is named Theon, is made by Plutarch to praise the Delphic oracle as follows:

οὐ δένα καθ' αὑτῆς ἔλεγχον ἄχρι νῦν παραδέδωκεν, ἀναθημάτων δὲ καὶ δώρων ἐμπέπληκε βαρβαρικῶν καὶ Ἑλληνικῶν τὸ χρηστήριον, οἰκοδομημάτων δὲ ⟨κατακεκόσμηκε⟩ κάλλεσι καὶ κατασκευαῖς Ἀμφικτυονικαῖς. ὁρᾶτε δήπουθεν αὐτοὶ πολλὰ μὲν ἐπεκτισμένα τῶν πρότερον οὐκ ὄντων, πολλὰ δ' ἀνειλημμένα τῶν συγκεχυμένων καὶ διεφθαρμένων. ὡς δὲ τοῖς εὐθαλέσι τῶν δένδρων ἕτερα παραβλαστάνει, καὶ τοῖς Δελφοῖς ἡ Πυλαία συνηβᾷ καὶ συναναβόσκεται διὰ τὰς ἐντεῦθεν εὐπορίας σχῆμα λαμβάνουσα καὶ μορφὴν καὶ κόσμον ἱερῶν καὶ συνεδρίων καὶ ὑδάτων οἷον ἐν χιλίοις ἔτεσι τοῖς πρότερον οὐκ ἔλαβεν.

---

[18] Inscription: SIG³ 829 A (on the date, see Pomtow ad loc., n. 1). Eusebius apud Syncellus 349 B (659, 13), on which see Groag, Reichsbeamten von Achaia (1939), 145 ff.; Pflaum, Les Carrières procuratoriennes équestres, 3 (1961), 1071.

[19] In 124/5, 128/9, and 131/2: see W. Weber, Untersuchungen zur Geschichte des Kaisers Hadrianus (1907), 156 ff., 205 ff., 268 ff.

[20] Hadrian and Delphi: E. Bourguet, De rebus Delphicis imperatoriae aetatis (1905), 72 ff. Statues erected to him: SIG³ 829, 835. ὤρθωσας τὴν πόλιν: inscription in Bourguet, op. cit. 84 f., l. 27.

Theon proceeds to compare Galaxium in Boeotia, to the inhabitants of which Apollo had shown his favour by producing a miraculous abundance of milk in their cattle. He continues:

ἡμῖν δὲ λαμπρότερα καὶ κρείττονα καὶ σαφέστερα σημεῖα τούτων ἀναδίδωσιν, ὥσπερ ἐξ αὐχμοῦ τῆς πρόσθεν ἐρημίας καὶ πενίας εὐπορίαν καὶ λαμπρότητα καὶ τιμὴν πεποιηκώς. καίτοι φιλῶ μὲν ἐμαυτὸν ἐφ' οἷς ἐγενόμην εἰς τὰ πράγματα ταῦτα πρόθυμος καὶ χρήσιμος μετὰ Πολυκράτους καὶ Πετραίου, φιλῶ δὲ τὸν καθηγεμόνα ταύτης τῆς πολιτείας γενόμενον ἡμῖν καὶ τὰ πλεῖστα τούτων ἐκφροντίζοντα καὶ παρασκευάζοντα ... ἀλλ' οὐκ ἔστιν [ἄλλως ὅτι] τηλικαύτην καὶ τοσαύτην μεταβολὴν ἐν ὀλίγῳ χρόνῳ γενέσθαι δι' ἀνθρωπίνης ἐπιμελείας, μὴ θεοῦ παρόντος ἐνταῦθα καὶ συνεπιθειάζοντος τὸ χρηστήριον.

κατακεκόσμηκε add. Schwartz.   παρασκευάζοντα ... lac. 25 litt. E, 30 B.
ἄλλως ὅτι del. Reiske.

The controversy that has centred on this passage mainly concerns the denotation of the phrase τὸν καθηγεμόνα ταύτης τῆς πολιτείας. Those who would see in it a reference to Hadrian regard him as this 'leader', and base their belief on the fact that in his reign Delphi, like many cities in the Roman world, enjoyed a revival abundantly attested by inscriptions.[21] But this hypothesis raises several difficulties. First, the earliest datable indication of Hadrian's benefactions to Delphi falls in 125, when Plutarch was about 80, and this is late for him to have noticed them in a published work.[22] Second, Plutarch would hardly have contrasted so casually the divine help of Apollo with the 'mortal help' of the emperor. Even if he advances elsewhere unfavourable views on the cult of living persons, he would not have expressed them in a passage intended to be a panegyric of

---

[21] So Bourguet, op. cit. 74; Pomtow, *ad SIG*³ 830 n. 6; Flacelière, *Rev. de Phil.* 3ᵉ sér. 8 (1934), 56 ff. and frequently since.

[22] *SIG*³ 835 B. Flacelière, art. cit. 64, asserts that the date of Plutarch's death 'ne doit pas être antérieure à 127', referring to W. Christ, *Geschichte der griechischen Literatur*⁴ (1905), 675. Christ's evidence was the identification of an Egyptian riot mentioned by Plutarch (*de Isid. et Osir.* 380 B f.) with that of Juvenal 15. 27 ff. (*consule Iunco*). Christ himself, however, had doubts about the identification (ib., n. 4) and in fact it is incorrect: see now Ziegler, 640 f. On the true date of Plutarch's death see below, p. 106.

Hadrian.[23] But the greatest weakness of the thesis that Hadrian is the 'leader' was only exposed in 1938. Since Reiske the belief had been unquestioned that the 'Pylaea' to which Plutarch refers as the site of 'temples, meeting-places, and fountains' was a suburb of Delphi. In 1938, however, this suburb was shown to have been a mirage: Plutarch is commemorating the new prosperity not of a suburb but, as the context suggests, of the other meeting-place of the Amphictyons, Thermopylae.[24] Thus a large part of the new building to which he refers is removed at a blow to Thermopylae, and Hadrian's benefactions to Delphi become a much weaker reason for construing this passage as a reference to him. Of course, if it were known that Hadrian was the first emperor to take an interest in Delphi, and that before him the shrine had been totally neglected, the conclusion that Plutarch wrote these words in his reign, if not in reference to him, would still be inescapable; but in fact Augustus, Claudius, Nero, Titus, Domitian (who restored the temple of Apollo), and Trajan are all known to have favoured the shrine.[25] In view, therefore, of the other obstacles to referring this passage to Hadrian, or indeed to any emperor, it is necessary to look elsewhere for the 'leader'.

Though this passage thus becomes irrelevant to the present inquiry, it is worth taking the search to its conclusion. There remain two possibilities. First, it might be suggested that the 'leader' is the god Apollo.[26] καθηγεμών is indeed a *vox propria* of deities. It is found applied to Artemis and Dionysus; Antiochus IV of Commagene used it of the μεγάλων δαιμόνων ἐπιφάνειαι that had assured him a

---

[23] Despite Flacelière, *REG* 63 (1950), 302. Though Plutarch several times castigates the worship of Hellenistic monarchs (K. Scott, *TAPA* 60 (1929), 117 ff), he never mentions the emperor-cult.

[24] Daux, *Rev. Arch.* 6ᵉ sér. 11 (1938), 3 ff., whose arguments are now accepted by Flacelière, *Plutarque: Dialogue sur les oracles de la Pythie* (1962), 80 f.

[25] Augustus: Plut. *de E Delph.* 385 F. Claudius: *SIG³* 801 D. Nero: Dio Cass. 63. 14. 2. Titus: *SIG³* 817. Domitian: *SIG³* 821 A (temple), C. Trajan: inscription in Bourguet, op cit. nn. 20, 70.

[26] In a seminar on Plutarch at Harvard in 1963 this interpretation was considered and rejected by Prof. G. W. Bowersock, who has nevertheless kindly allowed me to make it public.

happy reign;[27] and Plutarch himself uses it of Aphrodite (*Thes.* 18. 3). It is true that this interpretation would require taking the καίτοι sentence to contain two opposing ideas introduced respectively by καίτοι μέν and δέ, which is somewhat unusual: but this construction is found precisely in Plato, the source of so much in Plutarch.[28] However, there are other difficulties in the way of this interpretation that are not so easily disposed of. It makes the καίτοι and the ἀλλά sentences equivalent in meaning, since both will now contrast the work of Apollo with that of Polycrates, Petraeus, and Theon, when the ἀλλά ought to mark a break in the sense (though it is true that the text is defective at this point). Further, it makes Plutarch refer to Apollo as having 'planned and executed' works at Delphi, and to ascribe to him only 'most' of what had been done. This interpretation, like the first, is untenable: it is necessary again to look among mortals, though not to the emperors, for the 'leader'.

The only other known person who might qualify (if indeed Plutarch is referring to a well-known person) is none other than Plutarch.[29] He was for a very long time priest and epimelete of Delphi, and had celebrated it in his Pythian dialogues; after his death, Delphi joined with Chaeronea in raising a monument to him.[30] Moreover, he might well have been responsible for the conception and execution of building there, for in his home town also he supervised the construction of public buildings and even superintended 'the measuring out of tiles and the conveyance of cement and stones' (*praec. ger. reip.* 811 C). The chief objection to this interpretation is that it is uncharacteristically immodest of Plutarch to represent one of his friends praising him for his services to Delphi.[31] But if he allows his father in

[27] Artemis: *SIG*³ 559, l. 36. Dionysus: *CIG* 3067, l. 2, 3068 A, l. 5 (Teos); *SIG*³ 694, l. 46 (Pergamum). Antiochus: *OGIS* 383, ll. 85 ff. These and other examples in Flacelière, *Rev. de Phil.* 3ᵉ sér. 8 (1934), 61 n. 1.

[28] Denniston, *Greek Particles*² (1954), 558. The fact that μέν and δέ are both preceded by the same word, φιλῶ, would normally suggest that they introduced unopposed sentences (ib. 370).

[29] So Ziegler, 661, after Hirzel and others. For καθηγεμών of a political leader, cf. *praec. ger. reip.* 805 F.

[30] *SIG*³ 843.

[31] Note the uneasiness of Wilamowitz, *Glaube der Hellenen*, 2 (1932), 470 n. 4; cf. Flacelière, *REG* 63 (1950), 301 f.

another dialogue to speak of the road to justice 'which under the guidance of Plato my son is showing . . . to those who are willing not to resist but to follow and learn' (*de soll. anim.* 964 D),[32] he could perhaps allow Theon here to praise him for his services to Delphi, especially since he does not fail to acknowledge that his help would have been nothing without Apollo's. There is no difficulty, therefore, in supposing that like his friends Petraeus, who was epimelete of the Amphictyons,[33] and Polycrates, who was probably Helladarch,[34] Plutarch played a considerable part in the revival of Delphic prosperity, and might fairly have called himself the 'leader' of the new policy.

Thus the *de Pythiae oraculis* cannot be shown to be of Hadrianic date. But there remain several of Plutarch's works which, because they anticipate measures that the emperor carried out on his visits to Greece, or for other reasons, might be dated to his reign.

More than one of Hadrian's measures in Greece appear to be adumbrated in the writings of Plutarch; and since Plutarch is known to have lived to his reign and to have been his procurator, it is imaginable that these adumbrations contain advice or hints to the new emperor. Plutarch might certainly have been gratified, for example, when apparently in 125 Hadrian restored to Mantinea her original name in place of 'Antigonea', which commemorated Antigonus Doson's alliance with Aratus;[35] for Plutarch had deplored the name 'Antigonea' in the *Life of Aratus* (45. 8 f.). He might similarly have been pleased when Hadrian completed the Athenian temple of Olympian Zeus in 131/2,[36] for he had referred to the incompleteness of this temple in the *Life of Solon* (32. 2). Hadrian may also have been anticipated by Plutarch when in 124 he began to rebuild the temple of Apollo at Megara in marble.[37] Plutarch records

---

[32] That the speaker is Plutarch's father, however, is not quite certain: Ziegler, 644.

[33] *SIG*³ 825 A–C.

[34] *SIG*³ 846; but this may refer to his son (Pomtow, ad loc., n. 3).

[35] Pausanias, 8. 8. 12. On the date: Weber, *Untersuchungen zur Geschichte des Kaisers Hadrianus* (1907), 185.

[36] Weber, op. cit. 268 ff.

[37] Pausanias, 1. 42. 5; cf. Weber, op. cit. 180 f.

that Antony inspected the council-house at Megara, 'and moreover he measured out the temple of the Pythian god, intending to complete it, for so he promised the senate' (*Ant.* 23. 3 f.). It is usually assumed that Antony's promise concerned the temple of Apollo at Delphi,[38] but since the cult of Apollo Pythios is attested at Megara Plutarch may have meant the same temple as that rebuilt by Hadrian. Lastly, a connection between the author and the emperor might be seen in certain coins, issued only in this reign, that show the E which Plutarch celebrated in one of his dialogues.[39] But to assume that Plutarch used his published works to convey advice to the emperor is unnecessary. As an eminent Greek, he might perhaps have given advice to Hadrian privately; more probably these measures were such as any emperor with Hadrian's knowledge of Greek antiquities and his love of Greece would have carried out.

There remain only two works that have been dated at all plausibly to the reign of Hadrian. In the *amatorius*, a work certainly written after 96 (771 C), Plutarch mentions a person who had 'fallen' in Egypt (771 B), and this has been taken as a reference to the Jewish revolt that broke out there and in other provinces at the end of Trajan's reign.[40] But recent research shows that Roman troops fought with the insurgents a pitched battle, in which the man referred to by Plutarch could have fallen, as early as 115;[41] besides, there had been previous outbreaks in Egypt crushed by Roman force.[42] The treatise on old men in politics has also been dated to the reign of Hadrian because of Plutarch's reference in it to the 'many Pythiads' during which he had served Apollo (792 F).[43] If it were certain that Plutarch here referred to his duties as epimelete of the Amphictyons, this might be so: but he could equally well refer to his

[38] For instance, by von Gaertringen, *RE* 4: 2578; Daux, *Delphes au IIe et au Ier Siècle* (1936), 410 n. 1: against, Pomtow, *apud* von Gaertringen, ib.
[39] I. N. Svoronos, *BCH* 20 (1896), 36, No. 54; 46, No. 88.
[40] Cichorius, *Römische Studien* (1922), 406 ff.
[41] A. Fuks, *JRS* 51 (1961), 98 ff.
[42] Dio of Prusa 32. 72; perhaps Plut. *de Iside et Osir.* 380 B f. (on the date of this work, see above, n. 22, and below, p. 122).
[43] So West, *CP* 23 (1928), 266.

service in the priesthood of Apollo, and he may have held
this position since the 90s.[44]

Thus there is nothing in his works that shows Plutarch to
have outlasted Trajan: only the inscription and the passage
of Eusebius already referred to prove that he did, though
they do not indicate that he lived long past 117. That he
died soon after this date is suggested by evidence that has
hitherto been overlooked. There were at this time two
priests of Apollo at Delphi, each holding office for life.
Plutarch mentions a colleague called Euthydemus (*quaest.
conviv.* 700 E), who can be shown from inscriptions to have
been his senior partner, and to have been in office already
in the 80s.[45] It is therefore virtually certain that when
Plutarch acted on behalf of the Amphictyons in setting up a
statue of Hadrian early in the reign, he did so in virtue of
his seniority in the priesthood, Euthydemus by then having
died.[46] Hence it is of importance that when the Amphictyons voted to set up a similar statue to the emperor in 125,
and again directed one of the priests of Apollo to take
charge of it, the one who did so was not Plutarch but a
certain T. Flavius Aristotimus.[47] Unless the Amphictyons
had changed their practice of only a few years before,
Aristotimus had succeeded Plutarch as the senior priest,
and the author was by then dead.

III. THE CHRONOLOGY OF THE *PARALLEL LIVES*

Under this heading there are two questions to be studied, that
of the order and method in which the *Parallel Lives* were
composed (their relative chronology), and that of the dates at
which they were published (their absolute chronology).

The first is by far the more difficult. Through almost all
of the *Lives* are scattered cross-references, usually of the
form ὡς ἐν τοῖς περὶ τοῦ δεῖνος γέγραπται, which appear at

---

[44] Daux, *Chronologie delphique* (1943), 90.
[45] Daux, ib.
[46] Statue and date: above, n. 18.
[47] *SIG*³ 835 B.

first sight to provide evidence for the order in which the
Lives were published; from *Cato minor* 22. 4, for instance,
ὡς ἐν τοῖς περὶ Κικέρωνος γέγραπται, it seems to follow that
the *Cicero* was written before the *Cato minor*. But there
is a circumstance that brings the reliability of these cross-
references into question. Several times they appear to
contradict one another: *Dio* 58. 10 cites the *Timoleon* and
Timoleon 13. 10 and 33. 4 the *Dio*; *Brutus* 9. 9 cites the
Caesar and *Caesar* 62. 8 and 68. 7 the *Brutus*; and, while
Camillus 33. 10 cites the *Romulus*, and *Theseus* 1. 4 and
Romulus 21. 1 cite the *Numa*, *Numa* 9. 15 and 12. 13
conversely cite the *Camillus*. The old resort of excising all
or some of the cross-references will not do: many of them
are demonstrably genuine, and even the contradictory ones
bear the stamp of Plutarch's authorship.[48]

To meet this difficulty, it was suggested by J. Mewaldt
that the *Parallel Lives* were not all issued one pair at a time,
as had been generally assumed, but that certain pairs were
published in groups.[49] Plutarch might have issued one
group consisting of *Themistocles–Camillus*, *Lycurgus–Numa*,
and *Theseus–Romulus*, and another consisting of *Dio–Brutus*,
Aemilius–Timoleon, and *Caesar–Alexander*; and thus there
would have been no difficulty for the reader in consulting,
for example, the *Dio* while reading the *Timoleon* and vice
versa. With reference to the first group, Mewaldt's thesis
cannot stand without modification, for in the introduction
to the *Theseus*, Plutarch clearly speaks of the *Lycurgus–
Numa* as already published (τὸν περὶ Λυκούργου τοῦ νομοθέτου
καὶ Νομᾶ τοῦ βασιλέως λόγον ἐκδόντες, 1. 4).[50] There is no
evidence, however, that with regard to the *Dio–Brutus*,
Aemilius–Timoleon, and *Caesar–Alexander* Mewaldt's
theory is not correct; and as for the other set there is

---

[48] The fullest discussion of the 'self-citations' is that of C. Stoltz, *Zur relativen
Chronologie der Parallelbiographien Plutarchs* (1929), with a full list on p. 9. See
also Ziegler, 899 ff.; W. Bühler, *Maia* NS 14 (1962), 271 ff.; M. Brożek, *Eos* 53
(1963), 68 ff. After exhaustive analysis, Stoltz concluded that all the self-citations
were genuine except *Dio* 58. 10; *Brutus* 9. 9; and *Camillus* 33. 10: cf. Mewaldt,
Gnomon 6 (1930), 431 ff.

[49] *Hermes* 42 (1907), 564 ff.

[50] So Stoltz, op. cit. 72 ff.; Bühler, art. cit. 273; Flacelière's defence of Mewaldt
(*REG* 61 (1948), 68 f.) is not convincing.

evidence in support of it that has only recently been noticed. For the *Themistocles* opens with the words Θεμιστοκλεῖ δέ . . ., which those editors who observed it assumed to indicate a lacuna in the text. When it is considered, however, that the *Themistocles* is one of the *Lives* which Mewaldt supposed to have been published as part of a set, this opening becomes susceptible of another explanation.[51] Since the *Lycurgus–Numa* had already appeared, the *Themistocles–Camillus* must have been published simultaneously with the *Theseus–Romulus*. The *Themistocles* will therefore have followed directly on the *Romulus*, and it is appropriate that the reference to the begetting of Theseus that closes the *Romulus* (35. 7) should have been followed by the discussion of Themistocles' humble origins that opens the *Themistocles* (1. 1). It is true that those who read the *Numa* at publication would not have been able to make use of Plutarch's references to the *Camillus*, but Plutarch elsewhere alludes to a *Life* that was still in process of composition (*Caes.* 35. 2; 45. 9), and the interval before the appearance of the *Camillus* could have been very short.

The cross-references, therefore, even the contradictory ones, may be used as an approximate guide to the relative chronology of the *Parallel Lives*. They are not numerous enough for the entire order of composition to be determined, but with their help and that of other indications certain conclusions can be reached.

It is probable that the whole series, perhaps with an introduction addressed to Plutarch's friend, Q. Sosius Senecio, to whom the *Lives* are dedicated, was begun with the lost pair of *Epaminondas* and *Scipio* mentioned in the catalogue of Lamprias;[52] and from Plutarch himself it is known that the *Demosthenes–Cicero* constituted pair v (*Dem.* 3. 1), the *Pericles–Fabius Maximus* pair x (*Per.* 2. 5), and the *Dio–Brutus* pair xii (*Dio* 2. 7). Hence it is possible to place with only slight uncertainty in the series the two already mentioned sets of simultaneously published *Lives*. The group consisting of the *Lycurgus–Numa*, *Theseus–Romulus*, and

---

[51] See the Budé editors, *Plutarque, Vies*, ii (1961), 217.

[52] Thus Ziegler, 897, e.g. Probably the younger Africanus is meant, Ziegler, 896.

Themistocles–Camillus must occupy, with the *Lysander–Sulla*, the places between v and x; for the *Theseus* (27. 8) cites the *Demosthenes* (v), and the *Lysander*, which cites the *Lycurgus* (17. 11),[53] is itself cited by one of pair x, the *Pericles* (22. 4). As for the group *Dio–Brutus*, *Aemilius–Timoleon*, and *Alexander–Caesar*, the first is explicitly stated by Plutarch to be pair XII, and must have been followed—it is not certain in which order—by the *Aemilius–Timoleon* and the *Alexander–Caesar* as XIII and XIV. Moreover, since the *Caesar* in its turn refers to the *Pompey* as if it were soon to appear (35. 2; cf. 45. 9), the *Agesilaus–Pompey* will have formed pair XV, and this is corroborated by the *Pompey*'s reference (16. 8) to the *Brutus*. So far, therefore, the following order seems assured.

I	*Epaminondas–Scipio*
II–IV	
V	*Demosthenes–Cicero*
VI	*Lycurgus–Numa*
VII–IX	*Theseus–Romulus*
VII–IX	*Themistocles–Camillus*
VII–IX	*Lysander–Sulla*
X	*Pericles–Fabius Maximus*
XI	
XII	*Dio–Brutus*
XIII–XIV	*Aemilius–Timoleon*
XIII–XIV	*Alexander–Caesar*
XV	*Agesilaus–Pompey*
XVI–XXIII	

Henceforth it is only possible to proceed with much less certainty. Since pairs I and v–x are known, a *Life* which is cited by any of those between v and x inclusive, and is not one of them, must be placed in II–IV. In this position, therefore, belong the *Cimon–Lucullus*, of which the *Cimon* is cited by the *Theseus* (36. 2) and the *Pericles* (9. 5), and the *Pelopidas–Marcellus*, since the *Marcellus* is twice cited by the *Fabius Maximus* (19. 2; 22. 8).

At the other end of the series, in XVI–XXIII, five pairs

---

[53] This refers to the *Lycurgus*, not to the spurious *Instituta Laconica* (Stoltz, op. cit. 101 f.).

belong with certainty. The *Nicias–Crassus* and the *Alcibiades–Coriolanus* appear to have been published within a short time of each other, since the *Alcibiades* (13. 9) refers to the *Nicias*,[54] and the *Nicias* (11. 2) in the present tense to the *Alcibiades*. Since there is no place in I–XV for two pairs published closely together, these two must belong in XVI–XXIII; and with this agrees the fact that the *Coriolanus* (39. 11) refers to the *Numa* (VI), and the *Nicias* (28. 4) to the *Lysander* (VII–IX). Also in XVI–XXIII belong three pairs that refer to the *Lives* published simultaneously, or nearly so, in XII–XV. These are the *Demetrius–Antony*, of which the *Antony* (69. 2) refers to the *Brutus* (XII), the *Phocion–Cato minor*, of which the *Cato minor* (54. 10; 73. 6) refers to the *Pompey* (XV) and the *Brutus* (XII), and the *Phocion* (29. 1) to the *Demosthenes* (V),[55] and the *Pyrrhus–Marius*, of which the *Marius* (6. 4) refers to the *Caesar* (XIII–XIV).

There remain five pairs of *Lives* so far unplaced to fill one position in II–IV, XI, and three positions in XVI–XXIII; these are the *Sertorius–Eumenes*, the *Solon–Poplicola*, the *Philopoemen–Flamininus*, the *Aristides–Cato maior*, and the double pair *Agis–Cleomenes–Gracchi*. From the place in II–IV the last two pairs are excluded by the fact that both cite the *Philopoemen–Flamininus* (*Cato maior* 12. 4; *Agis–Cleomenes* 45. 9, which also (33. 5) cites the *Lycurgus*). The *Solon–Poplicola* seems excluded too by Plutarch's statement in the so-called σύγκρισις that 'there is something peculiar to this comparison that is not really applicable to any of those so far written' (*Popl.* 24. 1).[56] Either *Sertorius–Eumenes* or *Philopoemen–Flamininus* must therefore fill the vacant place in II–IV. The remaining possibilities are too numerous to be worth speculating upon, though the uncertainty of the *Agis–Cleomenes–Gracchi*'s position has some bearing on the question of the *terminus ante* of the whole series (see below, p. 114). The table on p. 109 can now be completed as follows.

---

[54] The reference seems clear, though Plutarch does not mention the *Nicias* by name (Mewaldt, *Hermes* 42 (1907), 573; Stoltz, op. cit. 22).

[55] Again, Plutarch does not mention the *Demosthenes* by name (Stoltz, ib.).

[56] So Flacelière, *Rev. de Phil.* 3ᵉ sér. 23 (1949), 132.

I	*Epaminondas–Scipio*
II–IV	*Cimon–Lucullus*
II–IV	*Pelopidas–Marcellus*
II–IV	Either *Sertorius–Eumenes* or
	Philopoemen–Flamininus
V	*Demosthenes–Cicero*
VI	*Lycurgus–Numa*[57]
VII–IX	*Theseus–Romulus*
VII–IX	*Themistocles–Camillus*
VII–IX	*Lysander–Sulla*
X	*Pericles–Fabius Maximus*
XI	*Sertorius–Eumenes, Solon–Poplicola*, or
	Philopoemen–Flamininus; if the last belongs in
	II–IV, then also *Aristides–Cato maior* or *Agis–*
	Cleomenes–Gracchi
XII	*Dio–Brutus*
XIII–XIV	*Aemilius–Timoleon*
XIII–XIV	*Alexander–Caesar*
XV	*Agesilaus–Pompey*
XVI–XXIII	Either *Sertorius–Eumenes* or *Philopoemen–*
	Flamininus or *Solon–Poplicola*; either *Agis–*
	Cleomenes–Gracchi or *Aristides–Cato maior* or
	both; certainly *Alcibiades–Coriolanus* (after
	the *Solon–Poplicola, Cor.* 33. 2), *Nicias–*
	Crassus, Phocion–Cato minor (after the
	Aristides–Cato maior, Cato min. 1. 1),
	Demetrius–Antony, and *Pyrrhus–Marius*

With the relative chronology of the *Parallel Lives* approximately established, it remains to determine as far as possible their date of composition. The following is a list of *termini post* and *ante*, where they occur. Since there is no reason to question the generally accepted date of *c.*45 for Plutarch's birth, and it has been argued above (p. 106) that he died

---

[57] Plutarch's words in the preface to the *Theseus* (1. 2), ἐμοὶ περὶ τὴν τῶν βίων τῶν παραλλήλων ἀναγραφὴν τὸν ἐφικτὸν εἰκότι λόγῳ ... χρόνον διελθόντι, have led some to consider the *Theseus–Romulus* one of the last pairs (thus Stoltz, op. cit. 134). But it is clear that Plutarch had already written *Lives* of persons from very diverse times; and in the same preface he implies (ἐδοκοῦμεν οὔκ ἂν ἀλόγως τῷ Ῥωμύλῳ προσαναβῆναι, 1. 4) that this pair followed immediately on the *Lycurgus–Numa*.

*c.*120, no *terminus* earlier than 68 or later than 117 has been included.

After 68:   *Philopoemen–Flamininus* (II–IV, XI, or VI–XXIII)

> *Flam.* 12. 13 refers to Nero's liberation of Greece in 67.

Demetrius–Antony (XVI–XXIII)

> *Ant.* 87. 9 refers to Nero as dead.

After 96:   *Lycurgus–Numa* (VI)

> *Numa* 19. 7 refers to Domitian's death.

Theseus–Romulus (VII–IX)

> *Rom.* 15. 7 refers to the *quaest. Rom.*, which was undoubtedly written after Domitian's death (276 E).

Themistocles–Camillus (VII–IX)

> *Cam.* 19. 12 again refers to the *quaest. Rom.*

Solon–Poplicola (XI or XVI–XXIII)

> *Popl.* 15. 3–6 refers to Domitian with a hostility which shows him to have died. The reference to Poplicola's death as an event of 600 years ago (*Popl.* 24. 3), taken strictly, produces a date of 97 or so, for Poplicola's death traditionally occurred in 503 BC (so Flacelière, *Rev. de Phil.* 3ᵉ sér. 23 (1949), 130 f.): but this cannot be pressed.

Aemilius–Timoleon (XIII–XIV)

> *Aem.* 25. 5–7 refers to the rebellion of Antonius Saturninus in winter 88–9. Here Plutarch speaks of Domitian neutrally; but the plain Δομετιανός suggests that he was no longer living, as indeed the position of the *Aemilius* in the series makes certain.

After 99:   *Dio–Brutus* (XII)

> *Brutus* 25. 6 refers to *quaest. conviv.* 693 F. The *terminus post* for this part of the *quaest. conviv.* is 99 (see below, p. 121).

Before 114:   *Cimon–Lucullus* (ii–iv)

At *Luc.* 36. 5 Plutarch observes of Lucullus that εἰ τοῦτο (the ability to win the affection of his troops) μετὰ τῶν ἄλλων ὑπῆρξεν αὐτῷ ... οὐκ ἄν εἶχεν ἡ Ῥωμαίων ἡγεμονία τὸν Εὐφράτην τῆς Ἀσίας ὅρον, ἀλλὰ τὰ ἔσχατα καὶ τὴν Ὑρκανίαν θάλασσαν. This cannot have been written after 114, when Trajan crossed the Euphrates, and established Armenia and Mesopotamia as Roman provinces. It is true that in 117 Hadrian gave up Trajan's conquests and made the Euphrates again Rome's eastern boundary in Asia: but these words could not have been written even then, for after that date Hadrian no less than Lucullus would have been a cause of Rome's not ruling east of the Euphrates.

Before 114 and   *Lysander–Sulla* (vii–ix)
after *c.*104:

At *Sulla* 21. 8 Plutarch says that 'almost 200 years' have passed since the battle of Orchomenus in 86 BC.

Before 116:   *Demosthenes–Cicero* (v)
Theseus–Romulus (vii–ix)
Dio–Brutus (xii)
Aemilius–Timoleon (xiii–xiv)
Agis–Cleomenes–Gracchi (xi or xvi–xxiii)

All these Lives can be assumed written before 116 or so from the mention of Q. Sosius Senecio, addressed either by name (*Demosth.* 1. 1; 31. 7; *Thes.* 1. 1; *Dio* 1. 1) or indicated by the author's use of the second person singular (*Aem.* 1. 6; *Agis–Cleom.* 2. 9; *Gracchi* 45. 7). Sosius was one of the first *consules ordinarii* of Trajan's reign in 99, held a command in one or both of the emperor's Dacian Wars (Syme, *JRS* 49 (1959), 28 f., suggests Moesia Superior *c.*100–3), and was again *consul ordinarius* in 107. A man so highly honoured would certainly be expected to proceed to the dignity of being proconsul of Africa or Asia, an honour that would have come to Sosius in about 116 (Syme, *Tacitus* (1958), 664 f.). There is, however, no trace of his name in the *fasti* of these provinces, and so it is almost certain that he died before 116, perhaps on the eve of Trajan's Parthian War (so Groag, *RE* 3 A, 1187; cf. Syme, op. cit. 476). This is a valuable indication of the date not only of the *Parallel Lives* but of other of Plutarch's works also (see below, pp. 121, 123).

Though the first pair of the series that can be dated definitely after 96 is thus not earlier than the *Lycurgus–Numa* (VI), the *Lysander–Sulla* (VII–IX) was written not long before 114. The whole series was probably begun after 96; it might be conjectured that Sosius' consulate in 99 furnished an occasion for Plutarch to dedicate the new undertaking to him.[58] The *terminus ante* is even less secure. The last pair that refers to Sosius may be the *Aemilius–Timoleon* (XII–XIV); more probably it is the *Agis–Cleomenes–Gracchi* (XI or XVI–XXIII). If the latter, the fact that Sosius was addressed four times in I–XIV (probably five, if the *Epaminondas–Scipio* were extant) and only once thereafter suggests that the last *Lives* were written after his death. The end of the series probably came only with Plutarch's death in *c.*120 (above, p. 106; for his apparent failure to write the *Life of Metellus Numidicus* promised in the *Marius* (29. 12) lends substance to Wilamowitz's conjecture that 'Plutarch wollte noch weiterschreiben, als der Tod ihn abrief'.[59]

[58] For similar dedications in consular years, see Syme, *Tacitus* (1958), 672.
[59] *Reden und Vortr.* 2⁴ (1926), 258; see above, p. 56.

IV. A CHRONOLOGY OF PLUTARCH'S
WORKS

The following is a list of Plutarch's datable works. The evidence of style or subject-matter has not been admitted: thus the declamatory works have not been included, despite the fact that they were *juvenilia* (Ziegler, 716 ff.), nor, for instance, has the *de genio Socratis*, despite its affinity with the *Pelopidas* (Ziegler, 842). The only evidence used is that of Plutarch's references to the circumstances of his own time, to his own earlier works, and to his own life. As with the *Parallel Lives*, and for the same reasons (pp. 111–12), no *terminus* earlier than 68 or later than 117 has been included.

This is a positive list, in that I have not troubled to draw attention to the *termini* sometimes wrongly assigned to certain works (except when these works could be included because of other *termini*): this negative task has been adequately performed by Ziegler (708 ff.). Two works, however, which Ziegler himself has dated for insufficient reasons are best dealt with immediately. In the dialogue *de facie in orbe lunae* one of the speakers mentions an eclipse of the sun that had happened ἔναγχος (931 D). Whatever the true date of this eclipse (see Ziegler, 709 ff.), the dialogue need not have been composed shortly after its occurrence (so Pohlenz, p. ix of his edition, 1955); besides, ἔναγχος need not even imply that a short time had elapsed between the eclipse and the putative date of the dialogue, for Plutarch uses it in the context of the relief of Cyzicus in 74 or 73 BC to refer to an event of 86 (*Luc.* 11. 6). Secondly, Ziegler has dated the *de defectu oraculorum* to *c.*100 on the ground that the Terentius Priscus to whom it is dedicated received Martial's Book XII in 101 (712). But Martial had two friends of this name, father and son, of whom he dedicated Book XII to the son; and Ziegler has elsewhere rightly conceded that Plutarch's friend could also be the father (694; cf. Stein, *RE* 5 A, 667 f.). Neither of these works has therefore been included in the following list.

After 68:   *de garrulitate*
            After Nero's death (505 C f.).

After 68;   *de fraterno amore*
before 107:
At 487 F f. Plutarch mentions two brothers, the most influential Greeks of his day, who quarrelled and were exiled by 'the tyrant'. As Groag first saw, this passage must be combined with the evidence of disturbance in Sparta late in Nero's reign, as a result of which C. Julius Spartiaticus, who had been a Roman knight and a procurator of the imperial house, was exiled (*Reichsbeamten von Achaia* (1939), 37 f.). The brother may well be C. Julius Laco, also a procurator of the imperial house (G. W. Bowersock, *JRS* 51 (1961), 117). Hence Nero's death is a *terminus post*. Groag's observation is ignored by Ziegler, who takes Domitian to be the tyrant mentioned and the *de fraterno amore* to have been written after 96 (800), and yet omits it from his chronology of Plutarch's works (708 ff.).

A *terminus ante* is provided by the dedication of the work to the brothers 'Nigrinus and Quietus' (478 B), for Quietus must be the elder Avidius Quietus, who died at some time between 98 and 107 (Groag, *PIR*² A 1410, again ignored by Ziegler, 691).

After 79 (?);   *Galba* and *Otho*
before 96 (?):
From an unflattering reference to Caecina Alienus (*Otho* 6), the friend of Vespasian who was executed in 79 on a charge of conspiracy, the work has been assumed later than that year (thus Syme, *Tacitus* (1958), 181; on Alienus see *PIR*² C 99). This may be correct, though Josephus also gives an unfavourable account of Alienus in the *Bellum Judaicum* (4. 634 ff.), which appears to

have been published in Vespasian's lifetime (see Chilver, *JRS* 46 (1956), 204).
A similar *terminus post* is implied by the
reference to the γῆρας of Verginius
Rufus (*Galba* 10). Since Rufus was born
in 14/15 (Pliny, *Epp.* 2. 1. 4), and γῆρας
suggests that he was over 60 (see below on the *an seni respublica gerenda sit*,
p. 122), this gives a *terminus* of about 75.
The fact that Plutarch's *Lives of the
Caesars* ended with Vitellius suggests
that they were written before the end of
the Flavian dynasty in 96 (so E. G.
Hardy, *Plutarch's Lives of Galba and
Otho* (1890), xxviii f.; Wilamowitz,
Reden und Vortr. 2⁴ (1926), 269 above,
pp. 65–6).

After 80 (?):   *de audiendis poetis*

Written when Plutarch's son Soclarus
was old enough to be influenced by
poetry (15 A), and so at least about 10.
Plutarch married young, when both his
and his wife's parents were still alive
(*amat.* 749 B), and he had at least five
children (*consol. ad uxorem* 608 C): in
*c.*70, therefore. Soclarus may have been
the eldest child, who died (ib. 609 D),
though the fact that this child is given
no name by Plutarch suggests that it
died very young or was stillborn. If
Soclarus was not this child, he must
have been born after the composition of
the *consolatio ad uxorem*, since the
names of the other four children are
known, and in that case the present
work will have been written at least
after 100 (on the confusing evidence
about Plutarch's family, see Ziegler,
641 ff., criticized by Flacelière, *REG* 63
(1950), 302).

After 81 (?);   *de sera numinis uindicta*
before 107:   After 81 if Titus is the 'good' emperor
                       whose death is alluded to at 566 E; cer-
                       tainly after the eruption of Vesuvius in
                       79 (ib.). The dedication to 'Quietus'
                       (548 A) provides the *terminus ante* (see
                       above, p. 116, on the *de fraterno
                       amore*).

After 81 (?):   *de sollertia animalium*
                       The reference to ὁ γέρων Οὐεσπασιανός
                       (974 A) might appear only to yield a
                       terminus post of 79. But Plutarch not
                       infrequently uses γέρων to distinguish
                       the older of two namesakes (see Wytten-
                       bach on *de Alex. magni fort.* 330 E): thus
                       Μέτελλος ὁ γέρων (*de garrul.* 506 D) distin-
                       guishes Metellus Numidicus from Me-
                       tellus Pius, and, as G. W. Bowersock
                       has recently shown, Αἰμιλιανός ὁ γέρων
                       (*de def. orac.* 419 E) is not the Aemili-
                       anus just referred to there, but his
                       father, Epitherses Aemilianus (*CQ* NS
                       15 (1965), 268 f.). If, therefore, ὁ γέρων
                       Οὐεσπασιανός here means 'the elder Ves-
                       pasian', the work was probably written
                       after the death of Titus in 81 (Domitian
                       did not bear the name 'Vespasian').

After 81:   *de tuenda sanitate*
                       After Titus' death (123 D).

Between *c.*85   *consolatio ad uxorem*
and *c.*95:   Written after the loss of their fifth child
                       (608 C). Plutarch married in about 70
                       (see above, on the *de audiendis poetis*),
                       and hence this work was written in
                       about 90.

Between *c.*90   *praecepta coniugalia*
and *c.*100:   Addressed to 'Pollianus and Eurydice'
                       (138 A). G. W. Bowersock has shown
                       that Poliaenus was the son of Plutarch's
                       contemporary, Soclarus of Tithora, and

father of his friend Clea; Pollianus could therefore have married *c*.95 and his daughter have grown up to be a friend of Plutarch *c*.115 (*CQ* NS 15 (1965), 267 f.).

After *c*.90; *de adulatore et amico*
before 116: After the death of Nero (56 F, 60 E). The work is addressed to (C. Julius) Antiochus Philopappus (48 E), whose tomb in Athens was constructed between 114 and 116 (*ILS* 845); and if he was about 50 at his death, as Mommsen supposed (*Ges. Schr.* 4 (1906), 90), he would first have been of an age to enter Plutarch's circle in about 90.

After 92; *de cohibenda ira*
before 100 (?): See above, pp. 96–7.

After *c*.95: *de E Delphico*
After the death of Nero (385 B). More than one of Plutarch's sons adult (385 A); on the date of his marriage see above, p. 117, on the *de audiendis poetis*.

After *c*.95: *de animae procreatione in Timaeo*
Dedicated to Plutarch's sons Autobulus and Plutarch in recognition of their interest in Plato (1012 A f.); cf. on the *de E Delphico*.

After *c*.95: *de Pythiae oraculis*
Certainly after the eruption of Vesuvius in 79, which is referred to by one of the interlocutors as of recent occurrence (398 E). This must be a deliberate anachronism, however, for another of the interlocutors, the young Diogenianus, was the son of a friend of Plutarch (395 A: Ziegler, 673), and presumably of roughly the same age as Plutarch's sons. The reasons for which the work has been dated to the reign of Hadrian are insufficient (above, pp. 100–4).

After 96:   *de curiositate*
Domitian dead (522 D f.).

After 96;   *amatorius*
The Flavian house ended (771 C). It cannot be inferred from 771 B that the work was written after 115 (above, pp. 105–6).

After 96;
before 114:   *praecepta gerendae reipublicae*
An event mentioned that happened ἔναγχος ἐπὶ Δομετιανοῦ (815 D): on the word ἔναγχος, see above, p. 115. For the *terminus ante*, see below, on the *de capienda ex inimicis utilitate*.

After 96;
before 114:   *de capienda ex inimicis utilitate*
Written after the *praecepta gerendae reipublicae* (86 C). The recipient, Cornelius Pulcher, is clearly to be identified with a notable Greek of this period (*PIR*² C 1424). G. W. Bowersock has shown that the opening sentence, which refers to an important administrative post held by Pulcher, provides a *terminus ante* of 114 (*CQ* NS 15 (1965), 269 f.).

After 96:   *de exilio*
Written to a wealthy Sardian (599 E, 607 E), who is probably the Menemachus to whom on his entry into politics Plutarch addressed the *praecepta gerendae reipublicae* (so Stein, *RE* 15: 837 f., Ziegler, 819).

Between *c*.96
and *c*. 120:   *Parallel Lives*
See above, p. 114.

After 97 (?):   *adversus Colotem*
Addressed to a 'Saturninus' (1107 D), who could be L. Herennius Saturninus, proconsul of Greece in 97/98 or 98/99 (*PIR*² H 126). It is possible (not certain, as assumed in *PIR*) that the work was dedicated to Saturninus in his proconsulship.

After 99; | *quaestiones convivales*
before 116:

This work contains several convergent indications of date.

The reference to Avidius Quietus' 'province' (632 A), in which, as Plutarch testifies, he had been an honest proconsul, can only indicate Greece (thus Groag, *PIR²* A 1410). Quietus is known to have been proconsul when Cyllus was epimelete of the Amphictyons at Delphi, and so after 91 (*SIG³* 822: West, *CP* 23 (1928), 263), and before his consulship in 93 (N. Alfieri, *Athenaeum* 26 (1948), 117, 130 f.), and so in 90/91 or 91/92. Further, if the words with which Plutarch speaks of Avidius to Sosius Senecio, μέμνησαι γάρ, imply that Avidius was dead, this gives a *terminus post* between 98 and 107 (see above, p. 116, on the *de fraterno amore*).

The reference to (L. Cassius) Petraeus as agonothete at Delphi (674 F) gives a *terminus post* of 99, since Petraeus first took office in that year (West, art. cit. 264 f.).

The reference to Favorinus' activity as a philosopher would suggest an even later date (734 D ff.: see below, on the *quaestiones Romanae*). A secure *terminus ante* is provided by the dedication of all nine books of this work to Sosius Senecio, who died before 116 (see above, p. 114).

After 100 (?): | *de laude ipsius*

If the Herculanus to whom the work is addressed (539 A) is the eminent Spartan, C. Julius Eurycles Herculanus (so Stein, *RE* 8: 549, No. 1, *dubitanter*; against, Groag, *RE* 10: 585), it belongs fairly late in Plutarch's life, for

Herculanus is attested as priest of the emperors in 116–17 (*IG* 5. 1, 380) and died not long after 130 (*SIG³* 841).

After *c.*105: *quaestiones Romanae*
Certainly later than 96 (276 E). Since Favorinus is quoted for his opinion (271 C) and was born in about 80 (E. Mensching, *Favorin von Arelate* (1963), 1 n. 2), he must by now have been a mature man.

After 107: *de primo frigido*
Mentions οἱ νῦν μετὰ τοῦ Καίσαρος ἐπὶ τοῦ Ἴστρου διαχειμάσαντες (949 E). The work being dedicated to Favorinus (945 F), the reference is probably to Trajan's Second Dacian War (so Ziegler, 713).

After *c.*107: *de tranquillitate animi*
See above, pp. 97–9.

After *c.*110: *an seni respublica gerenda sit*
Plutarch refers to his γῆρας (783 B f.). The age implied by this word and its cognates need not be very great: Plutarch calls Cicero a γέρων in 43 (*Cic.* 46. 1), when he was 63. If Plutarch was born in about 45, this work could have been written as early as 105. His reference to the 'many Pythiads' in which he had served Apollo (792 F), if it refers to his priesthood, might suggest a date of 110 or later; it cannot be used to prove a Hadrianic date (above, pp. 105–6).

C.115: *de Iside et Osiride*
The Clea to whom the work is dedicated (351 C) has been shown by G. W. Bowersock to be the daughter of Plutarch's friends Pollianus and Eurydice, for whom he wrote the *praecepta coniugalia* (see above, pp. 118–19), and so the granddaughter of his contemporary, Soclarus

of Tithora. Hence the work was written very late in his life.

C.115:   *mulierum uirtutes*
Dedicated to Clea (242 E), on whom see above, on the *de Iside et Osiride*.

Before 116:   *de profectibus in uirtute*
Dedicated to Sosius Senecio (75 B), on whom see above, pp. 113–14.

V. CONCLUSIONS

From these dates certain conclusions may be drawn about Plutarch's literary activity. The view that most of his writing was done after 96 is strikingly confirmed. The only works that can be placed with certainty before that date on historical grounds are the *Lives of the Caesars* and the *consolatio ad uxorem*; after 96 were written the *Parallel Lives* and at least fifteen of the *moralia*, including the nine books of the *quaestiones convivales*. The inference is inescapable that, like Tacitus, Plutarch felt constrained to silence during the reign of Domitian, towards whose memory he later displayed cordial dislike.

These figures also support the thesis advanced above (p. 106) that Plutarch did not outlive Trajan by much. The latest *terminus post* is 115, and it would be surprising, if Plutarch lived for many years beyond that date, that he left no clear indication of it.

Plutarch concentrated the greater part of his activity as a writer into the last twenty-five years of his life. The reason for this burst of energy, as for his earlier silence, is not hard to guess. Plutarch, like others, had had to wait for the day 'ubi sentire quae uelis et quae sentias dicere licet' (Tacitus, *Hist.* 1. 1).

4

Plutarch's Adaptation of his Source-Material

C. B. R. PELLING

In an earlier article, I argued that six of the Roman Lives—
Crassus, *Pompey*, *Caesar*, *Cato*, *Brutus*, and *Antony*—were
prepared as a single project, and rest upon the same store
of source-material.[1] If this is so, it affords a unique
opportunity to investigate Plutarch's techniques. There are
substantial variations among these six versions, both crude
inconsistencies of fact and subtler differences of interpretation. It no longer seems adequate to assume that these are
simply inherited from differing source-material; they must
arise from Plutarch's individual literary methods. Their
analysis should therefore illuminate those methods. How
much licence did Plutarch allow himself in rewriting and
manipulating detail for artistic ends? And what considerations would lead him to vary his treatment in these ways?

In the first part of this paper, I examine the literary
devices which Plutarch employed in streamlining his material: conflation of similar items, chronological compression
and dislocation, fabrication of circumstantial detail, and the
like. In the second, I turn to the differences of interpretation
and emphasis among these Lives. These suggest some wider
conclusions concerning Plutarch's biographical practice,
which are developed in the final section: in particular, the
very different aims, interests, and conventions which are
followed in different Lives, and the flexible nature of this
biographical genre.

I am most grateful to Mr D. A. Russell, Dr J. L. Moles, and Mr R. H. A.
Jenkyns for their helpful criticisms of this paper.

[1] 'Plutarch's method of work in the Roman *Lives*', *JHS* 99 (1979), 74–96; see
below, pp. 265–312 (cited in what follows as *Method*).

I. COMPOSITIONAL DEVICES

I start with some devices for *abridging* the narrative: first, various forms of simplification.

A characteristic technique here is the *conflation* of similar items. (i) At *Caes.* 7. 7 Plutarch found it tedious to distinguish the three final senatorial debates on the Catilinarians. He was, after all, concerned with Caesar's role, and that was confined to the final session. He thus gives the impression that the culprits were exposed (3 Dec.), and their punishment decided (5 Dec.), at the same debate. But he certainly knew that the sittings of 3 and 5 Dec. were distinct (cf. the earlier *Cicero*, 19. 1–4 and 20. 4–21. 5), and he seems also to have known of the sitting of the 4th (*Crass.* 13. 3).

(ii) At *Cato* 43 Plutarch clearly distinguishes the *lex Trebonia* of 55 BC, giving Crassus and Pompey their provinces, from the subsequent *lex Licinia Pompeia*, which continued Caesar in Gaul. In that Life Plutarch needs to keep the bills separate, for they brought different reactions from Cato:[2] he publicly opposed the *lex Trebonia*, whereas the *lex Licinia Pompeia* provoked his personal appeal to Pompey, warning him of the dangers which Caesar threatened. *Pompey* 52. 4 makes much less of this: ἔπειτα νόμους διὰ Τρεβωνίου δημαρχοῦντος εἰσέφερον . . . , giving commands to Caesar, Crassus, and Pompey. *Pompey* thus associates Trebonius with all three commands; in *Cato* Plutarch links him with the grant to Crassus and Pompey, but correctly omits him from the continuation of Caesar's command. *Pompey* groups all three commands together, naming Caesar first; *Cato* gives the correct sequence, with Caesar's command being granted after the other two. *Crass.* 15. 7 similarly takes all three commands together, though Plutarch does not there mention Trebonius.[3]

---

[2] *Caes.* 14. 2 and *Cato* 32–3 form a similar case, which I discuss at *Method* 77 (with n. 21); see below, p. 271. *Caesar* treats two bills together; *Cato* has to distinguish them, as Plutarch there wishes to trace Cato's reactions to both. (In this paper, *Cato* refers to the *Cato minor*.)

[3] For similar conflations, cf. e.g. *Ant.* 5. 8, conflating at least two meetings of the senate in early 49 (Plutarch knows better at *Caes.* 30–1); *Ant.* 14. 3, with

Similar is Plutarch's technique of chronological *compression*, the portrayal of distinct events as closely linked in time. When two items were linked causally or thematically, it would have been clumsy to point to a long interval between them; hence Plutarch often connects such events in a way which suggests chronological closeness. There are many examples, and only two need be mentioned here.[4] (i) At *Cato* 51 he treats Cato's proposal to surrender Caesar to the Germans. He tells the same story, with less detail, at *Caes.* 22. 4–5. In *Caesar* he places the item in its correct chronological position, the year 55; *Cato* delays it to the context of the outbreak of the Civil War, where it can conveniently be linked with Cato's further attacks on Caesar's command. The vague sentence at *Cato* 51. 6 conceals a time-lag of five years: ἐκυρώθη μὲν οὐδέν, ἀλλ' ἐλέχθη μόνον ὅτι καλῶς ἔχει διάδοχον Καίσαρι δοθῆναι. (ii) At *Caes.* 21. 8 Plutarch explains why Cato was absent from a debate in spring, 56 BC:[5] ἐπίτηδες γὰρ αὐτὸν εἰς Κύπρον [the triumvirs] ἀπεδιοπομπήσαντο. That naturally suggests a tactic to safeguard this specific piece of legislation, and one would conclude that Cato had only recently departed. In fact, Plutarch knew that Cato had been despatched during Clodius' tribunate, 58 BC (*Pomp.* 48. 9, *Cato* 34, and the earlier *Cic.* 34. 2). But, as those passages show, Plutarch thought that Cato's removal was designed to protect *any* legislation which the dynasts might introduce. Here he again wrote as if this logical link corresponded to a chronological closeness.

Method 77 (below, p. 273); *Caes.* 30. 6, where the outburst of 'Lentulus' combines two remarks made by Marcellus, *Pomp.* 58. 6 and 10 (below, p. 154); and *Cic.* 15. 4–5, combining (i) the two reports from Etruria and (ii) the *tumultus* decree and the *s.c.u.* Note also that in *Coriolanus* he appears to combine details of the battles of Regillus and of the Naevian meadow: Russell, *JRS* 53 (1963), 23–4; see below, p. 363.

[4] Similar instances are collected in A. N. Sherwin-White, *CQ* 27 (1977), 177–8; cf. also T. J. Carney, *JHS* 80 (1960), 26–7, for similar cases in *Marius*.

[5] The debate concerned the grant of *stipendium* for Caesar's troops. It presumably took place after Luca, but before the debate on the consular provinces in (?) June: cf. Cic. *prov. cons.* 28. Plutarch's notice of Cato's absence is often regarded as a blunder: so e.g. Garzetti, ad loc., and C. Luibheid, *CPh* 65 (1970), 89 n. 13. But Cato seems to have returned from Cyprus at almost exactly this time, in spring or early summer, 56 (S. I. Oost, *CPh* 50 (1955), 107–8). There is no reason to think that he reached Rome before the *stipendium* debate, and Plutarch's version can stand.

Such telescoping is similar to simple chronological *dis-*
placement; and this brings us to techniques which, without
necessarily abridging the narrative, serve to organize it in a
more elegant and pleasing manner. Displacements may
serve to organize into logical compartments, or to give
smooth transitions: (i) At *Pompey* 62. 1 Plutarch briefly
tells the story of Caesar and the tribune Metellus: Metellus
refused to allow Caesar to open the treasury, and Caesar
bluntly threatened him with death. In *Pompey* the story is
placed before Caesar's pursuit of Pompey to Brundisium
(62. 2 is explicit on the chronological sequence). The same
story is told at greater length at *Caesar* 35: there Plutarch
puts it in its correct chronological place, after Pompey has
sailed from Brundisium and Caesar has returned to Rome.
Caesar can afford to be accurate: its narrative is here con-
trolled by Caesar's own movements, and the episode fits
neatly into the narrative shift from Brundisium to Spain (36).
Pompey organizes its narrative around Pompey's person: it
is there convenient to group together all Italian events and
place them before Brundisium. Pompey's embarkation then
moves the narrative decisively to the East.

(ii) The early chapters of *Caesar* show a more elaborate
reordering. It is elegant and pleasing to group together
Caesar's early foreign adventures: the trip to Nicomedes (1.
7), the pirate adventure (1. 8–2. 7), the study in Rhodes (3).
The return to Rome (4. 1) can then restore the reader to an
uninterrupted treatment of domestic politics. But two separate antedatings were necessary to produce this. Plutarch
associates the pirate adventure with the trip to Nicomedes
(80/79); a later date, in 75 or 74, is certain.[6] The journey to
Rhodes is then dated τῆς Σύλλα δυνάμεως ἤδη μαραινομένης—
presumably 79/8; in fact, a date of 76 or later is very

---

[6] See now A. M. Ward, *AJAH* 2 (1977), 26–36 (correcting *CPh* 70 (1975),
267–8). Suet. *Div. Iul.* puts the pirate episode after the Dolabella trial, and this is
confirmed by the precise reference of Vell. ii. 42. 3. Caesar there refers the matter
to the proconsul of Bithynia and Asia, who seems to be called *Iuncus* or *Iunius
Iuncus* (both emendations are due to Nipperdey: *Iunium cum* codd.). This can only
be the Ἰουγκος of *Caes.* 2. 6, who apparently held this unique combination of
provinces for the first part of 74. (See Ward, *AJAH* art. cit.; Broughton, *MRR* ii.
98, 100; D. Magie, *Roman Rule in Asia Minor* (Princeton, NJ, 1950), 1126–7,
1204.) Caesar was held by the pirates for 38 days: his capture should therefore be
late 75 or 74.

probable.[7] Both episodes therefore belong after the Dolabella and Antonius trials, datable to 77/6, which Plutarch
treats in ch. 4. He doubtless knew the true sequence, for Suetonius' account, clearly resting on similar source-material,[8]
is correct. But Plutarch's arrangement is more elegant,
and it has one further effect. Caesar's rhetorical successes at
Rome are now placed after the study in Rhodes, and it is
natural to infer that they are the result of that teaching: a
theme which alike suits Plutarch's Hellenism and his interest in παιδεία. (We might compare the emphasis on Cicero's
Greek teachers at *Cic.* 3–4.)

(iii) This last instance suggests that displacements may
also make, or reinforce, a causal or logical point; this, too, is
frequent. *Cato* 30. 9–10 puts great stress on Cato's rejection
of a marriage-connection with Pompey: in this Life, it is
that which began the train of events which led to war.
When, immediately afterwards, Plutarch comes to the affairs of 59 BC, he places Pompey's betrothal to Julia at the
beginning of the account (31. 6). This emphasizes the
point, but is another displacement: *Caes.* 14. 7 and *Pomp.*
47. 10 put this later, and a date in spring or early summer
is confirmed by Cic. *Att.* ii. 17. 1 (*ista repentina adfinitatis
coniunctio*).[9]

I pass to a different form of displacement, the *transfer* of
an item from one character to another: this is an extreme
form of technique often visible elsewhere, the suppression

---

[7] Suet. *Div. Iul.* 4 again places this after the Dolabella trial, connecting it with
the pirate adventure. If that connection is historical, the date should again be
75/4.

[8] H. Strasburger, *Caesars Eintritt in die Geschichte* (Munich, 1938), 72–3.
Strasburger demonstrates the uniform nature of the tradition for Caesar's early
years.

[9] Ch. Meier, *Hist.* 10 (1961), 69–79. Such displacements are very frequent. For
further examples, cf. e.g. *Ant.* 12. 6 and *Caes.* 60. 6, discussed at *Method* 86 n. 88
(below, p. 290); *Ant.* 21, where material from the *Second Philippic* is delayed to a
point after Cicero's death (*Method* 90), see below, p. 298; *Pomp.* 64. 5, where
Plutarch displaces the arrival of Labienus in order to include him in his survey of
Pompey's new supporters (contrast *Caes.* 34. 5); *Caes.* 11. 5–6 and 32. 9, using
material which the source apparently attached to Caesar's quaestorship (cf. Suet.
Div. Iul. 7–8); *Pomp.* 48. 9–12, where the *amoibaia* material is brought forward
from 56 BC (cf. Dio, xxxix. 19, Cic. *Q. fr.* ii. 3. 2), as Plutarch wishes to connect it
with events two years earlier; and apparently several displacements in his account
of senate-meetings before the outbreak of war (see excursus, pp. 151-4 f.).

of the role of a complicating extra character.[10] (i) At *Ant.* 5.
10 Antony and Cassius are given the speech to Caesar's
troops before the crossing of the Rubicon; at *Caes.* 31. 3
Plutarch says that Caesar incited the troops himself. Comparison with Appian (ii. 33. 133) and Caesar (*BC* i. 7)
suggests that the *Caesar* version accurately reproduces the
source. (ii) At *Pomp.* 58. 6 Marcellus is given a proposal
which Plutarch knows to be Scipio's, and a remark (Caesar
as a λῃστής) which he elsewhere gives to Lentulus (*Caes.* 30.
4, 6). This last instance seems only one of several such
transfers in the accounts of the outbreak of war. These are
discussed in the excursus at the end of this paper.

We have so far been concerned with ways in which
Plutarch has streamlined his narrative. The effect has usually been to abbreviate his source-material, or at least to
arrange it in as simple and elegant a manner as possible,
avoiding duplications, side-tracks, or distracting explanations. The opposite technique is also visible: the *expansion*
of inadequate material, normally by the fabrication of circumstantial detail. Russell's analysis of *Coriolanus* has demonstrated how much licence Plutarch allowed himself in
introducing such inventions.[11] The present group of Lives
do not lend themselves so conveniently to this investigation:
when one Life has more detail than another, it is rare that
we can be *certain* that it is the leaner, not the fuller, account
which accurately reproduces the source. But some instances
of fabrication seem adequately clear. (i) At *Caes.* 9. 2–10. 11
Plutarch tells of Clodius and the Bona Dea. He had already
told this story in *Cicero* (28–9), and there are great similarities between the two versions: as I have argued elsewhere,
it is likely that he based the *Caesar* account on his earlier
version.[12] But *Caesar* does have many picturesque details
absent from the *Cicero* model. The doors of the house are
open; the maid runs off to fetch Pompeia; Clodius is too

---

[10] For instances of this, cf. *Method* 77 (below, p. 273); for transfers, *Method* 79
n. 41 (below, p. 276). Add *Brut.* 24. 7, where the watchword 'Apollo' at Philippi
is transferred from Antony to Brutus.

[11] *JRS* 53 (1963), 21–8, esp. 23–5, see below, pp. 357–72, esp. 361–5. For
similar instances in *Marius*, cf. Carney, *JHS* 80 (1960), 28–9; in *mul. virt.*, P. A.
Stadter, *Plutarch's Historical Methods* (Cambridge, Mass., 1965), 138–9.

[12] *Method* 90, with n. 120 (below, p. 299).

nervous to stay where he is left; Aurelia's maid is playful—
ὡς δὴ γυνὴ γυναῖκα παίζειν προὐκαλεῖτο, καὶ μὴ βουλόμενον εἰς
τὸ μέσον εἷλκε . . .; Aurelia is formidable and decisive; the
wives return and gossip to their husbands, and it is the
menfolk who cry out for vengeance. Yet none of this new
detail is very substantial, and the main lines of the account
remain unmistakably close to the *Cicero* version. Plutarch
may have had good information for this new detail, but it
is much more likely that he is using his imagination to
supplement an unsatisfactory spare original.

(ii) In my earlier article I discussed Plutarch's use of the
Second Philippic in the early chapters of *Antony*, and tried
to show how he has revised that material to bring out
points important to the Life: for instance, Antony's susceptibility to the wiles of others.[13] We can also see him supplementing the *Philippic* with circumstantial detail, for which
it is hard to believe that he has any independent authority.
Ant. 9. 6 has Antony vomiting on his *tribunal*, an item in
which the *Philippic* had revelled (63): Plutarch adds, dis-
creetly, τῶν φίλων τινὸς ὑποσχόντος τὸ ἱμάτιον. *Ant.* 11 has the
squabbles between Antony and Dolabella, and clearly rests
on *Phil.* ii. 79 ff.; again, circumstantial detail is added (e.g.
τότε μὲν αἰσχυνθεὶς τὴν ἀκοσμίαν ὁ Καῖσαρ ἀπηλλάγη. μετὰ δὲ
ταῦτα προελθὼν ἀναγορεῦσαι τὸν Δολοβέλλαν . . .). The unexpected night-time return of Antony to Fulvia is similarly
elaborated (*Ant.* 10. 8–9 ~ *Phil.* ii. 77–8). Finally, *Ant.* 13
repays examination. Antony has just failed in his clumsy
attempt to crown Caesar at the Lupercalia. That episode
strengthened the conspirators' hand, and they considered
approaching possible allies. Some suggested inviting
Antony, but Trebonius opposed this: he mentioned an
earlier occasion on which he had himself sounded Antony.
His remarks again seem based on the *Second Philippic*
(34): (Antony), *quem et Narbone hoc consilium cum C.
Trebonio cepisse notissimum est et ob eius consili societatem
cum interficeretur Caesar, tum te a Trebonio uidimus seuocari.*
In Plutarch, the passage is transformed. Antony now shares
a tent with Trebonius as his travel-companion; Trebonius

broaches the subject ἀτρέμα πως καὶ μετ᾽ εὐλαβείας; and
Plutarch stresses (what was a very easy inference) that
Antony neither joined the plot nor revealed it to Caesar.
The details give the anecdote conviction and interest, but
they are again not very substantial. They are much more
likely to come from Plutarch's imagination than from any
independent authority.

   This instance brings us to a final category, which we may
call the *fabrication of a context*: the devices by which Plutarch sought to incorporate additional details, often those
which sat awkwardly with his principal version. (i) The
whole context in *Ant.* 13 is interesting. This is a poor piece
of narrative, and the Trebonius item fits uneasily into its
context.[14] The explanation of the awkwardness is clear
enough: Plutarch is fitting the item from the *Philippic* into
the framework drawn from his main Pollio-source, and the
joints creak. The main source had described the conspirators' approaches to possible allies (App. *BC* ii. 113 ff., *Brut.*
11–12, etc.): this was the best peg he could find for Trebonius' sounding of Antony, and he inserted the item here. But
the insertion involved fabrication of detail. The *Philippic*
mentioned the Narbo conversation, and Trebonius' distrac-
tion of Antony on the Ides; that is all. Neither the *Philippic*
nor any other source confirms that the conspirators *now*
considered sounding Antony, nor that Trebonius told his
colleagues of his earlier conversation. Those items seem to
be Plutarch's fabrication, as he developed a context for the
startling item of Antony's knowledge of the plot.

   (ii) The battle with Vercingetorix, shortly before Alesia,
provides a second example. *Caes.* 26. 7–8 comments on the
ferocity of the battle: (Caesar) ἔδοξε δὲ κατ᾽ ἀρχάς τι καὶ
σφαλῆναι. καὶ δεικνύουσιν Ἀρβέρνοι ξιφίδιον πρὸς ἱερῷ κρεμάμενον,
ὡς δὴ Καίσαρος λάφυρον. Caesar himself smiled at the sight
of this dagger, and would not allow it to be removed.
Plutarch's narrative of the Gallic Wars is mostly drawn

---

[14] The suggestion that Antony should be approached comes awkwardly after
his subservient antics at the Lupercalia; disturbingly little is made of the astonish-
ing item of Antony's knowledge of the plot; the 'renewed discussions' at 13. 3 are
also clumsy; and it is odd that Trebonius is not named in the final sentence
(ἐνίους: cf. *Method* 79 n. 41; see below, p. 276).

from Caesar's *commentarii* (though he certainly did not know Caesar's work at first hand).[15] But Caesar's account of this battle (*BG* vii. 66–7) does not include the ξιφίδιον anecdote, nor does it suggest that the Romans at first had the worse of the fighting. Hence some have assumed that Plutarch's notice goes back to an early and independent source.[16] But the ξιφίδιον item must be derived from a source (perhaps an oral source) much nearer to Plutarch's own day: note the present δεικνύουσιν.[17] That anecdote was hard to reconcile with Caesar's own version, which left no room for such a 'spoil'. Plutarch needed to find a stage in the battle when Caesar ἔδοξε . . . τι καὶ σφαλῆναι, and it was natural to put this at 'the beginning'. The revision of his material again arises from the need to find a context for a disparate item.[18]

So much for the compositional devices. We should not, of course, assume that their employment was always a wholly conscious process. Sometimes, doubtless, Plutarch did revise his narrative in the most calculated manner, struggling to reshape the source-material before his eyes. At other times, the flow of his narrative would carry him on more quickly, and it seems that he sometimes relied on his memory.[19] Conflation, compression, and imaginative embroidery would then arise easily and unconsciously: such is the nature of story-telling.

II. DIFFERENCES OF INTERPRETATION

The most straightforward differences of interpretation among these Lives concern the *motivation* of actions. For

---

[15] Cf. *Method* 84 n. 69, 89 with n. 108 (below, pp. 286, 296). The contact with Appian's *Celtica* suggests that Plutarch drew his account from the Pollio-source: *Method* 84–5 (below, pp. 287–8).

[16] Especially Gelzer, *RE* 8 A (1912), 998, and E. Thevenot, *Les Éduens n'ont pas trahi* (Coll. Latomus, 1950), 132, 151.

[17] *Method* 90 (below, p. 300).

[18] A further 'fabrication of a context' seems to be *Brut.* 19, where Plutarch alone attests a senate-meeting for 18 Mar. 44. He appears to have introduced this separate session in order to include disparate material from a secondary source: *Method* 86 n. 90 (below, p. 291).

[19] *Method* 91–6 (below, pp. 300–12).

instance, *Pomp.* 57. 7 tells of the rumours spread in Italy in 50 BC, when Caesar returned to Pompey the troops he had borrowed three years earlier. These were brought by Appius Claudius, who encouraged Pompey to believe that, if it came to war, Caesar's troops would immediately desert to the republican side. Here there is no suggestion that Appius had been bribed by Caesar to do this: he is simply mistaken, reflecting the false Italian confidence which the context in *Pompey* is stressing. *Caes.* 29. 5 has the same item, though Appius is not here named; but here there is a clear hint that οἱ τούτους Πομπηΐῳ κομίζοντες *deliberately* spread false rumours, and were acting in Caesar's service.[20] That fits the themes of the *Caesar* context, which is making much of Caesar's ubiquitous corruption. Pollio may have mentioned both possible explanations, for the parallel passage in Appian has the men acting εἴθ' ὑπ' ἀγνοίας εἴτε διεφθαρμένοι (ii. 30. 117). In each Life Plutarch selected the interpretation which suited the run of his argument.

A more elaborate variation concerns Pompey himself during the fifties: how alert was he to the dangers which Caesar threatened? Different Lives give different answers. *Cato* stresses Pompey's blindness to the menace: that is not surprising, for in that Life he provides the foil to Cato's own mantic foresight.[21] At 43. 10, for instance, Cato 'often warned Pompey' of the danger: ταῦτα πολλάκις ἀκούων ὁ Πομπήϊος ἠμέλει καὶ παρέπεμπεν, ἀπιστίᾳ τῆς Καίσαρος μεταβολῆς διὰ πίστιν εὐτυχίας τῆς ἑαυτοῦ καὶ δυνάμεως. It is only after the consulship of 52 BC that Pompey becomes alert, and wistfully recalls Cato's wisdom (49. 1–2)—but even then he is ὄκνου καὶ μελλήσεως ἀτόλμου πρὸς τὸ κωλύειν καὶ ἐπιχειρεῖν ὑπόπλεως. *Caesar* passes quickly over the politics of the fifties, but its summaries seem to reflect the same analysis: here, too, Pompey is blind. 'For the entire time of his campaign' Caesar deceived him, and he did not notice the growth of Caesar's political strength (20. 3); as war

[20] I defend and elaborate this interpretation of the *Caesar* passage in 'Notes on Plutarch's *Caesar*', *RhM* 127 (1984), 43–5.

[21] Cato's foresight is stressed at *Cato* 31. 7, 33. 5, 35. 7, 42. 6, 43. 9, 45. 7, 49. 1–2, 51. 4–5, 52. 1–3; it is given a divine tinge at 35. 7, 42. 6, and 43. 3, and is contrasted with Pompey's blindness at 43. 9, 49. 1–2, and 52. 3.

approached, he had 'recently' come to fear Caesar, having until then despised him (28. 2).

Pompey itself has a different, more subtle analysis. There, too, Pompey is certainly outsmarted (51. 1): he does not possess Caesar's grasp of urban politics, and Caesar ἐλάνθανεν ὑπὸ δεινότητος ἐν μέσῳ τῷ δήμῳ καὶ τοῖς κυριωτάτοις πράγμασι καταπολιτευόμενος Πομπήϊον. But Pompey here realizes the danger earlier, even if he does not meet it. By the time of Crassus' death, he too ὑπαλείφεται τῷ χεῖρέ θ' ὑποκονίεται (53. 9); in those years τότε δὲ τὸν Καίσαρα δοκῶν οὐ προήσεσθαι τὴν δύναμιν, ἐζήτει ταῖς πολιτικαῖς ἀρχαῖς ὀχυρὸς εἶναι πρὸς αὐτόν, ἄλλο δ' οὐδὲν ἐνεωτέριζεν, οὐδ' ἐβούλετο δοκεῖν ἀπιστεῖν, ἀλλ' ὑπερορᾶν μᾶλλον καὶ καταφρονεῖν (54. 2). Plutarch goes on to narrate the events of 54 BC. In other words, Pompey's alertness to the danger is put several years earlier than in *Cato*, and his neglect is now a matter of conscious policy rather than political blindness. It is then only in the last months before the war, with his joyful reception in the cities of Italy, that he genuinely comes to misjudge the danger: he then lays aside caution, and comes to unqualified disdain of Caesar's strength (57. 5–6). This enthusiasm of the Italian cities is consequently given extraordinary emphasis: οὐδενὸς μέντοι τοῦτο λέγεται τῶν ἀπεργασαμένων τὸν πόλεμον αἰτίων ἔλαττον γενέσθαι (57. 5). This whole reading is quite individual to *Pompey*, and no other Life gives such emphasis to that moment.[22]

The different emphasis here is partly to be explained by biographical relevance, for the complexity of Pompey's changing views is naturally most apposite in his own Life; equally naturally, the other versions may simplify. But there is more to it than this. His alertness to the menace suits the Life's stress on his εὐλαβεία;[23] it also contributes to the tragic texture of the second half of the Life. The outbreak

---

[22] *Caesar* (28. 2, 29. 5, 33. 5) and *Cato* (49. 1, 52. 4) make related points much less extravagantly; in neither Life does Plutarch think this Italian joy worth mentioning. To judge from Appian (*BC* ii. 28. 107–8), Pollio did not make much of it.

[23] *Pomp.* 57. 6 stresses that it was his εὐλαβεία which had earlier guided his εὐτυχήματα to safety. Plutarch presumably has in mind such instances as 8. 5, 13. 2–3, 13. 9, 19. 8, 21. 5–7, 22. 4, 26. 1, 27. 3, 33. 5, 36. 3, 40. 8–9, 43. 3; cf. also 2. 10, 20. 8, 39. 2, 42. 4.

of war is presaged by this joy in Italy, an elegant contrast to
the bleakness which will be Pompey's fate: this θέαμα
κάλλιστον ... καὶ λαμπρότατον will eventually yield to the
very different tableaux of the final chapters.[24] 'Garlands and
flowers' now introduce the events which lead to Pompey's
fall, and, as *Pompey* has recast matters, they also causally
contribute to that fall. A false confidence is produced in
Pompey, and he casts off that εὐλάβεια which has hitherto
protected him. He is now utterly vulnerable to Τύχη, another
of the Life's major themes.[25] Some of this could be formally
stated in Aristotelian terms—the ἁμαρτία, the events following παρὰ τὴν δόξαν δι' ἄλληλα, and so on; but there is no need
to labour the point. The tragic elements are manifest.[26]

There is a further aspect to Pompey's tragedy, and this
may be introduced by another question of interpretation,
Plutarch's treatment of Clodius. Was he acting independently, or was he a triumviral agent? In particular, the exile
of Cicero, which is treated in several Lives: was that simply,
or largely, Clodius' own desire, or was it a matter of
triumviral policy? There is no clear and consistent answer,
but the differences among the Lives are illuminating.[27]

[24] Especially the scenes of Pompey's death, 78–80; Plutarch's technique is
there extremely visual, describing events from the viewpoint of Cornelia and the
rest of Pompey's followers, still at sea. The Italian reception is also intended to
evoke the procession of ch. 45, a previous turning-point of Pompey's life.

[25] Esp. 21. 3, 21. 8, 41. 4, 42. 12, 46. 2, 50. 3, 53. 8–10, 57. 6, 73. 8, 74. 5–6, 75.
1–2, 75. 5, 82(2). 1.

[26] Talk of 'tragic influence' is of course facile and problematic. Sensitivity to
the 'tragic' elements of the human condition has never been confined to one genre
of literature, nor any single art-form, nor even to art itself. Truly 'tragic' elements
in a writer spring from his humane sensibilities and sympathies; literary allusive-
ness is secondary. (When the stylistic elements become primary, we are close to
'tragic history' in the debased Hellenistic sense.) I here suggest only that, in
Plutarch's best writing, his tragic sensibilities are given literary depth and reso-
nance by the adoption of motifs from Tragedy, the literary genre. Cf. esp. P. de
Lacy, *AJP* 73 (1952), 359–71; note also the cautious remarks of Russell, *Plutarch*
(London, 1973), 123, and A. E. Wardman, *Plutarch's Lives* (London, 1974), 168–
79.

[27] In using terms such as 'triumvirate' or 'independent agent', I do not suggest
that these categories are appropriate for illuminating historical fact; I do suggest
that it was in categories such as these that Plutarch approached and understood
the period. I omit the earlier *Cicero* from this analysis; the later Lives are better
informed on the fifties than *Cic.*, and we need not assume that Plutarch then had
the same view of events. *Cic.* in fact represents Clodius as largely independent,
with his hostility to Cicero dating from the Bona Dea affair. That emphasis suits

Pompey does imply some arrangement between Clodius
and Pompey, but in this Life, surprisingly, Clodius seems
the dominant partner. Pompey needs support to defend his
eastern *acta* (46. 7), and is forced to flee to 'demagogues
and youths': ὧν ὁ βδελυρώτατος καὶ θρασύτατος Κλώδιος
ἀναλαβὼν αὐτὸν ὑπέρριψε τῷ δήμῳ, καὶ παρ' ἀξίαν ἐν ἀγορᾷ
κυλινδούμενον ἔχων καὶ περιφέρων, ἐχρῆτο τῶν πρὸς χάριν ὄχλου
καὶ κολακείαν γραφομένων καὶ λεγομένων βεβαιωτῇ (46. 8)—
and he even demanded and obtained a reward, the sacrifice
of Cicero, as if he were doing him service rather than
bringing him shame. 'As if' he were doing him service—
but all these demagogic acts are done on Clodius' initiative,
who uses Pompey merely as a βεβαιωτής. Nor has Pompey
any wish of his own for Cicero's exile; it is solely Clodius'
pressure which achieves this. The analysis evidently represents Pompey as more powerful than Clodius, and Pompey's
backing is needed to secure what Clodius desires. But the
moving and active spirit is quite clearly Clodius, not
Pompey. By ch. 48, Clodius is quite out of hand. He has
cast out Cicero, he has sent Cato to Cyprus, and he then
turns on Pompey himself. In this Life he is, most certainly,
an independent agent.

Cato is rather different. Here Clodius serves the interests
of the triumvirs, and receives the exile of Cicero as his part of
the bargain: ἐπὶ μισθῷ τῇ Κικέρωνος ἐξελάσει πάντα πρὸς χάριν
ἐκείνοις πολιτευόμενον, 33. 6. In *Pompey* (48. 9) Plutarch
made Cato's mission to Cyprus the work of Clodius himself
(. . . καὶ Κάτωνα προφάσει στρατηγίας εἰς Κύπρον ἀπέπεμψε),
and that mission even worked against Pompey's interest.
Cato 34. 3 agrees that this was Clodius' idea, but the
context (33. 6, 34. 1) again makes it evident that he was
serving the policy of the triumvirs.[28] The exile of Cicero
remains the result of Clodius' pressure rather than the

the Life's interest in Cicero's private affairs, especially gossip relating to Terentia
(e.g. 20. 3, 29. 2–4, 30. 4, 41. 2–3). The triumvirs are at first friendly to Cicero,
and their feelings change only when Caesar is offended over his offered *legatio*
(30. 4–5). Caesar then 'strengthens' Clodius, and dissuades Pompey from helping
Cicero. There is no more extensive deal between the triumvirs and Clodius, only
this casual backing for Cicero's exile.

[28] So S. I. Oost (n. 5), 109 n. 3: 'Plut. *Cat. min.* 34 surely can only mean that
the triumvirate was behind the silencing of Cato'.

dynasts', but that is all. Later in the fifties, Clodius temporarily detaches himself—but he soon 'slips back to Pompey',
αὖθις εἰς Πομπήϊον ὑπορρυείς (45. 2). This is a much more
subservient figure than the Clodius of *Pompey*.

The brief notice of *Caesar* 14. 17 is different again. This
time only Cicero's exile is in point, and there is no mention
of any other services. But here, and here alone, Cicero's exile
is not only the wish of Clodius: Plutarch's language strongly
suggests that Caesar wanted this as much as Clodius. 'The
worst deed of Caesar's consulship was the election of Clodius
to the tribunate, and he was elected ἐπὶ τῇ Κικέρωνος καταλύ-
σει. Caesar did not leave Italy before, in company with
Clodius, he had defeated Cicero and forced him into exile.'
Again, there is no hint of this reading in *Pompey* or *Cato*.[29]

It is not hard to see why *Caesar* and *Cato* take the lines
they do. *Caesar* is denouncing the acts of 59 BC, and the
disapproval has a crescendo: Clodius' election, especially
shameful after the Bona Dea affair, marks the climax. It is
natural to blacken Caesar still further by suggesting that
Cicero's exile, too, was his doing. *Cato* controls a great deal
of its narrative by polarizing the struggles of the fifties:
Cato is always the champion of the republic, the triumvirs
(especially Pompey and Caesar) are always the threat.[30] It
is natural to fit Clodius, too, into this scheme.

The *Pompey* rewriting is more interesting. The Life has
just begun an important new movement. 46. 1–4 has
stressed that Pompey's earlier career enjoyed success to
match Alexander: how fortunate, if he had died now! For
the future brought him envy in his successes, and irretriev-
able disaster. He came to use his power οὐ δικαίως for
others, and gave them strength while reducing his own
glory: ἔλαθε ῥώμῃ καὶ μεγέθει τῆς αὐτοῦ δυνάμεως καταλυθείς.
For Caesar rose through Pompey's strength to challenge
the city, and eventually he destroyed Pompey himself.

Clodius is then introduced (46. 8), and, thanks to Plutarch's rewriting, he plays out in miniature much of what is
to come. Pompey gives strength to Clodius, and is the

---

[29] Though the *Caesar* version is closer to that of *Cicero* (n. 27), and may be a
simplification of that Life's account.
[30] For an instance of this, cf. *Method* 77 (below, p. 271).

βεβαιότης of his measures; but Clodius 'uses' Pompey (46.8), as shortly Caesar will 'use' him (47.8), for sheer demagogy. This weakens Pompey's reputation (e.g. καταισχύνων, 46. 8), and finally the strength given to Clodius is used against Pompey himself (48. 9–12). Pompey himself is slow to see what is happening (48. 8, cf. ἔλαθε in 46. 3). Here there is a more specific foreshadowing of later events, for Pompey is too wrapped up in his marriage with Julia to notice the political currents (48. 8), and this is what leaves him vulnerable to Clodius. Just so will he neglect affairs later in the fifties, first with Julia (53. 1) and then with Cornelia (55. 3–4, cf. 2. 10). With Clodius, events do not go too far; with the help of the senate, Pompey can retrieve his position. Against Caesar, too, he will need the senate's help, and he will return to their side. But Caesar will not be so manageable.

The treatment of Clodius is one of several passages in the Life which bring out Pompey's *passivity*. In the politics of the fifties, he is seldom in control: it is extraordinary how little in the Life's narrative is initiated by Pompey himself. We hear a good deal of his advisers, both good and bad (49. 4, 54. 5, 54. 9, 57. 7–8); his friends, too, are emphasized, excusing his blunders (47. 8), discussing his policy with him (49. 3), or giving some indication of his wishes (54. 4). He himself reveals little; he is a man to whom things happen.[31] Commands are voted to him; he is not said to press for them, or even to desire them.[32] When pressed, he may answer questions (47. 6–7, 51, 7–8, 60. 6, 60. 8)—but normally his answers reveal a further lack of sureness, and he has little dignity or control. After the outbreak of war, no one allowed him to think for himself; all men rushed to Pompey and filled him with their own transient emotions and fears. καὶ τἀναντία τῆς αὐτῆς ἡμέρας ἐκράτει βουλεύματα

---

[31] There is of course considerable historical acumen in Plutarch's portrayal: 'nosti hominis tarditatem et taciturnitatem' (Cic. *fam.* i. 5b. 2), and cf. e.g. Gelzer, *Pompeius²* (Munich, 1959), 158–9, 170–1, 175. Gelzer (164) also finds it useful to contrast Pompey's phlegmatic conduct of politics with 'die alte Energie' on campaigns. But such matters are beyond the scope of this paper.

[32] Esp. 49, 54, 55. 12, 61. 1: contrast the Life's earlier stress on his φιλαρχία, esp. 30. 7–8. Pompey of course wants to retain his pre-eminent position (53. 9–10), but the nearest approach to desire for a *specific ἀρχή* is the hint of 54. 8, where he thanks Cato for his support.

(61. 4–5), for Pompey was the prey to every false rumour; hurriedly, he left the city to its fate. For ten years, we have seen this indecisive man, one who is out of his depth in the political currents: he is a general lost in politics (a theme introduced earlier in the Life, 23. 3–6). It is, indeed, only on campaign that he acts with his old briskness and success. His *cura annonae* (50) shows a different, stronger Pompey than the man we have just seen humiliated by Clodius; his swift departure from Brundisium (62) shows him a match for Caesar, again different from the man who has just been the feeble victim of others' emotions (61). In Rome and at peace, he is fully himself only with his wives, Julia and then Cornelia, who themselves distract him from public affairs. It is a powerful and sympathetic psychological portrait—and the other Lives' accounts of the fifties have little hint of it.[33]

Pompey's lack of decision is reflected in the Life's treatment of his motives, and here again there is a difference of interpretation between *Pompey* and the other Lives. *Caesar* and *Cato* stress his calculated ambitions in the years from 54 to 52 BC. *Caes.* 28. 7 is explicit, ἔργῳ παντὸς μᾶλλον ἐπέραινεν ἐξ ὧν ἀναδειχθήσοιτο δικτάτωρ; while Cato's speech at *Cato* 45. 7 shows his usual foresight, . . . ἐξ ὧν οὐ λέληθε δι' ἀναρχίας μοναρχίαν ἑαυτῷ μνηστευόμενος. Pollio seems to have had something to say about this, for Appian has a similar passage (*BC* ii. 19. 71, 20. 73). But such calculation is foreign to the *Pompey*, and that Life cuts the analysis away: simply ἀναρχίαν ἐν τῇ πόλει περιεῖδε γενομένην (54. 3), he let it happen—though he himself has just been said to rely on the city's ἀρχαί, not on ἀναρχία (54. 2). There is no suggestion of any conscious plotting. And, as we saw earlier, Pompey's view of Caesar in Gaul is fairly similar: he realizes the danger, and yet he does nothing. He is, indeed, a man to whom things happen—and he lets them.

In all this there is a pervasive contrast with Caesar. Pompey is politically inert; Caesar is always at work, even when men do not realize. His furtive δεινότης undermines

---

[33] The other Lives reflect the dilatoriness and indecision at the outset of the war (*Caes.* 33. 4–6 and, less strongly, *Cato* 52. 4, 53. 3); but there is no similar attempt to prepare this theme in the accounts of the fifties. The psychological depth of *Pompey* contrasts with the crude passage at *Cato* 49.1, where in 52 BC Pompey ἦν ὄκνου καὶ μελλήσεως ἀτόλμου πρὸς τὸ κωλύειν καὶ ἐπιχειρεῖν ὑπόπλεως.

Roman politics, even when he is absent in Gaul (51. 1); he shows a deviousness quite alien to Pompey's simple and generous nature (cf. 49. 14). Caesar's flair for urban politics quite outwits Pompey (. . . ἐν μέσῳ τῷ δήμῳ καὶ τοῖς κυριωτάτοις πράγμασι καταπολιτευόμενος Πομπήϊον, 51. 1). This contrast is again a peculiarity of the *Pompey* (though this is a matter of technique rather than interpretation). In *Caesar* Pompey is certainly outwitted (20. 3), but that Life concentrates more on the similarities than the differences of the pair. Both aim at μοναρχία (cf. 28. 5–7), and both aim to destroy the other (28. 1). *Pompey* has something of this (53. 9–10, cf. 67. 2, 67. 4–5), but states it less sharply: the points of contact are here much less emphatic than those of contrast.

More important is the preparation which all this affords for the tragedy of Pharsalus. When the war begins, Pompey again seems to have regained his stature. His strategy of leaving Italy is correct: Plutarch elaborately defends it.[34] The army admires him, and he inspires all with his own vigour (64. 3). At Dyrrhachium, he outmanœuvres Caesar, and forces him into all manner of hardship; meanwhile 'every wind blows' for Pompey, bringing provisions, reinforcements, and funds (65. 6–7). His strategy of delay, avoiding a pitched battle, is again evidently correct (66. 1); Plutarch defends it in the concluding *Comparison* (84(4). 6). All this is consonant with Pompey's history of decisive generalship and unbroken military success. But now, fatally, his two worlds of politics and warfare are coming together. Even in this decisive campaign, his political failings are felt, and it is these which bring him to defeat. He is destroyed by his inability to lead or persuade his senatorial lieutenants. In politics, he has never been able to manage men like these, and he cannot manage them now. He still sees things more clearly

[34] *Pomp.* 64 treats the forces which Pompey gathered during 49 BC, and Plutarch's argument seems intended to justify the strategy of leaving Italy. Some praised Pompey's departure, though Caesar and Cicero uttered dismissive remarks (63. 1–2); but Caesar showed in his actions that he particularly feared τὸν χρόνον (63. 3–4); ἐν δὲ τῷ χρόνῳ τούτῳ μεγάλη συνέστη Πομπηΐῳ δύναμις (64. 1). The strength which Pompey now acquired contrasts forcefully with his initial weakness (57. 6–9, 60. 6.8). Plutarch's approval of the strategy seems clear; though, in a different train of thought, he later criticizes the decision to abandon *Rome* (*Comparison* 83(3). 6–8, cf. 61. 6–7).

than they (66. 6), but he cannot resist them. He abandons the task of a general, and, conscious of the folly, leads his army to its fate: the moment inspires Plutarch to great eloquence, 67. 7–10 and *Comparison* 84(4). His political unsureness becomes his decisive failing, and leaves him vulnerable to Fortune: he has no control, and events bear him inexorably to his fall.

We are, once again, close to tragedy; and Plutarch's style and imagery adopt an appropriate tone. The Caesarian troops take their positions ὥσπερ χορός (68. 7)—and indeed the startling ch. 70, where participants reflect on human blindness and greed, is very much in the manner of a choral ode. Pharsalus itself is later said to be the θέατρον (*Comparison* 84(4). 6)—there, a theatre which Pompey should have avoided.[35] It is a theatre where the armies play out events to an inevitable conclusion. The Pompeian dandies are no match for Caesar's veterans (69. 4–5, 71. 7–8). The empty luxury found in Pompey's camp closes the account of the battle (72. 5–6), elegantly returning to the vital theme, the manic optimism of Pompey's staff: οὕτω ταῖς ἐλπίσι διεφθαρμένοι καὶ γέμοντες ἀνοήτου θράσους ἐπὶ τὸν πόλεμον ἐχώρουν. And Pompey the Great, now μάλιστα δ' ὅμοιος παράφρονι καὶ παραπλῆγι τὴν διάνοιαν (72. 1), is involved inescapably in their fate.

III. BIOGRAPHICAL THEORY AND PRACTICE

Plutarch introduces the pair *Alexander* and *Caesar* with one of his clearest programmatic statements. The reader of those two Lives should not expect a detailed narrative of all the well-known historical events. 'For it is not histories we are writing, but Lives. Nor is it always his most famous

---

[35] At 84(4). 6 the θέατρον image is also woven into the texture of the *athletic* imagery which pervades the Life (cf. esp. 8. 7, 17. 2, 20. 2, 41. 2, 51. 2, 66. 4, 84(4) *passim*): Pharsalus is 'the stadium and theatre for the contest': 'no herald called Pompey to come and fight, if he would not leave the crown for another'. A good example both of the systematic elaboration of Plutarch's imagery, and of the interaction of different systems. For the 'theatre' motif, we might compare the theatrical imagery in another Life rich in tragedy, the *Antony*: *Dtr.* 53. 10, *Ant.* 29. 4, 45. 4, 54. 5. *Antony* here echoes and develops the imagery of *Demetrius*: cf. de Lacy (n. 26), 371.

actions which reveal a man's good or bad qualities: a clearer insight into a man's character is often given by a small matter, a word or a jest, than by engagements where thousands die, or by the greatest of pitched battles, or by the sieges of cities' (*Alex.* 1. 1–2). The point recurs elsewhere: Plutarch feels no responsibility to give a continuous history of events, which the reader can find elsewhere.[36] His interest is character, ἦθος. Compare the first chapter of *Nicias*: Plutarch is 'not as stupid as Timaeus, who tried to rival Thucydides': he has merely tried to collect some less familiar material, οὐ τὴν ἄχρηστον ἀθροίζων ἱστορίαν, ἀλλὰ τὴν πρὸς κατανόησιν ἤθους καὶ τρόπου παραδιδούς.[37] Why this interest in character? Plutarch's answer is again clear: he hopes that his readers might be led by examples of virtue to become better men themselves.[38] He hopes that a few examples of wickedness, carefully introduced, may deter his audience from evil.[39] And he has himself tried to become a better man for his biographical studies, 'using history like a mirror, and somehow improving and moulding my own life in imitation of their virtues' (*Aem.* 1. 1). The theory is clear and consistent. Biography will often concentrate on personal details, and may abbreviate its historical narrative; its concern will be the portrayal of character, and its ultimate purpose will be protreptic and moral.

That is the theory; and the practice often closely corresponds. *Pompey* itself is one example. Everything centres on Pompey's own character, on motifs such as the tension between home life and public affairs or between politics and warfare; on the strengths and weaknesses which bring success and then defeat. The explanations of such matters are sought in Pompey's own personality, and there is no attempt to relate them to any wider historical background. It is also a moralistic Life: Pompey's good qualities—the σωφροσύνη of his personal life, or his diligent provincial administration—receive due praise; his political

[36] *Galba* 2.5, *Fab.* 16. 6.
[37] On the *Nicias* passage, cf. Wardman, *CQ* 21 (1971), 257–61, and op. cit. (n. 26), 154–7. For the interest in ἦθος, cf. esp. *Pomp.* 8. 6–7, *Demosth.* 11. 7; for Plutarch's terminology, Russell, *G&R* 13 (1966), 139–54; see above, pp. 75-94.
[38] Cf. esp. *Per.* 1–2, *Aem.* 1.
[39] *Dtr.* 1, cf. *Cim.* 2. 2–5.

unscrupulousness seldom escapes censure.[40] Passing morals
are intrusively pointed (the most striking example being the
'choric' reflections before Pharsalus).[41] And the insight
into the vulnerability of a great man carries an awareness of
human fragility which is 'moralistic' in the deepest sense.

Cato is also close to the theory. The Life underlines
Cato's unbending and upright character, ἦθος ... ἄτρεπτον
καὶ ἀπαθὲς καὶ βέβαιον ἐν πᾶσιν (1. 3). Cato's austere and
energetic demeanour on campaign, his ostentatiously just
administration, his immaculate conduct as a candidate for
office, his magnanimity in accepting a personal defeat:
these are the points which are stressed.[42] The tradition
richly illustrated Cato's courageous resistance to unscrupu-
lous and violent opponents: Plutarch revels in it. There
were a few bad points, too, and Plutarch, true to his theory,
observes them carefully: his unbending opposition to
Pompey's agents was perilous, although well-intentioned
(26. 5); his unpretentious dress and demeanour detracted
from his dignity as praetor (44. 1); his divorce and remar-
riage of Marcia was at least questionable (52. 8). But the
general picture is altogether favourable. The climax is
reached with Cato's last days. He is determined on suicide,
but his first thought is for the safety of the people of
Utica.[43] They doubt the wisdom of resisting Caesar; but
even they come to understand and marvel at the constancy
of Cato's virtue (64. 3).

'Small matters', too, receive the stress which the *Alexander* prologue suggests. The Life is studded with anecdotes:
the infant Cato's meeting with Poppaedius Silo, the trium-
phant entry of Demetrius into Antioch, the circumstances
in which Cato received Ptolemy, the complicated snub of

---

[40] Personal life: *Pomp.* 18. 3, 40. 8–9, 53. 2. Administration: 39. 4–6, cf. 27. 6–
7, 28. 5–7. More praise: 10. 10–14, 20. 6–8, 49. 14. Criticism: esp. 10. 3–5, 29, 30.
8, 38. 1, 40. 6, 44. 4–5, 46. 3, 47. 8, 53. 9–10, 55. 6–10, 67. 7–10. And the
Comparison, as always, is rich in praise and blame.

[41] 28. 5, man as naturally responsive to kindness; 29. 5, the culpable φιλοτιμία
of Achilles; 53. 10, Fortune cannot meet the demands of human nature, for greed
is insatiable; 70, blindness and greed; 73. 11, φεῦ τοῖσι γενναίοισιν ὡς ἅπαν καλόν.

[42] Campaigns: *Cato* 8. 2–3, 9. 5–10, 12. 1. Administration: 16–18, 21. 3 ff., 35–
8, 44, 48. 8–10. Candidatures: 8. 4–5, 20–1, 42. 3–4, 49. 2–6. Rebuff: 50.

[43] *Cato* 58. 5, 59. 4–8, 65. 2, 65. 6–7, 70. 6–7.

Juba.[44] Cato's quarrel with Munatius is described at length (37), and Plutarch concludes in language very reminiscent of the *Alexander*: 'I have treated this episode at length because I think that this, no less than his great and public deeds, reveals and illustrates his character' (37. 10). This is indeed a very 'personal' Life. Cato's love for his brother is emphasized; the difficulties of his womenfolk are a recurrent theme; his fondness for drink is not concealed.[45] There is little interest in the historical background: he can relate the formation of the first triumvirate without even mentioning Crassus.[46] Cato's resistance to the dynasts is not brought into any political scheme: he is one man working on his own. The controlling interest is ethical, not political, and passing ethical truths are duly pointed.[47]

Cato, then, and *Pompey* are all Plutarch's theory could demand: personal, moralistic, non-historical. They are also not very typical. Consider, for instance, *Caesar*. Plutarch there generates a great interest in the historical background, and is particularly careful to keep the theme of the coming tyranny before our eyes.[48] The early chapters introduce the theme. 3. 2–4 digresses to mention the later period in Caesar's life when, 'striving to become first in power and in armed conflict', he allowed the highest rank of eloquence to escape him.[49] Abusive political opponents charge him with challenging the state and aiming at tyranny (4. 8, 6. 3, 6. 6); but the people encourage his ambitions, and promise their support (5. 8–9, 6. 9). Later in the Life, little touches show Plutarch's careful emphasis. At 29. 5 the rumour spreads in Italy that Caesar's men are likely to desert: οὕτως γεγονέναι τὸν Καίσαρα πλήθει στρατειῶν λυπηρὸν αὐτοῖς καὶ φόβῳ μοναρχίας ὕποπτον. The parallel passage in *Pompey* (57.7) does not

---

[44] 2. 1–5, 13, 35. 4–6, 57.

[45] Brother: 3. 8–10, 8. 1, 11. 1–8, 15. 4. Women: 24. 4–25. 13, 30. 3–10, 52. 5–9; cf. 73. 2–4, on the sexual predilections of Cato's son. Drink: 6. 1–4, but cf. the rejection of the slander at 44. 2. [46] 31–3; cf. *Method* 95 (below, p. 310).

[47] 7. 3, 52. 7–9, on married life; 9. 10, on 'true virtue'; 44. 12–14, on justice; 46. 8, on senseless extravagance; 50. 3, on the wise man's constancy.

[48] Cf. W. Steidle, *Sueton und die antike Biographie* (Munich, 1951), 13–24, echoed by C. Brutscher, *Analysen zu Suetons Divus Julius u. d. Parallelüberliefe- rung* (Bern, Stuttgart, 1958), 27–31, 89–91; Garzetti's comm. on *Caesar*, xliii–xlix.

[49] I discuss the precise interpretation of this sentence in *RhM* 127 (1984), 43–5.

mention μοναρχία; nor, to judge from Appian (*BC* ii. 30. 116), did Pollio make much of this. At *Caes.* 30. 1 Caesar accuses the optimates of building Pompey's tyranny while they destroy Caesar himself; the parallel *Pompey* 58. 5 does not mention 'tyranny'. The affair with Metellus (*Caes.* 35. 6–11) is also brought into the scheme: Plutarch ventures into *oratio recta* to bring out a vital point, Caesar's outburst ἐμὸς γὰρ εἶ καὶ σὺ καὶ πάντες ὅσους εἴληφα τῶν πρὸς ἐμέ στασιασάντων. Plutarch does not need to labour the point:[50] these are the words of a tyrant. Such hints thoroughly prepare the way for the final chapters. Caesar's rule became 'an acknowledged tyranny' (57. 1); and yet the pressures of that rule forced him to his death.[51] He had spent his life in seeking absolute power, and saw only its name, and the perils of its reputation (69. 1).

Caesar became tyrant; Plutarch asks himself how it happened. His answer is again clear and emphatic. From the beginning, Caesar is the champion of the *demos*. They support him, and he rises; he loses their favour, and he falls.[52] Early in his life, it is the people who encourage him to become first in the state (6. 9). He fosters them with shows and games, and they seek 'new commands and new honours' with which to repay him (5. 9). This generosity to the *demos* indeed purchases the greatest prizes cheaply (5. 8, cf. 4. 8); and the optimates are quite deceived (4. 6–9, 5. 8). The theme continues through the Life: even the brief notices of the politics of the fifties are underpinned by references to the *demos*.[53] It is when Caesar loses this popular support that his fortunes waver, and the reactions of the *demos* are important in explaining this fall; but, after his death, the popular fervour again erupts.[54]

----

[50] The pedestrian Dio xli. 17. 2–3 makes the same point more crudely.

[51] Here, once again, there are elements of tragedy: cf. *Method* 79 (below, p. 275). As so often, a major Shakespearian theme may be seen as a brilliant elaboration of a Plutarchian idea.

[52] Cf. *Method* 78 (below, pp. 273–4).

[53] Thus Caesar's meddlings in Rome are 'demagogy' (20. 2): the unprecedented fifteen-day *supplicatio* was largely the response to ἡ πρὸς ἐκεῖνον εὔνοια τῶν πολλῶν (21. 2); the reaction of τὸ πλῆθος to Favonius' outburst is traced (21. 8–9); the popular emotions at Julia's death are emphasized (23. 7). Other Lives differ: see n. 55.

[54] I have said something of this at *Method* 78–9, and tried to show that this reading involved some reworking of material (below, pp. 273–5).

This *demos–tyrannis* analysis dominates *Caesar*, and it is essentially a *historical* interest. Other Lives occasionally differ in detail from this analysis,[55] and, more important, they are simply less interested in offering *any* such explanation of events. This interest leads in *Caesar* to the suppression of themes and emphases which elsewhere typify Plutarch's work. Caesar's own ἦθος, for instance, remains rather shadowy: there is none of the psychological interest of *Pompey*, and there are few personalia of the type we see in either *Pompey* or *Cato*. Pompey's home life was stressed in his Life, and Cato's womenfolk in his; here there is very little on Caesar's three or four marriages. And Caesar's personal, especially sexual, habits might afford vast scope for a biographer: one need only glance at Suetonius' *Divus Iulius*. Plutarch welcomes such material elsewhere, but here he suppresses it.[56] Even Cleopatra is treated rather perfunctorily (49. 1–3). There are indeed remarkably few of those 'small matters which illustrate a man's character' which the preface to *Alexander and Caesar* had promised.[57]

Nor is it a very moralistic Life: we can indeed see Plutarch avoiding points he elsewhere thinks important to an estimate of Caesar. In other Lives he gives Caesar credit, the

[55] For instance, *Pompey* is more interested in Pompey's relations with the senate (above, pp. 139–42). Thus *Pomp.* 51. 1–3 gives no stress to the *demos* in its account of Caesar's urban machinations: it is there 'aediles, praetors, consuls, and their wives' who are stressed. The *Pompey* account of Luca closes with Pompey's clash with Marcellinus (51); the parallel *Caes.* 21 ends by stressing the reaction of the *demos. Pompey* gives no hint that the *demos* theme is important for an understanding of the period, and there are other places where it cuts away references to the people: *Cato*, for instance, has more of the popular, as well as the senatorial, opposition to Pompey (e.g. *Cato* 42. 3–4, 42. 7, 43. 6–7). *Cato* itself has material which would be a great embarrassment to the tidy account of *Caesar*, particularly some popular enthusiasm for Cato himself and the optimate cause (e.g. 44. 12–14, and the passages mentioned above). That again suits the emphasis of *Cato*, for the popular reaction reflects Plutarch's own enthusiasm for Cato. Once again, Plutarch has in each Life selected the political analysis to suit his interests and themes. For the different emphases of *Brutus* and *Caesar* in describing Caesar's death, cf. *Method* 78–9 (below, pp. 273–5).

[56] Cf. e.g. *Caes.* 8. 2, where Plutarch suppresses the ἐπιστόλιον ἀκόλαστον brought to Caesar during the Catilinarian debate: contrast *Cato* 24. 1–3, *Brut.* 5. 2–4, *Caes.* 49. 10 makes little of Caesar's affair with Cleopatra; and the initial mention of Nicomedes (1. 7) is very tame. Contrast such passages as *Sull.* 2. 2–7, *Pomp.* 2. 5–10, *Cim.* 4. 6–10, *Crass.* 1. 2 ff.

[57] But there are a few: esp. 17, and e.g. 38, 49. 7–8.

πρᾳότατος ἰατρός of the evils of his generation (*Ant.* 6. 7, *Brut.* 55(2). 2): not a word of this in *Caesar* itself. Little stress is given to Caesar's ἐπιείκεια in the Civil Wars:[58] for instance, his generous treatment of the troops of Afranius and Petreius is stressed at *Pomp.* 65. 3, but omitted at *Caes.* 36. 2. Other obvious merits are neglected: Caesar's φιλεταιρία, for instance, or his devotion to his troops. Nor does Plutarch make negative moral points. There is not a breath of disapproval for Caesar's vulgar demagogy, or his extravagance, or his debts.[59] The moralist does occasionally show through, but these hints are sparse, and seldom important.[60]

But *Caesar* is no more typical than *Cato*. Consider another Life, the *Antony*. In many ways this is closer to Plutarch's theory. There is certainly little interest in the history, and the struggle of Antony and Octavian is not related to any wider background. The origins of the war of Actium are described in terms of antagonistic personalities: in particular, the antagonism of Cleopatra and Octavia.[61] The battle itself is narrated very hazily, and all centres on the personal demeanour of Antony and Cleopatra. It is, indeed, a very personal Life. The narrative often stops for powerful characterizing surveys: not just of Antony, but also of Cleopatra, of Fulvia, of Octavia, even of the incidental Timon of Athens.[62] A fund of anecdotes illustrates Antony's character, κομπώδη καὶ φρυαγματίαν ὄντα καὶ κενοῦ γαυριάματος καὶ φιλοτιμίας ἀνωμάλου μεστόν (2. 8). His luxurious private life is a dominant motif, and 'small matters' figure as prominently as the *Alexander* preface would suggest.[63] The Life is also at times extremely moralistic, as

[58] Plutarch does make something of this (34. 7, 48. 3–4, 54. 5, 57. 4–6), but might easily have made more.

[59] Contrast Plutarch's disapproval of vulgar demagogy at *Cato* 46. 8, 49. 6, *Aem.* 2. 6, *praec. reip. ger.* 802d *al.*, *Brut.* 10. 6; of extravagance and debt at *praec. reip. ger.* 802d, 821f, 822c–823e, and *de uitando aere alieno*.

[60] Cf. 14. 16–17, 29. 5, 48. 5, 56. 8–9. Note 54. 6, a much more measured description of Caesar's *Anticato* than the vituperative *Cato* 11. 7–8, 36. 5, 54. 2.

[61] *Ant.* 35. 2–4, 53–4, 56. 4, 57. 4–5, 59.3, 72. 3. Other ancient accounts make far less of Octavia, and this theme seems to be Plutarch's own elaboration.

[62] Antony: 4, 9. 5–9, 24. 9–12, 43. 3–6. Cleopatra: esp. 27. 3–5, 29. 1–7. Fulvia: 10. 5–10. Octavia: cf. 54. 3–5. Timon: 70.

[63] e.g. dress and demeanour, 4. 1–5, 17. 3–6; dream, 16. 7; comment on Megarian *bouleuterion*, 23. 3; comment on the repeated tribute, 24. 7–9; detail of the feasts, 28; fishing anecdote, 29. 5–7; dice and fighting cocks, 33; etc.

indeed the introduction to *Demetrius and Antony* leads us to expect.[64] Antony's private luxury is criticized; so is his autocratic behaviour in public.[65] The proscriptions are strongly stigmatized (19–20). The final *Comparison* is heavy with 'crude and prudish' moralism.[66] And it is tempting to characterize the entire Life as 'basically . . . a simple cautionary tale'.[67]

Yet it is perhaps not so simple. Most of these instances have been drawn from the first third of the Life, before the entrance of Cleopatra (25. 1). Cleopatra herself is introduced as Antony's τελευταῖον κακόν—but the story is immediately seized by a new narrative and descriptive vigour, and the nature of Plutarch's moralism becomes rather different. There are no more intrusive moralizing remarks; no more explicit denunciations of the actions he describes. Antony and Cleopatra vie with each other in the extravagance of their entertainment (26–8); Plutarch might have done more than mildly rebuke Antony for time-wasting (28. 1, cf. 30. 1). Cleopatra is the mistress of every type of κολακεία (29. 1), and contrasts tellingly with Octavia's σεμνότης (31. 4, 53. 5); but it is an essentially *artistic* contrast, and no moral is drawn. Cleopatra and Antony behave disgracefully at Actium, 'betraying' the whole army (cf. 68. 5). Plutarch makes little ethical capital of it: contrast his remarks on Pompey's behaviour at Pharsalus (*Pomp.* 67. 7–10). By the end of the narrative, the interests of writer and audience are far from crude moralism. Octavian is allowed no praise for his noble conduct towards Cleopatra (82. 2, 84. 3, 86. 7); and it is indeed a surprise, when we come to the *Comparison*, to discover that Plutarch disapproved of the manner of Antony's death.[68] Praise and blame are alike irrelevant to the narrative: Plutarch, like his readers, is quite carried away by the vigour and splendour of the death scenes.

---

[64] *Dtr.* 1, esp. 1. 6.

[65] 9. 5–9, 21. 1–3, cf. 56. 8; 6. 6–7, 15. 4–5, 24. 5–10.

[66] Russell (n. 26), 142.

[67] Russell (n. 26), 135.

[68] 93(6). 4. What little ethical colouring there is in the narrative is favourable to Antony: 67. 9–10, 75. 3.

Plutarch is here doing more than pointing the fate of the κόλαξ, or noting the effects of the corruption of ἔρως. His concern is the tragic depiction of a noble and brilliant nature, a man torn by psychological struggle and cruelly undone by his flaws: by his weakness of will, by his susceptibility to others, by his sad and conscious submission to his own lowest traits. There is moralism here, certainly, just as there is usually moralism in tragedy; but it is a subtle and muted type of moralism. It is the moralism of a sympathetic insight into human frailty; the moralism which, like the tragic aspects of *Pompey*, points a truth of human nature. We are some way from the ethical colouring of *Cato*, with its crude and explicit protreptic and censure.

One further point is important. Antony disappears from the narrative at 78. 1 (his death is never explicitly stated). The last ten chapters are all Cleopatra's. Plutarch often concludes a Life with a brief death-notice, giving the hero's age when he died and summarizing his achievement. Here there are two heroes, and they are given a joint notice (86. 8–9). In the last analysis, *Antony* fits Plutarch's biographical theory only a little better than *Caesar*. Its moralism soon becomes more subtle and less strident, as it is overlaid by the interest in literary artistry; and, by the end, it is not really a biography at all. After the entrance of Cleopatra, the Life becomes a dramatic set-piece.[69]

A writer's programmatic statements can sometimes be a poor guide to his work, and some Lives fit Plutarch's theory better than others. Any account of the Lives must bring out their *versatility*. It must find room for *Caesar*, which is not moralistic, nor personal, but is certainly historical. It must include Lives which break away from the constrictions of a single man's life, as *Antony* moves its attention to Cleopatra, or as *Brutus* often divides its interest between Brutus and Cassius.[70] It must find room for different *types* of moral interest: the explicit praise and blame of

[69] The Life is correspondingly rich in theatrical imagery: see n. 35.
[70] 'This *Life* is, to a large extent, the story not of one man but of two, Brutus and Cassius', Wardman (n. 26), 174. The complexities of this Life are well analysed in J. L. Moles's dissertation, '*A Commentary on Plutarch's Life of Brutus*', D. Phil. thesis (Oxford, 1979).

Cato, or the subtler and more tragic insights of *Antony*. Other Lives again—*Crassus*, perhaps, or *Sertorius*, or even *Cicero*—are simply less ambitious and less richly textured. This biographical genre is an extremely flexible one, and admits works of very different patterns.

It is arguable that these different emphases go deeper, and illuminate more puzzling aspects of Plutarch's work. He is, indeed, a curiously uneven writer. Sometimes he is impressively critical of his sources, sometimes absurdly credulous. His historical judgements are sometimes sensible and sophisticated, sometimes childlike and innocent. His characterization often impresses with its insight; it some-times irritates with its triviality and woodenness. His style and imagery are usually sober and restrained, but occasion-ally florid, extravagant, even melodramatic. Might such irregularities be related to the different directions and inter-ests of the Lives? That inquiry would indeed be delicate and complicated; and yet, perhaps, it would have its rewards.

EXCURSUS

The most bewildering example of Plutarch's simplifications and displacements is seen in his accounts of the senatorial debates at the outset of the war: *Caes.* 30–1, *Pomp.* 58–9, and *Ant.* 5. The historical accuracy of these accounts has been thoroughly examined by K. Raaflaub,[71] and only a few points need be considered here.

The *Pompey* account mentions the debate of 1 Dec. 50, but omits that of 1 Jan. 49: *Caesar* and *Antony* have the 1 Jan. debate, but not that of 1 Dec. Plutarch seems quite clear that these are different sessions, in different years. Thus at *Pomp.* 59. 2 he explicitly notes that Lentulus was *consul designatus*, and then at §5 marks the moment when he assumed the consulship; at *Caes.* 30. 6 and 31. 2, Lentulus is consul throughout. In *Pompey* it is Curio (tribune until 9 Dec. 50) who proposes that both Caesar and Pompey should

---

[71] *Chiron*, 4 (1974), 306–11. Further references, both to ancient sources and to secondary literature, may be found in Raaflaub's paper.

disarm: this proposal is of course historically well attested for the 1 Dec. debate. But in *Antony*, and apparently in *Caesar*,[72] it is Antony, tribune from 10 Dec. onwards, who makes this proposal. No other ancient source suggests that this proposal was made on 1 Jan., nor that Antony put it forward at any time. Some features of the chronology seem to be distinguished in consequence of the Lives' focus on different sessions. Curio's enthusiastic reception by the *demos* follows the *Pompey* session (58. 9), but precedes that in *Caesar* (30. 2); the same is true of Antony's insistence on reading a letter from Caesar to the *demos* (*Pomp.* 59. 3–4, *Caes.* 30. 3, *Ant.* 5. 5).[73] It does seem probable that Plutarch, in selecting these different sessions for emphasis in the three Lives, was not simply confused. His choice was deliberate, and we shall examine his reasons in a moment.

Yet the course of the debates themselves is extraordinarily similar. All three Lives have the sequence of votes (though *Pompey* simplifies a little): first, those who wished Pompey to disarm; then those who wished this of Caesar; finally, those who preferred the disarmament of both.[74] Both *Pompey* and *Caesar* have similar *apophthegmata* of the presiding consul: Caesar as a ληστής, and the need for arms rather than words.[75] In both cases, the senatorial reaction is to change their clothes as a mark of grief (*Pomp.* 59. 1, *Caes.* 30. 6). It is natural to suspect that these similarities arise from some deliberate conflation and displacement by Plutarch, and, in the case of the consular *apophthegmata*, some conscious displacement seems clear: in *Caesar* Lentulus is

[72] *Caes.* 30. 5 has τῶν περὶ Ἀντώνιον, but this seems the later Greek usage, equivalent merely to 'Antony': cf. Holden on *Them.* 7. 6, Hamilton on *Alex.* 41. 5. Antony is certainly already tribune at the time of the *Caesar* debate (30. 3).

[73] Though there may well be further confusion (or conflation) here. Raaflaub (309) may be right to suspect that Plutarch's notice in *Pompey* combines Caesar's terms of 1 Jan. 49 with the occasion, some weeks earlier, of *Ant.* 5. 3–4.

[74] *Pompey* (the one Life which refers to the 1 Dec. 50 debate, when the triple sequence of votes certainly took place) in fact gives this sequence least clearly. There Plutarch mentions only two votes, first that Caesar should disarm, secondly that both should do so; and he makes Curio introduce both motions, suppressing the role of the consuls. But *Pompey* does correctly have 22 senators oppose the final motion; *Antony* and *Caesar* have all those present support 'Antony'.

[75] *Caesar* conflates the two *apophthegmata*, and gives them to Lentulus (30. 6); *Pompey* keeps them separate (58. 6, 10), and assigns them to Marcellus. See above, p. 130.

the consul, and he is given the remarks which in *Pompey* belong to Marcellus. It is likely enough, too, that the change of clothes belongs after the *Caesar–Antony* debate, in early January, while *Pompey* has displaced this to a month earlier.[76]

What are we to make of the rest, and particularly the similar sequences of votes in the two sessions, and the similar role of the two tribunes? No doubt, as Raaflaub remarks, the two debates did cover similar ground, and no doubt the Caesarian tribunes were active in both.[77] But it requires great faith to believe that the *Caesar* account is accurate, and that Antony genuinely revived Curio's ploy a month later and gained a similar response. That is Raaflaub's view; but what we have seen of Plutarch's technique shows that this is a flimsy structure to build on his evidence. It is easier to assume that, for certain reasons, Plutarch chose to stress different debates in different *Lives*; but, once he had made this choice, he felt free to select the most spectacular items from *either* debate, and exploit them in the single context he had imposed. Such transfers and displacements are anyway visible here, as we have seen: he has surely done the same with Curio's proposal and its fate. In *Caesar* and *Antony* he delays this to the new year, and this involved transferring it to the new year's tribune, just as the *apophthegmata* needed to be transferred to the new year's consul. Plutarch need have no historical basis for this, and provides no evidence for Antony's true behaviour on 1 Jan.

Why, then, did Plutarch stress different sessions in the three *Lives*? First, both *Antony* and *Caesar* make much of the tribunes' flight to Caesar's camp (*Caes.* 31. 2–3, *Ant.* 5. 8–9): in both *Lives*, this flight gives the transition to the crossing of the Rubicon. (*Pompey* omits this flight, and Plutarch there prefers to link events by a different device.)[78]

---

[76] So Raaflaub 308–9. Dio xli. 3. 1 is a poor witness, but he confirms the *uestis mutatio* for the 1 Jan. 49 context: Raaflaub (n. 71), 307. Ed. Meyer, *Caesars Monarchie*³ (Stuttgart, Berlin, 1922), 284 n. 1, assumed that the *Caesar–Antony* and *Pompey* versions were doublets, and this has been the general view: *contra*, T. R. Holmes, *Roman Republic* (Oxford, 1923), ii. 330 n. 2.

[77] Raaflaub (n. 71), 307.

[78] The device of the false rumour (60. 1–2), followed by the truth (60. 2 ff.). False rumours are important in *Pompey*: above, pp. 134, 140 f. The importance of the tribunes' flight in *Caesar* and *Antony* explains a fact which puzzled Raaflaub

The transfer of Curio's proposal to Antony evidently tidies the sequence, and aids the focus on the tribunes of 49: not merely is their proposal rebuffed, they are even driven out of the senate-house and forced to the camp of Caesar. Secondly, *Pompey* makes much more of the republican opposition to Caesar, and particularly the relation of the optimate extremists with Pompey. In that Life the canvas is large enough to admit the role of Marcellus, Lentulus, and Cato; *Caesar* has only Lentulus. As Marcellus is given three speeches in *Pompey* (58. 6, 58. 10, 59. 1), it is worth while to distinguish him from Lentulus; once that distinction is made, the marking of the separate consular years is no great cumbrance. *Caesar* conflates, and the concentration of all these events into a single consular year is a natural consequence. Thirdly, the suppression of the December debate in *Caesar* leaves, as the first events of the sequence, Curio's enthusiastic reception by the *demos*, and Antony's reading (βίᾳ τῶν ὑπάτων) of Caesar's letter to the people: these are themes which cohere closely with that Life's emphasis on the *demos* of Rome.

(307), that Antony's proposal (in *Caes.–Ant.*) failed while Curio's (in *Pomp.*) succeeded. Curio's ploy *must* be successful, for Plutarch there wishes to pass to an exulting sequel, the joy with which the *demos* greeted him (58. 9). Antony's proposal *must* fail, for the sequel there is the humiliating flight.

5

Plutarch's Comparison of Pericles and Fabius Maximus

PHILIP A. STADTER

The purpose of Plutarch's *Parallel Lives* was to make clear the moral qualities of the heroes who are being described. Two fundamental practices distinguish Plutarch's method: he used the heroes' deeds and words as evidence for their moral qualities or virtues, and he compared two people with the same or similar qualities to determine the exact nature of those qualities in the individual. The comparative method is essential to Plutarch's technique. Plutarch's parallel lives are indeed *parallel*. Plutarch designed his pairs of lives to be read together: he regularly called them βίοι παράλληλοι, and in his prefaces he speaks of each pair as being united in one book. He tells us, for instance, that the lives of Pericles and Fabius Maximus, with which I will be concerned here, form the tenth book or βιβλίον of his *Lives* (*Per.* 2. 5).

The fundamental design has been frequently misunderstood. The authenticity of the συγκρίσεις found at the end of most pairs of lives was attacked in the nineteenth century, especially because they seemed to point out the differences between the heroes rather than the similarities. Yet the importance of comparisons in contemporary rhetorical theory and practice provided Plutarch with a conceptual background for comparing heroes. Further investigation revealed, in fact, that the συγκρίσεις are balanced by the introductions, so that the introductions usually stress the congruences, the conclusions the differences of the heroes.[1]

---

[1] See F. Leo, *Die griechisch-römische Biographie nach ihrer literarischen Form* (Leipzig, 1901), 149–52; A. Stiefenhofer, 'Die Echtheitsfrage der biographischen Synkriseis Plutarchs', *Philologus* 73 (1914–16), 462–503; F. Focke, 'Synkrisis', *Hermes* 58 (1923), 327–68. The integrity of the συγκρίσεις as a part of each pair is

Harmut Erbse more recently demonstrated on the basis of
the *Demosthenes* and *Cicero* that Plutarch does not limit his
comparison to the introduction and conclusion but makes
much of the various events of his heroes' lives which parallel
each other.[2] This insight, that Plutarch's comparative
method is used throughout the pair of lives and not just at
the beginning and end, needs further consideration, especially in the case of lives which, unlike the *Demosthenes–
Cicero* pair, are not obviously similar.

Plutarch's purpose in using the comparative method is
nowhere better explained than in the introduction to his
short treatise *De mulierum virtutibus*, 243 B–D:

In fact, there is no better way of learning the similarity and
difference of male and female virtue than by putting lives beside
lives and deeds beside deeds, just as if they were works of art, and
considering whether the μεγαλοπραγμοσύνη of Semiramis has the
same mark and character as that of Sesostris, or the σύνεσις of
Tanaquil as that of King Servius, or the φρόνημα of Porcia and
Timocleia as that of Brutus and Pelopidas, according to the most
important common feature and faculty. The virtues take on
certain differences—peculiar colours, so to speak—because of the
underlying habits, bodily constitution, food and way of life. For
in fact Achilles was courageous in a different way from Ajax, and
Odysseus' φρόνησις was different from Nestor's. Cato and Agesilaus were not just in the same way; Eirene was not like Alcestis in
her love for her husband, nor was Cornelia like Olympias in her
highmindedness.

Although Plutarch in this treatise is interested in comparing
women with men, in this paragraph we have, *mutatis
mutandis*, a kind of programme for the parallel lives, suggesting how each book, each pair of lives will explore a virtue
or group of virtues and how it manifests itself in two men

also clear from the MSS, as was first brought out by the Lindskog–Ziegler edition
by printing the συγκρίσεις continuously with the text of the second life, as the
introduction is printed with the first.

  [2] H. Erbse, 'Die Bedeutung der Synkrisis in den Parallelbiographien Plutarchs',
Hermes 84 (1956), 398–424. Erbse rightly sees that Plutarch attempts to base his
comparisons not on externals but on important similarities in *Charakter* and
Lebenslauf. Cf. also B. Bucher-Isler, *Norm und Individualität in den Biographien
Plutarchs* (Bern, Stuttgart, 1972 = *Noctes Romanae*, 13), 74–8.

and by comparison and contrast reveals its peculiar presence in each.[3] In the process, we might expect each life to be influenced and subtly shaped by its mate, as Plutarch searches to bring out the similarities and differences of his heroes. A proper evaluation of these reciprocal influences thus becomes essential for the true understanding of any life.

Unfortunately, because of our division of Greek and Roman history, each life of a pair is regularly studied and analysed separately with little or no regard for the life which is parallel to it, and usually without even mentioning the comparisons set after both. In this essay I will consider some aspects of the relation between the *Pericles* and its parallel life, the *Fabius Maximus*.[4]

There is no need to point out the basic differences between the situation of the two heroes.[5] Pericles was leading statesman in a democracy when Athenian imperialism was at its height; Fabius, just one member of a ruling senatorial oligarchy at a time when Rome was facing the greatest crisis of its history. The structure of the two lives is also radically different. The *Fabius* very early comes to the zenith of Fabius' career, in chapters 4–13, which describe how Fabius by his delaying tactics successfully kept Hannibal at bay in 217 BC. The rest of the life moves summarily through the remaining years of the war, though there is a secondary peak at the conquest of Tarentum in 209 (cc. 21–2), and concludes with Fabius' difficulties with Scipio and his eventual death. The *Pericles*, on the other hand, recites a long history of the Athenian statesman's education (cc. 4–6), his struggle for power against first Cimon (cc. 9–10) and then Thucydides (cc. 11–14), and only arrives—almost at

---

[3] Plutarch's theory of virtue as taking different forms in different people is framed in opposition to Stoic ethical theory. For Plutarch's contrast with the Stoics on this point see D. Babut, *Plutarque et le Stoicisme* (Paris, 1969), 318–66. For his use of Peripatetic terminology, see A. Dihle, *Studien zur griechischen Biographie* (*AbhGött* 3, Folge 37, 1956), 60–87.

[4] Thus, in a sense, answering the question of K. Ziegler, *Plutarchos von Chaironeia* (Stuttgart, 1949), 262 (= *RE* s.v. Plutarchos, 21 [1951], 899), 'was haben ... Perikles und Fabius Maximus ... in Wahrheit miteinander gemein?'

[5] Several distinctions are brought out in the σύγκρισις, *Fab.* 28–30.

the end of the life—to the moral height of Pericles' career in his conduct of the first years of the Peloponnesian War (cc. 29–35). His death, of course, follows immediately. However, despite these obvious differences, there are a large number of similarities. A study of these will show how Plutarch used the comparative method in this pair of lives.

First of all, the nicknames of the two leaders. In chapter 1 of the *Fabius* that hero was called Ovicula, 'Little Sheep'. The regular *agnomen* of Fabius, used by Cicero, Pliny, and the Fasti Capitolini, was Verrucosus. Plutarch, however, has encountered Ovicula[6] and reports it to us, explaining that Fabius was given the name because of his self-control (πρᾳότης) and his general dignity (βαρύτης).[7] Pericles also was given a nickname, 'Ολύμπιος, which the biographer ascribes especially to his style of speaking (*Per.* 8. 3–4).[8] At the end of the life, Plutarch reconsiders the name and decides that although it sounded affected and pompous, the name was especially appropriate to Pericles because he shared in that calmness and quiet which we properly associate with the home of the gods. By drawing attention to these two distinctive nicknames, Plutarch has been able to comment on a similar quality in the two men, a calm and dignified self-control.

A second similarity between the two lives is found in the emphasis on one-man rule. Plutarch goes to some lengths to bring out the fact that both men acted as monarchs in politics, despite the great difference of the constitutions under which they lived. Fabius, of course, was made a dictator. 'The times needed an unrestrained *monarchy*, which they called a dictatorship' (*Fab.* 3. 7). The powers of the office were tyrannical (*Fab.* 4. 2), and in fact the tribune Metilius accused Fabius of trying to overthrow the populace and set up an unrestrained monarchy and of exercising

---

[6] Known to us otherwise only from *De vir. ill.* 43. 1.

[7] I prefer βαρύτητα of the MSS (= *gravitas*) to Cobet's emendation, βραδυτῆτα.

[8] On the traditional opinion of Pericles' oratory, see W. R. Connor, 'Vim quamdam incredibilem: A Tradition concerning the Oratory of Pericles', *ClMed* 23 (1962), 23–33.

a tyranny (*Fab.* 8. 4 and 9. 2). Pericles also struck many as being a monarch. From the beginning he was suspected of tyrannical inclinations because of his resemblance to Peisistratus (*Per.* 7. 1) and had to avoid suspicion on this account (ὑποψία τυραννίδος, *Per.* 7. 3). His adviser Damon was ostracized for being φιλοτύραννος (*Per.* 4. 3). After his last great opponent Thucydides son of Melesias was expelled, the chorus of 'tyrant' was heard on all sides, especially from the comic poets (see *Per.* 16. 1 and 3. 5). The historian's dictum was true: 'it was a democracy in name, but in fact rule by the leading man' (*Per.* 9. 1). This condition was not limited to one year, as was Fabius', but lasted almost to his death. Only after he died did the citizens realize that what had been called μοναρχία and τυραννίς was really the bulwark, σωτήριον ἔρυμα, of the state (*Per.* 39. 4). Here Plutarch brings out certain similarities between the position and way of acting of his two statesmen.

A third case concerns the respective heroes' handling of their fellow citizens. In chapter 33 of the *Pericles* we are told, following Thucydides (2. 13. 1), how the foresighted statesman warned the Athenians that Archidamus might decide to spare his (Pericles') land, thus laying him open to slander and sowing division in the city. Pericles therefore promised that any land which should be spared by Archidamus he himself would give over to the city. The difficulty is surmounted before it arises, and we hear nothing more of it. The same problem presents itself in the *Fabius* but with a different outcome. In chapter 7 Hannibal carefully spares the lands of Fabius while he is ravaging the other farms near Rome so as to influence the passions of the Romans against Fabius. His plan proves successful, and the resulting outcry in the city was one of the causes of the continuing attacks on Fabius' policies. Plutarch has found two incidents of basically similar nature, which were handled differently by his two heroes, and presented them to us in such a way that we can see the differences which can exist between two men who share basically the same virtues. In this case, Plutarch has brought out Pericles' greater foresight.

Plutarch draws attention to various other resemblances

or parallels between Pericles and Fabius: their lack of superstition in religious matters,[9] their honesty (δικαιοσύνη),[10]
their use of oratory as an ὄργανον πειθοῦς,[11] their caution in
war,[12] their strength in facing deaths in their family,[13] etc.
But for Plutarch the great similarity between the two statesmen, that which subsumes all the others, was their ability
to endure the stupidities of the mass of common citizens
and their own colleagues,[14] that is, the virtue of πραότης.
This virtue is defined by Aristotle (*Eth. Nic.* 1125ᵇ26 ff.) as
a mean with regard to feeling (ὀργή). The man who is πρᾶος
controls his emotions, being neither without feeling nor
carried away by feeling. Rather, all is subject to λόγος.
Plutarch used the term in much the same sense, as has been
shown by Hubert Martin,[15] to describe 'a self-restraint
which avoids excess of every kind, whether physical or
emotional, whether within the individual or in his relations
with other people'. It is of the essence of the concept of
πραότης that one be under pressure from feeling, ὀργή,
whether in oneself or outside, and be able to resist it and
control it by the use of reason. Plutarch saw this quality as
being exemplified in different ways by both Pericles and
Fabius Maximus. He notes its manifestation in many aspects of their lives; their nicknames, as we have seen, their
way of walking,[16] their caution in war,[17] and so on. The

---

[9] Pericles was καθυπέρτερος δεισιδαιμονίας (*Per.* 6. 1, cf. the anecdote of the
eclipse, *Per.* 35. 2, and his shame at wearing a charm when mortally ill, *Per.* 38.
2). Fabius on being made dictator performs religious rites οὐ δεισιδαιμονίαν
ἐνεργαζόμενος, ἀλλὰ θαρρύνων εὐσεβείᾳ τὴν ἀρετήν (*Fab.* 4. 4, cf. 5. 1). Fabius, of
course, shows much more respect for religious obligations than Pericles: cf. *Fab.* 4
and 18.

[10] The honesty of Pericles: *Per.* 15. 3, 16. 3; of Fabius: *Fab.* 7. 5–8; of both:
Per. 2. 5, *Fab.* 30. 5–6.

[11] *Per.* 8. 1–4, 15. 2–3; *Fab.* 1. 7–9.

[12] The leading quality of both as generals was ἀσφάλεια. See *Per.* 18. 1: ἐν δὲ
ταῖς στρατηγίαις εὐδοκίμει μάλιστα διὰ τὴν ἀσφάλειαν. The idea lies behind *Per.* 18,
19. 3, 20. 3–4, 21, 38. 4. Fabius' cautiousness does not need to be emphasized, but
see *Fab.* 5. 3 (ἄτολμος), 5. 4, 10. 7, 19. 3, 25. 3, 26. 3–4.

[13] *Per.* 36. 6–9, *Fab.* 24. 6.

[14] See *Per.* 2. 5: τῷ δύνασθαι φέρειν δήμων καὶ συναρχόντων ἀγνωμοσύνας.

[15] 'The Concept of Praotes in Plutarch's *Lives*', *GRBS* 3 (1960), 65–73; this
quotation is from p. 73.

[16] *Per.* 5. 1, πραότης πορείας (this chapter is devoted to demonstrating Pericles'
general self-control); *Fab.* 17. 7, πρᾴῳ βαδίσματι.

[17] See above, n. 12.

word πρᾳότης and its cognates are used more frequently in this than in any other pair of lives.[18]

Both Pericles and Fabius are presented throughout especially as men who control themselves and thus can control the state in difficult times. Anaxagoras lifted up Pericles' thoughts and taught him dignity and self-control, inward and outward, including a proper attitude toward superstition, and a lofty oratory (*Per.* 4–6, 8). His rivalry with Cimon and Thucydides son of Melesias forced Pericles to cater more to the people (*Per.* 9–14), but afterward he asserted his natural aristocratic temperament (*Per.* 15). When on his own he emerges as doctor to the ills of the state (*Per.* 15. 1, 34. 5), using his rhetoric as a Platonic ψυχαγωγία (*Per.* 15. 2). As monarch he encourages the city to μέγα φρονεῖν through initiatives like the Congress Decree (*Per.* 17), but he also checks it when it inclines to excess in the years before the Peloponnesian War.[19] His great moment comes at the time of the first Peloponnesian invasion of Attica. In this passage in chapter 33 we find that Plutarch, following the example of Thucydides, describes the contest as one between reason and emotion, γνώμη and ὀργή.[20] Pericles kept calming them (κατεπράϋνε), and he would not call them into assembly from fear that he might be forced to do something against his judgement (παρὰ γνώμην). Like the helmsman of a ship who resists the anguished cries of the passengers and exercises his skill (τέχνη), Pericles kept the city closed up for safety and exercised his own judgement (λογισμοῖς). Pericles' ability to exercise control over the Athenians is emphasized by his words contrasting trees and men, by the helmsman-simile reminiscent of Plato,[21] and by the account of the attacks made on Pericles at this time, by friends, foes, and comic poets. The whole is rounded off forcefully: πλὴν ὑπ' οὐδενὸς ἐκινήθη τῶν τοιούτων ὁ Περικλῆς, ἀλλὰ πρᾴως καὶ σιωπῇ τὴν ἀδοξίαν καὶ τὴν ἀπέχθειαν

[18] Sixteen times. The next highest appears to be the Gracchi–Agis and Cleomenes set, with six.
[19] κατέχειν ἐπειρᾶτο, 18. 2; οὐ συνεχώρει . . . οὐδὲ συνεξέπιπτεν, 20. 3; κατεῖχε, 21. 1; ἔργον ἦν κατασχεῖν, 27. 2.
[20] Thuc. 2. 22. 1: ἐκκλησίαν οὐκ ἐποίει αὐτῶν οὐδὲ ξύλλογον οὐδένα, τοῦ μὴ ὀργῇ τι μᾶλλον ἢ γνώμῃ ξυνελθόντας ἐξαμαρτεῖν.
[21] Cf. *Resp.* 488, esp. the stress on the need for τέχνη in a helmsman.

ὑφιστάμενος . . . ἔμεινεν οἰκουρῶν καὶ διὰ χειρὸς ἔχων τὴν πόλιν
(*Per.* 34. 1). Pericles is presented as truly πρᾶος, able to
endure the outcry of the people in silence and self-control,
as he had endured the taunts of the boor in the anecdote
recounted at the beginning of the life (*Per.* 5. 2).

Using a simile from medical practice, Plutarch describes
Pericles as a doctor who is blamed by his patients for the
disease (*Per.* 34. 5) after the outbreak of the plague causes
new frustration. By sending out expeditions against the
Peloponnese he attempts to heal, calm, and encourage the
Athenians.[22] He was deprived of his office but almost at
once called back because no other general was equal to the
task: οὐδεὶς βάρος ἔχων ἰσόρροπον οὐδ' ἀξίωμα πρὸς τοσαύτην ἐχέγ-
γυον ἡγεμονίαν ἐφαίνετο (*Per.* 37. 1).

Fabius' great moment comes after the disaster of
Flaminius at Trasimene, when he is chosen dictator, as ἰσόρροπον ἔχοντα τῷ μεγέθει τῆς ἀρχῆς τὸ φρόνημα καὶ τὸ ἀξίωμα
τοῦ ἤθους.[23] Fabius' policy of delay, although feared by
Hannibal, is mocked by the Romans, who like the Athenians
under Pericles wish to fight their enemies at once. The
account of Fabius' firmness in controlling the Romans and
especially his colleague Minucius is told at some length and
reinforced by anecdotes such as that in 5. 6–8, where
Fabius when informed of Minucius' taunts replies that he
would indeed be a coward if he abandoned his own judgement from fear of mocking and insults.[24] Hannibal's success
in using the trick of the cattle to get out of a difficult
position and his refusal to ravage Fabius' fields increased
the opposition of the Romans so that they would not honour
Fabius' agreement ransoming prisoners. But ὁ Φάβιος τὴν μὲν
ὀργὴ ἔφερε πράως τῶν πολιτῶν (*Fab.* 7. 7) and freed the
prisoners with his own money. The apophthegm of Diogenes, ἀλλ' ἐγὼ οὐ καταγελῶμαι, is used by Plutarch to put
in relief Fabius' ability to endure the insulting treatment of
Minucius: ἔφερεν ἀπαθῶς καὶ ῥᾳδίως (*Fab.* 10. 2). This self-
control is shown finally when, after Minucius had fallen
into Hannibal's trap and been saved by Fabius, the latter

[22] *Per.* 35. 1 ἰᾶσθαι, 35. 4 παρηγορεῖν καὶ ἀναθαρρύνειν.
[23] Cf. *Per.* 37. 1 quoted above.
[24] ἐκπέσοιμι τῶν ἐμαυτοῦ λογισμῶν, cf. ἐχρῆτο τοῖς αὐτοῦ λογισμοῖς at *Per.* 33. 6.

did not remonstrate: οὐδὲν ὑπερήφανον οὐδ' ἐπαχθὲς εἰπὼν περὶ τοῦ συνάρχοντος (*Fab.* 13. 1). Throughout Fabius' legendary cautiousness is united with his ability to control himself and others: ἀσφάλεια is seen as one aspect of his πρᾳότης.

Fabius' first dictatorship was the chief occasion for demonstrating his πρᾳότης, but references to this leading characteristic continue in the rest of the life. It is apparent after Cannae (*Fab.* 17. 7), when he shared management of the war with Marcellus (*Fab.* 19. 4), and in his treatment of the allies (*Fab.* 20). The anecdotes and personal comments in chapter 20 emphasize the importance of the virtue of πρᾳότης in the leader.

Unlike Pericles, however, to Plutarch's mind the Roman shows a shift away from πρᾳότης to less admirable virtues, especially φιλοτιμία. After the conquest of Tarentum, he erred in having the Bruttians slain: δοκεῖ φιλοτιμίας ἥττων γενέσθαι (*Fab.* 22. 5);[25] the same quality reappears in his opposition to Scipio: what began as ἀσφάλεια and πρόνοια continued as φιλοτιμία and φιλονικία (*Fab.* 25. 3). Plutarch at any rate seems to think that his sense of caution overwhelmed his judgement, and πρᾳότης is no longer apparent.[26]

In his βιβλίον of the lives of Pericles and Fabius Maximus, Plutarch developed the similarities and differences he saw between two men in whom the quality of πρᾳότης was outstanding. The concept of comparison was ever present in his selection of incident and anecdote, as well as in the overall development of the lives. When the biographer discourses at length on Pericles' philosophical education or his caution as a general, or dilates on Fabius' dealings with Minucius while skimping the details of his confrontation with Hannibal, the reason lies in his desire to illustrate the πρᾳότης of each. A peculiar feature of the *Pericles* which has often puzzled commentators may be explained in the same way. Plutarch chooses to follow the comic poets and later historians in treating the attacks against Pericles and his

[25] Plutarch also criticizes his decision to remove a colossal statue of Heracles from Tarentum, which seemed out of place and made even Marcellus seem a man πρᾳότητι καὶ φιλανθρωπίᾳ θαυμαστόν (*Fab.* 22. 8).
[26] Note the repetition of ἐπισφαλές at *Fab.* 26. 3, 4.

friends, despite Thucydides' silence on the subject. Yet this is not strange if we think that Plutarch saw these attacks as strengthening the picture—which he had received from Thucydides—of Pericles as a man who was always able by the cool skill of reason to dominate the tempestuous passion of his critics. In fact Plutarch must have thought that the stronger the criticism to which Pericles was subjected, the greater the πρᾳότης in being able to rise above it. In a similar way our biographer is at pains to develop as vividly as possible the opposition of Minucius, the senate, and the tribunes to Fabius. One life strengthens and explains the other, as we understand one hero by comparison with the other. The two lives were written as a unit, and the reader—whether historian, student of biography, or amateur—should never forget the fact.

Finally, if *Pericles* emerges from Plutarch's *Life* immeasurably a greater man than Fabius, it is in no small part due to this same juxtaposition, which while illuminating the πρᾳότης of each, reveals that only Pericles possessed that sense of greatness—φρόνημα or μεγαλοφροσύνη—which could envision and build the Acropolis temples and make Athens the leading city of Greece.[27]

---

[27] The φρόνημα of Pericles is a secondary theme in the *Life*, and it or its compounds appears frequently: φρονέω μέγα 13. 3, 17. 1, 28. 7; φρόνημα 4. 6, 5. 1, 8. 1, 10. 7, 17. 4, 31. 1, 36. 8, 38. 1, 39. 1; μεγαλοφροσύνη 14. 2, 16. 7, 17. 4. φρόνημα is associated with Pericles in Thucydides: Thuc. 2. 43. 6, 2. 61. 3, 2. 62. 3. The word appears rarely in the *Fabius*: 3. 7, 18. 4 (applied to Rome); φρόνιμος: 24. 6.

6

Plutarch's *Parallel Lives*: The Choice of Heroes

JOSEPH GEIGER

Wenn es uns scheinen will, als wären doch die größten
Männer von Hellas und Rom so ziemlich alle in
Plutarchs Heldenschau vertreten, so ist das vielmehr
gerade die Wirkung seiner schriftstellerischen Lei-
stung: die von ihm behandelten Männer sind eben
durch ihn in den Vordergrund des Interesses der
Nachwelt gerückt, viele, die es nicht minder verdient
hätten, im Dunkeln geblieben; es wäre nicht schwer,
eine Liste von Männern aufzustellen, die mindere
Popularität genießen und von deren Persönlichkeit wir
weniger wissen, weil Plutarch an ihnen vorübergegan-
gen ist—carent quia vate sacro.

K. Ziegler *RE* 21: 898 = *Plutarchos* (Stuttgart, 1949), 261.

Few, if any, will disagree with the verdict of the highest
twentieth-century authority on Plutarch by questioning the
significance of his choice of heroes for our understanding
and evaluating the history of Greece and Rome. Yet while
Plutarch's aims and methods of composition, including the
choice of certain types of men had been given adequate
attention[1] little of it has been paid to his preference for
certain individuals and omission of others. No doubt the
main reason for this neglect is the inherent difficulties of
the problem. The following attempt does not propose to

I wish to thank Prof. D. Asheri, Mr E. L. Bowie, and Prof. C. P. Jones for their
advice and criticism; I alone am responsible for the remaining faults.

[1] e.g. J. R. Hamilton, *Plutarch, Alexander, A Commentary* (Oxford, 1969),
xxxvii ff.; D. A. Russell, *Plutarch* (London, 1972), 100 ff.; A. Wardman, *Plutarch's
Lives* (London, 1974), 21 ff.; S. S. Averincev, 'The Choice of Heroes in Plutarch's
Parallel Lives and the Ancient Biographical Tradition', *VDI* 92 (1965), 51 ff. (in
Russian).

ignore, or belittle, these difficulties, but to cover the ground with a view to hitherto unnoticed openings.

Ziegler himself, in what follows the above quotation, contents himself with a cursory view of the problem, touching on only two of the aspects pertaining to it: he notes that Plutarch, in accordance with the classicistic tendencies of his time, shows a marked preference for Greeks from Classical times and places. Secondly, discussing the composition of the pairs, Ziegler praises the choice of some pairs while he condemns Plutarch for others, where he, according to Ziegler, forced together unlike yokefellows by means of rhetorical arts, the implication probably being that some of these pairings were forced on Plutarch by his choice of heroes. The first of Ziegler's points is, as shall be shown in detail below, far from being as simple as it may seem at first glance; the second does not provide a profitable avenue (though, let it be said, Ziegler's own views of what do and what do not constitute matching pairs do sometimes betray a lack of understanding of Plutarch's literary methods).[2]

Nevertheless these two approaches are significant for the two main aspects of our problem. On the one hand, proper historical understanding must place Plutarch against his background in order to appreciate the influences of his age and of the literary genre which he was using, while on the other hand, we should be careful not to ignore the vital part played by the author's own interests and preferences. Chance is an important, but not an exclusive factor: the arrangement of the gallery of heroes of which Ziegler speaks in such convincing terms is not purely the random selection of an individual, but also the choice forced on this individual by his circumstances. Understanding the composition of the mosaic of the Parallel Lives involves not only the mind of the artist, but also the materials available as well as the rules and conventions of his art.

Unfortunately Plutarch himself is far from outspoken on the subject. Nor does his earlier practice reveal his motives: The Lives of the Emperors from Augustus to Vitellius which he composed earlier than the Parallel Lives—prob-

---

[2] See e.g. Part III of this paper.

ably under the brief reign of Nerva[3]—followed one of the most conventional themes in Greek biographical writing.[4] There are no clues for the time of the composition of other biographies that did not form part of the Parallel Lives and which are mostly lost, though that of Scipio Africanus must have been written before the commencement of the work on the series:[5] yet it would stand to reason that most of these were out of the way when Plutarch embarked on the great undertaking of the Parallel Lives. For the choice of the subjects of some of these single Lives purely personal motives seem to have been decisive: the extant *Aratus* was expressly composed for the instruction of the descendants of the hero (*Arat.* 1),[6] *Daiphantus* (*Lamprias catalogue*, No. 38; cf. *mul. virt.* 244 B = frg. 11)[7] and the *Pindar* (*Lamprias catalogue*, No. 36; cf. frg. 9) must have been outcomes of his local interests.

Turning to the Parallel Lives, similar considerations can be noticed. The suggestion that the only lost pair, the *Epaminondas–Scipio*, formed the opening book and as it were the flagship of the series, has as a main reason Plu-

---

[3] J. Geiger, 'Zum Bild Julius Caesars in der römischen Kaiserzeit', *Historia.* 24 (1975), 444 ff.
[4] Histories of countries by means of series of biographies of their rulers were written by e.g. Pha(e)nias of Eresus (Wehrli, *Die Schule des Aristoteles*, ix), Baton of Sinope (*FGrHist* 268), Charon of Carthage (*FHG* iv. 360), Euagoras of Lindos (*FGrHist* 619), Nicandros of Chalcedon (*FGrHist* 700), Menander of Ephesus (*FGrHist* 783), Timagenes of Alexandria (*FGrHist* 88), Athenaeus of Naucrates (*FGrHist* 166), and the authors of Jewish histories Justus of Tiberias (*FGrHist* 734), Demetrius (*FGrHist* 722), and Eumolpus (*FGrHist* 723).
[5] The *Lamprias catalogue* lists both a Life of Scipio Africanus (No. 28) and a pair *Epaminondas–Scipio* (No. 7). The problem of the proper assignment of these Lives to the elder and the younger Africanus has been a matter of considerable dispute (see résumé in Sandbach, Loeb *Moralia*, xv. 74). To the points already discussed should be added that the *Scipio Africanus* must have been written before the series was planned, since it is inconceivable that no room would have been found in the Parallel Lives for both Scipios. Thus the question should be not which of the two Romans would have been more aptly compared with Epaminondas, but rather which of the two would have excited Plutarch's imagination even before he conceived the plan of the Parallel Lives. The application 'Scipio Africanus' presupposes a certain uniqueness fitting for a single biography but hardly acceptable after a series of which a 'Scipio' was one.
[6] F. W. Walbank, *Aratus of Sicyon* (Cambridge, 1933), 16, maintains, apparently on no evidence, that the *Aratus* was composed later than the Lives of Agis and Cleomenes.
[7] Cf. P. A. Stadter, *Plutarch's Historical Methods* (Cambr., Mass., 1965), 137 f.

tarch's glowing admiration for his Boeotian compatriot,[8] evident in the Life of Pelopidas, in the *de genio Socratis*, as well as in the number of references to him in other works of the *Moralia*, which is second only to that of Alexander the Great. Local patriotism is explicitly the cause of the inclusion of Lucullus, of whom Plutarch pledges to leave a more beautiful portrait than the one at Chaeronaea, erected to him by a grateful city (*Cim.* 2). Personal considerations might have played sometimes a more subordinate role the value of which would be difficult to assess: certainly Themistocles was a natural choice even if his descendant and namesake were not a fellow student of the young Plutarch (*Them.* ad fin.) and the memories of his grandfather were at most but a complementary reason for writing a Life of Antony (*Ant.* 28). Nevertheless these facts provide us with some rare glimpses at the influences bearing on the decisions of the author.

The necessity of adhering to the strict framework of the Parallel Lives must have forced Plutarch more than once to include a biography so that he could provide a pair to another Life. Presumably at the outset of the series there existed a rudimentary plan for part of it, some of which like the *Demosthenes–Cicero*, the fifth pair (*Demosth.* 3. 1), would have been traditional or self-evident.[9] Yet Plutarch states that he expanded the series out of the delight and moral profit he derived from it (*Aem. Paul.* 1) and probably at this stage he would have had to look around for likely companions for the biographies he wanted to write. In a number of cases indeed Plutarch states his starting-point and the fact that he is looking around for an accompanying pair (*Thes.* 1. 3; *Agis* 2. 6; *Cim.* 3. 1; *Sert.* 1. 11; *Publ.* 1. 1; *Nic.* 1. 1; *Phil.* ad fin. and *Flam.* init.) yet this does not necessarily mean that the need to provide a pair for a hero on whose inclusion he already decided was the sole reason

   [8] Cf. Wilamowitz, *Reden und Vorträge*[4] ii (1926), 260; see above, p. 58.
   [9] The comparison of Demosthenes and Cicero goes back of course to Cicero himself: e.g. his calling his orations against Antony 'Philippics': ad *Brut.* 2. 4. 2; cf. Plu. *Cic.* 24. 6. For the comparison of the two orators by Caecilius of Caleacte see Plu. *Demosth.* 3. 2. For a comparison contemporary with Plutarch see Juvenal 10. 114 ff.

for the choice of his counterpart. In the following we shall have an opportunity to assess the value of some of these passages.

It seems that the above is the entire explicit evidence concerning Plutarch's choice of his heroes. To this main difficulty and the concomitant inability to reconstruct the author's mental processes two further points should be added: one, already mentioned in passing, is the fact that Plutarch did not work according to a fixed and complete plan. We have seen that he admitted to expanding the series because of the satisfaction he derived from it (*Aem. Paul.* 1. 1); also his statement (*Thes.* 1) that the Lives of Theseus and Romulus, and by implication Lycurgus and Numa, lie respectively beyond the pale, and on the borderline of, the verifiable facts of history, and that he came to write them only after he had traversed these, imply that this was a possible expansion of the original plan he may have had; the explanation of the inclusion of the book *Demetrius–Antony* (*Demetr.* 1) with the need to add one or two negative to the many positive examples seems also to have been an afterthought.

The other difficulty is the notorious problem of the relative chronology of the Parallel Lives without which there can be no clear picture of our problem. Jones's tentative results (*JRS* 56 (1966), 66 ff.; see above, p. 106 ff.) must be regarded with due caution, resting as they do on the conclusions of Stoltz.[10] Yet evidently the progress of the series cannot be divorced from the chronological framework, however tentative it may be.

It will seem that our problem lies well guarded behind a high wall of stony silence: in what follows one or two avenues will be shown to give some access to the exploration of those dark areas.

[10] C. Stoltz, *Zur relativen Chronologie der Parallelbiographien Plutarchs* (Lund, 1929). I have criticized Stoltz's method in my paper 'Munatius Rufus and Thrasea Paetus on Cato the Younger', *Athenaeum*, 57 (1979), 48–72.

I. PLUTARCH ON HELLENISTIC HISTORY

An interesting facet of the choice of Plutarch's heroes is his inclusion of subjects from the Hellenistic Age. It has been noticed[11] that Philostratus' sophists of the Second Sophistic did not treat historical subjects later than the time of Alexander the Great, and though this restriction is not as perfect as it seems to be assumed[12] it is fairly typical of the times. An important feature of these times—whatever the reason for it[13]—was the nostalgia for the glorious past of Hellas, which meant, in the first place, Athens and Sparta of the Classical Age and the life and times of Alexander. There is little sign of interest in the Diadochi and subsequent times, no glorification of deeds and heroes later than Alexander: the historical *exempla* as well as the rhetorical themes and hypotheses treated the well-known episodes and incidents of history down to the death of Alexander, the main features of which formed an important component of the common literary culture of the time. The classics of ancient history, Herodotus, Thucydides, and Xenophon, but also Theopompus and Ephorus were widely read: one may remember the anecdote told by Plutarch himself (*garr.* 514 C) how in tiny Chaeronaea a man, who had read only a few books of Ephorus was nicknamed 'Epaminondas'. A public whose chief cultural entertainment seems to have been listening to speeches recounting the glories of the battles of Marathon, Plataea, and Eurymedon[14] must have been reasonably well acquainted with the main historical facts relating to these events.

Plutarch's choice of his Greek heroes reflects well his peculiar stance of being both a child of his own age and of standing on the edge of the main cultural movements of

[11] Hamilton, op. cit. xxii.

[12] Sophists discussing themes later than Alexander: Gell. 17. 21. 3; Plu. *Philop.* 2 fin. (where Perrin (Loeb) translates erroneously ἐν ταῖς σχολαῖς = in the schools of philosophy).

[13] On this important and controversial topic see E. L. Bowie, 'The Greeks and their Past in the Second Sophistic', *Past and Present*, 46 (1970), 3 ff. and F. Millar, 'Herennius Dexippus: The Greek World and the Third Century Invasions', *JRS* 59 (1969), 12 ff.

[14] See e.g. Plu. *praec. reip.* 814 C; Lucian. *rhet. praec.* 18.

Atticism and Sophistic. There is no need to reproduce here
Plutarch's view of rhetoric[15] nor to emphasize those features of his language and style which set him apart from the
reigning Atticism of his time.[16] Yet it is significant and
characteristic of Plutarch that in the choice of his Greek
heroes he displays an attitude of detachment without opposition or spite, of maintaining an individual outlook without
necessarily dismissing the mainstream of contemporary opinion. It has been noticed[17] that Plutarch chose, in conformity
with the taste of his times, most of his Greek heroes from
the well-known areas of classical history; yet here as often,
the exceptions are more significant than the rule.

The bulk of the Greeks is from Classical Athens—with
small contributions from Sparta and Thebes: Solon,
Themistocles, Aristides, Cimon, Pericles, Nicias, Alcibiades, Demosthenes, Phocion, Lysander and Agesilaus,
Epaminondas (whose Life is lost) and Pelopidas; to these
should be added the two liberators of Sicily, Dion and
Timoleon; the Athenian and Spartan of mythical and semi-
mythical times, Theseus and Lycurgus have been accounted
for as probable expansions of Plutarch's original intent to
concentrate on biographies of historical personages (see
above); it is to the remaining heroes from the Hellenistic
era that we now must turn our attention. These include,
besides Aratus, who is not part of the series, but may be as
well taken into account as relevant for our purposes,
Eumenes of Cardia, Demetrius Poliorcetes, Pyrrhus of
Epirus, the Spartan kings Agis IV and Cleomenes III who
are paired off with the Gracchi, and 'the last of the Greeks'
Philopoemen. To begin with it is interesting to note that
Plutarch, normally so sparing with comments on his choice,
gives one in almost every one of these cases: we have seen
that the *Aratus* was written for the benefit of the hero's
descendants (*Arat.* 1), Eumenes to provide a pair for Sertorius (*Sert.* 1. 11), Demetrius with Antony as deterrent
examples (*Demetr.* 1), Agis and Cleomenes to be coupled

[15] R. Jeuckens, *Plutarch von Chaeronea und die Rhetorik* (Diss. Strassburg,
1907); Ziegler, *Plutarchos* (Stuttgart, 1949), 291 ff.
[16] Ziegler, op. cit. (above, n. 15), 294 ff.; Russell, op. cit. (above, n. 1), 18 ff.;
W. Schmid, *Der Atticismus* (Stuttgart, 1887), i. 3, 26.
[17] Bowie, op. cit. (above, n. 13), 14.

with the Gracchi (*Agis* 2. 6); in the case of Philopoemen it
is ostensibly Flamininus who is sought out as accompani-
ment for Philopoemen (*Flam.* 1. 1), but there might be
good reasons to believe that despite Plutarch's turn of
phrase it was from Flamininus that the author started in his
composition.[18] It is remarkable that these comments are so
much more rare in the biographies of the Greeks from the
Classical period.

Of course a major factor in Plutarch's choice of his
subjects must have been the material available to him.
Thus it is not possible to discuss our problem without
recourse to the problem of Plutarch's sources. It will not be
necessary to revise here the endless discussions of Plutarchian *Quellenforschung*, but some of its generally accepted
results will serve to throw some light on our problem.

The historical picture of the hundred and fifty years that
passed between the death of Alexander the Great and the
battle of Pydna was dominated by the accounts of three
historians: Hieronymus of Cardia,[19] describing the fifty
years from the death of Alexander to that of Pyrrhus; for
the next fifty years from Pyrrhus' last campaign to the
beginning of Polybius Phylarchus is the 'maßgebende
autor';[20] and finally Polybius dominates the scene for the
period of Rome's great expansion. Hieronymus is generally
acknowledged as a historian of the highest order, an equal
of Polybius.[21] Though Phylarchus seems not to have attained the high standards either of his predecessor or of his
continuator the partisan criticism directed against him by
Polybius seems to be greatly exaggerated.[22] The seven

---

[18] Polybius was the main source of both biographies: see R. M. Errington,
Philopoemen (Oxford, 1969), 228 ff.; H. Peter, *Die Quellen Plutarchs in den Biographien der Römer* (Halle, 1865), 80 ff.; A. Klotz, 'Die Quellen Plutarchs in der
Lebensbeschreibung des T. Quinctius Flamininus', *RhM* 84 (1935), 46 ff.; the
belief of R. E. Smith, 'The Sources of Plutarch's Life of Titus Flamininus', *CQ*
38 (1944), 89 ff. in a biographical source is totally unfounded. Plutarch must have
read Polybius mainly for the sake of his Roman Lives, so that *Philopoemen* might
easily have been a by-product.

[19] *FGrHist* 154; on Hieronymus and Plutarch: ibid. IID, p. 544.

[20] *FGrHist* 81; ibid. IIC, p. 133; cf. T. W. Africa, *Phylarchus and the Spartan
Revolution* (Univ. Calif. Publ. Hist. 68, 1961); cf. Jacoby, *FGrHist* IIC, p. 134.

[21] T. S. Brown, 'Hieronymus of Cardia', *Am. Hist. Rev.* 52 (1946–7), 684 ff.

[22] See E. Gabba, 'Studi su Filarco', *Athenaeum*, 35 (1957), 3 ff.; 193 ff.

Hellenistic Lives of Plutarch deal with the careers of the
chief characters of these historians: Eumenes, Demetrius
Poliorcetes (together with his father Antigonus Monophthalmos, who also plays a considerable part in the Plutarchian
biography), and Pyrrhus are the protagonists of Hieronymus; Phylarchus eulogizes Agis, Cleomenes, and the Spartan Revolution, while the Achaeans Aratus and Philopoemen—the latter the subject of a special encomiastic work[23]
—are the principal heroes among the Greek characters of
their compatriot.

This is not to maintain that these historians were the
only sources of Plutarch in his Hellenistic biographies:
what we are concerned with is the choice of his protagonists.
The most likely reconstruction of his course of action is to
assume that he would embark upon the writing of a biography with all that such work involved in reading, research,
etc. after he had decided on the subject from preliminary
reading and knowledge: indeed it is such a course of action
that suggests itself to us from Plutarch's own description of
his reading of Latin sources (*Demosth.* 2). Thus, for example, though in the *Aratus*, Aratus' Memoirs have been
used in addition to Phylarchus and Polybius[24], probably this
book came to Plutarch's attention only through reading
Polybius,[25] as there is no sign that any other writer in
antiquity was acquainted with it;[26] similarly, whatever the
share of Aristocrates of Sparta and other, unidentified
sources in the Life of Philopoemen it is clear that Plutarch
took his departure from Polybius.[27] Most instructive is the
case of Eumenes of Cardia: the paradox that his career is
the best known among those of his contemporary Diadochi
is due to his compatriot, and probably relative, Hierony-

[23] Plb. 10. 21. 5.

[24] On the sources of the *Aratus* see Walbank, op. cit. (above, n. 6), 15 ff. and
the editions and commentaries of W. H. Porter (Cork, 1937) and A. J. Koster
(Leiden, 1937).

[25] Professor Jones has kindly suggested to me that it may have been Plutarch's
friends descended from Aratus who have brought the Memoirs to his attention.

[26] For the rediscovery of not unimportant authors in this period cf. Arrian's
rediscovery of Ptolemy: Arr. *Anabasis* 1 praef.; Jacoby, *FGrHist* IIB, p. 499.

[27] Cf. Errington, op. cit. (above, n. 18), 236 ff.

mus:[28] thus he is included not only in the Parallel Lives
but also in the only other extant series of biographies of
Greek generals by Cornelius Nepos.[29]

Indeed the degree of Plutarch's originality in the choice
of heroes from the Hellenistic age is best demonstrated by a
comparison with Nepos. Among Plutarch's heroes of the
Classical Age only Solon, Pericles, Nicias, Demosthenes,
and Alexander are not included in Nepos' selection. Among
these Alexander's exclusion, like that of other kings, is
explicitly accounted for by Nepos (*reg.* 2. 1); most probably
Demosthenes, but perhaps also Solon, Pericles, and Nicias
might have been included in categories other than generals.[30] Thus the difference between the Hellenistic biographies of the two writers is the more striking: from among
the seven Hellenistic subjects of Plutarch's Lives only one,
Eumenes, appears in Nepos as well—and is, in fact, the
only figure from post-Classical Greece to do so. Nepos'
classical canon is remarkable for a man who was both a
Roman and lived before the age of Atticism: Plutarch's
originality, whether in relation to the traditions of the
literary genre or to his age is a feature of his writing that
should not be overlooked.

Another possible criterion to test Plutarch's attitude towards his heroes is to collect and compare his numerous
references to them outside his biographical writing. The
results here could hardly be more significant.

Of the Hellenistic heroes Agis is never mentioned in the
Moralia, Aratus and Eumenes score one reference each,
Cleomenes two, Pyrrhus and Philopoemen four each, and
Demetrius is nine times mentioned. The seven together are
thus mentioned twenty-one times, or an average of three

[28] Cf. H. D. Westlake, 'Eumenes of Cardia', *Bull. John Rylands Libr.* 37 1
(1954), 309. Eumenes was the son of a Hieronymus; Arr. *Ind.* 18. The relationship
was first suggested by U. Köhler (Sitz. Ber. Akad. Berlin, 1890), 558 n. 1.

[29] For Nepos' dependence on Hieronymus cf. Westlake op. cit. (above, n. 28),
313. The dissertation of J. R. Bradley, 'The Sources of Cornelius Nepos: Selected
Lives' (Harvard, 1968), I know only from his report in *HSCP* 73 (1969), 308 f.

[30] The work might have included books on Greek orators (comprising Lives of
Demosthenes, possibly Pericles and Nicias) and Solon could have been included
in a book on Poets, Philosophers, or Lawgivers. But one cannot be too cautious on
this subject: see my caveat in: Cornelius Nepos, *De regibus Exterarum Gentium*
(Latomus 38 1979, 662–9).

times. It will not be surprising that this is significantly less
than the references to the rest of the Greek heroes, though
the size of the gap should not go without drawing attention
to it. Allowance has been made for the fact that some of
these characters occupy special positions in certain works of
the *Moralia*: the fifty-seven quotations from and references
to Demosthenes' speeches have been ignored together with
the nine quotations from Solon; also disregarded are the
references to Alexander the Great in the two Declamations
about his Fortune, the references to Solon in the Banquet
of the Seven Sages, and to Epaminondas and Pelopidas in
the *de genio Socratis*. Even so the eighteen subjects rate 409
mentions, or nearly twenty-three on average. Only Timoleon (five mentions) and Theseus (eight) rate less than
Demetrius, the most often referred to of the Hellenistic
heroes, while Nicias (nine) equals his score: but even Timoleon surpasses the other six Hellenistic subjects. It becomes
plain that though Plutarch chose his heroes from all periods
of Greek history, those of Hellenistic times were step-
children only.

These facts can be supported by another set of statistics,
relating to the references to the subjects of the Roman
Lives in the *Moralia*. Plutarch's Greek culture, late start in
reading Latin (*Demosth.* 2), as well as the subject-matter of
many of his essays make it self-evident that there will be far
fewer references in the *Moralia* to Roman than to Greek
matters. His historical *exempla*, literary reminiscences, allusions, and quotations most naturally derive from the Greek
culture whose typical representative he is: it is not an unfair
assumption that a very great proportion of the references to
Romans in the *Moralia* are but a by-product of his work on
the Parallel Lives. This assumption may be supported by
the observation that the bulk of these references is, as a
matter of fact, paralleled in the biographies, while in the
references to the Greeks in the *Moralia* there is much more
that is not included in the Lives.[31] Thus the twenty-five

---

[31] One example will suffice: in the prologue to the *Alexander–Caesar* (*Alex.* 1)
Plutarch discusses the abundance of material and the choice the biographer is
bound to make. Indeed he refers to Alexander in the *Moralia* (except the two
Declamations) sixty-five times: many of these references contain material not

Romans (including the two Scipios whose Lives have been
lost) are referred to 175 times, or seven times on average, in
the *Moralia*. But we do arrive at surprising results if we
divide the Romans into two groups, the first comprising
Antony, Flamininus, the two Gracchi, Marius, and Sertorius, the second all the others. There are no common
denominators for either group, except that the first group
are paired off with Hellenistic Greeks in the Parallel Lives,
and the second with the rest. Yet the first group rate an
average of 2.66 mentions only in the *Moralia*, the second
8.3, or more than three times as many. The picture is much
the same if we disregard the specialist essays *de fortuna
Romanorum* and *Quaestiones Romanae*, the respective figures
being 1.66 and 5.8, the ratio between the two approx. 1:3.5.
(Interestingly there is a close resemblance between the
frequency of the references in the *Moralia* to the Hellenistic
heroes and to their Roman counterparts.) It is impossible to
explain this phenomenon otherwise than with reference to
Plutarch's technique of composition. Thus, for example,
the fact that Tiberius Gracchus is never mentioned, and
Gaius only twice in the *Moralia* can hardly be explained
either by their lack of historical significance or of pre-emi-
nence in Latin letters and historiography: but recalling the
record of Agis and Cleomenes, who form together with the
Gracchi a book of the Parallel Lives a pattern seems to
emerge. The statement of Plutarch (*Agis* 2. 6) that he set
out from the Gracchi and found Agis and Cleomenes as a
fitting pair to contrast with them still need not be doubted:
but it now seems that the whole book must have been
composed at a very late stage of the series (and at a time
probably most of the essays of the *Moralia* have been
published)—a view that is, by the way, totally consistent
with C. P. Jones's relative chronology. A similar situation
can be discerned in regard to the *Sertorius–Eumenes*: Sertorius (admittedly not on the highest plane of historical significance) is referred to only once in the *de fortuna Romanorum*,

included in the Life (cf. also Hamilton, op. cit. (above, n. 1), p. xxxi). Caesar is
mentioned in the *Moralia* seven times: there is nothing in these passages to
suggest that Plutarch's acquaintance with the career of Caesar exceeded what is
included in the Life.

Eumenes a single time in an anecdote that recurs also in the Life (*garr.* 506 E; *Eum.* 6–7). Again there is an indication (*Sert.* 1. 11) that the Roman was the starting-point of the pair, and again C. P. Jones's scheme would accept this pair as one of the last of the series. We have seen that the introduction to the *Demetrius–Antony* (*Demetr.* 1) seems to indicate that this book was added after the completion of the bulk of the series that comprised morally excellent heroes—and this book, too, belongs according to Jones to the last part of the series.

The combined evidence thus seems to indicate that the books of Parallel Lives that included biographies of Greeks from the Hellenistic age probably did not form a part of Plutarch's original plan, but were added to the series when the success of the work and his personal satisfaction made such an extension desirable. Plutarch's procedure seems to have been to turn in the first place to the most important historians dealing with the Hellenistic age and pick from them such characters as might have seemed suitable for the series. These histories served as points of departure only: but an extensive analysis of Plutarch's sources in these Lives is not within the scope of the present paper. Still, let it be said that this procedure seems to be well in line with other facts pertaining to Plutarch's use of historical and biographical sources.

II. NEPOS, PLUTARCH, AND THE SUBJECTS OF THE ROMAN *LIVES*

We have seen that most, and perhaps all, the subjects of the Greek Lives of the Classical period were also included in the *de viris illustribus* of Cornelius Nepos. Plutarch was acquainted with Nepos (*Marc.* 30; *comp. Marc. Pel.* 1 = *Marc.* 31; *Luc.* 43; *TiGr.* 21) and the suggestion that he might have turned to him for guidance in choosing the subjects of his Roman Lives seems so attractive, that it is surprising to find that apparently it has never been put forward. Plutarch's limitations both in Latin and in his acquaintance with Roman history are self-evident and have been mentioned above. On the other hand, not only did he know Nepos' *de viris illustribus*, but this is the only collection of the sort known to us to have included a large number of Roman subjects.[32] The fact that the Lives were brief and written in an easy style could have been but further attractions. What work, indeed, could Plutarch's description in *Demosth.* 2 presuppose more convincingly than Nepos' Lives? Of course the correspondence need not have been total, nor, obviously, was Nepos the only source of influence on Plutarch: we have seen that, for instance, personal reasons may have influenced his choice, as was the case with Lucullus (see above). Yet the almost total silence of Plutarch on a considerable number of his Roman heroes in the *Moralia* suggests that Plutarch's acquaintance with the careers of some of these men might have been minimal before he set to work on them for his Parallel Lives: the theme might have suggested itself only after reading a short work devoted to the subject, such as Nepos' Lives.

   Before turning to a more detailed analysis of the connections between Plutarch's Roman Lives and Nepos some general considerations will perhaps be not entirely out of place. Almost the first facts that present themselves in a survey of Plutarch's Roman subjects is that these are Lives of Republican heroes, with a heavy preponderance of the Late Republic from the Gracchi to Brutus and Mark Antony. Neither of these facts is self-evident or self-explanatory. Though Plutarch completed the Lives of the Emperors before the Parallel Lives we must beware of the notion, based perhaps on Suetonius and the *Historia Augusta*, that biography under the Empire must have been exclusively biographies of emperors. After all, would it have been impossible for Plutarch to compose Lives of M. Agrippa, Germanicus Caesar—or, indeed, Agricola or Thrasea Paetus?[33] It might be pure coincidence that the last Roman

[32] Varro's *Imagines*, acquaintance with which is not attested for Plutarch, would hardly include enough material even for biographical degustation. The inclusion in this work of kings, statesmen, and generals is an unproved conjecture of F. Ritschl, *Opuscula*, iii (Leipzig, 1877), 519 f.
[33] Cf. A. Momigliano, *The Development of Greek Biography* (Cambridge, Mass., 1971), 99 f.

in the Parallel Lives, Antony, is also the last general who could conceivably figure in Nepos' work (and I have tried to argue elsewhere that Nepos did, as a matter of fact, include a Life of Antony in his book on Roman generals),[34] but it is the very number of coincidences that throws doubt upon their being such. To view the predilection for Late Republican subjects as something in the nature of things would mean accepting the very fallacious argument from which Ziegler warns us. Though of course any number of explanations can be found for this preference, for a certain period one should not discard the possibility that a Late Republican or Early Augustan author, such as Nepos, expanding his work as he was nearing his own times, is responsible for it. Another important point is the possible influence of Nepos' arrangement of Greeks and Romans on Plutarch's method of confrontation and comparison.[35] Nepos seems to have compared the Greek and Roman generals as groups (Nepos, *Hann.* 13. 4): it would be otiose to point out the difference between this and Plutarch's method of σύγκρισις, though this need not mean that the latter could not get its inspiration from the former.

But all these are general considerations rather than definite proof. Of course we know so little about the lost books of Nepos' work—and even part of this depends on Plutarch—that we can scarcely hope to advance beyond mere speculation as to their contents. Nevertheless a survey of what we know and of what we may surmise might be useful.

First the explicit references to Nepos in Plutarch. The reference to Nepos concerning Lucullus' death (*Luc.* 43) is revealing: the manner of the death of his heroes is something of an obsession with Nepos[36] and there can be no doubt that the passage in question must come from a Life of

---

[34] 'An Overlooked Item of the War of Propaganda between Octavian and Antony', *Historia*, 29 (1980), 112 ff.

[35] L. E. Lord, 'The Biographical Interests of Nepos', *CJ* 22 (1926–7), 499; cf. A. J. Gossage, *Plutarch*, in T. A. Dorey (ed.), *Latin Biography* (London, 1967), 75 n. 48.

[36] All biographers are interested in the manner of death of their heroes; yet in Nepos the subject is a *sine qua non* even in the very brief biographical sketches in the chapter *de regibus*.

Lucullus contained in Nepos' book on Roman generals. Plutarch's main source in the central part of this Life is Sallust,[37] and it is doubtful how much besides our notice depends on Nepos: but the relevant fact is that both series did contain Lives of Lucullus. Next, Marcellus. Here Plutarch refers twice to Nepos (*Marc.* 30, *comp. Marc. Pel.* 1 = *Marc.* 31), both times in 'Zitatennester'. Nevertheless the notion that these references are at second hand can be maintained only with an old-fashioned and doctrinaire approach to Plutarchian *Quellenforschung.*[38] Again it is noteworthy that one of the references is to Marcellus' death and funeral, a well-known preoccupation of Nepos.[39]

The last reference to Nepos in Plutarch (*TiGr.* 21) concerns a statement about the family relationships of the Gracchi (Gaius married the daughter of Brutus rather than of Crassus):[40] again, without entering into the notoriously difficult problem of Plutarch's sources in the Life of the Gracchi it seems clear that the information comes from a Life of Gaius Gracchus, or of both brothers. This is not to say that he (or they) was included in the book on Roman generals, as another part of the *de viris illustribus*, such as a book on Roman orators, might have been Plutarch's source (cf. n. 30 above).

Another Roman whose life was described by both biographers is Scipio Aemilianus. Nepos' Life is not directly attested: but it seems certain that the information concerning the topography of Carthage was contained in a biography of its conqueror.[41] Another passage pertaining to the same Life is contained in the Nepos fragment from the

[37] Peter, op. cit. (above, n. 18), 106 ff.
[38] Peter, op. cit. (above, n. 18), 74 ff. cf. A. Klotz, 'Die Quellen der plutarchischen Lebensbeschreibung des Marcellus', *RhM* 83 (1934), 289 ff.
[39] Cf. Nepos, *Ages.* 8. 7; *Eum.* 4. 4; 13. 4; *Phoc.* 4. 4.
[40] For a conjecture that would absolve Nepos from a mistake here see F. Münzer, *Römische Adelsparteien und Adelsfamilien* (Stuttgart, 1920), 270 f.
[41] Serv. *ad. Aen.* 1. 368 = frg. 9 *vir. ill.* Peter = frg. 49 Malcovati. It does not matter in this context (cf. O. Metzer, *NJbb* 155 (1897), 291 n. 3), to what layer of our present text of Servius the statement belongs. Obviously the information depends ultimately on Polybius, where it must have occurred in the description of the campaign of Scipio Aemilianus: cf. App. *Lib.* 117. 554–5; 135. 639; Zonaras, 9. 29. On the other hand, the two notices from Suet. *poet.* 6. 1; 6. 3 = frg. 12, 13 Peter = 52, 53 Malcovati belong to a Life of Terence rather than Scipio.

Milan palimpsest of Fronto concerning a letter about some *res Numantina*.[42]

Another subject common to Nepos and Plutarch was the elder Cato. As is well known Nepos composed a full-length ('volumen') Life in addition to the brief sketch extant from the book on Roman historians (Nepos *Cato* 3. 5), and even those most anxious to invent imaginary Roman biographies as intermediary sources could not deny Plutarch's acquaintance with Nepos' Life.[43]

Next, Cicero. Nepos wrote a Life of Cicero in at least two books (Gell. 15. 28. 1 = frg. 38 Malcovati), though the extant fragment from the book *de historicis Latinis* (frg. 57 Malcovati) looks rather like an apology for not including a *Cicero*, presumably taken from the preface, or the conclusion, of the book. Still it seems highly probable that, as in the case of Cato, a shorter biography, based on a longer work, was included in the series, most probably in the book on Roman orators—if there was such a book.

Lastly, Antony. Plutarch's Life of Antony is the longest biography in the series and one of his most splendid achievements of character drawing and description, incorporating an unusual amount of personal observations and digressions.[44] I have suggested elsewhere (cf. n. 34 above) that Nepos has written a Life of Antony and it is not impossible that Plutarch took from here his theme and perhaps also some of the details of the Life.

These seven Lives are the only ones from Nepos' work about which we know anything at all and which may have suited Plutarch's subject-matter;[45] the fact that all seven became subjects of Plutarchian biographies does certainly underline the general considerations that have been ad-

---

[42] First identified by E. Hauler, 'Neues aus dem Frontopalimpsest', *WSt* 31 (1909), 268 f. He reaffirmed his first position in *WSt* 55 (1937), 196 ff., rejecting the conjecture of C. Cichorius, *Röm. Studien* (Leipzig, Berlin, 1922), 102 ff.; cf. also F. Münzer, *NJbb* (1923), 38 ff. The allocation is accepted by van den Hout, p. 120 of his edition (Leiden, 1954).

[43] See R. E. Smith, 'Plutarch's Biographical Sources in the Roman Lives', *CQ* 34 (1940), 5; id., 'The Cato Censorius of Plutarch', ibid. 105 ff.; cf. D. Kienast, *Cato der Zensor* (Heidelberg, 1954), 10 ff.

[44] For a sympathetic appreciation cf. Russell op. cit. (above, n. 1), 134 ff.

[45] For a Life of Terence cf. n. 41 above; Suet. *rhet.* 3 (on. L. Voltacilius Pitholaus) includes material from Nepos (frg. *vir. ill.* 16 Peter; 56 Malcovati).

vanced in favour of the hypothesis that Plutarch may have
turned to Nepos' *de viris illustribus* for guidance in the
matter of the choice of the subjects of his Roman Lives.[46]
Nevertheless the limited amount of information available
should render us the more cautious not to try and reconstruct the contents of Nepos' book on Roman generals from
Plutarch's Parallel Lives.

Another approach to the choice of Plutarch's Roman
heroes is to scrutinize the feasible alternatives available to
him. This is possible if we investigate the references in the
Moralia to Roman generals and statesmen not included in
the Parallel Lives. The results are unequivocal. Even the
two specialist works, *de fortuna Romanorum* and *Quaestiones
Romanae* do not go beyond a very restricted number of
well-known and fairly general historical examples: the triumvir Aemilius Lepidus is mentioned a single time (*fort. Rom.*
319 E), together with Cicero, Hirtius and Pansa (the only
reference to that unfortunate pair), and Mark Antony in an
enumeration of Augustus' enemies. Others fare even worse:
Cincinnatus is mentioned only fleetingly (*fort. Rom.* 317 D:
Φαβρίκιοι ... καὶ Κάμιλλοι καὶ Δέκιοι καὶ Κικιννᾶτοι καὶ Μά-
ξιμοι Φάβιοι καὶ Κλαύδιοι Μάρκελλοι καὶ Σκιπίωνες), while C.
Flaminius' name occurs only because of the circus
Flaminius, built by Φλαμινίου τινὸς τῶν παλαιῶν (*quaest.
Rom.* 66, 280 A). Nor do great Republican personages who
do not occur in these two works fare better: Regulus is
mentioned once in a commonplace notice on captives (*Hdt.
mal.* 857 A), and once each Ap. Claudius the Censor (*praec.
reip.* 794 D) and M. Livius Drusus tr. pl. 91 (*praec. reip.*
800 F). Others are mentioned only because of their links
with subjects of the biographies: M. Lucullus only as caring
for his brother in the latter's last years (*an seni* 792 C), L.
Valerius Flaccus only in his connection with Cato the
Censor (frg. 49), C. Laelius as the friend of Scipio Aemilianus (*an seni* 797 D; *praec. reip.* 806 A); Cassius—if indeed
the reference at *quaest. conv.* 9. 1. 737 BC is to him—though
he plays a very prominent role in the Life of Brutus is

---

[46] One might compare with this correspondence the list of Republican heroes
in the 'Heldenschau' Verg. *Aen.* 6. 818–47 and 855–9, only half of which are
subjects of Plutarch's Lives.

referred to only in this place. Some persons occur in the *Moralia* only in anecdotes that are plainly repetitions from the Lives: thus Plutarch repeats an anecdote about Murena (*inim. ut.* 91 DE) from *Cato min.* 21; a saying of Metellus Nepos (*de laude ips.* 542 A) recurs from *Cic.* 26. 6. Clearly Plutarch was not shy of repeating stories—nor is he to blame considering the bulk of his extant writings. Thus an anecdote with a *bon mot* about Cn. Domitius Ahenobarbus and the orator Crassus[47] is told three times (*inim. ut.* 89 A; *praec. reip.* 811 A; *soll. an.* 976 A). Even the few Romans who occur in the *Moralia* two or three times (none more often!)[48] are referred to in such general terms or commonplace contexts that it would be impossible to assume that Plutarch was intimately acquainted with their careers: about Fabricius we hear that, like Epaminondas, he died childless (*tranq. an.* 467 E) and that he was buried in the forum (*quaest. Rom.* 79 283 A) beside a bare mention (Φαβρίκιοι) at *fort. Rom.* 317 D; Mucius Scaevola is a commonplace example (*fort. Rom.* 317 D; *coh. ira* 458 A) like Horatius Cocles (*fort. Rom.* 317 D; *praec. reip.* 820 E); also the references to Catilina (*praec. reip.* 809 E; 818 D; *de laude ips.* 540 F) and Clodius (*exil.* 605 F; *garr.* 511 DE) do not indicate that to Plutarch they were anything but examples of worthless rogues.

The inference from this short survey is that Plutarch's acquaintance with Republican history and its heroes was commonplace and superficial. There is no indication that he could have chosen subjects for additional biographies without engaging in special research before deciding on their suitabililty. This raises again the question of a guide whom Plutarch followed in his choice of Roman heroes. Nepos or another such guide, if available, looks like the easiest solution of Plutarch's difficulties and one that seems to harmonize well with his methods of composition.[49]

[47] Cf. Münzer, op. cit. (above, n. 40), 108.
[48] This does not include Varro, who is referred to as a source about half a dozen times in the *Quaestiones Romanae*.
[49] NB: If Nepos' book on Roman generals was of approximately the same size as that on foreign generals (twenty-two Lives) it consisted of roughly the same number of biographies as the books of Plutarch's Parallel Lives.

III. THE *LIVES* OF AEMILIUS PAULUS AND
TIMOLEON[50]

In the preceding two sections I have tried to put forward some profitable lines of investigation concerning the choice of Plutarch's heroes. Still, in some cases we probably shall never be able to guess his particular reasons, in others we shall be able to do so only after a detailed analysis. It is the purpose of the present section to assail such a case and to put to the test some of our assumptions.

It has been stated already that the pair *Aemilius Paullus–Timoleon* did not form part of the original plan of Plutarch but was added at a later stage when the success of the series caused him to expand it (*Aem. Paul.* 1). What can be ascertained about Plutarch's motives at that particular time? How far was he acquainted with the careers of the two men and what was his attitude towards them? What were the sources available to him? Was either of the two Lives the starting-point to which his counterpart was added? What, finally, were the considerations that enabled him to adapt the stories of the two men to the series and to what extent did he succeed in doing so?

Unfortunately it is not possible to date the *Aemilius Paullus–Timoleon*. The series was begun perhaps in 99 and probably continued into the first years of Hadrian:[51] the relatively late date of the book in the series gives only a very approximate idea about the time of its composition.

As we have seen above, Timoleon, mentioned only five times in the *Moralia*, is the least often referred to of Plutarch's Greek heroes, save those of Hellenistic times (but not Demetrius Poliorcetes). It is worth while to subject these references to some scrutiny.

Only one of the five places indicates expressly its source:

---

[50] For the approach of this chapter cf. P. A. Stadter, 'Plutarch's Comparison of Pericles and Fabius Maximus', *GRBS* 16 (1975), 77 ff. (see above, pp. 155 ff.) and my own Hebrew essay, 'Plutarch's Lives as Literature', *Eshkoloth*, NS 1 (1975–6), 42 ff.

[51] C. P. Jones, 'Towards a Chronology of Plutarch's Works', *JRS* 56 (1966), 70 (above, p. 114).

at *quaest. conv.* 6. 3. 673 D (= *FGrHist* 566 F 116), we are
told on the authority of Timaeus the story of the omen of
the celery, also narrated at *Tim.* 26. 1 (and retold in *Polyaen.
Strat.* 5. 12. 1). Timaeus was Plutarch's main source in the
Timoleon (see below): the *quaest. conv.*, dedicated to Sosius
Senecio, are roughly contemporary with the Parallel Lives
(see Jones, op. cit. 72 f. and above, p. 121 f., and cf. J.
Geiger, *SCI* 1 (1974), 139). There is no way of ascertaining
which is the primary and which the secondary place of the
story, though the probabilities are that where it is incidental
and anecdotal it is only secondary to the place where it is part
and parcel of the narrative and derives from its main source.

At *praec. reip.* 808 A Timoleon, who joined the killers of
his brother after he could not persuade him to give up the
tyranny, is one of a number of historical examples of statesmen who preferred the common good to personal considerations: the information here given is fairly general and every
educated person must have been familiar with it; also the
praec. reip. is roughly contemporary with the Lives (cf.
Jones, op. cit. 72 and above, p. 120) and thus the mention
might have been a reminiscence of the extensive version at
Timol. 4–5.

Two places repeat the story of Timoleon's dedicating a
shrine (or altar) to Automatia, and, in the second version,
also consecrating his house to Agathos Daimon (*praec. reip.*
816 E; *de laude ips.* 542 E). Also this last place may be more
or less contemporary with the *Timoleon* (Jones, op. cit. 73
and above, pp. 121–2), where the story also recurs (36. 6).
Apparently all the versions of this story including Nepos'
Timoleon derive directly from Timaeus.[52]

The last reference to Timoleon, at *sera num. vind.* 552 F,
contains information, also quoted at *Timol.* 30. 4, about
the seizure of the temple of Apollo at Delphi by the merce-
naries who were later to join the Sicilian expedition. The
terminus ante quem of the *sera num. vind.*, dedicated to
Quietus, is 107 (Jones, op. cit. 71 and above, p. 118); this
does not exclude the possibility that Plutarch composed
at about the same time this work and the Life of Timo-

[52] Cf. M. Sordi, 'Timoleonte', coll. Σικελικά, ii (Palermo, 1961), 81 f.

leon. Yet even if it was earlier than the Life the informa-
tion in this Delphic dialogue could have derived from
Plutarch's wide knowledge of local history (cf. Ziegler,
Plutarchos, 24 ff.).

This short survey clearly indicates why Timoleon was
not included in the initial plan of the series. Plutarch was
never specially attracted to the figure and story of Timoleon
and possibly was not acquainted with them beyond the
rudimentary knowledge of a good general education. Yet
the *Timoleon* is one of the most eulogistic biographies in the
Parallel Lives: the sudden conversion from almost total
neglect to enthusiasm invites examination.

It is well known that Timaeus of Tauromenium (*FGrHist*
566) who 'exalted Timoleon above the illustrious gods'
(Plb. 12. 23. 4; cf. Marcell. *vita Thuc.* 27 = *FGrHist* 566 T
13; Cic. *fam.* 5. 12. 7) was the main source of the Lives by
Plutarch and by Nepos as well as of the whole subsequent
tradition of the subject.[53] Characteristically Plutarch is the
only writer who has frequent references to Timaeus in a
time when the ruling fashion of Atticism held him in
disfavour[54] and even the somewhat later work of Arrian
may well have been written under the influence of Plutarch.[55] Perhaps the most significant aspect of Plutarch's
choice is the direction he took in search for biographical
material: whatever the assumptions of latter-day adherents of
Ed. Meyer, it is to a historical work that Plutarch turned, not to

[53] See H. D. Westlake, 'The Sources of Plutarch's Timoleon', *CQ* 32 (1938),
65 ff.; N. G. L. Hammond, 'The Sources of Diodorus Siculus XVI. II. The
Sicilian Narrative', ibid. 137 ff.; vol. 4 of kokalos (1958) dedicated to Timoleon;
T. S. Brown, *Timaeus of Tauromenium* (Un. Cal. Publ. Hist. 55, Berkeley, LA),
M. Sordi, op. cit. (above, n. 52); R. J. A. Talbert, *Timoleon and the Revival of
Greek Sicily* (Cambridge, 1974).
[54] Cf. F. Jacoby, *FGrHist.* IIIB, p. 526; Talbert, op. cit. (above, n. 53), 42.
[55] Arrian's first exercises in historiography were histories (not biographies) of
Dion and Timoleon: *FGrHist* 156 T 4a (= Phot. *Bibl.* 93, p. 73a 35 Bekker); for
the dating cf. P. A. Brunt's Loeb Arrian i, pp. XII f.; A. B. Bosworth, 'Arrian's
Literary Development', *CQ* 22 (1972), 167. The suggestion that he turned to the
stories of Dion and Timoleon under Plutarch's influence accords well with the
latter's popularity at that time: cf. R. Hirzel, *Plutarch* (Das Erbe der Alten, IV;
Leipzig, 1912), 74 ff. and (for Polyaenus) P. A. Stadter, op. cit. (above, n. 7)
passim; on Arrian's use of Plutarch see R. B. Steele, 'Plutarch's Alexander and
Arrian's *Anabasis*', *CP* 11 (1916), 419 ff.

a (hypothetical) previously written biography.[56] Nor should anybody doubt that this is the rule rather than the exception: Occam's razor can be applied more successfully to adherents of *Mittelquellen* than to most other perpetrators of erroneous creeds. Plutarch must have been acquainted with Timaeus before he decided to embark on a biography of Timoleon: he used him both in his *Nicias* and *Dio*, the latter of which formed part of the twelfth book of the Parallel Lives (*Dio* 2. 7), and thus was certainly written before the *Aemilius Paullus–Timoleon*. Unfortunately the references to Timaeus in the *Moralia* do not contain chronological clues that would enable us to ascertain whether they can be dated before the Lives.

Timoleon is coupled with Aemilius Paullus. In his case also the *Moralia* give little to hold on to. Very possibly the first mention is at *fort. Rom.* 318 B, if we are to concur with the widely accepted, if unproven, dating of the rhetorical exercises as *juvenilia*. It is remarkable that Aemilius Paullus appears here among historical examples of Romans possessed of Fortune: he returned from Macedonia with his troops entirely unharmed. Since this is contradicted both by a reliable historical account (Livy 44. 42) and by Plutarch himself in the Life (21)—not to mention common sense—it will be reasonable to conclude that the former, inexact, notice is a generalized reminiscence of the story of Aemilius Paullus, with which no doubt every educated person—and certainly one who knew his Polybius—was acquainted. Next *conj. praec.* 141 A. The dictum about putting away a wife like a shoe that hurts is here referred to 'a Roman (ὁ Ῥωμαῖος): it recurs in *Aem. Paul.* 5 (and Jerome, *adv. Iovin.* 1. 148 = *PL* ii. 292). Whether the saying is rightly or wrongly attributed to Paullus the reference in the *Moralia* certainly does not testify to any special interest in the hero.[57] Also the mention at *tranq. an.* 475 A is a historical example of the most general kind—and roughly contempo-

[56] Such a biography was surmised by Westlake, op. cit. (above, n. 53), followed in the main (though with reservations) by Talbert, op. cit. (above, n. 53), 22 ff.; Brown, op. cit. (above, n. 53), 85 even put a name to it; rejected by Talbert, op. cit. 195. See also my *Cornelius Nepos and Ancient Political Biography* (Stuttgart, 1985).
[57] Jones, op. cit. (above, n. 51), 71, and see this volume, pp. 118–19, dates the *conj. praec.* very tentatively to *c*.90–*c*.100.

rary with the latter part of the Parallel Lives (Jones, op. cit. 62 f. and above, pp. 97 f.). The information at *quaest. conv.* 1. 2 615 EF on Paullus' dinner-parties after the Macedonian campaign might derive from the again roughly contemporary Life (28. 5). The last two references only mention Scipio Aemilianus as Paullus' son (*cum princ. phil.* 777 B; *praec. reip.* 810 B). Clearly none of these places indicates any special interest in, or acquaintance with the career of Aemilius Paullus prior to the composition of the Life. There is no need for a detailed analysis of the Life to see that Polybius—on whose personal relations with the family of Aemilius Paullus there is no need to dwell—must have been its starting-point: its very focusing upon a single period of this life—when the hero was already 60 years of age—shows how absurd it is to assume a 'biographical source' for Plutarch.[58]

Which Life was Plutarch's starting-point and what made him join Timoleon and Aemilius Paullus in one book? It will be expedient to start with the second of the two questions. Ziegler (*Plutarchos*, 262 = *RE* 21. 898) after conceding that some of the couples are convincing and successful, goes on to say that others are joined artificially and by force: 'Was haben Aristeides und der alte Cato, Perikles und Fabius Maximus, Timoleon und Aemilius Paullus in Wahrheit miteinander gemein? Nur mittels rhetorischer Künste konnten Ähnlichkeiten zwischen solchen Männern konstruiert werden . . .'. For our present purpose it will be sufficient to answer the question regarding the pair under review. As we have seen, the tradition about Timoleon was uniform and went back to the eulogies of Timaeus. The prominent feature of this tradition was Timoleon's Fortune.[59] Plutarch put his tradition to good use and made τύχη the Leitmotiv of the entire Life. There is no need to bring examples as practically every incident in the biography is ascribed to Timoleon's τύχη, the turning-points

---

[58] On the sources of the *Aemilius Paullus* see H. Peter, op. cit. (above, n. 8), 86 ff.; R. E. Smith, 'Plutarch's Biographical Sources in the Roman Lives', *CQ* 34 (1940), 1 ff., esp. 4, on account of the existence of a very small number of isolated notices on Paullus' career that apparently do not derive from Polybius surmises an intermediary biographical source.

[59] M. J. Fontana, 'Fortuna di Timoleonte, Rassegna delle fonti letterarie', *Kokalos*, 4 (1958), 3 ff.

being μεταβολαὶ τύχης: towards the end of the Life we are
even assured that Timoleon's blindness was due to a congeni-
tal illness and was not the effect of τύχη (37. 7)!

The connection of Timoleon and τύχη was traditional
and well established. Less well known is Aemilius Paullus'
connection with Fortuna. Yet Plutarch makes him refer to
τύχη in his *contio* after his triumph in 167 (*Aem. Paul.* 36.
3 ff.). That this was not an invention of Plutarch's is clear
from all the parallel reports of the speech.[60] Moreover
Paullus dedicated a statue of Athene by Phidias at the
temple of Fortuna Huiusce Diei, and it is even possible that
it was he who was responsible for the erection of the
shrine.[61] Thus Plutarch had a starting-point that had at
least some foundation in historical fact. Still, the joining of
the two heroes and the composition of the whole book
around the central feature of Fortuna is a literary device—
'rhetorical art' according to Ziegler—and it is as such that
we have to evaluate it. Incidentally it is quite possible that
such an evaluation can provide the key to a well-known
crux regarding our book: the *Aemilius Paullus–Timoleon*,
together with the *Sertorius–Eumenes* and the *Coriolanus–Alcibiades* are the only books of the Parallel Lives where the
Roman biography is placed first.[62] It is possible to attempt
at least in our case to ascribe the order of the Lives to their
literary structure. Each of the two Lives demonstrates the
government of τύχη centred on a single episode in the life of
the hero—the battle of Pydna and the liberation of Sicily

[60] Livy 45. 41; Val. Max. 5. 10. 2 (a verbatim passage of the speech); Vell. 1.
10. 3–5; App. *Mac.* 19 (this last source missing in Malcovati *ORF*³ 101).

[61] Plin. *NH* 34. 54: *(Pheidias fecit) et aliam Minervam quam Romae Paulus
Aemilius ad aedem Fortunae Huiusce Diei dicavit*; cf. ibid. 60. K. Latte, *Röm.
Religionsgesch.* (Munich, 1960), 179: 4 misinterprets this passage to mean that
Pliny referred to the location of the statue in his time without acknowledging that
the dedication was to the goddess. This must be due to some confusion on
account of the existence of two temples of the same deity in different parts of the
city, since Q. Lutatius Catulus dedicated an Aedes Fortunae Huiusce Diei on the
day of the battle of Vercellae (30 July): Plu. *Mar.* 26. 3; 8; *CIL* i² pp. 217, 219,
323. On the location of the two temples see S. B. Platner and T. Ashby, *Topogr.
Dict.* 216; the suggestion that the first shrine was erected by Aemilius Paullus:
Otto, *RE* 7: 32; Roscher, i. 1514; I have not seen Aust, *de aedibus sacris* 26, where
the suggestion was apparently first made.

[62] Cf. K. Ziegler, *Die Überlieferungsgeschichte der vergleichenden Lebensbe-
schreibungen Plutarchs* (1907), 29 ff.

respectively. In both cases there is a μεταβολὴ τύχης. In the first case the victory is followed by domestic catastrophe (the death of Paullus' sons); in the second, the command of the Sicilian expedition is given to Timoleon after a long period in the political wilderness which followed on the domestic catastrophe of his having to collaborate in the murder of his brother the tyrant. This last episode is told in the Timoleon at some length, and in the (for ancient prose) quite extraordinary technique of flashback. Thus the interlude of the murder of Timophanes is put between the two dramatic climaxes of the book. The first half of the book passes from success to catastrophe, the second from disaster to victory: it is possible that Plutarch departed from his usual arrangement for the sake of the effect this provided.

To return to the main issue. Literary considerations played their part not only in the composition of the book of the Lives of Aemilius Paullus and Timoleon, but also enabled the inclusion of the book in the series. A Greek and a Roman were to be found whose careers were significant enough to rank among the other great statesmen and generals of the Parallel Lives and well attested enough to provide the skeletons of biographies. Yet this in itself was not sufficient for Plutarch's moralistic purposes. Only the discovery of an angle that could serve these purposes enabled the incorporation of the two Lives in the series. It is as well to stress that the common denominator of the two Lives, stories centred on τύχη, on virtue and fortitude overcoming the blows of Fate, had a solid foundation in historical tradition and that Plutarch's sharp eye only discovered the literary use to which this historical tradition could be turned.

7

Plutarch, *Alcibiades* 1–16

D. A. RUSSELL

The first part of Plutarch's *Alcibiades*, down to the point at which preparations for Sicily begin (17. 1), has only the roughest chronological framework. It is largely made up of anecdote and reflection, and the order seems to be determined mainly by literary considerations. Hence its special interest for the study of Plutarch's methods. Why is the material arranged as it is? And what, if any, is Plutarch's original contribution? These are dangerous questions—the first because it is human to claim the presence of design where there is really only accident, and the second because to answer it properly would require unattainable completeness in our knowledge of the sources. Nevertheless, it is perhaps worth making the attempt.[1]

Alcibiades is indeed one of the best documented of Plutarch's subjects. Perhaps that is why he put off the daunting synthesis till a comparatively late stage in the enterprise of the *Parallel Lives*.[2] It involved drawing on a vast range of reading. There were the historians, among whom Xenophon proved especially useful for the later phases of the war;[3] the orators—Andocides, Antiphon, Lysias, Isocrates, Demosthenes; and the learned commentaries which had accumu-

---

[1] A first version of this paper was read to the Cambridge Philological Society early in 1965. I am indebted to Professor K. J. Dover and to Mr R. Littman.

[2] There are several reasons for thinking this. (i) *Cor.* and *Alc.* are warning examples; the decision to write one or two such συζυγίαι is announced as an innovation in *Demetr.* 1; (ii) it might have been more natural to couple Coriolanus with Themistocles (cf. Cic. *Brutus* 41–3), but this could not be done if Themistocles had already been used; (iii) *Nicias* and *Lysander*, the overlapping Lives, are probably earlier: so, with reservations, C. Stoltz, *Zur relativen Chronologie der Parallelbiographien Plutarchs*, 16 ff.; it may be added that the cross-reference to *Alc.* in *Nic.* 11. 2 may be seen to be an interpolation from the fact that it refers not to the corresponding passage of *Alc.* (13), but to a somewhat later situation (16. 2).

[3] R. Dippel, *Quae ratio intercedat inter Xenophontis historiam Graecam et Plutarchi vitas quaeritur* (Gressen, 1898).

D. A. Russell

there were the Socratics; as Plutarch himself points out (1.
3), the involvement with Socrates added much to Alcibiades' δόξα: we even know the names of his nurse and pae-
dagogus. Moreover, the whole material had been handled
long before in a biographical way: that is, the historical
events had been selected and marshalled around the character and fortunes of the hero. To see this, there is no need to
speculate about Hellenistic biography; we have only to look
at Nepos' *Alcibiades* and observe how much richer it is than
the run of his work. His first chapter consists of an elaboration on the theme of what Plutarch calls Alcibiades' ἀνωμαλία,
his mixture of virtue and vice, activity and idleness. The
closing chapter shows a treatment of the τόπος of Alcibiades'
adaptability to circumstances which we know also from
Satyrus[5] and which is used by Plutarch (who never puts
character-summaries at the end) in the dramatically appropriate place (23), i.e. where Alcibiades first goes into exile
and so first really has to be a 'chameleon'. Moreover, there
are within Nepos' narrative itself features which, if we
knew them only in Plutarch, we should be tempted to put
down as Plutarchian: the account of the feelings of the
Athenians towards Alcibiades on his return[6] and the high-
lighting of the reversal of fortune which followed those
happy days: *haec Alcibiadi laetitia non nimis fuit diuturna.*[7]
Plutarch was less 'on his own' in designing this life than in
many others. Selection rather than construction was his
problem.

I. BOYHOOD AND PRIVATE LIFE: 1–9

Alcibiades is the second Life of a pair,[8] but there is no
formula of transition. Plutarch begins abruptly with his

[4] Plutarch's direct reading of comedy was not extensive: H. Schläpfer, *Plutarch und die klassischen Dichter* (Zürich, 1950), 57 ff.
[5] There is no good reason for thinking that Satyrus' anecdotes about Alcibiades (Athenaeus 534) come from a formal Life.
[6] Nepos, 6. 2, Plu. 32. 4 ff.
[7] Nepos, 7. 1, Plu. 34. 1.
[8] It is unusual for the Roman to come first, but the reason is presumably chronology: cf. *Demosth.* 3. 5 λεκτέον δὲ περὶ τοῦ πρεσβυτέρου πρότερον.

hero's ancestry. This is learning displayed not only to satisfy curiosity but to give dignity and formality to the prooimion; Alcibiades' family goes back to heroic times, as Coriolanus' did to King Ancus. Unhappily, the facts are not all right: the Clinias who fought at Artemisium was Alcibiades' great-uncle, not his father.[9] Anyway, as Plutarch makes haste to remind us, Alcibiades' fame rests even more on his association with Socrates than on his family connections.

Physical appearance (1. 4–5), voice (1. 6–8), ἦθος (2. 1): there is a similar arrangement of the preliminaries in *Alexander* and *Marcellus*, variations elsewhere.[10] It is natural that κάλλος should have pride of place: cf. Pl. *Alc. I.* 104 A πρῶτον μὲν κάλλιστός τε καὶ μέγιστος. As often, Plutarch supports his point by a scholarly note (1. 7), culled from the compilations of κωμῳδούμενοι. It is the interpretation of character (2. 1) that raises the first real problem. It accords indeed with Plutarch's usual way of talking: ἦθος is acquired principally in education, and is therefore changeable, while φύσις is an endowment, not always revealed at first, but constant, and difficult to change. What is in question here is rather the justification of the diagnosis in the ensuing narrative. What *are* the μεταβολαί? There is the ἀνωμαλία τῆς φύσεως of 16. 9, the innate discordance which made Alcibiades behave virtuously and viciously by turns; and there is the description of his chameleon-like skill at adapting himself to his surroundings in 23. 4. These passages—both parts of the inherited account—support ἀνομοιότητας πρὸς αὐτό and μεταβολάς, but not, it seems to me, the comment ὡς εἰκὸς ἐν πράγμασι μεγάλοις καὶ τύχαις πολυτρόποις; this suggests the effect of chance and event on a normal personality,[11] rather than the anomalies and versatility of an exceptional one.

The key to an understanding of Alcibiades is τὸ φιλόνικον καὶ φιλόπρωτον, one of the commonest passions in Plutarch's

---

[9] Herod. 8. 17. If we adopt E. Vanderpool's stemma (*Hesperia*, 21: 5 ff.), he would be the great-grandfather. Anyway, Plutarch's version is unacceptable (ibid., n. 9).

[10] F. Leo, *Die griechisch-römische Biographie*, 180 ff., attempts to enumerate the variant orders; he is too schematic.

[11] Cf. *Per.* 38. 2, *Sert.* 10, *Sulla* 30. 5. I discuss briefly the problem of Plutarch's view of character-change in 'On Reading Plutarch's Lives' in *Greece and Rome* (1966); see above, pp. 81–6.

repertoire. Its importance here is illustrated by three excellent and well-chosen anecdotes: how the child Alcibiades 'bit like a lion'; how he lay down in front of a wagon; and how he refused to learn the aulos. In the following narrative, Plutarch often returns to this key characteristic, or to its near but less specific synonym φιλοτιμία. In 6. 3 it is φιλοτιμία—laudable compared with love of pleasure—which exposes Alcibiades to a peculiarly subtle form of flattery; Socrates' attack on his self-esteem attempts to redress the balance. In 23. 8, Alcibiades contemptuously says that he seduced Timaea οὐχ ὕβρει οὐδὲ κρατούμενος ὑφ' ἡδονῆς, but to beget a line of Spartan kings. In 27. 6, he goes, φιλοτιμού-μενος, to show off his success to Tissaphernes, and is clapped into prison: an unlikely motive for a political move, but Plutarch wants to represent this striking, if temporary, disappointment as the result not so much of a miscalculation as of an emotional weakness. There is a similar case in 34. 3; if indeed Alcibiades' reason for staying in Athens all the summer of 407 was to wait for the mysteries, this was because he thought the demonstration he had in mind politically important; to say, as Plutarch does, φιλοτιμία τις οὐκ ἀγεννὴς προσπεσοῦσα κατέσχεν αὐτόν, is again to relate a complex decision to a simple emotional cause. Another example of this common procedure may be found in the account of Alcibiades' conduct in warning the Athenians at Aegospotami of their impending danger (36. 6, 41. 6). Here, however, the emotion involved is slightly different. A hostile—and realistic—view would be that he was trying to stage a come-back; Plutarch thinks of it rather as the forgiving act of a true patriot. His Alcibiades, unlike his Coriolanus, bore no grudges (33. 2, 41. 6 (= *Comparatio* 2. 6)).

Some shape is given to the three childhood stories in 2 by ἐπεὶ δ' εἰς τὸ μανθάνειν ἧκε (2. 5),[12] which marks a new stage of education. All show Alcibiades in a favourable light, as a proud and spirited boy.[13] But this order is followed by something like chaos. The two stories (3) from Antiphon's

[12] Cf. *Cato Minor* 1. 3–6 εὐθὺς ἐκ παιδίου . . . ὡς οὖν εἰς τὸ μανθάνειν ἧκε.
[13] (i) To Ziegler's references for the flute anecdote add Proclus on *Alc. I*, p. 91 Westerink. (ii) τοῖς Ἀθηναίοις (228. 26 Ziegler) should probably be deleted as a gloss: cf. *Pericles* 38. 4.

λοιδορίαι form a sort of footnote; the first of them, which is
a love story, has not even been integrated into the general
context of ἐρωτικά to which Plutarch now turns.
With this new topic (4. 1), tone and style change abruptly.
In elaborate periods, Plutarch recounts the victory of Socrates, the true friend and lover, over the flatterers and sycophants. Alcibiades' εὐφυΐα (cf. 6. 1) made him cleave to
Socrates: with him alone he 'lowered his wing like a beaten
cock'.[14] But the grand vein quickly gives way again (4. 5) to
an anecdote: the rough treatment of Anytus. We have
another version of this in Athenaeus, from Satyrus.[15] This
differs both in wording and in substance. In wording,
Satyrus has what seems to be the more pointed form of
Anytus' repartee. When someone says that Alcibiades ἀγνώ-
μονα εἴη πεποιηκώς, he answers, Οὐ μὰ Δί' ἀλλ' εὐγνώμονα.
Plutarch, both here and (with minor variants) in *Eroticus*
762 c, has his characteristic double expressions: ὑβριστικῶς
καὶ ὑπερηφάνως . . . ἐπιεικῶς μὲν οὖν καὶ φιλανθρώπως. In substance, Satyrus (and Plutarch in the *Eroticus*) omits the
preliminary episode that Anytus had himself asked Alcibiades to dinner; he does, however, add that Alcibiades gave
the silver to his needy friend Thrasyllus instead of keeping
it for his own use. In both these respects, the version in the
Life makes Alcibiades' conduct seem more outrageous. It
thus makes the general point more plainly, and contrasts
more markedly with what follows—the case of the favoured
metic. If this effect of contrast is deliberate, we should
think of 4–6 at least as planned as a whole. The metic affair
(5) is one for which we have no other evidence; there is,
however, no reason to doubt its early origin,[16] despite its
Plutarchian language.[17]

[14] For 4. 4 and *Eroticus* 762 E, see Flacelière, ad loc. To his references add that
the slightly unexpected τὸ Σωκράτους πρᾶγμα (230. 11 Ziegler) is from *Alc. I* 104 D
4.
[15] Athen. 534 E ff.: see above, n. 5, W. von Uxkull-Gyllenband, *Plutarch und
die griechische Biographie* (Stuttgart, 1927), 30 ff.
[16] Cf. Andoc. *de mysteriis* 134 ff., where A. takes credit for bidding 36 talents
for the taxes when the regular τελῶναι had expectations of getting them for the
usual sum of 30.
[17] Note the pairs γελάσας καὶ ἡσθείς . . . ἑστιάσας καὶ φιλοφρονηθείς . . . συστρεφό-
μενοι καὶ ἀγανακτοῦντες . . .

Socrates' love had to contend against numerous and powerful rivals (6. 1), whose weapon was flattery and especially the temptation of high political hopes. The situation is envisaged much as in *Alcibiades I*. The thought that Alcibiades might hope to surpass Pericles' reputation occurs there (105 B) as well as here (6. 4). The very end of the dialogue too expresses the general position as Plutarch sees it: ὀρρωδῶ δὲ ... τὴν τῆς πόλεως ὁρῶν ῥώμην, μὴ ἐμοῦ τε καὶ σοῦ κρατήσῃ. But the whole chapter, especially 6. 1, echoes the Alcibiades of Plato's *Symposium*:

(i) τῶν λόγων ... τὴν καρδίαν στρεφόντων καὶ δάκρυα ἐκχεόντων is from 215 E: ἥ τε καρδία πηδᾷ καὶ δάκρυα ἐκχεῖται ὑπὸ τῶν λόγων.

(ii) δραπετεύων ... ἐκυνηγεῖτο is from δραπετεύω ... καὶ φεύγω (216 B 5).

(iii) πρὸς μόνον ἐκεῖνον ἔχων τὸ αἰδεῖσθαι is from πέπονθα δὲ πρὸς τοῦτον μόνον ἀνθρώπων ... τὸ αἰσχύνεσθαι ὁντινοῦν (216 B 1–5).

(iv) ἐνδεής at the end of the chapter[18] picks up 216 A 5: ἀναγκάζει γάρ με ὁμολογεῖν ὅτι πολλοῦ ἐνδεὴς ὢν αὐτὸς ἔτι, as well as *Alc. I* 104 A 2.

With all this is combined the evidence of Thucydides. Plutarch quotes 6. 15. 4: τὸ μέγεθος τῆς κατὰ τὸ ἑαυτοῦ σῶμα παρανομίας ἐς τὴν δίαιταν. This he says 'raises a suspicion' that Alcibiades was easily tempted into pleasure. One would think that evidence of this was unnecessary; certainly the character-sketch at a later stage (16) leaves no doubt about Alcibiades' τρυφή, which was notorious. Nor is it likely that Plutarch is thinking with chronological strictness of the early period in Alcibiades' life and using Thucydides for this; if he were doing that, indeed, he would probably be wrong, since the reference in 6. 15. 4 is clearly to 415 *and to the closing period of the war*, not to the earlier phase.[19] None the less, Plutarch attaches great weight to what Thucydides says. He is aware that the historian's restraint in personal

---

[18] In a favourite simile, found at least seven times in the *Moralia*: see Wyttenbach on *de adulatore et amico* 73 C.

[19] See K. J. Dover, *Thucydides Book VI*, 1965, pp. 23–4.

detail and comment makes his lightest word deserve consideration. So with Hyperbolus (13. 4): μέμνηται μὲν ὡς
ἀνθρώπου πονηροῦ καὶ Θουκυδίδης. He is aware too of the
singularity of Thucydides' judgement compared with later
tradition: the historian makes no moral judgement, but
simply states as a fact that Alcibiades' behaviour gave rise
to the suspicion that he was aiming at tyranny and that in
consequence the feelings of individuals made them forget
his excellence as a leader and led to the ruin of Athens. The
παρανομία was wholly irrelevant, except for the impression
it created. It is regrettable that the vulgar could not rise to
the enlightened tolerance which would have saved the
country. Plutarch cannot talk like this; for him the τρυφή,
even if it is an expression of φιλοτιμία rather than φιληδονία,
as he tries for the moment to maintain, is morally reprehensible.

The more fragmented, anecdotal style resumes its sway
from 7. 1. Of the stories now told, the one about the retort
to Pericles (7. 2) belongs to the mythology of the causes of
the war. The Potidaea story (7. 3–5) is from Plato,[20] though
the details of the ἀριστεῖα (garland and panoply) are not
given in the *Symposium*, and have probably come from
Isocrates 16. 29. It is, however, modified in an interesting
way. In Plato, Alcibiades asks the generals to make the
award to Socrates, but Socrates persuades them to follow
their natural inclinations and give it to Alcibiades himself.
In Plutarch, the sequence of events is simpler: by rights the
prize belonged to Socrates; the generals want to give it
Alcibiades διὰ τὸ ἀξίωμα;[21] Socrates urges them to do this
'because he wanted to foster Alcibiades' ambition in noble
causes'. The motive is new; it presupposes a distinction
between the kind of φιλοτιμία on which Alcibiades' flatterers
battened and the ambition to be brave; and the effect of it is
to put Socrates in a more clearly pedagogic relation to
Alcibiades than in the *Symposium*—more in fact in the style
of *Alcibiades I*. It is difficult to catch the tone of this
argument about military decorations; but Plato's Alcibiades
seems clear in his mind that his position gave him a natural

---

[20] *Sympos.* 220 E.
[21] Plato's word, and cf. Thuc. 5. 43. 2: ἀξιώματι προγόνων.

right, which he takes some credit for having disclaimed.
Plato thus depicts a more subtle situation; Plutarch is cruder
and his motivations unlikely.

Alcibiades is now to be married. Plutarch's account of
this (8) reveals features both of his handling of sources and
of his own opinions. The insult to Hipponicus (8. 1) was, it
seems, *before* Delium: καὶ ταῦτα μὲν ὕστερον ἐπράχθη (7. 6)
shows unusual chronological scruple. It looks as though
Plutarch believed that Hipponicus fell in that campaign:
so—with the additional detail that he was general—ps.-
Andoc. 4. 13.[22] In any case, Plutarch believes Hipponicus
to have died between the marriage and the birth of the first
child. When, thereupon, Alcibiades claims the promised
second ten talents, Callias 'fearing a plot' offers his property
to the demos if he should die childless. Hipparete then runs
away to her brother's, distressed at her husband's attentions
to his ἑταῖραι. Alcibiades treats the affair with insouciance,[23]
but when she has to attend before the archon to register the
separation (ἀπόλειψις), he turns up too and takes her home,
unopposed by her friends. Plutarch passes a favourable
comment on the law which allows a husband these opportunities; he disapproves in fact of divorce and second marriages, which he regards as un-Hellenic, a disagreeable
feature in Roman *mores*.[24] His approval here is based on a
false notion, if it is true[25] that registration of ἀπόλειψις was
not compulsory but only expedient in order to provide
certified evidence in future proceedings for the recovery of
the dowry. It should, however, be added that Plutarch's
wording is not quite clear. He may mean simply that the
registration, if desired, had to be made in person; but I
doubt if many readers would have so interpreted him had it
not been for the external evidence. And what is the connec-

---

[22] We cannot disprove these statements. The allusion to Callias in the Κόλακες
of 421 as newly inheriting does not exclude the possibility that he may have
inherited two or three years before (A. R. Burn, *CQ* NS 4 (1954), 139; D. M.
MacDowell, *CQ* NS 15 (1965), 42 n. 1).

[23] ἐτρυφῶντος, a favourite word; cf. 23. 8, 32. 2, 36. 2; Holden on *Themistocles*
18. 4.

[24] Cf. *praecepta coniugalia* 144 A; L. Goessler, *Plutarchs Gedanke über die Ehe*
(Zürich, 1962), 75.

[25] See J. W. Jones, *Law and Legal Theory of the Greeks*, 182; evidence is
Demosthenes 30. 17 and 26.

tion between the genitive absolute τοῦ δ' Ἀλκιβιάδου ...
ἐντρυφῶντος and the main clause? Was it *because* Alcibiades
made it plain he didn't care, that the fact of the divorce had
to be made public?

In ps.-Andoc. 4. 15, the corresponding narrative is con-
ventionally coloured to illustrate πλεονεξία and ὑπερηφανία.
The enormous dowry was not enough: Alcibiades must
needs have ἑταῖραι in the house, and his poor wife 'went to
the archon according to the law'. Then he showed his
mind; he took a party of his friends and kidnapped her in
the agora, in flagrant contempt of the law. Nor was this
enough; he plotted the murder of Callias, as Callias himself
told the Assembly when he offered his property to the
demos in the event of his dying childless 'because he was
afraid of being killed for his property'.

Most of the points in which Plutarch's account differs
from this are in the direction of a more favourable picture
of Alcibiades' behaviour. Plutarch does not assert that he
did in fact conspire to kill Callias, but only that Callias
feared it. Nor does he make him take his friends with him
to fetch Hipparete home; he uses force (συναρπάσας implies
this), but there is no gang violence. These differences are
explicable on the hypothesis that Plutarch is discounting
the λοιδορία of the orator; but there are others which are
not. Plutarch makes Hipparete run away *to her brother's*, yet
it is *before* this that Callias becomes alarmed; the orator
makes her go *to the archon*, and it is *after* this that Alcibiades
plots against Callias. Neither of these makes a convincing
story; but if we combine Plutarch's version of the procedure
with the orator's chronology, a more coherent story begins
to appear. Hipparete goes to the head of her family (her
κύριος), who is alarmed at the possible revenge of her powerful and impulsive husband, and thereupon makes the demos
his heir, failing children. Now Hipparete's desertion of her
husband has put Callias in a position to claim the return of
the dowry; if he dies and leaves no son, will not the demos
inherit also the claim against Alcibiades? It might be
thought to secure him against attack, if the consequence of
an attack would be that his brother-in-law would be faced
with a claim from the demos which it would be ruinous to

pay and politically disastrous to refuse. This is of course speculation; but if something like this is the original of the story, both authors have distorted—and neither is dependent on the other.[26]

II. ENTRY INTO POLITICS, 10–16

After an isolated *apophthegma*,[27] we come at last to Alcibiades' political career. All this is still unchronological: πρώτην ... πάροδον (10. 1), μεγάλας ... κλισιάδας (10. 3), and ἐπεί δ' ἀφῆκεν αὐτόν (13. 1) look as if they gave a time-sequence, but this is illusory. Of the three episodes introduced by these phrases, the first is undatable and sounds as though it may be comic in origin; the second is a general account of Alcibiades' excellence as an orator;[28] and the third (13. 1) relates to a period preceding the Olympic ἱπποτροφίαι of the intervening passage (11–12).

12. 1 again raises the question of Plutarch's relation to ps.-And. 4. That he knew of this speech follows from 13. 3; that he knew it directly is another matter. In 12. 1, Plutarch describes the services rendered to Alcibiades by various allied states. They are related also by pseudo-Andocides (30) and by Satyrus in Athenaeus (534 D). The three accounts vary somewhat. That of Satyrus is peculiar in failing to attach the story to the Olympic θεωρία: Alcibiades enjoys these benefits whenever he goes abroad. (The uprooting of an anecdote from its context like this seems not uncommon; we saw it in 7. 3, and it happens again at 13. 3, where Plutarch fails to refer the story about the gold plate, which he knows to have been in the pseudo-Andocides, to its proper setting at Olympia. This curious phenomenon could result from the use of collections of anecdotes stripped of their historical context—as in the extant *Apophthegmata*—and then inaccurately reconstituted into a continuous narrative.)

---

[26] The problem of ps.-And. 4 has been often handled; see esp. A. R. Burn, *CQ* loc. cit.

[27] Cf. *Mor.* 186 D.

[28] Cf. Nepos, 1. 2. We do not know from what work of Theophrastus the point about Alcibiades' hesitant delivery is taken; perhaps περὶ ὑποκρίσεως.

Apart from this, each of the three versions has a point at which it differs from the other two. Plutarch is unique in omitting the description of the marquee as a Persian one; Satyrus is unique in saying that Cyzicus, not Chios, supplied the victims; the speech is unique in making the marquee double the size of the public one. If we postulate an original account from which the others deviate by omission or misunderstanding, then it is clear from this that the account in Satyrus either is this original or at least is nearest to it. The only thing wrong with it is that it is so implausibly separated from the Olympic θεωρία. This could be Athenaeus' own error. We can also see that 'Andocides' does not depend on Plutarch—the Persian marquee is proof enough of this—but for proof of the contrary proposition, that Plutarch is independent of 'Andocides', we must wait for the ensuing anecdote (12. 3).

Here, in Plutarch's version, Diomedes—ἀνὴρ οὐ πονηρός, Ἀλκιβιάδου δὲ φίλος—persuades Alcibiades to buy the Argive state chariot on his behalf. Alcibiades does so, but treats it as his own and takes no notice of Diomedes. In the speech (26), Alcibiades uses his influence with the agonothetai to deprive Diomedes—πολίτην ὄντα καὶ ⟨οὐ⟩ τὸν ἐπιτυχόντα—of his chariot. No mention of Argos or the Argives; and although the story is told in a way as hostile to Alcibiades as possible, the victim has only the claims of a πολίτης, or an important πολίτης, not the stronger ones of a φίλος.

Further confirmation comes from the Hyperbolus episode which follows. Accepting (as we must) the priority of *Nicias* to *Alcibiades*, we have to say that the principal addition to Plutarch's knowledge between the two Lives relates to the part played by Phaeax. Yet he knows little enough about it. Though he now (13. 1) gives Alcibiades two rivals, Phaeax and Nicias, the ostracism itself (13. 4–7) is told without reference to Phaeax, who appears simply in a variant account (13. 8), as he does in *Nicias* 11. 10. This variant account is from Theophrastus; since it takes the contenders to be Phaeax, Alcibiades, and Hyperbolus, it cannot be derived from ps.-And. 4. The situation is consistent with two possibilities: either Plutarch never read ps.-And. 4, or he read it but rejected its view of events and questioned its

authenticity (φέρεται, 13. 3). The inaccuracy of the reference
in 13. 3 inclines one to the former view; and I would
suspect that *all* Plutarch's knowledge of Phaeax is derived
from nothing more direct than commentaries on classical
authors—on Demosthenes 21 and on comedy: we should
note the references to comedy in 13. 2, 13. 4, and 13. 9.[29]

But the most striking fact about 13–15 is that the ostracism is dealt with *before* the dispute between Nicias and
Alcibiades over the Spartan ambassadors. This reverses the
order of the *Nicias*, and of history. In fact this chapter is
not chronologically arranged narrative. Plutarch is still concerned to define Alcibiades' position rather than to relate
what happened to him. The hero is still μειράκιον (13. 1, as
in 7. 3), though he was 33 or 34 in 417, and he has
established himself as one of the three leading δημαγωγοί.
His wealth, eloquence, courage, and ambition have been
illustrated. There remains his political and strategic skill:
the Hyperbolus affair and the duping of the Spartan ambassadors illustrate the former, the various episodes in 15 the
latter.

The episode of the ambassadors comes in its essentials
from Thucydides. This is the point at which the historian
(5. 43) first introduces Alcibiades, going out of his way to
say a word about him and to make it clear that even in his
austere judgement φιλοτιμία was a key motive in the young
man's actions and that his emotions were a fact of political
import. Plutarch himself in the πολιτικὰ παραγγέλματα
(804 E) cites the sudden accession to power of Alcibiades τὰ
Μαντινικὰ συστήσας as an example of the quick success that
evades φθόνος. This is an important moment; it is also the
first political scene which could be treated in detail. Plutarch
restrains moral comment; he treats the ἀπάτη simply on the
level of expediency, just as he did that of Themistocles and
the walls (*Themist.* 19).[30] His account contains one addition
and one omission which are of interest. (i) In 14. 4–5

[29] On Plutarch's use of comedy and its commentators, see Uxkull-Gyllenband,
op. cit. 17–30, esp. 22–3.
[30] Contrast the judgement of Grote, also a moralist in his way: 'an unblushing
combination of imprudence and fraud ... in the vein of Fielding's Jonathan
Wild'.

Alcibiades directs certain charges against Nicias, εἰκότα κατηγορῶν. They are that he had been lax at Sphacteria, as general and afterwards in giving back the prisoners, and that he had not pressed Athenian objections to Spartan alliances with Corinth and Thebes, while giving Sparta a power of veto on new Athenian allies. These accusations are not in Thucydides or in *Nicias*; they may therefore be amplifications of Plutarch's own—if so, they exemplify a procedure which is rare in well-documented Lives, common enough in 'thin' ones. (ii) A feature of Thucydides' account, reproduced by Plutarch in the *Nicias*, is that after the discomfiture of the ambassadors there is an earthquake, the assembly is adjourned, and Nicias at the resumed meeting succeeds in having a delegation sent to Sparta, though this proves fruitless. In the *Alcibiades*, this delay is omitted; it is clearly of more importance for Nicias, because it gives him a second chance, than for Alcibiades. Still, the compression is striking; and so is the omission of the earthquake, of all things, in a writer deeply interested in omens and prodigies. Compare, however, the departure of the fleet for Sicily in 17. The corresponding narrative in *Nicias* 13. 1–5 has no less than three details of this kind: Alcibiades produces oracles to forecast victory, someone mutilates himself on the altar of the Twelve Gods, and ravens attack certain Athenian treasures at Delphi. All that remains in the *Alcibiades* of the complex of which these episodes form part is the essential omen of the Adonia. In general, this change of emphasis can be accounted for by the requirements of the *Nicias*, where the hero is δεισιδαίμων and the story punctuated by omens and portents; but the omission of Alcibiades' trick, a notable piece of δεινότης, remains surprising. Cynicism about religion, it seems, is no part of the hero's character: in 407, genuine piety entered into his decision to protect the Mystai: καλὸν . . . ἐφαίνετο τῷ Ἀλκιβιάδῃ καὶ πρὸς θεῶν ὁσιότητα καὶ πρὸς ἀνθρώπων δόξαν (34. 5).

In 15, Alcibiades is seen on the international stage. The arrangement is still not chronological. The proposal for Long Walls at Patrae (15. 6) was made in 419 (Thuc. 5. 52), two years before the similar move at Argos. The connection of 15. 7–8 with the context is purely by subject: the point is that Alcibiades was not simply a sea-power man, he also enjoined on the Athenians expansion by land. This looks like an apologia designed to make him acceptable to critics of the naval democracy and believers in the hoplite virtues; such a defence would be in place in his own lifetime or in the fourth century. The point is made by a curious misinterpretation of the ephebic oath,[31] which we also know from Cicero,[32] and which involves a gross error. It is clear from the inscription that ὅροι τῆς πατρίδος as well as πυροί, κριθαί, etc., are among the θεοὶ ἵστορες who witness the ephebus' promise. Someone has simply taken ὅροι τῆς πατρίδος as the subject, and πυροί and the rest as predicates. Result: the patriotic appeal to claim all land where corn grows as Athenian. Could Alcibiades himself have made such a point? This cannot, I think, be ruled out; the misinterpretations of the poets by sophists—for instance, Plato's handling of Simonides in *Protagoras*—show the same kind of grammatical sharp practice.

The following chapter (16) is a summary, marking a pause before the more continuous narrative to come. It begins with elaborate rhetoric and closes with a formula summarizing the main point: οὕτως ἄκριτος ἦν ἡ δόξα περὶ αὐτοῦ διὰ τὴν τῆς φύσεως ἀνωμαλίαν.

First, Plutarch handles some traditional details allusively and in a highly literary fashion: the plurals give 'elevation'.[33] One of the facts mentioned—the gold shield with Eros the Thunderer—appears in Athenaeus (534 E), where both the situation (καὶ στρατηγῶν δὲ ἔτι καλός) and the metre of Ἔρως κεραυνὸν ἠγκυλημένος strongly suggest an origin in comedy. Of the other points we know nothing; throughout this chapter Plutarch is putting pieces together in his own way, and showing more compositional ambition than in any earlier part of the Life. Thus the description of the popular reaction to all this display (16. 2) is made up partly of topics used in *Nicias* 11, and partly of a pair of quotations from the *Frogs*, a play dating from a time ten years after the

[31] See Tod, *GHI* ii. 303 ff. and references.
[32] *De republica* 3. 15. For a kindred τόπος, see Plu. *de exilio* 601 A.
[33] 'Longinus' 23.

period which should here be in question. Alcibiades is a source of alarm to the ἔνδοξοι, but popular with the demos and easily forgiven, for they are indulgent to youth and wealth, a good-humoured folk who love a young lord.[34] As examples of their indulgence Plutarch gives a number of anecdotes from the traditional stock. Two of these are known to us also from Demosthenes;[35] more important, all the first three occur in ps.-Andoc. 4, and in the same order. They are treated in a way which, once again, suggests a common source rather than Plutarch's use of the speech. (i) In Plutarch, the painter Agatharchus is allowed to go, and indeed rewarded, when he has painted Alcibiades' house; in 'Andocides' (17) he has to escape after three months—it is like running away from the King of Persia.[36] Plutarch's story is differently coloured: it illustrates impulsiveness and generosity. In Demosthenes there is yet another turn: Agatharchus, he understands, had been caught doing something wrong. Demosthenes is trying to show that Alcibiades, despite his family and wealth, couldn't get away with offences less serious than those of Midias; Plutarch's point is just that he did get away with all this. We see Plutarch steering a judicious course between opposing rhetorical exaggerations. (ii) It is from 'Andocides' that we know something of the Taureas affair: the man had tried to get one of Alcibiades' choir-singers disqualified as an alien. Plutarch does not go into this—either because he is ignorant or because the further details might suggest that there were two sides to the question—but takes it for granted that Alcibiades was in the wrong and that the motive was φιλοτιμία. (iii) The story of the Melian woman, a striking anachronism in 'Andocides' and a proof that the author cannot be writing near the actual time, is told by Plutarch with no factual discrepancy but once again with a different interpretation. Since he writes φιλάνθρωπον ἐκάλουν he must either have come across the anecdote in a defensive context or be misunderstanding some piece of bitter irony—unless

---

[34] Cf. *praec. ger. r.p.* 799 C: the Athenians welcome τῶν λόγων τοὺς παιγνιώδεις καὶ γελοίους.

[35] 21. 147.

[36] Cf. Alcibiades' own predicament, 28. 1.

indeed he is using the common τόπος of the revaluation of moral words to invent a detail on his own.

The theme of ἄκριτος δόξα continues to the end of the chapter, illustrated now by stories not found in 'Andocides'. Aristophon the painter appears (as Aglaophon) in Athenaeus; the story is there anchored to the Olympic θεωρία.[37] That the older people should be critics is natural—it is part, for example, of Thucydides' narrative that the young supported Alcibiades and war, and that there was a conflict of generations. Plutarch, however, has moved tacitly from his earlier contrast (16. 2) of demos and notables to this new one. The apophthegm of Archestratus (16. 8)[38] does not support the main theme, but only the view of Alcibiades as τυραννικός; the Timon story,[39] with which the chapter closes, contains nothing in itself to support it, but the sequel of οἱ μὲν ἐγέλων, οἱ δ' ἐβλασφήμουν brings it into place. There was no settled opinion about Alcibiades.

The foregoing analysis is intended to show, in sufficient but not exhaustive detail, the texture of Plutarch's anecdotal composition. I hope that his overriding aims appear clearly: they are characterization and variety of writing. The result is a loose structure, alarming in its incoherence.[40] The 'pieces' of which such a composition is made up are of very various sizes. Some are fairly extensive, like the story of Alcibiades and the ambassadors. Some are small, like the apophthegm of Archestratus. Large or small, they need not be correctly placed in date in relation to their neighbours. Again, they are of very different origins. Some are taken from continuous writing, and their historical or rhetorical context is remembered: the Spartan ambassadors; Delium and Potidaea. Others have passed through the stage of inclusion in a collection of *apophthegmata* or a learned note, with the result that their context has been obscured or

---

[37] τούτοις (p. 243. 5 Ziegler) ought to refer either to more than one fact or at least to some vaguer circumstances; Plutarch may have in mind, but have failed to record, the other picture mentioned in Athenaeus—that of Olympias and Pythias garlanding Alcibiades.

[38] From Theophrastus; see *Lysander* 19.

[39] Cf. *Antony* 70.

[40] New paragraphs, besides those in Ziegler, seem appropriate in eleven places: 2. 2, 2. 3 ἔτι δέ, 2. 5, 7. 3, 7. 6, 15. 4, 15. 6, 15. 7, 16. 7, 16. 8, 16. 9.

forgotten: such are the conversation with Pericles (7. 3) and
the story of the gold plate (13. 3). These *déracinés*, which
may find a new and inappropriate home, are a special
danger to the historian. Thirdly, Plutarch's use of the units
varies. Some are worked into a coherent scheme as *exempla*,
like the childhood anecdotes (2) or the stories of Agatharchus and Taureas (16. 5). It sometimes happens that these
groups have historical coherence, as the Olympia stories in
12 have—but note the stray, 13. 3. More often, the coherence is logical, not historical: 15. 6–7, Patrae and the ephebic
oath. And sometimes there is no scheme at all, only juxtaposition: 9 (the dog's tail) and 16. 8 (Archestratus) exemplify
this. Passages like 3 (Antiphon's λοιδορίαι) and 5 (the metic
lover) also interrupt the natural sequence, but they do have
a loose attachment to their surroundings, the former as
παιδικὰ ἀπομνημονεύματα, the latter in a general erotic context. Finally, there are the places where the material is
fairly thoroughly worked into a reflective or descriptive
piece: 6, 16, cf. 23. When this happens, Plutarch is at his
most characteristic: familiar similes and allusions abound
and the sentence structure becomes more varied and complex. Some such categorization of the items which make up
Plutarch's narrative is an essential tool in the analysis and
interpretation of his work.

8

Tragedy and Epic in Plutarch's *Alexander*

J. M. MOSSMAN

Achilles is the poetic paradigm of a hero, Alexander his real-life counterpart as well as his descendant. This idea is a commonplace of all our sources for Alexander's life. There are numerous examples of it: Diodorus says at xvii. 1. 4:

ἐν ἔτεσι γὰρ δώδεκα καταστρεψάμενος τῆς μὲν Εὐρώπης οὐκ ὀλίγα, τὴν δὲ Ἀσίαν σχεδὸν ἅπασαν εἰκότως περιβόητον ἔσχε τὴν δόξαν καὶ τοῖς παλαιοῖς ἥρωσι καὶ ἡμιθέοις ἰσάζουσαν . . . Ἀλέξανδρος οὖν γεγονὼς κατὰ πατέρα μὲν ἀφ' Ἡρακλέους, κατὰ δὲ μητέρα τῶν Αἰακιδῶν οἰκείαν ἔσχε τὴν φύσιν καὶ τὴν ἀρετὴν τῆς τῶν προγόνων εὐδοξίας.[1]

Diodorus xvii. 97. 3 extends the parallelism to a specific incident: Achilles' fight with Scamander, Alexander's lucky escape from drowning.[2] Arrian's account of Alexander's landing at Sigeum (i. 11–12) strongly suggests that Alexander himself encouraged the parallel:

θῦσαι δὲ αὐτὸν καὶ Πριάμωι ἐπὶ τοῦ βωμοῦ τοῦ Διὸς τοῦ Ἑρκείου λόγος κατέχει, μῆνιν Πριάμου παραιτούμενον τῶι Νεοπτολέμου γένει, ὃ δὴ ἐς αὐτὸν καθῆκεν . . . οἱ δέ, ὅτι καὶ τὸν Ἀχιλλέως ἄρα τάφον ἐστεφάνωσεν· Ἡφαιστίωνα δὲ λέγουσιν ὅτι τοῦ Πατρόκλου τὸν τάφον ἐστεφάνωσε· καὶ εὐδαιμόνισεν ἄρα, ὡς λόγος, Ἀλέξανδρος Ἀχιλλέα ὅτι Ὁμήρου κήρυκος ἐς τὴν ἔπειτα μνήμην ἔτυχε.

---

[1] Cf. Plut. *Alex.* 2. 1. An earlier draft of this paper was delivered at the conference of the International Plutarch Society held at the Canadian and American Schools of Classical Studies in Athens, 26–8 June 1987. I am most grateful to the Society and to the organizers of the conference. I owe a special debt to Dr C. B. R. Pelling and Mr E. L. Bowie, whose perceptive criticisms were invaluable, to the very useful remarks of an unnamed referee, and to Mark Edwards for his generous interest and stimulating conversation.

[2] D.S. xvii. 97. 3: σωθεὶς δὲ παραδόξως τοῖς θεοῖς ἔθυσεν ὡς μεγίστους ἐκπεφευγὼς κινδύνους καὶ πρὸς ποταμὸν ὁμοίως Ἀχιλλεῖ διαγωνισάμενος.

Compare also Diodorus xvii. 17. 3. The sacrifice is a public act affirming his lineage.

Plutarch in the *de Alexandri Magni fortuna aut virtute* (*Mor.* 327f–328a) makes it clear that Alexander's love of Homer was well known (though for the purposes of his argument he subordinates Homer to philosophy here):

ἀλλὰ τοῖς μὲν γράφουσιν, ὡς Ἀλέξανδρος ἔφη ποτὲ τὴν Ἰλιάδα καὶ τὴν Ὀδύσσειαν ἀκολυθεῖν αὐτῶι τῆς στρατείας ἐφόδιον, πιστεύομεν, Ὅμηρον σεμνύνοντες· ἀνδέτισφῆι Ἰλιάδα καὶ τὴν Ὀδύσσειαν παραμύθια πόνου καὶ διατριβὴν ἔπεσθαι σχολῆς γλυκείας, ἐφόδιον δ' ἀληθῶς γεγονέναι τὸν ἐκ φιλοσοφίας λόγον . . . καταφρονοῦμεν;

Compare also the *Life*, 8. 2 and 26. 2.

Elsewhere in the treatise there are comparisons of some length between Alexander and a number of Homeric heroes: for example 331cd, which also stresses Alexander's knowledge of Homer and his espousal of Homeric ideals:

Καὶ μὴν εἴ ποτε γένοιτο τῶν Ὁμήρου σύγκρισις ἐπῶν ἐν ταῖς διατριβαῖς ἢ παρὰ τὰ συμπόσια, ἄλλον ἄλλου στίχον προκρίνοντος, αὐτὸς ὡς διαφέροντα πάντων ἐνέκρινε τοῦτον,

ἀμφότερον βασιλεύς τ' ἀγαθὸς κρατερός τ' αἰχμητής
(*Il.* iii. 179; cf. Xen. *Mem.* iii. 2. 2)

ὃν ἄλλος ἔπαινον τῶι χρόνωι προέλαβε, τοῦτον αὐτῶι νόμον κεῖσθαι λογιζόμενος, ὥστ' εἰπεῖν Ὅμηρον ὅτι τῶι αὐτῶι μέτρωι τὴν μὲν Ἀγαμέμνονος ἀνδραγαθίαν κεκόσμηκε, τὴν δ' Ἀλεξάνδρου μεμάντευται.

The description is indeed of Agamemnon—Helen says it in the Teichoskopia. Later in the section we find another Achilles comparison.

καί τινος αὐτῶι τῶν ἐγχωρίων ὑποσχομένου τὴν Πάριδος λύραν εἰ βούλοιτο δώσειν 'οὐδέν' ἔφη 'τῆς ἐκείνου δέομαι· τὴν γὰρ Ἀχιλλέως κέκτημαι, πρὸς ἣν ἐκεῖνος ἀνεπαύετο

ἄειδε δ' ἄρα κλέα ἀνδρῶν (*Il.* ix. 189)

ἡ δὲ Πάριδος πάντως μαλακήν τινα καὶ θήλειαν ἁρμονίαν ἐρωτικοῖς ἔψαλλε μέλεσι.'

At 343ab we find a more elaborate system of comparisons: Alexander is more self-restrained in dealing with his female captives than Agamemnon, more magnanimous to Darius than Achilles was to Hector, more generous than Achilles because he enriched even his enemies, whereas Achilles accepted gifts from his friends in compensation after his anger had passed, more reverent than Diomedes, and more deeply mourned by his relatives than Odysseus, for Odysseus' mother died of grief, but the mother of Alexander's greatest enemy loved him so much that she chose to share his death.

We should notice two points here: firstly, that there are *two* points of comparison with Achilles, one with each of the other heroes; secondly, that although this type of comparison is a commonplace of encomium, particularly when the subject of the encomium claims to be related to a hero like Achilles or to a god,[3] at 343ab the scale of the passage and the detailed references to the poems perhaps suggest a more conscious identification with the heroes as they appear in the Homeric epics.

Plutarch's source for Alexander's love of Homer is presumably Onesicritus. It is interesting that, although most Onesicritus material is treated more lightly in the *Life* than in the *de Alexandri Magni*, notably Onesicritus' picture of Alexander as the philosopher man of action, the material on Alexander's love of Homer and literature generally is given just as much weight.[4]

Since Alexander's association with Homer was well known, and since he does seem to have encouraged such Iliadic parallelism,[5] and since a certain encomiastic strain

---

[3] Cf. e.g. Theocritus, xvii. 53 ff.: Ἀργεία κυάνοφρυ, σὺ λαοφόνον Διομήδεα | μισγομένα Τυδῆι τέκες, Καλυδώνιον ἄνδρα, | ἀλλὰ Θέτις βαθύκολπος ἀκοντιστὰν Ἀχιλῆα | Αἰακίδαι Πηλῆι· σὲ δ᾽ αἰχμητὰ Πτολεμαῖε | αἰχμητᾶι Πτολεμαίωι ἀρίζηλος Βερενίκα.

[4] A. Momigliano, *The Development of Greek Biography, Four Lectures* (Harvard, 1971), 82–3 shows the importance of accounts of education to Greek biography, and this may explain Plutarch's selection of material. But in that case it is perhaps surprising that he did not make more use of Onesicritus in the early part of the *Life*: cf. J. R. Hamilton, *Plutarch, Alexander: A Commentary* (Oxford, 1969), lvii. Onesicritus' ὡς Ἀλέξανδρος ἤχθη is paralleled by the Ἀλεξάνδρου ἀγωγή of Marsyas of Pella, another companion of Alexander.

[5] This cannot of course be deduced from the *de Alexandri Magni* but the conjunction of Diodorus and Arrian is convincing.

212   *J. M. Mossman*

inherent in epic poetry encouraged such comparisons to become well rooted in the later encomiastic tradition, it comes as no surprise to find Plutarch developing and exploring the epic dimension of Alexander in the *Life*. It is considerably more unexpected to find him introducing *tragic* atmosphere as a counterbalance to the epic view, as I would argue he does. This may seem surprising because, as Phillip de Lacy has pointed out ('Biography and Tragedy in Plutarch', *AJP* 73 (1952), 159 ff.), although tragedy obviously has an important place in Plutarch's literary background, allusions to it usually imply an adverse moral judgement and in literary contexts it is used as a term of censure in his writings.[6] This view is associated with Plutarch's Platonism, as de Lacy has shown.[7]

A distinction needs to be made, however, as we shall see, between the sensationalism of so-called 'tragic history' which Plutarch dislikes so much and the sustained tragic patterning and imagery which is a perfectly respectable feature of both biography and history. Plutarch himself not infrequently chooses to characterize some of the subjects of the *Lives* and their actions by using such tragic imagery: Dionysius, Pompey, Lysander, Antony, and Demetrius are examples.[8] Some of these we will discuss more fully below.

[6] Plutarch and tragedy: the material is false: *de Aud. Poet.* 16a–17e *passim*; tragedy contrasted with historical truth: *Theseus* 1. 3–4, 2. 3, 15. 2, 16. 3–4 (cf. Plato, *Minos* 318de, 320e–321b); cf. *Romulus* 8. 9. Theopompus condemned as 'tragic' for giving a false account: *Demosthenes* 21. 2; Phylarchus ditto, cf. *Themistocles* 32. 4; Herodotus, cf. *de Mal. Herod.* 870c; Ctesias, *Artaxerxes* 6. 9; others, cf. *Alexander* 75. 5. Also of philosophical arguments: *de Pyth. Or.* 399e–400c; *Adv. Col.* 1119c, 1123b. The audience is deceived: *de Aud. Poet.* 15cd, 16a–17c, esp. 17c. So are the poets: 17d. Tragedy = pretence: in philosophy *Mor.* 528bc (*de genio Socratis*), 724d (*Quaestiones Conviviales*); in wild stories *Mor.* 926c (*de facie in Orbe lunae*) cf. *Lucullus* 11. 2; putting extra tragoedia in oracles cf. *de Pyth. Or.* 407b. The actor pretends: *Mor.* 50e (*Quomodo Adulator ab Amico Internoscatur*): cf. Ps.-Plut. *de Liberis Educandis* 13b; *Non posse suaviter vivi* 1102b. Against actors: cf. *Sulla* 2. 3–4, 36. 1; *Galba* 16. 3; *Apophthegmata Laconica* 212f (cf. *Agesilaos* 21. 8); *Solon* 29. 7; *Demosthenes* 28. 3–29. 7; *An Seni Resp.* 785a. Tragedy = madness and anger: *de Cohib. Ira* 462b. Tragedy vs. philosophy *Mor.* 545 f.; = naughty stories *de Aud. Poet.* 27 f. Cf. also A. E. Wardman, *Plutarch's Lives* (London, 1974), 168–79.

[7] Art. cit. 167–8. For Plutarch's Platonism in general cf. e.g. R. M. Jones, 'The Platonism of Plutarch' (Diss. Menasha, Wis., 1916).

[8] Deception = 'constructing a tragic machine', cf. *Them.* 10. 1; *Lysander* 25. 2, 26. 6; Numa's meetings with the Muses etc. a 'drama': *Numa* 8. 10; cf. *Marius* and the Syrian prophetess: *Marius* 17. 5. Pomp and circumstance to deceive the

De Lacy comments: 'Plutarch's tragic figures are not his great heroes, such as Alexander and Epaminondas; they are his villains: the elder Dionysius, Antony, and Nero.' As I hope will become clear, this is an inadequate description of the way in which Plutarch uses tragedy. Central to the *Alexander* is the tension, first made explicit as early as 4. 5–8 (an important passage), between Alexander's hot temper and his self-control;[9] his θυμός is the source of great achievements, but also of disaster, when, combined with heavy drinking, it breaks down his σωφροσύνη. Plutarch often chooses to illustrate this tension by interweaving and contrasting epic and tragic elements throughout the *Life*.[10] In short, I would argue that in the *Alexander* Plutarch is interested not only in what Alexander does, but in what he does to himself, and that just as he may use epic colouring to chronicle Alexander's great deeds, so he also uses tragic colouring to delineate the darker side of Alexander's character.

In putting forward this argument we shall encounter one fundamental methodological problem: identifying and dis-

---

eye: *Aratus* 15. 3 'tragedy and scene-painting'; *Pompey* 31. 10; *Nicias* 21. 1; *Lucullus* 21. 6; *de Cupid. Div.* 527ef, 528b. Tyrants and tragedy: *Demosthenes* 22. 5 (cf. *de Alex. Mag.* 337d); *Lucullus* 21. 3; *Poplicola* 10. 3; *Antony* 54.5 (cf. *de Alex. Mag.* 329f: Persian dress 'tragic'). Nero: *Quomodo Adul.* 56e: cf. also *Galba* 14. 2–3; *Quaest. Conviv.* 717c; *Pelopidas* 34. 1; *Quomodo Adul.* 63a; *Praecepta Rei p. Gerendae* 823e. Opposition of tragic to military: *Eumenes* 2. 2; *Otho* 5. 8. Tragic calamities: *QC* 714e; *Galba* 1. 7–8, 12. 5; *Crassus* 33 *passim*, esp. 33. 7; *Marius* 27. 2; *Pompey* 9. 3–4.

[9] 4. 5–8 (Plutarch is speculating as to the cause of Alexander's pleasant body-odour: he concludes that the κρᾶσις of Alexander's body was responsible, πολύθερμος οὖσα καὶ πυρώδης, and continues by saying): Ἀλέξανδρον δ᾽ ἡ θερμότης τοῦ σώματος ὡς ἔοικε καὶ ποτικὸν καὶ θυμοειδῆ παρεῖχεν. Ἔτι δ᾽ ὄντος αὐτοῦ παιδὸς ἥ τε σωφροσύνη διεφαίνετο . . . This passage is heavily influenced by philosophy: it refers to Theophrastus' *de Odoribus* and is akin to such works as the *Airs, Waters, Places*, and θυμοειδής is a Platonic word; cf. *Rep.* 375c, 411c, 456a. As Wardman has pointed out (A. E. Wardman, 'Plutarch and Alexander', *CQ*, NS 5 (1955), 96–107), θυμός and *ira* are frequently cited in Hellenistic philosophy (e.g. by Plutarch himself in the *de Cohibenda Ira, Mor.* 458b) as denoting bad qualities, which Alexander is used to exemplify; though in the *Life*, as in epic and often in tragedy, θυμός is more ambiguous.

[10] The alternation of motifs is a favourite technique of Plutarch's: one may compare the early chapters of the *Antony*, where Antony's military virtues are dwelt on alternately with his submissiveness first to Fulvia, then to Cleopatra. On this cf. C. B. R. Pelling, 'Plutarch's Method of Work in the Roman Lives', *JHS* 99 (1979), 90 (below, p. 298).

tinguishing 'epic' and 'tragic' tone. Since antiquity the intimate nature of the connection between tragedy and epic has been recognized.[11] Aristotle in the *Poetics* lays great stress on it: cf. 1448^{b}34–1449^{a}1, 1449^{b}9–20, 1456^{a}10–19, 1459^b–1460^{a}5, 1461^{b}26 ff. However, Aristotle also makes it clear that there is a difference between the two: this is perhaps most clearly formulated at 1449^{b}16–20:

μέρη δ' ἐστὶ τὰ μὲν ταὐτά, τὰ δὲ ἴδια τῆς τραγωιδίας· διόπερ ὅστις περὶ τραγωιδίας οἶδε σπουδαίας καὶ φαύλης, οἶδε καὶ περὶ ἐπῶν· ἃ μὲν γὰρ ἐποποιία ἔχει, ὑπάρχει τῆι τραγωιδίαι, ἃ δὲ αὐτῆι, οὐ πάντα ἐν τῆι ἐποποιίαι.

The remarks of Stephen Halliwell (*The Poetics of Aristotle, Translation and Commentary* (London, 1987), 81) are helpful and perceptive; 'Epic poetry ... developed from the original impulse to portray and celebrate the actions of outstanding or noble men; but the essence of tragedy, *both in its Homeric* [my italics] and in its later Attic form, involves such characters in great changes of fortune, or transformations, which arouse pity or fear in those who contemplate them.' Halliwell is right to remind us that tragic feeling lies at the very heart of the *Iliad*: it is not by any means the exclusive preserve of Attic drama, but can be traced in Herodotus and, as Macleod pointed out ('Thucydides and Tragedy', *Collected Papers* (Oxford, 1983), 140), in Thucydides: '... his theme, like the tragedians', is suffering on the grand scale, and ... like them, he is not afraid to represent it as the utmost of human experience'. None the less, in the *Alexander*, theatrical imagery or a tragic quotation or an obvious reminiscence or quotation from Homer will usually be sufficient to pin down a passage firmly as 'epic' or 'tragic'.

In the chapters following 4. 5–8 the epic tone prevails: for example we are told that Lysimachus called himself Phoenix, Alexander Achilles, and Philip Peleus, and the taming of Bucephalas is narrated. Horse-taming is a very

---

[11] For recent, perceptive accounts of this relationship cf. R. B. Rutherford, 'Tragic Form and Feeling in the *Iliad*', *JHS* 102 (1982), 145–60, and J. Gould, 'Homeric Epic and the Tragic Moment', in T. Winnifrith *et al.* (eds.), *Aspects of the Epic* (London, 1983).

Iliadic activity: heroes are given the epithet ἱπποδάμος, 'tamer of horses'. Achilles of course has divine horses, so it is appropriate that there should be something distinguished about Alexander's. In ch. 8 we hear more of Alexander's love of Homer: (8. 2)

καὶ τὴν μὲν Ἰλιάδα τῆς πολεμικῆς ἀρετῆς ἐφόδιον καὶ νομίζων καὶ ὀνομάξων, ἔλαβε μὲν Ἀριστοτέλους διορθώσαντος ἣν ἐκ τοῦ νάρθηκος καλοῦσιν, εἶχε δ' ἀεὶ μετὰ τοῦ ἐγχειριδίου κειμένην ὑπὸ τὸ προσκεφάλαιον, ὡς Ὀνησίκριτος ἱστόρηκε (*FGrH* 134 F 38).

In the chapters describing the end of Philip's life the tragic tone is uppermost: in contrast to the campaigns at the start of ch. 9 we hear of αἱ δὲ περὶ τὴν οἰκίαν ταραχαί, the stuff of tragedy, Olympias' βαρυθυμία and Philip's drunkenness sketching the origins of, and foreshadowing, Alexander's own proclivities in these directions. Philip's drunken attempt to attack Alexander is a doublet of the death of Cleitus: here Philip stumbles, and the incident comes to nothing εὐτυχίαι δὲ ἑκατέρου—Cleitus dies δυστυχίαι τινι . . . τοῦ βασιλέως. Philip's troubles arise διὰ τοὺς γάμους καὶ τοὺς ἔρωτας. The quotation from the *Medea* (288)

τὸν δόντα καὶ γήμαντα καὶ γαμουμένην

attributed to Alexander is thus an apposite one to complete the mood: compare also, for example, *Med.* 626 ff.[12]

The destruction of Thebes is a display of θυμός (tempered by the story of Timocleia, which prefigures Alexander's chivalry to Darius' household): Plutarch suggests that Alexander forgave Athens μεστὸς ὢν ἤδη τὸν θυμὸν, ὥσπερ οἱ λέοντες (cf. *Demosthenes* 23. 5). The simile must look back to the portent of Alexander's birth at 2. 4 and is important for what follows, for lions are very much associated with Alexander as Dionysus.[13] It is immediately followed by 13. 4:

[12] Eur. *Med.* 626 ff.: ἔρωτες ὑπὲρ μὲν ἄγαν | ἐλθόντες οὐκ εὐδοξίαν | οὐδ' ἀρετὰν παρέδωκαν | ἀνδράσιν.
[13] Cf. E. E. Rice, *The Grand Procession of Ptolemy Philadelphus* (Oxford, 1983), 112–13: Athenaeus 201f: there were twenty-four extremely large lions in the procession with statues of Alexander and Ptolemy. For lions' role in Dionysiac cult cf. the lion in the Hellenistic Dionysiac procession in the dromos of the Memphian Serapeum and the frieze of the Great Altar of Pergamum. Lions are frequent on later sarcophagi depicting Dionysus' Indian Campaign, either as part

ὅλως δὲ καὶ τὸ περὶ Κλεῖτον ἔργον ἐν οἴνωι γενόμενον, καὶ τὴν πρὸς
Ἰνδοὺς τῶν Μακεδόνων ἀποδειλίασιν, ὥσπερ ἀτελῆ τὴν στρατείαν
καὶ τὴν δόξαν αὐτοῦ προεμένων, εἰς μῆνιν ἀνῆγε Διονύσου καὶ νέ-
μεσιν.

This is the first of several connections between Alexander
and Dionysus, always (with the single exception of 17. 9,
crowning Theodectas' statue in his cups) with sinister force.
In the *Life* Dionysus comes to represent the traits in Alexander which lead him to take his most disastrous actions: his
drinking and his temper.[14] Olympias is also particularly
associated with Dionysus: cf. 2. 9,

ἡ δ' Ὀλυμπιὰς μᾶλλον ἑτέρων ζηλώσασα τὰς κατοχάς, καὶ τοὺς
ἐνθουσιασμοὺς [i.e. the Orphic rites and the orgies of Diony-
sus] ἐξάγουσα βαρβαρικώτερον, ὄφεις μεγάλους χειροήθεις ἐφείλ-
κετο τοῖς θιάσοις . . .

This special link with Dionysus constitutes a bold reinterpre-
tation of the relationship between Alexander and the god:
the Diadochi usually made the connection a complimentary
one to Alexander and hence to his current royal successor:
Dionysus is seen as the world-conqueror, the bringer of
joy, rather than as the Dionysus of the *Bacchae* of Euripides.[15] Plutarch also makes a similar link between Dionysus

of his triumph or drawing the god's chariot. Lions and Alexander: cf. Curt. Ruf.
v. 1. 21 (A. fights a lion in Bactria) and viii. 1. 14 (he is given presents of lions by
the Babylonians). Lions are royal animals in the East. A. hunts lions on the
Alexander sarcophagus; a Delphian statue of Craterus records that C. saved A.'s
life on a lion-hunt (*FD* III (4), 137). A. wore the lion-skin as Heracles: Ath. 537f.

[14] The two are closely associated by Plutarch, as we have seen, at 4. 7–8: they
are seen as springing from the same natural cause.
[15] Clearly in the *Bacchae* both elements are present; but the terrifying aspect is
uppermost in the end. For Alexander as Dionysus in Alexandria cf. Rice, 43, 48
(Dionysus' Indian triumph in the light of Alexander's successes in the East), 67
(Alexander as new Dionysus following in the god's footsteps, identifying land-
marks associated with the god. Cf. Arrian, v. 1. 1 ff., vi. 28. 1 ff., vii. 20. 1 ff., *Ind.*
i. 1 ff., v. 8 ff.). The key text is Athenaeus 200d–201c, the procession of Dionysus
(cf. Rice *passim*, esp. 83–6 and P. M. Fraser, *Ptolemaic Alexandria* (Oxford, 1972),
202–6, 211): Alexander is more the hero of the procession than Dionysus. Dionysus
in military contexts: cf. Eur. *Cyc.* 5 ff., *Ba.* 13–20. The Ptolemies connect
themselves with A. through Dionysus: cf. the genealogy in Satyrus. The procession
is 'the indirect celebration of A. through the glorification of D.' (Rice). Rice sums
up: (191–2) 'The importance of the emphatic presentation of Alexander as the
Neos Dionysos who followed in the footsteps of the god and succeeded as an
equal conqueror in the east can hardly be over-estimated. These scenes from the

and Antony in the *Antony*, with the same sort of effect. To those familiar with the Alexandrian identification, this view of Dionysus as a malevolent force in Alexander's make-up would have been very striking.

The epic tone, as one would expect, is reintroduced with the beginning of the expedition and Alexander's arrival at Troy. The parallelism with Achilles is very strong here, with Alexander's reverence for Achilles' tomb and the anecdote about the lyres (15. 8–9), for which compare *Mor.* 331d above. Coming at the very beginning of the expedition, this acts as a declaration of Alexander's heroic intentions: the pun on his name and Paris' helps to drive home the point. This Alexander will be as completely different from the mythological one as Achilles was: his preoccupations will be with glory and conquest; he will shun the pleasures of the palace and the bedroom with which Paris is particularly associated in Homer. The heroics in the battle of the Granicus should be read in this context (there is a similar arrangement in Arrian). 16. 7 is significant: Alexander has wonderful armour like Achilles:

ἦν δὲ τῆι πέλτηι καὶ τοῦ κράνους τῆι χαίτηι διαπρεπής, ἧς ἑκατέρωθεν εἰστήκει πτερὸν λευκότητι καὶ μεγέθει θαυμαστόν.

In the incident of Philip the Acarnanian and the cup of medicine (ch. 19) we find the exception to the usual use of tragic imagery in the *Life*: for, as Plutarch depicts θαυμαστὴν καὶ θεατρικὴν τὴν ὄψιν of Philip reading the letter accusing him of trying to poison Alexander and Alexander simultaneously drinking the cup which may be poisoned, we find tragic imagery used to illustrate Alexander's best qualities, with admirable economy, in one action: Alexander's trust in his friends, his fondness for the grand gesture, and his physical courage are all brought out. The scene is at once a fine exercise in the sort of character-drawing described in

Dionysiac procession give support to the claims that this picture of Alexander had an Alexandrian origin ... the Ptolemaic kings adopted and publicised this view of Alexander, and shared in the glory of this vision themselves through their claim to a blood-relationship with both A. and D. This in turn enhanced their position as the legitimate heirs of Alexander in Egypt and endowed them with a convenient legitimisation of the divine status of their dynasty.' Cf. also P. Goukowsky, *Essai sur les origines du mythe d'Alexandre* (Nancy, 1978–81), ii *passim*, esp. 79 ff. For the similar link in the *Antony*, cf. esp. *Ant.* 24.

1. 2–3 and simply a tremendous stage-picture. Its economy and ἐναργεία, realized particularly by the skilful narration in 19. 4, fully justify the epithet θεατρικήν.[16]

As Alexander's successes mount up, we find more Homeric reminders—Lysimachus as Phoenix once again at 24. 10, and the placing of the *Iliad* in the precious coffer of Darius at 26. 2 leading into the dream of Homer telling Alexander to found Alexandria in the proper site at 26. 4–5. The 'arming scene' at 32. 8–11 before Gaugamela certainly owes something to those in the *Iliad*, with its careful descriptions of the appearance of the armour and weapons, who made them, and who gave them to the wearer: we may compare for example *Il.* xi. 16 ff.

The burning of Persepolis (ch. 38), however, continues the theme of dubious deeds committed by Alexander while drunk. Dionysus is very much in our minds here: the palace is burned by a band of revellers κώμωι καὶ βοῆι, with Alexander in a garland (38. 5–6). The remark at 23. 1 ἦν δὲ καὶ πρὸς οἶνον ἧττον ἢ ἐδόκει καταφερής, despite Plutarch's careful discussion and rejection of the extremity of the prevailing view in chapter 23, is not really borne out by his narrative. Once again, as after Thebes, repentance speedily follows: cf. 38. 8.

Alexander's relationship with his friends is carefully dwelt on throughout the *Life* (right from 5. 4), and their difficulty in adapting to foreign ways forms a major theme. The transplanting of Greek plants by Harpalus at 35. 15, with limited success (ivy will not grow in the πυρώδης Babylonian soil), is a metaphor for this. Chs. 47 and following skilfully sketch deteriorating relationships with what may conveniently be thought of as a series of scenes. They contrast with 40–42—Alexander's amazement at his friends' extravagance—where one is only just aware of trouble on the horizon and the present is all sweetness and light.

The affair of Philotas and Parmenio leads into the more

[16] It is perhaps possible that the use of θεατρικήν here rather than τραγικήν is significant, either because Plutarch is thinking of another genre, mime, for instance, or because he does not want to label the episode directly as tragic, as, after all, it does turn out happily; if either of these possibilities is correct, then this is an exception which proves a rule.

traumatic episode of Cleitus, who, we remember, saved
Alexander's life at the Granicus. Plutarch's introduction is
extremely interesting: at first sight the affair is ἀγριώτερα,
he says, but if we consider τὴν αἰτίαν καὶ τὸν καιρόν, we see
that it happened οὐκ ἀπὸ γνώμης, ἀλλὰ δυστυχίαι τινι . . . τοῦ
βασιλέως, ὀργὴν καὶ μέθην πρόφασιν τῶι Κλείτωι δαίμονι
παρασχόντος (50. 2). In other words both men suffered from
forces beyond their control. One is reminded of Alexander's
conviction that this incident was part of Dionysus' revenge
for the burning of Thebes. This and the evil omen, the
sacrifices ordered by Alexander (in vain) for the safety of
Cleitus, and the sinister dream linking Cleitus and Philotas,
and the fact that Cleitus goes to his final feast straight from
his unfinished sacrifice all reinforce the impression that
both men are caught in some inexorable divine plan, a
favourite theme of tragedy, exemplified by the *Oedipus
Tyrannus*. Of course it is not a theme confined to tragedy:
historians may make use of such story-patterns too: compare, for example, Hdt. i. 35 ff., the story of Adrastus; but
it is one particularly characteristic of it. The quarrel is
reported with a high proportion of direct speech, which
adds vividness. The climax comes when Alexander loses
control: οὐκέτι φέρων τὴν ὀργὴν. Despite the precautions
taken by Aristophanes, the pleadings of his friends and the
reluctance of the trumpeter, and despite Cleitus' removal,
the killing still occurs: the emphasis on the precautions
taken intensifies the idea of inevitability: it happened despite
everything that mortal man could do. Cleitus' re-entry and
continued defiance, marked by the tragic quotation, seem
to be so irrational as to be the work of his *daimon*. The
terrible remorse which instantly follows the deed emphasizes his horror and how alien it is to Alexander's true
intentions and feelings: his attempt at self-destruction, his
extreme grief, and the seer's reminder of τήν τε ὄψιν ἣν εἶδε
περὶ τοῦ Κλείτου, καὶ τὸ σημεῖον, ὡς δὴ πάλαι καθειμαρμένων
τούτων (52.2), all reinforce the initial impression that here
we are in the world of tragedy, with inexorable divine forces
working on the characters of men to produce disaster which
brings bitter regret. As in a number of tragedies, the gods
work through the men themselves and their characteristics:

in Alexander's case through his propensity for drink and his θυμός. In tragedy Dionysus works on Pentheus' prurience, and Hera, Iris, and Lyssa on Hercles' great strength and force in the *Heracles Mainomenos*. It may well be no accident that the Cleitus episode, with its pattern of madness/murder—remorse—consolation is highly reminiscent of the *Heracles*: Heracles is of course Alexander's other ancestor and is closely associated with him.[17]

A comparison between Plutarch's account of this incident and Arrian's is instructive: Arrian has no evil omens, no dream: Cleitus makes no unfinished sacrifice, though Alexander fails to sacrifice to Dionysus as is usual on that day. Arrian interrupts Cleitus' tirade with his own criticisms of Cleitus, and has almost none of Plutarch's elaborate precautions: Alexander's friends merely try to hold him back and fail. Cleitus' voluntary return is mentioned as an alternative version of Aristobulus, who, however, left the drinking bout without a context, according to Arrian. Cleitus does not use a tragic quotation. It seems very likely from this that Plutarch has carefully constructed his version from various sources to produce the maximum tragic effect.

The consolations of the philosophers Callisthenes and Anaxarchus bring no real relief: for the narrative continues with the destruction of Callisthenes and the Pages' conspiracy which are brought about by too great reliance on the doctrines of Anaxarchus: his words at 52. 6–7 are specifically said to have a bad effect on Alexander: τὸ δὲ ἦθος εἰς πολλὰ χαυνότερον καὶ παρανομώτερον ἐποίησεν ... καὶ τοῦ Καλλισθένους τὴν ὁμιλίαν ... προσδιέβαλε.

As to Anaxarchus' actual words (also in Arrian), Dike is the πάρεδρος of Zeus as early as Pindar (*Ol.* viii. 21 ff.) and Sophocles (*OC* 1381 ff.). But for the idea that the king can

---

[17] Most frequently in art, e.g. on his coins, and on the Alexander sarcophagus. Shakespeare (*Henry V* iv. vii) makes Fluellen compare Henry's rejection of Falstaff with the death of Cleitus: 'Alexander—God knows, and you know—in his rages, and his furies, and his wraths, and his cholers, and his moods, and his displeasures, and his indignations, and also being a little intoxicates in his prains, did, in his ales and his angers, look you, kill his best friend, Cleitus ... I speak but in the figures and comparisons of it; as Alexander kill'd his friend Cleitus, being in his ales and his cups, so also Harry Monmouth, being in his right wits and his good judgements, turn'd away the fat knight with the great belly doublet; ...'.

do no wrong we must turn to Hdt. iii. 31 (of Persia) and to Creon in the *Antigone* (666–7):

ἀλλ᾽ ὃν πόλις στήσειε, τοῦδε χρὴ κλύειν
καὶ σμικρὰ καὶ δίκαια καὶ τἀναντία.[18]

Plutarch transplants in time the downfall of Callisthenes and the Pages' conspiracy to act as an illustration of the deterioration in Alexander's morals (cf. 56. 1)—they really belong to the spring of 327. On the present arrangement the episodes grow organically one out of the other (Arrian too saw the benefits of this plan and also adopted it, apologizing for the change at iv. 14): Callisthenes is first played off against Anaxarchus in the aftermath of the death of Cleitus: his character is then developed. He is represented as an honest, upright, and independent, if rather irritating, character. Plutarch's portrait of him is far more favourable than Arrian's who calls him ὑπαγροικότερον and refers to his ὕβρις καὶ σκαιότης and his ἄκαιρος παρρησία καὶ ὑπέρογκος ἀβελτερία (iv. 10. 1, 12. 6–7). The episode of the speeches (ch. 53) does not show Alexander in a good light, for it is by his request that Callisthenes speaks against the Macedonians and alienates both them and Alexander himself. The quotation from the *Bacchae* which Alexander applies to Callisthenes is by no means really complimentary: it is from Teiresias' speech to Pentheus (and thus indicates an interesting role-reversal when it is put into Alexander's mouth in this context) and continues: (278)

σὺ δ᾽ εὔτροχον μὲν γλῶσσαν ὡς φρονῶν ἔχεις
ἐν τοῖς λόγοισι δ᾽ οὐκ ἔνεισί σοι φρένες.

The story of the kiss (ch. 54) confirms Callisthenes as the proud philosopher, Alexander as the demanding monarch. The treatment of the Pages' conspiracy, far less detailed than Arrian's account, keeps Callisthenes rather than Hermolaüs and the boys in the forefront of our minds, and it is his fate that is dwelt on rather than theirs. His miserable

[18] For discussion on Plutarch's views on ruler-cult cf. K. Scott, 'Plutarch and the Ruler Cult', *TAPA* 60 (1929), 117–35; G. W. Bowersock, 'Greek Intellectuals and the Imperial Cult in the Second Century AD', *Entr. Hardt.* 19 (1972), esp. 187–90; S. R. F. Price, *Rituals and Power* (Cambridge, 1984), 116–17.

end is immediately contrasted with that of Demaratus and his magnificent funeral: we are reminded that Alexander can be loyal and generous to his friends.

The expedition into India moves into the epic sphere again after these dark interludes: Alexander's courage is to the fore, contrasted with the cowardice of Sisimithres in 58. His generous behaviour to Taxiles and Porus recalls his earlier munificence: the death of Bucephalas and the dog Peritas remind us of his gentleness. Then there is his Achillean withdrawal into his tent in protest at his soldiers' reluctance to advance and his relenting to their pleas. The climax of this epic phase of the narrative is of course the battle in the Malli township, where he leapt from the wall into the mêlée: τιναξαμένου δὲ τοῖς ὅπλοις, ἔδοξαν οἱ βάρβαροι σέλας τι καὶ φάσμα πρὸ τοῦ σώματος φέρεσθαι (63. 4). (Cf. also Mor. 343e.)

This is surely to be compared with Achilles' appearance in the closing books of the Iliad, shining in his divine armour: cf. Il. xix. 375 ff.:[19] note the repeated use of σέλας (375, 379) and that the flashing light comes from the movement of the armour. Alexander is never more like Achilles than this, in his magnificent courage: it is a fine touch to mark the resemblance with so plain a reference to his Iliadic model. Arrian, too, makes such a reference, though, as one would expect, in less romantic fashion:

δῆλος μὲν ἦν Ἀλέξανδρος ὢν τῶν τε ὅπλων τῆι λαμπρότητι καὶ τῶι ἀτόπωι τῆς τόλμης . . .

he says at vi. 9. 5.

The hardships of campaign and exploration are contrasted with the unlikely Bacchanalian revel in Carmania in ch. 67. We are not here concerned with its historical credentials: its function in the scheme of Plutarch's narrative is, I think, to introduce a darker phase of the Life. Dionysus, as we have seen, is scarcely a propitious deity for Alexander in

---

[19] Homer, Il. xix. 375 ff.: ὡς δ᾽ ὅτ᾽ ἄν ἐκ πόντοιο σέλας ναύτηισι φανήηι | καιομένοιο πυρός, τό τε καίεται ὑψόθ᾽ ὄρεσφι | σταθμῶι ἐν οἰοπόλωι· τοὺς δ᾽ οὐκ ἐθέλοντας ἄελλαι | πόντον ἐπ᾽ ἰχθυόεντα φίλων ἀπάνευθε φέρουσιν· | ὡς ἀπ᾽ Ἀχιλλῆος σάκεος σέλας αἰθέρ᾽ ἵκανε | καλοῦ δαιδαλέου· περὶ δὲ τρυφάλειαν ἀείρας | κρατὶ θέτο βριαρήν· ἡ δ᾽ ἀστὴρ ὡς ἀπέλαμπεν | ἵππουρις τρυφάλεια, περισσείοντο δὴ ἔθειραι | χρύσεαι, ἃς Ἥφαιστος ἵει λόφον ἀμφὶ θαμειάς.

Tragedy and Epic in Plutarch's Alexander   223

Plutarch's account: it is ominous, therefore, to hear at 67. 7:

τῶι δὲ ἀτάκτωι καὶ πεπλανημένωι τῆς πορείας παρείπετο καὶ
παιδιὰ βακχικῆς ὕβρεως, ὡς τοῦ θεοῦ παρόντος αὐτοῦ καὶ
συμπαραπέμποντος τὸν κῶμον.

Note ἀτάκτωι and πεπλανημένωι pointing the contrast between this and the usual military discipline and swiftness
with which Alexander moves.

Further, his public display of affection towards Bagoas,
which we must be meant to contrast unfavourably with his
earlier σωφροσύνη and his outrage in ch. 22 when Philoxenus
and Hagnon offer him boys, occurs when he is drunk: 67. 8
λέγεται δὲ μεθύοντα αὐτὸν θεωρεῖν ἀγῶνας χορῶν . . .

Alexander's difficulties multiply in the next chapter: he
has ignored the advice of the Gymnosophist Calanus in
65[20] and spread his realm too far, and rebellion is rife (68.
2–3). Troubles at Macedon, Oxyartes' death by Alexander's
own hand, Abuletes' punishment (all in ch. 68) are succeeded by the episode of Cyrus' tomb, whose inscription
ἐμπαθῆ σφόδρα τὸν Ἀλέξανδρον ἐποίησεν, ἐν νῶι λαβόντα τὴν ἀδηλό-
τητα καὶ μεταβολήν: a distinctively tragic theme. Calanus'
death and funeral, with its disastrous aftermath, follow: his
prophecy that he would soon see the king at Babylon and
the deaths from drinking at the funeral continue the feeling
of impending doom. Even Alexander's marriage to Stateira
scarcely lightens the tone; and the misunderstanding with
the Macedonian veterans at 71. 1 ff., though it is resolved,
is an unhappy incident. Arrian, we should note, gives the
Macedonians less reason to complain by omitting the thirty
thousand boys who in Plutarch are the cause of the trouble:
vii. 8–11.

The death of Hephaestion (ch. 72) after eating casseroled
fowl and drinking ψυκτῆρα μέγαν οἴνου while his physician
was at the theatre and Alexander's mourning for him follow.

[20] The Calanus incident, and Alexander subsequently ignoring his advice, is
typical of a *topos* which goes back to Herodotus and (e.g.) Croesus' encounter with
Solon (Hdt. i. 29–32); on the other hand, despite Alexander's heedlessness of
Calanus' counsel, Plutarch obviously does wish to portray him as being well
disposed towards philosophers, as we see from 7–8, 14, and 64. There are
certainly traces of Onesicritus in 64–5: Alexander *philosophus* is being hinted at
here, and it is Onesicritus who visits the sophists in 65.

Here we are irresistibly reminded of Achilles' mourning for
Patroclus: the destruction of the Cossaeans is an ἐναγισμός
for Hephaestion's shade (72. 4), recalling Achilles' human
sacrifice in *Il.* xxiii. 175–7. Here, it might be said, we have
an example of an epic reminiscence being used to develop
the darker side of Alexander's character. This is an exception, however, which proves a rule: Achilles in his mourning
for Patroclus is very much a forerunner of the great tragic
heroes, as Rutherford (art. cit. (n. 11), 145–6) has pointed
out: we have a reference here to the most tragic part of epic.
At the same time it is appropriate that here the ethos is not
purely tragic: for Alexander's mourning for Hephaestion is
not part of the self-destructive side of his nature in the
same way that the murder of Cleitus is.

The portents of Alexander's own death follow immediately on from this (contrasting bitterly with Stasicrates'
elaborate plans for Mount Athos). The effect of the portents
on Alexander is traumatic: 74. 1 αὐτὸς δὲ ἠθύμει καὶ δύσελπις
ἦν πρὸς τὸ θεῖον ἤδη καὶ πρὸς τοὺς φίλους ὕποπτος. This was the
man who drank Philip of Acarnania's medicine προθύμως
καὶ ἀνυπόπτως! Suspicion, fear, and excessive belief in prodigies possess him: 75. 1–2. The trusting man is paranoid, the
brave man a prey to fear, the man who created his own
portents (24. 6–7) sees omens in the tiniest occurrence. The
calamities of tragedy sometimes bring about similar collapses:
Creon the 'hard man' crumbles quickly into submission in
the *Antigone*; the strong man Heracles must be led away
like a child, as he once led his own children, by Theseus;
under the influence of the god Pentheus' puritanism gives
way to the streak of prurience which was always in him.

And it is Dionysus, once again, who dominates Alexander's death. 75. 5, where Plutarch rejects some of the more
romantic versions of Alexander's end (notably that found in
Diodorus), is interesting (and very typical of the style of his
criticism of tragic history elsewhere: cf. n. 6): he says: ταῦτά
τινες ᾤοντο δεῖν γράφειν ὥσπερ δράματος μεγάλου τραγικὸν ἐξό-
διον καὶ περιπαθὲς πλάσαντες. We shall have reason to mention
the 'tragic historians' involved in a moment. The point of
Plutarch's criticism of his sources here is not, I think, that
they saw Alexander's life as a δρᾶμα μέγα and he did not:

Plutarch himself, as I have tried to show, thought it appropriate to illustrate Alexander's life by means of sustained dramatic patterning, as well as seeing matter for straightforward dramatic spectacle in it, for example in the Philip of Acarnania scene. The emphasis, I think, must be on πλάσαντες: there was no need to fabricate a pathetic end to Alexander's life, says Plutarch: and he substitutes for the absurdities of the 'tragic' historians an account which far exceeds theirs in pathos and which has the additional merit of being true—or at least culled from the royal journals. The unforgettable picture of the soldiers filing past Alexander's couch far surpasses the fictions of the sources Plutarch has rejected.

One should not pass from the description of Alexander's death without mentioning a very striking parallel from the end of the *Demetrius*, a life whose whole structure, as de Lacy notes, seems to be conceived in terms of a tragedy: at Demetrius' death we are told that the Macedonian δρᾶμα is at an end. The more oblique link between Alexander and δρᾶμα reflects the less schematized, more complex play which Plutarch makes with tragedy in this *Life*.

For one cannot say simply that tragic colouring means automatically that Plutarch is 'attacking' Alexander. It very often means that Alexander's darker side is to the fore, but the theatrical imagery in the episode of Philip of Acarnania is used to pack some of Alexander's best qualities into one memorable scene. I use the word 'scene' advisedly, for as I hope has become clear, there are scenes in the *Alexander*: great set-pieces told with tremendous ἐναργεία which more than anything else constitute the ingredients of the εἰδοποιία described in chapter 1.

We must now consider tragic history, and whether we should be surprised to find Plutarch, its arch-enemy, apparently succumbing to its charms. The answer to this question, it seems to me, is that put forward by Walbank in his articles on the origins of tragic history:[21] 'tragic' history

[21] Cf. F. Walbank, 'Tragic History: A Reconsideration', *BICS* 2 (1955), 4–14; 'Tragedy and History', *Historia*, 9 (1960), 216–34, repr. *Selected Papers*, ch. 15, 224–41; C. B. R. Pelling, 'Plutarch's Adaptation of his Source-Material', *JHS* 100 (1980), 127–40, esp. 132 n. 26 (see above, pp. 125–54); and D. A. Russell, *Plutarch* (London, 1972), 123.

constitutes no more than a souping-up of the facts for a cheap thrill; although it sometimes made use of theatrical imagery, it has nothing to do with sustained tragic patterning in the sense in which it may be observed in the *Alexander*, the *Demetrius*, or the *Antony*, where it is also extremely important. There is no inconsistency in Plutarch's despising this debased genre and adopting the techniques we have observed perfectly deliberately in his own work for a serious artistic purpose. It is also possible that Plutarch considered that biography, with its greater concentration on individuals, was a more suitable *genre* in which to set up such patterning than history; hence his remarks at 1. 2–3.

Plutarch is sparing in this use of such tragic frameworks, however: he does not, for example, use it in the *Caesar*,[22] which seems surprising: the tragic colouring in the *Demetrius* continues into the *Antony*. It seems clear that something about Alexander's career suggested that it would be a fruitful approach to take, and that Caesar's did not: Alexander was a patron of the arts and a lover of literature (4. 6) and Caesar was not: and Alexander saw himself in epic terms and Caesar did not (the nearest he comes is *Caesar* 11. 2). But perhaps the most decisive reason was that tragic patterning could not fit into Plutarch's conception of Caesar's downfall: for Plutarch, external factors destroyed Caesar, whereas internal forces worked on Alexander, as they did on Demetrius and Antony; Plutarch evidently felt it more appropriate to explain Caesar's end in terms of historical causation and politics, and Alexander's vicissitudes in terms of tragedy, epic, and divine wrath. Onesicritus gave Plutarch the epic strand and the general literary ethos of Alexander's life; the interweaving and

---

[22] For Caesar destroyed by external factors, cf. Pelling, art. cit. 136–7 (above, pp. 115–18). He also notes how material on Caesar's personal (especially sexual) habits, extensively used elsewhere, is largely suppressed in the *Life*. There is a strong atmosphere of divine threat in the last chapters of the *Caesar* (the many omens, the accounts of how Caesar is *nearly* warned more than once of the conspiracy, culminating in Pompey's statue as it were presiding over his death), which could be seen as comparable to the handling of the Cleitus incident in the *Alexander*; but this is never pinned down as tragic in the same manner: an important difference, I think.

balancing of epic and tragic is Plutarch's own original contribution to the tradition: individual versions of incidents are combined, where they exist, to produce the desired result: the elements may spring from others but the product is Plutarch's own.

Possibly, too, Plutarch was inclined towards working with these tragic overtones by Herodotus' account of the Persian Wars, in which there are many tragic elements. The works cover some of the same geographical area, and in many ways Alexander's conquest of Persia is seen as a reversal of, and a reply to, the Persian attempts on Greece: hence Demaratus the Corinthian's remarks at 37. 7. There are a number of Herodotean elements in the *Life*: the relationship of Amyntas and Darius recalls a number of wise but disregarded Greek councillors in Herodotus, for instance, and both works show careful Oriental colouring when dealing with Persian affairs. Above all, there is the episode with the statue of Xerxes at 37. 5, where Alexander, seeing a fallen statue of Xerxes, deposed by looting soldiers, debates whether to set it up again:

πότερόν σε᾽ εἶπε ᾽διὰ τὴν ἐπὶ τοὺς Ἕλληνας στρατείαν κείμενον παρέλθωμεν, ἢ διὰ τὴν ἄλλην μεγαλοφροσύνην καὶ ἀρετὴν ἐγείρωμεν;᾽ τέλος δὲ πολὺν χρόνον πρὸς ἑαυτῶι γενόμενος καὶ σιωπήσας, παρῆλθε.

Xerxes, the tragic king who wept at the ephemeral nature of his great army in Herodotus (vii. 46), is presented in an encounter with Alexander, who, just as he later empathizes with Cyrus (ch. 69), silently ponders the fate of Xerxes. The episodes both form part of the large theme of the contact and conflict between Greek and Persian which Plutarch, like Herodotus before him, found fascinating. I do not find the idea that Plutarch had Herodotus in mind and wanted to elaborate and expand the intimations of tragedy in that author incongruous; as Russell has pointed out (op. cit. (n. 21), 60 ff.), Plutarch's indignation against Herodotus in the *de malignitate Herodoti* is distinctly artificial, and surely assumed for rhetorical purposes.[23]

---

[23] The handling of the material in the *Themistocles* perhaps supports this.

In no other prose author,[24] though, are the poetic genres, tragedy and epic, used in so sophisticated and refined a way to illuminate the tensions within a character. This illustrates not only the different preoccupations of history and biography (Plutarch is concerned with Alexander's internal development more than with his external career, as he makes clear from the beginning) but also just how good Plutarch is at what he does: using the genres in this way Plutarch can produce an account of Alexander, that most complex of characters, which is one of the most memorable he ever wrote, rich in ambiguity, contradiction, and irony and thus magnificently real.

---

[24] With the possible exception of Heliodorus, whose use of stage-terms is extensive and complex. On this cf. J. W. H. Walden, 'Stage-terms in Heliodorus' *Aethiopica*', *HSCP* 5 (1894), 1–43.

9

Hellenic Culture and the Roman Heroes of Plutarch

S. C. R. SWAIN

Plutarch of Chaeroneia stands almost alone among Greeks of the Roman Empire in displaying in his works an extensive knowledge of, and interest in, Rome and Romans. The knowledge of Roman history and the many notes on Roman institutions and usages seen in the *Lives* together with the work specifically devoted to Roman customs, the *quaest. Rom.*, and the celebration of Rome's good fortune, the *de fort. Rom.*, testify to his great sympathy with the Roman way of life. For us Plutarch is a unique bridge between Greece and Rome. But what sort of bridge does he himself envisage between Rome and his own world? In particular, how far does Plutarch believe that Romans share his own Hellenic culture? In answering this question I shall argue that in his presentation of Romans Plutarch often shows himself to be conscious that Hellenic culture had been imported to Rome and could never be fully taken for granted among Romans as it could among Greeks, and that as a consequence it is worth while for him as a student of character to consider how well and with what benefit Romans absorb it.

I. HELLENIC INFLUENCE AT ROME

Plutarch's interest in Hellenic culture at Rome is restricted almost entirely to effects on the individual. If we leave this area aside for the moment, it will be found that he is silent

For helpful suggestions and criticisms of this paper I am indebted to E. L. Bowie, J. L. Moles, and C. B. R. Pelling.

on wide areas where we would see Hellenic influence at
work in Roman life, from portrait statues to imitation of
Alexander and claims to divinity by Republican grandees.[1]
The silence extends to influences which the ancients often
noticed themselves. The generally accepted topos of the
Greek origin of the Latin language has almost no attraction
for him (cf. *Marc.* 22. 7, *Numa* 13. 9–10).[2] Similarly, he
makes surprisingly little effort to discover Greek *aitia*
behind Roman customs.[3] In *Marc.* Plutarch does address
the effect of Hellenic art introduced by Marcellus on the
Roman society of the time, but his remarks there are designed principally to complement the favourable characterization of the hero, as we will see, for it is the benefits of
Hellenism which are highlighted, while hardly anything is
made of the suggestion voiced by the older citizens that
Hellenic civilization was challenging traditional Roman culture (*Marc.* 21. 6). Only at *Cato Maj.* 23. 2–3 is a direct
Roman attack on Hellenic culture as a destructive influence
at Rome cited and refuted.[4] Plutarch's silence on these

---

[1] For statues, cf. *Cato Maj.* 19. 5–6, *praec. ger. reip.* 820b (Rome began to be
full of portrait statues in the time of Cato the elder; Plutarch knows of earlier
Greek statues at Rome, cf. *Numa* 8. 20 with Pliny, *HN* xxxiv. 26). The similarity
of Greek and Roman portrait statues is noted by Dio of Prusa (lxxii. 5), who also
says nothing on Greek origins (contrast Pliny, *HN* xxxiv. 27). The Roman
fascination with Alexander (bibliography in P. A. Stadter, *Arrian of Nicomedia*
(Chapel Hill, NC, 1980), 211 n. 14) might have been exploited rather more by
Plutarch regarding Pompey's craving for power and plans for world conquest
(*Pomp.* 38. 4–5; comparison is made on other levels at 2. 2–4, 34. 7–8, 46. 1–4), the
eastern adventures of Antony (cf. *Ant.* 37. 5), and Caesar's monarchy and divinity
(cf. *Caes.* 11. 6, *Ant.* 6. 3, *Alex.* 28).

[2] Greek origin: E. Gabba, in *Studi Rostagni* (Turin, 1963), 188–94, F. della
Corte, *La filologia latina dalle origini a Varrone*[2] (Florence, 1981), 169–75. Plutarch's caution towards Juba's suggestion of Greek influence in Latin at *Numa* 13.
9–10 (ὁ Ἰόβας ... γλιχόμενος ἐξελληνίσαι ... εἴ γε δὴ δεῖ πρὸς τὴν Ἑλληνικὴν διάλεκτον
ἐξάγειν) should be remembered when he mentions Juba in connection with the
statement that Greek and Latin were mixed together in ancient Italy (*Numa* 7.
10–11 (cf. *Marc.* 5. 5, *quaest. Rom.* 40, 274c, *Rom.* 15. 4). Greek etymologies are
uncommon in Plutarch, and when they do occur (e.g. *quaest. Rom.* 277d, 280a–b)
we may attribute them to his sources, since the idea is ridiculed at *quaest. conv.*
viii. 6, 726d–727a.

[3] The closest he comes is to cite Greek parallels (e.g. *quaest. Rom.* 5. 264f; 37.
273d).

[4] Cato said that 'the Romans would lose their empire when they had become
infected with Greek letters. But time, in which the city's empire reached its
greatest extent and Greek learning and culture as a whole became familiar, shows
that this gloomy forecast was empty.'

matters is attributable partly to a lack of interest, partly to a lack of awareness, coupled with a genuine appreciation of Rome's separate development.[5] He must, though, have known of Romans' special fears about social and moral decay as the Greek disease.[6] His silence here must be deliberate. Indeed, in the case of Lucullus, who spectacularly combined intellectual and material Hellenism, he implicitly denies Greek responsibility.[7] Yet there is nothing which directly links Antony's moral decline with his sojourns in Asia,[8] and in *Sulla* Plutarch avoids the connection Sallust made easily between Asia's *loca amoena voluptaria* (*BC* 11. 5–7) and Sulla's army, and portrays Sulla and his men as corrupting, rather than being corrupted by, Greece (12. 9–14).

One other Greek at least was aware of this possible link. Cato the elder's reproach of Roman luxury, that a fish sold at Rome for more money than an ox,[9] goes back to Polybius (xxxi. 25. 5a), who introduces it while tracing the origins of Roman luxury to the adoption of Greek εὐχέρεια during the Second Macedonian War (xxxi. 25. 4).[10] Plutarch knows that Romans had linked the decline of Greece with particular Greek cultural practices (*quaest. Rom.* 40. 274d–e). Why

[5] *Flam.* 11. 7 ἐναύσματα μικρὰ καὶ γλίσχρα κοινωνήματα παλαιοῦ γένους ἔχειν δοκοῦντες [sc. οἱ Ῥωμαῖοι] should not be pressed: *Flam.* 11 does represent Plutarch's thoughts, but the words are dramatized as those of the Greeks following Flamininus' proclamation of Greek liberty at Corinth. Lack of interest must also account for the silence of Plutarch and other Greeks on the Roman origin of contemporary cultural intrusions in Greece such as pantomime and gladiatorial games, for these activities were closely connected with the Roman imperial festivals (S. R. F. Price, *Rituals and Power: The Imperial Cult in Asia Minor* (Cambridge, 1984), 89).

[6] Cf. *graecari, pergraecari, congraecare*.

[7] Cf. *Luc.* 41. 2 for the Greeks who were troubled by Lucullus' excessive hospitality ὄντως Ἑλληνικόν τι παθόντας. On Lucullus, see N. Petrochilos, *Roman Attitudes to the Greeks* (Athens, 1974), 85.

[8] Asian Greeks are not differentiated from peninsular Greeks in the *Ant.*: when Plutarch talks of Antony behaving properly to the Greeks 'at least at first' (23. 2), he is talking of all the Greeks, and Antony's later bad behaviour is his carousing in Asia at the expense of the Asian cities (24 ff.). This and other aspects of *Ant.* are discussed in *QUCC*, 34 (1990), 151–7.

[9] *Cato Maj* 8. 2 = *reg. et imp. apophth.* 198d, *quaest. conv.* iv. 4, 668b–c.

[10] From the Polybian passage come also Athenaeus, *deipn.* 274f–275a and Posidonius, F 211c Theiler (Diodorus Siculus, xxxvii. 3. 6). See also Polybius, ix. 10 on the moral damage caused to Rome by acquiring the rich artefacts of Syracuse.

then does he ignore the connection made between Roman
degeneration and Greek culture?

Plutarch has much to say on the kind of corruption
which stems from great wealth. But he does not hold that
moral degeneracy is a necessary consequence of money.[11]
Human nature, not money, is what matters. At *Cato Maj.*
18. 4–5 he discusses love of wealth purely as a disease of
man imposed upon the soul by 'the vulgar beliefs of the
outside world'.[12] There is no hint that love of money by
Romans is a phenomenon arising from contact with Greece
or Asia. By the first or second century AD it would have
required a great deal more imagination than Sallust had
needed to envisage Greece as capable of corrupting the
heroes of the Republic. Rather, Plutarch thinks of Greece
and Asia at that time as impoverished and humiliated.[13]
And he notes critically the vast increase in wealth and
luxury from Republican to Imperial times at Rome itself.[14]
As for Polybius' εὐχέρεια, he applies the term equally to
Greeks and to Romans (*Nic.* 8. 6, *Crass.* 7. 7).

Plutarch's exposition of moral and political corruption is
concerned in fact only with power. There is a notable
similarity in the way he sets out the development and effect
of power in Greek and Roman history:[15] for example, the
idea that the people arrogate power to themselves as the
power of the state grows,[16] or the idea that in the early days
of empire the δῆμος is still basically virtuous.[17] The parallels
between early fifth-century Athens and second-century
Rome (both seen as aristocratic) and the later emergence of
pernicious democratic elements, together with a departure

[11] Cf. e.g. *Art.* 24. 9, *Cam.* 2. 6.

[12] Cf. further *Nic.–Cras. synk.* 1. 4, *de cupid. divit.*, *On Wealth frr.* 149–51.

[13] *Sulla* 12. 5–14, 25. 4–5, *Sert.* 24. 5, *Luc.* 7. 6–7, 20. 1–4, *Cim.* 1. 3–2. 2, *Ant.*
24. 5–8, 62. 1, 68. 6–8.

[14] *Marius* 34. 4, *Luc.* 39. 2, *Publ.* 15. 3–6.

[15] For Plutarch's similar presentation of day-to-day politics in Greece and
Rome, cf. H. Aalders, *Plutarch's Political Thought* (Amsterdam, 1982), 28, 30, 35,
37, and particularly on his fondness for the βουλή-δῆμος opposition see C. B. R.
Pelling, in *Past Perspectives: Studies in Greek and Roman Historical Writing*, ed. I.
Moxon, J. Smart, A. Woodman (Cambridge, 1986), esp. 175 ff (below, pp.
339 ff.).

[16] *Them.* 19. 5, *Arist.* 26. 2, *Cato Maj.* 14. 4, 27. 3.

[17] *Arist.* 22. 1, 4, *Cato Maj.* 16. 8, esp. *Aem.* 10. 1, 11. 3–4, *Aem.–Tim. synk.*
2. 2.

from the ancestral constitution, are clear.[18] In earlier times
political disputes are still moderate.[19] Later, the underlying
split between the people and the ruling class becomes apparent.[20] The truly able leader must control the δῆμος,
resist their impulses,[21] and prevail over their sycophants.[22]
Similar phraseology helps to identify common trends. For
example, at *Them.* 4. 5 Plutarch wonders whether Themistocles destroyed τὴν ἀκρίβειαν καὶ τὸ καθαρὸν τοῦ πολιτεύματος,
and at *Cato Maj.* 4. 2 explains that ἤδη τότε τῆς πολιτείας τὸ
καθαρὸν ὑπὸ μεγέθους οὐ φυλαττούσης. Pericles has to 'impose
a bridle' on the people (*Per.–Fab. synk.* 1. 4), which is what
Scipio Nasica wants to do at *Cato Maj.* 27. 3. The pattern
Plutarch works with is the familiar one: 'power corrupts'.
Compare *Cato Maj.* 4. 2 again where the degeneration of
the government is introduced early on: in the second century 'the state had already become too large to preserve its
integrity, but control in many spheres and over many men
brought a mixture of many customs and the acceptance of
all kinds of ways of life'. *Per.* 15. 1, 2 offer good parallels.
Again, Sparta gives up her hegemony when she sees her
generals corrupted by 'the magnitude of their powers'
(*Arist.* 23. 7). The corruption of Roman society is caused δι'
ὄγκον ... καὶ δύναμιν (*Arist.–Cato Maj. synk.* 1. 3), not by
luxury, eastern promise, or Hellenic culture.

II. HELLENIC INFLUENCE ON ROMANS

Plutarch ignores Roman myths about the effect of Hellenism on Roman society. His interest lies in the effect of
Hellenism on Romans as people. The attainment of Hellenic
culture and education occupies a central position in his

[18] e.g. *Arist.* 2. 1, *Aem.* 38. 2, 6; *Cim.* 15. 1–2, *Per.* 7. 8, *Gracchi* 16. 1, 26. 3–4,
Caes. 14. 2
[19] *Cim.* 17. 9, *Gracchi* 20. 1.
[20] *Per.* 11. 2–3, cf. e.g. *Alc.* 13. 5, *Nic.* 6. 1, *Phoc.* 34. 6; *Gracchi* 20. 1, *Mar.* 35.
1, *Caes.* 6. 1 ff., cf. e.g. *Pomp.* 25. 7, *Cic.* 33. 2. The opposition between the
people and the establishment is also the background to politics in the very early
period (*Thes.* 24–5, 32. 1–2), *Sol.*, *Rom.* (13. 7, 27. 8–9), *Numa* (2. 3, 5), *Publ.*,
Cor., *Cam.*).
[21] *Per.* 15. 1, 20. 3, *Aem.* 11. 2, 38. 2. 6.
[22] *Alc.* 19. 7, 34. 10, *Phoc.* 32. 3, *Luc.* 42. 8, *Cato Min.* 18. 3.

thought as a moralist and a biographer because of its importance to character formation.[23] Plutarch's ideas here, as set
out especially in de virt. mor., are Aristotelian. The soul has
a rational and an irrational part (442a–c). Character (ἦθος) is
the quality which the irrational takes on through habit (ἔθει)
as it is moulded by the rational, enabling the rational to
control the passions (443c–d).[24] The ἕξις ('established state')
of the soul is the condition of the irrational ἐξ ἔθους ἐγγενο-
μένη, κακία μέν, ἂν φαύλως, ἀρετὴ δ', ἂν καλῶς, ὑπὸ τοῦ λόγου
παιδαγωγηθῇ τὸ πάθος (443d). Education is a crucial part of
this habit-forming,[25] for Plutarch also envisages λόγος
('reason') co-operating with νόμος ('law' or 'custom') as an
external force—παιδεία—keeping the passions in check
(452d). As he puts it at de soll. anim. 962c. 'λόγος is im-
planted by nature, but σπουδαῖος λόγος καὶ τέλειος is the
product of care and instruction'. Similarly, when the soul
has acquired bad habits a course of (re-)training is needed
to restore it.[26]

It is no surprise that Plutarch should be interested in the
question of how education affects individuals; the surprise
is that he approaches the question differently for Greeks
and for Romans. The evidence assembled in the following
pages, which is drawn mostly from the Parallel Lives,
suggests that Romans are far more likely to be scrutinized
from the angle of education than Greeks, and that when
Greeks are scrutinized in this respect the examination is far
less thorough. The only plausible explanation of this situation is that Plutarch feels that good education cannot be
assumed for Romans as it can for Greeks, since παιδεία had
not been available from the start at Rome but had been
introduced later on (as a result of contact with Greece). As
a consequence an effective method of evaluating character

[23] Educational works in the Moralia include de aud. poet., de ad., de prof. in
virt., max. cum princ. phil. esse dis., ad princ. indoct.; lost works include Lamp. Cat.
106 The proper use of school exercises, 233 Introductions to philosophy, frr. 128–33
from The necessity of educating one's wife. The relationship between character and
education is discussed more fully by me in Phoenix 43 (1989), 62–8.
[24] τὴν ποιότητα ταύτην καὶ τὴν διαφορὰν ἔθει λαμβάνει τὸ ἄλογον ὑπὸ τοῦ λόγου πλαττό-
μενον. For ἦθος/ἔθος, cf. de sera num. vind. 551e, Aristotle, EN 1103ᵃ17 f., Plato,
Laws 792e.
[25] It is aided by age, de sera num. vind. 552d, Fab. 3. 7, Them. 2. 7.
[26] Cf. de vit. pud. 530e, de sera num. vind. 551d, de gen. Socr. 584e.

in the *Lives* of Roman heroes is to ask with what benefit they had absorbed Greek culture.[27] The picture which emerges from the *Parallel Lives* may be introduced by material in the *Moralia*, which shows a similar approach to Romans who are Plutarch's contemporaries. Here Plutarch is not concerned with character, but he does seem to expect a somewhat lower standard of culture from Romans than from Greeks, and to suggest the importance for Romans of acquiring and utilizing Hellenic culture. As we would expect, in the *Moralia* Roman examples in essays concerned with cultural, social, and philosophical issues are quite rare. It is worth making this point because Plutarch takes his illustrations of statecraft readily from both Greece and Rome (*de cap. ex inim. util., an seni resp. ger. sit., praec. ger. reip.*). Works dedicated to Plutarch's Roman friends are for the most part intellectually undemanding, while in the after-dinner conversations of the *quaestiones convivales* Plutarch's Roman hosts/guests seem to be wary of falling short intellectually and to be ready to defer to the dominant Hellenism.

Several of Plutarch's works are dedicated to Romans. Sosius Senecio, recipient of the *Parallel Lives*, is also the dedicatee of *de profectibus in virtute* and the *quaestiones convivales*.[28] Paccius, an unknown, receives on request *de tranquillitate animi*.[29] The brothers Avidius Nigrinus and Avidius Quietus are honoured with *de fraterno amore*, and Quietus with *de sera numinis vindicta*.[30] Herennius Saturninus receives *adversus Colotem*.[31] Further, two of Plutarch's

---

[27] As D. A. Russell, *Plutarch* (London, 1973), 132 observes with regard to the hero Marius who rejects the benefits of Hellenism, 'Most Romans, for Plutarch, had a potentiality for barbarism.'

[28] C. P. Jones, *JRS* 60 (1970), 98–104, *Plutarch and Rome* (Oxford, 1971), 54–7. The suggestion that Sosius Senecio in fact hailed from the East (R. Syme, *Historia*, 17 (1968), 101 n. 127 = *Roman Papers*, ii, ed. E. Badian (Oxford, 1979), 688 n. 3, Jones (1970), 103) is insecure. The only probable basis is the phrase τὴν ἐκ προγόνων εὔνοιαν εἰς τὴν πόλιν in a *titulus honorarius* (*IGRR* iv. 779) cited by Jones from the Phrygian town of Apameia honouring Sosius' daughter. The words are more likely to refer to Sosius' father-in-law, Sex. Iulius Frontinus, than to Sosius himself. The argument for discounting eastern origin will be elsewhere set out by me more fully.

[29] Jones (n. 28), 59–60.

[30] Jones (n. 28), 51–3.

[31] Jones (n. 28), 57, 63.

S. C. R. Swain

dialogues have Roman interlocutors: Sextius Sulla and Minicius Fundanus share *de cohibenda ira*, and Sulla takes part
in *de facie quae in orbe lunae apparet*.[32] It has been pointed
out that Greek authors of the late second to early first
centuries BC and later did not dedicate difficult works to
Roman patrons.[33] Plutarch's dedications, though not to
patrons, are comparable. *De prof. in virt.*, *de tranq. an.*, *de
frat. am.*, the *quaest. conv.*, *de sera num. vind.*, are not
difficult works. The same is true of *de cohib. ira*. Only *de
fac. quae in orbe lun. app.* and *adv. Col.* require any philosophical understanding. Sextius Sulla, who speaks in the
former, is 'a man who lacks neither learning nor charm' (*Rom.*
15. 3); Saturninus, recipient of the latter, is hailed as φιλόκαλον
και φιλάρχαιον (*adv. Col.* 1107e). But it is unlikely that
Saturninus, a career soldier, or even the amiable Sulla are ever
thought of by Plutarch as philosophers (Romans are in fact
hardly ever so described).[34] The level of understanding
attributed to them is more a mark of honour than of reality.

Sextius Sulla appears also in the *quaest. conv.* He is
clearly a good friend of Plutarch, for we find him hosting a
dinner to welcome Plutarch back to Rome after a long
absence (*quaest. conv.* viii. 7–8). Here as elsewhere in the
quaest. conv. Greek culture dominates. The *cena adventicia*
(viii. 7. 727b τὸ ὑποδεκτικόν) is hijacked by the guests into a
discussion of Greek philosophy without mention of the
Roman music and poetry traditional to it.[35] Plutarch, whose
modesty is not always apparent in the *quaest. conv.*, tells us
that his words gave the others (not all Romans) λόγων ἄδειαν
('licence to speak', 7. 728b).[36] Sulla, though, in alluding to
the myth of Tereus, Procne, and Philomela, is careful to
accord with Greek convention in making Philomela the
swallow rather than the nightingale as Romans usually did
(7. 727d–e).[37] This may be out of deference to Plutarch or

---

[32] Sulla: Jones (n. 28), 60; Fundanus: Jones 58–66.

[33] E. Rawson, *Intellectual Life in the Late Roman Republic* (London, 1985), 57.

[34] See n. 69 with text.

[35] A traditional Roman occasion—R. Nisbet and M. Hubbard, *A Commentary
on Horace: Odes Book 1* (Oxford, 1970), 401–2, on Horace *Odes* i. 36 (*Et ture et
fidibus iuvat*); music and poetry—O. Murray, *JRS* 75 (1985), 47.

[36] Modesty: v. 2. 674f–675b, v. 3. 677b (see below).

[37] Roscher, iii. 2. 2347, 3024.

from his own inclination, or one may suggest that in writing the question up Plutarch substituted what he considered to be the correct version.

There is a parallel to this in the presentation of Sosius Senecio, one of the two major Roman dining companions. At i. 5. 623c Sosius quotes Sophocles' lines about Thebes: ὁμοῦ μὲν θυμιαμάτων ... ὁμοῦ δὲ παιάνων τε καὶ στεναγμάτων (*OT* 4–5). This is one of Plutarch's favourite quotations,[38] and he always takes the lines as a pointed paradox ('hymns of joy and lamentations'). This reading was surely not Sophocles' own (in his city 'paeans' must mean 'prayers for deliverance'), though it may have become the standard one (cf. Athenaeus, *deipn.* 420f).[39] Sosius uses the paradox to illustrate the confused soul of the lover, and Plutarch also uses it of the soul at *de superstit.* 169d and *de virt. mor.* 445d. It seems likely that Plutarch's interpretation and application of the lines have come to be Sosius' own. This would fit in with his general presentation as a man of good average intelligence who is familiar with the major Greek poets and philosophers, and no more.[40] Sosius appears in no question which requires serious independent thought.[41] Typical of his characterization is the question where Plutarch, displaying his own erudition by citing an obscure author, abandons the dramatic representation to explain to Sosius that 'the Prokles I mean was a fellow-student of Xenocrates in the Academy' (v. 3. 677b).[42] We should not forget that this Roman soldier at some point confides in Plutarch his problems in attaining true virtue and elicits from him a guide on how to make progress towards it (*de prof. in virt.* 75a ff.).[43]

---

[38] 95c, 169d, 445d, *Ant.* 24. 3.

[39] Cf. C. B. R. Pelling, *Plutarch: Life of Antony* (Cambridge, 1988), 178–9.

[40] He cites Homer, Pindar, Sophocles, Menander, Theophrastus, Hecataeus of Abdera, and knows something of the Stoics (ii. 3. 637a, cf. *de prof. in virt.* 75d) and Epicureans (v introd. 672d).

[41] He appears six times on six separate occasions (i. 1, i. 5, ii. 1, ii. 3, iv. 3, v. 1).

[42] For Prokles, see Müller, *FHG* ii. 342 Menecrates fr. 2 with note; F. Fuhrmann, *Plutarque: Œuvres morales* (*Coll. des univ. de France*); ix/2 (Paris, 1978), 169. Suspension of dramatic representation: Fuhrmann ib.

[43] The date of *de prof. in virt.* is unknown (before 116—C. P. Jones, *JRS* 56 (1966), 73; and see above, p. 123), though Plutarch may imply that Sosius is still a νέος (i.e. under 30 or so; cf. 79a, 85c–d).

The presentation of Plutarch's other main Roman companion, Mestrius Florus, is comparable.[44] Florus, who is about Plutarch's age,[45] emerges as a more educated man than Sosius. Plutarch describes him as having a philosophical nature (viii. 10. 734d). He likes the philosophers, especially Plato.[46] He is φιλάρχαιος (vii. 4. 702d), and Plutarch uses the speculations of his son and his son-in-law on archaic Roman customs in the *quaest. Rom.* (vii. 4. 702d–704b; *quaest. Rom.* 64, 279d, 75, 281f). But Florus defers wholly to Hellenic culture in the questions. He demands 'a good Hellenic answer' to a query at v. 10. 685a. He pretends to be in love with a Greek dinner guest, Tyndares, at viii. 2. 718f–719a. And in the discussion about σκιαί (vii. 6), which is pursued at his request (707c), the answers about this prevalent Roman habit (707a, 708b) draw exclusively on Greek literature without commenting on the origin of the term. Like Sosius Florus tends only to ask questions, not to answer them.[47]

Plutarch expects his Roman dining companions to use Hellenic culture in the conversations while paradoxically presenting them as being not fully and absolutely at ease with it. He is convinced of the need to encourage them to acquire it more completely (*de prof. in virt.*). With this experience of his Roman friends, it is quite understandable that he is interested in examining how far and with what benefit Hellenic culture is absorbed by his Roman heroes in the *Lives*, who are also thought of, with their Greek pairs, as guests whom he is entertaining (*Aem.* 1. 2 συνδιαιτήσει καὶ συμβιώσει . . . ἐπιξενούμενον ἕκαστον . . . ὑποδεχόμενοι).[48]

---

[44] For Florus see Jones (n. 28), 48–9. He obtained for Plutarch his Roman citizenship (*SIG³* 829A). Florus appears in thirteen questions on ten separate occasions (i. 9; iii. 3, 4, 5; v. 7; v. 10; vii. 1; vii. 2; vii. 4; vii. 6; viii. 1, 2; viii. 10).

[45] Jones (n. 28), 49.

[46] He also mentions Aristotle, Protagoras, Pyrrhon, and the historian Phylarchus.

[47] Sosius: see i. 1. 613d, ii. 1. 629f, v. 1 (no speech); Florus: i. 9 (no speech), iii. 5. 651f, 652b, v. 10. 684e, vii. 1. 698e, vii. 2. 701a, vii. 4. 702e, vii. 6. 707c, viii. 10 (no speech); note, though, that Sosius does speak in i. 5. 623a–d, ii. 3. 636e–638a (a long speech), and iv. 3. 666d–667a, and Florus speaks in iii. 3 and iii. 4. 650a, 651c–e (the same meal as iii. 5), v. 7. 680c–f, viii. 1. 717d–e, and viii. 2. 719a–c (the same meal as viii. 1).

[48] Note that two of the surviving single *Lives*, *Galba* and *Otho*, concern men who lived during Plutarch's lifetime. Plutarch is not interested in the education of

III. HELLENIC EDUCATION IN THE ROMAN
LIVES

I turn now to the evidence on Romans and Hellenic education afforded by the *Parallel Lives*. I shall outline first Plutarch's understanding of the advent of Hellenic education at Rome, and the differing approaches which he adopts towards Romans and Greeks in relation to education. Then as examples I shall take *Coriolanus*, showing a hero suffering from the absence of παιδεία in early Rome, *Marius*, which with its pair *Pyrrhus* shows clearly the contrasting approach to Romans and Greeks, and finally *Marcellus* and *Lucullus*, which illustrate in different ways Plutarch's interest in bringing out the benefits of Hellenic culture.[49]

Plutarch traces the beginning of Hellenic culture at Rome in *Marcellus*.[50] We tend to think of Marcellus as an archetypal Roman soldier, but Plutarch tells us at the beginning of his *Life* that he was also 'an enthusiast for Hellenic learning and literature' (1. 3). The silence on Greek culture in the biography of his contemporary, Fabius Maximus, serves to highlight the unexpected presentation. The emphasis on Hellenism may be Plutarch's development of Marcellus' description of Archimedes, in which he alludes to the culture of the *symposion* (17. 2). It is probably encouraged by Posidonius' narrative of Marcellus' campaign in Sicily. Marcellus' Hellenism is closely associated with Plutarch's stress in the *Life* on the propriety and Hellenic character of Roman religion at the time (3. 6), a stress which ties in with themes in the paired *Pelopidas* (*Pel.* 21. 5–6). Plutarch's interest in Marcellus' Hellenism leads him to extenuate his

these heroes, though he does observe the consequences for Rome of not having educated leaders in the period after Nero's death at *Galba* 1. 3–4 (cf. A. Georgiadou, *ICS* 13/2 (1988), 349–65).

[49] I am not concerned with Romulus, Publicola, or Camillus, whose *Lives* offer nothing on the subject, nor with Numa, who is a semi-divine, semi-mythological hero, and something of a special case (but see n. 75).

[50] Cf. Porcius Licinus fr. 1 Buechner: *Poenico bello secundo Musa pinnato gradu* | *intulit se bellicosam in Romuli gentem feram*; but Plutarch (or his source) is unlikely to have been affected by this tradition (for which see F. Leo, *Geschichte der römischen Literatur*, i (Berlin, 1913), 388, 436).

war crimes in Sicily (*Marc.* 20). He is keen to applaud him
for introducing Rome to 'Hellenic grace' in the form of
works of art taken from Syracuse (21. 4), and to be able to
present to us the hero who 'taught the Romans to give
honour and admiration to the beauties and marvels of
Greece' (21. 7). The special stress on Hellenism in *Marc.*,
is paralleled well in *Lucullus*, where the hero's education
and culture are accorded great prominence (cf. esp. 1. 4–8,
42. 1–4), no doubt principally because of his political aid to
Chaeroneia and Greece during the Mithridatic War (7. 4–7,
20. 1–6; *Cim.* 1–2). In Lucullus' age Hellenic education is
no surprise in itself. In Marcellus' Rome Plutarch is
aware that Hellenic culture is not readily available. Hence
Marcellus, despite his Hellenic tastes, is not fully educated
and succumbs to a fatal ambition in old age (28. 6). One
may compare Flamininus. He is 'a naturally good man'
(2. 5) who is 'humane in appearance, a Hellene in voice
and in language' (5. 7); but he too lacks a proper Hellenic
education (1. 4), and he too later becomes the victim
of φιλοτιμία (20–1). The surrender to ambition is closely
connected with insufficient παιδεία, for φιλοτιμία is particularly dangerous to statesmen unless regulated by education.[51]

Aemilius Paullus is the first hero we hear of who is said
to receive 'a native and ancestral education' (*Aem.* 6. 8),[52]
and also the first to set aside the traditional pursuits of
Roman youth (litigation and levies) in order to win a
'reputation for courage, justice, and trust' (2. 6). The Hellenic tone of this has no doubt been invented by Plutarch
on the basis of what Polybius says about the upbringing

[51] Particularly dangerous for statesmen: *Ag./Cleom.* 2. 3, *Arist.–Cato Maj.*
synk. 5. 4, *praec. ger. reip.* 819f–820f. 825f (note that φιλοτιμία can be a good thing;
see n. 61); regulated by education: *de virt. mor.* 452d τὰ πάθη τῶν νέων . . . φιλοτιμίαν.
ὧν ἐμμελῆ καὶ σωτήριον ἀφὴν ἁπτόμενος ὁ λόγος καὶ ὁ νόμος εἰς τὴν προσήκουσαν ὁδὸν
ἀνυσίμως καθίστησι τὸν νέον. See generally A. Wardman, *Plutarch's Lives* (London,
1974), 115–24. Note that Plutarch thinks that Romans are particularly prone to
one form of ambition, φιλαρχία—at any rate 16 of the 18 instances of the word in
the *Lives* concern Roman heroes (and of these 5 are to do with Pompey).
[52] It is not clear what Plutarch means by this—probably military training (cf.
Cor. 1. 6), probably also (forensic) oratory which he thinks of, perhaps anachronistic-
ally, as characterizing even early Rome (*Publ.* 2. 1, *Cor.* 27. 1, 39. 6, *Fab.* 1. 7–9,
Luc. 1. 3); see below, p. 248.

and education of Aemilius' son, Scipio Aemilianus (xxxi. 25–30). Scipio rejects similar traditional activities of Roman youth (xxxi. 25. 8, 29. 8–12) in favour of securing a reputation for σωφροσύνη and καλοκἀγαθία (28. 10), and it is likely that Plutarch has simply transposed the education given to the son by the father to the father himself (though he is careful not to fabricate details of specific teachers or syllabuses).[53] Plutarch's assumption that Hellenic παιδεία is available to Aemilius' sons at Rome (*Aem.* 6. 8–9) is clearly based on Polybius xxxi. 24. 6–7, where Polybius tells Scipio shortly after 167 that he will not lack tutors in the subjects which interest him owing to the present influx of teachers from Greece.[54] One suspects in fact that Polybius' Greek educators are anachronistic: certainly at this time Aemilius himself had to import a teacher for his sons from Athens.[55] But Plutarch, while generally aware of the timescale of the introduction of Hellenic culture, would not have argued with him.[56] Plutarch's own statement that a real influx of 'philosophies, sophistries, and casuistry'[57] had already occurred by the time of the Cimbric wars (*de fort. Rom.* 318e, 322d) is basically correct, even if there were no major scholars at Rome for a while after Polybius and Panaetius.[58]

By the late Republic Plutarch can of course take the

[53] Similarly there are no details about the education of Cato the elder who is well versed in Greek life and letters (*Cato Maj.* 2. 3–6, 4. 1, 8. 4, 8. 14, 9. 3, 13. 1, 20. 3, 24. 8) in spite of apparent hostility (22, 23. 1–24. 1); he is merely described as an 'opsimath' (2. 5).

[54] πολὺ γὰρ δή τι φῦλον ἀπὸ τῆς Ἑλλάδος ἐπιρρέον ὁρῶ . . . τῶν τοιούτων ἀνθρώπων. The date is indicated by Scipio being 18 (xxxi. 24. 1)—see F. Walbank, *A Historical Commentary on Polybius* iii (Oxford, 1979), 497 ad loc. It is reasonable to assume that παιδεία was also an important element in Plutarch's lost *Scip. Aem.*, but impossible to estimate how important (cf. *Luc.* 38. 4 on Scipio's unreasonable ambition in later years).

[55] This was Metrodorus, *pictor idemque philosophus* (Pliny, *HN* xxxv. 135).

[56] Cf. *Arat.* 38. 12—Phylarchus is not trustworthy 'unless supported by the testimony of Polybius'.

[57] λόγοι, σοφίσματα, στωμυλία; for στωμυλία ('clever talk', 'philosophers' claptrap') cf. *de aud.* 42e, *Cim.* 4. 5.

[58] Cf. Rawson (n. 33), 5. Plutarch will mention the presence of Greek scholars at Rome (Polybius, *Cato Maj.* 9. 2–3; Blossius, *Gracchi* 8. 6; Philon, *Cic.* 3. 1; Panaetius? *Scip. Aem.*), and knows of their stimulating effects on Roman philosophy (Lucullus' support of Antiochus against Cicero's support of Philon *Luc.* 42. 3–4), but is not interested in who was where at what time.

availability of Greek education for granted, and is free to explore its effects. There is a good deal on particular teachers and studies.[59] One might expect that the education of Roman heroes would in most cases simply be assumed. But Plutarch's treatment of the subject differs wildly. In some *Lives* there is little on it, in others a lot. The amount of information Plutarch inherits from sources does not seem greatly to determine the extent and relevance of education in a *Life*. For example, there was obviously a good deal more material available on education for Cicero than for Lucullus, yet education is of great importance in the *Lives* of both men. There is a variety of factors at work. One certain reason for examining a hero from this angle is his degree of contentedness and freedom from ambition (cf. 143 (below, 261)). To take Lucullus and Cicero, it is explicitly stated that Lucullus overcomes φιλοτιμία and is happy to give up politics for study because he has benefited from παιδεία (*Luc.* 1. 6, 42. 4), whereas Cicero's early political career is dominated by φιλοτιμία and a yearning for δόξα which continues despite attempts to reason himself out of it (6. 4–5). In the personal crisis of exile Cicero's education again fails to help him (32. 5–7), and the attentions of philosophers are unable to console him after his daughter's death (41. 8).[60] Similarly, Marius' unhappy ambition in old age is clearly associated by Plutarch with his rejection of Hellenic values (*Marius* 1. 3–4, 45. 10–46. 5).

However, Plutarch by no means feels that ambition is always or necessarily a bad thing.[61] After Marius Caesar is his most ambitious Roman (*Caes.* 58. 4–5); but no link is made between φιλοτιμία and education, perhaps because Caesar's ambition—while not finally satisfying (cf. 69. 1)— is not destructive to him. In fact there is very little informa-

---

[59] Note that we do not really have anything in the *Lives* on what Romans rejected in Greek education: at *quaest. Rom.* 274d–e Plutarch remarks on their strong aversion to athletics (cf. H.-I. Marrou, *Histoire de l'education dans l'antiquité*[6] (Paris, 1965), 363–6), and at *Cic.* 5. 2 notes τὰ Ῥωμαίων τοῖς βαναυσοτάτοις πρόχειρα καὶ συνήθη ῥήματα Γραικὸς καὶ σχολαστικός.

[60] For excessive grief as a sign of ineffective education, cf. *Cato Min.* 11. 3 ἐμπαθέστερον ... ἢ φιλοσοφώτερον (Cato's reaction to Caepio's death), *consol. ad uxor.* 608c, 609b, 611a (the need for 'correct reasoning').

[61] Cf. *de cap. ex inim. util.* 92d, *de virt. mor.* 452b, *Ages.* 5. 5, *Lys.* 2. 4.

tion at all on Caesar's education, which is not due simply to
the loss of the early chapters, since the theme is not developed later,[62] but rather to Plutarch's overriding interest in
the political background.[63] Pompey and Crassus are also
ambitious men and are not criticized for it in respect of
education or anything else, perhaps because there is no
element of κακοήθεια to their ambition (*Pomp.* 49. 14; *Crass.*
7. 5).[64] As with Caesar there is nothing substantial on
education in their *Lives*, which may again be due to the
dominance of other themes.[65] In the case of Crassus Plutarch does at least suggest that his φιλοπλουτία was due to
'an instability and discordance of character' (*synk.* 1. 4),
which is often indicative of deficient education.[66] Sulla is
another late Republican hero who displays ἀνωμαλία in
character (*Sulla* 6. 14–15, 30. 6); but again no connection is
made between his failings and education, probably because
Plutarch develops other themes rather than because Sulla's
success in life makes moralizing about deficient education
otiose.[67] With Antony, a particularly complex creation,
Plutarch may have felt that his degeneration could not be
crudely attributed to poor education (and in *Ant.* he is not
so interested anyway in Helleno-Roman contrasts).[68]

More interesting are Cato the younger and Brutus. Cato

[62] Loss of early chapters: C. B. R. Pelling, *CQ* 23 (1973), 343–4.
[63] There is a little on Caesar's rhetorical education under Apollonius Molon (3.
1, corresponding to Alexander's tuition under Aristotle, *Alex.* 7–8). Note how
Plutarch uses Caesar's study with Apollonius to introduce his prosecutions of
Cornelius Dolabella and Antonius Hybrida (4. 1–3), whereas in fact these unsuccessful trials (in 77–6) were followed by the stay on Rhodes (75; Suetonius *DJ* 4.
2; M. Gelzer, *Caesar: Der Politiker und Staatsmann*[6] (Wiesbaden, 1960), 20–1).
[64] Contrast Marius (*Marius* 25. 8) and Cicero (*Cic.* 5. 6).
[65] Note *Pomp.* 8. 7: Plutarch has no time to dwell on Pompey's early life.
Pompey is pictured as having an interest in literature and philosophy (10. 8, 42.
9–11, 52. 5, 75. 4–5); see Rawson (n. 33), 104–9. Crassus 'is said to have had an
encyclopaedic knowledge of history, and was also something of a philosopher,
holding with the doctrines of Aristotle' (3. 6); cf. *Cic.* 25. 4 (interest in Stoic doctrine).
[66] Cf. *Arat.* 10. 5 τὴν δὲ τοιαύτην ἀνωμαλίαν ἔνδεια λόγου φιλοσόφου . . . ἀπεργά-
ζεται. Note that Crassus' wide education (*Crass.* 3. 6; see n. 65) is only alleged
(λέγεται).
[67] Note that Sertorius like Sulla undergoes a change of character (*Sert.* 10. 5–7,
Sulla 30. 6), but Plutarch has nothing in this *Life* on education and affirms that
Sertorius' προαίρεσις and φύσις were in fact noble.
[68] Plutarch does comment drily on Antony's 'schooling' in uxoriousness and
pleasure (10. 6 διδασκάλια . . . πεπαιδαγωγημένον, 29. 1 διεπαιδαγώγει).

is one of a very few Romans—politicians or scholars—who
is ever called 'philosopher'.[69] He is not described thus in
his own *Life*, and I have argued elsewhere that his importance to Plutarch is principally as a statesman.[70] However,
in the *Life* Plutarch does present him as having a wide
interest in philosophy, particularly Stoic philosophy. Education is not connected with routine flaws in *Cato*. Rather,
Plutarch uses Stoicism to illustrate the flaws of Cato's
statemanship, and he goes as far as to blame Cato's philosophical principles for the outbreak of the Civil War (30. 9–
10, 49. 6, 50. 2; *Phoc*. 3. 2). Plutarch is also interested in
philosophy in *Brutus*, where Brutus' education is tempered
especially by Platonism (1. 3, 2. 2–3). It is probably because
of his Platonism that Brutus' rigid principles, which in
reality have a strong Stoic colour like Cato's, are never
criticized in the context of his own political failures.[71]

There is an important difference between the *Lives* of the
Roman and the Greek heroes. Although Plutarch can
assume that his Greek heroes have a Greek education, the
effects of this παιδεία are not regularly explored to any great
extent. This is the more surprising because in most of the
Parallel Lives Plutarch is careful to interweave themes developed in one *Life* with those in the other.[72] This is the case

[69] *Cato Maj*. 27. 7, *Brut*. 2. 1, *Pomp*. 40. 2. The only other examples seem to
be the astrologist, scholar, and philosopher P. Nigidius Figulus (*an seni resp. ger.
sit* 797d; used at *quaest. Rom*. 268f; cf. *Cic*. 20. 3), and the polymath M. Terentius
Varro (*Rom*. 12. 3; used on several occasions, cf. E. Valgiglio, in *Atti del congresso
internazionale di studi Varroniani* (Rieti, 1976), 571–95).

[70] Cf. Swain, 'Plutarch's Lives of Cicero, Cato, and Brutus', *Hermes*, 118
(1990), 192–203.

[71] A good illustration of Plutarch's suppression of Stoicism in *Brut*. is the
contrast between his silence on Antiochus of Ascalon's Stoic leanings at *Brut*. 2. 3
and his interested comments at *Cic*. 4. 2 and *Luc*. 42. 3–4 (cf. D. Babut, *Plutarque
et le Stoïcisme* (Paris, 1969), 198–200). Brutus was formally a Platonist, which is of
course the basis for the comparison with Dion (cf. *Dion* 1). On his actual tendency
towards Stoicism, see J. L. Moles, *QUCC* 25 (1987), 64–5. It may be thought
surprising that we find nothing in *Gracchi* on the limitations of idealism in
politics: the reason is probably that the Gracchi are destroyed not by a blind
reforming zeal like Cato, but by a φόβος ἀδοξίας (*Ag.*/*Cleom*. 2. 7) which Plutarch
considers to be no bad thing (ib. ἐκ προφάσεως οὐκ ἀγεννοῦς, cf. 30. 4–5).

[72] The standard exploration of this aspect of Plutarch's methodology is P. A.
Stadter, *GRBS* 16 (1975), 77–85 (above, pp. 155–64) (on *Per.–Fab*.); see also H.
Erbse, *Hermes*, 84 (1956), 398–424; C. B. R. Pelling, in *Miscellanea Plutarchea:
Atti del II convegno di studi su Plutarco* (Ferrara, 1986), 83–96: F. Frazier, *RPh* 61

in *Pyr.–Marius*; but only in the Roman *Life* is education
introduced to explain failings common to both heroes (even
though Plutarch does know something of Pyrrhus' education, *Pyr.* 1. 4, 8. 3, 6). In *Demosthenes–Cicero* Demosthenes
like Cicero suffers an exile which he bears μαλακῶς (*Demosth.* 26. 5), and the death of a daughter which he bears well
(22. 3). Demosthenes is 'uneducated in the subjects which
are suitable and proper for a free-born child' (4. 4). Yet
Plutarch makes no attempt to connect his education or lack
of it with his ability to resist emotion.[73] Again, in
Coriolanus–Alcibiades Alcibiades' failings may be pointed
out by Socrates (*Alc.* 6. 5), but in the rest of the *Life*
Plutarch never refers back to his education under the philosopher (4) even when he notes 'the instability of his
nature' (16. 9), whereas he strongly implies that Coriolanus'
lack of παιδεία is the root cause of his failings (*Cor.* 1. 3–6,
15. 4–5). Where a Roman's education is greatly emphasized
(Marcellus, Aemilius, Lucullus), the education of his Greek
counterpart may be largely ignored (cf. *Pel.* 4. 1–2; *Tim.* 6.
1; *Cim.* 4. 5): education is not regularly a vital feature in the
pairings. Perhaps, indeed, it is only in *Philopoemen–Flamininus* that Hellenic influences lead to the same result (of
benefiting Greece). But even here in the individuals' own
lives we have something of the same pattern: Philopoemen's
education is stressed (*Phil.* 1. 2–5, 4. 6–8), but is not then
clearly connected with the good or bad in his character,
whereas Flamininus' lack of any deep education is the
implicit cause of his later ambition (cf. p. 240 above).

   In general, where there is important material on Greeks'
education (*Alc.* 4; *Alex.* 7. 2–8. 5; *Sol.* 3. 6–6. 7; *Dion, Per.,
Them., Arat.*, see below), Plutarch very rarely uses it to
explore or illustrate virtue and vice. Dion has much contact
with philosophy. At *Dion* 47.4 he says that he has long
practised in the Academy to overcome φιλονικία and will
not kill the demagogue Heracleides; typically Plutarch does
not comment on his education when he records his continu-

(1987), 65–75; D. H. J. Larmour, *TAPA* 118 (1988), 361–75; my papers in *ICS*
13. 2 (1988), 335–47; *Historia*, 38 (1989), 314–34.

   [73] Cf. Erbse (n. 72), 399–400, 406–13 on the closely paralleled structure of
Demosth.–Cic., and 406–7 on the exposure of both heroes to φιλοτιμία.

ing contentiousness and later murder of his enemy (52. 5,
53. 5). *Pericles*, with a good deal on education (4–6. 1) and
culture (esp. 12. 1, 13. 5, *synk*. 3. 7), merits a few more
words. Pericles is an ambitious man (10. 7) and indulges in
political rivalry (11. 3), but his ambition is entirely free of
πάθος (10. 7), as is also his public speaking (5. 1), and his
chief characteristics, πρᾳότης and φιλανθρωπία, are elsewhere
thought of by Plutarch as means between the passions
brought about by λόγος (*de virt. mor.* 445a, 451e). Further,
Plutarch plays down Pericles' φιλονικία (29. 8, 31. 1 before
the Peloponnesian War) and the surrender of his ἀρετή to
πάθη during the plague (38. 2). All of this could be indirectly
attributable to education and culture. However, had Pericles
been Roman, the attribution would surely have been as
explicit as in *Luc.* and *Marc.*: the significance of culture and
education in his resistance to passions, which Plutarch
emphasizes so greatly, would have been brought out into
the open in a Roman *Life*. In *Per.* Plutarch's major interest
in Pericles' education seems to be in his beautification of
Athens, which is extolled for two long chapters in the *Life*
(12–13) and saluted proudly at the end of the *synkrisis* (3.
7). In those Greek *Lives* where a clear causal connection is
suggested between education and character the theme is
again barely developed or explored. In *Themistocles* and
Aratus Plutarch attributes ἀνωμαλία to deficient λόγος and
παιδεία (*Them*. 2. 3, 7) or an ἔνδεια λόγου φιλοσόφου (*Arat*. 3.
3, 10. 5). At first this seems a deeper, more illuminating
point than the analysis of a similar instability in *Sulla* (cf.
p. 243 above), but still one notices how little is made of it:
again one feels that in most Roman *Lives*, if not in *Sulla*
itself, the early identification of such a cause would have
been followed by a more insistent and explicit tracing of the
theme through the narrative (as we will see in *Cor.* and
Marius).[74]

Naturally it is not always true that Plutarch has more on
Romans' education. The paradox indeed is that there is
often more material about education on the Greek side of a
pair than on the Roman (*Alex.–Caes., Cor.–Alc., Lyc.–*

---

[74] In the case of Sulla it should be remembered that Plutarch offers no reason
for the instability in the first place.

Num., Per.–Fab., Phil.–Flam., Sol.–Publ., Them.–Cam.),
but that Plutarch does little with it. In a number of Roman
Lives (*Aem., Brut., Cato Maj., Cato Min., Cic., Cor., Luc.,
Marc., Marius*) concerns about education and culture
emerge prominently in a manner which is unrepresentative
of the source-material and independent of thematic struc-
tures which run through a pair as a whole. Plutarch seems
ready to examine Romans' education and culture in a way
he does not think of doing with Greeks. He is aware that
Greek culture had been imported to Rome, had never been
fully naturalized, and hence cannot simply be taken for
granted. He frequently recalls this difference between
Greece and Rome and makes use of it as an interesting
criterion for analysing the character of his Roman heroes.

IV. CORIOLANUS

The Rome of the *Coriolanus* is certainly pre-Hellenic.[75] It
is a pure age without corruption (*Cor.* 14. 3–6), the era of
peasant-patriarchs (24. 8). Plutarch's *Coriolanus* is a noble
savage. His nature is γενναία and ἀγαθή, and he displays
strong natural qualities of ἐγκράτεια, δικαιοσύνη, and ἀνδρεία
which stem from his ἀπάθεια towards pleasure, labour, and
money (1. 4, cf. *synk.* 5. 2). However, he suffers from
insufficient παιδεία (1. 3) and his φύσις is a εὐγενὴς χώρα
lacking the farmer's due care (ib., cf. *Arat.* 10. 5). Alcibiades, the paired hero, is luckier in having Socrates to look
out for him when he is like 'a tree in blossom shedding and
destroying its own fruit' (*Alc.* 4. 1, cf. *Cato Maj.* 3. 3). As
at *Marius* 2. 4 (see p. 251 below), Plutarch affirms that the
greatest benefit man can enjoy from the Muses is to ἐξη-
μεροῦσθαι τὴν φύσιν ὑπὸ λόγου καὶ παιδείας τῷ λόγῳ δεξαμένην τὸ
μέτριον καὶ τὸ ἄγαν ἀποβαλοῦσαν (*Cor.* 1. 5). Coriolanus, however, has no Hellenic learning. Nor does he have the opportunity. Plutarch knows that Hellenic culture had not

---

[75] Although Plutarch presents Numa as enjoying contacts with Pythagoras in
the regal period (cf. *Numa* 8. 22, 5), Numa's 'most beautiful and most just system'
quickly fails because it lacked the cohesive force that is παιδεία (*synk.* 4. 12, cf.
Numa 1. 3).

reached Rome by Coriolanus' day. He observes that in those times the Romans concentrated on the aspect of ἀρετή which concerns warfare: 'evidence for this is found in the fact that they call ἀρετή by the one term they have for ἀνδρεία, and the word they specifically use for ἀνδρεία serves as the generic term' (1. 6).[76] This is a simple Rome where environmental conditions mould character.[77]

The good old antique virtues are not sufficient in all walks of life. Plutarch takes over from Dionysius of Halicarnassus[78] a picture of political activity in Coriolanus' Rome which is sometimes out of step with his own presentation of more simple social conditions. In this climate Coriolanus' anti-social nature, like that of Marius, leads to political ineptitude (*synk.* 4. 7–9, 5. 1; *Marius* 32. 2). He is especially prone to φιλοτιμία (4. 1–3), and lacks the mixture of τὸ ἐμβριθὲς καὶ τὸ πρᾷον which is an indispensable part of political virtue and a mixture made by λόγος and παιδεία (15. 4, cf. *Brut.* 1. 3). Owing to his simple ways (15. 5, *synk.* 2. 1) he makes the mistake of believing that to win all is a sign of ἀνδρεία, whereas really it is ἀσθένεια and μαλακία (15. 5). One recalls a number of passages in the *Moralia* where Plutarch ascribes to ignorance and self-deception and flattery the dangerous practice of extenuating failings by giving them the names of virtues.[79] Education, leading to self-awareness, is the only antidote for such troubled natures.

Despite his lack of education Coriolanus is a brilliant orator (27. 1, 39. 6), if not a good extempore speaker (20. 6, cf. *Alc.* 10. 4). It has been noted already that Plutarch thinks of rhetoric as characteristic of even early Rome;[80] in the case of Coriolanus he may also be influenced by Dionysius' verdant speeches, or by a desire to compare Coriolanus with Alcibiades, who aims at popular support through oratory (*Alc.* 10. 3–4). In other respects Plutarch keeps to his

---

[76] Cf. Polybius, xxxi. 29. 1: ἀνδρεία is 'a most important item . . . particularly at Rome'.

[77] Cf. educational conditioning in Sparta at *Lys.* 2. 4, *Ages.* 5. 5.

[78] The main source (quoted at *synk.* 2. 4); see D. A. Russell, *JRS* 53 (1963), 21–8 (below, pp. 357–72).

[79] *de adul. et amico* 56b–f, *de cohib. ira* 462f, *animi an corp. affect. sint peiores* 500e–501b, *de vit. pud.* 529d, fr. 161 from the *Letter on friendship*; cf. *Alc.* 16. 4.

[80] See n. 52.

picture of a Rome lacking education. Later Romans may be
scrutinized from the angle of παιδεία (which is taken to be
available to them): for example, Cicero's surrender to emotion during his exile is taken as an opportunity to comment
on his claims to be an educated man (*Cic.* 32. 5–7). Coriolanus has no pretensions to education. Plutarch can only
underline its absence at the beginning of the *Life*. Thus
there is no comment when Coriolanus goes into exile at 21.
1 ἐμπαθὴς ὑπ' ὀργῆς καὶ βαρυφροσύνης, or when his πάθος at
seeing his mother turns him from his reasoning (34. 3; a
similar change of mind at *Tim.* 6.1 is felt—unusually in a
Greek *Life*—to reveal a deficiency of λόγος and φιλοσοφία).
But though Plutarch cannot openly use education as a tool
to analyse Coriolanus' character and must rather examine
him on moral grounds alone as he does with Alcibiades (15.
4–5, 18. 3, 21. 1–2, 35. 5, *synk.* 5. 1–2), he does at least
imply strongly that Coriolanus' failings should be connected with his lack of Hellenic culture (1. 3–6, 15. 4, 21.
1).

<h2 style="text-align:center">V. PYRRHUS–MARIUS</h2>

Marius differs from Coriolanus in that Plutarch can and
does insist that he is culpable for rejecting the Hellenic
education which is available to him. To understand Plutarch's attitude it is well first to consider the paired *Pyrrhus*,
which offers interesting correspondences with the themes
we are concerned with.

I concentrate on Pyrrhus in the West. His adventures in
Italy and Sicily are bracketed by two forceful comments on
the misuse of fortune (13. 1, 26. 1–2), which is a major
failing both in him and in Marius. In Italy Pyrrhus encoun-
ters Romans who are paragons of virtue. The meeting is
fertile ground for moral exploitation.[81] One of Plutarch's
sources for the narrative, Dionysius of Halicarnassus (cf.
17. 7, 21. 13), makes use of it as part of his broader aim of

[81] Note that Plutarch detests the Hellenistic monarchs of which Pyrrhus is a
prime example (7. 3, 12. 2–12), if better than most (8. 2, *Demetr.* 41. 4–5); cf.
Arist. 6. 2–5, *Demetr.* 3. 3–5, 42. 8–11, *ad princ. indoct.* 780f.

showing that the Romans lived by a high moral code.
Plutarch's intention is rather to highlight Pyrrhus' faults.
To this end Romans are given a good press. The Tarentines
have gone to war with them 'owing to the reckless depravity
of their demagogues' (13. 4), and their love of luxury is
brought out forcefully in the tale of Meton.[82] The moralizing becomes still more obvious in the next chapter as
Pyrrhus' agent Kineas vainly demonstrates to the king that
power will win him no happiness.

From the very start Pyrrhus has a high opinion of his
Roman enemies: 'when we have conquered the Romans
there is no barbarian or Greek city there which will be a
match for us' (14. 6). His respect for them increases still
more on seeing their discipline before the battle of Siris:
(16. 7). 'he was amazed, and addressing the nearest of his
friends, said, "Megakles, the formation of the βάρβαροι is
not βάρβαρος—but we shall know from their actions"'. After
the battle Pyrrhus is 'very proud . . . to have overcome the
Romans' great power' (17. 10). He next sends Kineas to
Rome to see if the Romans will come to an agreement.
'While he was on this mission he made it his business to
make a thorough investigation of their way of life and to
discover the ἀρετή of their system of government' (19. 6).
He duly reports to Pyrrhus that the senate is 'a council of
many kings',[83] and that the masses are like the 'Lernaean
Hydra' (19. 6–7). In the next chapter Pyrrhus comes face to
face with Fabricius, who is 'a good man and a good soldier,
but extremely poor' (20. 1). Plutarch follows Dionysius
(xix. 14) in having Pyrrhus try to corrupt Fabricius finan-
cially. Plutarch's Roman, without recourse to Dionysius'
long moralizing speech, functions perfectly as an embodiment of poverty and hence as a foil to the king. This
emerges particularly in the story of Pyrrhus' banquet (20.
6–7): 'all sorts of topics were discussed, particularly Greece
and her philosophers, and Kineas, happening to mention
Epicurus, went through their doctrines . . . about placing
the highest good in pleasure . . . but while he was still

---

[82] τις ἀνὴρ ἐπιεικής 13. 6–11; cf. Dionysius, xix. 8.
[83] The one true valuation ever made of the senate according to Livy, ix. 17. 14;
for Kineas' visit, cf. Livy, *Per.* 13.

speaking, Fabricius cried out and said, "O Hercules, may Pyrrhus and the Samnites cherish these notions as long as they are at war with us!"' Plutarch, aware that Greek παιδεία had not yet come to Rome, passes by the opportunity of portraying Fabricius as cultured and knowledgeable about Greece and philosophy in order to emphasize his native virtue.

Fabricius is a man content with little, he is modest, yet is held in the highest esteem at Rome (20. 1). His virtue (and the Romans'—21. 4, 11) appears especially in the warning he sends to Pyrrhus about his doctor (21. 1–5). In the *Pyr.* Fabricius and his countrymen effectively expose the king's character. They also have a wider function within the pair as a whole: as Romans of virtue they form an important contrast with the following subject, Marius.

Marius lives to a miserable old age where he is prey to an insatiable ambition and a craving for fame (*Marius* 34. 5–6, 45. 10–12; *Luc.* 38. 3; *Sulla* 7. 2). In 2 Plutarch tells us why he ends up this way: he is wilfully ignorant of Greek culture. 'It is said that he did not study Greek literature and did not employ the Greek language for serious subjects, thinking it risible to study literature whose teachers were other people's slaves' (2.2). Plutarch goes on (2. 4) to record Plato's advice to the sullen Xenocrates, that he should sacrifice to the Graces, 'and if someone had persuaded Marius to sacrifice to the Greek Muses and Graces . . ., he would not have been beached on the shore of a most cruel and savage old age'.[84] That Marius' attitude to culture is of great importance in the *Life* is shown by the final words of 2: 'these matters should be examined straight away in the facts themselves'.[85]

In assessing Marius' attitude towards Greek culture Plutarch has been influenced by comments such as survive at Valerius Maximus, ii. 2. 3 (*senectutem tuam . . . victor devictae gentis facundia politiorem fieri noluisti . . . litterarum gloriosissimum contemptorem*) or Sallust *BJ* 63. 3 (*non Graeca*

---

[84] 'Greek Muses', cf. *Cor.* 1. 5; for Plato's advice, cf. *conj. praec.* 141f, *amat.* 769d. For 'beached' (ἐξοκείλας), cf. 45. 10, *Luc* 38. 3 (of Marius).

[85] Cf. similarly *Flam.* 2. 5, *Arat.* 10. 5, *Per.* 2. 5, 9. 1, *Cim.* 3. 3, *Ag./Cleom.* 2. 9, *Phoc.* 3. 9, *quaest. conv.* vii, introd. 697e.

facundia ... sese exercuit; cf. Marius' own words at 85. 32).[86] This traditional picture, whatever its truth, suits Plutarch's interpretation of Marius as a man who lacks control when in contact with power. 'By nature he was virile and fond of war, his παιδεία being that of the soldier rather than the civilian, and he showed extreme temper when in positions of power' (2. 1). We are reminded of Coriolanus (*Cor.* 1. 2 ff.) and Flamininus (*Flam.* 1. 4) with their military upbringing. But there is a difference, for Plutarch considered that Greek culture had been available to Romans from before the time of Marius' birth (cf. *Aem.* 6. 8–9). Unlike Coriolanus or Flamininus, Marius in Plutarch's eyes does have the opportunity to benefit from Hellenism (one can only reject openly what is offered openly). In fact his traditional education most probably included tuition in Greek 'at the level of the *grammaticus Graecus*'.[87] Plutarch ignores this (which he might have assumed had he not factually known it) and says that Marius' life at Arpinum displayed 'a boorish view towards smart urban life, but was proper and resembled the upbringing of the ancient Romans' (3. 1). Valerius Maximus praises Marius for refusing to pursue Greek rhetoric in his old age; Plutarch strongly implies that Marius is hostile to Greek learning from the very start of his life. The facts of the narrative, which reveal Marius' acquaintance with Greek modes of thought, do not bear him out.[88]

It is no surprise that without παιδεία Marius succumbs to ambition in old age (*Luc.* 38. 3, cf. 1. 6). The senile Marius acts φιλοτίμως πάνυ καὶ μειρακιωδῶς (34. 5; cf. 29. 6).[89] His

[86] Plutarch cites Val. Max. at *Brut.* 53. 5, *Marc.* 30. 5; Sallust at *Lys.–Sulla synk.* 3. 3, *Luc.* 11. 6, 33. 3 (Sallust may have been used in translation, cf. *Suda* Z 73 Adler). There is no evidence that Posidonius' unfavourable account of Marius (cf. J. Malitz, *Die Historien von Posidonios* (Munich, 1983), 394 ff.) has affected Plutarch's position here.

[87] T. Carney, *A Biography of C. Marius, PACA* Suppl. i (1961), 14.

[88] Carney (n. 87), 12–14 pointing to 2. 2 (Greek games given at the dedication of Marius' temple of Honos and Virtus), 8. 5 (Marius says he has fastened an ἀλάστωρ on Metellus), 29. 5 (Marius describes Metellus by quoting from Pindar (this is rather Plutarch speaking)), 45. 9 (Marius speaks of Hellenistic τύχη). It would certainly have jarred with Plutarch's presentation if he had recorded Marius' appearance after Vercellae as *Neos Dionysus* (Carney 12 n. 70).

[89] Cf. Marcellus (*Marc.* 28. 6 μειρακιῶδες ... καὶ φιλοτιμότερον πάθος) and Flamininus (*Flam.* 20. 1 νεανίζοντα τῷ πάθει).

lack of education comes out in politics too. We have seen that Plutarch does not associate with Coriolanus' lack of philosophical λόγος a corresponding absence of oratory. Marius, however, is unsuccessful in politics because he does not have oratorical λόγος (6. 3; cf. 28. 1–2, 32. 2).

In the last chapters of the *Life* Plutarch makes himself quite clear in his comments on Marius' use of fortune. Having attacked Marius' ambition (45) he contrasts the dying Plato who 'sang the praises of his δαίμων and his τύχη because firstly he had been born a man, and not a beast with an irrational nature, and secondly a Greek, and not a barbarian, and in addition to this, that his birth had fallen in the times of Socrates'. This picks up the advice which Plutarch says Marius should have followed at 2. 3–4, and Plutarch stresses here most obviously the need for Greek culture ('a Greek, and not a barbarian'). This is backed up by observing the soul's need of a foundation made firm by λόγος and παιδεία (46. 5).

In *Marius* the hero's wilful ignorance of Greek learning is closely linked with his inability to withstand changes in fortune and his insatiable ambition. We have seen that Plutarch includes a note on Marius' traditional and antique education at Arpinum. It suits him well to emphasize Marius' rusticity and opposition to newer ways. But Marius falls between two stools. He has been brought up with ταῖς πάλαι Ῥωμαίων τροφαῖς (3. 1), then succumbs, perhaps to bribery (28. 8), certainly to luxury (34. 3, 6). Men with whom Marius is contrasted appear as examples of good old-fashioned Roman integrity (Catulus (23. 5), Metellus (28. 6), Octavius (42. 7)). The distinctive and antique Roman virtues (political and military honesty) exemplified by a Fabricius do not require Greek παιδεία to bring them out. In a Marius such virtues are undermined by love of glory and ambition exacerbated by power, to which Marius' nature was especially vulnerable (2. 1). Marius is unable to combat his passions by the only effective method, education, because he has utterly rejected this path.

Plutarch might have made the point that although Pyrrhus was a Greek and therefore has had a Greek education (cf. *Pyr.* 1. 4; 8. 3, 6 φιλοσοφῶν ἀεί in military science), he does not benefit from it in the least. But he almost always takes the παιδεία of Greeks for granted, and moral failing (or success) is explained without reference to education. Romans are seen differently. Hence Plutarch does not simply take the traditional picture of Marius as uneducated and boorish, leaving him noble but exposed (like Coriolanus). His Marius consciously repudiates παιδεία, as he makes quite clear in 2. Plutarch invites us to measure Marius' moral defects during his life directly against his lack of Hellenic culture (2. 4), and at the end of the biography, where Marius' shortcomings come to a head, he once more invokes Plato to confirm his correct identification of where Marius goes astray.

VI. MARCELLUS

By contrast with *Marius* the *Marcellus* shows a hero who benefits himself and others with Hellenic culture. Marcellus is 'by nature fond of war ... but in other respects his character was σώφρων and φιλάνθρωπος, and he was an enthusiast for Hellenic learning and literature ..., though owing to his occupations he was unable to attain the levels of practice and knowledge that he desired' (1. 2–3). As Alan Wardman remarks, 'the reader who is used to a stereotype of Marcellus as the warlike Roman ..., will be surprised'.[90] As Wardman notes, Rome's atrocities in Sicily under Marcellus are not brought out by Plutarch at all. Rather, Marcellus 'seems at that time to have been the first to show the Greeks that the Romans were δικαιοτάτους' (20. 1).[91] At 20. 2 Plutarch feels he can say that 'if Henna or Megara or the Syracusans met with any action which was οὐκ ἐπιεικές, the blame for this seems to have lain with the sufferers rather than the perpetrators'. Even Livy says of the massacre at Henna that 'Henna was held *aut malo aut necessario facinore*' (xxiv. 39. 7). Plutarch continues his narrative by giving

---

[90] Wardman (n. 51), 130.

[91] Note the v. *l.* at *Marc.* 20. 1 δικαιοτέρους ('juster'); Plutarch should not be taken as intending a comparison with Greeks (the Romans were now 'very just' or 'juster' than they had been).

details of what happened to the pro-Roman Nicias at Engyium and of Marcellus' leniency to the town (20. 2–11).

These comments on Roman policy in Sicily come immediately after the storming of Syracuse (18–19) and before notes on Marcellus' taking of spoils from the city (21). Polybius condemns this action on grounds of morality and expediency (ix. 10). Livy too is scathing about the taking of the *signa tabulasque*, feeling that Marcellus had set a precedent for despoiling temples (xxv. 40. 1–3), and at xxvii. 16. 7–8 he says of the art treasures which Fabius Maximus took from Tarentum that 'they almost equalled the Syracusan *ornamenta*; but Fabius refrained from this type of plunder *maiore animo* than Marcellus'.[92]

Plutarch is presumably responding to Livy's comparison when he suggests in *Fab.* that Fabius at Tarentum was ἀτοπώτερος than Marcellus, 'or rather showed that that man was quite remarkable for his πρᾳότης and his φιλανθρωπία (as has been written in his *Life*)' (*Fab.* 22. 8). Plutarch means that Marcellus did not incur the charges of 'treachery and brutality', which Fabius does at Tarentum (22. 5), for Marcellus acted with moderation (*Marc.* 19. 6) in not harming the free citizens.[93] The moral attributes of πρᾳότης and φιλανθρωπία (*et sim.*) are brought out in *Marc.* too (1. 3, 10. 6, 23. 8, 28. 1), and at 1. 3 are closely associated with Hellenic παιδεία.

Marcellus differs from his contemporaries, who gave no proof of εὐγνωμοσύνη, φιλανθρωπία, or πολιτικὴ ἀρετή (20. 1). In 21 Plutarch records his transportation of *objets d'art* to Rome with an approval, though cautious, unexpected in one so keen on Greece's heritage: 'until then Rome neither knew nor possessed any stylish or outstanding design work, and she showed no love for such grace and refinement' (21. 2). The warlike appearance of Rome at that time is con-

---

[92] The example Livy gives in this passage, which is partially the basis of *Marc.* 21. 4–5 (see below), is of Fabius leaving behind the colossal statues of the gods; Pliny (*HN* xxxiv. 40) reports that Fabius left the colossus of Jove because he could not move it, and did in fact take the statue of Heracles (as Plutarch notes, *Fab.* 22. 8).

[93] Πρᾳότης and φιλανθρωπία do not refer to Marcellus' taste in art as is sometimes asserted. Cf. Cicero, ii. *Verr.* 4. 120–1, on Marcellus' *humanitas* in sparing Syracuse and not denuding it entirely of treasures (unlike Verres).

trasted with the 'Hellenic grace' (21. 4) imported by Marcellus. Plutarch then (21. 4–5) includes a comparison made by older Romans between Marcellus and Fabius: Fabius had left the gods' statues at Tarentum, whereas Marcellus had taken them from Syracuse, and (21. 6) Marcellus had made the city odious and corrupted the δῆμος, previously used only to 'fighting or farming', by 'filling them with leisure and chatter, so that they spent a great deal of the day urbanely discussing art and artists'.

Plutarch knows that it was not until much later that Greek learning and ideals established themselves among the Romans, and if we may judge from *Cato Maj.* and *Aem.* believed that the Roman people were basically well-behaved for a good many years after Marcellus (see above, n. 17). At *Marc.* 21. 4 ff. he is perhaps building on Polybius when he talks of moral corruption, but he places the criticisms in the mouths of the older citizens and we need not seek his own views. On occasion Plutarch does express criticism of the fate of Greek artefacts at Rome (cf. *Demetr.* 22. 7, *Publ.* 15. 4). But in *Marc.* he is very far from excoriating his hero, and at the end of 21 we read that Marcellus 'would talk with pride of these things, even to Greeks, saying that he had taught the Romans to give honour and admiration to the beauties and marvels of Greece which they had not known how to do' (21. 7). Any disapproval on Plutarch's part has been muted: Rome needed art at this time, and if she could be taught genuine appreciation by a man whose own motives could be seen as sincere, that might pass.[94]

Where does Plutarch get the idea that Marcellus, the 'sword of Rome',[95] is a *connoisseur* of art and a frustrated *littérateur*? Posidonius may be the source. He probably affects Plutarch's projection of Marcellus' campaign in Sicily (the tale of Nicias in 20 comes from him, *FGrH* 87 F 43). But there is no real reason to ascribe to Posidonius the remarks on Marcellus' Hellenism (1. 3) along with those which Plutarch attributes on the origin of Marcellus' name

---

[94] Cf. C. B. R. Pelling, 'Plutarch: Roman Heroes and Greek Culture', in M. Griffin, J. Barnes (eds.), *Philosophia Togata*, (Oxford, 1989), 202 'the criticism [21. 4 ff.] . . . seems very mild'.

[95] For 'sword of Rome', cf. 9. 7; *Fab.* 19. 4; Posidonius, *FGrH* 87 F 42ab.

(1. 1–2).⁹⁶ Nor is there good cause to believe that Plutarch's approval of Marcellus' use of Syracusan art comes from him.⁹⁷ The slant is Plutarch's own. He may have developed the idea of Marcellus' παιδεία from his famous remark about Archimedes (17. 2), recorded first by Polybius (viii. 6. 6, cf. Athenaeus, *deipn.* 634b), that Archimedes was a geometrical giant who was using Marcellus' ships like wine-glasses and ejecting his σαμβῦκαι (instruments both of music and of war) from the party. Marcellus' references in Plutarch's version to Briareos and to 'the hundred-handed giants of mythology' are additional. The original comment demonstrates an ability to pun in Greek on the Greek culture of the *symposion,* and Plutarch may have felt that a man who could do this might supply an apt allusion from Greek mythology (here Hesiod, *Theog.* 147 ff.). This specific instance perhaps explains the general reference to Greek λόγοι at 1. 3 (Plutarch does not—or cannot—find another concrete example). The general assumption will have reinforced what Plutarch knows from Posidonius about the campaign in Sicily, and encouraged his presentation of Marcellus' view of Syracusan art in 21 in terms of cultural rather than financial gain.

Another reason for thinking that the emphasis on Hellenism is Plutarch's own is that it chimes with the stress in the *Life* on the proper and Hellenic character of Roman religion, a stress which is demonstrably his. In the sphere of religion Plutarch suggests that the Romans of Marcellus' time are already like Greeks. His comments are made as a result of the live burial of two Greeks and two Gauls before the Insubrian invasion of 225. The Romans, says Plutarch, made an innovation in their sacrifices. For although their

⁹⁶ As is done by Edelstein–Kidd, fr. 261, and Theiler, F 92 (but not Jacoby, *FGrH* 87 F 41), and accepted by Malitz (n. 86), 363; Theiler, ii. 89 notes that *Marc.* 1. 3 is Plutarch's addition. On Plutarch's relationship with Posidonius I have not seen M. Mühl, *Posidonios und der plutarchische Marcellus: Untersuchungen zur Geschichtsschreibung des Posidonios von Apamea* (Berlin, 1925), reviewed by F. Münzer, *Gnomon,* 1 (1925), 96–100.
⁹⁷ Though note that Posidonius knows of (and presumably approved of) dedications from the spoils at Lindos on his adopted Rhodes (and elsewhere), *Marc.* 30. 6–8, *FGrH* 87 F 44; it is possible that he approved of the dedication of much of the booty which was brought to Rome (cf. Livy, xxv. 40. 3, Cicero, ii *Verr.* 4. 121).

rites contain nothing βαρβαρικόν or ἔκφυλον, but as far as possible in their attitudes to the divine they act Ἑλληνικῶς and πρᾴως, at the time when the war fell upon them they were forced to obey certain oracles from the Sibylline Books' (3. 5–6). At *Them.* 13. 3 (cf. *Arist.* 9. 2; *Pel.* 21. 3) there is no attempt to defend a similar sacrifice of Persians as an act of faith. In *Marc.* a defence has to be made, for Greeks are among the victims.

Plutarch argues from the premiss that the Romans are not barbarians (he is explicit about this at *Flam.* 5. 6 ff.), and therefore cannot practise barbarian rites. In the following chapters of *Marc.* (4, 5) he very carefully stresses their commitment to proper and ancestral religion, ending with the statement at 5. 6 that they kept to τὰ πάτρια and did not become involved in δεισιδαιμονία.[98] This theme offers an obvious link between *Marc.* and the pair *Pel.*, where Plutarch, doubtless expressing his own view (cf. *de Stoic. repug.* 1051b–d), condemns those who held that there were evil daimons which delighted in the βάρβαρος καὶ παράνομος θυσία of human sacrifice (*Pel.* 21. 5–6).[99] Given the emphasis on religious scruples it is no surprise to find Marcellus himself stepping down from the consulate owing to ill omens (*Marc.* 12. 2). And his death, like that of Pelopidas (*Pel.* 31. 3–4), is anticipated by his disregard of obviously bad signs (29. 9–11). In Plutarch's writings there are a number of passages where Roman superstition is noted.[100] It is even pointed out once in *Marc.* (6. 11). The main stress in the *Life*, though, is on the correctness of Roman religion and its similarity to Greek practice.[101]

[98] For barbarous rites contrasted with approved ancestral practice see *de superstit.* 166b and *de fac. quae in orbe lun. app.* 935b; cf. also *amat.* 756c where the god Eros is οὐδ᾽ ἔπηλυς ἔκ τινος βαρβαρικῆς δεισιδαιμονίας.

[99] Cf. *Ages.* 6. 7–8, *de superstit.* 171b–e; for 'barbarous and abnormal' views about deities, cf. *de Is. et Osir.* 358e–f, *de def. orac.* 418e. On barbarian and Hellenic religious practices in Plutarch's eyes, cf. Aalders (n. 15), 20, A. Nikolaides, *WS* 20 (1986), 233–5.

[100] *Sulla* 12. 7, 35. 3, *Numa* 10. 4, 22. 12. *Caes.* 63. 11, *Brut.* 39. 6, *Cam.* 19. 12, *quaest. Rom.* 83, 283f–284c (a later sacrifice of two Greeks and two Gauls ordered by the Sibylline Books for ἀλλοκότοις τισί δαίμοσι καὶ ξένοις; in *Marc.* Plutarch cannot invoke strange daimons, but must insist on propriety in Roman religion to match *Pel.* and protect Marcellus' Hellenism).

[101] Note *Fab.* 4. 4. also plays down Roman superstition during the Hannibalic War; this ties in with *Per.* (cf. 6. 1).

Plutarch's suggestion that Roman religion in Marcellus' age is essentially Hellenic in character is clearly intended to support his proposition that Marcellus is highly interested in Hellenic culture and that the people of Rome are receptive to its introduction. Religion aside, the suggested Hellenism of Marcellus and the Romans owes little to the themes and concerns of *Pel.* There the education of Pelopidas is in doubt (cf. 3. 6–7, 4. 1–2), and Plutarch takes no interest in the subject in his *Life*. This contrast between *Pel.* and *Marc.* is reflected more glaringly still in *Cim.–Luc.*, where despite the existence of close thematic ties between the *Lives* Plutarch firmly denies to Cimon the Hellenic education which he attributes so forcefully to Lucullus. We will see below that the availability of Greek education to Lucullus is assumed by Plutarch and that there is nothing in his *Life* on Greek teachers or specific studies. In *Marc.* Plutarch is aware that Greek culture is not established at Rome until Marcellus himself introduces it (21). Marcellus' education is incomplete—Plutarch points to the constant wars fought by his generation as an excuse (1. 2–5, cf. *Cor.* 1. 6–2. 1, *Flam.* 1. 4)—and this is the implied cause of his fatal ambition in old age (28. 6, cf. Flamininus, Marius). Plutarch has nevertheless gleaned from his sources enough to build up a distinctive and novel characterization and to suggest that in a noble warrior lies hidden a scholar and a gentleman. This characterization is guided by his preoccupation with Hellenic education and culture.

VII. LUCULLUS

As surprising as the Hellenic characterization of Marcellus is the emphasis on Hellenism in the biography of Lucullus, for like Marcellus Lucullus is usually remembered for something other than his devotion to Hellenic culture, that is his luxury.[102] In the introduction to *Cimon–Lucullus* Plutarch tells us that he has chosen Lucullus as a subject because of

[102] To avoid cross-references I have preferred to repeat here some material on Lucullus from the paper 'Plutarch's Characterization of Lucullus', *RhM* 135 (1992), 307–16.

his aid to Chaeroneia during the Mithridatic War: 'though
we are separated by many generations, we believe that the
gratitude [for his actions] extends even to us who are alive
now' (2. 2). Plutarch continues by asserting that his character portrait is independent of this gratitude, and that he will
not ignore Lucullus' flaws; on the other hand 'we should
not point out [failings] in our narrative superfluously and
with excessive zeal, but as it were in a tone of apology for
human nature if it produces no character which is purely
good and indisputably set on virtue' (2. 5). This line of
thought may be paralleled.[103] That it is voiced here as part
of the introduction to a biography where the hero's luxury
and extravagance are to be underplayed suggests a conscious
attempt by Plutarch to make his audience well disposed
towards his favourable presentation.

Both Lucullus and Cimon are presented in the pair as
great benefactors of the Greeks. Lucullus restores the
people of Cyrene (*Luc.* 2. 4–5). He frees the cities of Asia
from the depredations of Roman tax gatherers (which Plutarch stresses, 7, 6–7, 20. 1–6, 23. 1–2). He fights barbarians,
liberating Greeks from Mithridates at Kabeira and from
Tigranes at Tigranokerta (18. 1, 29. 5). He is distressed
when he cannot save the city of Amisos from fire during the
war and is prevented from fulfilling his 'ambition of displaying his goodness to the Greeks' (19. 4–5; 32. 6). And his
harsh treatment of the people of Mytilene is excused in a
way which recalls Marcellus in Sicily (4. 2–3, *Marc.* 20).
Similarly, Cimon's exploits are among the few which mag-
nify Athens (*Cim.* 8. 2, 10. 6, 13. 5–7, *synk.* 1. 5) without
harming Greece (11. 2; 18. 1), and he enjoys a προεδρία
among generals for his deeds against barbarians (13. 3;
synk. 2. 1), which were not to be matched (19. 3–4; cf.
Flam. 11. 6).

Since Cimon is one of Greece's greatest benefactors, it
might be thought that Plutarch would suggest that he is
acquainted with Hellenic culture. After all, in the final
words of his biography he is ὁ Ἑλληνικὸς ἡγεμών (19. 5).
There is nothing except a casual remark on his ability to

---

[103] 'We should not point out failings'—see *de Herod. Mal.* 3. 855c–d; 'no
character which is purely good'—*de laude ips.* 545e, *Sulla* 30. 6, *Sert.* 10. 5–7.

sing (9. 1, cf. *Per.* 5. 3). Plutarch may be hampered by a
lack of information; but since he records Cimon's later
beautification of Athens (13. 7), he does not have to accept
Stesimbrotus' report that Cimon was entirely uneducated
(4. 5), still less to confirm it by appending a quotation from
Euripides which he uses at *Marc.* 21. 6 to illustrate the
state of the Roman δῆμος before the introduction of Hellenic
culture.[104]

By contrast, Lucullus' education and culture are much
emphasized. At *Luc.* 1. 4–9 we learn that he was fluent in
Latin and Greek, in forensic and other types of oratory,
and had from childhood enjoyed a liberal education ἐπὶ τῷ
καλῷ (1. 5, cf. *synk.* 1. 4). He even wrote a history of the Social
War in Greek for a wager (1. 7–8). By nature Lucullus is
φιλότιμος (*synk.* 1. 8), but when he is older and has leisure
time it is his practice of theoretical philosophy that enables
him to curb ambition against Pompey (1. 6, 42. 4; cf. 5. 5).
Hellenism is the key to Lucullus' moral outlook. His
δικαιοσύνη and φιλανθρωπία are explicitly associated with his
education (29. 6). Moreover his qualities are often under-
lined in the context of his dealings with Greeks (2. 1–2, 4.
2, 18. 9, 19. 4, 20. 1, 23. 1, 29. 6, 42. 1). Here is where *Luc.*
departs from *Cim.*: both heroes are praised greatly by Plutarch for their attitude towards Greece, but only with Lucullus is this attitude associated with the possession of Hellenic
culture and education.

On his return to Rome Lucullus presents something of a
problem to Plutarch, for he gives up an active life for a
sedentary one. Plutarch offers two reasons for this: either
he realized that public life was now corrupt and out of
control, or 'as some say' he had had enough of glory and
had decided to indulge himself in luxurious living (38. 2).
Plutarch mentions that 'some people' favourably contrasted
Lucullus' decision to withdraw from politics with the unsea-
sonable ambition of Marius, Cicero, and Scipio Aemilianus
(38. 3–4). This accords with the notice at 1. 6 on Lucullus'
ability to control ambition during his retirement through

---

[104] 'φαῦλον, ἄκομψον, τὰ μεγιστ'ἀγαθόν' (Euripides, *Likymnios* fr. 473 N²).
Plutarch refuses to believe Stesimbrotus on Themistocles (a pupil of Anaxagoras
and Melissus, *Them.* 2. 5), and criticizes him also at *Per.* 13. 16, 26. 1.

262   *S. C. R. Swain*

the study of φιλοσοφία, and is developed at 42. 4–43. 1.[105]
For the moment Plutarch explores the alternative explanation. He records Pompey's and Crassus' criticisms of Lucullus' luxury (38. 5), and dwells on the subject for the next
three chapters (39–41). Having established the facts, Plutarch then sets about restoring Lucullus' reputation by
focusing on his cultural attainments, again picking up the
first chapter of the *Life*. On his return to Rome Lucullus
sets up a library (42. 1).[106] Greeks benefit especially. 'The
Greeks had unrestricted access to the covered walkways
and study-rooms, and would make visits there, as if to some
caravanserai of the Muses, and spend the day in each
other's company' (42. 1). Not only scholars, but also politicians came there, so that the house was 'really both a home
and a Greek town hall for those who arrived in Rome' (42. 2).
Plutarch goes on to report Lucullus' fondness for philosophy,
and his particular adherence to Plato and the Old Academy
as represented by Antiochus of Ascalon (42. 3–4). He explains
Lucullus' role in the dialogue Cicero named after him.[107]

In the *Moralia*, apart from a reference to his closeness to
his brother (*de frat. amore* 484d–e) and to his rise to power
under Sulla (*praec. ger. reip.* 805e–f), it is Lucullus' luxury
and time-wasting that are singled out (*ad princ. indoct.*
782f; *an seni resp. ger.* 785f–786a, 792b–c). There is nothing
on his cultured retirement (792b βίον ἄπρακτον καὶ δίαιταν
οἰκουρὸν καὶ ἄφροντιν). His luxury is familiar in the *Lives* too
(*Cato Min.* 19. 8, *Pomp.* 2. 12, *Marius* 34. 4).[108] In his own

---

[105] Lucullus' infighting with Pompey 42. 4 ff. is less serious than at *Pomp.* 46.
5–6, 48. 2, 4, 7 and *Cato Min.* 31. 1, 7.

[106] Plutarch veils the fact that the books were booty (ἥ τε χρῆσις ἦν φιλοτιμοτέρα
τῆς κτήσεως); see J. van Ooteghem, *L. Licinius Lucullus* (Brussels, 1959), 184.

[107] Plutarch seems to know the basic argument of Cicero's *Lucullus* (*Acad.
Priora*); there is an unattributed quotation from it at *Cic.* 24. 5 (ii. 119), and C. P.
Jones, *Hermes*, 110 (1982), 254–6 argues correctly for an intransitive sense to
ἀντετάττετο at 42. 3, so that Lucullus himself 'opposed' Cicero as in Cicero's work.
But Plutarch is unaware of *Acad. Post.* (in which Lucullus' part was disparagingly
transferred to Varro; Cicero, *ad Att.* xiii. 12. 3, 13. 1, 16. 1, 19. 5, Ooteghem (n.
106), 25–7), and it is hard to say whether he had actually read *Acad. Priora*
himself (as is suggested by Babut (n. 71), 198–200).

[108] Cf. Velleius Paterculus, ii. 33. 4 (*profusae huius . . . luxuriae primus auctor*),
Athenaeus, *deipn.* 274e–f, 543a, resting on Nicolaus, *FGrH* 90 F 77ab ('foremost
guide of the πολυτέλεια which now flourishes', 'pioneer of τρυφή among the
Romans').

Life, though, it is his Hellenism, cultural and political, that is introduced and stressed heavily throughout. Cicero also chooses to emphasize the Hellenic culture of Lucullus (along with that of Catulus and Hortensius) in *Acad. Priora*.[109] It is difficult to say whether Plutarch knew his work well enough to have been influenced by his suggestion of Lucullus' learning.[110] It seems rather that his stress on Lucullus' Hellenism is his own. It has been pointed out that Lucullus' predilection for the Old Academy and for Antiochus of Ascalon has been introduced by him.[111] The Hellenism may appear especially adventitious because it is not related to any period of study in Greece.

In *Cim.* Plutarch establishes Cimon as a benefactor of Athens and of Greece, in brief, 'the Hellenic general' (19. 5). In *Luc.* he responds to this theme as fully as he can. Lucullus like Cimon fights barbarians and aids Greeks. Both are Hellenists. With Lucullus alone Plutarch feels compelled to account for this Hellenism. There are two reasons why this is so. One is that Plutarch tends to work up themes in the second *Life* of a pair which he has introduced in the first *Life*.[112] In *Luc.* he establishes the basis for the hero's Hellenic ideals. Assuming an education ἐπὶ τῷ καλῷ (*Luc.* 1. 5) he gathers together relevant information (the library, the history of the Social War, the appearance in Cicero's *Lucullus*), inferring what he does not really know (the love of the Old Academy and of Antiochus), and carefully integrates Lucullus' virtues with his relations with

---

[109] *Esp.* ii. 4; see Rawson (n. 33), 57, 81. The emphasis is quite hypocritical—see n. 107.

[110] See n. 107. Plutarch's φιλοσοφίαν δὲ πᾶσαν μὲν ἠσπάζετο καὶ πρὸς πᾶσαν εὐμενὴς ἦν καὶ οἰκεῖος (42. 3) may reflect Cicero's *cum omni litterarum generi tum philosophiae deditus* (ii. 4), though both statements look like generalizations. Note, however, J. Glucker, *Antiochus and the Late Academy* (Göttingen, 1978), 27: 'Lucullus the philosopher is a creation of Cicero'.

[111] See Glucker (n. 110), 21–7, Rawson (n. 33) 81, both observing that Antiochus was more useful to Lucullus as a guide to eastern affairs than to philosophy. Note that Cicero's Lucullus becomes attached to Antiochus not through love of the Old Academy but because Antiochus enjoys the best reputation among the philosophers of his day (ii. 4, 113). Note further that Lucullus' generous sentiments about the grammarian Tyrannion (*Luc.* 19. 8–9) are also really Plutarch's own (see J. Christes, *Sklaven und Freigelassene als Grammatiker und Philologen im antiken Rom* (Wiesbaden, 1979), 29).

[112] Cf. Pelling (n. 72), 94.

Greeks. The second reason is that Lucullus is a Roman: as such he might have lacked Hellenic manners. Plutarch is surely correct in trying to pinpoint why he differs in his attitude to Greece from so many of his contemporaries (cf. *Sulla* 12. 9–14). His conclusion is that Lucullus' actions are deeply rooted in his possession of Hellenic παιδεία.

The examples of Coriolanus, Marius, Marcellus, and Lucullus show different aspects of Plutarch's interest in the education and culture of his Roman heroes. We should remember that he does not explore their culture as an end in itself. The *Parallel Lives* were composed πρὸς ἐπανόρθωσιν ἠθῶν (*Aem.* 1. 3),[113] and Plutarch's interest in the παιδεία of his Roman heroes is a subordinate part of his general concern about the relation between education and character development. He feels that since Hellenic education cannot be taken for granted among Romans, it may be applied as an effective criterion for bringing out their character. We should not imagine that Plutarch is sneering at heroes who lacked παιδεία like Coriolanus or Marius, or patronizing those like Marcellus and Lucullus whom he presents as possessing it.[114] Plutarch examines the character of all his heroes, Greek and Roman, not to applaud or to condemn them, but to improve and correct the morals of his audience. He bids us, not them, take notice of the benefits Hellenic culture has to offer and of the detriment which may be occasioned by its absence.

[113] See Jones (n. 28 (1971)), 103–9 (103 n. 1 citing earlier literature), Wardman (n. 51), 18–26.

[114] I see no reason to agree with R. Flacelière, *AC* 32 (1963), 33–4: 'Naturellement Plutarque se fait un malin plaisir de montrer . . . que la plupart de ceux-ci [Roman heroes] étaient pénétrés de culture grecque'.

10

Plutarch's Method of Work in the Roman *Lives*

C. B. R. PELLING

This paper is concerned with the eight Lives in which Plutarch describes the final years of the Roman Republic: *Lucullus, Pompey, Crassus, Cicero, Caesar, Cato, Brutus,* and *Antony.*[1] It is not my main concern to identify particular sources, though some problems of provenance will inevitably arise; it is rather to investigate the methods which Plutarch adopted in gathering his information, whatever his sources may have been. Did he, for instance, compose each biography independently? Or did he prepare several Lives simultaneously, combining in one project his reading for a number of different works?[2] Did he always have his source-material before him as he composed? Or can we detect an extensive use of memory?[3] Can one conjecture what use, if any, he made of notes?[4] And can we tell whether he usually drew his material from just one source, or wove together his

---

[1] I am grateful to Mr D. A. Russell, to Mr J. L. Moles, and to Mr P. J. Parsons for their helpful scrutiny and criticism of this paper. The following works will be referred to by author's name alone: H. Peter, *Die Quellen Plutarchs in den Biographien der Römer* (1865); C. Stoltz, *Zur relativen Chronologie der Parallelbiographien Plutarchs* (1929); A. W. Gomme, *A Historical Commentary on Thucydides,* i (1945); C. Theander, *Plutarch und die Geschichte* (1951); J. R. Hamilton, *Plutarch, Alexander: A Commentary* (1969); C. P. Jones, *Plutarch and Rome* (1971). Except where stated, *Cato* will refer to *Cato minor.*

[2] Simultaneous preparation is suggested by Gomme, 83 n. 3, and Brożek, *Eos,* 53 (1963), 68–80; cf. Stoltz, 18–19 and 67. Mewaldt had already postulated simultaneous preparation in arguing for simultaneous publication: *Hermes* 42 (1907), 564–78.

[3] A large use of memory is suggested by Zimmermann, *RhM* 79 (1930), 61–2; cf. Russell, *JRS* 53 (1963), 22 (see below, p. 359); Jones, 87; Hamilton, xliii–xliv; Gomme, 78–81; P. A. Stadter, *Plutarch's Historical Methods,* 138.

[4] Plutarch seems to have kept some 'commonplace book' in his philosophical studies (*Mor.* 464f, cf. 457d), but that tells us little of his methods in the Lives. For varying views of the importance of notes, cf. works cited in previous note.

narrative from his knowledge of several different versions?[5]

I start from an important assumption: that, in one way or another, Plutarch *needed* to gather information before writing these Lives; that, whatever may be the case with some of the Greek Lives, he would not be able to write these Roman biographies simply from his general knowledge. The full basis for this assumption will only become clear as the discussion progresses: for example, we shall find traces of increasing knowledge within these Lives, with early biographies showing only a slight knowledge of some important events, and later ones gradually filling the gaps. It will become probable that Plutarch knew comparatively little of the *detail* of Roman history before he began work on the Lives, and that considerable 'research'—directed and methodical reading—would be necessary for their composition.

This thesis must not be overstated: Plutarch would have read the standard Greek histories of the Roman world some time before he began the Lives. If the *de fortuna Romanorum* is a youthful work, he already knew Dionysius of Halicarnassus, and probably Polybius, at that time.[6] A knowledge of the outline of Roman history was a natural expectation in an educated Greek of the day. But at the same time it is clear that the Roman Lives have, in important respects, a different texture from the Greek; and one striking aspect of this is relevant here. No one can doubt that Plutarch had all his life read widely and sensitively in Greek literature, and that, even before he started work on the Lives, his memory was full of anecdotes concerning the Greek heroes he described.[7] In writing *Pericles*, for instance, he could exploit his recollections of the comic poets, of philosophers (especi-

[5] A combination of different sources is strongly argued by Theander, esp. 42 ff.; cf. Stadter, op. cit. 125–40.

[6] Most of that work is clearly drawn from Dionysius (note especially the inherited error at 318e–f); non-Dionysian material seems largely derived from oral traditions at Rome, especially those associated with surviving monuments. (On this type of material cf. Theander, 2–32, and *Eranos* 57 (1959), 99–131.) Plutarch quotes Polybius 'in the second book' at 325f, and elsewhere book-numbers seem to imply first-hand knowledge of a work: Jones, 83.

[7] For Plutarch's wide reading, cf. esp. Ziegler, RE s.v. 'Plutarchos', 914–28.

ally Plato), of Theophrastus, of Ion of Chios.[8] In no sense
had he read these authors 'for' the *Pericles*; he had read
them for their own sake, and probably read them many
years before. But they filled his mind with recollections and
allusions, and these furnished some valuable supplements
to his historical sources: he could fill a whole chapter with
anecdotes of Aspasia which 'just came to mind' as he wrote.[9]

Matters were different when he turned to Rome. He had
learnt his Latin fairly late in life;[10] he evidently did not
read Latin literature for pleasure, and therefore had no
such ready fund of Latin recollections. We might have
expected some quotations from Augustan poetry in
Antony—in the descriptions of Cleopatra, perhaps, or the
notices of Roman public opinion;[11] there are none. Plutarch
never mentions Virgil; nor Catullus, relevant for *Caesar*;
nor Ennius, though *cunctando restituit rem* would have been
a useful ornament for *Fabius*.[12] Not only did Plutarch lack
that general knowledge of the Roman past which a literary
background could give: a man who had not read Ennius or
Virgil would be unlikely to know his Livy, his Pollio, or his
Sallust.[13] It is reasonable to assume that the reading of the
great Roman historians was work which still lay in front of

[8] Comic poets: *Per.* 3. 5–7, 8. 4, 13. 8–10, 24. 9–10, *al.* Plato: 7. 8, 13. 7, 24. 7,
cf. 8. 2, 15. 2. Other philosophers: 4. 5, 7. 7, 27. 4, 35. 5. Theophrastus: 38. 2.
Ion: 5. 3, 28. 7. Some of these quotations may be inherited; it is hard to believe they *all*
are. Cf. E. Meinhardt, *Perikles bei Plutarch* (Frankfurt, 1957), 9–22 and *passim*.

[9] ἐπελθόντα τῇ μνήμῃ κατὰ τὴν γραφήν, *Per.* 24. 12.

[10] *Dem.* 2. 2. On the weary question of Plutarch's Latinity, Rose, *The Roman
Questions of Plutarch* (1924), 11–19, is still the soundest treatment.

[11] Cleopatra: Latin quotations would have been apposite especially (but not
only) at 27. 2–5, 56. 6–10, and in the description of Actium (esp. 66. 5–8); note
also 29. 1, 36. 1–2, and 62. 1, where quotations from Plato and Euripides, rather
than Latin poetry, lend stylistic height. Roman public opinion: e.g. 36. 4–5, 50. 7,
54. 5, 55, 57. 5.

[12] The reference to Horace at *Lucull.* 39. 5 is an exception, so isolated that one
suspects the quotation to be tralatician; but it at least shows that quotations from
Latin poets were not excluded by any generic 'rules'. Had Plutarch known his
Horace, a mention of him might be expected in *Brutus*, perhaps at 24. 3, perhaps
in the account of Philippi. The contrast between *Caesar* and Suet. *Div. Iul.* is here
eloquent, for Suet. is rich with material similar to that used by Plutarch for
Pericles: quotations from contemporary pamphlets and lampoons, Calvus, Catullus, Curio, etc. Plutarch has nothing like this in *Caesar*.

[13] He may have glanced at Pollio or Livy when engaged on his *Life of Augustus*,
but even this is unlikely: 'the *Lives of the Caesars*, to judge from the remains, were
not the fruit of deep research' (Jones 80).

Plutarch, reading which he would have to conduct 'for' the Roman Lives.

The first section of this paper will examine the possibility that several Lives were prepared simultaneously. Various arguments will suggest that six of these eight Lives— *Pompey, Crassus, Caesar, Cato, Brutus,* and *Antony*—belong closely together, and were probably prepared as a single project. The second section will consider the manner in which Plutarch collected his information from the sources.

I. SIMULTANEOUS PREPARATION

(a) Increasing knowledge

Lucullus and *Cicero* seem to be the earliest of these eight Lives. *Demosthenes–Cicero* formed the fifth pair in the series of *Parallel Lives* (*Dem.* 3. 1), and it seems likely that *Cimon–Lucullus* should be placed even earlier.[14] The *Parallel Lives* were clearly produced over a considerable period of time, and it is natural to think that Plutarch read more widely during their production; it is therefore not surprising that, in *Lucullus* and *Cicero*, he seems less knowledgeable than in the later Lives. The second half of *Cicero*, in particular, is scrappy and ill-informed, and leaves a very different impression from the detailed later accounts. It is sometimes possible to see specific cases of ignorance: for instance, Plutarch had presumably not yet discovered the item of *Crass.* 13. 3–4—Cicero inculpating Caesar and Crassus in the Catilinarian conspiracy, but in a work published after both were dead.[15] Plutarch would surely have

---

[14] Jones, *JRS*, 56 (1966), 67–8 (above, pp. 109–11), places *Cim.–Luc.* in one of positions II–IV; Theander, *Eranos* 66 (1958), 12–20, in position IV; cf. Stoltz, table at p. 135. The principal indication is that *Pericles*, which occupied position X (*Per.* 2. 5), itself quotes *Cimon* (9. 5); *Dem.–Cic.* occupied position V, and, on Jones's analysis, positions VI–IX are already filled by other pairs. For reservations about this type of analysis, see below, p. 281; but the early position of *Lucullus* is adequately demonstrated by its content.

[15] Presumably the 'Theopompean' *de consiliis*: so e.g. Strasburger, *Caesars Eintritt in die Geschichte*, 108; and Brunt, *CR* 7 (1957), 193.

mentioned this in the context of *Cic.* 20. 6–7, where he
discusses Caesar's guilt: he would have welcomed the eru-
dite allusion to Cicero's own works (cf. 20. 3). Again, had
he yet known of Cicero's support for Pompey's *curatio
annonae* (*Pomp.* 49. 6), he would probably have included it;
after underlining Pompey's part in securing Cicero's recall
(*Cic.* 33. 2–4), he would naturally mention Cicero's grateful
recompense. *Lucullus* offers fewer possibilities of comparison with later Lives; but, at least; the confrontation of
Lucullus and Pompey in Cilicia is very curtly dismissed at
Luc. 36. 4. Plutarch is better informed by the time of
Pompey (31. 8–13). Finally, a very clear case is afforded by
the accounts of the triumviral proscriptions. In the brief
notice of *Cic.* 46. 5, Plutarch clearly states that Lepidus
wished to save his brother Paullus, but sacrificed him to the
wishes of Antony and Octavian. By the time of *Antony* (19.
3), Plutarch had discovered a different version: that Lepidus
was the man who wished to kill Paullus, and the other two
acceded to his wishes. That version came from a source
which he could trust, and in *Antony* he prefers it: he notes
the *Cicero* version merely as a variant.[16]

Such signs of increasing knowledge are not surprising; it
would indeed be odd if Plutarch had *not* read more widely
as the series progressed. What is striking is that *Cicero* and
Lucullus stand so firmly isolated from the other, later Lives.
We should expect to discover that Plutarch's knowledge
continued to increase as his reading widened—that *Pompey*,
for instance, showed more familiarity with the period than
Caesar, for we know that *Pompey* was the later Life to be
written;[17] but it is very difficult, and probably impossible,
to detect such a further increase in knowledge. The full
support for this negative thesis cannot, of course, be set out
here: only a detailed comparison of every parallel version in
every Life could establish this. But it may be helpful to
examine two specific examples, taking sequences of events
which Plutarch several times describes in detail: first, the

---

[16] The *Antony* version is shared by App. *BC* iv. 12. 45 (cf. Dio, xlvii. 6. 3), and
probably derives from Asinius Pollio.
[17] *Caes.* 35. 2 refers to the projected *Pompey* in the future tense, ὡς ἐν τοῖς περὶ
ἐκείνου γραφησομένοις τὰ καθ' ἕκαστον δηλωθήσεται. Cf. below, pp. 277–82.

formation of the triple pact in 60 BC, and the ensuing consulate of Caesar; and, secondly, Caesar's assassination.

(i) Plutarch accepted the view of Asinius Pollio: it was the pact of Crassus, Pompey, and Caesar which set Rome on the path to civil war.[18] It was inevitable that several Lives should treat this alliance, and continue to narrate Caesar's consulate: and Plutarch duly gives accounts at *Luc.* 42. 6–8, *Cic.* 30. 1–4, *Caes.* 13–14, *Pomp.* 47–8, *Cato* 31–3, and *Crass.* 14. 1–5. It is immediately clear that the four later accounts, especially those of *Caesar, Pompey,* and *Cato,* are better informed than those of *Lucullus* and *Cicero.* The *Lucullus* version is very skimpy: a brief and misleading reference to the formation of the pact, a mention of the fracas in the assembly, then a rather fuller treatment of the Vettius affair. All this is substantially different from the later accounts: Crassus is never again associated with Cato or Lucullus, as he is here (42. 4); Vettius is never again mentioned. *Cicero* also passes swiftly over these events: no mention of the triple alliance, no formal treatment of the year 59—though a place could easily have been found among the antecedents of Cicero's exile, as *Caes.* 14. 17 shows. Only a very few items are exploited, and those are misleading: the story of *Cic.* 30. 3–5, Cicero's request for a legateship in Caesar's army, has something behind it, but this version is very garbled;[19] the anecdote of *Cic.* 30. 5, Caesar denouncing Cicero in the assembly, is another garbling, this time of the story of Dio, xxxviii. 17. 1–2. Neither item is exploited in the later Lives. Equally, Plutarch does not yet seem to know some material which he was later to exploit: he would surely have mentioned the story of *Cato* 32. 8–10, Cicero prevailing on Cato to take the oath.

In the four later Lives, Plutarch is much richer in narrative detail; he has evidently discovered a new store of material in the interval since *Lucullus* and *Cicero.* Moreover, these later accounts are extremely similar to one another—

---

[18] For Pollio's view, Hor. *Carm.* ii. 1. 1; cf. *Caes.* 13. 4–6, *Pomp.* 47. 4, *Cato* 30. 9.

[19] Cf. *Cic. Att.* ii. 18. 3, 19. 5.

the similarities often extend to verbal echoes;[20] and all seem to be based on the same material. Naturally, different Lives select different material for emphasis, as Plutarch tailors his material to suit the Lives' subjects and aims; but literary technique can explain all the variations, and there is no indication that he made any fresh discoveries during these Lives' composition. Literary technique would naturally lead him to be fuller in *Pompey* than in *Caesar* on Pompey's ill-judged remark in the assembly—*Pompey* finds room to speculate on his motives (47. 6–8); while *Caesar* understandably emphasizes Caesar's brushes with Considius and Cato, which were not relevant for *Pompey. Caesar* passes over the role of Lucullus, eschewing the complicating individual; but *Pompey* has made much of the Lucullus–Pompey feud, and therefore includes the material (48. 2, 7, cf. 4). In *Caesar* Plutarch finds it useful to treat the two agrarian bills together (εὐθὺς εἰσέφερε νόμους . . ., 14. 2); but in *Cato* it is necessary to treat them separately, for each led to distinct acts of heroism on Cato's part which Plutarch wishes to include.[21] The first provoked Cato's refusal to swear to the bill (32. 4–11), the second the disgraceful episode of the imprisonment (33. 1–4). In this Life, Cato himself dominates all the opposition to Caesar; the role of fellow-opponents—Bibulus, Lucullus, Considius—is abbreviated or suppressed. Finally, *Crassus* understandably has the briefest treatment. Crassus had the smallest (or least public) role in these events, and Plutarch is by then hurrying on to the more rewarding theme of the Syrian command.

---

[20] Verbal similarities: e.g. *Caes.* 14. 2 stigmatizes the νόμους οὐχ ὑπάτῳ προσήκοντας, ἀλλὰ δημάρχῳ τινὶ θρασυτάτῳ; cf. *Pomp.* 47. 5, παρεκβαίνων τὸ τῆς ἀρχῆς ἀξίωμα, καὶ τρόπον τινὰ δημαρχίαν τὴν ὑπατείαν καθιστάς, and *Cato* 32. 2, ἃ γὰρ οἱ θρασύτατοι δήμαρχοι καὶ ὀλιγωρότατοι πρὸς χάριν ἐπολιτεύοντο τῶν πολλῶν, ταῦτ' ἀπ' ἐξουσίας ὑπατικῆς αἰσχρῶς καὶ ταπεινῶς ὑποδυόμενος τὸν δῆμον ἔπραττε. *Crass.* 14. 4, like *Cato* 33. 5, speaks of the Gallic command establishing Caesar ὥσπερ εἰς ἀκρόπολιν; *Caesar* and *Pompey* are close to each other in their descriptions of Pompey and Crassus in the assembly (*Caes.* 14. 3–6, *Pomp.* 47. 6–8); and so on.

[21] It is thus unnecessary to assume, with Taylor, *AJP* 72 (1951), 265 (cf. Meier, *Hist.* 10 (1961), 72–3), that Plutarch went to a new source when composing *Cato*, and there found the distinction of two separate bills. Note the plural νόμους in *Caesar*; but Plutarch there finds it stylistically useful to speak as if the bills were debated simultaneously. The procedure of Appian (*BC* 2. 10. 35) is exactly similar. Such conflations are common in Plutarch: cf. Pelling, 'Plutarch's Adaptation of his Source-Material', *JHS* 100 (1980), (above, p. 126).

The complex events of 60–56 are dismissed in a single chapter.

One further point confirms the close connection of these accounts: all show similarities with the version of Cassius Dio (xxxvii. 54–xxxviii. 12), and the similarities are best explained in terms of shared source-material. *Pompey* and *Caesar* have the story of Pompey and Crassus in the assembly; Dio has it too, and gives a similar emphasis to Pompey's outburst.[22] *Pompey* and *Cato* have the assault on Bibulus; so does Dio, with similar details.[23] *Caesar* and *Cato* are close to Dio in the stress and interpretation given to the election of Clodius, and in the emphasis they lay on the attempt to imprison Cato.[24] Suetonius, too, shows some contact with this tradition: in particular, his versions of the attempted imprisonment and of the dynastic marriages are close to both Plutarch and Dio.[25] The natural explanation is to suppose that all Plutarch's later accounts are informed by the same source or sources, and that this material was also available to Suetonius and Dio; and this supports the hypothesis that Plutarch's four later versions are all based on the same store of material.

(ii) Caesar's assassination is naturally treated most lavishly in *Brutus* (7 ff.) and in *Caesar* (62 ff.). *Cicero* had mentioned these events briefly (42); *Antony* (13–15) has a little material on the murder, then rather more on the immediate sequel.

Cicero adds little to this analysis. Its account is brief and shows no signs of great background knowledge; but brevity is only to be expected, for Cicero's role was so small. *Antony* is more interesting, but here too the differences are explained by literary technique. For instance, it is no surprise that *Brutus* and *Caesar* omit the story of *Ant.* 13. 2, Trebonius resisting the proposal to kill Antony, for this

[22] *Pomp.* 47. 6–8, *Caes.* 14. 3–6; Dio, xxxviii. 4. 4–5. 5.

[23] *Pomp.* 48. 2, *Cato* 32. 3; Dio, xxxviii. 6. 3.

[24] Clodius: *Caes.* 14. 16–17, *Cato* 32. 10, 33. 6; Dio, xxxviii. 12. 1–2. Cato's imprisonment: *Caes.* 14. 11–12, *Cato* 33. 1–4; Dio, xxxviii. 3. 2–3. The two authors give this story a different context, but seem to reflect the same original item. It was probably narrated 'out of time' in the shared source, and both authors chose to exploit it where they thought best. Cf. Marsh, *CJ* 22 (1927), 508–13, and Meier, art. cit. 71–9.

[25] Suet. *Div. Iul.* 20. 4 (imprisonment); 21 (marriages).

item is only a peg for the more interesting tale, drawn from the *Second Philippic*—Trebonius had earlier tried to involve Antony in the plot, and Antony had kept the secret.[26] This is an anecdote of some interest for Antony himself, but it tells us little of Caesar or Brutus, and is naturally omitted from their Lives. When *Antony* comes to the sequel of the assassination, Plutarch understandably wishes to simplify the confusing sequence of events. Two senate-sittings are conflated (14. 3); *Brutus* 19 distinguishes them. The role of complicating individuals is suppressed: nothing on Lepidus, nor on Plancus, nor even on Cicero's plea for amnesty. All three are mentioned in other Lives.[27] Nor does Plutarch mention the items of *Brutus* 20. 1, Antony's request for a public funeral and for the opening of Caesar's will. But none of this abbreviation is hard to understand. Plutarch's emphasis in *Antony* is simple: the brilliance of Antony's conciliation, the nobility of the solution he could bring— these Plutarch describes in his most affective language (14. 4). Yet this solution is swiftly and characteristically upset by Antony's impulse to play for popularity at the funeral (14. 5). Had the request for a public funeral been included, Antony's demagogy might no longer seem a sudden impulse: it is therefore omitted. The other individuals who pressed for peace would equally complicate the picture: they are therefore cut away. There is certainly no need to suppose that he is less well informed here than in *Brutus* or *Caesar*.

Brutus and *Caesar* themselves pose a more complicated problem. Again, the two accounts show close similarities of language and content where they overlap;[28] but these two Lives have very different interests and aims, and the selection of material differs greatly. *Caesar* is a very historical Life. It has explained Caesar's career in terms of his popular support: from the beginning, he is the champion and the favourite of the *demos*, and he easily deceives the short-sighted optimates.[29] But as tyrant he loses his popularity,

[26] Cic. *Phil.* ii. 34. For Plutarch's use of this speech, see below, pp. 297–9.

[27] Lepidus: *Caes.* 67. 2. Plancus: *Brut.* 19. 1. Cicero: *Cic.* 42. 3, *Brut.* 19. 1.

[28] Cf. Stoltz, 75–81

[29] *Caes.* 4. 4–5, 5. 3, 5. 8–9, 6. 3–7, etc.; deceived optimates at 4. 6–9, 5. 8, 6. 7, 7. 5, etc. Cato alone saw the truth (13. 3), though Cicero had earlier felt suspicions (4. 8–9). By 14. 6 it is too late, and the optimates can only grieve.

and it is then that his fortunes waver;[30] and he loses this
less by his own errors than by the failings of his friends.[31]
This focus on the *demos* continues in the closing chapters.
Their reactions are carefully traced in chs. 60–1 (where
Plutarch seems to reinterpret and distort his source-material);[32] then *Caes.* 62. 1 makes οἱ πολλοί turn to Brutus,
whereas in *Brutus* itself it seems not to be artisans, but 'the
first of the citizens', who give Brutus his encouragement.[33]
Caesar, then, seeks the origins of the assassination in
Caesar's own actions and those of his friends, and the effect
of these on the *demos*. Such a reading naturally reduces the
interest in the peculiar motives and characters of the conspirators; indeed, an extended treatment of Brutus and
Cassius is delayed to a point where Caesar's fall already
seems inevitable.[34] It is therefore natural for *Caesar* strictly
to follow biographical relevance, and to suppress most of
the material of *Brutus* which deals with the conspirators'
side of events. *Caesar* mentions the long-nurtured resentment of Cassius only briefly;[35] and the delicate approaches
to possible conspirators, fully described in *Brutus*, have no
place in *Caesar*.[36]

Brutus, in contrast, is a more moralistic life than *Caesar*:
'tyrannicide' is the elevating theme which links it to its pair

[30] *Caes.* 56. 7, 60. 1, 60. 5, 61. 9–10, 62. 1: below, n. 32.

[31] *Caes.* 51, where the διαβολή earned by the friends—ἐπὶ τούτοις γὰρ ἐδυσφόρουν
Ῥωμαῖοι, 51. 3—prepares for this loss of popular support; cf. also 57. 2, 57. 7, 60.
8, 61. See also below, p. 284 and n. 66.

[32] The popular reactions to the regal salutation are traced at 60. 3; to the
excessive honours at 60. 5 (rather uneasily, Plutarch represents them as shocked at
the insult to the senate); to the Lupercalia affair at 61. 6; to the tribunes'
imprisonment at 61. 9–62. 1. App. *BC* ii. 107–9 and Suet. *Div. Iul.* 78–9, both
apparently from the same source, have no such emphasis; nor does *Ant.* 12. App.
ii. 109. 458 further gives a different reading of the people's reaction at the
Lupercalia. Plutarch stresses their resentment at the attempts to crown Caesar;
for Appian, their dominant emotion was applause for his rejection of the crown.
For the rather different account of Nic. Dam. (*FGrH* 90) *vit. Aug.* 68–79, cf.
Jacoby, ad loc.

[33] *Brut.* 10. 6: this was apparently the version and emphasis of the source (cf.
App. *BC* ii. 113. 472).

[34] *Caes.* 62, using material treated earlier in the corresponding account in
Brutus.

[35] *Caes.* 62. 8. As the text stands, a cross-reference directs the reader to *Brutus*
for a fuller treatment, here as at 68. 7; cf. *Brut.* 9. 9, similarly referring to *Caesar*.
See below, pp. 277–82.

[36] *Brut.* 11–12.

Dion. It is less concerned with the historical background
than *Caesar*,[37] and here Plutarch has nothing of the *demos*-
motif, nothing even of the sequence of outrages (such as the
Lupercalia) which provoked such unrest.[38] He here prefers
more ethically promising themes: the anecdotes of Porcia,
the thoughtful justice with which Brutus tried his cases on
the morning of the Ides, or the constancy with which he
bore the πολλὰ θορυβώδη. The pure motives of Brutus are set
off by the brooding resentment of Cassius, μᾶλλον ἰδίᾳ
μισοκαῖσαρ ἢ κοινῇ μισοτύραννος (8. 5)—and Cassius is a far
blacker and more complex character here than in *Caesar*.
This material could have had no place in *Caesar*: it is
relevant to the conspirators alone, and *Caesar* is anyway not
that sort of moralistic Life. There is no hint of increasing
knowledge here.

The treatment of the Ides itself largely follows biographical relevance. *Caesar* describes events from Caesar's own
viewpoint: the warnings of the soothsayers, of Calpurnia,
and of Artemidorus; then the visit of D. Brutus, with his
cogent arguments that Caesar must attend the senate, despite the warnings: τίνας ἔσεσθαι λόγους παρὰ τῶν φθονούντων;
How close Caesar came to escape!—and yet eventually he
had no choice, the pressures of rule forced him to attend:
that is the tragic emphasis of *Caesar*. *Brutus* has no such
theme. The delay on the morning of the Ides is there
narrated from the conspirators' viewpoint, one of those
θορυβώδη which Brutus impressively overcame. The focus
rests on the forum and the conspirators; a message is heard
that Caesar is approaching (16. 1), but the narrative switches
to him only at the moment of his death. Plutarch here
concentrates on Brutus' own role in the killing: Caesar
surrendered to his blows when he saw Brutus, too, among

---

[37] Appian's account suggests that the shared source (below, pp. 286–8) was
much richer in historical analysis: e.g. *BC* ii. 113. 474, detail of the conspirators'
background and connections; ii. 120. 505–7, an analysis of the urban plebs.
Plutarch here suppresses most of this: *Brut.* 12 is more interested in men who
were not involved than in men who were. A terse μιγάδες at *Brut.* 18. 12, and a
dismissive ἐν πλήθεσι φορὰς ἀσταθμήτους καὶ ταχείας φερομένοις at 21. 2, are the only
reflections of the analysis of the plebs.
[38] *Brut.* 9. 9 refers to *Caesar*: above n. 35, and pp. 277–82 below.

his foes;[39] Brutus, too, was wounded. In the sequel, *Brutus* naturally has more detail of the conspirators' movements; *Caesar* stresses the general reaction to Caesar's death—and, particularly, the recrudescence of the popular fervour which the Life has carefully traced.

A difficulty remains: the two Lives show one positive discrepancy. Both mention that Antony was delayed outside the senate-house: but who did the delaying? *Brutus*, correctly, says Trebonius (17. 2); but *Caesar* says that it was D. Brutus Albinus (66. 4). It is almost certain that Plutarch's principal source here named Trebonius: that is the version of Appian, and his account is so similar to Plutarch that they must share the same source-material.[40] It is possible that Plutarch has deliberately distorted his narrative in *Caesar* by transferring the act to D. Brutus: such techniques are not unknown in his work.[41] But it is easiest to assume that this is a simple error: perhaps an error of memory, if he did not have his source before his eyes when he wrote;[42] perhaps one of those slips which find their way into the most careful writing. At least, this cannot be a case of increasing knowledge, or not a significant one: his main

---

[39] *Caes.* 66. 12 notes this item as a λεγόμενον; *Brutus* is less punctilious. For a similar case, cf. Cinna's dream: ὥς φασι at *Caes.* 68. 3, but no qualification in the more excited *Brut.* 20. 9.

[40] App. *BC* ii. 117. 490: presumably from Pollio, cf. pp. 286–8 below.

[41] e.g. at *Ant.* 5. 10 Antony and Cassius are given the rabble-rousing speech in Caesar's camp, though at *Caes.* 31. 3 Plutarch knows that Caesar made the speech himself (cf. Caes. *BC* i. 7); at *Pomp.* 58. 6 Marcellus is given a proposal which Plutarch knows to be Scipio's, and a remark he elsewhere gives to Lentulus (cf. *Caes.* 30.4, 6: see K. Raaflaub, *Chiron*, 4 (1974), 308–9). Something similar seems to have happened at *Ant.* 5. 6: there Antony is allowed to propose on 1 Jan. 49 that both Caesar and Pompey should disarm, while at *Pomp.* 58. 8 Plutarch knows that this was proposed a month earlier by Curio (*contra* Raaflaub, art. cit. 306–11, who believes that Antony genuinely revived Curio's ploy at that time). In the present instance, note that D. Brutus has already had a considerable role in *Caesar*, whereas Trebonius has not been mentioned. Elsewhere we can see similar simplifications: for instance, the two names at 67.4 seem to represent a longer list in the principal source, as App. *BC* ii. 119. 500 suggests; and Plutarch may have felt that he had too many individuals already. Note that *Ant.* 13. 4 has a vague ἐνίους in this context, though we should expect Trebonius to be named: he has already figured largely in that chapter. That looks like deliberate fudging, and may be the work of a man who is conscious of the inconsistency between his other two versions.

[42] Cf. Russell's explanation of similar errors in *Coriolanus*, *JRS* 53 (1963), 22 (below, p. 359). On the possible use of memory, below, pp. 304–7.

source seems to have contained the truth, and it cannot be the case that he first discovered the correct version later than *Caesar*. Whether misremembering or distortion, it at least seems to be misremembering or distortion of an accurate original.

As in the example of the accounts of 60–59, biographical technique can explain the differences in the later Lives; and it could also again be argued that they rest on similar source-material. However, the analysis of the sources is here more complicated, and will be left until the second part of the paper.[43]

No further examples will here be pursued, but in other parts of their narrative, too, close similarities among the six later Lives are abundant, and there are no hints of increasing knowledge.[44] Such differences and discrepancies as are found are always explicable, either as conscious literary devices or as simple and natural errors.[45] The impression is unmistakable: Plutarch's knowledge of the period increases greatly between *Lucullus* and *Cicero* and the other Lives—and then it seems to stop, with all the later Lives being based on the same store of knowledge. If this is so, it is natural to suspect that the later Lives were prepared simultaneously.

(b) Cross-references

The suggestion of simultaneous preparation would be more plausible if it could be shown that Plutarch worked in this way elsewhere; and some indications of this are afforded by his cross-references—the fifty or so notices, normally in the form ὡς ἐν τοῖς περὶ ... γέγραπται, which are scattered

---

[43] Below, pp. 290–2.

[44] The exceptionally curious may find further examples analysed in my doctoral dissertation on *Caesar* (Oxford D.Phil. thesis, 1974). Other parallel accounts where we might expect to find increasing knowledge and do not: the accounts of Luca, *Caes.* 21. 3–6, *Pomp.* 51. 4–5, *Crass.* 14. 6–7; the analysis of Roman κακοπολιτεία, *Caes.* 28, *Pomp.* 54, *Cato* 47; the debates before the outbreak of the war, *Ant.* 5, *Caes.* 30–1, *Pomp.* 58–9; Pharsalus, *Caes.* 42–6, *Pomp.* 68–73.

[45] For the literary devices see 'Plutarch's Adaptation', 127–31, and above, 126–33; for the errors, cf. below, pp. 306–7.

278   C. B. R. Pelling

among the Lives.[46] In discussing these, we should first
note that simultaneous preparation need not imply simultaneous *publication*—still less simultaneous composition of
final drafts, as Mewaldt once proposed.[47] The final biographies are individual works of art, and Plutarch must have
given his total attention to each in turn: if several Lives had
been prepared together, he would presumably complete the
final drafts one after another in fairly quick succession.
Therefore no argument against simultaneous preparation
can be drawn from *Caes.* 35. 2, where Plutarch refers to his
projected *Pompey* in the future tense: this shows only that
the final draft of *Pompey* was written later than that of
Caesar. *Caes.* 35. 2 might rather support the notion of
simultaneous preparation, for it shows that Plutarch has
already considered in some detail the range of material and
the presentation of the later Life: he can already refer to it
as a justification for abbreviating his present treatment. It
is no surprise that he can already regard himself as engaged
upon *Pompey* as well as *Caesar*, and can a few chapters later
refer to *Pompey* in the present tense: δηλοῦμεν ἐν τοῖς περὶ
ἐκείνου γράμμασιν, 45. 9.

This is relevant to the problem of the contradictory
cross-references. The future tense of *Caes.* 35. 2 and the
present of *Caes.* 45. 9 are the exception: nearly all the cross-
references have perfect tenses, γέγραπται. Such references
appear to provide evidence for the relative chronology of
the Lives. For instance, from *Cato* 54.9, ταῦτα μὲν οὖν ἐν τοῖς
περὶ Πομπηΐου γέγραπται, it seems to follow that *Cato* is later
than *Pompey*; *Pomp.* 16. 8 should suggest that *Pompey* is
later than *Brutus*; and so on. But some of the references
seem to contradict one another. *Caes.* 62. 8 and 68. 7 cite
Brutus; *Brut.* 9. 9 cites *Caesar*. *Tim.* 13. 10 and 33. 4
cite *Dion*; *Dion* 58. 10 cites *Timoleon*. *Cam.* 33. 10 quotes
Romulus, and *Thes.* 1.4 and *Rom.* 21. 1 quote *Numa*; but
Numa twice quotes *Camillus*, at 9. 15 and 12. 13. Simple
excision or emendation does not seem adequate to solve the

[46] The full list is given by Stoltz, 9. Study of the cross-references led Brożek,
for reasons similar to those given here, to suggest simultaneous preparation of
several Lives (*Eos*, 53 (1963), 68–80); cf. also Gomme, 83 n. 3.

[47] *Hermes* 42 (1907), 564–78, at 567–8; refuted by Stoltz, 63–8.

problem.[48] Nor does Mewaldt's suggestion, that several
Lives were *published* simultaneously, seem satisfactory;[49]
that theory anyway implies a simplified idea of ancient
'publication', for it is hard to see why Plutarch should not
have circulated a work among friends and pupils as soon as
it was complete.

However, Mewaldt may still have been on the right
track, for simultaneous *preparation* is more likely to afford
an explanation. It certainly seems that the 'publication'
dates of the three pairs *Lyc.–Numa*, *Them.–Cam.*, and
Thes.–Rom. were close to one another:[50] and this is precisely
what we should expect, if these pairs had been prepared
together. This would be a sensible procedure, for *Numa*,
Camillus, and *Romulus* would all involve research of a very
similar type, perhaps based on the same sources.[51] The
same applies to *Dion* and *Timoleon*; and we have already
noticed the close similarities between *Caesar* and *Brutus*,
which suggest that they are based on the same material.

[48] The analysis of Stoltz strongly defended the authenticity of the other, non-
contradictory cross-references. Stoltz doubted the authenticity of *Dion* 58. 10,
Brut. 9. 9, and *Cam.* 33. 10, but even here hesitated to delete. The language of
these three cross-references seems no less Plutarchian than that of the others: cf.
Mewaldt, *Gnomon* 6 (1930), 431–4. Note also the forceful argument of J. Geiger's
doctoral dissertation: 'Should one believe that on some 1000 folio pages an author
has made 45 references to other places in his work: in addition to these 3 other
references, through interpolation, corruption or otherwise, have made their way
into the text: and all three of them had the bad luck to have one at least of the
genuine references, so sparsely sown in the text, to testify to their false pretensions?' ('A Commentary on Plutarch's *Cato Minor*' (Oxford D.Phil. thesis 1971);
cf. his article 'Munatius Rufus and Thrasea Paetus on Cato the Younger',
Athenaeum, 57 (1979), 48–72).

[49] Stoltz, 58 ff.; in particular, the aorist ἐκδόντες at *Thes.* 1. 4 clearly implies
that *Lyc.–Numa* had already been published. Flacelière's defence of Mewaldt
(*REG* 61 (1948), 68–9) is countered by Hamilton, xxxvi–xxxvii. Jones, *JRS* 56
(1966), 67 (above, pp. 107–8), adopts a modified form of Mewaldt's theory, but is not
convincing.

[50] The language of *Thes.* 1. 4 seems to imply that *Romulus* was written soon
after *Numa*: so Jones, *JRS* 56 (1966), 68 n. 57 (above, p. 111) and Bühler, *Maia*
14 (1962), 281. Nor can *Numa* and *Camillus* be far apart. *Numa* twice quotes
Camillus; but *Numa* itself seems to be an early Life, for *Pericles*, one of the tenth
pair (*Per.* 2. 5), quotes *Lysander*, and *Lysander* quotes *Lycurgus* (*Per.* 22. 4, *Lys.*
17. 11, with Stoltz 101–2). Some reservations concerning this type of argument are
given below, and conclusions as precise as those of Jones (art. cit. 66–8, and above,
pp. 106–11) are not possible; but this whole group of Lives does seem early.

[51] The *Quaestiones Romanae*, partly based on similar source-material, seem to
have been composed at about the same time: Jones, art. cit. 73 (above, p. 122).
They are quoted at *Rom.* 15. 7 and *Cam.* 19. 12.

If each of these groups was the product of simultaneous preparation, two alternative explanations of the contradictory cross-references are possible. (i) Suppose, *exempli gratia*, that *Dion–Brutus* was composed earlier than *Alexander–Caesar*. The second pair would then be issued only a short time afterwards; there might then be only a small number of copies of *Dion–Brutus* in existence, circulating among Plutarch's acquaintances. It is quite possible that Plutarch himself subsequently inserted the cross-reference at *Brut.* 9. 9; ancient publication is a much more continuous process than its modern equivalent.[52] The same would apply to the offending references in the other groups. (ii) But it is probably better to assume that the references were already included in Plutarch's first 'published' version. By the time he wrote *Brutus*, he was fairly sure of what he would include in *Caesar*; he may even have had some sort of draft for the later Life.[53] He might refer to this later treatment as easily as, in *Caesar* itself, he would refer to the planned *Pompey*—or as easily as a modern editor, producing a work in fascicles, would refer to a passage in a future volume with the same formula as he would use for one already published. The use of the perfect γέγραπται in such references is still odd, especially in view of the scrupulous future tenses at *Caes.* 35. 2 (and at *Mar.* 29. 12 and *de mal. Hdt.* 866b); but it is not really much odder than the characteristic epistolary use of past tenses, relating an action to the viewpoint of the reader.[54]

---

[52] Cf. Ziegler, RE s.v. 'Plutarchos' 901, with *Hermes* 66 (1931), 268–9.

[53] For the possible nature of such a 'draft', see below, pp. 308–9. This may help to explain the oddity of *Tim.* 13. 10, referring to a passage of *Dion* which does not seem to exist. Plutarch may have included the relevant passage in an early version of *Dion*, but excised it from his final draft, forgetting to alter the reference in *Timoleon*: so Brożek, art. cit. 76–7. Plutarch may equally, if *Tim.* is the earlier Life, have intended at that time to include the passage in the planned *Dion*, but later have altered his mind or forgotten.

[54] Plutarch elsewhere uses such phrases and tenses as Γάιος δὲ Μάρκιος, ὑπὲρ οὗ τάδε γέγραπται, in the introduction to a Life (*Cor.* 1. 1, cf. *Cic.* 1. 5, *Agis* 3. 3, *Ti. Gr.* 1. 7); but an epistolary flavour is there felt especially strongly (cf. *Arat.* 1. 5). *Flam.* 16. 6, in mid-Life, is a closer parallel. See Stoltz, 86. It is of course possible that *Caesar* was expected sooner after *Brutus* than *Pompey* after *Caesar*; if a longer delay was anticipated in the second case, the future tenses at *Caes.* 35. 2 are more explicable.

It is worth digressing to point an important consequence of this. Whatever their explanation, the contradictory cross-references remain important; for (as J. Geiger has observed in an important dissertation)[55] they greatly impugn the reliability of the other cross-references as a criterion for establishing the sequence of the Lives. On at least three occasions, the cross-references do *not* refer back from a later to an earlier Life; and it is hardly likely that these are the only such 'forward-looking'—or 'sideways-looking'—references. In these three instances, other cross-references happen to show that the natural chronological inference would be false. Most of the other references have no such control; many stand as the only such indication of the sequence of two Lives, with no references elsewhere to confirm or impugn the chronological inference. *Cato* 54. 9 uses a perfect tense to refer to *Pompey*: but there, too, Plutarch might have added the reference subsequently or (more probably) might be using a past tense to refer to a projected Life. It is likely that a past tense should refer to a Life which, if not already in circulation, was at least expected soon; but that is all. It is clear that the relative chronology can only be established within wide limits, and that attempts to establish a detailed sequence on this basis are not plausible.[56]

A convenient solution, then, is offered to the problem of the cross-references if we assume that Plutarch often combined his preparation of several Lives. If the contradictory cross-references were included in Plutarch's original versions, it seems that when composing one Life he already had a firm idea of what a later Life would contain; in that case, the instance of *Caes.* 35. 2, where Plutarch has already considered the content of the projected *Pompey*, would not be an isolated example. Even if some of the references are subsequent additions made by Plutarch himself to the text, they still confirm that he issued a sequence of closely related Lives in quick succession. This in itself does not prove that they were prepared together, but it is certainly

[55] See n. 48.
[56] Thus the detailed argument of Jones, art. cit. 66–8 (above, pp.106–11), is not cogent.

just what we should expect if they had been so prepared. If
he followed the procedure of simultaneous preparation elsewhere, for instance in the cases of *Romulus*, *Numa*, and
Camillus, it is natural to suppose that he might do the same
with *Caesar*, *Pompey*, *Cato*, and the rest; and it is no
surprise to find that one set of contradictory cross-references, those of *Caesar* and *Brutus*, relates to this group.

(c) 'Cross-fertilization'

A further indication may be combined with that of the
cross-references. It is natural to expect signs of 'cross-fertilization' in the Lives—Plutarch discovering an item when
working for one Life, then remembering it and exploiting it
in his later writings. For instance, it was presumably when
working for *Cicero* that Plutarch came across the story of
Cic. 34, Cicero's attempt to destroy the records of Clodius'
tribunate: he remembered this, and repeated it, in the later
Cato (40). *Cicero* had mentioned the devotion felt by P.
Crassus for Cicero—Publius even managed to reconcile
him to his father Marcus (*Cic.* 33. 8): that is remembered,
and used, in *Crassus* (13. 5). The *Numa* had involved
Plutarch in some reading about the complexities of the
Roman calendar; he later exploited some of this knowledge
at *Caes.* 59. 3–4. There are a fair number of such cases,
identifiable with some probability. Again, one would expect
these to give an indication of the Lives' relative chronology.

We duly find such cross-fertilization among this group of
Roman Lives: for instance, *Pomp.* 10. 7–9 makes an astute
criticism (and one which suggests first-hand knowledge) of
the writings of C. Oppius, a work which Plutarch surely
read for the *Caesar*.[57] But these indications are found in a
very bewildering fashion, one which seems to exclude the
possibility of 'earlier' and 'later' research. For instance,
there are two anecdotes included in both *Pompey* and *Cato*
which seem to be cases of this phenomenon. The first is the
story of Demetrius of Antioch: the popular courting of this
freedman of Pompey, and Cato's dignified reaction (*Cato*
13, *Pomp.* 40). The second is the tale of Pompey's offer of

---

[57] For Oppius, see below, p. 289.

intermarriage with Cato: Pompey offered to marry Cato's elder niece himself, and give the younger niece to his son; the women were delighted with the proposal, and they resented Cato's refusal—but they later recognized that he had been wise (*Cato* 30, *Pomp.* 44). Both stories are likely to come from the reading for *Cato*: both focus on Cato as the wise and sober champion of political rectitude, while Pompey is in the first story incidental, in the second the butt and villain of the piece.[58] The items are presumably gleaned from that 'Catonian' literature which was abundant in the early Empire;[59] the prominent role of Munatius Rufus in the intermarriage story suggests that it is ultimately drawn from his *Memoirs*, whether or not Plutarch knew them directly.[60] The natural conclusion would be that *Pompey* is later than *Cato*, and exploits material gathered for the earlier Life;[61] yet, if the earlier analysis of the cross-references is correct, the reference to *Pompey* at *Cato* 54. 9 shows that *Pompey* was at least already planned and expected soon, if not already written, and its range of material had already been considered. A similar case is found in *Brutus*: *Brut.* 33, telling the story of Theodotus the Chian, seems certainly based on material collected for *Pompey* (cf. *Pomp.* 77).[62] This should suggest that *Brutus* is the later Life; yet *Pompey* refers to *Brutus* at 16. 8, and it is anyway difficult to find room for *Agesilaus–Pompey* before *Dion–Brutus*, the twelfth pair to be published.[63]

Even if the cross-references are neglected in this argument, the bewilderment is no less; for the last chapter of *Cato* exploits material which seems to have been gathered for *Brutus*.[64] This poses a familiar type of dilemma: the

[58] So Geiger, diss. cit., with additional arguments.

[59] For such literature, see e.g. Afzelius, *Class. et Med.* 4 (1941), 198–203.

[60] So Geiger, diss. cit.: perhaps transmitted by Thrasea Paetus, cf. below, pp. 289–90 and n. 84. (Geiger's arguments are repeated in his article 'Munatius Rufus and Thrasea Paetus on Cato the Younger', *Athenaeum*, 57 (1979), 48–72.

[61] Geiger tends towards this view, but prefers to think that the *Pompey* passages are based on notes taken for *Cato*, or a draft (not the final version) of *Cato*.

[62] Presumably from Pollio, as the contact with App. *BC* ii. 84–5 suggests.

[63] Cf. Jones, art. cit. 66–8 (see above, pp. 106–11), with the reservations expressed above.

[64] *Cato* 73. 6 = *Brut.* 13, 53. 5: some of this is apparently from Nicolaus of Damascus, as *Brut.* 53 suggests.

Demetrius and intermarriage stories suggest that *Pompey* is
later than *Cato*; the tale of Theodotus suggests that *Brutus*
is later than *Pompey*; yet the Porcia anecdote suggests that
Cato is later than *Brutus*. The natural escape from the
dilemma is to suppose that all three Lives were prepared
together: in that case, each might exploit the whole range of
the reading which Plutarch had undertaken. Let us take
another example: the explanation of Caesar's fall found in
Brutus (35. 4)[65] and again in *Antony* (6. 7)—Caesar himself
behaving in an equitable manner, but destroyed by the
excesses of his friends. This seems to be taken over from
Caesar, where it formed an important part of the Life's
political analysis;[66] and *Brutus* seems further to take over
some material from the preparation for *Antony* (28. 1, 50 =
Ant. 22. 6, 69. 2), despite the cross-reference to *Brutus* at
Ant. 69. 1. This implies a sequence of *Caesar*, then *Antony*,
then *Brutus*. Yet the last chapter of *Caesar* shows knowledge
of material which seems certainly gleaned from the reading
for *Brutus*; and some of the assassination account in *Caesar*
seems informed by the work of Bibulus and the memoir of
Brutus' friend Empylus, both works which were surely
read 'for' the *Brutus*.[67] The conclusion should again be the
same: *Caesar*, *Antony*, and *Brutus* were prepared together,
and then issued, together with their pairs, in quick succession. We cannot know what precise sequence their publication followed.

The conclusion should by now be firm. Nothing has
been found to counter the assumption that *Cicero* and
Lucullus were composed early in the sequence, and they

[65] The *Brutus* passage is corrupt as it stands: (the Ides of March), ἐν αἷς Καίσαρα
ἔκτειναν, οὐκ αὐτὸν ἄγοντα καὶ φέροντα πάντας ἀνθρώπους, ἀλλ᾽ ἑτέρων †δύναμιν ὄντα
ταῦτα πρασσόντων. It is important for the logic of the passage to have some
reference to 'friends': cf. the point of 35. 5, ἄμεινον ἦν τοὺς Καίσαρος φίλους ὑπομέ-
νειν ἢ τοὺς ἑαυτῶν περιορᾶν ἀδικοῦντας. Perhaps ἑτέρων conceals ἑταίρων. Ziegler's
speculative δύναμιν ὑπομένοντα ταῦτα πρασσόντων presumably captures the sense.

[66] Above, p. 274. Neither *Brutus* nor *Antony* is so interested in political
analysis, and in *Brutus* the notice is purely incidental. It is hardly likely that he
would have elaborated this (rather unusual, though hardly profound) analysis for
those Lives alone; but, once it had been developed for *Caesar*, it might readily be
taken over. For a similar instance in *Brutus*, cf. 18. 3: Plutarch there refers to
Antony's ὁμιλία καὶ συνήθεια πρὸς τὸ στρατιωτικόν, which seems to be borrowed
from one of the major themes of *Antony*.

[67] Below, pp. 290–2.

stand apart from the six later Lives; but those six Lives—
Pompey, Cato, Crassus, Caesar, Brutus, and *Antony*—stand
closely together, and show peculiarities which are best explained in terms of simultaneous preparation.[68] One last
point: five of the six Greek pairs of these Lives—*Agesilaus,
Dion, Phocion, Alexander,* and *Demetrius*—come from the
fourth and very early third centuries. The earlier Greek
Lives had been fairly widely spread, but had tended to
concentrate on the fifth century and earlier. These are
Plutarch's historical interests of the moment: the fall of the
Roman Republic, and the fourth century of Greece.

II. THE COLLECTION OF MATERIAL

(a) The range of first-hand sources

However, it is still unclear what 'simultaneous preparation'
really implies. If, for instance, most or all of the material of
these Lives was derived from a single narrative source,
'simultaneous preparation' would simply be a grand way of
saying that Plutarch read through the whole of this source
before beginning to compose. If, on the other hand, it
could be shown that he consulted a wider range of
material—or even if the Lives were largely based on earlier
biographies, as nineteenth-century researchers tended to
assume—the hypothesis of simultaneous preparation would
be far more substantial. It is not my concern to give a
comprehensive discussion of the Lives' sources, but it may
be possible, even in a brief and selective study, to gain
some notion of the width or narrowness of his research. He
quotes some twenty-five sources by name in the six later

---

[68] I omit *Sertorius* from this analysis because it relates to the very beginning of
the relevant period, and because its content affords little basis for comparison
with other Lives. It may well be later than this group of Lives: B. Scardigli, *SIFC*
43 (1971), 33–41, argues for a late date, and a significant detail may confirm this.
The early chapters of *Demetrius* point Demetrius' εὐφυΐα . . . πρὸς ἐπιείκειαν καὶ
δικαιοσύνην (4. 5), and Plutarch makes the most of what anecdotes he can find:
note the expansive treatment of the tales of chs. 3–4. Yet he omits Demetrius'
pressure to save the life of Eumenes (early 316), an item which he knows at *Eum.*
18. 6. This looks like a case of increasing knowledge: if so, *Sert.–Eum.* should be
later than *Dtr.–Ant.*

Lives, and a further half-dozen in *Lucullus* and *Cicero*; but
it is clear that he does not know all these authors at first
hand, and no criterion will tell us exactly which sources he
knows directly, and which quotations are tralatician.[69] The
purpose of this discussion will simply be to establish an
inescapable *minimum* of *types* of literature which we must
assume that Plutarch knew at first hand.

First, it is clear that the six later Lives are not based
merely on a sequence of earlier biographies. The great
similarities among these Lives, both of language and of
content, have already been noted: these are odd in themselves, if Plutarch had consulted only a series of individual
biographies, but perhaps not inexplicable.[70] More important is the regular contact which these Lives show with the
narratives of other authors. Time and again, we find an
identical narrative structure and articulation in Plutarch
and in another account; or a regular tendency to reproduce
the same items; or even a series of verbal echoes. One
example of such contact is Plutarch's closeness to Dio in
narrating Caesar's first consulate.[71] Similarly, from the year
58 onwards, Plutarch's later accounts show regular contact
with the version of Appian, both in *Bellum Civile* and in
the fragments of *Celtica*. Most of the parallels between the
two authors can be traced in Kornemann's convenient tabu-
lation, and there is no need to labour the point here.[72] Dio,
too, often shows contact with this tradition;[73] so, rather

[69] Cf. Jones, 84–6. For a particularly clear example, *Caes.* 22. 1–5, where the
citations of Tanusius Geminus and of Caesar's *commentarii* seem inherited: App.
Celt. fr. 18, certainly from the same source, retails them in the same manner.
Caes. 44. 8 and *Pomp.* 69. 7 provide a similar case: both again quote Caesar, but so
does App. *BC* ii, 79, clearly from the same source. See Peter, 120–3. Note also
Brut. 41. 7 = App. *BC* iv. 110. 463, both quoting Augustus.

[70] See the remarks on the ὑπόμνημα stage of composition, below, pp. 308–9.

[71] Above, p. 272.

[72] *Jb. für cl. Phil.* Suppl. 22 (1896), 672–91; cf. Peter, 125, and many works
since then (bibliography at Schanz–Hosius ii⁴ 28–9).

[73] The following list is very selective: Dio, xxxix. 31–2 ∼ App. *BC* ii. 17–18 ∼
Pomp. 51–3, *Crass.* 15, *Cato* 41–3; Dio, xxxix. 39. 5–7 ∼ App. ii. 18. 66 ∼ *Crass.*
16. 7–8; Dio, xl. 52–5 ∼ App. ii. 23–4 ∼ *Pomp.* 55. 6–11, *Cato* 48. 5–10; Dio, xli.
41. 1 ∼ App. ii. 40 ∼ *Cato* 53. 2–3, *Pomp.* 61. 2; Dio, xli. 46 ∼ App. ii. 56–8 ∼
Caes. 38; Dio, xlii. 3–4 ∼ App. ii. 84–6 ∼ *Pomp.* 77–80, *Brut.* 33; Dio, xlii. 40. 4–
5 ∼ App. ii. 90. 377 ∼ *Caes.* 49. 7–8; Dio, xlii. 57 ∼ App. ii. 87. 367 ∼ *Cato* 57–
8; Dio, xliii. 10–12 ∼ App. ii. 98–9 ∼ *Cato* 62–71; Dio, xliii. 12. 1, 13. 4 ∼ App.
ii. 99. 414 ∼ *Caes.* 54. *Cato* 36. 5; Dio, xliv. 8–11 ∼ App. ii. 107–10 ∼ *Caes.* 60–

more rarely, does Suetonius.[74] One possible explanation of
this systematic contact might be that the later writers had
read Plutarch himself; and it is indeed quite likely that
these authors, especially Appian, did know Plutarch, and
that some of the verbal parallels arise from echoes of Plutarch's own words.[75] It is, however, impossible to think
that all the points of contact are explicable in this way, that
Appian, Suetonius, and Dio all systematically used Plutarch
as a historical authority. It is easy to show that both Appian
and Dio would have to know all of Plutarch's six versions.
Such a combination of biographies would be an odd procedure for any historian; for both of them, independently,
it is quite impossible. So regular a contact must arise from
a shared inheritance from a common source, whether or not
the later authors knew that source directly; and, again, it
must surely be a *historical* source which Appian and Dio
are using, not a combination of biographies.

This is one occasion where the source—at least, the
ultimate source—can be identified: it is surely Asinius
Pollio. It was suggested earlier that Plutarch encountered a
rich store of new information after *Cicero* and *Lucullus*, but
before the later group of Lives. This new material appears

1, *Ant.* 12; Dio, xliv. 12 ~ App. ii. 112. 469 ~ *Caes.* 62, *Brut.* 9–10 ~ Suet. *Div.
Iul.* 80. 3; Dio, xlvi. 49 ~ App. iii. 95. 392–3 *al.* ~ *Brut.* 27; Dio, xlvii. 47.8 ~
App. iv. 114–17 ~ *Brut.* 44–5; Dio, xlviii. 38 ~ App. v. 73 ~ *Ant.* 32; Dio,
xlviii. 39. 2 ~ App. v. 76 ~ *Ant.* 33. 6–7. The similarities will be inherited from
Pollio, but Dio is very unlikely to have known Pollio at first hand: he will have
found his account transmitted in Livy (cf. below, p. 301 and n. 124). Two further
points are worth making. (*a*) The persistence of the Dio–Plutarch–Appian contact
well past Philippi supports the view that Pollio continued his history to include at
least the mid-thirties, and possibly Actium as well: so E. Gabba, *Appiano e la
storia delle guerre civili* (1956), 242–3, *contra* J. André, *La Vie et l'œuvre d'Asinius
Pollion* (1949), 46–51. (*b*) F. Millar, *A Study of Cassius Dio*, 56, tentatively
suggests that Dio used Plutarch's *Brutus* as a source. This will now be seen to be
unlikely: Dio's relation to *Brutus* is parallel to his relation to the other five later
Lives, and is best explained as a shared inheritance from a historical source.

[74] e.g. Suet. *Div. Iul.* 29. 1 ~ App. *BC* ii. 26. 100–1 ~ *Caes.* 29. 3, *Pomp.* 58.
2; Suet. 30. 4 ~ *Caes.* 46. 2; Suet. 31–2 ~ App. ii. 35 ~ *Caes.* 32; Suet. 36 ~
App. ii. 62. 260 ~ *Caes.* 39. 8; Suet. 44. 2–3 ~ App. ii. 110 ~ *Caes.* 58; and
many points of contact in the account of the assassination.

[75] For Appian's possible knowledge of Plutarch, Gabba, *Appiano* 225–8. Such
verbal parallels as App. ii. 14. 51 ~ *Caes.* 14. 8 and App. ii. 27. 106 ~ *Caes.* 30. 2
may thus be explained: see Kornemann, art cit. 577 for further close verbal
similarities. It is also possible that the elaborate comparison of Alexander and
Caesar which concludes *BC* ii is indebted to the (lost) Plutarch *synkrisis*.

to begin with the years 60–59: it is natural to suppose that Plutarch has encountered Pollio's work, beginning *ex Metello consule*, or at least a work based on this.[76] Many more indications point the same way: these have long been recognized, and there is no point in going over old ground here.[77] We shall never know whether Plutarch knew Pollio at first hand, or at least in translation;[78] but, even if he did not, it at least seems certain that he derived Pollio's account from a historical, rather than a biographical, intermediary. All six of these Lives include material from this provenance, and it is hard to believe that Plutarch consulted six different biographers, each one of which chanced to be dependent on the same original account. It must be a historical source, and this seems to have been his principal authority for the fifties, forties, and thirties. For that period, something like three-quarters of his material shows contact with the detailed account of Appian, and seems to be owed to this source.

However, it cannot be this 'Pollio-source' alone which informs these Lives. Plutarch must have supplemented this, at the very least, from *some* biographical material. In cases where Plutarch has no such biographical source, it is normally the opening chapters of the Life which make this clear: for instance, *Fabius*, where he finds little to say about his subject's early life, and reaches his first consulate by the beginning of ch. 2; or *Camillus*, which is similar; or *Coriolanus*, where his source's few hints about Coriolanus' youth are laboriously expanded.[79] In the present group of Lives,

---

[76] Therefore it is odd that the contact with Appian only begins with the year 58. It is possible that Plutarch drew his accounts of Caesar's consulate from a different source, perhaps Livy: the closeness to Dio's account has been observed, and Livy is likely to be Dio's source. But it is more likely that Appian, who is capable of exploiting a variety of sources (Gabba, *Appiano* 109–15), did not turn to the common source until ii. 15. 54. N. Barbu, *Les Sources et l'originalité d'Appien dans le deuxième livre des Guerres Civiles* (1934), 28–40, 81–8, argued on different grounds for a similar view. In that case, Plutarch and Dio both reflect Pollio's version: Dio probably inherited it from Livy.

[77] Cf. e.g. Kornemann, art. cit.; Peter, 124 ff.; A. Garzetti, comm. on *Caesar* (1954), xxii–xxxiii; Gabba, *Appiano*, esp. 119–51, 229–49; André, op. cit. 41–66.

[78] Sallust's *Histories* were translated into Greek in the early second century (*Suda* Z 73 Adler, cf. Jones, 86), and nothing precludes the possibility that Pollio was translated as well. But *Caes.* 46. 2 should not be used as evidence for this: Häussler, *RhM* 109 (1966), 339–55, is convincing.

[79] Russell, *JRS* 53 (1963), 23–5 (below, pp. 361–3).

too, we occasionally find something similar: for instance, the early chapters of *Crassus* are unusually generalized and feeble, as Plutarch makes the most of a few odd tales—tales of his marriages, of his φιλοπλουτία, of his φιλοτιμία, and so on. By ch. 4 we have reached the time of the Sullan civil wars, and material which could come from a historical source.[80] *Antony*, too, suffers from some early discomfort. Plutarch there wishes to introduce some dominant themes as soon as possible—in particular, military excellence compromised by debauchery and weakness of will; but, as we shall see, he can do no better than elaborate some hints from the *Second Philippic*. However, the other Lives are considerably richer in early detail. *Caesar* is one example: much of its early material has the flavour of a biographical source—the escape from Sulla, the trip to Nicomedes, the pirate adventure, the study under Apollonius, the early rhetorical successes at Rome. It is probable, too, that the initial lacuna contained some further details of Caesar's boyhood.[81] Some material later in the Life, especially in 17, appears to have a similar provenance: and there Plutarch quotes the work of C. Oppius for one of the anecdotes, and seems to draw several more from the same origin.[82] Plutarch elsewhere criticizes Oppius in a way which suggests first-hand knowledge of his writings, and it is likely that all this biographical material is drawn from him.[83] The other Lives are similarly rich in biographical items. *Cato* is especially full of such personalia, and that material is likely to derive from the memoirs of Munatius Rufus; Munatius' account was probably transmitted to Plutarch in the biography of

[80] Probably Fenestella: cf. *Crass.* 5. 6. All the material of the first chapters may come from the same author: we know that Fenestella mentioned the fate of the Vestal Licinia (fr. 11 P; cf. *Crass.* 1. 4–6). See Peter, 109.

[81] I have attempted to reconstruct some elements of the lost preface from Zonareas' excerpt in *CQ* 23 (1973), 343–4. Flacelière (Budé edn. *Alex.–Caes.* 130) suggests that *Caesar* is complete as it stands, but this is quite unconvincing: cf. Briscoe, *CR* 27 (1977), 177–8.

[82] Oppius is quoted at 17. 7; comparison with Suet. *Div. Iul.* 53 leaves no doubt that Oppius lies behind 17. 9–10; and he is again mentioned in the anecdote of 17. 11.

[83] *Pomp.* 10. 7–9 criticizes Oppius' bias. Oppius' work is never precisely described as a biography (cf. Strasburger, *Caesars Eintritt in die Geschichte* 30–3), but content is here more important than form. For the fragments of Oppius' work, Peter, *HRR* ii. 46–9, LXIII–LXIV.

Thrasea Paetus.[84] *Pompey* shows similar traces of the work of Theophanes.[85]

Brutus, too, is rich in personal detail, but here it may be misleading to think of a straightforward biography as a source. This will become clearer if we revert to the example of Caesar's murder, and try to detect the provenance of that material. A large proportion of Plutarch's narrative shows contact with Appian, and the two authors are often very close indeed.[86] This is no surprise: the contact is presumably due, as usual, to a shared inheritance from Pollio. But the amount of non-Appianic material in Plutarch's accounts is appreciably greater than usual—comparison, for instance, with the earlier chapters in *Caesar* leaves no doubt of this;[87] and this is odd, for Appian's account of these events is impressively full and detailed. It seems that Plutarch is here contaminating his Pollio-source with a larger supply of extraneous information. It will be useful to list some of these extraneous items: they include the earlier quarrels of Cassius and Brutus (*Brut.* 7. 1); the ἀναμενεῖ τοῦτο τὸ δέρμα Βροῦτος story (*Brut.* 8. 3, *Caes.* 62. 6); Caesar's special fear for τοὺς ὠχροὺς καὶ ἰσχνοὺς ἐκείνους (*Brut.* 8. 2, *Caes.* 62. 10, *Ant.* 11. 6); Cassius' personal reasons for enmity with Caesar (*Brut.* 8. 6–7, cf. *Caes.* 62. 8); Caesar baring his neck to a hostile crowd, and bidding his enemies strike (*Caes.* 60. 6, *Ant.* 12. 6);[88] the stories of Porcia (*Brut.* 13, 15. 6–9, 23. 4–7); the version that it was Artemidorus who handed

[84] Cf. Peter, 65–9; Flacelière, Budé edn. *Phoc.–Cato* 65–6; Geiger, 'Munatius Rufus and Thrasea Paetus on Cato the Younger', *Athenaeum*, 57 (1979), 48–52; above, pp. 282–3.

[85] Cf. Peter, 114–17; Flacelière, Budé edn. *Ages.–Pomp.* 154–6.

[86] e.g. Appl. *BC* ii. 109. 455 ~ *Caes.* 57. 7; App. ii. 110 (cf. iii. 25, 77) ~ *Caes.* 58; App. ii. 107. 445 ~ *Caes.* 60. 4; App. ii. 108–9 ~ *Caes.* 61; App. ii. 112. 466–7 ~ *Caes.* 62. 4–6, *Brut.* 7–8; App. ii. 115–16, 149. 619 ~ *Caes.* 63–5, *Brut.* 14–16; App. ii. 117 ~ *Caes.* 66, *Brut.* 17; and perhaps App. ii 112. 469 ~ *Caes.* 62. 7, *Brut.* 9–10 (though in this case Mr. Moles may be right in sugesting that App.'s account is itself indebted to Plutarch; if so, it is likely that App. is incorporating the items from memory, without having Plut.'s words before his eyes).

[87] Cf. Garzetti, comm. on *Caesar*, xxviii–xxix.

[88] The item is given a different context in Plutarch's two accounts. *Caesar* attaches it to the story of Caesar's failure to rise before the approaching magistrates, while *Antony* links it with the Lupercalia episode. It may be that the item was given no context in the source; it is more likely that Plutarch deliberately displaces it in *Antony*, where he does not use the 'approaching magistrates' story.

Caesar a letter revealing the conspiracy (*Caes.* 65. 1–4, where the rival version of App. *BC* ii. 116. 486 is mentioned as a variant); and several details of the senatorial proceedings in the days following the murder—honours for the tyrannicides, *Brut.* 19. 1; a separate session on the day after their descent from the Capitol, and the details of their provinces, *Brut.* 19. 4–5; and the decision 'to honour Caesar as a god', *Caes.* 67. 8.

Some of this material may have been transmitted by Appian's source, and suppressed by Appian himself: it would surprise no one familiar with Appian's technique if, after exploiting the story of Brutus' contention with Cassius over the urban praetorship, he dispensed with the similar item of the pair's earlier quarrels.[89] But one cannot believe that the source contained *all* these items. That source seems elsewhere to have had less taste for personalia and anecdote than this material suggests; and, in particular, Appian's account of the senatorial debate of 17 March is too detailed and well informed to be reconciled with the errors and confusions of Plutarch's extraneous material.[90] These mis-

[89] Urban praetorship: *BC* ii. 112. 466–7. But Appian is interested in the conspirators' motives, and does not portray them favourably: cf. ii. 111. If he had had the story of *Brut.* 8. 6–7 before his eyes he would have used it.

[90] (*a*) Honours were not voted to the tyrannicides, as Plutarch claims: this apparently reflects the proposal of Ti. Claudius Nero (Suet. *Tib.* 4. 1), but Appian knows that this was not carried (*BC* ii. 127. 530 ff.—apparently not put to the vote). App.'s version was doubtless that of the Pollio-source. (*b*) 'They voted to honour Caesar as a god' seems another error: there is no mention elsewhere of divine honours granted at this juncture, though many had already been voted during Caesar's lifetime (Weinstock, *Divus Julius*, esp. 281 ff., 287 ff.). Plutarch seems to imply consecration, which was in fact decreed on or about 1 Jan. 42 (Weinstock, 386). (*c*) Plutarch's notice of the provinces granted to the tyrannicides (*Brut.* 19. 5) is no less confused: Sternkopf, *Hermes* 47 (1912), 340–9. (*d*) Plutarch alone attests a separate session of the senate, held mainly in honour of the assassins and in the presence of some of them, on the day after their descent from the Capitol (*Brut.* 19. 4–5). This is surely an error (so Sternkopf, art. cit. 348–9; Motzo, *Ann. Fac. Fil. Lett. Cagliari* (1933), 26–31; *contra* e.g. Gelzer, *Cicero*, 327). We should assume that Plutarch found, perhaps in Empylus, a notice of such an honorific session, and combined this as best he could with the Pollio-source. He knew from that source that the assassins had not been present at the 17 Mar. session, for the sons of Antony and Lepidus had been sent as hostages to persuade the conspirators to descend from Capitol, and the source had clearly placed this mission *after* the 17 Mar. debate (*Brut.* 19. 2, App. ii. 142. 594; misleadingly streamlined at *Ant.* 14. 2–4). If these honours, voted in the assassins' presence, were to be introduced at all, a separate session was inevitable.

takes surely come from elsewhere, and Plutarch has grafted them on to the more responsible version he found in the Pollio-source.

The nature of this extra material suggests a source favourable to the tyrannicides: particularly eloquent is the exaggeration of the honours and support they received from the senate. The Porcia stories seem to be drawn from the βιβλίδιον μικρὸν ἀπομνημονευμάτων Βρούτου of her son Bibulus. Plutarch mentions and quotes the work in telling these very tales (*Brut.* 13. 3, 23. 7), and there is no reason to doubt that he knew this source at first hand.[91] But Bibulus may not have provided all the items: the debate in the senate, the past of Cassius, the Artemidorus story—these seem alien to such ἀπομνημονεύματα Βρούτου. Here we should rather think of the work of Empylus of Rhodes, mentioned at *Brut.* 2. 4 in terms which strongly suggest first-hand knowledge: Empylus left a μικρὸν μέν, οὐ φαῦλον δὲ σύγγραμμα περὶ τῆς Καίσαρος ἀναιρέσεως, ὃ Βροῦτος ἐπιγέγραπται. A work περὶ τῆς Καίσαρος ἀναιρέσεως—even one entitled 'Brutus'— suggests a wider scope than mere ἀπομνημονεύματα Βρούτου.[92] Plutarch seems also to have read Brutus' own letters, or at least a selection of these: these would furnish some background material and some adorning quotations.[93] But Brutus' letters hardly provided the mass of the picturesque and inaccurate extraneous material: that is surely owed to Bibulus and Empylus.

Elsewhere, too, Plutarch shows knowledge of similar mem-

---

[91] Cf. Theander, *Eranos* 57 (1959), 120–8.

[92] Empylus: *FGrH*, No. 191; mentioned as an orator by Quint. x. 6. 4. He was a companion of Brutus (*Brut.* loc. cit.), and an enthusiastic treatment is to be expected. He does not sound a reliable man for the details of senatorial decisions; and a Rhodian orator might well be attracted by the role of the Cnidian 'sophist' Artemidorus (*Caes.* 65. 1).

[93] Cf. *Brut.* 2. 4–8, 21. 6, 22. 4–6, 24. 3, 28. 2, 29. 8–11, 53. 6–7; *Cic.* 45. 2, 53(4). 4. The information which Plutarch derives from these letters is independent of the historical tradition, and (at least in the case of the *Latin* letters) seems excellent. Various collections of Brutus' letters were published: Schanz–Hosius i⁴ 397. Plutarch's quotations, when comparable with extant letters, are close enough to suggest first-hand knowledge: esp. *Brut.* 22. 4–6 ~ Cic. *ad Brut.* 24, 25 (i. 16, 17); cf. A. Sickinger, *de linguae Latinae apud Plutarchum et reliquiis et vestigiis* (diss. Freiburg, 1883), 81–3; Peter, 140–1. The letters may have been read for *Cicero* (below, p. 296); but there is no indication that Plutarch knew Cicero's letters to Brutus—note ὥς φασιν at *Brut.* 26. 6. See also below, p. 305 and n. 140.

oirs; and he seems especially to favour such literature at the
richest and most intense moments of his narrative—moments, indeed, of an intensity similar to the assassination of
Caesar. These, of course, are precisely the moments when
Pollio's account might well seem too austere for Plutarch's
purposes, and it might appear necessary to seek picturesque
detail from elsewhere. The battle of Philippi is one example.
As *Brutus* approaches the battle, we again find a sudden
increase in non-Appianic material, and it again seems clear
that Plutarch is supplementing the Pollio-source from other
accounts. The extraneous material includes most of the
omens of 39 and 48; Cassius and Brutus discussing the
ethics of suicide, 40; the mission of Clodius, who just failed
to warn Brutus of the vital success at sea, 47; most of the
account of Brutus' death, 51–2; and many details of the
fighting in both battles. This material does not read like
Pollio, and in at least one case is inconsistent with Pollio's
account.[94] It surely comes from elsewhere, and its provenance is not hard to guess. Plutarch quotes the memoirs of
Messala Corvinus several times for the details of the fighting, and then the obscure work of P. Volumnius for the
omens and the story of Brutus' death; and both Messala
and Volumnius have a tellingly prominent role in these
events.[95] They, surely, were the sources (at least the ultimate sources). It is of course possible, if Plutarch drew
Pollio's account from a historical intermediary, that it was
this writer rather than Plutarch who combined Pollio with
Messala and Volumnius—but it is much more likely that
the combination is due to Plutarch himself: this seems

[94] Ch. 47, the fine story of Clodius, cannot be reconciled with App.'s insistence
that both sides knew of the sea-battle and its outcome, *BC* iv. 122. 513. App. and
Dio agree that Brutus was forced into battle by the reproaches of his officers and
men (an obvious reminiscence of Pompey at Pharsalia), and this was doubtless
Pollio's version. Plutarch might well prefer the Clodius anecdote: the tragic
elements, both of Brutus struggling against an adverse destiny and of his coming
so close to being saved, are important to him; and the picture of Brutus which
Plutarch has favoured—e.g. ὄρθιον τὴν γνώμην ... διαφυλάττων, 29. 3—would sit
uneasily with Pollio's description of a man persuaded into a civil battle against his
better judgement.
[95] For Messala: 40. 1 ff., 40. 11, 41. 5, 42. 5, 45. 1, 45. 7, 53. 1, 53. 3. For
Volumnius: 48. 1 ff., 51. 1, 51. 3–4, 52. 2. For their works: Peter, 137–9, and
HRR ii. 52–3, 65–7, and LXVII–LXVIII, LXXVIII–LXXXIII.

another instance in which he found the Pollio-source lacking in biographical and dramatic detail, and chose to supplement it from other, more promising, versions.

Plutarch's two accounts of the Parthian Wars are likely to be similar instances: the campaign of Carrhae, described at *Crassus* 17–33, and the later war of Antony (*Ant.* 33–50). Pollio, whose concern was the civil wars, is unlikely to have been so detailed on Crassus' war: it is more likely that Plutarch has consulted at least one supplementary source, though it is hard to suggest names.[96] Names are easier when it comes to Antony's Parthian campaign, on which Plutarch again lavishes considerable dramatic art: the recurrent evocation of Xenophon's *Anabasis*, in particular, is surely Plutarch's own skilful addition.[97] Pollio, again, is unlikely to have treated the campaign in detail, and Plutarch has probably consulted at least one other version.[98] The most likely source is Q. Dellius, the infamous *desultor bellorum civilium*. We know that he wrote of the war, and he was clearly an important authority: at *Ant.* 59. 6 Plutarch refers to him as Δέλλιος ὁ ἱστορικός, and expects his readers to recognize the man. It is not surprising that the one item attested for Dellius' Parthian account is consonant with Plutarch's version (*Ant.* 49. 4–5 ~ *FGrH* 197 fr. 1). Once

[96] Suggestions have included Nicolaus (Heeren, Gutschmid); Strabo (Heeren); an unevidenced memoir of C. Cassius (Flacelière); Timagenes (Regling, arguing for a combination of Timagenes with Livy); and, implausibly, Dellius (Adcock). The possibility of two sources should certainly not be dismissed. Some aspects of Plutarch's version show close contact with the Livian tradition: e.g. 17. 8 ~ Dio, xl. 13. 3–4; 17. 9 ~ Oros. vi. 13. 1–2; 19, 23. 1 ~ Obs. 64, Dio, xl. 18–19, Val. Max. i. 6. 11; etc. Yet most of Plutarch's details of the fighting cannot be reconciled with Dio or the other Livian sources, even when we take into account Dio's tendency to revamp battle-descriptions according to his own stereotypes. If there is some supplementation of Livy from another authority, it is more likely to be due to Plutarch himself than to any intermediate source. Such a combination was argued (though crudely) by K. Regling, *de belli Parthici Crassiani fontibus* (diss. Berlin, 1899).
[97] Most obviously at the explicit 45. 12, and at 49. 5; but the impression is reinforced elsewhere. The description of the χωρά as εὐδαίμων (49. 6) uses a favourite *Anabasis* locution; so does the mention of κώμας οἰκουμένας (41. 3). The echoes need not be derived from Dellius (cf. Jacoby on *FGrH* 197 fr. 1): such allusion is very much in Plutarch's manner.
[98] It is again possible that two versions are here combined: some of Plutarch's details look like doublets. Cf. 41 ~ 46–7, 45. 3–6 ~ 49. 1 (Flor. ii. 20. 7 attaches the item of 49. 3 to the context of 45); and perhaps 47. 6 ~ 49. 6.

again, we shall never be quite certain that Plutarch knew Dellius at first hand; but it does seem very likely. Much of the rest of *Antony*, too, appears indebted to sources other than Pollio, particularly the imaginative final scenes. Pollio's history probably concluded with Actium (or even before), and Plutarch would anyway now have to go elsewhere.[99] The physician Olympus is quoted at 82. 4, and perhaps provided some of the material; but there are clearly other possible sources, and it is likely that Plutarch consulted several authorities for these moving events.[100] One of these may again have been Dellius: it is possible that he extended his history to include Actium and Alexandria, or wrote a further work on those campaigns.[101] Few of the participants were better qualified—and it would be no surprise if some of the treatment were extravagant or scandalous.

It would be easy to extend this list: it seems likely, for instance, that Plutarch knew the work of Livy. At *Caes.* 47 he quotes Livy for some omens which accompanied Pharsalia: the item is unlikely to have been included in the Pollio-source, who had already finished with omens (cf. 43. 4). Nor did Pollio exhaust Plutarch's taste for portents when he approached the Ides of March: at *Caes.* 63. 9 he adds, as a variant, Livy's version of Calpurnia's dream. In other Lives, too, traces of Livy can be found—in *Pompey* and in *Crassus*, at the very least.[102] Perhaps Plutarch found these items in an excerpt of Livy, or in another writer's

---

[99] On the terminus of Pollio's history, above, n. 73

[100] Cf. Russell, *Plutarch*, 140; J. Griffin, *JRS* 67 (1977), 25–6.

[101] Strabo xi. 523e refers to ὁ Δέλλιος (Casaubon: ἀδέλφιος codd.) ὁ τοῦ Ἀντωνίου φίλος συγγράψας τὴν ἐπὶ Παρθαίους αὐτοῦ στρατείαν, ἐν ᾗ παρῆν καὶ αὐτὸς ἡγεμονίαν ἔχων. Jacoby (on *FGrH*, No. 197) concludes that this historical work was limited to this campaign, but this is by no means certain: A. Bürcklein had some reason to suggest that Dellius continued his work at least as far as Actium (*Quellen und Chronologie der röm.-parth. Feldzüge* (diss. Leipzig, 1879)). *Ant.* 59. 6–7 certainly seems to imply that the tale of Dellius' desertion in 32 is drawn from his own work (note the present φησιν): the item is more likely to come from a memoir or history than from the *epistulae ad Cleopatram lascivae* (Sen. *Suas.* i. 7). If Plutarch expected his readers to recognize Δέλλιος ὁ ἱστορικός, it seems unlikely that his historical fame rested on the description of just one campaign. Plutarch also mentions Dellius' role in Antony's first meeting with Cleopatra (*Ant.* 25–6): it is not unlikely that those splendid chapters are also indebted to Dellius himself. Cf. Russell, *Plutarch*, 136.

[102] For *Crassus*, see n. 96; for *Pompey*, Peter, 117 n. 1 and 119, and note the suggestive similarities between *Pompey*'s closing chapters and Lucan *BC* viii.

quotation or adaptation; but elsewhere, in Plutarch's treatment of earlier Roman history, it is likely enough that he
knew Livy's accounts at first hand.[103] In the present group
of Lives, one could further suggest the use of Sallust, of
Fenestella, and perhaps of others.[104] But it is more profitable to turn from these secondary sources to those occasions
on which Plutarch seems to know some contemporary material of the period.

Here there is a contrast between the early *Cicero* and the
later group of Lives. *Cicero* seems to show knowledge of
many of Cicero's own writings. A large portion of the
account of Catiline seems to be based on the περὶ ὑπατείας;
there are also quotations from the letters and speeches; and
there is more besides.[105] Nor is it just Cicero himself:
Plutarch seems to know some of Brutus' letters, and he also
mentions Antony's reply to the *Second Philippic*; and it
appears likely that part of the account is drawn from the
work of Tiro, both the biography and the *de iocis*.[106] Once
read for *Cicero*, this material might be recalled, and exploited, in later Lives.[107] Yet it is striking that Plutarch
seems rarely to have felt the need to undertake any *further*
research of this type. There is no sign, for instance, that he
knew Caesar's *commentarii* at first hand, though he certainly
knew of their existence (*Caes.* 22. 2).[108] He refers to the
speeches of Caesar, of Crassus, of Cato, of Brutus, and of
Antony—but there is no suggestion that he has read them,

[103] Cf. Theander, 72–8. For a possible explanation of the sparseness of these
traces of Livy in the present group of Lives, see below, p. 310.
[104] Sallust seems to inform the early chapters of *Pompey* (cf. Peter 112–14), and
has clearly influenced the earlier *Lucullus* (and underlies most of *Sertorius*:
Scardigli, *SIFC* 43 (1971), 33–64, esp. 41 n. 2). For Fenestella, see n. 80. Of other
secondary sources Nepos, Strabo, Nicolaus, Timagenes, and Valerius Maximus
are the most likely to be known at first hand.
[105] περὶ ὑπατείας: cf. Lendle, *Hermes*, 95 (1967), 90–109, esp. 94–8. *Caes.* 8. 4
clearly implies that Plutarch knew the work at first hand, and *Crass.* 13. 4
similarly seems to show him taking a pride in his own researches. Letters: *Cic.* 24.
6–9, 36. 6, 37. 3–4, 40. 3. Speeches: 6. 3, 24. 6, 33. 8, 48. 6, 50(1). 4. More
besides: 5. 6, 20. 3, 24. 4–6. In general, cf. Flacelière, Budé edn. *Demosthenes–
Cicero*, 56–61.
[106] Brutus: 45. 2, 53(4). 4 (cf. n. 93). Antony: 41. 6. Tiro: cf. Peter 129 ff.;
Flacelière, op. cit. 57.
[107] Most clearly at *Pomp.* 42. 13, 63, 2; *Phoc.* 3. 2; and cf. n. 93.
[108] The quotations at *Caes.* 22. 2 and 44. 8 seem inherited: above, n. 69.

though many were in circulation.[109] At *Cato* 23. 3 he notes only that '*they say that* this is the only speech of Cato to survive'. Letters of Caesar and of Antony were available: Plutarch makes no use of them.[110] (He does use those of Brutus, but these had probably been read for use in *Cicero*.)[111] Perhaps Plutarch simply did not have access to all this material (though this argument should not be over-stressed);[112] we should still have expected him to look up the works in a library during his visits to cultural centres, especially Athens. The reason is presumably a simple one: that Plutarch was so pleased with the Pollio-source that he excused himself from any further research into primary sources. *Cicero* clearly had no such satisfactory narrative source, and Plutarch must himself have felt the inadequacy of some of his material: hence, for instance, the unusual number of *apophthegmata*, which could usefully fill out the second half of the Life. It is very likely that, when preparing *Cicero*, he had undertaken this wide reading of primary sources for precisely this reason: there was no satisfactory chronological and synoptic source, and the narrative would otherwise have fallen to pieces. After he had read Pollio's account, the problem was solved, and the later Lives could be built around this.

Only once do we find the later Lives making extensive use of primary sources.[113] The first thirty chapters of *Antony* show a resounding similarity to the *Second Philippic*, so close that we should assume a direct use of the speech, and a use primed by recent re-reading.[114] Here Plutarch naturally wished to foreshadow and introduce the Life's important themes: themes such as Antony's luxury, his weakness of will, and his susceptibility to subtle schemers,

[109] *Caes.* 3. 2–4, *Crass.* 3. 3–4, *Cato* 5. 3–4 and 23. 3, *Brut.* 2. 5, *Ant.* 2. 8. For the survival of their speeches until Plutarch's day, cf. Schanz–Hosius I⁴ 336, 388–9, 396–7, 400, 490.

[110] For Caesar's letters, Suet. *Div. Iul.* 56. 6, Gell. xvii. 9. 1–2; for Antony's, Suet. *Div. Aug.* 7. 1 *al.*, Ov. *ex.P.* i. 1. 23, Tac. *Ann.* iv. 34.

[111] Above, n. 93.

[112] Cf. Garzetti, *RSI* 65 (1953), 80; Hamilton, xliii, n. 6.

[113] For a second, less important example, *Crass.* 13. 4: above, pp. 268–9.

[114] For use of the *Second Philippic* in the early parts of *Antony*, Flacelière, Budé edn. *Demetrius–Antony*, 89–90, with a qualification I make in my review, *CR* 29 (1979).

offset by his natural nobility and brilliance (especially as a
soldier and general), and by the popularity which these
qualities could excite. Ability and popularity could emerge
from the historical sources, when they touched on the first
episodes of Antony's life: the campaign in Syria, for instance, of ch. 3, or his authoritative demeanour after the
Ides of March (14–15), or his command at Philippi (22); or
even, with some straining, his exploits in the Pharsalus
campaign.[115] But the historical sources would have less to
say about the more private themes; nor, it appears, did
Plutarch know a satisfactory biography of Antony.[116] He
had probably read the *Second Philippic* some time ago,
when preparing *Cicero*; if he recalled that it contained
suitable material, he might naturally go back to it, and
exploit its rich fund of obloquy. It is no surprise that he
revises Cicero's material in a way which will suit the
economy of the Life. In ch. 2, for instance, he represents
Antony as far more of Curio's dupe than Cicero (*Phil.* ii.
44–7) had done: Cicero had portrayed Antony as no less
debauched than Curio himself—but Plutarch will later
make much of Antony's vulnerability to others' wiles, first
to Fulvia (10. 5–6), then of course to Cleopatra and her
κόλακες. It is useful to anticipate the theme here. Again, some
of the *Second Philippic* material is delayed until after
Cicero's death (*Ant.* 21, exploiting *Phil.* ii. 67–9). No other
account suggests that Antony's excesses were especially
evident at that stage, just after the proscriptions, but Plutarch finds it useful to exploit the themes here, with 22
proceeding to stress the glory of Antony's command at
Philippi and his noble treatment of Brutus' corpse. Private
excesses and yet brilliant ability: the contrast is programmatic, and excellently prepares the emergence of Cleopatra,
Antony's τελευταῖον κακόν (25. 1). Such adaptations of the
Second Philippic are eloquent, for they suggest that Plutarch
did know the work at first hand: the rewriting is so clearly
tailored to the interests and themes of the present Life.

---

[115] *Ant.* 8. 1–3 seems to be making the most of slight information: 8. 1 is a
great overstatement of the items of Caes. *BC* iii. 46 and 65, while 8. 2–3 seems a
simple inference from Antony's command of the left wing at Pharsalia.
[116] Above, p. 289.

Whoever revised the original material did so in the service of precisely those points which Plutarch will later stress: and the reviser is clearly more likely to be Plutarch himself than any intermediate source.[117]

These Lives, then, are not just informed by the Pollio-source; an admixture of biographies, memoirs, histories, and even first-hand contemporary material gives depth and colour to Pollio's account. And two last types of material should be mentioned. First, there is a sense in which Plutarch, when composing the six later biographies, would sometimes be using his own earlier work as his source. Some points remembered from *Cicero* and *Numa* have already been mentioned,[118] but there are times when the whole narrative of the later Lives is so close to the language and articulation of *Cicero* that we should assume that he looked again at his earlier version, and wrote the later accounts on its basis. One example might be the account of the final Catilinarian debate;[119] another, the account of the *Bona Dea* scandal in late 62.[120]

Secondly, it is very likely that oral traditions and sources played a considerable role. At the beginning of *Demosthenes* Plutarch lists the advantages to the historian of living in a great city: not merely an abundance of books, but also access to 'those stories which the written sources have

[117] If the preparation of these six Lives was simultaneous, it is not surprising that reflections of this rereading of the *Second Philippic* are found elsewhere, especially at *Caes.* 51. 2; cf. also *Pomp.* 58. 6, on Antony's friendship with Curio.

[118] Above, p. 282.

[119] *Caes.* 7. 7–8. 4 and *Cato* 22. 4–24. 3 ~ *Cic.* 20. 4–21. 5: esp. *Caes.* 7. 8–8. 1, *Cato* 22. 5 ~ *Cic.* 21. 1–2; *Caes.* 8. 1, *Cato* 22. 6 ~ *Cic.* 21. 3 (Silanus); *Caes.* 8. 2, *Cato* 23 ~ *Cic.* 21. 4 (Cato inculpating Caesar).

[120] *Caes.* 9–10 ~ *Cic.* 28–9. The adaptation has two curiosities. (*a*) At *Cic.* 28. 4 the codd. have Clodius indicted by an unnamed τις; *Caes.* 10. 6 specifies εἷς τῶν δημάρχων (whence Barton proposed τις ⟨τῶν δημάρχων⟩ in *Cic.*, which Ziegler accepts). But the *Caes.* version seems a mistake. The affair was raised in the senate by the praetorian Q. Cornificius, while Clodius' formal prosecutor was L. Cornelius Lentulus Crus, the pr. 58 and cos. 49. If Lentulus was now tribune, it is odd that this is not mentioned elsewhere (e.g. at *Cic. Att.* i. 14. 6, i. 16. 3). It is easier to assume that *Caes.* is here in error; in that case, we should retain the manuscript reading at *Cic.* 28. 4. Plutarch has here carelessly misread his earlier account. (*b*) At *Caes.* 10. 3 Plutarch uses the vigorous and rare word διαπτοηθεισῶν; he had also used the word, in a quite different context, in the account of the 63 Bona Dea incident (*Cic.* 20. 2). If he had recently reread *Cicero*, the use of the same phrase in *Caesar* may unconsciously reflect that passage.

passed over, but which are still recalled in the popular memory' (*Dem.* 2. 1). He would have discovered some of these stories himself, during his visits to Rome and elsewhere; others would have been passed on to him by his Roman friends and acquaintances.[121] At *Caes.* 26. 8 Plutarch tells an anecdote of Caesar's final battle with Vercingetorix: at the beginning things did not go well with the Romans, καὶ δεικνύουσιν Ἀρβέρνοι ξιφίδιον πρὸς ἱερῷ κρεμάμενον, ὡς δὴ Καίσαρος λάφυρον. The Arverni 'still point to' the ξιφίδιον: that item cannot be derived from a source. Plutarch heard of the ξιφίδιον and its associated local tradition, and skilfully wove it into his narrative.

The *Antony* is likely to be especially rich in this material: indeed, two substantial anecdotes are explicitly attributed to oral tradition within Plutarch's own family, the sumptuous banqueting in 41 BC and the hardships of Greece after Actium (28. 3–12, 68. 6–8). 'Greece', indeed, plays an important role in *Antony*. Antony's love for Greece is emphasized shortly after Philippi, τοῖς μὲν οὖν Ἕλλησιν οὐκ ἄτοπος οὐδὲ φορτικὸς συνηνέχθη τό γε πρῶτον . . . (23. 2), and the theme soon recurs (33. 7). But that τό γε πρῶτον has introduced an ominous note, and the eventual sufferings of Greece, τῆς πολλὰ δὴ τλάσης Ἑλλάδος (62. 1, quoting Euripides), are given a corresponding emphasis in chs. 62 and 68. Antony's love of Athens may remain unshaken (72. 1)—but to this extent has Greece, too, been reduced by Antony's Eastern extravagance and luxury. Little of this Hellenic material or this emphasis emerges in the other ancient accounts. It is likely that the development of the theme is Plutarch's own, with its material drawn from surviving oral traditions.

(b) The method of writing

This treatment has inevitably been selective, but it should be enough to suggest that Plutarch drew on a fairly wide range of material. Yet this conclusion poses its own problems. For it is still clear that the greater portion of these Lives is based on the Pollio-source alone: even on those

---

[121] It is a great merit of Theander, 2–32, to emphasize this point: cf. *Eranos* 57 (1959), 99–131.

occasions (such as Caesar's murder) where Plutarch has other sources, it is still Pollio's account which provides the basic narrative articulation, and Pollio's account which provides most of the facts. The extraneous material is not more than one quarter of the whole of Plutarch's narrative. This wide reading of other sources is surprisingly unproductive: it seems to provide only a few stray supplements and additions, and occasionally to replace the Pollio-source where that account was unsuitable. This is undeniably odd: if a modern researcher had read so widely, he, would weave items from all these sources into a composite and independent narrative, owing little more to any one account than to any other; as a matter of course, he would apply the technique of 'breakdown and reconstruction' (as T. J. Luce calls it)[122] of his sources' accounts. Plutarch has no hint of this.

Yet this problem is not confined to Plutarch, nor to biography. Time and again, we find Greek and Roman historians claiming a wide range of reading, and deserving to be believed; yet, time and again, we find them demonstrably basing their narrative of individual episodes on a single source. Cassius Dio is one example: he claims to have read 'nearly every book' on Roman history—but, as he goes on to say, he 'did not write up all his material, but only a selection'.[123] We can see what he means. It is evident that, at least in his treatment of Republican history, he is generally content to draw his material from a single source at a time. His account of the sixties, fifties, forties, and thirties regularly shows close contact with the Livian tradition, and there can be no doubt that Livy has provided the basis of Dio's narrative, and nearly all his material.[124] There are times when Dio's faithfulness to a source can be traced in

---

[122] *Livy: The Composition of his History* (1977), 143. It will become clear that my approach to Plutarch is very similar to Luce's treatment of Livy.

[123] Fr. 1. 2 (Boissevain): ⟨ἀνέγνωκα⟩ ⟨συνέλεξα coni. Millar⟩ πάντα ὡς εἰπεῖν τὰ περὶ αὐτῶν τισι γεγραμμένα, συνέγραψα δὲ οὐ πάντα ἀλλ' ὅσα ἐξέκρινα. So at liii. 19. 6 he refers to 'the many books which I have read'.

[124] This is, I trust, not controversial: the similarities may be traced in Schwartz, RE iii. 1697–714. The non-Livian material seems to increase after Caesar's death: ib., 1711–14. Thus the systematic contact with Plutarch and Appian (above, n. 73) is best explained by the assumption that Dio found Pollio's account transmitted by Livy.

detail: for instance, his accounts of Caesar's campaigns are ultimately based on Caesar's *commentarii*, and there is little indication of the use of any supplementary material;[125] while his account of Catiline shows contact with Plutarch's *Cicero*, which can only be explained if both authors derive from a common source (probably the περὶ ὑπατείας).[126] It is very unlikely that Dio is following either Caesar or Cicero directly—in both cases the material was probably transmitted by Livy;[127] but the similarities at least show that Dio knew the works in a full and close copy, and was himself reluctant to intrude material from elsewhere.

Or consider Livy himself. He claimed to have read widely: he can, for instance, speak of the 'very many Greek and Roman authors' whom he has read.[128] Nor is there any strong reason to doubt these claims.[129] Yet, when we can obtain some control of his use of sources, he has one principal authority for each section of his account, and uses the rest of his reading merely to supplement this principal narrative source. This is most clear in the later surviving books, when Polybius informs nearly all Livy's account of events in Greece and Asia. there are intrusions from Roman sources into these Polybian sections, but those intrusions are very limited.[130] In the earlier books, too, we often see systematic contact with the version of Dionysius of Halicarnassus, which demonstrates that, for individual episodes,

---

[125] Cf. Schwartz, RE iii. 1706–9, though not all his arguments are strong. As I argue in CR 32 (1982) 146–8, additions to, or revisions of, Caesar's material can always be explained by Dio's own techniques.

[126] The similarities are analysed in my doctoral thesis on *Caesar* (diss. Oxford, 1974), App. 1; cf. Hermes 113 (1985), 311–29 and n. 105 above.

[127] For Caesar being transmitted by Livy, Schwartz, RE iii. 1706–8; for Cicero, Schwartz, *Hermes*, 32 (1897), 581 ff.; H. Willrich, *de coni. Cat. Fontibus* (1893), 45–51.

[128] xxix. 27. 13; cf. e.g. vi. 12. 2–3, xxvi. 49. 2–6, xxix. 25. 2, xxxiii. 30. 6–11. At xxxii. 6. 8 he refers to *ceteri graeci latinique auctores, quorum quidem ego legi annales . . .*: thus he admits that he has not read everything, but evidently claims to have read several accounts other than that of Valerius Antias (quoted at xxxii. 6. 5 ff.). In general, cf. Steele, *AJP* 25 (1904), 15–31.

[129] Luce, op. cit. 158–84, has strong arguments to defend Livy's wide reading. In particular, cf. Tränkle, *Cato in der vierten und fünften Dekade des Livius* (Abh. Mainz, 1971), in defence of Livy's first-hand knowledge of Cato.

[130] Cf. Tränkle, *Livius und Polybios* (1976), esp. 28 ff., 59–72.

they both depend on a single authority.[131] Everything here supports Luce's conclusion: Livy read widely, but nevertheless followed a single source for a single section; within these sections, he would occasionally add supplementary items from other sources, but he would not use a number of versions to weave together a coherent and independent account of his own.[132] Moreover, the contact with Dionysius in the early books is as important for Dionysius as it is for Livy: Dionysius quotes widely among his authorities (some thirty names in the first few books)—but he, too, seems generally to be faithful to a single source in narrating an episode. And even Tacitus seems to be similar. He was quite evidently a conscientious and wide-ranging researcher; but, on the few occasions when we can control his own choice of items—most clearly in the first two books of the *Histories*[133]—he seems generally to draw the mass of his information from a single source at a time.

This seems less strange if we remember the circumstances in which these writers composed. It is known, and it is not surprising, that authors often collected all their material and read all their literature before beginning to compose.[134] What is more surprising is the lengths to which some authors took this procedure. Cassius Dio first spent ten years collecting his material, and then took twelve years to write it up; Dionysius took twenty-two years to familiarize himself with the Latin language and gather the material for his history.[135] If Plutarch chose to read all the materials for

[131] Schwartz, RE v. 939, 946–60; for the coincidences between Livy and Dionysius in their accounts of the early Republic, Tränkle, *Hermes* 93 (1965), 311–37. Plutarch offers a useful control: *Romulus, Numa,* and *Poplicola* are at times close to this tradition; elsewhere (e.g. in describing the birth of Romulus and Remus, *Rom.* 2 ff.) they show what divergences were possible.

[132] Luce, op. cit. 139–84, esp. 143–50 and 172 n. 73; cf. Tränkle, *Livius und Polybios* 20: 'ein kontinuierliches Verweben mehrerer Darstellungen wird man ihm höchstens in Ausnahmefällen zutrauen dürfen'.

[133] Cf. esp. Syme, *Tacitus,* 180–90, 674–6: subsequent bibliography at Jones, 74 n. 15. Townend, *AJP* 85 (1964), 337–77, plausibly argues for the use of several sources in these books of the *Histories*; but the overwhelming predominance of a single source within a single expanse of narrative remains unimpugned.

[134] Lucian *quom. hist.* 47–8, quoted below (p. 308), with the passages collected by G. Avenarius, *Lukians Schrift zur Geschichtsschreibung* (1956), 71–104, esp. 88.

[135] Dio, lxxii. 23. 5, with Millar, *A Study of Cassius Dio,* 32–40; D.H. *Ant. Rom.* i. 7. 2. It is thus plausible to suggest that Livy, too, read widely in his sources before beginning to compose: Luce, op. cit. 188–93.

his six Lives before beginning to write, his methods were not unusual. The curious fidelity to a single source for individual episodes is most easily understood if we make a simple assumption: that, following this initial wide reading, an author would generally choose just one work to have before his eyes when he composed, and this work would provide the basis of his narrative. In Plutarch's case, this work would normally be the Pollio-source; but when this was in some way unsuitable—for the early life of a figure, perhaps, or for the Parthian Wars—it would temporarily be replaced by another work, such as Oppius or Dellius. Items from the earlier reading would more widely be combined with the principal source but a writer would not normally refer back to that reading to verify individual references, and would instead rely on his memory, or on the briefest of notes. Alternatively, it may be that an author, immediately before narrating an episode, would *re*read one account, and compose with that version fresh in his mind.[136] This procedure might better explain such cases as the confusion between Albinus and Trebonius at *Caes.* 66, which can now be a simple slip of the memory. On either view, the important point is to explain the peculiar position of one source by the peculiar use to which it was put. Stray facts and additions would be recalled from the preliminary reading, but it would be a very different matter to recall the detail of an episode's presentation, and combine versions independently and evenly.

Such a procedure seem less perverse in view of the physical difficulties of working with papyrus rolls. These were hefty and unmanageable things; and indexing, chapter-headings, and even line- and column-numbering were rudimentary or non-existent.[137] It would be easy to read a roll continuously, at the stage of the preliminary

[136] Cf. Russell, *JRS* 53 (1963), 22 (below, p. 359), who suggests a similar procedure for Plutarch in *Coriolanus*; Luce, op. cit. 210 ff., who makes a similar suggestion concerning Livy.

[137] Cf esp. Birt, *Das antike Buchwesen* (1882), 157 ff.; Schubart, *Das Buch bei den Griechen und Römern*[3] (1962), 66–71. The relevance of such points was clearly seen by Nissen, *Kritische Untersuchungen über die Quellen der vierten und fünften Dekade des Livius* (1863), 78–9; cf. Briscoe, *Commentary on Livy xxxi–xxxiii* (1973), 10.

reading; but reading was a two-handed business,[138] and it would be difficult to have more than one roll under one's eyes during composition itself. Even if (for example) a slave held a second roll for an author to compare accounts, or the author himself used a book-rest, combining versions would still be awkward. If two accounts did not deal with events in the same sequence—if, for instance, one narrated chronologically, while the other ordered events thematically—it would be a cumbrous business to roll back and forth to find the parallel account. There were probably no chapter-headings to help. Systematic comparison of two accounts might still be possible; no doubt it was sometimes done.[139] But it would be very inconvenient, and it would not be surprising if authors preferred to rely on their memory.

And signs of the use of memory are duly found, especially when Plutarch exploits a non-chronological genre, such as speeches or letters—the sort of literature in which he had read widely before writing *Cicero*. In genres such as these, the relevant information might be found anywhere in the roll, and one would hardly expect a writer always to check his references. Plutarch's memory is inevitably sometimes imprecise: thus a story from *pro Plancio* is garbled and emasculated at *Cic.* 6. 3–4, and the quotations from Brutus' letters at *Brut.* 22 provide a pastiche of several different passages from two different letters.[140] We should not infer that Plutarch did not know the works at first hand,[141] but he is certainly unlikely to have had them under his eyes

---

[138] Birt, *Kritik und Hermeneutik des antiken Buchwesens* (1913), 303–4.

[139] e.g. Strabo, xvii. 790, who does seem to have collated two (closely similar) versions. And, of course, systematic comparison of texts was regular in the case of διόρθωσις, with textual variants being noted in a margin: cf. e.g. Allen, *PBSR* 5 (1910), 76–80. In such cases, either a book-rest or a slave's assistance (e.g. by dictating one version) was presumably used. But comparison of versions must have been more complicated for a historian, who had to deal (*a*) with a wider range of texts; (*b*) with texts which might order their material in different sequences, (*c*) with variants which were generally more substantial, and (*d*) with variants which were more difficult to note. (This footnote is indebted to discussion with Mr Parsons.)

[140] Cf. above, n. 93. *Brut.* 22. 4–6 has a medley of points taken from Brutus' two letters, and these points recur in an order quite different from the original. Apart from one explicit quotation (οἱ δὲ πρόγονοι . . .), itself easily memorable, the passage looks like a paraphrase from memory.

[141] As Peter, 130, argued in the case of the *pro Plancio* passage.

when composing. Elsewhere, too, we can detect the use of
memory when Plutarch seeks to supplement the material
before him. In the *Comparison of Nicias and Crassus* (2. 3)
he mentions an anecdote which he had forgotten to include
in the narrative of *Crassus* itself: ὅπερ ἡμᾶς ἐν τῇ διηγήσει
παρελήλυθε. Had that story been included in the source
before his eyes, he would hardly have omitted it: this is
rather an item culled from the wider preliminary reading.
But for the slip of his memory, he would silently have
inserted it into his main source's narrative.

A different type of example is found in the account of the
Gallic Wars. *Caes.* 22. 1–5 tells of Caesar's slaughter of the
Usipetes and Tencteri: 400,000 barbarians were killed. Both
Cato (51. 1) and the *Comparison of Nicias and Crassus* (4. 2)
briefly mention the same incident, and both give the figure
as 300,000. There is no need to emend; still less, to give the
lower figure any authority.[142] In *Cato* and in the *Comparison* Plutarch has not referred back to the source, and has
misremembered the detail. But here the detail seems to
have been given by Pollio himself, for Appian too has a
figure of 400,000 dead (*Celt.* fr. 1. 12, 18. 1). In writing
Caesar, Plutarch presumably worked carefully through the
Pollio-source's account of the war, and had it before him in
composing; in *Cato* or in *Crassus*, he would skim this part
of the narrative, and wind through the roll quickly.[143] It is
not surprising that he did not hunt carefully for the reference, but preferred to add it from memory. A similar case
is *Brut.* 27. 6, where Plutarch says that 'two hundred' were
proscribed: this is apparently another misremembering, for
Ant. 20. 2 gives 'three hundred', and this was apparently
Pollio's figure (App. *BC* iv. 7. 28). In composing *Antony*,
he presumably read Pollio's version thoroughly; but the
proscriptions were less central for *Brutus*, and he might
again wind through the account more quickly.

---

[142] As Gelzer does: *Festgabe P. Kirn* (1961), 49 n. 19. The number may
originally be derived from Caes. *BG* iv. 15. 3, who claims that the enemy had
totalled 430,000; Pollio may have reasoned that very few escaped.

[143] Or, if we assume that Plutarch composed just one ὑπόμνημα for all six Lives
(below, pp. 308–9), he presumably worked carefully through this part of the ὑπόμνημα when composing *Caesar*, and turned the pages (or tablets) more quickly
when writing *Cato* or *Crassus*.

Elsewhere, of course, his memory would furnish him with items recalled from much further back, items which he had encountered in a different context, and had probably known for years: perhaps from the reading for *Cicero*, perhaps from his work for other Lives or essays, perhaps simply from his general knowledge.[144]

This reconstruction implies that he made little use of notes, for notes on different authors, made in a codex of parchment, of papyrus, or of wax-tablets, might easily be combined into an independent pastiche. He might perhaps have taken such notes when working in libraries during his visits to cultural centres—enjoying that 'abundance of every type of book' which he talks about at *Dem.* 2. 1. He would then have known that he might not use the material for months or years; note-taking would be a natural safe-guard.[145] It is much harder to believe that he took detailed notes when composing from books which were at hand.[146] He used the Pollio-source so extensively that note-taking would be superfluous: it would be far more convenient to have the account under his eyes during composition. It might seem more sensible to take notes on his preliminary reading, works such as Volumnius or Messala or Bibulus; but we should be careful not to exaggerate the time taken in composing these Lives, which (as we shall see) have their signs of haste. The whole process probably took only a few months, and the preliminary reading would still be rela-tively fresh in his mind when he came to compose. Even in old age, he doubtless retained an extraordinarily good memory, and an extensive use of notes might well seem an unnecessary and time-consuming luxury. If he took notes at all, they would probably form the briefest *aide-mémoire*, with headings and a few important details of some good

---

[144] From the reading for *Cicero* or other Lives: above, p. 282. From general knowledge, or from research for other works: e.g. the digression on the Bona Dea festival, *Caes.* 9. 4–8 (perhaps drawn from work for the *Quaestiones Romanae*; cf. 268de); and perhaps such cases as *Ant.* 33. 2–4 and 34. 9, absent from other ancient narratives of these events, but exploited by Plutarch in *de fortuna Romano-rum* (319d–320a).

[145] Cf. Gomme, 78.

[146] Cf. Hamilton, xliv. The elder Pliny's studious practice, *nihil enim legit quod non excerperet*, is noted as a peculiarity: Plin. *Ep.* iii. 5. 10.

stories: they were perhaps similar to the extant *Apophtheg-mata*, whether or not those works are genuine. Such notes were perhaps taken in notebooks of wax-tablets, rather than papyrus or parchment: so Quintilian advises his pupils, in the interest of speed and fluency;[147] and such notes would have only a temporary use, so that reusable tablets would be a sensible economy. (Writers such as Dio or Dionysius, and perhaps Livy, who needed more long-term notes, might more naturally use parchment or papyrus.)[148]

More extensive notes seem to belong at a later stage of composition, the production of the ὑπόμνημα. The most usual method of writing seems to be that reflected by Lucian *quom. hist.* 47–8:[149] the historian should first collect his material from the most reliable sources,

καὶ ἐπειδὰν ἀθροίσῃ ἅπαντα ἢ τὰ πλεῖστα, πρῶτα μὲν ὑπόμνημά τι συνυφαινέτω αὐτῶν καὶ σῶμα ποιείτω ἀκαλλὲς ἔτι καὶ ἀδιάρθρω-τον· εἶτα ἐπιθεὶς τὴν τάξιν ἐπαγέτω τὸ κάλλος καὶ χρωννύτω τῇ λέξει καὶ σχηματιζέτω καὶ ῥυθμιζέτω.

This ὑπόμνημα, this 'inartistic and uncoordinated draft', was clearly an important stage of the composition, but it is hard to know how close to the final version it would be.[150] Its precise form surely varied from author to author. Some ancient writers speak of it as if it were a mere collection of chapter-headings, others as if it were a fairly finished version, merely needing to be 'translated' into the correct literary style.[151] Plutarch, too, doubtless wrote some

---

[147] *Inst. Or.* x. 3. 31. In general, cf. Roberts, *PBA* 40 (1954), 170–5.

[148] In these cases, however, the possibility of marginal jottings in the main source's account should be considered—very much after the manner of διόρθωσις: this is especially likely with Livy. The elder Pliny may be exceptional, but he not merely *excerpebat* but also *adnotabat* (Plin. *Ep.* 5. 10), i.e. noted things in a margin, which would be a convenient way of assembling minor divergences, for instance in numbers. Livy's (though not Plutarch's) supplements to his main source are often of this type. But in this case the problems of using two rolls simultaneously would remain, and we should assume either a book-rest or some assistance from a slave. (This note is again indebted to Mr Parsons.)

[149] See Avenarius' collection of parallel passages, *Lukians Schrift zur Geschichts-schreibung*, 85–104.

[150] Cf. the remarks of Millar, *A Study of Cassius Dio*, 33.

[151] The following references are drawn from Avenarius, op. cit. 85–9. Ammonius, *CIAG* iv. 1887, ὑπομνηματικὰ δὲ καλοῦνται ἐν οἷς τὰ κεφάλαια μόνα ἀναγρά-φονται, suggests a very unfinished version. But there seems to have been a theory

sort of ὑπόμνημα before proceeding to the final versions of these Lives, but we cannot know its form. He may have written several ὑπομνήματα, one for each Life, but he may well have preferred to construct just one ὑπόμνημα which would serve for all six works. We should certainly remember this stage of composition when we consider the extreme verbal similarities among the accounts. Some of them are doubtless inherited from Pollio, but the six Lives may also represent elaborations of the same draft, and it would be natural for the language of that draft to leave its mark on each of Plutarch's versions.

On this theory, then, there were three stages. (*a*) The preliminary reading, which would embrace the whole range of Plutarch's sources. (*b*) The production of the ὑπομνήματα (or ὑπόμνημα): this would normally be guided by the Pollio-source, but when that account was unsuitable Plutarch might prefer another authority, such as Oppius or Dellius. (*c*) The writing of the finished versions.

The discussion has so far been simplified in an important respect: for Plutarch would certainly have his slave and freedman assistants. Plin. *Ep.* iii. 5, describing how the elder Pliny spent his studious days, shows how greatly he exploited such aides: he would have a *lector* to read to him while he was in the bath, or taking a walk; a *notarius* would be at hand in case he wished to dictate. Pliny was perhaps exceptional, but Plutarch may well have enjoyed some similar assistance. It is likely that much of the first stage, the preliminary reading, was read out *to* Plutarch by a *lector*: we cannot be sure that Plutarch himself read silently, and this procedure might be less time-wasting than it seems.[152] It is likely that any preliminary notes, and then the ὑπόμνημα itself, would be dictated to a slave or freedman; as reading a roll required both hands, dictation would be the most convenient method. It is likely, too, that the final

that Thuc. viii represents a ὑπόμνημα rather than a final composition (Marc. *vit. Thuc.* 44), which suggests that a ὑπόμνημα could be much more finished; the same impression is given by Jos. *c.Ap.* i. 50. Mr Parsons observes that *FGrH* 533 fr. 2 may be a ὑπόμνημα: if so, it seems close to its final form.

[152] But, on silent reading, note the cautious remarks of Knox, *GRBS* 9 (1968), 421–35.

version, after Plutarch had considered it carefully, was
dictated as well.[153] And slaves, or more likely freedmen,
might prove useful in other ways. Some authors used them
very widely: Josephus exploited 'helpers in the Greek language' to aid the production of his final draft.[154] Plutarch
did not need ghost writers; but he may certainly have used
freedmen as research assistants, to consult the more recherché sources, report interesting stories from them, and perhaps produce epitomes.[155] The sparse traces in the Lives of
such writers as Livy and Strabo may well be owed to such
helpers. A whole factory of work may lie behind every
ancient writer's production, and we should not expect a
master to 'acknowledge' his servants' help.[156]

Such helpers would greatly ease the production of the
Lives; and, artistically finished and systematically researched though they are, we should not exaggerate the
diligence of Plutarch's methods. Time and again, we find
signs of hasty production: the awkward intrusion of the
item 'which I had forgotten to include in the narrative' in
the *Comparison of Nicias and Crassus*; the confusions over
the casualty figures or the number proscribed; the muddle
over Trebonius and Albinus. Sometimes he forgets what he
has, or has not, included: at *Brut*. 13. 3 he mentions Porcia,
who θυγάτηρ μὲν ὥσπερ εἴρηται Κάτωνος ἦν—but he has *not* in
fact mentioned this at 2. 1, though he doubtless meant to. A
different type of example is found in *Cato*, which contrives
to describe the triple alliance of 60 BC without mentioning
Crassus; then Plutarch introduces Crassus into the account
of Luca as if his role were quite familiar (41. 1). Elsewhere,
at *Tim*. 13. 10, he refers to a passage in *Dion* which does not
exist: he probably meant to include the item in *Dion*, but
finally omitted to do so. Other, more trivial, awkwardnesses
are frequent: two examples will suffice. At *Caes*. 24. 3 he
does not make it clear that Κικέρων is Quintus, not Marcus:
the reader, or listener, unfamiliar with the period would

---

[153] On dictation, Herescu, *REL* 34 (1956), 132–46.

[154] *c.Ap.* i. 50; cf. H. Thackeray, *Josephus* (1929), 100–24.

[155] Cf. Quint. *Inst. Or.* x. 1. 128, on Seneca: 'ingenium facile et copiosum,
plurimum studii, multa rerum cognitio, in qua tamen aliquando ab iis quibus
inquirenda quaedam mandabat deceptus est'.

[156] Jones, 84–7, has a sensible and useful discussion of such assistants.

flounder. And at *Ant.* 19. 1 the mention of οἱ τρεῖς, coming just after a sentence which links Caesar, Antony, and Cicero, would bemuse an audience which did not know of the alliance of Caesar, Antony, and Lepidus.[157] Plutarch's research for these six Lives was systematic, sensible, and quite extensive; but the whole production might still be a comparatively speedy process. Even allowing for the parallel composition of the pairs to each Life, the whole business probably occupied months rather than years.

Finally, I stress that this analysis has been confined to a few Roman Lives; and these anyway provide a special case, for so extensive a use of simultaneous preparation cannot be traced elsewhere. It is not at all clear how much one can generalize from this study to infer his procedures elsewhere, especially in the Greek Lives. Methodical reading was necessary before writing the Roman Lives, but at least some of their Greek counterparts could be produced much more easily. In many Greek instances, particularly those drawn from the fifth century, he might be able to dispense with the preliminary general reading, for he would already be sufficiently familiar with the material. He might still have a historical source before his eyes: in writing *Themistocles*, for instance, he seems to have been heavily dependent on Herodotus and Thucydides. He would certainly still exploit his memory to add supplementary items, but it would be more usual for these to be remembered from years before, and they would often be facts which he had known since his youth. The whole process of composing a fifth-century Life could be far less methodical, and it might be misleading to speak of 'research', or of 'reading *for* a biography', at all.[158] Equally, some of the later Greek Lives—*Philopoemen*, perhaps, or *Timoleon*, or *Pyrrhus*—might be more similar to the Roman biographies: periods where his general knowledge might carry him less far, where more systematic research would be necessary.[159] As so often in the

---

[157] It was understandable that Stegmann, followed by Flacelière, should conjecture ⟨καὶ Λέπιδον⟩ at *Ant.* 19. 1; but that is more likely to correct the author than his text.

[158] In such Lives, the picture of Gomme, 77–81, is likely to be more accurate; cf. above, pp. 266–7.

[159] This point is owed to Mr Russell.

study of the Lives, each group of biographies must have posed different problems, and may have been approached in different ways.[160]

It is perhaps not too ambitious to hope that this study has a more general application. Far too often, we tend to specify 'the source' of a passage, in Plutarch or elsewhere, with no further qualification; yet this tells us little. What sort of source, and how was it used? Was it a work read for the writer by an assistant? Was it a work read some time before, and perhaps noted, in a library? Was it a work read in the preliminary stage of general reading? Or was it before the author's eyes in composition? All these classes of material contribute to Plutarch's work, but all contribute very differently; and, until we know *how* an author used a particular source, we know very little indeed.

POSTSCRIPT (1994)

On the whole this article has provoked acquiescence rather than dissent,[161] but it has been strongly criticized by T. W. Hillard in *Antichthon* 21 (1987), 19–48, and by W. Steidle in *GrB* 17 (1990), 163–85. I am grateful to the editor for allowing a brief reply.

My article argued for simultaneous preparation of six *Lives*, but acknowledged that *Cicero* and *Lucullus* belonged to an earlier stage, when Plutarch was less well-informed about the period. Hillard and Steidle attack different aspects of the thesis. Hillard rejects the notion of simultaneous preparation; Steidle takes issue with the idea of expanding knowledge, and claims that the *Cicero* shows the same awareness of the period as the later *Lives*. Both scholars rest part of their case on general considerations. Hillard feels that the notion of simultaneous preparation does not leave enough room for the independent artistic creation of each

---

[160] For another aspect of the differences among the Lives, cf. Wardman, *CQ* 21 (1971), 254–261.

[161] Not that every point has stood up well; cf. e.g. J. W. Rich, in *History as Text* (ed. A. Cameron, London, 1989), 91 n. 19 for correction of my remarks on Cassius Dio (p. 91 of the original article = pp. 301–2 above).

Life; Steidle suggests that the frequent cross-references imply that the series was conceived from the outset as a coherent entity, and that even when writing *Cicero* Plutarch was consciously assuming knowledge, or avoiding treatment, of material which he would treat elsewhere.

They are unlikely both to be right. The implication of Steidle's argument would be to include *Cicero* in the group of *Lives* researched and prepared together, and it is precisely that notion which Hillard rejects. It is, I hope, also plain that the general arguments do not take us far. Simultaneous *preparation* is of course compatible with an acceptance that the finished biographies are individual artistic and thematic creations; the final drafts were presumably written separately and in sequence.[162] Most scholars are used to working on material which they will later write up in several separate papers or books. And Plutarch may well have already envisaged his early biographies as part of a series of works which would mutually supplement one another.[163] It does not follow that he already knew exactly which biographies he would go on to write,[164] still less that he had already completed all the relevant reading and research.

Steidle's detailed criticisms centre on pp. 75–6 of the original article (= pp. 268–9 above), where I suggest that Plutarch's knowledge of the period increased between *Cicero* and the later group of *Lives*. He is sceptical of arguments from silence from *Cicero*, arguing (quite correctly) that artistic reasons can often explain omissions;[165] in particular, he claims (1) that Plutarch could already have known of the λόγος in which Cicero inculpated Caesar and Crassus, for in *Cic.* he already knows that both men were suspected, and he has the same view of Caesar's long-term

---

[162] Cf. p. 80 = p. 278 above.

[163] The idea of a mutually supplementing series is plausible enough; cf. esp. Stoltz, 42–55, who observed that a cross-reference to a second *Life* is often used to explain or excuse a brief treatment of a topic.

[164] Thus *Thes.* 1. 4 implies that he decided to write *Thes.–Rom.* only after publishing *Lyc.–Numa*. We need not necessarily take that literally, but such a picture of composition could not have seemed implausible to his audience. Cf also *Aem.* 1, 1 and Geiger, above. pp. 169, 77.

[165] But at 166 he misrepresents my argument about the triumviral chapters.

ambitions (*Cic.* 15, 20);[166] (2) that in *Cic.* Plutarch could readily have passed over Cicero's support for Pompey's *cura annonae* (*Pomp.* 49. 6), for it does not illuminate Cicero's ἦθος; (3) that the discrepancies over Paullus' death between *Cic.* and the later *Lives* (p. 76 = 269) are of the same type as certain discrepancies *within* the group of later *Lives* (such as those I discuss on pp. 93–4 = 306); (4) that my description of the second half of *Cicero* as 'scrappy and ill-informed' is subjective and hasty, for *Cic.* is no more ill-informed than *Brut.* or *Ant.* on the fifties, and Plutarch's weight falls on the same high-spots of Cicero's career as are stressed by other ancient authors—the consulship, the exile and the return, the final years. He adds (5) that *Cicero* shares some errors with the later *Lives*, which he thinks odd if Plutarch's knowledge genuinely expanded.

I find these points unconvincing. (1) Of course Plutarch already knew about the suspicions about Crassus and Caesar; the *Cicero* account is already quite well-informed about the conspiracy, and Caesar's long-term ambition was a familiar commonplace. The knowledge of Cicero's own later inculpating λόγος is what is in point. My argument was that *Cic.* 20, discussing variant versions of Caesar's guilt and Cicero's attitude towards him, could naturally have mentioned that work if Plutarch already knew of it. It would have been a striking point to make, and it would have fitted the tone of the context. Notice that Plutarch has already referred to Cicero's own work once in that chapter, at 20. 3—presumably in that case the περὶ ὑπατείας.

(2) I do not understand why Steidle thinks Cicero's support for Pompey would have cast no light on his ἦθος: it might evidently have illuminated his gratitude for Pompey's part in his return, and could readily have contrasted with the vindictiveness towards Clodius (*Cic.* 34). It certainly seems to illuminate Cicero's ἦθος more than Pompey's, despite its appearance at *Pomp.* 49. 6.

---

[166] J. L. Moles (*Plutarch: Cicero* (Warminster, 1988), 28, *Hermes* 120 (1992), 247, and in H. D. Jocelyn (ed.), *Tria Lustra: Classical Essays for John Pinsent* (Liverpool, 1993)) also thinks that Plutarch knew this λόγος at the time of *Cic.*, and indeed drew on it for *Cic.* 20. 6–7. I am not convinced: App. *BC* 2. 6. 20 suggests that such material figured in the mainstream historical tradition.

(3) There is some force in Steidle's third point, but those discrepancies among the later *Lives* tend to be easier to explain, either in terms of slips of memory (pp. 93–4 of the original above, pp. 306) or of the various compositional devices which I discussed in my 1980 paper (above, pp. 126–33).[167] The Paullus instance seems different: at *Ant.* 19. 3 Plutarch carefully calls attention to the existence of variant versions, and there is evidently no carelessness there; he prefers a different version in *Ant.* and explicitly rejects the one he had followed in *Cic.*, but there seems no artistic or compositional reason why he should have preferred one version rather than another in either *Life*. As we know that *Ant.* is the later *Life*, it seems most economical to suppose that he had simply come across a version which he thought more reliable.

(4) It is hardly surprising that *Brut.* and *Ant.* are skimpy on the fifties; neither Brutus nor Antony was then a major actor. The 'scrappiness' of the second half of *Cicero* is different. It is not the concentration on the familiar high-spots which is relevant, but the perfunctory nature of the transition between them, for instance the speed with which he advances from 56 to 52 at *Cic.* 35. 1 (cf. now J. L. Moles, *Plutarch: Cicero* (Warminster, 1988), 47 and 183). Steidle's appeal to other ancient authors does not wholly support his case: Appian and Velleius are too thin on the fifties to allow any conclusions, but we might notice Dio 39. 18. 1 and 20. 2, tracing through the saga of Cicero's house and various clashes involving Cicero, Milo, and Clodius in the mid-fifties; or 39. 59. 2–60. 1, on Cicero's brushes with the triumvirs in 55; or 39. 62–3, on his part in the various Gabinius trials.

(5) The persistence of certain errors in the later *Lives* is evidently inconclusive. Expanding knowledge need not mean perfect knowledge. In any case, not all of Steidle's examples are cogent. He puts particular weight on the

[167] Thus the discrepancy concerning the amnesty of 17 Mar. 44 (Steidle, 169)—was it urged by Antony (*Ant.* 14. 3), by Antony, Plancus, and Cicero (*Brut.* 19. 1), or by Antony and Cicero (*Cic.* 42. 3)?—is easy enough to explain in terms of the 'law of biographical relevance', given that Antony's role as consul had to be stressed in each *Life*, and *Brut.* had no reason to highlight any one of the proposers rather than another.

misdating of Octavian's arrival in Rome at *Brut.* 22. 1; *Cic.* 43. 8 also misdated it, though not to the same point. But Steidle neglects *Ant.* 16. 1, where the arrival is put in the correct chronological sequence. In fact, it is probably wrong to think of the *Brut.* and *Cic.* passages as 'mistakes': in each case the positioning of the item allows Plutarch to switch the narrative focus to Octavian, and he does this at whatever point seems most convenient in each *Life*. The procedure of Appian, *BC* 3. 9. 30 is very similar. In that case, the instance provides no evidence either way for the present issue.

Much of the rest of Steidle's article is devoted to a treatment of Plutarch's narrative in *Cicero* and *Pompey*, emphasizing his readiness to abbreviate and adapt for artistic purposes. We differ on several details, but his general point is common ground between us, and is, I think, no longer controversial.

The thrust of Hillard's article is to stress that the character of each *Life* was largely determined by the available source-material. I think he underestimates Plutarch's capacity to rewrite and remould material; but even if he is right, it does not affect the issue of simultaneous preparation. That thesis can still allow that particular material affects the texture of particular *Lives*; the available material on Cato, for instance, has certainly influenced Plutarch's portrayal of the man in *Cato minor*. My argument was simply that, even if such reading was conducted primarily 'for' one *Life*, we can often detect traces of it elsewhere, and in patterns which are most easily explicable if we think that all the preparation of the later six *Lives* was complete before any one of them was written up (cf. pp. 82–3 = 282–5). Hillard does not address this point.

Hillard argues that I underestimate the impact of biographical material on the *Lives*. It may well be that in 1979 I made too much of the Pollio-source, though this still seems to me the most economical thesis; but the persistent verbal contact with Appian, and to a lesser extent with Dio, anyway seems to point to an important mainstream historical source, whether or not this was Pollio.[168] How far an

---

[168] Cf. p. 84 (= p. 286–7).

individual *Life* can be based on such a source will evidently
vary; but it is misleading to speak as if the availability of
biographical matter is the only factor to influence Plutarch's
choice of source-material. Just as important will be the
question how far a person's story intersects with, and in
extreme cases is identical with, the central political and
military history of the period. Plutarch may well have
known just as much 'biographical' material on Pompey and
Caesar as on Crassus and Brutus; but the story of Pompey
and Caesar fundamentally *is* the central history of the
period, and therefore biographical material leaves much
less distinctive a mark on Plutarch's version.

Hillard also points out that the arguments for simultaneous preparation are not equally strong for each of the six
Lives; in particular, not many of the arguments bear on
Crassus.[169] I accept that point, and the case for including
Crassus among the six is less strong than for the others. In
itself that is hardly surprising: Crassus' part in the history
of the period was less conspicuous than that of any of the
others, and his *Life* consequently offers less material for
direct comparison with the other *Lives*. The speed with
which Plutarch passes from 59 to 56 (*Crass.* 14) allows no
inferences as to his knowledge of the mainstream history of
the period: Crassus' own part in those years was simply too
difficult to trace, no matter how much Plutarch knew.[170]
Still, the *Lives'* relative chronology suggests that *Crassus*
was written at much the same time as the other relevant
Lives,[171] and that might create a presumption in favour of
including it among the six. If so, a negative argument
becomes more telling: it is hard to see any material in the
other *Lives* which might naturally have found a place in
Crassus but is omitted, or any material in *Crassus* which
might naturally have been included in other *Lives* but is
not. In that case, it is easiest to assume that it rests on the
same body of knowledge and research. That impression is

---

[169] The same point is made by B. Scardigli, *Plutarco: Agide e Cleomene–Tiberio e
Caio Gracco* (Milan, 1991), introd. 47.

[170] It is therefore not parallel with the perfunctoriness of the second half of
Cicero, pace Steidle, 166.

[171] C. P. Jones, *JRS* 56 (1966), 68 (= p. 111 of this collection).

confirmed by the series of verbal parallels between *Crassus* and the other five later *Lives*;[172] *Crassus*, like the others, shows some contact with the narrative of Appian, which suggests awareness of the same mainstream historical source;[173] there are even some signs of cross-fertilization, for *Crass.* 7. 5 uses the story of the young Caesar's adventure with the pirates, an item which would naturally come from the reading 'for' *Caesar*. The cumulative case for including *Crassus* among the six is therefore a substantial one.

[172] Cf. *Crass.* 11. 10–11 ~ *Pomp.* 21. 3, 12. 1–3 ~ *Pomp.* 22. 1–3, 12. 4–5 ~ *Pomp.* 23. 1–2, 14. 4 ~ *C. min.* 33. 5, *Caes.* 14. 2, 15. 2–4 ~ *Pomp.* 51. 6–52. 1, and the instances collected in the next note.

[173] The 'Pollio-source', in the terms of the 1979 paper. Cf. esp. 15. 6–7 ~ App. *BC* 2. 17. 64 as well as *Pomp.* 52. 1–3, *C. min.* 41. 3–42. 1; 16. 4–8 ~ App. *BC* 2. 18. 66; 37(4). 2–3 ~ *Celt.* fr. 18 as well as *Caes.* 22. 4.

I I

Plutarch and Roman Politics

C. B. R. PELLING

Is Plutarch really interested in Roman politics? After all, he is writing biography, not history; and there are certainly times when he disclaims any interest in describing historical background. That sort of thing, he says, may be left to the writers of continuous histories;[1] it is often the little things, the words and the jests, which reveal a man's character, not the great battles or the sieges of cities.[2] *'Often'* the little things, we should notice: often, not always. Plutarch's biography is a very flexible genre, and his interest in historical background is one of the things which vary. Sometimes he does write very personal Lives, sketching the historical setting in only the vaguest lines: the *Crassus*, for instance; or the *Antony*, which somehow or other describes the politics of the two years from summer 44 to summer 42 without even mentioning Brutus and Cassius; or the *Cato minor*, where he contrives to describe the formation of the triple alliance of 60 BC without naming Crassus. But there are other Lives where his interest in history is very clear indeed, and he is evidently concerned to present the same sort of analysis as those 'writers of continuous history'—though he naturally sets about it in rather different ways. The *Caesar* is a good example. Plutarch is there very concerned to *explain* Caesar's rise to tyranny—the 'absolute power', as he says in the last chapter, 'which he had sought all his life—

Versions of this paper were read at Leeds and Manchester, to the 1982 meeting of the American Philological Association in Philadelphia, and to the Oxford Philological Society; I am grateful to all these audiences for their patient hearings and many helpful comments. Particular thanks are due to Andrew Lintott, David Stockton, Philip Stadter, Owen Watkins, and Peter Scott for their scrutiny and detailed criticism of the paper as it was nearing its final draft.

[1] *Fab.* 16. 6, cf. *Galba* 2.5.
[2] *Alex.* 1. 2.

and he saw only its name, and the perils of its reputation'
(*Caes.* 69. 1, cf. 57. 1). What forces carried him to this
power? Plutarch's answer is a clear one. From the beginning, Caesar is the champion and the favourite of the
Roman *dēmos*. When they support him, he rises; when he
loses their favour, he falls. In the early chapters, the *dēmos*
encourage him to become first in the state.[3] When Caesar
revives the flagging 'Marian faction', this too is brought
into the same analysis: his opponents denounce the display
of Marian *imagines* as 'an attempt to win over the *dēmos*' (6.
1–3), while the admirers of the display encourage him to
great ambitions: the *dēmos*, they say, will support him as he
goes on to conquest and supremacy (6. 7).[4] Caesar spends
lavishly on the people, and they seek 'new commands and
new honours' to repay him (5. 9, cf. 4. 4–9)—an interesting
foreshadowing of the spectacular and odious honours they
vote him, and resent voting him, at the end of his life.
Plutarch comments that, at the beginning, Caesar's outlays
are purchasing the greatest of prizes cheaply (5. 8, cf. 4. 8);
and, at first, the *optimates* are wholly deceived (4. 6–9, 5. 8).
It is only gradually that 'the senate' comes to realize the
danger; and it is indeed 'the senate', described like that,
which is seen as Caesar's enemy.[5] Caesar is duly victorious,
and becomes tyrant—and it is then that he begins to lose
his crucial popular support. The Lupercalia outrage, for
example, is carefully presented at 60–1 in a way which
dwells on the people's reactions, and especially their final
dismay; and we can see, I think, that this is a passage where
he is *re*writing and *re*interpreting what stood in his source.[6]
(Appian, Suetonius, and Plutarch's parallel account in

---

[3] *Caes.* 6. 7, cf. 5. 1–3, 8. 4–5, 14. 2–3, 14. 6.

[4] For the 'Marianism' see 5. 2–3, 6. 1–7; and then note 19. 4 (with 18. 1) for the
continuation of the theme in the military narrative. The stress is an interesting
one, and seems individual to Plutarch; neither Suet. *DJ* 11 nor Vell. 2. 43. 4 give
anything like so charged and coloured an account of the Marian display as *Caes.* 6.
For the historical importance of Caesar's 'Marian' links see Syme (1939), 65, 89–
90, 93–4, Strasburger (1938), 131, 136–7.

[5] *Caes.* 7. 4, 14. 3, 21. 7, 60. 5, 64. 2, cf. 10. 6–7. His enemies may also be
described as the ἀριστοκρατικοί (13. 5, 14. 6), or the καλοὶ κἀγαθοί (14. 3), or the
ἄριστοι (7. 4): cf. below, pp. 339–40.

[6] See Pelling (1979), 78 (above, p. 274), where Plutarch's adaptation of his
source-material is analysed in more detail.

Antony all seem to draw on the same source-material as the *Caesar*—probably the account of Asinius Pollio—but none of these versions carries the same popular emphasis.) It is duly οἱ πολλοί who turn to Brutus and Cassius. Caesar is now left vulnerable, and is killed; but the popular fervour then immediately erupts once more, and the victim is the luckless 'Cinna the poet' (68).[7]

So intense an interest in historical explanation is not of course typical; but it is not wholly isolated, either. The Lives of the *Gracchi*, for example, again show Plutarch very eager to relate the brothers' policies and destinies to the attitudes of the urban *dēmos*. The *Marius* and the *Cicero* are both concerned to explain their subjects' rises—what forces and what combinations of support enabled such men to overcome the obstacles which, Plutarch knew, confronted a new man at Rome.[8] So, in a different way, is the *Cato maior*, though the sort of explanation he there offers is rather more sonorous and less convincing: the Roman people were greater in those days and worthier of great leaders, and so they joyfully chose a man of austerity to be their consul and rejected the demagogues who were his rivals (*C. mai.* 16. 8, cf. *Aem.* 11. 3–4). Less *our* sort of historical explanation, perhaps—but still a historical generalization intended to make a surprising success more intelligible. But other Lives are naturally less interested in historical themes. The *Sulla* is conspicuously less interested in history than the *Marius*: when historical points are made in the *Sulla*, they are rather inorganic, introducing notions which are simply useful for our *moral* estimate of Sulla's character. Generals by now *had* to spend large sums on bribing their armies, and so it was not surprising that Sulla was harder on Greece than men like Aemilius Paullus or Titus Flamininus—though Sulla himself must equally take some blame for encouraging and accelerating the decline (*Sulla* 12. 9–14). Rome was by now so decayed a city that Sulla found it easier to stand out there than Lysander at Sparta (*Sulla* 40 (1). 2–7). We are some

[7] For the historical interests of the *Caesar*, and some further aspects of Plutarch's presentation of his analysis, see Pelling (1980), 136–7 (above, pp. 145–8).

[8] *Mar.* 6, *Cic.* 11. 2–3; and for a new man's difficulties, *C. mai*, 16. 4–5.

way from the simple interest in making careers historically intelligible which we find in the *Marius* or the
Caesar.

And, when Plutarch's mind is not primarily focused on
history, he is capable of saying some very odd things. The
Crassus, for example, is a peculiarly lightweight and anecdotal Life. Plutarch evidently decided—wisely enough—that
it was simply impossible to write a serious historical biography of Crassus. The weight of that Life falls on the great
narrative set-pieces—the exciting escape from Marius and
Cinna, the war against Spartacus, then the great Parthian
disaster. The political aspects are dismissed very quickly: a
notably trivial account of the consulship of 70 BC, then all
the political history of 60–56—about which Plutarch by
now knew a great deal[9]—dismissed in a single woolly chapter (14). The most substantial political analysis is in fact
introduced in a digression, placed just before the Spartacus
war. It is evidently supposed to provide some guide to the
entire twenty years which followed. 'Rome was divided into
three powers [δυνάμεις—a very odd phrase), those of Pompey,
Caesar, and Crassus: for Cato's reputation was greater than
his power, and he was more admired than effective. And
the wise and sound part of the state supported Pompey,
while the excitable and reckless followed the hopes aroused
by Caesar; Crassus stood in the middle, exploiting both
sides, continually changing his position in the state, not
reliable in his friendships nor irreconcilable in his feuds,
readily abandoning both gratitude and hostility when it was
expedient for him to do so' (7. 7). That is an extraordinary
thing to say. It would be hard to find *any* period when this
analysis—Pompey as the establishment figure, Caesar the
popularis, Crassus the inconsistent trimmer—bore much
relation to reality; least of all does it fit the part of the Life
where we find it, when we are still deep in the seventies.
Plutarch knows very well that Caesar only became important ten years later: he makes that clear in both the *Pompey*

---

[9] See Pelling (1979), and above, pp. 265 ff., where I argue that *Crassus* was
prepared at the same time as *Caesar*, *Pompey*, *Cato minor*, *Brutus*, and *Antony*.
The first three of those Lives all give much more detailed accounts of the politics
of the early fifties.

and the *Caesar*.[10] He knows very well that Pompey never really enjoyed the confidence of this 'wise and sound part of the state' (as he puts it here): indeed, in the *Pompey* he makes it clear that it was only late in the fifties—after Crassus' death, and hence beyond the scope of the *Crassus* itself—that the *optimates* came to any real understanding with Pompey, and that it was the *popular* support for Pompey which was important in the first period of his life, down to 60 BC.[11] The account in the *Pompey* of the shared consulship of 70 BC makes the contrast with the *Crassus* passage very clear. In the *Pompey*, Plutarch *is* concerned to explain the historical background, and he says that 'Crassus had the greater strength in the senate, whereas Pompey enjoyed great power among the people' (*Pomp.* 22. 3)— note, incidentally, that characteristic *boulē–dēmos* analysis again. That is evidently quite irreconcilable with the *Crassus* passage, which made Pompey the establishment figure and Crassus the trimmer. In the *Crassus* he is prepared to give the different analysis—much cruder and less satisfactory though it is—simply because it aids the characterization of the Life. Crassus is there the shrewd manipulator, unscrupulously exploiting everyone he can in the interests of his own ambition and (particularly) greed. 'The middle', now supporting one side and now the other, is evidently the right place for him. That view of Crassus himself is, of course,

[10] Thus, in *Caesar*, his authority 'increased slowly' (4. 5), and it was only 'late' (4. 7) that his opponents realized the danger; in 61 he flees before his creditors to Crassus, who finds him useful for his own opposition to Pompey (11. 1); in 60 Pompey and Crassus are still 'the greatest powers in the state' (13. 3). It is the alliance with Pompey in 60 which brings Caesar to real power (28. 2–3, cf. *Pomp.* 57. 6). (It is true, as Strasburger (1938), 71, 75–6, 85–9 insists, that Plutarch exaggerates the extent and importance of Caesar's early popular *support*; but this does not lead him to exaggerate Caesar's early *power* as greatly as Strasburger's discussion would suggest.) In *Pompey*, Caesar again only comes to prominence with the alliance of 60, which brought him 'gratitude, and power for the future' (47. 1); it was Pompey's power which raised Caesar against the city, and finally against Pompey himself (46. 3–4, cf. 57. 6).

[11] *Optimates* come to an understanding, 54. 5–9, 59. 1–2, etc.: the accord reached in 57 BC (49. 6) is very transient. Early popularity: 1. 3–4, 2. 1, 14. 11, 15. 1, 21. 7–8, 22. 3–4, 22. 9, 25. 7–13, 30. 4. This stress disappears in the second half of the Life, for Pompey is then the tool of other, more subtle and degraded demagogues, Clodius and Caesar; it is then *their* popularity which is stressed (46. 7, 47. 5, 48. 3, 48. 9, 51. 1, 53. 6, 58. 4). Cf. the firm division of the 'two parts' of Pompey's Life at 46. 1–4, and Pelling (1980), 133–5 above, pp. 138–42.

not without some truth; but it is a far less plausible matter to make *Caesar and Pompey* the two 'powers' between which he oscillated. There, if he thought about it, Plutarch must have realized that he was falsifying and trivializing historical reality.

It is easy enough to find further examples of the same sort of thing. It can be shown, I think, that his view of Clodius varies from one Life to another, depending on the interests and emphases of each Life; in one Life he is an independent figure, bullying the passive Pompey into submission and disgrace; in another, he is relatively meek and subservient, demurely following the triumvirs' will.[12] It can be shown that Plutarch's view of the origins of the Civil War is not always quite the same;[13] and that Pompey's awareness of the menace of Caesar in Gaul is greater in the *Pompey* itself than in the other Lives.[14] All this makes the analysis of his political views and interpretations a rather delicate question. We should not expect him always to be consistent, and we must always be aware that he may be bending his analysis to suit the themes of a particular Life; and we should give more weight to some Lives than to others. It is the Lives where he is most interested in historical analysis—the *Caesar*, perhaps, and the *Marius*

[12] Pelling (1980), 132–3 above, pp. 136–9.

[13] The analysis is set out in its simplest form in *Caesar*, and that Life's treatment is discussed below. In *Cato minor*, affairs are taken further back than the alliance of 60 BC, to Cato's rejection of the proffered marriage-link with Pompey: *that* was the start of it all (30. 9–10), for Pompey was driven to marry Julia instead. The marriage of Julia and Pompey is advanced to the very beginning of the narrative of 59 BC in order to emphasize the point (31. 6, contrast *Caes.* 14. 7–8, *Pomp.* 47. 9); and Cato's own insight concerning the 60 BC alliance, stressed at *Caes.* 13. 6 and *Pomp.* 47. 4, is here muted and delayed. The *Cato* explains all in terms of personal factors and personal rebuffs, while the *Caesar* represents the alliance of Pompey and Caesar in purely political terms. That treatment excellently suits the *Cato*, which shows little interest in politics but a considerable concern with the affairs of Cato's womenfolk (24. 4–25, 13, 30. 3–10, 52. 5–9). *Pompey* is different again. Pollio's view is retained (47. 3–4, cf. 51. 1–2, 53. 8–10, 54. 3); but Plutarch here gives the crucial importance to Pompey's own reactions and attitudes during the fifties (see Pelling 1980), 131–5 above, pp. 133–42). In particular, the joyous Italian reaction in 50 BC, when Pompey recovered from illness, is given extraordinary weight, for this engendered his false confidence: οὐδενὸς μέντοι τοῦτο λέγεται τῶν ἀπεργασαμένων τὸν πόλεμον αἰτίων ἔλαττον γενέσθαι (57. 5). No other Life gives such emphasis to this moment.

[14] Pelling (1980), 131–2 above, pp. 134–6. Though more aware, he is also more passive: ibid. 133–5 (above, pp. 138–42).

and the *Gracchi*—which should provide the kernel of our estimation. We should not be surprised if the views developed in those Lives are muted or trivialized elsewhere.

One further difficulty should be noted. No one, I hope, would now regard Plutarch as a mere excerptor, meekly copying out the analyses of his sources. (Scholars have, in fact, been relatively swift to realize that Plutarch has a mind and a literary hand of his own. That procedure of scholarly enlightenment is only just beginning with Appian and Cassius Dio.) Yet it is equally clear that Plutarch *sometimes* adopts ideas and interpretations very closely indeed. Take the analysis of the origins of the Civil War, which we find in its simplest form in the *Caesar*. It was not the enmity, but the friendship, of Pompey and Caesar which caused the war: the year 60 was the start of it all. They first combined to destroy the aristocracy, and their final estrangement only sealed the Republic's fate. Cato alone saw the truth. Caesar was always ambitious for tyranny, and purchased his way to power with his Gallic wealth. Pompey was his dupe, first disingenuous, then vacillating, then the prey of conflicting senatorial interests and ambitions. The deaths of Crassus and Julia removed vital obstacles to war; and the parlous state of politics at Rome—its κακοπολιτεία, so acute that many recognized monarchy as the only solution—was the background which made it all possible.[15] It is certainly a powerful analysis; but it is hardly Plutarch's own. Much of it recurs in a tellingly similar form in Appian[16] (and of course elsewhere), and it is surely derived originally from the work of Asinius

[15] *Caes.* 28, cf. e.g. 13. 4–6, 23. 5–7. For the variations in other Lives see n. 13. The analysis is clearest in *Caesar* because Plutarch there brings together so many of the themes in the single powerful survey (28); that analysis, returning the reader decisively to urban politics after the account of the Gallic campaigns, combines many motifs which are exploited earlier in the narratives of the other Lives.

[16] Cf. esp. Gaul as the training-ground for Caesar's army: App. *BC* 2. 17. 62 with *Caes.* 28. 3, *Pomp.* 51. 2; κακοπολιτεία: App. 2. 19. 69–70, with *Caes.* 28. 4, *C. min.* 44. 3, *Pomp.* 54. 3; Pompey's disingenuous behaviour and true ambitions: App. 2. 19. 71, 2. 20. 73 with *Caes.* 28. 7, *C. min.* 45. 7, *Pomp.* 53. 9–10, cf. Pelling (1980), 134 above, pp. 140–1; monarchy the only remedy: App. 2. 20. 72 with *Caes.* 28. 5–6, *C. min.* 47. 2, *Pomp.* 54. 7 (and also *Brut.* 55(2). 2, an interesting variation of the idea). For Pollio's view, and for other ancient analyses of the Republic's fall, see Pohlenz (1927), Syme (1950), Lintott (1971), 493–8.

Pollio. Of course, we are free to criticize it. Pollio, wishing
to give his work a powerful beginning, surely exaggerated
the importance of the electoral pact of 60 BC, thus giving
rise to that long legend of the 'first triumvirate' (as we used
to call it). Horace speaks of 'gravis principum amicitias' as a
theme of Pollio's work (*Odes* 2. 1. 3–4): Pollio perhaps laid
too much stress on the personal relationships of the great
men, and made them too far-sighted and clear-cut in their
ambitions. The treatment of Roman κακοπολιτεία tends to
confine itself to violence and bribery in Rome itself—especially the violence and bribery initiated by the great men or
their followers; there is no hint that Pollio gave any wider
sweep of the empire, armies, and provinces. But, whatever
we say, we are really making points about Pollio more than
Plutarch: Plutarch simply recognized, and welcomed, the
intellectual distinction and power of the analysis.

   Such passages as this certainly help us to see which
analyses Plutarch found plausible and welcomed as illuminating and intelligible; and, thus far, they can be used as
evidence for his own historical understanding. But, in the
end, they will tell us less than those passages where we can
see his *individual* judgements and assumptions at work,
where we can see him imposing his own views and interpretations on the events he is describing: particularly, where
we can see him *re*interpreting what his sources offered—as,
for instance, in the *Caesar*'s account of the Lupercalia
incident, where (as we saw) he seems to be revising and
rewriting Pollio's account to concentrate on the reactions of
the *dēmos*; or in the early chapters of that Life, where he
goes out of his way to stress the people's encouragement to
Caesar to become 'first in the state'.[17] (We can there contrast the early chapters of Suetonius' biography, which are
evidently based on very similar source-material, but have
no such emphasis on the popular theme.)[18] In those passages we see Plutarch *himself* labouring to make his material
intelligible. And in those passages, most insistently, his

[17] Above, pp. 319–21.
[18] The uniformity of the tradition for Caesar's early years is demonstrated by
Strasburger (1938), 72–3, though the elaborate source-analysis which Strasburger
develops is not at all plausible.

analysis concentrates on the *dēmos* theme, the popular support which Caesar enjoyed—a theme, incidentally, which is rather lost from sight when Plutarch is reproducing Pollio's analysis of the causes of war.

In a Life such as the *Caesar*, what Plutarch leaves out can tell us as much about his assumptions as what he puts in. We should not, of course, expect him to say much about Caesar's family relationship to (say) the Aurelii or the Aemilii Lepidi, two highly influential *gentes* at the period of Caesar's early career;[19] however much importance we ourselves may choose to attach to such links (at least in explaining the *first* steps in a young man's career), these are not the sorts of connection which ancient writers regularly stress. But Plutarch might surely have said more about Caesar's various attempts to conciliate senatorial opinion or foster senatorial connections—at 5. 7, for instance, he does not mention that Caesar's bride Pompeia was Sulla's grand-daughter, though this has clear biographical interest.[20] And it is certainly striking that Plutarch has nothing on Caesar's relations with the great men, Crassus and Pompey: nothing, in this Life, on Caesar's support for the *lex Gabinia*, or his pressure for Pompey's recall from the East, or his association with Pompey's lieutenant Metellus Nepos; nothing on Caesar's alleged involvement with Crassus during the Catilinarian affair. All of these are items which Plutarch certainly knew.[21] But, in this Life, Caesar

[19] For Caesar's connection with these *gentes* see Suet. *DJ* 1. 2; for their power see Münzer (1920), 312 f., 324 ff. Note Aemilii Lepidi as consuls in 78/7, Aurelii Cottae in 75/4—precisely the period when Caesar's career was beginning.

[20] He probably knew the item: cf. Suet. *DJ* 6. 2, probably from the same source.

[21] He mentions Caesar's support for the *lex Gabinia* at *Pomp.* 25. 8, but not in *Caesar* (Dio, 36. 43. 2–4, describing Caesar's support for the *lex Manilia* in very similar terms, is probably a doublet: Strasburger (1938), 63, 100–1); Plutarch had already described Caesar's agitation together with Metellus in the earlier *Cicero* (23. 1–4), and makes a great deal of it at *C. min.* 27–9, but at *Caes.* 9. 1 he blandly states that 'Caesar's praetorship was not at all turbulent'; at *Cic.* 23. 5 he had also mentioned Caesar's proposal to recall Pompey from the East, and repeats the story (in a slightly different form) at *C. min.* 26. 2, but again does not mention this in *Caes.* He mentions Caesar's involvement with Crassus at *Crass.* 13. 4 (with some pride in his learning). In *Caesar*, apart from the casual mention of Pompey at 5. 7, the introduction of both Crassus and Pompey is delayed until 11. 1.

is his own master and agent. He gains his support—that
vital popular support—wholly in his own right. Here, as
elsewhere, Plutarch gives little indication of the personal
attachments, alliances, and deals which most modern scholars would want to stress—however transient, or however
firmly based, we might regard them as being; here, as
elsewhere, it is the *dēmos* theme which dominates.

Now no one would regard Plutarch's analysis as wholly
false. Of course, Caesar *was* a great *popularis*, recognized as
such in his own day;[22] and the support of the urban *dēmos*
was important to him. What is wrong with the analysis is
simply what it leaves out. It is one strand among several
important for explaining Caesar's career and success, and it
is the exclusiveness of Plutarch's focus on it which is so
striking. And it is a type of analysis which recurs time and
again. In Life after Life, in much the same way in every
period, we have the urban *dēmos* against the senate. There
are just these two forces in politics: they can be described as
ἀμφότεροι at (for instance) *Marius* 4. 7. 'The senate wanted
peace, but Marcellus stirred up the people for war' (*Marc.*
6. 2); 'Appius Claudius always had the senate and the best
men with him—it was his family tradition—while Scipio
Africanus was a great man on his own account, but also
always enjoyed great support and enthusiasm among the
people' (*Aem.* 38. 3); Marius 'was a formidable antagonist
of the senate, for he was playing the demagogue with the
people' (*Mar.* 4. 6); in 70 BC people criticized Pompey for
'giving himself more to the people than the senate' (*Pomp.*
21. 7), and, as we saw, 'Crassus had more strength in the
senate, while Pompey was very powerful with the people'
(*Pomp.* 22. 3); in 66 it was the 'favour of the people and the
flattery of the demagogues' which gave Pompey the command against Mithridates, while 'the senate and the best
men' felt that Lucullus was being terribly slighted (*Lucull.*
35. 9); in 59 Caesar cried out that 'he was driven to court
the people against his will, because of the violence and
recklessness of the senate' (*Caes.* 14. 3); by 50 Cato was

[22] Cf. esp. Cic. *Cat.* 4. 9, *de prov. cons.* 38–9, *Phil.* 2. 116, 5. 49; Caelius, *apud*
Cic. *ad fam.* 8. 6. 5. See Strasburger (1938), esp. 129 ff., and C. Meier (1965) *RE*
Supplementband 10, cols. 580, 582, 590.

making no progress with the people, who 'wanted Caesar to be greatest', but he 'persuaded the senate, who were afraid of the people' (*C. min.* 51. 7); in March and April 44 Brutus and Cassius 'had the goodwill of the senate', and turned to courting the people (*Brut.* 21. 2–3).[23] These two forces or factors in politics are not quite parties: Plutarch never suggests that there was any organized group of politicians who systematically devoted themselves to promoting the people's interests (though he sometimes talks of 'the demagogues' in terms which have some analogies with this).[24] But, at least, the senate and people almost always act each in their unified and corporate ways, and Plutarch is surprised if the two sides act in concert—if they unite to support Cicero for the consulship, for instance, or if the aristocratically minded Aemilius is as popular as any demagogue (*Cic.* 10–11, *Aem.* 38. 6). Other, complicating factors—the *equites*, perhaps, or the Italians, or the veterans—tend to be left out of things, as Plutarch prefers to leave his picture simple and unblurred.

In some ways, Plutarch is hardly alone in this. Nothing could be more natural at Rome than to contrast 'the senate' and 'the people'; this mode of analysis is frequent enough in Roman historiography (we shall see that later), and, of course, with its clear analogies to classical Greek stereotypes of the ὀλίγοι and the δῆμος, it was particularly congenial to the *Greek* historians of Rome. The Greek equivalents are clearest in Polybius, who makes the senate and the people two of the three vital factors in his vision of the Roman 'mixed constitution': just as the consuls contribute the elements of monarchy to this, so the senate inject those of aristocracy and the people those of democracy.[25] It is not surprising that this schematism leaves no room for the *equites*, for example: at 6. 17, very uneasily, he has to

---

[23] Cf. also e.g. *Marc.* 10. 2 (Nola), *C. mai.* 16. 4, *Mar.* 9. 4, *Pomp.* 25. 7, 46. 5, 49. 3–6, 49. 11, 52. 2, 59. 3, *Lucull.* 38. 2, *C. min.* 22. 6, 26. 1, 28. 6, 29. 3, 32. 1, *Cic.* 33. 2, 33. 6, 43. 4; and the detailed analyses of *Caesar, Gracchi,* and *Fabius* elsewhere in this paper. Note the isolated exception at *Mar.* 34. 2, where Plutarch is aware that the views of the *dēmos* were divided.

[24] e.g. *Aem.* 38. 6, *Ant.* 2. 6, *Lucull.* 35. 9, *C. min.* 31. 2.

[25] Plb. 6. 11–18, 43–58.

include the equestrian *publicani* among 'the people'.[26] As
Clemence Schultze points out, Dionysius of Halicarnassus
is similarly fond of *boulē–dēmos* antitheses in describing the
history of the early and middle Republic.[27] Appian begins
his *Civil Wars* with the remark that 'at Rome there was
frequent conflict between the senate and people, as they
clashed over legislation and debt-cancellations and land-
distributions and elections'; and Cassius Dio, too, readily
adopts the *boulē–dēmos* antithesis as a favourite device for
analysing late republican history, and equally stresses popular support as the key to Caesar's rise.[28] And yet with these
other authors—but not really with Plutarch—there is normally more to it than that. There is often a measure of
thoughtfulness in the way these categories are applied, as
possibly with Dionysius and certainly with Polybius. The
latter has evidently expended an extraordinary amount of
intellectual effort in isolating the elements of the Roman
constitution which correspond to the Greek stereotypes—
and of course concludes that the particular *blend* of monar-
chic, aristocratic, and democratic factors, though not necessarily any of the factors themselves, is really *unlike* any
Greek constitution, and indeed superior to anything the
Greeks could offer.[29] It is hard to think that Plutarch's
application of the *boulē–dēmos* categories is anything like so
reflective. In the other authors, too, there is usually some
sense of historical change. Polybius, like Dionysius, stresses
that it took considerable time for the distinctive Roman
blend of monarchy, aristocracy, and democracy to develop;[30] and Appian, in his introductory survey, tends to
regard *boulē–dēmos* strife as the main strand in *earlier*

[26] See e.g. Walbank (1957), ad loc., or Brunt (1965*a*), 119: 'by the people he of
course means the Equites'. Nicolet (1966), 322–3 does not quite bring out the
importance of Polybius' schematism.

[27] Schultze (1986), 130–1, 139–40.

[28] *Boulē–dēmos*: e.g. 36. 24. 1–2, 36. 24. 5, 36, 37. 1, 36. 38. 3–5, 36. 43. 2–5,
36. 51. 3, 37. 26. 3, 37, 29. 3, 37. 41. 3, 37. 42. 3, 37. 43. 1, 37. 51. 3, 37. 56. 5, 38.
1. 1, 38. 12. 4–13. 1, 38. 15. 3, 38. 16. 3, 38. 16. 6, and so on. Popular support for
Caesar: 36. 43. 2–4, 37. 22. 1, 37. 37. 2–3, 37. 56. 1–2, 38. 11. 3–6, 39. 25. 1–3, 40.
50. 5, 45. 6. 1, 45. 11. 2. Cf. Brutscher (1958), 43–6. But, as Strasburger (1938),
98–106 observes, he does make considerably more than Plutarch of Caesar's
associations with Pompey during the sixties.

[29] Plb. 6. 43–58.

[30] Plb. 6. 10. 13–14, 51. 5; for Dionysius see Schultze (1986), 130–2, 139.

Roman history—before the Gracchi. The Gracchi marked
the introduction of violence into politics;[31] afterwards
Appian concentrates much more on the theme of the 'returning general', with his discontented army which needed to
be settled.[32] The analysis recurs later in Appian's history,
and his use of the *boulē–dēmos* antithesis is correspondingly
sparing.[33] He, like Cassius Dio, shows much more awareness than Plutarch that the *boulē–dēmos* contrast often
breaks down, and other strands of explanation need to be
employed. Thus both Appian and Dio have rather more of
the veterans, for example, and the *equites*;[34] thus Appian
knows that Pompey can be both 'a friend of the people',
φιλόδημος, and thoroughly responsible in his behviour towards the senate;[35] thus Dio can introduce the interesting
and revealing descriptions of Cato, and then of Brutus and
Cassius, as 'lovers of the people' (δημερασταί);[36] and he can
talk—admittedly in a rather bewildering way—of the various 'associations' (ἑταιρεῖαι) which Pompey and Crassus
respectively brought to the alliance of 60 BC.[37] What
strikes one about Plutarch is how rarely such complicating
factors are adduced, and how relentlessly and exclusively he
presses the simple *boulē–dēmos* antithesis—indeed, how
often he reduces and simplifies other modes of explanation
so that he can phrase them in these terms. We are certainly
here confronting an *individual* feature of Plutarch's
technique.

Particularly striking and illuminating are the Lives of the
Gracchi. There we find analyses very similar to those given
in the *Caesar*, and there, too, elements which complicate
the simple picture tend to be cut away. Tiberius is greeted

[31] App. *BC* 1. 2. 4, cf. Plut. *Gracch.* 20. 1.
[32] App. *BC* 1. 1–6, esp. 1. 2. 4 ff.
[33] 'Returning general' theme: cf. 1. 55. 240, 1. 60. 269–70; 5. 17 brings out the
importance of finding a *settlement* of such an army. Sparing use of *boulē–dēmos*
antithesis: e.g. 1. 21. 87–9, 1. 38. 169, 1. 69. 316–17, 1. 107. 502.
[34] Below, pp. 344–6.
[35] App. *BC* 2. 20. 72.
[36] Dio, 37. 22. 3, 43. 11. 6, 47. 38. 3 (with Rawson (1986), 115). Dr Lintott
notes that Dio's view of Helvidius Priscus is interestingly similar (65. 12. 2), and
suggests that Dio's interpretation of Helvidius' philosophical ideals may have
influenced his portrayal of Cato.
[37] Dio, 37. 54. 3, 37. 57. 2; for the use of ἑταιρεία cf. Nic. Dam. *Vit. Aug.* 103,
105.

by popular acclaim (*Gracch.* 7. 3–4, 8. 10, 10. 1), and his
policies are aimed at the urban *dēmos*.[38] The senate—or,
more usually in this Life, 'the rich'[39]—naturally respond
with hostility. Led on by the people's enthusiams, Tiberius
manages to depose Octavius—but, at that, his popular support begins to waver (15. 1). He finds himself forced into
policies which are more extreme (16. 1), but the people
remain cool: the enraged opponents of the bill seize their
chance, and Tiberius is killed. But, by the time of his
death, the popular fervour is beginning to erupt once more
(21)—exactly, one remembers, as it did when Caesar was
killed, and Cinna the poet became the victim. Indeed, the
whole sequence is closely similar to the pattern developed
in the *Caesar*: popular support brings success, popular
cooling drives a man to fatal mistakes, popular fervour
reasserts itself at the end. A few years later, and the whole
pattern starts again with Gaius: we see the great initial
popularity, and Gaius responding to it with a collection of
popular measures; then we have the wavering of popular
support, this time caused less by any mistake of Gaius than
by the shrewdness of his opponents, who use M. Livius
Drusus to outbid Gaius' proposals. Gaius is forced to more
extreme tactics; the opponents take their chance, and he
dies; the popular fervour returns after his death.[40] Once
again, all is focused on the urban *dēmos*, whose support
brings success and whose indifference brings failure and

---

[38] *Gracch.* 8. 10, 9. 3, 10. 1, 12. 6, 13. 4, 13. 6

[39] *Gracch.* 10. 9, 11. 1, 11. 4, 12. 6, 18. 3, 20. 3. These 'rich' dominate the
senate (11. 4, though cf. 18. 3), and indeed seem closely equivalent to the political
grouping which Plutarch normally describes simply as 'the senate': cf. 14. 3, 16. 2,
21. 1–4. Plutarch here calls them 'the rich' simply to phrase the conflict in the
relevant terms, i.e. economic ones. When political rather than economic divisions
come to be more relevant, he naturally reverts to describing Tiberius' opponents
as 'the senate' (20–1). Economic considerations were less central to his treatment
of Gaius, and his antagonists are again usually 'the senate': 26. 1, 27. 1–2, 29. 3–6,
30. 1–2, 30. 6–7, 32. 5, 33. 3, 35. 2.

[40] Initial popularity: *Gracch.* 22. 7. Demagogic proposals: 24. 5, 25. 1, and
especially 26, the bills which he introduced τῷ δήμῳ χαριζόμενος καὶ καταλύων τὴν
σύγκλητον (26. 1); 27. 5. People rejoice: 25. 4, 27. 1, 28. 1. Γνωριμώτατοι launch
Livius Drusus: 29. 4, 31. 3–4. People waver: 30. 7 ('the people became more
gently disposed to the senate'), 32. 4, 37. 7. Gaius more extreme: 33. Death: 36–8.
Popular hatred of Opimius: 38. 8–9, 39. 2; and demonstrations for Gaius after
death: 39. 2–3.

death; and the pattern of the *Caesar* comes back in the *Gracchi*, and comes back twice.

What is more, we can see that Plutarch has removed material which does not fit. Consider *Gracch*. 8, where Plutarch is setting out the background of the troubles. That chapter seems clearly to come from the same source as Appian, *BC* 1. 7,[41] but we can see that Plutarch and Appian have selected rather different strands to stress. Appian, as is well known, makes a great deal of the *Italian* strand. The problem is the εὐανδρία or δυσανδρία of the Italian race, and Tiberius tries to favour the poor—including the allies, it is clear[42]— throughout Italy. One particular concern is that, on the large estates, landowners prefer slave to freeborn labour, because the freeborn are eligible for military service; and this *military* strand is given great stress. Now Plutarch does seem to know of this type of explanation, and it is reasonable to infer that something like this stood in the shared source. Plutarch does mention, for instance, that 'the poor did not enlist enthusiastically for military service', and that they 'did not care to bring up their young, so that shortly *all Italy* would be afflicted by a shortage of free men'; and he records Tiberius' resonant speech, proclaiming the plight of those who 'fight and die for Italy'.[43] But none of this is brought to the centre of the analysis, and the isolated mention of 'all Italy' remains rather opaque. All Plutarch's weight falls on the urban *dēmos*, whom Tiberius is trying to benefit and placate. The public land had been distributed 'to the destitute and landless *citizens*', and these had now been dispossessed. Tiberius tries to reverse the process.[44]

[41] The sequence and selection of material in the two authors is tellingly similar. The usual view (and surely the right one) is that they share a source (cf. Gabba (1958), on App. *BC* 1. 7. 26): see esp. Tibiletti (1948), 206–9 (who seems right against Gabba on 1. 7. 28), Shochat (1970), 34 ff., with extensive bibliography at n. 31, Badian (1972), 707. The principal dissenter is Göhler (1939), 74–5, but his strongest argument rests on precisely the difference of interpretation—Appian stressing the Italians, Plutarch the urban poor—which is here explained in terms of Plutarch's individual techniques.

[42] See esp. *BC* 1. 7. 28, 1. 8. 32, 1. 18. 74, 1. 21. 86–7, with Gabba's notes; Göhler (1939), 76–82.

[43] *Gracch*. 8. 4, 9. 5. Cf. Gabba (1956), 37 n. 1, Shochat (1970), 36–7, Richardson (1980), 2.

[44] *Gracch*. 8. 1, 9. 2; for the stress on the *dēmos* see n. 38.

the citizens *in Rome* as the beneficiaries of his measures: a
conventional γῆς ἀναδασμός, in fact, in very Greek terms.
(That indeed is the charge of his enemies: he is introducing
a γῆς ἀναδασμός and starting a revolution, 9. 3) Later,
Appian speaks of 'the countrymen' (1. 10. 41) coming to
Rome to support Tiberius, and then of the country citizens
who might come to vote for his re-election (1. 14. 58): in
each case there may be some confusion in Appian's detail,
but something like these notices surely stood in the shared
source.[45] Plutarch again cuts the details away, reducing
everything to the urban *dēmos*. His treatment of Gaius is
very similar, again concentrating purely on the popular
elements. The laws—including the συμμαχικός law, extend-
ing the citizenship to the allies—all have one absolutely
straightforward aim, and Plutarch has no doubts about it:
Gaius is trying to win the goodwill of the *dēmos* (*Gracch.*
26, esp. 26. 2). Once again, too, there are hints that Plutarch
is recasting and simplifying his source-material. There is,
for instance, his casual mention that the Italians gave Gaius
their support, or the notice of the accusations that he and
Fulvius Flaccus were stirring up the allies to revolt.[46]
Passages like those certainly suggest that Plutarch's source
had rather more material on the Italians (as indeed does
Appian). But in Plutarch this material again remains tan-
gential and unexplained. The centre of the analysis remains the urban *dēmos*, wooed in a stereotyped way by
Gaius, a stereotyped demagogue. That stress on the *dēmos*
certainly fits the structure of the Lives—and not merely
the structure of the Lives, but of the double pair. The
Gracchi are compared with Agis and Cleomenes, and all
four are seen as demagogues, even if they are initially
idealistic ones: that is the whole point of the comparison
(*Agis and Cleomenes* 2. 7–11, cf. *Gracch.* 42(2) and 44(4)).
But it certainly seems clear that Plutarch is drastically
simplifying and recasting in order to produce this clear-cut
popular focus.

It is worth spending a moment on the significance of this

[45] For countrymen coming to Rome in 133, cf. Diod. 34/5. 6. 1.
[46] *Gracch.* 24. 1–2, 33. 1 (Italian support); 24. 1–2, 31. 3 (accusations of stirring
revolt).

for the Roman historian. The tendency of *Appian*'s account of the Gracchi is often examined closely, and we are frequently warned to beware of the 'pan-Italic motif' in Appian *BC* 1;[47] and scholars have often sought to exploit Plutarch against Appian in order to discredit that 'Italian' material. Most influentially, Badian, when arguing that Tiberius' land-grants were to be limited to Roman citizens, has explicitly defended Plutarch's authority: Plutarch's emphasis on the urban *dēmos*, he thinks, represents an earlier and more authentic stage in the tradition than Appian, and all these Italians were sneaked into the tradition by Appian's imediate source (who, he thinks, was a *popularis* historian of the late republican or Augustan period).[48] More recently, Bernstein has sought to reconcile Plutarch and Appian by suggesting that Tiberius first intended to include the Italian allies in his grants (Appian)—but then changed his plan and confined the distribution to Roman citizens (Plutarch).[49] What is worrying about all this is how little attention is being paid to *Plutarch*'s methods—how often he is the dumb partner in the comparison with Appian. If we can see, as we surely can, that it is absolutely characteristic of Plutarch to reduce complicated descriptions to the simple *boulē–dēmos* categories, then surely it is much more likely that *he* is the one who is sneaking the Italians *out of* his account, not Appian, or Appian's immediate source, who is sneaking them *in*. If it is right to assume a shared source, it is surely likely to be Appian, not Plutarch, who is preserving its spirit.

If this is so, it becomes much harder to discard Appian's evidence for this 'Italian' strand, and harder, in particular, to reject his statement that Tiberius intended the Italian

[47] Particularly by Badian: see Badian (1958), 172, and Badian (1972), 701 n. 100, 717 and n. 146, 731 n. 183. Gabba (1956) discusses 'il motivo alleato' with great care, but is much more ready than Badian to believe that it may bear some relation to historical reality.

[48] Badian (1958), 168–74, cf. Badian (1972), 731 and n. 183; he was following and developing some suggestions of Gelzer (see esp. Gelzer (1929), 299–303). See also e.g. Earl (1963), 20–3, and Nagle (1970) 373–6, for similar arguments.

[49] Bernstein (1978), 137–59. Bernstein also argues that reflections of this change of plan can be seen in Appian's own narrative: this is no place for a discussion, but his argument is not at all cogent. Cf. Astin (1979), 111 f., Richardson (1980), 2–3.

allies to share in the grants of land.[50] 'Italian' needs further
definition, of course: who were these people? Not just the
rural citizens, it seems, unless Appian has wildly misunderstood his source;[51] but Latins and allies, or just allies? And
were they to receive the citizenship as well as their parcel of
land, as Richardson suggests?[52] Those are real questions,
and perhaps there is not sufficient evidence to give firm
answers. And it may well be that this whole 'Italian' strand
did not figure quite so prominently in Tiberius' propaganda
and programme as Appian would suggest. It is certainly
very important to Appian's vision of the whole period to
stress Italian discontent, for he is already preparing and
developing the themes which will return in his treatment of
the Social War: all that is traced with great sensitivity by
Gabba and by Cuff.[53] Appian might well want to make the
most of any Italians he found—and that anyway suits his
way of doing history. He is not particularly 'Italophile' (it
is not a question of that, as again Cuff has shown); but he *is*
unusually sensitive to social factors in his history, and
particularly the relevance of the countryside in providing
support.[54] But 'making the most of any Italians he found'
is one thing, widespread fabrication is another. It is foreign
to anything we know about Appian, or anything we can
infer about his source-material, to believe that this strand
has no foundation at all in historical reality. There is certainly nothing in Appian's account to justify the dismissive
attitude shown, for instance, by Badian. When he discards

[50] Naturally, not all the material relevant to this complicated issue can be
discussed here: any serious treatment would have to consider the terms of the *lex
agraria* of 111 BC, as well as the various (largely enigmatic) statements made by
Cicero. I here limit myself to those arguments drawn from the divergence of the
narratives of Plutarch and Appian—arguments, it is true, which most scholars
have felt to be of particular importance in discussing this question. For fuller
recent discussions see Shochat (1970) and (1980), Richardson (1980) (Italians
included in the grants); Brunt (1971), 76 n. 1, Sherwin-White (1973), 217–18, and
Stockton (1979), 40–6 (cautious, but not excluding Italian participation); Nagle
(1970), Badian (1972) (Italians excluded); and Bernstein (1978) (discussed above).
[51] Cf. Göhler (1939), 76–82 (showing that by 'Italians' Appian certainly means
Italian allies), Cuff (1967).
[52] Richardson (1980).
[53] Gabba (1956), Cuff (1967).
[54] This emerges with particular clarity in Book 5 (which, *pace* Gabba, is surely
not drawn from the same source as the early parts of Book 1): cf. esp. 5. 12–14, 5.
23. 90, 5. 27. 106. See also Cuff (1983).

the 'chatter about the opposition between "the rich" and "the poor"' which he finds in both Plutarch and Appian as 'no more than a stereotype of *stasis*, a purely literary device of little use to the historian',[55] Badian obscures the extremely important differences between Plutarch and Appian here. As far as Plutarch is concerned, the historian is right to be sceptical: the rich–poor antithesis is more than *a* stereotype, it is a version of *his* distinctive stereotype, and we can indeed see that he is simplifying a complex reality in order to make it fit. But Appian really is rather different. For him the rich–poor conflict is just one strand in a much more complex reality: town and country, Roman and Italian are in fact much more important to his analysis. The categories are of course rough ones,[56] but that need not in itself arouse suspicions. The most complex political divisions regularly embrace contrasts which can perfectly fairly, if roughly, be described in such terms. The blend of factors may be confusing, but it is certainly not stereotyped: Gabba is indeed right to comment on the *un*stereotyped and *un*conventional nature of Appian's analysis in this part of *BC* 1.[57] It is very hard to believe that the Italian material is simply drawn from the air.

To return to Plutarch: something similar has probably happened in his account of Saturninus and Glaucia, which he gives at *Marius* 28–30. *Marius* is of course another Life in which Plutarch is extremely interested in historical analysis, and he is most concerned at that point to analyse Marius' wavering popular support. Once again, it is likely that he is drawing his material from the same source as Appian, who gives a parallel account at *BC* 1. 28–33.[58] But, once again, the emphases of the two authors are very different. Appian is very clear that it was 'the Italians' who supported Saturni-

[55] Badian (1972), 707; cf. the criticisms of De Ste Croix (1981), 359.
[56] As Badian (1972), 717 f. and n. 149 rightly insists.
[57] Gabba (1956), 62.
[58] This is likely, though less certain than in the case of the accounts of the Gracchi. The exile of Metellus is certainly described in extremely similar terms by both authors (App. *BC* 1. 29, Plut. *Mar.* 29), and must surely come from a common source. It is possible that one or the other has turned to a different source for the political background—but, in view of Plutarch's capacity for recasting material, there is no *need* to resort to that assumption.

nus, and were to benefit from his land-bill. The urban
dēmos (πολιτικὸς ὄχλος, 1. 30. 133) oppose Saturninus
fiercely, and in this they are at one with the senate. When
Saturninus tries to drive Metellus into exile, the Italians
again support him (1. 31. 139–40), and again threaten to
come to blows with the city-dwellers; and, once Saturninus
is overthrown, the *dēmos* and the senate, again at one,
gratefully seize their chance to press for Metellus' recall. (I
take it that Appian means 'the Italian allies' when he speaks
of the 'Italian' or 'rustic' support for Saturninus; even if, as
many suppose, he means the 'rural citizens', the fact remains
that he is drawing a firm distinction between countrymen
and city-dwellers.)[59] All that is much too complicated for
Plutarch. He turns Saturninus, like the Gracchi, into a very
conventional demagogue. Saturninus aims at the 'destitute
and turbulent mob' (πλῆθος ἄπορον καὶ θορυβοποιόν, 28. 7, cf.
29. 9): it is clearly the urban *dēmos* which supports him (29.
7, 29. 11, 30. 2), and the senate which is opposed. The
land-bill seems aimed, once again, at the urban *dēmos*: not
a word of those 'countrymen' or 'Italians' of Appian. (Nor
indeed, in this context, of Marius' veterans, though he has
mentioned them in the preceding chapter (28. 7); more of
that later.) This leaves the final popular surge *against*
Marius (30. 5) and the popular pressure for Metellus' recall
(31. 2) harder to explain—but Plutarch is not too concerned:
mobs, after all, are fickle. Appian's version of all this is
much more subtle and sophisticated, whatever its relation
to historical reality;[60] if he and Plutarch do share a source,
it is surely likely that it is Appian, not Plutarch, who is
retaining more of the complexities of the source's analysis.
And, once again, we see Plutarch's reductionism, his readiness to simplify the most complex events into simple *dēmos*

[59] See Badian (1958), 207 n. 2, Göhler (1939), 80 f. (Appian means allies);
Shochat (1970), 40 and n. 44, Gelzer, (1929), 298, Brunt (1965*b*), 106 (rural
citizens); Lintott (1968), 178–81 (Appian confused).

[60] Historians normally accept that Saturninus proposed some distribution to
Italians, but argue (or imply) that only Italian *veterans*—particularly those of
Marius' army—were to benefit: Göhler (1939), 197–203, Badian (1958), 203–8,
Gabba (1951), 178–9 and (1956), 75–6. I suspect that this needs reconsideration.
The veterans were clearly of central importance (cf. *Mar.* 28. 7, App. *BC* 1. 29.
132), and would doubtless be the first to be settled; but there seems no reason to
assume that only veterans were to receive benefits.

and *boulē* conflict, and his readiness to cut away material which would complicate and blur that simple stereotype.

I mentioned previously the γῆς ἀναδασμός of Tiberius as described 'in very Greek terms', and it is naturally tempting to take this suggestion further. This whole *boulē–dēmos* analysis does remind one irresistibly of the way Plutarch talks about Greek politics, and the stereotypes of Greek political thought: not, perhaps, the *boulē*, but at least the *oligoi*, who are predictably and violently opposed to the fickle *dēmos*. Before he came to write the *Parallel Lives*, Plutarch evidently had an extremely thorough knowledge of Greek history and literature, whereas his knowledge of detailed Roman history was probably scanty; is Plutarch here imposing Greek concepts on Roman reality, bending Roman history to fit stereotypes which did not wholly match the reality? It is interesting to note that Gomme made the converse suggestion, which is equally attractive— that Plutarch sometimes imposed Roman stereotypes on Greek history: Nicias buying the goodwill of the *dēmos* with expensive shows, for instance, or Cimon as the soldier who is lost when it comes to the tricks of domestic politics.[61] And certainly the similarity of the terms used for the Greek and Roman worlds was sometimes very *useful* to Plutarch, making his parallels all the closer. Just as Dion and Brutus have to kill similar tyrants, so Pericles and Fabius have to confront similar mobs and similar demagogues; and the corruption of good programmes into rank demagogy can link Agis and Cleomenes with the Gracchi.

Certainly, the similarities of Plutarch's language to that in his Greek Lives do seem very close. The opponents of the Roman *dēmos* may be described in various ways, though they can usually be seen to be equivalent to (or at least to dominate) the senate: they are the ἀριστοκρατικοί,[62] or the γνώριμοι,[63] or the καλοὶ κἀγαθοί,[64] or the χαρίεντες,[65] or the

[61] Gomme (1945–81), 1. 72–4.
[62] *Caes.* 13. 5, 14. 6, *Aem.* 38. 2, 38. 6, *Tit.* 18. 2, *Mar.* 28. 6, *C. min.* 26. 4, *Pomp.* 30. 3–4, *Lucull.* 38. 2, *Cic.* 10. 1, 33. 2, cf. 22. 2
[63] *Aem.* 31. 2, *C. mai.* 16. 4, *Gracch.* 24. 2, 29. 6, 30. 7, *Pomp.* 4. 8, *Brut.* 24. 4.
[64] *Caes.* 14. 3, *Cic.* 11. 2, 29. 4.
[65] *Gracch.* 40. 3, *Pomp.* 4. 8, *Brut.* 24. 4, *C. min.* 27. 8, cf. 49. 3.

ὀλιγαρχικοί,⁶⁶ or the ἀξιόλογοι,⁶⁷ or the δοκιμώτατοι,⁶⁸ or the
δυνατώτατοι,⁶⁹ or the κράτιστοι,⁷⁰ or simply the πρῶτοι or
ἄριστοι.⁷¹ Those, indeed, are precisely the terms in which
Plutarch is accustomed to speak of Greek politics.⁷² The
sort of analysis he gives in *Caesar* or the *Gracchi*—the hero
wins popular support, then forfeits it, then it is finally
reasserted—has considerable parallels with, say, the *Pericles*.
Just as in Greece, an individual tries occasionally to become
first man in the state; then, particularly if that individual is
hoping to exploit his popularity with the *dēmos*, Plutarch
usually assumes that he hoped for or achieved a τυραννίς, a
δυναστεία, a μοναρχία. These accusations were of course
thrown around in the real world of Roman politics, and it is
perhaps natural that Plutarch should say such things of
Sulla, Marius, Cinna, Saturninus, Cicero, Caesar, or
Pompey; It is more striking that he should casually note
that 'C. Gracchus had by now acquired a sort of monarch's
strength', or record the suggestion that 'Cassius was seeking
to secure a δυναστεία for himself, not freedom for his fellow
citizens'.⁷³ If a man's aim is specified more closely, it is
rarely any more informative than 'revolution'—μετάστασις
or σύγχυσις τῆς πολιτείας: so, naturally enough, of the Catilinarians and of Caesar; so also, though, of Saturninus; and
even, once again casually, of the supporters of Pompey in
the late sixties—'a sizeable part of the *dēmos* wanted

⁶⁶ *Gracch.* 32. 4, 35. 2, *Cic.* 9. 7.
⁶⁷ *Mar.* 9. 4, cf. *Otho* 3. 3.
⁶⁸ *Marc.* 27. 4.
⁶⁹ *Fab.* 8. 4, *Gracch.* 13. 2, 20. 1, *Lucull.* 37. 3, *Pomp.* 25. 7, *Caes.* 10. 6; cf.
Mar. 9. 4, 30. 5, *Gracch.* 24. 3.
⁷⁰ *Mar.* 30. 2
⁷¹ *Fab.* 8. 4, *Marc.* 27. 4, *Aem.* 38. 2–3, *C. mai.* 16. 4, *Mar.* 14. 14, 29. 7, 34. 6,
Lucull. 35. 9, 37. 3, *Pomp.* 16. 3, 49. 3, 51. 6, *Crass.* 4. 1, *Caes.* 7. 4, *C. min.* 27. 8,
Brut. 27. 5, 29. 3.
⁷² A representative selection of Greek passages: *Arist.* 2. 1, 26. 2, *Cim.* 10. 8,
15. 1–2, *Nic.* 2. 2, 11. 2, *Alc.* 13. 5, 21. 2, 26. 2, *Dion* 28. 1; and esp. *Per.* 7. 3–4, 9.
5, 10. 7.8, 11. 1–3 (with Meinhardt (1957), 38, and Andrewes (1978), 2), 15. 1. In
general see Rhodes (1981) on [Arist.] *AP* 2. 1.
⁷³ Sulla: *Sull.* 30. 5–6 (etc.), *Pomp.* 9. 3, *Brut.* 9. 2, *Cic.* 17. 5, 27. 6. Marius:
Mar. 46. 6, *Sull.* 30. 5, cf. *Pomp.* 81(1). 2. Cinna: *Mar.* 41. 2, *Sull.* 22. 1, *Cic.* 17.
5, *Caes.* 1. 1. Carbo: *Sull.* 22. 1. Saturninus: *Mar.* 30. 1. Cicero: *Cic.* 23. 4.
Caesar: *Caes.* 4. 8, 57. 1, 64. 5, 69. 1, *C. min.* 55. 4, 58. 7, 66. 2, *Ant.* 12. 5, *Brut.*
12. 3. Pompey: *Pomp.* 25. 3, 30. 3–4, 43. 1, 54. 5, *Caes.* 41. 2, *Lucull.* 38. 2, *C. min.*
47. 2. C. Gracchus: *Gracch.* 27. 1. Cassius: *Brut.* 29. 5.

Pompey's return because they looked for a revolution' (*C. min.* 27. 1, cf. *Pomp.* 43. 5); and notice the charges laid against the ruling class during the Hannibalic War: 'they were exploiting the war to destroy the *dēmos* and introduce an absolute monarchy' (*Fab.* 8. 4).[74] This assumption that political aims and achievements are regularly to be explained in terms of constitutional change is really very Greek. Plutarch has little idea of the characteristic Roman desire to be first within the system, rather than change it. When he writes of Marius or of Pompey, he writes of their φιλαρχία, their quest for offices or commands;[75] he has no notion of an ambition for a position of prestige and respect within an appreciative state. There is certainly little feel for the importance of such ideas as *dignitas* or *auctoritas*. He does, perhaps, have rather more feeling for the Roman passion for *gloria*: he certainly seems clear enough, for instance, that T. Flamininus was eager to avoid handing the war with Philip over to a successor, and was prepared to make peace rather than see this. 'He was fiercely ambitious for honour, and was afraid that he might forfeit his glory if another general were sent to the war' (*Titus* 7. 2, cf. 13. 2); Plutarch does not find that at all remarkable or perplexing.[76] But, usually, when he speaks of such ambition for glory, he does so with considerable bitterness and hostility: in particular, this was the decisive failing of the Gracchi (*Agis and Cleomenes* 2), and it was an important aspect in which the elder Cato fell short of Aristides (*C. mai.* 32(5). 4). Plutarch has certainly not felt his way into the values of Roman public life, and gives no sense of the respect and value Romans accorded to a competitive quest for glory.[77]

  Where Greek analogies of Roman institutions exist, Plutarch is quite good: he does, for instance, seem to understand

[74] Catilinarians: *Cic.* 10. 2, 10. 5. Caesar: *Caes.* 4. 9, 13. 4, *Cic.* 20. 6. Saturninus: *Mar.* 30. 1. On *Fab.* 8. 4 see below, p. 350.
[75] Marius: *Mar.* 2. 4, 28. 1, 31. 3, 34. 6, 45. 4–12. Pompey: *Pomp.* 30. 7–8. (There is little on Pompey's wishes—for commands or for anything else—in the second half of that Life: see Pelling (1980), 133 (above, p. 139) and n. 32.)
[76] This ascription of motive derives from Polybius (18. 10. 11–12, 18. 39. 4). Livy, interestingly, finds the charge embarrassing and plays it down: see Livy 32. 32. 5–8 and 33. 13. 15, with Briscoe (1973), 22 n. 4, and notes on both passages. For a powerful modern discussion see Badian (1970), 295 ff.: note esp. 310 ff., with some trenchant remarks on Roman views of *gloria*.
[77] Wardman (1974), 120 brings this out well.

a fair amount about political activity in the lawcourts, and his
discussion of political trials at *C. mai.* 15 is sensible enough.
Things in Greece were perhaps not so very different—or at
least *less* different than they were in many other aspects of
political life.[78] When Greek equivalents are absent, he is in
trouble. It may be a particular institution which defeats him:
the tribunate, for instance, was a very curious thing to a
Greek of the Roman Empire, and Plutarch several times
incorrectly explains the tribunicial veto, speaking as if a
tribune could only veto the acts of a fellow tribune.[79] Certain
aspects of the early days of January 49 BC are therefore beyond
him: at *Ant.* 5. 10 he can only refer to the infringement by the
optimates (τῶν ἀπὸ βουλῆς) of the tribunes' freedom of speech,
and gives no hint of the overriding of their veto.[80] Or it may
be a convention of political life which he finds difficult, or
tends to obscure. He certainly knows the importance of the
Roman political family, and of family traditions: the Claudii,
for instance, and the Metelli are by tradition aristocratically
minded (*Aem.* 38. 3, *C. min.* 26. 4). He sees the importance of
kinsmen, too, in persuading Aemilius Paullus to stand for the
consulship at a time of national crisis (*Aem.* 10. 2). But he
does not seem to sense the extent of the authority exercised by
the *very* great families, the Scipiones or the Metelli or even
(despite *Gracch.* 1) the Sempronii. When he seeks to explain
the early electoral successes of Marcellus, it never occurs to
him to mention the importance of the *family* (*Marc.* 2): the
answer must be found in his military promise. The senate are
the ἀριστοκρατικοί; Plutarch has no notion of the importance
of *nobilitas*, and makes no attempt to distinguish grades of
aristocracy within the senate itself. When the terms εὐγενής or
εὐπατρίδης do occur, they often seem rather to refer to the
patriciate.[81] All that scarcely conveys the flavour of the
realities of Roman aristocratic society.

[78] The important political aspect which Plutarch does *not* see concerns the
composition of the juries. To understand this he would need to show more grasp
of the *equites* than he does: see below, p. 344.

[79] *Ant.* 5. 8, *Gracch.* 10. 3, *C. min.* 20. 8—though, oddly enough, he gets it
right at *QR* 81 (*Mor.* 283c).

[80] *Caes.* 35. 6–11, Caesar's clash with the tribune Metellus, is another case
where Plutarch does not bring out the importance of the veto.

[81] See esp. *Sull.* 1. 1, γένει μὲν ἦν ἐκ πατρικίων, οὓς εὐπατρίδας ἄν τις εἴποι, and
Ant. 12. 3. Most men so described are in fact both *nobiles*—whether on Gelzer's

And Greek stereotypes could certainly not accommodate so unfamiliar an institution as *clientela*. Plutarch's definition of *patronus* at *Fab.* 13. 6 is feeble and inadequate; and, when he mentions a *cliens–patronus* relationship, it is normally to explain the adhesion or obligation of *one* individual—normally a fairly important individual: Marius to Metellus or to C. Herennius, for example, or Mucius (if that was the man's name) to Ti. Gracchus.[82] He has no feel for the electoral or military significance of a *large body* of clients.[83] Thus the senatorial opponents of Ti. Gracchus can arm only 'their slaves and friends' against him (*Gracch.* 18. 3); thus—though he knows Pompey was always welcome in Picenum, that he liked being there 'because people liked him so much', and that his popularity was inherited from his father (*Pomp.* 6. 1)—he can still describe Pompey's raising of a private army in the eighties without any explicit mention of *clientela*. Nor is he alert to the importance of *clientelae* which are foreign—though he *is* always very interested in his subjects' achievements in the provinces, and in particular the justice and humanity of their administration. (A rather distinctive feature, this, and one which marks him out from Greek historians more steeped in Roman life and Roman historiography, Appian and Cassius Dio; and Plutarch, incidentally, has few illusions about the savagery and rapacity which typified most Roman governors.)[84] But,

definition or on Mommsen's, revived by Brunt (1982)—and *patricii*: P. Clodius (*Caes.* 9. 2, *Cic.* 28. 1), Cornelius Lentulus at Cannae (*Fab.* 16. 7), Valerius Flaccus (*C. mai.* 3. 1), P. Cornelius Dolabella in AD 69 (*Otho* 5. 1), the house of the Servii (*Galb.* 3. 1). But the terms are clearly vague ones: cf. *Popl.* 18. 3, *Cam.* 33. 4, *Cic.* 40. 2. Note *Sert.* 25. 2, on Perperna's εὐγένεια (Perperna was not *patricius*, but he was *nobilis*, Gelzer (1969), 51 n. 457); and *C. mai.* 16. 4, where the εὐπατρίδαι monopolize the consulship (clearly *nobiles*, for he knows that one plebeian had to be elected, 16. 2). Plutarch simply follows any source which refers to high birth, and has no awareness of subtle distinctions.

[82] *Mar.* 4. 1, 5. 7–9, *Gracch.* 13. 2: cf. *Cor.* 21. 4, *Pomp.* 4. 7, *C. min.* 34. 6.

[83] *Cor.* 13. 5 is an exception, but relates to a very different political climate.

[84] For Plutarch's interest see e.g. *Fab.* 20. 1, *Marc.* 20, *Tit.* 2. 3–5, 5. 1–2, 12. 6, *C. mai.* 6. 2–4, 10. 4–6, *Aem.* 6. 6–7, 28. 6 ff., 39. 7–9, *Gracch.* 3. 1, 23. 2, *Lucull.* 20, 29, *C. min.* 34–40, *Pomp.* 10. 2, 28, 39, 50, *Caes.* 11–12, *Cic.* 6. 1–2, 36, 52(3). As emerges most clearly from *Pompey*, he tends to be more interested in mildness of everyday administration and equity in routine jurisdiction than in the great administrative *settlements*. For his awareness of general rapacity see esp. *C. mai.* 6. 2–4, *Cic.* 52 (3). 3, *C. min.* 12. 3–6, *Brut.* 6. 10–12, and the other instances collected by Jones (1971), 100.

still, he can describe the links of Aemilius Paullus with various foreign nations in extremely wondering terms, and regard his continuing concern for their welfare as a quite remarkable trait (*Aem.* 39. 8–9); and, still, he can describe the enthusiasm shown by the Spaniards for Ti. Gracchus as simply 'inherited from his father', with no hint that there was any more formal bond of duty or obligation (*Gracch.* 5. 4–5).

Very often, he modifies unfamiliar ideas and forces to ones he can understand: again, usually to the familiar *boulē–dēmos* antithesis, by the same characteristic reductionism. He of course knows that the equestrian order existed, but he rarely brings it into his political analysis: he can, for instance, mention Sulpicius' 'anti-senate' of 600 *equites*, but there is no deeper analysis of Marius' equestrian support.[85] (He has therefore, very uneasily, to represent Marius as a curious sort of incompetent trimmer, spasmodically courting the *dēmos* 'against his true instincts' (28. 1), but tending to drift away from them at inexplicable moments (e.g. 30).) When Tiberius or Gaius Gracchus or Pompey proposes to give the knights a share in the juries for the lawcourts, in each case Plutarch knows the political significance: in all three cases, they were trying to win the goodwill—of the *dēmos*![86] His treatment of the *publicani* is similar: resentful *publicani* determine to do down Lucullus in Roman politics—but the only way they can do so is by using 'demagogues' (*Lucull.* 20. 5). In all this Plutarch contrasts with Appian and Cassius Dio, who both (especially Appian) have a good deal of the equestrian order—perhaps, indeed, rather too much.[87] But there is no doubt that Plutarch has too little.

We can certainly see a similar reductionism in Plutarch's treatment of the army, particularly the army in politics. Here he is quite good on some aspects. He knows the perils

---

[85] *Mar.* 35. 2; other casual mentions of *equites* at e.g. *Mar.* 30. 4, *Cic.* 10. 5, 13. 2, 31. 1, *Pomp.* 14. 11 (where again note that Plutarch stresses the enthusiasm of the *people* at Pompey's equestrian demonstration). Brunt (1965a), 130, is therefore right to notice the absence of *equites* from Plutarch's account of Marius, but wrong to find this surprising or significant.

[86] *Gracch.* 16. 1, 26. 2, *Pomp.* 22. 3.

[87] Dio: esp. 38. 12. 4, 38. 13. 1, 38. 16. 2–3, 38. 16. 6; casual references are also more frequent than in Plutarch, e.g. 40. 49. 4, 40. 60. 4, 40. 63. 3, 41. 7. 1, 42. 51. 5, 43. 25. 1, 44. 6. 1, 44. 9. 1. Appian: esp. *BC* 1. 22. 91–7, 1. 35. 157–36. 162, 1. 37. 165–8, 1. 100. 468, 2. 13. 47–8.

presented by the returning generals, dangerous men at the
head of devoted armies: he digresses on these in the *Sulla*
(12), and the theme recurs—though not very insistently—in
the *Pompey*.[88] But what do these returning armies *want*? Here
he is less good, and he certainly does not understand their
imperative need for *land*. He knows that the veterans were in
some way connected with the land-bills of 59 BC; he even
knows that Pompey 'filled the city with soldiers' to pass the
measure; but still he does not see the connection. The bills are
aimed 'to win the goodwill of the mob'; they distribute land 'to
the poor and destitute'.[89] His treatment of Saturninus' land-
bill is exactly similar. There too he knows that Marius
introduced his soldiers into the assemblies to help Saturninus
(*Mar.* 28. 7)—but the land-bill is still, as we saw, aimed at
captivating and benefiting the urban *dēmos*. Just as he strips
away the Italian allies from his analysis, so also with the
veterans: once again, everything is reduced to a simple,
conventional γῆς ἀναδασμός, aimed at the urban mob. As he is
so blind to the veterans' interest in land, it is hardly surprising
that he seems to miss the point of the Marian military reforms.
He knows that Marius introduced a new type of recruit into
the Roman army, but makes a revealing error when he
mentions this: Marius is recruiting 'destitute men and *slaves*'
(*Mar.* 9. 1). He clearly does not realize that it is a different type
of *citizen*, the man without capital or land, who is involved: it
is clear that his stereotype of the *dēmos* is too simple to admit
of subtle distinctions between *assidui* and *proletarii*. In the
Sulla, similarly, when he digresses on the theme of the
'returning general' he does not bring out that Sulla's army
included these new, landless types of recruit. He does not see
that this army was in important ways different from the forces
of Flamininus, Acilius, and Aemilius Paullus, with whom he
compares it (*Sull.* 12. 8–14); and that these differences were
central in explaining the new bond between general and
troops, and the violent consequences this produced.

Indeed, he is not really very interested in the soldiers at

[88] *Sull.* 12. 12–14, *Pomp.* 20. 1, 21. 5–7, 43. 1–3.
[89] τὸ στρατιωτικόν somehow involved: *C. min.* 31. 2. City filled with soldiers:
Pomp. 48. 1. Mob's goodwill as the aim: *Caes.* 14. 2. Land distributed to the poor
and destitute: *C. min.* 31. 5, 33. 1, *Pomp.* 47. 5. *Dēmos* enraptured: *Pomp.* 48. 2.

all. Very often, he simply leaves them out completely when
he is describing politics. In the turbulent days of spring
and summer 44 BC, he rarely mentions the veterans; it is
again usually the urban *dēmos* for whose favour Brutus,
Octavian, and Antony contend.⁹⁰ Plutarch certainly has
little notion that the veterans might have *genuine* loyalties,
worth discussing and analysing: 'the armies', he says in an
aside in the *Brutus* (23. 1), 'were on sale—it was just like an
auction: they gave themselves to the highest bidder [. . .]'.
When he comes in *Antony* to describe the treaty of Brundisium, it is simply the 'friends' of Antony and Octavian who
urge them to come to terms, and cement their alliance with
the marriage agreement.⁹¹ Appian, again probably drawing
on similar material, makes it very clear that it was the
veterans who began this pressure on their leaders to agree
on peace.⁹² Indeed, the entire history of the Triumvirate
reads very differently in our other accounts, and especially
in their treatment of the soldiery: Appian, in particular, has
a great deal more on the impact of their veterans and their
loyalties on political life, even though he seems to be using
similar source-material. Cassius Dio has his blind spots
with the soldiers, but he too knows that their loyalties were
not wholly for sale; Nicolaus of Damascus, also, is more in
tune with historical reality.⁹³ Plutarch cuts the theme away,
and again it is the urban *dēmos* which matters.

It is perhaps time to return to the question of the *origins* of
these assumptions of Plutarch. I have been dwelling on the
'Greekness' of it all, and suggesting that he is imposing his
own categories, drawn from Classical Greek history and
political thought, on Roman realities which do not wholly

⁹⁰ *Brut.* 18. 10–14, 20. 1, 20. 4–11, 21. 2–6, 22. 3, *Ant.* 14. 5, 16. 6–8. Scanty
references to the soldiers: *Ant.* 16. 6–8, *Brut.* 21. 4, 22. 3, 23. 1.
⁹¹ *Ant.* 30. 6–31. 3.
⁹² App. *BC* 5. 63–4.
⁹³ App. *BC* 2. 119. 501, 2. 120. 507, 2. 125. 523, 2. 135. 565, 3. 6. 18, 3. 11. 38–
12. 41, 3. 21. 78, and so on, esp. 5. 17 (see e.g. n. 52): a glance at the *index locorum*
of Botermann (1968) reveals how much of the evidence for the political loyalties
and impact of the veterans is drawn from Appian. Dio's blind spots on the
veterans: see Botermann (1968), 30, but note e.g. 45. 7. 2, 45. 12–13, bringing out
both their genuine loyalties and their capacity to be influenced by largesse. Nic.
Dam.: see *Vit. Aug.* 41, 46, 56, 95, 99, 103, 108, 115–19, 121, 130–3, 136–9.

fit. But, of course, we must not overstate the differences
between Greek and Roman political stereotypes. That
boulē–dēmos analysis, for instance: is it so very different
from Sallust's view of the 'duas partis' of the Roman state,
the *pauci* (or *nobiles* or *potentes* or just *senatus*) and the
plebs?[94] Sallust, too, often omits the *equites* from his analysis; and Sallust too dwells on the *plebs*, the 'artisans and
rustics', as the decisive force which carried Marius to the
consulship.[95] The incautious reader might well assume—
just as Plutarch often seems to assume[96]—that the poorest
citizens could genuinely dominate the wealth-based *comitia
centuriata*. Livy as well sometimes describes events in similar terms, with the senate (or *nobiles*) striving valiantly to
resist stereotyped popular fury.[97] Cicero, in his tendentious
little account in the *pro Sestio*, feels he can get away with
speaking of the two great traditions in the Roman state, the
optimates and the *populares*; and he then describes the
Gracchi in terms very similar to Plutarch, affirming that
they introduced laws which were welcome to the people but
hateful to the *boni*.[98] Tacitus, too, can refer to 'assidua

---

[94] Cf. esp. Sall. *BJ* 41, *BC* 37–8, *Hist.* 1. 6–13M, and (if authentic) *ad Caes.* 2.
5. 1. For Sall.'s usage see Hanell (1945), Syme (1964), 17 f., 171 ff., Hellegouarc'h
(1963), esp. 110 ff., 430, 438, 442 ff., 512. Sallust is, of course, heavily indebted to
Thucydides in his use of these categories, and applies them to Roman politics
with little intelligence or insight.

[95] See *BJ* 73. 6–7 ('[. . .] plebes sic accensa [. . .] opifices agrestesque omnes'),
84. 1 ('cupientissuma plebe consul factus'). For the general omission of the *equites*
(though note 65. 4) see Syme (1964), 173: 'a serious omission [. . .] if nothing
worse'.

[96] e.g. *Pomp.* 15. 1, 22. 2, *C. min.* 21. 3.

[97] Though he admittedly tends to confine such analyses to the early books,
where such categories are natural enough for the description of the struggle of the
Orders (see e.g. Hellegouarc'h (1963), 430 with nn. 1 and 7, 436 with n. 2, 515–
16). His use of such categories to describe Roman politics is extremely sparing in
the third, fourth, and fifth decades (except in Book 22, esp. 22. 34. 1–35. 3, 22. 40.
1–4: rather a special case, as I suggest below). Such instances as 21. 63. 4, 31. 6. 4,
or 43. 14. 2–3 are in fact fairly isolated. Interestingly, he is far readier to use such
terms for non-Roman states, e.g. Capua (23. 2. 3, 4. 2–4, etc.), or 'all the states of
Italy' (24. 2. 8), or Carthage (e.g. 34. 62. 1), or the states of Greece (35. 34. 3), or
Phocaea (37. 9. 4).

[98] *Sest.* 103, cf. *de leg. agr.* 2. 10, 81 (and *de off.* 2. 78–81, where his language
very much suggests a γῆς ἀναδασμός). But, once again, this should not be overstated.
Hellegouarc'h (1963), 512, could reasonably comment on the *rarity* with which
Cicero employs *patres–plebs* or *nobiles–plebs* antitheses, or speaks of the *plebs* as a
political group.

senatus adversus plebem certamina' as a conspicuous feature of the last phase of the Republic.[99] And all that quest for tyranny and revolution: was this not the stuff of political abuse, and occasionally of reality, in the late Republic—'uterque regnare vult', and so on?[100] Is there not a real chance that here—just as in the case of Pollio's explanation of the war which we noticed earlier—Plutarch is simply following the analysis of some Latin sources, and the similarity of his language and interpretation to the ways he speaks of Greek politics is just a fortunate coincidence?

There may be something in that objection. It is certainly true that he may not have found any very clear *correctives* to his natural assumptions in the Roman historical tradition, and so it is not surprising that the later Lives are not conspicuously more sophisticated in their historical interpretations than the ones which he had written earlier.[101] But it is also true that few Roman writers (and few Greek writers, as we noticed earlier) apply the *boulē–dēmos* analysis quite so relentlessly and quite so exclusively as Plutarch does. Consider, for example, the wide group of people whom Cicero would class as *optimates* in the *pro Sestio*, or the various different classes of supporters who contributed to Marius' *honestissuma suffragatio* in Sallust.[102] And there is some way between abusive *allegations* that individuals are aiming for tyranny, uttered by political opponents with ferocity and passion, and Plutarch's casual *assumption* that such allegations are regularly true. But it anyway seems clear that Plutarch is not simply taking over categories which he finds in his sources; on the contrary, he is regularly reinterpreting his material in order to bring out these favoured categories, and is not at all the slave of the tradition. We saw a certain amount of this earlier, in examining his recastings of Pollio in describing Caesar, and of an unidenti-

[99] *Dial.* 36. 3. Cf. his conspectus of all republican history at *Ann.* 4. 32–3, especially 'plebis et optimatium certamina' (32. 1), '[. . .] plebe valida vel cum patres pollerent' (33. 2).

[100] Cic. *ad Att.* 8. 11. 2; see passages collected by Hellegouarc'h (1963), 560–5, and Seager (1972), 335 n. 11.

[101] Not that it is a particularly easy matter to establish the relative chronology of the Lives. Jones (1966) (see above, pp. 95 ff.) gives the best discussion, but needs to be treated with some caution: see Pelling (1979), 80–2 (above, pp. 277–82).

[102] *Sest.* 97–8, 132–9, esp. 138; Sall. *BJ* 65. 5.

fiable source in telling the story of the Gracchi. And the recastings will emerge even more clearly if we go back to an earlier period of Roman history, where we can compare Plutarch with his source-material—or something very like his source-material—rather more closely.

If we had to pick a piece of Roman historiography to remind us of Greek *dēmos* and demagogue stereotypes, we might well choose Livy 22. Minucius and Varro, in turn, are the Cleon-like demagogues, mobilizing the uncontrollable forces of the vulgar mob; on the other side, we have the sober and sensible Fabius and Paullus, and the sober and sensible senate. And this is a place where we can compare Plutarch very closely: for his narrative in *Fabius* is often very similar indeed to Livy—so similar that we should either assume that he is using Livy directly, or an earlier authority to whom Livy, too, kept very close.[103] In either case, Livy can give us a very good idea of the content of Plutarch's source-material. What is interesting is the way in which Plutarch takes those *dēmos* and demagogue stereotypes even further than Livy:[104] even this very Greek

---

[103] The extreme closeness of much of *Fabius* to Livy is quite clear, but several passages seem to show accurate knowledge of non-Livian detail: e.g. the 15,000 prisoners at Trasimene, 3. 3; the deception at Rome when news of the Trebia arrived, 3. 4; the 4,000 men of 6. 4. Such elements suggest either that Plutarch knew Livy's source rather than Livy himself (so Peter (1865), Soltau (1897), etc., suggesting Coelius Antipater; Klotz (1935), suggesting Valerius Antias); or a systematic, though small-scale, supplementation of Livy from a closely parallel account. (There is larger-scale supplementation at e.g. *Fab.* 15, 20, 26, but those passages are not woven so closely into the Livian material, and can easily represent additions from Plutarch's own memory and general reading.) Some parts of Plutarch show knowledge of those parts of Livy which are most likely to be Livy's own contribution (e.g. the arguments of Herennius Balbus, 22. 34 and *Fab.* 8. 4; the Camillus echo at 22. 3. 10 and *Fab.* 3. 1; the words of Fabius, 22. 18, 8 and *Fab.* 8. 1); and it is on balance more likely that Plutarch knows Livy himself, not his source. It may well be that a slave or freedman assistant was sent to consult (say) Coelius or Polybius, and report back to Plutarch any significant variations from Livy's account, or useful extra details: we too readily ignore the possibility of such 'research assistants' (see Jones (1971), 84–7, and Pelling (1979), 95 and above, pp. 309–10). At all events, even if it is Livy's source, not Livy himself, who is Plutarch's main authority, Livy's general closeness to Plutarch suggests that he is generally remaining very faithful to the source which, on this hypothesis, he and Plutarch share.

[104] Hoffmann (1942), 38–9, brings out this feature of Plutarch's narrative very well, though he is surely wrong in attributing the recasting of the material to Plutarch's source, not Plutarch himself.

passage of narrative was insufficiently reduced to the *boulē–dēmos* terms which he wanted. In Plutarch, much more than Livy, Fabius is initially created dictator by a mindless surge of popular panic—precisely the sort of mindless surge which he himself will later have to confront; Livy, like Polybius, had simply dwelt on the confusion in Rome at the time, and had not given any such *popular* stress.[105] In Plutarch, Fabius gives a speech to the *dēmos* as soon as he is appointed, reassuring them and quelling their panic; in Livy it was not delivered to the *dēmos*, but to the senate.[106] When Fabius is deceived by the oxen stratagem, and again when Minucius wins his initial delusive successes, it is the popular enthusiasm for Minucius—and the popular fears for his safety, if Fabius got his hands on him—which Plutarch stresses; on both occasions, Livy had concentrated on the attacks on Fabius delivered in the senate.[107] When Fabius is attacked, the demagogue Metilius claims that the senate 'had provoked the whole war to destroy the *dēmos* and impose an absolute monarchy' (8. 4). 'To impose a monarchy'? That sounds very odd, and very much like Plutarch himself: and, sure enough, Livy has nothing like this. Plutarch seems in fact to be borrowing from a passage rather later in Livy, when Varro accuses the nobles of 'using the war to gain control of the *comitia*'.[108] 'To gain control of the *comitia*' is rather milder, and much more plausible: Plutarch is again rewriting the Roman original to stress his own favoured theme. This *boulē–dēmos* analysis is indeed very important to *Fabius*—and not just to the Life, but to the whole pair. Stadter[109] has shown that the comparison of Pericles and Fabius is very elaborate, and the two men's reactions to hostile mobs and hostile demagogues are an important element in the pairing. Later in the *Fabius*—and this is a most interesting development—we see related themes coming back when Fabius is in decline, woefully jealous of the successes of the young Scipio. Fabius may still be urging his distinctive caution, but he is also

[105] *Fab.* 3. 6–7, cf. Livy, 22. 8, Plb. 3. 86–7.
[106] *Fab.* 4. 4, cf. Livy, 22. 9. 7.
[107] *Fab.* 7. 5–7, 9. 1, cf. Livy, 22. 23. 5–7, 22. 25. 12.
[108] Livy, 22. 34. 9.
[109] Stadter (1975) (above, pp. 155–64).

showing exactly those characteristics which we earlier saw in the demagogues: he is overcome by petty φιλονικία, scoring political points rather than prosecuting the war, 'crying out' (βοῶν) in the assembly, desperate to mobilize popular pressure against a great general.[110] As Pericles in old age gains a stature lacking from his demagogic youth, so Fabius' demagogic decline compromises the dignity which he has won in the years of his greatness: the pair as a whole shows an extremely elegant 'hour-glass structure' (to use the term of E. M. Forster).[111] And once again the neatness of the analysis seems to be Plutarch's own. We would be hard put to it to find any similar thematic links between Fabius' greatness and decline in the treatment of Livy.

In *Fabius*, then, Plutarch certainly does *not* seem to be at the mercy of his sources. Even where they offered an analysis which must have been congenial to him, he was not content to take it over: skilfully, he took it much further. One can trace the same individuality in other passages, and can see how reluctant he was to take over blindly the themes which his Roman sources developed. We might conclude by looking at some passages where he shows his awareness of the characteristic motifs of Roman historians: the importance of *metus hostilis*, for example, in keeping Rome morally upright, or the nature of moral decline from ancestral simplicity, or the disastrous effect of foreign culture. As Jones has stressed,[112] Plutarch often takes over some of these views himself, in a not very original way: in particular, he has some splendid passages of routine nostalgia, reflecting wistfully on the days before ambition and greed overtook the state.[113] But there are also passages

---

[110] φιλονικία: *Fab.* 25. 3–4 (cf. 22. 5). Political point-scoring rather than fighting the war: esp. 25. 3–4 (where χρήματα δοθῆναι πρὸς τὸν πόλεμον οὐκ εἴασε, 25. 3, closely reverses the story of 7. 5–8). Shouting: 26. 1, contrast 7. 5, 14. 2. Even in his distinctive πρᾳότης he is now outdone by Crassus (25. 4): that is prepared already at 22. 8, when Marcellus emerges as more πρᾷος than Fabius. On the nature of the tradition see Hoffmann (1942), 92–3: the *contrast* of Fabius and Scipio seems well founded in the historical tradition, but the personal pettiness of Fabius seems individual to Plutarch's account.

[111] Forster (1962), 151, discussing Anatole France's *Thais*.

[112] Jones (1971), 99–100.

[113] e.g. *Pomp.* 70, *C. mai.* 4. 2, 16. 8, 28(1). 2–3, *Aem.* 11. 3–4, *Sull.* 1. 5, 12. 8–14, *Phoc.* 3. 3.

where he gives such Roman ideas as *metus hostilis* a rather individual twist; and one can indeed see that some of the most cherished Roman beliefs would have been hateful to him. *Metus hostilis*, vital to keep the state morally healthy? Plutarch found such glorification of war extremely distasteful, surely: on a related theme, he insists with some feeling that triumphs would far more appropriately be given for the arts of *peace* (*Marc.* 22. 9–10, cf. *Pomp.* 13. 10–11). And the disastrous effect of external, especially Greek, culture? He clearly knows the idea (cf. *C. mai.* 4. 2)[114]—but it was hardly a theme to appeal to him! He feels that Romans should have learnt a lot more from Greece (*Mar.* 2); and he indeed criticizes the elder Cato most forthrightly for his prophecy that Greek influences would be fatal to Rome. 'Time shows that he was wrong; for the time of Rome's greatest achievements was the time when it was most ready to welcome Greek studies and Greek culture' (*C. mai.* 23. 3). When Plutarch does echo such Roman *topoi* he is therefore keen to adapt them, and the nature of these adaptations is again extremely suggestive. Marcellus was criticized for bringing back the treasures of Syracuse and corrupting— corrupting whom? Corrupting the Roman *dēmos*, turning them from farming and warfare to luxury and idleness, filling them with laziness and chatter, so that they spend most of the day discussing arts and artists . . . (*Marc.* 21. 6)! It is a very mild form of criticism, and Plutarch is clearly on Marcellus' side.[115] He has just been stressing the great superiority of Greek culture, and bringing out the wretchedly primitive character of Rome at the time: as he makes Marcel-

---

[114] When the theme is first introduced at *C. mai.* 4. 2, Plutarch simply talks of Rome 'not preserving her purity because of her very size: her control of so many affairs and so many peoples was exposing her to many different customs and examples of many different sorts of life'. Nothing specifically on *Greece* there— probably because Plutarch is so far reluctant to cast any shadow of hesitation or doubt on Cato's moral insight. It is only at 22. 4–23. 2 that Cato's hostility to Greek culture is specifically stressed and criticized: at that stage of the Life Plutarch is tracing with more subtlety the manner in which Cato's strengths and flaws both spring from the same basic traits. By then we have come to appreciate the man's moral force, and respect his concern for old-fashioned Roman virtue: we now see the excesses which this attitude can bring.

[115] Contrast the much more sombre emphasis of Plb. 9. 10 and Livy, 25. 40. 2.

lus say, he is *educating* these people. So much for that *topos* of Greek influence; even that is fitted into the *dēmos*-emphasis, and given a very individual turning. The same sort of thing emerges with *metus hostilis* in the famous passage at the end of *Cato maior*, when Scipio Nasica is arguing that Carthage should remain standing: 'for Nasica saw that the *dēmos* was going wildly astray through their *hubris*, and were hard for the senate to control [. . .] he wished the fear of Carthage to remain a bridle on the recklessness of the mob' (*C. mai.* 27. 3).[116] Again, quite characteristic: the Roman idea is given a very individual twist, and itself tied into the distinctive *boulē–dēmos* analysis.

The emphasis on the *dēmos* is clearly Plutarch's own: the great preconception with which he came to write about the Roman Republic. And, of course, no one would want to suggest that he was wholly wrong. The reduction of so many other forms of analysis to this theme is disquieting, and so is the assumption that the analysis is equally applicable to every period; but few of us would doubt that Plutarch captured something very important about the late Republic by describing it in this way. It was not Plutarch, it was Sir Ronald Syme, who described the end of the Republic as 'the Greek period of Roman history, stamped with the sign of the demagogue, the tyrant, and the class war'.[117]

REFERENCES

Andrewes, A. (1978): 'The Opposition to Pericles', *JHS* 98. 1–8.
Astin, A. E. (1967): *Scipio Aemilianus* (Oxford).
——(1979): Review of Bernstein (1978) in *CR* 29. 111–12.
Badian, E. (1958): *Foreign Clientelae* (Oxford).

[116] Contrast the parallel passage at Diodorus, 34/35. 33. 4–5, doubtless inspired by the same source (probably Posidonius). Diod. has no such emphasis on the *dēmos*, and speaks more vaguely of external fear as a stimulus to concord: indeed, his Nasica brings in concepts such as 'the need to rule Rome's subjects with equity and good repute', and the threat to Rome from dangerous *allies*. For recent discussions of Nasica's insight see Astin (1967), 276–80, and Lintott (1972), 632–8: Gelzer (1931), 272–3 and others were clearly quite wrong to see the hand of *Polybius* in influencing Plutarch's stress on the *boulē* and *dēmos*.
[117] Syme (1939), 441.

354   *C. B. R. Pelling*

Badian, E. (1970): *Titus Quinctius Flamininus, Philhellenism and Realpolitik*, Semple Memorial Lecture (Cincinnati).
—— (1972): 'Tiberius Gracchus and the Beginning of the Roman Revolution', in *ANRW* i. 1. 668–731.
Bernstein, A. H. (1978): *Ti. Sempronius Gracchus: Tradition and Apostasy* (Ithaca, NY).
Botermann, H. (1968): *Die Soldaten und die römische Politik in der Zeit von Caesars Tod bis zur Begründung des Zweiten Triumvirats* (Zetemata, 46: Munich).
Briscoe, J. (1973): *A Commentary on Livy xxxi–xxxiii* (Oxford).
Brunt, P. A. (1965a): 'The Equites in the Late Republic', *Second International Conference on Economic History 1962* (Aix-en-Provence), 117–49. (Repr. in *The Crisis of the Roman Republic* (Cambridge, 1969), ed. R. Seager, 83–117.)
—— (1965b): 'Italian Aims at the Time of the Social War', *JRS* 55: 90–109.
—— (1971): *Italian Manpower* (Oxford).
—— (1982): 'Nobilitas and novitas', *JRS* 72: 1–17.
Brutscher, C. (1958): *Analysen zu Suetons Divus Julius und der Parallelüberlieferung* (Berne).
Cuff, P. J. (1967): 'Prolegomena to a Critical Edition of Appian, *BC* i', *Historia*, 16: 177–88.
—— (1983): 'Appian's *Romaica*: A Note', *Athenaeum*, 61: 148–64.
Earl, D. C. (1963): *Tiberius Gracchus: A Study in Politics* (Collection Latomus, 66: Brussels).
Forster, E. M. (1962): *Aspects of the Novel* (Harmondsworth).
Gabba, E. (1951): 'Ricerche sull'esercito professionale romano da Mario ad Augusto', *Athenaeum*, 29: 171–272.
—— (1956): *Appiano e la Storia delle Guerre Civili* (Florence).
—— (1958): *Appiani Bellorum Civilium Liber Primus*, Edition and commentary (Florence).
Gelzer, M. (1929): Review of F. Taeger, *Tiberius Gracchus* in *Gnomon* 5: 296–303. (Repr. in his *Kleine Schriften*, ii (1963), 73–80.)
—— (1931): 'Nasicas Widerspruch gegen die Zerstörung Karthagos', *Philologus*, 86. 261–99. (Repr. in his *Kleine Schriften*, ii (1963), 39–72.)
—— (1969): *The Roman Nobility*. Trans. by R. Seager (Oxford).
Göhler, J. (1939): *Rom und Italien* (Breslau).
Gomme, A. W., Andrewes, A., and Dover, K. J. (1945–81): *Historical Commentary on Thucydides*, 5 vols. (Oxford).
Hanell, K. (1945): 'Bemerkungen zu der politischen Terminologie des Sallustius', *Eranos*, 43: 263–76.

Hellegouarc'h, J. (1963): *Le Vocabulaire latin des relations et des partis politiques sous la République* (Paris).

Hoffman, W. (1942): *Livius und der zweite Punische Krieg* (Berlin).

Jones, C. P. (1966): 'Towards a Chronology of Plutarch's Works', *JRS* 56: 61–74, reprinted above, pp. 95–123.

—— (1971): *Plutarch and Rome* (Oxford).

Klotz, A. (1935): 'Über die Quelle Plutarchs in der Lebensbeschreibung des Q. Fabius Maximus', *RhM* 84: 125–53.

Lintott, A. W. (1968): *Violence in Republican Rome* (Oxford).

—— (1971): 'Lucan and the History of the Civil War', *CQ* 21: 488–505.

—— (1972): 'Imperial Expansion and Moral Decline in the Roman Republic', *Historia*, 21: 626–38.

Meier, C. (1965): 'Populares' §§III and IV in *RE* Supplementband 10, cols. 580, 582, 590.

Meinhardt, E. (1957): *Perikles bei Plutarch* (Diss., Frankfurt).

Münzer, F. (1920): *Römische Adelsparteien und Adelsfamilien* (Stuttgart).

Nagle, D. B. (1970): 'The Failure of the Roman Political Process in 133 BC', *Athenaeum*, 48: 372–94.

Nicolet, C. (1966): *L'Ordre équestre: L'Époque républicaine (312–43 av. J.-C.)*, vol. i (Paris).

Pelling, C. B. R. (1979): 'Plutarch's Method of Work in the Roman Lives', *JHS* 99: 74–96, reprinted above, pp. 265–312.

—— (1980): 'Plutarch's Adaptation of his Source-Material', *JHS* 100: 127–40, reprinted above, pp. 125–54.

Peter, H. (1865): *Die Quellen Plutarchs* (Halle).

Pohlenz, M. (1927): 'Causae civilium armorum', in *Epitymbion H. Swoboda dargebracht* (Reichenberg), 201–10. (Repr. in his *Kleine Schriften* (Hildesheim, 1965), ii. 139–48).

Rawson, E. (1986): 'Cassius and Brutus: The Memory of the Liberators', in *Past Perspectives: Studies in Greek and Roman Historical Writing* (Cambridge), 101–19.

Rhodes, P. J. (1981): *A Commentary on the Aristotelian Athenaion Politeia* (Oxford).

Richardson, J. S. (1980): 'The Ownership of Roman Land: Tiberius Gracchus and the Italians', *JRS* 70: 1–11.

Schultze, C. (1986): 'Dionysius of Halicarnassus and his Audience', in *Past Perspectives: Studies in Greek and Roman Historical Writing* (Cambridge), 121–41.

Seager, R. (1972): 'Cicero and the Word *popularis*', *CQ* 22: 328–38.

Sherwin-White, A. N. (1973): *The Roman Citizenship*, 2nd edn (Oxford).

Shochat, Y. (1970): 'The Lex Agraria of 133 BC and the Italian Allies', *Athenaeum*, 48: 25–45.

——(1980): *Recruitment and the Programme of Tiberius Gracchus* (Collection Latomus, 169; Brussels).

Soltau, W. (1897): *Livius' Geschichtswerk* (Leipzig).

Stadter, P. A. (1975): 'Plutarch's Comparison of Pericles and Fabius Maximus', *GRBS* 16: 77–85, reprinted above, pp. 155–64.

Stockton, D. L. (1979): *The Gracchi* (Oxford).

Strasburger, H. (1938): *Caesars Eintritt in die Geschichte* (Munich).

Syme, R. (1939): *The Roman Revolution* (Oxford).

——(1950): *A Roman Post-Mortem*, Tod Memorial Lecture (Sydney).

——(1964): *Sallust* (Berkeley, Cambridge).

Tibiletti, G. (1948): 'Il possesso del'*ager publicus* e le norme *de modo agrorum* sino ai Gracchi', *Athenaeum*, 26: 173–236.

Walbank, F. W. (1957): *A Historical Commentary on Polybius*, vol. i (Oxford).

Wardman, A. E. (1974): *Plutarch's Lives* (London).

12

Plutarch's *Life* of Coriolanus

D. A. RUSSELL

I am concerned in this paper[1] with Plutarch's treatment of
the story of Coriolanus, not with the historical truth of the
legend or with its development before Plutarch's time. I
start from the hypothesis that the *Life* is, in its essentials, a
transposition into biographical form of the historical narrative in Dionysius of Halicarnassus, *Roman Antiquities*,
Books v to viii. This has long been the common view. It
was held and defended by Hermann Peter, Mommsen, and
Eduard Schwartz.[2] A careful reading of the two texts side
by side tempts me to call it certain, so exact and frequent
are the echoes.[3] It is at any rate probable enough to justify
an attempt to follow out its consequences by treating the
differences between Dionysius and Plutarch, in default of
other evidence, as Plutarch's constructions, to be explained
in terms of his literary purposes and methods. This is what
I shall do in the main part of this paper. I preface the
details, however, by a few more general considerations.

If Peter's view is right, *Coriolanus* affords a unique opportunity of studying Plutarch's methods. It was certainly rare
for him to base a whole Life on one authority: indeed, we
have no certain knowledge that he ever did it again. The
other Lives of early Roman worthies show no such single-
minded devotion, though some at least of them are earlier

[1] Read to the Oxford Philological Society in Nov. 1962. I should like to express
my gratitude to the Society for a welcome opportunity, friendly encouragement,
and helpful discussion. I owe special debts to Mr A. N. Sherwin-White, Mr R. G. M.
Nisbet, Mr J. P. V. D. Balsdon, Prof. A. Momigliano, and Mr R. Meiggs.
[2] H. Peter, *Die Quellen Plutarchs in den Biographien der Römer* (Halle, 1865),
7 ff.; Mommsen, *Römische Forschungen*, ii. 113 ff.; E. Schwartz, P-W s.v. Dionysios, col. 943.
[3] The parallels can usually be traced easily enough from the notes in Ziegler's
edition; but add the following: 1. 2 ~ Dion. Hal. 8. 51; 3. 1 ~ 7. 62, 8. 29; 4. 3 ~
8. 51 (?), 8. 29; 15. 1 ~ 7. 62; 21. 3 ~ 8. 41.

than *Coriolanus*.[4] It was therefore not ignorance or lack of
reading that caused what may well be a unique proceeding.
I should guess rather that it was the importance given to
the legend by Dionysius (contrast the brief account in
Livy), his unusually full and rich narrative, and especially
the elaborate character-sketch (8. 60–2) with which it ends.
This interpretation of Coriolanus' career was a natural
challenge to the biographer. I shall suggest later that Plutarch thought it in need of correction.

When we say that the *Life* is a transposition of this single
historical narrative, this must be understood with certain
fairly obvious limitations. (i) Of course there is a good deal
of alien matter. On a rough calculation, it is about 20 per
cent. Most of it can be identified at sight; it consists of
antiquarian and philosophical digressions and moral reflections. The longest pieces are those on cognomina (11),
inspiration (32), and miracles (38). These are typically Plutarchian themes.[5] (ii) Nor was Plutarch uncritical of Dionysius. An instructive instance is the episode in which Coriolanus tricks the Romans into a hostile act against the Volsci
by spreading a rumour that the latter were planning a
sudden coup at the games (Dion. Hal. 8. 2). Plutarch found
this a stumbling block. In the *Life* (26. 2), he says that the
Romans ordered the expulsion of the Volscian visitors 'as a
result of some suspicion or slander', and adds that 'some'
(ἔνιοι) say that it was by Coriolanus' trick that the slander
was spread. In the *Comparison of Coriolanus and Alcibiades*
(2. 4), Dionysius is mentioned by name (for once) as the
authority for this version, which Plutarch now apparently
accepts, adding, however, a motivation not in Dionysius,
namely that Coriolanus acted ὀργῇ χαριζόμενος—which made
his action all the more reprehensible. I think we probably
have here two stages in the interpretation of this ἀπάτη: in
the first, Plutarch thinks it out of keeping with Coriolanus'
simple, heroic nature, and leaves it as a variant version; in
the second, he accepts it and attributes it to his hero's

[4] *Publicola* is mentioned at 33. 2; *Numa* at 39. 11. On the problem of these
'cross-references' see Ziegler, P-W s.v. Plutarchos, col. 262 ff. (Sonderabdruck);
R. Flacelière, *Vies*, i. xxiv ff.; W. Bühler, *Maia*, 14 (1962), 272 f.
[5] Cf. (e.g.) *Romulus* 28, *Numa* 4, *Publicola* 15, *Camillus* 19.

principal vice, ὀργή, of which, as we shall see, he makes much more than Dionysius. He is here applying criteria of psychological probability to his source-narrative. Occasionally—very rarely indeed in this *Life*—he submits it similarly to the test of knowledge acquired from other sources.[6] He does not feel obliged to reproduce it unchanged. (iii) We must allow also for accidental errors. The most striking is the confusion over the names of Coriolanus' women-folk: the mother becomes Volumnia instead of Veturia, the wife Verginia instead of Volumnia. Similarly, there seems some mistake in the first name of the Volscian Tullus; the tradition of the text at 22. 1 points to Amphidius or Aufidius or the like, and it is not sound method to change this to Attius, as Ziegler does, to conform with Livy, Dionysius, and *Cicero*, 1. 2. Again, in 28 Plutarch gives the names of the peoples attacked by Coriolanus as Volscian commander in the order: Tolerini, Labicani, Pedani, Bolani. In Dionysius (8. 14 ff.) they are given, in the course of a lengthy narrative, in a different one: Tolerini, Bolani, Labicani, Pedani. How such errors arose is a matter for conjecture. Did Plutarch forget or make a mistake in his notes? I will only say that it seems to me prudent to come down on the side of memory. The process of composition is likely to have involved much less 'paper work' than the modern scholar likes to think. Even a very bookish ancient, like Plutarch, enjoyed what would nowadays be a phenomenally good memory. No doubt he made notes on Dionysius, or had them made for him; but their scale is something we cannot guess and should be careful not to exaggerate. It is perfectly possible that, when he came to his own writing, whole stretches of Dionysius' not very memorable prose were running in his head.[7] (iv) Plutarch

[6] The only certain case seems to be 39. 11, where Dionysius' statement (8. 62. 2) that the women mourned Coriolanus for a year is corrected in the light of *Numa* 12.

[7] It is perhaps worth drawing attention to passages where there is a strong verbal echo of very ordinary phraseology though the general sense has been a good deal modified: 9. 9, πολλῶν μὲν διαφθαρέντων πολλῶν δ' ἀλόντων from Dion. Hal. 6. 93, πολλοὺς μὲν ἀνῃρηκότες . . . πολλοὺς δ' αἰχμαλώτους ἄγοντες; 21. 3, ἐδήλωσε δὲ . . . τὴν διάθεσιν . . . εἰσελθὼν γὰρ οἴκαδε . . . from 7. 67, ἐδήλωσε τὴν γενναιότητα . . . ἐπειδὴ οἴκαδε ἀφικόμενος . . .

naturally felt no obligation to follow Dionysius' wording or
rhetorical treatment. Even if it stuck in his mind, he did not
apparently admire it greatly; generally speaking, he could
do much better. Thus he handles the fable of the belly and
the other parts of the body (6. 3–5) quite independently,
and wholly re-casts Coriolanus' political statement after his
rejection at the consular elections (16; Dion. Hal. 7. 22–4).
Again, Dionysius (8. 56. 2) made the miraculous voice
heard in the new temple of Fortuna Muliebris say ὁσίῳ
πόλεως νόμῳ, γυναῖκες γαμεταί, δεδώκατέ με. Plutarch in his
rhetorical piece *de fortuna Romanorum* (319A), usually believed to be early, had used a similar form of words; in
Coriolanus (37. 5) he gives a more euphonious version:
θεοφιλεῖ με θεσμῷ, γυναῖκες, δεδώκατε. The alliteration, the
rhythm, the solemn θεσμῷ, the avoidance of the clumsier
γυναῖκες γ α μ ε τ α ί for *matronae* show considerable care for
grandeur and elevation. (v) The most important cause of
Plutarch's deviations from Dionysius is of course the difference between the demands of βίοι and those of ἱστορία.[8]
Thus the scanty hints about Marcius' youth and upbringing
had to be expanded; education is an indispensable topic.
The enormous speeches in which Dionysius took such
pride had no place in a work on Plutarch's scale,[9] though
they formed a reservoir of argument and comment on
which the biographer could draw.[10] There was also a serious
problem of proportion: of the two great crises, the campaign
of Corioli and the exile of Coriolanus and its sequel, Dionysius' account of the former needed considerable expansion
(chapters 8 to 11 in Plutarch); in the latter, by contrast, he
had to be abridged and chastened. Finally, and most important of all, Plutarch had formed his own interpretation of
his hero's character and imposes it on the story; it is
primarily through him that it became what it was for
Shakespeare, a tragedy of ambition and anger.

[8] See Plutarch's own statement, *Alexander* 1: οὐχ ἱστορίας γράφομεν ἀλλὰ βίους,
οὔτε ταῖς ἐπιφανεστάταις πράξεσι πάντως ἔνεστι δήλωσις ἀρετῆς ἢ κακίας, ἀλλὰ πρᾶγμα
βραχὺ πολλάκις καὶ ῥῆμα καὶ παιδιά τις ἔμφασιν ἤθους ἐποίησε μᾶλλον ἢ μάχαι μυριόνεκροι
καὶ παρατάξεις αἱ μέγισται καὶ πολιορκίαι πόλεων.
[9] Volumnia's speech (35. 2–9) is about as much as he ever allows himself.
[10] So Coriolanus' speech in 8. 29 ff., and Veturia's in 8. 48–53, are drawn on
for the early life.

Only a very detailed commentary could show all the facts. They are very numerous, and many are trivial or ambivalent. What follows is a selection, arranged to illustrate certain rough principles. I shall speak of 'expansions', 'abridgements', and 'transpositions'. Theoretically, all the differences between any two narratives could be described by these three terms; wherever there is a difference, there must be a plus or a minus or a change of order. I begin therefore with examples of these, singly or in combination. There are also, and this is often more important, places where a fresh interpretation is put on accepted fact; these I reserve to the end.

(i) Nowhere is Plutarch's technique of expansion more in evidence than in the account of his hero's youth. Plausible explanations of this can be given. For one thing, Plutarch had abundant information concerning the education of Alcibiades, whom he had chosen as Coriolanus' parallel, and perhaps therefore felt that the companion piece also should be developed with some elaboration. For another—and I shall return to this—in so far as Coriolanus was an object lesson, he was a warning against certain defects in education.

The opening chapter, then, is made up of some facts about the family (non-Dionysian) and commonplaces on the disadvantages of orphans.[11] That great natures produce evil as well as good is basically a Platonic theme;[12] it is used by Plutarch also in the introduction to the Life of Demetrius, who, like Coriolanus and Alcibiades, is an example of vice and moral failure.[13] The second chapter concerns the hero's military education. Part of this is also commonplace, for example the conception of the body as the soldier's ὅπλον σύμφυτον.[14] That Marcius as a boy exercised himself in running and wrestling is not stated by Dionysius. As

[11] That Marcius was an orphan is stated in Veturia's speech, Dion. Hal. 8. 51.

[12] *Rep.* 491 D–E: οὐκοῦν . . . καὶ τὰς ψυχὰς οὕτω φῶμεν τὰς εὐφυεστάτας κακῆς παιδαγωγίας τυχούσας διαφερόντως κακὰς γίγνεσθαι. Similarly, ibid. 495 B.

[13] See P. de Lacy, *AJP* 73 (1952), 195 ff. *Dem.–Ant.* is probably earlier than *Cor.–Alc.*

[14] *Fabius* 1; Cic. *TD* 2. 37. Not proverbial, according to Otto, *Sprichwörter*, s.v. arma; but perhaps Roman rather than Greek.

there is no reason to suspect another source, it follows, on our hypothesis, that we have a speculative expansion of Plutarch's: this is what the boyhood of such a man must have been like. A historical instance, which may well be the pattern, is the boyhood of Philopoemen, a similar personality, which Plutarch describes (*Philopoemen* 3) in very similar terms.[15] A fictional expansion of the same theme is to be found in *Romulus* 6.

What follows (2. 2) seems also—again, on the initial hypothesis—to be a speculative embellishment. As evidence for the young man's excellence—if this is the force of γοῦν—we are told that his rivals in εὐψυχία and ἀρετή excused their own inferiority by attributing his success to physical strength. I suppose this means that they disparaged his merit by denying him special courage or skill. There appears to be no hint of this in Dionysius. Circumstantial as it is, the whole thing seems to be a piece of amplification, based on the story of Marcius' untiring exploits at Corioli and against Antium. And it is worth noting that the two motifs introduced here, Marcius' freedom from fatigue and the jealous rivals, occur elsewhere in the *Life*, also in expansions. Tirelessness appears at 9. 9: when Marcius refuses to give up the pursuit, he adds 'it is not for victors to feel tired'—a *sententia* not to be found in the corresponding passage of Dionysius (6. 9. 3). Envy appears at 10. 7–8: as in Dionysius, so also in Plutarch, the soldiers marvel more at Marcius' contempt for wealth than at his courage; but Plutarch adds out of his head that some were envious until they were disarmed by Marcius' refusal to profit by his success. I shall have a little more to say on envy later, in connection with 13. 6. It is one of the themes which distinguish Plutarch's reading of the whole story from his predecessor's.

The next section (3. 1–3) involves further expansions. Marcius' first campaign was an important epoch, comparable to that of Alcibiades as a μειράκιον at Potidaea (*Alcib.* 7. 3) and that of Camillus against the Volsci and Aequi (*Cam.* 2. 1). Plutarch learned of it from one of the speeches in

[15] *Philopoemen* is almost certainly earlier than *Cor.*; see the combinations summarized by Ziegler, P-W s.v. Plutarchos, col. 263–4 (Sonderabdruck).

Dionysius, that made by the exiled Coriolanus in reply to
the appeals of Minucius (8. 29): 'The first expedition on
which I served as a very young man was when we fought
against the kings when they attempted to return by force
(βίᾳ κατίοντας).' On this occasion he saved a citizen's life[16]
and won the oak crown.[17] When was this? According to 3. 5, it
was at the battle of Lake Regillus, the Dionysian date for
which is 496, only five years before Coriolanus' exile. But it
is not clear from Dionysius that this really was the campaign
in question, rather than that which followed soon after the
expulsion of the kings and is related in *Publicola* 9 from
Dionysius, 5. 14–17. Moreover, in 15. 1, Plutarch makes
Coriolanus display the wounds he has received in seventeen
years' campaigning; seventeen years back from 491 brings
us to the period just after the expulsion of Tarquin. The
figure 'seventeen' is nowhere in Dionysius. Either Plutarch
has embellished his story, or he has made a mistake. Either
he sets his hero's début at Lake Regillus, where the Dioscuri
appeared, to make it more impressive; or he confuses that
great occasion with the earlier battle of the 'Naevian
meadow', which was marked by nothing more extraordinary
than the miraculous voice which announced that the Etrus-
can casualties were more numerous than the Roman by
one.[18]

I pass to two examples of expansion in the account of the
capture of Corioli, or rather its sequels.

Corioli has fallen and is being plundered (9. 1–4; Dion.
Hal. 6. 92; 6. 93. 1). Marcius will not join in. There are still

[16] Note ὑπερασπίσας 3. 3, and Dion. Hal. 8. 29. 4.

[17] The account of the *corona civica* is one of several antiquarian digressions in
the *Life*. It corresponds to *Quaest. Rom.* 92, except that Plutarch now adds a
fourth explanation (ἔστι δέ κ.τ.λ.) and what is in effect a fifth (ἦν δὲ καί κ.τ.λ.). Cf.
the treatment of *Quaest. Rom.* 49 in *Cor.* 14: Plutarch in his antiquarian work gave
three explanations of why candidates did not wear tunics, in the *Life* he rejects
one of these. Cf. also 19 and *Quaest. Rom.* 42; 24 and *Quaest. Rom.* 70. *Quaest.
Rom.* clearly represents an earlier stage of knowledge of primitive Rome than the
Lives (cf. H. J. Rose, *Roman Questions*, pp. 46–8); whether or not Plutarch had the
writing of the *Lives* in mind when he made the collection we cannot say.

[18] But it is possible that ἐν ἐκείνῃ . . . ἀνιερώκασι is an interpolation. It is perhaps
worth observing that the effect of Plutarch's mistake, if it is one, is to make
Coriolanus much younger; and this seems more appropriate to the character of
iracundia which he gives him (cf. Ar. *Rhet.* 1389ᵃ9: (οἱ νέοι) . . . θυμικοὶ καὶ ὀξύθυμοι
καὶ οἷοι ἀκολουθεῖν τῇ ὀργῇ κ.τ.λ.).

enemies to fight, and he is eager to be at them. In Dionysius, no motives are given, except that 'he did not think it right to be left out of this battle either'. It is Plutarch who adds, from his own invention, that Marcius was angry at the greed displayed by his fellow-citizens in the sack of the captured town. This is of course in character; it accords with his ἐγκράτεια (1. 4) and with his habit of demanding his own high standards from everyone else (Dion. Hal. 8. 60. 1). But at this point it is new.

An innovation of a different kind follows in 9. 3. When Marcius comes up with Cominius' army, he finds the men 'girding up their togas and making unwritten wills'. There is nothing of this in Dionysius. Plutarch is drawing on his antiquarian knowledge. He knows of the *testamentum in procinctu*, and of the explanation according to which *in procinctu* means 'with the toga girded up, ready for battle'.[19] It is difficult not to regard this attempt at circumstantial detail as tasteless, even ridiculous—the clumsy touch of the second-rate historical novelist, anxious to instruct as well as to please.

After the battle came Marcius' reward (10–11. 2; Dion. Hal. 6. 94). This episode is important for Plutarch, for it culminates in the award of the cognomen Coriolanus and represents the hero's last unalloyed success, the peak of his fame before his faults began to tell. Hence considerable expansion of Dionysius' fairly short account; Plutarch gives the incident about half as much space again, not counting the digression on cognomina (11. 2–6). At the outset (10. 1), it is Plutarch who makes the consul piously give thanks to the gods. Next, an award of booty is made to Marcius. In Dionysius he is crowned with στέφανοι; Plutarch does not reproduce this. In Dionysius, he is offered ten captives, as

---

[19] Festus, p. 67 L: 'cum ex castris in proelium exitum est, procinctos, quasi praecinctos atque expeditos. nam apud antiquos togis incincti pugnitasse dicuntur'. Serv., *Aen.* 7. 612: 'veteres Latini cum necdum arma haberent praecinctis togis bellabant: unde etiam milites in procinctu esse dicuntur'. It was generally believed that such unwritten wills were in order in early times (Cic. *ND* ii. 9, with Pease's note). By the late Republic, unwritten wills of this kind were obsolete: in Caesar's camp before battle (*BG* 1. 39. 5) 'vulgo . . . testamenta *obsignabantur*'. In later times again unwritten dispositions before witnesses could be valid. Roby, *Roman Private Law* i. 216 f.; Girard, *Manuel de Droit Romain*, 796.

much silver as he can take, and many other ἀπαρχαί, quite apart from the horse and its trappings which alone he deigns to accept; in Plutarch, Cominius orders him to choose himself ten of everything (δέκα πάντα) before a distribution is made to the others. This recalls Greek rather than Roman practice; Plutarch perhaps has in mind the honour done to Pausanias after Plataea: πάντα δέκα ἐξαιρέθη τε καὶ ἐδόθη, γυναῖκες ἵπποι τάλαντα κάμηλοι, ὡς δὲ αὔτως καὶ τἆλλα χρήματα (Herod. 9. 81). Nothing like this seems to be known in Roman distributions of booty. Our historical novelist has mixed up his periods.[20]

Other changes follow. Marcius' request for his Volscian friend is emphasized in Plutarch by *oratio recta* (cf. 11. 1) and heightened by the new pathetic detail that his friend is ἐπιεικὴς καὶ μέτριος, once rich and now reduced to poverty.[21] This anonymous citizen of Corioli earned greater fame in later ages. 'I sometime lay . . . at a poor man's house; he us'd me kindly . . .' says Shakespeare's Coriolanus (I. ix. 82). Plutarch's impoverished rich man and Shakespeare's kindly man in the street are on the same level of historicity: both bear the characters which their authors think most likely to win sympathy.

The generous request is of course acclaimed. In Dionysius, the soldiers admire Marcius' contempt for wealth even more than his courage. Plutarch accepts this and expands it: 'They admired more highly the virtue through which he despised such rewards than that because of which he was judged worthy of them.' This is to give Marcius a distinctive mark of the Aristotelian μεγαλόψυχος.[22]

(ii) I pass over other simple instances of expansion, which are very numerous.[23] A somewhat different aspect of technique is illustrated by the narrative (13) of the period

---

[20] As he does again at 16. 5, where he makes Coriolanus speak of Ἑλλήνων οἱ ἀκρατέστατα (Naber: κράτιστα is nonsense, μάλιστα would be possible) δημοκρατούμενοι, though the democratic practices in question are those of late 5th- and 4th-cent. Athens.

[21] In the same say Titus Latinius, who is simply a countryman in Dionysius, is called καθαρὸς δεισιδαιμονίας by Plutarch (24. 2), to give credit to his improbable story.

[22] Ar. *EN* 1124ᵃ3 ff.; see also περὶ ὕψους 7. 1.

[23] 20. 9; 21. 5; and 31. 5, may be profitably compared with the corresponding parts of Dionysius.

between the sack of Corioli and Coriolanus' unsuccessful bid for the consulship.

In Dionysius (7. 12–13), the request from Velitrae for colonists is accepted (Plutarch 12), but the revolutionary disorders continue. Sicinius and Brutus play a part, but we hear nothing of Coriolanus' political position. When he is appointed to command in the field (7. 19), the only reaction of the plebs is confidence in such a distinguished general. His short and successful campaign ends the year. In the new consulship, dissension increases, and Coriolanus now comes to the front as an outspoken opponent of the plebs (7. 21). At this point we are told incidentally (7. 21. 2) that he had been a candidate at the recent consular elections.

Plutarch, as is natural, shifts the centre of interest to his hero. Coriolanus' political position is mentioned earlier, namely before the expedition. He takes with him against the Antiates a force consisting of his clients (πελάται) and volunteers. They win so much plunder that those who stay at home are jealous, and Coriolanus becomes increasingly unpopular.

What is said here about Coriolanus' πελάται is not invention. It comes from a later passage in Dionysius (7. 21. 3), where he is represented (in very Attic terms, not reproduced by Plutarch) as building up a ἑταιρεία with the object of δήμου κατάλυσις. The other new point, however, is not so easily explained. In Dionysius (7. 19. 4), the jealousy of those who did not take part in the expedition issues in dissatisfaction with the 'demagogues'; in Plutarch, it is directed against Coriolanus. Plutarch has no warrant for this change. He may have in mind the charge later levelled with fatal effect at the trial, that the booty had been unlawfully distributed among the general's friends (20. 5; Dionysius, 7. 63. 3). Or he may intend simply to show the build-up of φθόνος against the hero. This interpretation is perhaps supported by two passages already mentioned—2. 2, and 10. 7—where also the motif of φθόνος is added to the Dionysian situation. To these examples indeed may be added another, though it is somewhat different. Dionysius says nothing about the jealousy of the Volscian Tullus towards Coriolanus until near the end of the whole story (8.

57. 3), though he there says that it was of long standing.
Plutarch brings it forward to an earlier stage, namely Coriolanus' withdrawal of the Volscian army from the Fossae
Cluiliae (31. 1). No violence is done by this rearrangement
to the transmitted account;[24] no special motive is attributed
to Tullus, he is μηδὲν ἀδικούμενος, ἐν δ᾽ ἀνθρωπίνῳ πάθει
γεγονώς. But in giving his human feelings prominence,
Plutarch brings to the front something outside the range of
Dionysius' narrative, the power of the irrational and emotional in human affairs.

(iii) The second great crisis of Coriolanus' career, his
trial, is handled by Dionysius at great length, with enormous speeches. Plutarch abridges drastically.

This can be seen, for example, in the preliminaries. In
Dionysius (7. 36), the demagogue Sicinius yields to the
more moderate counsels of Brutus.[25] He advises the plebs
to go home and await the day of trial. 'And when we have
made the necessary preparations, we will appoint a time for
the man to defend himself.' Soon after, the patricians make
concessions about the food supply—a topic touched on
lightly by Plutarch, 16. 1—and obtain from the tribunes a
delay in the trial (7. 37. 2). They also contrive a further
postponement by using the opportune outbreak of hostilities
against Antium. This affair, however, cannot be spun out
for long, and on the return of the army Sicinius 'announced
a day on which he intended to hold the trial of Marcius' (7.
38. 1). Even this is not the end of the patricians' power of
delay. Discussions between the two sides follow, issuing in
what Dionysius (7. 58. 3) calls τὸ προβούλευμα . . . ὑπὲρ τῆς
δίκης.[26] This senatorial decision enables the trial to proceed.
At this point, and not before, Coriolanus is given μέχρι τῆς
τρίτης ἀγορᾶς to prepare his defence.

In Plutarch, all this is much compressed. It might indeed
be possible to reconstruct from Dionysius what his 'annalistic' sources thought about the legal situation. What power

[24] But if a historian seriously asked at what point Tullus began to be jealous,
and accepted Plutarch's account, he would be accepting a conjecture.
[25] Brutus = Plutarch's οἱ φίλοι καὶ οἰκεῖοι, 18. 5.
[26] Cf. Plu. 29. 3. On Dionysius' theory of the προβούλευμα, see E. Cary in the
Loeb *Dionysius*, vol. i, xxv ff.

368 D. A. Russell

could an assembly voting by tribes have over a senator? It
is out of the question to ask such things of Plutarch. In his
account, Coriolanus' vicissitudes are due to shifts of popular
feeling, not to uncertainties in the law. Sicinius first gives
notice to Marcius to appear εἰς τρίτην ἀγοράν at the moment
when he first consents to a trial in lieu of a lynching.²⁷
Plutarch explains εἰς τρίτην ἀγοράν, using the word νουνδίναι,
which is not in Dionysius.²⁸ It is within this one interval
that the Antiate War flares up and dies down, the patricians
discuss the affair, and Coriolanus duly comes to his trial.
Not only are twenty chapters of Dionysius compressed into
one, mostly by the omission of speeches, but the stages of
the original narrative are obscured, and the economic, legal,
and constitutional background concealed.

In many places, of course, Plutarch's compression of
Dionysius leads to immense literary gains. A notable instance is his account of the embassy of the women (34–6;
Dionysius, 8. 44–54). The mother's speech (35. 2–9) is
marked by a tautness and steady elevation quite different
from anything in Dionysius. The historian's speeches are
modelled on the Attic orators; Plutarch's has a different
ring and possesses σεμνότης and conciseness which faintly
recall the Latin historians. The scene too has been made
more picturesque. Coriolanus recognizes his mother himself, there is no messenger. Instead of interrupting her, he
stands silent after she has finished, so that she has to speak
again. The climactic moment is as in Dionysius, but much
better expressed. Plutarch's νενίκηκας εὐτυχῆ μὲν τῇ πατρίδι
νίκην, ἐμοὶ δ' ὀλεθρίον, which is neat and forceful, answers to
the muddled and ineffective antitheses of Dionysius (8. 54.
1): νικᾷς . . . οὐκ εὐτυχῆ νίκην οὔτε σεαυτῇ οὔτ' ἐμοί· τὴν μὲν γὰρ
πατρίδα σεσώκας, ἐμὲ δὲ τὸν εὐσεβῆ καὶ φιλόστοργον υἱὸν ἀπολώ-
λεκας.

(iv) I turn finally to what we may call reinterpretations—
passages in which Plutarch appears to be dissatisfied with

---

²⁷ Cf. Livy, 2. 35. 2: 'in exeuntem e curia impetus factus esset, ni peropportune
tribuni diem dixissent.' But there is no sign in *Coriolanus* of the use of Livy:
contrast *Camillus*.
²⁸ And should be added to Liddell and Scott.

Dionysius' account, not so much on factual grounds as in matters of ἤθη and πάθη, the biographer's proper sphere.

A fairly straightforward and self-contained instance is to be found at 29. 4, which corresponds to Dionysius 8. 21. The Senate, surprisingly enough, opposes a popular demand for Coriolanus' recall. Why? Dionysius suggests two reasons: (*a*) they wanted to test the true feelings of the demos and rouse them to greater enthusiasm for Marcius; (*b*) they wanted to free themselves from responsibility for any of Marcius' acts. Plutarch offers three reasons, all new: (*a*) the senators were inclined to oppose anything the demos wanted; (*b*) they thought it really in the better interests of the demos that Marcius should not come back, and wanted to save them from themselves; (*c*) they were by now angry with Marcius because he took out his resentment on the whole city, not only on those who had injured him. These guesses have a definite tendency. The second, which is also the most implausible, is, I suppose, due to Plutarch's inclination throughout the story to be favourable to the patricians, and so to attribute to them always the best motives—in this instance a highly unlikely degree of altruism. The other two are explanations in terms of sentiment rather than policy. The utilitarian calculation in Dionysius' motivation disappears; πάθη and the irrational come into view.

We saw something like this in the matter of Tullus' 'human feelings' (31. 1); I stress it here because the same kind of approach may also be seen in a much more central matter, namely the interpretation of Coriolanus' own character.

According to the character-sketch in Dionysius (8. 61–2), Coriolanus possessed great virtues: courage and capacity as a general, self-control, natural uprightness, μεγαλοφροσύνη and generosity as a bestower of largesse. But no man is perfect, and he had his faults. He lacked charm, affability, the power to please, the ability to give way and seek reconciliation. Above all, he was incapable of relaxing his absolute standards of δικαιοσύνη. This obstinate rigidity was his downfall. This was why he made no concessions to the plebs, and why he refused, in the last episode of his career, to avoid the anger of the Volsci by resigning from the command.

Most of this is of course in Plutarch too. The hero's

prowess, his self-control, his natural uprightness, his inability to flatter or placate, are all brought to notice in the first few sections of the *Life*. But Plutarch has deepened and varied the picture. If there is a single dominant theme in Dionysius' character-sketch, it is that Coriolanus is, in Aristotelian language (*EN* 1138ᵃ1) ἀκριβοδίκαιος, the opposite of ἐπιεικής. Plutarch dethrones this idea from its central place. He seeks the unity of Coriolanus' character in his πάθη, especially in φιλοτιμία and ὀργή.

In fact, he makes two new points, and both show this same tendency. (*a*) Coriolanus' failings were due to defective education (1. 4–5; 15. 4–5). He is a living demonstration of the fact that a good natural endowment can bear evil fruit. He needed the Muses to civilize him; he never learned the value of τὸ ἐμβριθὲς καὶ πρᾷον, gravity and gentleness, as a moderating influence on τὸ θυμοειδές and on αὐθάδεια. Essentially, this criticism is in Platonic terms: θυμοειδῆ . . . χρὴ . . . εἶναι, πρᾷον δέ (*Laws* 5. 731 B). But I think it may be useful to interpret it also in the light of the passage in Plutarch's *de genio Socratis* (579 D), where he gives what he says is Plato's reading of the oracle's command to the Delians to 'double the altar'. Men should keep company with the Muses, and use literature and mathematics to soothe and mollify their emotions, so that their dealings with one another may be not only not injurious but mutually beneficial. Study mathematics, and you will be civilized. In other words, Plutarch is saying of Coriolanus in our passage that what he lacked was Hellenic παιδεία; he remained a noble barbarian.[29] (*b*) But the principal key to Coriolanus' character, for Plutarch, is his inclination to anger. This springs from his φιλοτιμία (*Comparison* 5). Not at all prominent in Dionysius, it is a repeatedly emphasized feature in the *Life*.[30] We saw it in Plutarch's interpretation of the

[29] Plutarch's idea of the virtues and faults of early Rome appears elsewhere: see 1. 6, on the use of *virtus*, ἀνδρεία, as a general word for virtue; 24. 8, on primitive Roman simplicity; 25. 7, on Roman piety, now a thing of the past.

[30] Of course, it is a feature always implicit in the story. We must not say that it is new in Plutarch, only that he makes much more of it than does Dionysius. Cf. Cic. *Brutus* 41–3, where Coriolanus is treated as *plane alter Themistocles*, who *conatum iracundiae suae morte sedavit*. (This passage is important evidence for comparisons between Greek and Roman heroes before Plutarch; it is interesting that he preferred to pair Themistocles with Camillus.)

trick by which Coriolanus 'indulging his anger' provoked a
war between Rome and the Volsci (*Comparison* 2. 4). Another example is at 21. 1. The Dionysian Coriolanus (7. 67.
2), at the moment of his conviction and disgrace, 'was not
seen to weep ... or say or do anything unworthy of his
μεγαλοφροσύνη'. In Plutarch, he is 'undismayed and unhum-
bled' (ἀνέκπληκτος καὶ ἀταπείνωτος), the only unmoved figure
in the general atmosphere of sympathy (ἐν ... πεπονθόσιν
ἀσυμπαθὴς ἑαυτῷ μόνος). But his serenity is not now the
result of rational control or good temper. It is dumb anger
and depression (βαρυφροσύνη). 'Most people fail to understand', continues Plutarch, 'that this condition is distressful,
for when it changes to actual anger it catches fire, as it
were, and casts off its low spirits and lethargy; this indeed
is how angry people give the impression of being active,
just as a feverish man is hot, because the mind is in a state
of palpitation, distension, and swelling.' This little disquisition,[31] with its hint of polemic, lends emphasis to the
account of Coriolanus' *alta ira*. The divergence from the
interpretation of Dionysius is here clear and conspicuous.

In conclusion, I would again emphasize the status of
these comparisons and inferences: they depend on the assumption that Plutarch used no other source than Dionysius
for the events of the story. It may be urged that some of the
discrepancies discussed—for example, the transference of
φθόνος to Coriolanus in 12—are themselves such as to suggest a separate source rather than invention. There is then a
balancing of probabilities to be done. We must weigh the
chance of Plutarch's having used very sporadically a second
narrative which evidently went into a good deal of detail,
against that of his having handled Dionysius with a slightly
disconcerting degree of freedom. I am myself not convinced
that any of the divergences in the narrative itself require us
to assume a second source. I should therefore say that there
is a high probability that the differences from Dionysius
which we note give a useful indication of the degree of
originality and freedom which Plutarch allowed himself. It

---

[31] Cf. Plato, *Laws* 731; Plu. *de cohibenda ira* 7, 456 D (fever and anger);
Epictetus fr. XII Schenkl (a slow fever compared to the slow and deep anger of
μεγαλόθυμοι πρᾴως τινες; Coriolanus would be an example).

D. A. Russell

is important to see what this amounts to. We see that Plutarch read Dionysius with great care, and drew on the speeches as well as on the narrative. We find him in error sometimes about fact, perhaps even confusing two important battles more than ten years apart. We see his wide antiquarian and historical reading drawn on to supplement the story—most strikingly in the will-signing episode in 9. We can conjecture that he found Dionysius' interpretation of Coriolanus' character wanting, and made his own inferences—with perhaps hints from other writers—about the anger, jealousy, and pride which moved both Coriolanus himself and the subordinate persons of the story. But to extend the impressions we may form from such observations to other *Lives* would be an exceedingly difficult and delicate business. It remains only a hope, though I believe it to be a reasonable one, that when we ask concerning some statement in Plutarch whether it is fact or fiction, tradition or invention, the remembrance of *Coriolanus* may sometimes give a useful direction to our thoughts.

INDEX OF SOURCES

ANDOCIDES
de mysteriis, 134. ff.:
195 n.
see also Pseudo-
Andocides
ANONYM. *De vir. ill.*
43, 1: 158n.
APPIAN
BC 1: 335, 337
1. 1–6: 331 n.
1. 2. 4: 331 n.
1. 7: 333
1. 7. 28: 333 n.
1. 8. 32: 333 n.
1. 10. 41: 334
1. 14. 58: 334
1. 18. 74: 333 n.
1. 21. 86–7: 333 n.
1. 21. 87–9: 331 n.
1. 22. 33: 337
1. 22. 91–7: 344 n.
1. 28–33: 337
1. 29. 132: 337,
338 n.
1. 30. 133: 338
1. 31. 139–40: 338
1. 35. 162: 344 n.
1. 37. 165–8:
344 n.
1. 38. 169: 331 n.
1. 55. 240: 331 n.
1. 60. 269–70:
331 n.
1. 69. 316–17:
331 n.
1. 100. 468: 344 n.
1. 107. 502: 331 n.
2. 6. 20: 314 n.
2. 10. 35: 271 n.
2. 13. 47–8: 344 n.
2. 14. 51: 287 n.
2. 17–18: 286 n.
2. 17. 62: 325 n.
2. 17. 64: 318 n.
2. 18. 66: 286 n.,
318 n.

2. 19. 69–70:
325 n.
2. 19. 71: 140,
325 n.
2. 20. 72: 325 n.,
331 n.
2. 20. 73: 140,
325 n.
2. 23–4: 286 n.
2. 26. 100–1:
287 n.
2. 27. 106: 287 n.
2. 28. 107–8:
135 n.
2. 30. 116: 146
2. 30. 117: 134
2. 33. 133: 130
2. 35: 287 n.
2. 37 141. 2–3:
318 n.
2. 40: 286 n.
2. 56–8: 286 n.
2. 62. 260: 287 n.
2. 79: 286 n.
2. 84–6: 286 n.
2. 84–5: 283 n.
2. 87. 367: 286 n.
2. 90. 377: 286 n.
2. 98–9: 286 n.
2. 99. 414: 286 n.
2. 107–10: 286 n.
2. 107–9: 274 n.
2. 107. 445: 290 n.
2. 108–9: 290 n.
2. 109. 455: 290 n.
2. 109. 458: 274 n.
2. 110: 287 n., 290
2. 111: 291
2. 112. 466–7:
290 n., 291
2. 112. 469: 287 n.,
290 n.
2. 113 ff.: 132
2. 113. 472: 274 n.
2. 113. 474: 275 n.
2. 115–16: 290 n.

2. 116. 486: 291
2. 117: 290
2. 117. 490: 276 n.
2. 119. 500: 276 n.
2. 119. 501: 346 n.
2. 120. 505–7:
275 n.
2. 120. 507: 346 n.
2. 125. 523: 346 n.
2. 127. 530 ff.:
291 n.
2. 135. 565: 346 n.
2. 142. 594: 291 n.
2. 149. 619: 290 n.
3. 6. 18: 346 n.
3. 9. 30: 316
3. 11. 38–12. 41:
346 n.
3. 21. 78: 346 n.
3. 25: 290 n.
3. 77: 290 n.
3. 95. 392–
3: 287 n.
4. 7. 28: 306
4. 12. 45: 269 n.
4. 110. 463: 286 n.
4. 114–17: 287 n.
4. 122. 513: 293 n.
5. 17: 331 n.
5. 63–4: 346 n.
5. 73: 287 n.
5. 76: 287 n.
Celtica fr. 1. 12:
306
18: 286 n., 318 n.
18. 1: 306
Lib. 117. 554–5:
181 n.
Mac. 19: 189 n.
ARISTOTLE and
PSEUDOAR.
Athen. Pol. 2.
1: 340 n.
16, 6: 12
Eth. Nic. 1103^{a}14
ff.: 81 n.

1103ᵃ17 f.: 234 n.
1124ᵃ3 ff: 365 n.
1125ᵇ26 ff.: 160
1138ᵃ1: 370
1150ᵇ25: 91 n.
Poet. 1448ᵇ34–
    1449ᵃ1: 214
1449ᵇ9–20: 214
1450ᵃ35–ᵇ11: 10
1454ᵃ31–3: 70
1456ᵃ10–19: 214
1459ᵇ–1460ᵃ5: 214
1461ᵇ26 ff.: 214
Probl. 953ᵃ20: 91 n.
Rhet. 1360ᵃ37–9: 10
    1368ᵃ18–19: 10 n.
    1389ᵃ9: 363 n.
fr. 609 see PLUT.
    Quaest. Rom.

ARRIAN
Anab., 1 praef.:
    173 n.
1. 11–12: 209
4. 10. 1: 221
4. 12. 6–7: 221
4. 14: 221
5. 1. 1 ff.: 216 n.
6. 9. 5: 222
6. 28. 1 ff.: 216 n.
7. 8–11: 223
7. 20. 1 ff.: 216 n.
Ind. 1. 1 ff.: 216 n.
    5, 8 ff.: 216 n.
    18: 174 n.

ATHENAEUS FGrHist
156 T 4a: 186 n.
200ᵈ–201ᶜ: 216 n.
201ᶠ: 215 n.
274ᵉ–ᶠ: 262 n.
274ᶠ–275ᵃ: 231 n.
420ᶠ: 237
534ᵈ: 200
534ᵉ ff.: 195 n.
534ᵉ: 204
537ᶠ: 216 n.
543ᵃ: 262 n.
569ᵈᵉ: 2
634ᵇ: 257

CAESAR
BC 1. 7: 130, 276 n.
    3. 46: 298 n.
    3. 65: 298 n.

BG 1. 39. 5: 364 n.
    4. 15. 3: 306
    7. 66–7: 133
CATO CENS.
fr. 49: 182
CICERO
Acad. Pr. 2, 119:
    262 n.
    2, 4: 263 n.
ad Att. 1. 14. 6: 299 n.
    1. 16. 3: 299 n.
    1. 16. 15: 24
    2. 17. 1: 129
    2. 18. 3: 270 n.
    2. 19. 5: 270 n.
    8. 11. 2: 348 n.
    9. 10. 3: 20 n.
    13: 262 n.
ad Brut. 2. 4. 2.: 168 n.
    24, 25: 292 n.
ad Quint. fratr. 2. 3.
    2: 129 n.
ad fam. 1. 5b. 2:
    139 n.
    5. 12. 7: 186
Arch. 9. 21: 24
Brut. 15. 62: 19 n.
    29. 112: 5 n.
    41–3: 20 n.,
        191 n., 370 n.
    138–44: 20–1
    204: 13
    285: 20–1
    290: 20–1
Cat. 4. 9: 328 n.
de div. 2. 29.
    62: 19 n.
de leg. agr. 2. 10,
    81: 347 n.
de natura deorum 2.
    9: 364 n.
de officiis 2. 78–
    81: 347 n.
de orat. 2. 341: 17
    2. 57. 94: 13
    3. 36: 13
de republica 3.
    15: 204 n.
Lael. 42: 20 n.
Orator. 12, 39: 7
Philipp. Second
    Philippic: 296,
    297, 298, 2.

34: 131, 273 n.
2. 44–7: 298
2. 67–9: 298
2. 77–8: 131
2. 79 ff.: 131
Sest. 97–8: 348 n.
    103: 347 n.
    132–9: 348 n.
Prov. cons. 28: 127 n.
Tusc., 2. 37: 361 n.
    4. 2. 3: 19 n.
Verr. 2. 4. 120–
    1: 255 n.
    2. 4. 121: 257 n.
CIG 3067, l. 2: 103 n.
    3068, l. 5: 103 n.
CORNELIUS NEPOS
De histories lat. 181
De vir. illustr. 178, 182
    Ages. 8. 7: 180 n.
    Alcib. 1. 2: 200 n.
        6. 2: 192 n.
        7. 1: 192 n.
    Cato 3. 5: 181
    Epam. 4. 6: 17
    Eum. 4. 4: 180 n.
        13. 4: 180 n.
    Hann. 13. 4: 21, 179
    Pel. 1. 1: 10
    Phoc. 4. 4: 180 n.
    Proem. 1. 1: 17
    Reg. 2. 1: 174
    vir. ill. fr. 9 P.: 180 n.
    fr. 16 P.: 181 n.
CURTIUS RUFUS, Q.
    5. 1. 21: 216 n.
    8. 1. 14: 216 n.
DELLIUS
    FGrHist 197, fr.1:
        294 and n.
DEMOSTHENES
    21: 202
    21. 147: 205 n.
DIO, CASSIUS
    fr. 1.2: 301 n.
    36. 24. 1–2: 330 n.
    36. 24–5: 330 n.
    36. 37. 1: 330 n.
    36. 38. 3–5: 330 n.
    36. 43. 2–5: 330 n.,
        327 n.
    36. 51. 3: 330 n.
    37. 22. 1: 330 n.

37. 22. 3: 331 n.
37. 26. 3: 330 n.
37. 29. 3: 330 n.
37. 39. 2–3: 330 n.
37. 41. 3: 330 n.
37. 42. 3: 330 n.
37. 43. 1: 330 n.
37. 51. 3: 330 n.
37. 54–38. 12: 272
37. 54. 3: 331 n.
37. 56. 5: 330 n.
37. 57. 2: 331 n.
38. 1. 1: 330 n.
38. 3. 2–3: 272 n.
38. 4. 4–5. 5: 272 n.
38. 6. 3: 272 n.
38. 11. 3–6: 330 n.,
    344 n.
38. 12. 1–2: 272 n.
38. 12. 4–13: 330 n.
38. 13–1: 344 n.
38. 15. 3: 330 n.
38. 16. 3: 330 n.,
    344 n.
38. 16. 6: 330 n.,
    344 n.
38. 17. 1–2: 270
39. 18. 1: 315
39. 19: 129 n.
39. 20. 2: 315
39. 25. 1–3: 330 n.
39. 31–2: 286 n.
39. 39. 5–7: 286 n.
39. 59. 2–60. 1: 315
39. 62–3: 315
40. 13. 3–4: 294 n.
40. 18–19: 294 n.
40. 50. 5: 330 n.
40. 52–5: 286 n.
41. 3. 1: 153 n.
41. 17. 2–3: 146 n.
41. 41. 1: 286 n.
41. 46: 286 n.
42. 3–4: 286 n.
42. 40. 4–5: 286 n.
42. 57: 286 n.
43. 10–12: 286 n.
43. 11. 6: 331 n.
43. 12. 1: 286 n.
43. 13. 4: 286 n.
44. 8–11: 286 n.
44. 12: 287 n.
45. 6. 1: 330 n.

45. 7. 2: 346 n.
45. 11. 2: 330 n.
45. 12–13: 346 n.
46. 49: 287 n.
47. 6. 3: 269 n.
47. 38. 3: 331 n.
47. 47. 8: 287 n.
48. 38: 287 n.
48. 39. 2: 287 n.
56: 287 n.
63. 14. 2: 102 n.
65. 12. 2: 331 n.
72. 23. 5: 303 n.
DIO OF PRUSA
  or. 12: 69
    32. 72: 105 n.
    72. 5: 230 n.
DIODORUS
  1. 24. 4: 63 n.
  17. 1. 4: 209
  17. 7. 3: 210
  17. 97. 3: 209 and n.
  34/5. 6. 1: 334 n.
  34/5. 33. 4–5:
    353 n.
  37. 3. 6: 231 n.
DIOGENES LAERTIUS
  5. 47: 7
DIONYSIUS OF
    HALICARNASSUS
  ad Pomp 6. 4: 18 n.
  Ant. Rom. 1. 7. 2:
    303 n.
    5. 14–17: 363
    5. 48: 22 n.
    6. 9. 3: 362
    6. 92: 363
    6. 93: 359 n.
    6. 93. 1: 363
    6. 94: 364
    7. 12–13: 366
    7. 19. 4: 366
    7. 21. 3: 366
    7. 22–4: 360
    7. 36: 367
    7. 37. 2: 367
    7. 38. 1: 367
    7. 58. 3: 367
    7. 60–62: 22 n.
    7. 62: 357 n.
    7. 63. 3: 366
    7. 67: 359 n.
    7. 67. 2: 370

    8. 2: 358
    8. 14 ff.: 359
    8. 21: 369
    8. 29 ff.: 360 n.
    8. 29: 357 n., 363
    8. 29. 4: 363 n.
    8. 41: 357 n.
    8. 44–54: 368
    8. 48–53: 360 n.
    8. 51: 357 n.,
      361 n.
    8. 54. 1: 368
    8. 56. 2: 360
    8. 57. 3: 366–7
    8. 60–2: 358
    8. 60. 1: 364
    8. 61–2: 369
    8. 62. 2: 359 n.
    Exc. books 16–21:
      250, 251
    Life of Isaeus 1: 62 n.

DURIS
  FGrHist 76 f1: 14 n.,
    15
EMPYLLIUS
  FGrHist 191, T: 292
EPICTETUS
  fr. 12: 372 n.
EURIPIDES
  Bacch. 13–20: 216 n.
    278: 221
  Cycl., 5 ff.: 216 n.
  Med. 288: 215
    626 ff.: 215 n.
EUSEBIUS
  ap. Syncell. 349b
    (659, 13): 100 n.
FESTUS, p. 67 L:
    364 n.
FLORUS
  2. 20. 7: 294 n.

GELLIUS
  1. 14. 1: 20 n.
  3. 10. 17: 20 n.
  6. 1. 3: 20 n.
  15. 28. 1: 181
  17. 9. 1–2: 297 n.
  17. 21. 3: 170 n.

HERACLITUS
  fr. 119: 84 n.

HERODOTUS
  1. 29–32: 223 n.
  1. 35 ff.: 219
  1. 107–35: 3
  3. 1–66: 3
  3. 31: 221
  7. 46: 227
  8. 17: 193 n.
  9. 81: 365
HESIOD
  Theog. 147 ff.: 257
HIERONYMUS
  adv. Jovin. 1, 148:
    187
HIERONYMUS OF CARDIA
  FGrHist 154: 172 n.
HOMER
  Il. 3. 179: 210
    9. 189: 210
    11. 16 ff.: 218
    19. 375 ff.: 222 n.
    23. 175–7: 224

HORACE
  AP 105–27: 70
  Odes 2. 1. 1: 270 n.
    2. 1. 3–4: 326
HYPERBOLUS 13.4: 197

ILS 845: 119
    1030: 96 n.
    8819: 99 n.
    8971: 99 n.
    9349: 99 n.
    9485: 99 n.
ISOCRATES
  16. 29: 197

JOSEPHUS
  BJ, 4. 634 ff.: 116
  c.Ap., 1. 50: 309 n.,
    310 n.
JUVENAL
  3. 60: 78
  10. 114 ff.: 168 n.
  15. 27 ff.: 101 n.

LAMPRIAS
  Catalogue 36: 167
    38: 167
    106: 234 n.
    113: 52. n.
    233: 234 n.

LIKYMN
  h. 473 n.: 261 n.
LIVY
  1. 46. 4: 98 n.
  1. 48-49: 22 n.
  2. 35. 2: 368 n.
  6. 12. 2–3: 302 n.
  8. 40. 4: 19 n.
  9. 17. 14: 250
  21. 63. 4: 347 n.
  22: 347 n., 349 and
    n., 350 n.
  22. 9. 7: 350 n.
  23. 2. 3: 347 n.
  23. 4. 2–4: 347 n.
  24. 2. 8: 347 n.
  24. 39. 7: 254
  25. 40: 352 n.
  25. 40. 1–3: 255
  25. 40. 3: 257 n.
  26. 49. 2–6: 302 n.
  27. 16. 7–8: 255
  29. 25. 2: 302 n.
  29. 27. 13: 302 n.
  31–3: 304 n.
  31. 6. 4: 347 n.
  32. 6. 8: 302 n.
  32. 32. 5–8: 341 n.
  33. 13. 15: 341 n.
  33. 30. 6–11: 302 n.
  34. 62. 1: 347 n.
  35. 34. 3: 347 n.
  37. 9. 4: 347 n.
  43. 14. 2–3: 347 n.
  44. 42: 187
  45. 41: 189 n.
LUCAN
  Bellum Civile
    8: 295 n.
LUCIAN
  de conscr. hist.
    53: 90 n.
  quom. hist. 47–8:
    308
  rhet. praec.
    18: 170 n.

MARCELLINUS
  vita Thucydidis
    27: 186
    44: 309 n.
MARCUS AURELIUS
  To Himself 1: 74

MENECRATES
  FHG II, fr. 2: 237 n.
MESSALA CORVINUS
  Peter HRR: 293 n.

NICOLAUS OF DAMASCUS
  FGrHist 90
  vit. Aug. 4: 70
    41: 346 n.
    46 346 n.
    56: 346 n.
    68-79: 274 n.
    95: 346 n.
    99: 346 n.
    103: 331 n. 346 n.
    105: 331 n.
    108: 346 n.
    115-19: 346 n.
    121: 346 n.
    130-3: 346 n.
    136-9: 346 n.
  Hist. 77ab: 262 n.

OBSEQUENS
  liber prod. 64: 249 n.

OGIS 383, ll. 85 ff.:
    103 n.

PAP. OXYR.
    1367: 62 n.
OROSIUS
  6. 13. 1-2: 294 n.
OVID
  ex ponto 1. 1. 23: 297
PAUSANIAS
  1. 42. 5: 104 n.
  4. 16: 65 n.
  4. 32: 65 n.
  8. 8. 12: 104 n.
  10. 1: 65 n.
PHOTIUS
  Bibl. 93, p. 73a
    35: 186 n.
  176, p. 121a 35: 14
  176, p. 121a 41: 15
PHYLARCHOS
  FGrHist 81 (comm.)
    p. 133: 15
PINDAR
  Ol, 21 ff.: 220
PLATO
  Alcibi. I 104 A: 193

104 A 2: 196
104 D: 195 n.
105 B: 196
Laws 731: 372 n.
731 B: 370
792 E: 234 n.
Minos 318 DE: 212 n.
320 E–321B: 212 n.
Rep. 375C: 213 n.
411 C: 213 n.
456 A: 213 n.
488 CE: 161 n.
491 DE: 361 n.
495 B: 361 n.
Symposium 215E: 196
216 A 5: 196
216 B 1–5: 196
220 E: 197 n.
PLINY THE ELDER
Natural History
34. 26: 230 n.
34. 27: 230 n.
34. 40: 255 n.
34. 54: 189 n.
34. 60: 189 n.
35. 135: 241 n.
PLINY THE YOUNGER
Ep. 1. 13: 78 n.
2. 1. 4: 117
3. 5: 309
3. 5. 10: 307 n.,
308 n.
5, 16: 96
5: 96
16: 96
PLUTARCH (and
PSEUDO-PLUT.)
ad princ. indoct.
234 n.
780 F: 249 n.
782 F: 262

adversus Colotem:
120, 235
1107 D: 120
1107 E: 236
1119 C: 212 n.
1123 B: 212 n.

Aemilius Paullus
1: 143 n., 168, 184
1. 1: 23, 143, 169
1. 2: 238
1. 3: 264

1. 4: 23
1. 6: 113
2. 6: 148 n., 240
5: 187
6. 6–7: 343 n.
6. 8–9: 241, 252
6. 8: 240
10. 1: 232 n.
10. 2: 342
11. 2: 233 n.
11. 3–4: 232 n.,
321, 351 n.
21: 187
25. 5-7: 112
28. 5: 188
28. 6 ff.: 343 n.
30: 82 n.
31. 2: 339 n.
36. 3 ff.: 189
38. 2–3: 340 n.
38. 2: 233 n.,
339 n.
38. 3: 328, 342
38. 6: 233 n., 329
and n.
39. 7–9: 343 n.
39. 8–9: 344

Aemilius Paullus/
Timoleon/Synk
2. 2: 232 n.

Agesilaus
5. 5: 242 n., 248 n.
6. 7–8: 258 n.
7–8: 93
7: 93
13: 77 n.
21. 8: 212 n.
33. 1: 14 n.

Agesilaus/Pompey/
Synk
81(1). 2: 340 n.
82(2). 1:136 n.
83(3). 6-8: 141 n.
84(4): 142, and n.
84(4). 6: 141

Agis and Cleomenes
2: 341
2. 3: 240 n.
2. 6: 168, 172, 176
2. 7–11: 334
2. 7: 244 n.
2. 9: 113, 251 n.

3. 3: 280 n.
33. 5: 110
see also *Gracchi*
Synk

Alcibiades
1. 3: 192
1. 4–5: 193
1. 6–8: 193
1. 7: 193
2: 194, 207
2. 1: 193
2. 2: 206 n.
2. 3: 206 n.
2. 5: 206 n.
3: 194, 207
4–6: 195
4: 245
4. 1: 195, 247
4. 4: 195 n.
4. 5: 195
5: 195, 207
6: 207
6. 1: 195, 196
6. 3: 194
6. 4: 196
6. 5: 245
7. 1: 197
7. 2: 197
7. 3–5: 197
7. 3: 200, 202, 206
and n., 207, 362
7. 6: 198, 206 n.
7-8: 93
8: 198
8. 1: 198
9: 207
10. 1: 200
10. 3: 200
10. 4: 248
11–12: 200
12: 207
12. 1: 200
12. 3: 201
13: 191 n.
13. 1: 200, 201,
202
13. 2: 202
13. 3: 200, 202,
207
13. 4–7: 201
13. 4: 197, 202
13. 5: 233 n.
13. 8: 201

13. 9: 110, 202
14. 4–5: 202–3, 249
15: 87 n., 202, 203
15. 4: 206 n.
15. 6: 87 n.
15. 6–7: 207
15. 6: 203, 206 n.
15. 7–8: 203
15. 7: 206 n.
16: 196, 204, 207
16. 2: 191 n., 204, 206
16. 4: 248 n.
16. 5: 207
16. 7: 206 n.
16. 8: 206 and n., 207
16. 9: 193, 206 n., 245
17. 1: 191
18. 3: 249
19. 7: 233 n.
21. 1–2: 249
23: 85 n., 192, 207
23. 3f: 105
23. 4: 193
23. 8: 194, 198 n.
26: 201
27. 6: 194
28. 1: 205 n.
32. 2: 198 n.
32. 4 ff.: 192 n.
33. 2: 194
33. 10: 107 and n.
34. 1: 192 n.
34. 3: 194
34. 5: 203
34. 10: 233 n.
35. 5: 249
36. 2: 198 n.
36. 6: 194
41. 6: 194

Alcibiades/Coriolanus/ Synk
2. 1: 248
2. 4: 248 n., 358, 370
2. 6: 194
4. 7–9: 248
5: 370
5. 1–2: 249
5. 1: 248

5. 2: 247

Alexander
1: 79 n., 86 n., 175 n., 225, 360 n.
1. 1–2: 143
1. 2–3: 217–18, 226
1. 2: 10 n., 27 n., 319 n.
2. 1: 209 n.
2. 4: 215
2. 9: 216
4. 5–8: 213, 214
4. 6: 226
4. 7–8: 216 n.
5. 4: 218
7–8: 223 n., 243 n.
7. 2–8. 5: 245
8. 2: 210, 215
13. 4: 215–16
14: 223 n.
15. 8–9: 217
16. 7: 217
17. 9: 216
19: 217
19. 4: 218
22: 223
23. 1: 218
24. 6–7: 224
24. 10: 218
26. 2: 210, 218
26. 4–5: 218
28: 230 n.
32. 8–11: 218
35. 15: 218
37. 5: 227
37. 7: 227
38: 218
38. 5–6: 218
38. 8: 218
40–2: 218
41. 5: 152 n.
47: 218
50. 2: 219
52. 2: 219
52. 6–7: 220
53: 221
54: 221
56. 1: 221
63. 4: 222
64–5: 223 n.
67: 222

67. 7: 223
67. 8: 223
68: 223
69: 227
71. 1 ff.: 223
72: 223
72. 4: 224
74. 1: 224
75. 1–2: 224
75. 5: 212 n., 224

amatorius: 120
749 B: 51, 117
755 E: 51 n.
756 C: 258 n.
762 C: 195
762 E: 195 n.
770 C: 98 n.
771 B: 105
771 C: 105

an seni respublica gerenda sit: 235
783 Bf: 122
785 A: 212 n.
785 F–786 A: 262
792 B–C: 262
792 C: 182
792 F: 105, 122
794 B: 98 n.

animi an corp.
500 E–501 B: 248 n.

Antony
2: 298
2. 6: 329 n.
2. 8: 148, 297 n.
3: 298
4: 148 n.
4. 1–5: 148 n.
5: 151, 277 n.
5. 5: 152
5. 6: 276 n.
5. 8–9: 153
5. 8: 126 n., 342 n.
5. 10: 130, 276 n., 342
6. 3: 230 n.
6. 6–7: 149 n.
6. 7: 148, 284
8. 1–3: 298 n.
9. 5–9: 148 n., 149 n.
9. 6: 131
10. 5–10: 148 n.

10. 5–6: 298
10. 6: 243 n.
10. 8–9: 131
11: 131
11. 6: 290
12: 274 n., 287 n.
12. 3: 342 n.
12. 5: 340 n.
12. 6: 129 n., 290
13–15: 272
13: 132 n.
13. 2: 272
13. 3: 132
13. 4: 276 n.
14–15: 298
14. 2–4: 291 n.
14. 3: 126 n., 273, 315 n.
14. 4: 273
14. 5: 273, 346 n.
15. 4–5: 149 n.
16. 1: 316
16. 6–8: 346 n.
16. 7: 148 n.
17. 3–6: 148 n.
19–20: 149
19. 1: 311
19. 3: 269, 315
20. 2: 306
21: 129 n., 298
21. 1–3: 149 n.
22: 298
22. 6: 284
23. 2: 231 n., 300
23. 3 f.: 105
23. 3: 148 n.
24 ff.: 231 n.
24: 217 n.
24. 5–10: 149 n.
24. 5–8: 232 n.
24. 7–9: 148 n.
24. 9–12: 148 n.
25–6: 295
25. 1: 149, 298
26–8: 149
27. 2–5: 267 n.
27. 3–5: 148 n.
28: 148 n., 168
28. 1: 149
28. 3–12: 300
29. 1–7: 148 n.
29. 1: 149, 243 n., 267 n.

29. 4: 142 n.
29. 5–7: 148
30. 1: 149
30. 6–31. 3: 346 n.
31. 4: 149
32: 287 n.
33. 50: 294
33: 148
33. 2–4: 307 n.
33. 6–7: 287 n.
33. 7: 300
34. 9: 307 n.
35. 2–4: 148 n.
36. 1–2: 267 n.
36. 4–5: 267 n.
37. 5: 230 n.
41. 3: 294 n.
43. 3–6: 148 n.
45: 12: 294 n.
45. 4: 142 n.
49. 4–5: 294
49. 5: 294 n.
49. 6: 294 n.
50. 7: 267 n.
53–4: 148 n.
53. 5: 149
54. 3–5: 148 n.
54. 5: 142 n., 213 n., 267 n.
55: 267 n.
56. 4: 148 n.
56. 6–10: 267 n.
56. 8: 149 n.
57. 4–5: 148 n.
57. 5: 267 n.
59. 3: 148 n.
59. 6–7: 295 n.
59. 6: 294
62: 300
62. 1: 232 n., 267 n.
66. 5–8: 267 n.
67. 9–10: 149 n.
68: 300
68. 5: 149
68. 6–8: 232 n., 300
69. 1: 284
69. 2: 110, 284
70: 148 n., 206 n.
72. 1: 300
75. 3: 149 n.
78. 1: 150

82. 2: 149
82. 4: 295
84. 3: 149
86. 7: 149
86. 8–9: 150
87. 9: 112
see also *Demetrius/ Antony/Synk*

apophthegmata Laconica
208 B–215B: 12 n.
212 F: 212 n.

apophthegmata regum
186 D: 200 n.
190F–191Dp: 12 n.
198D: 231 n.

Aratus
1: 167, 171
1. 5: 280 n.
3. 3: 246
10. 5: 243 n., 246, 247, 251 n.
15. 3: 213 n.
38. 2: 9 n.
38. 12: 241 n.
45. 8: 104
49–53: 9 n.

Aristides
2. 1: 233 n.
5: 87 n.
6. 2–5: 249 n.
7. 8: 79 n.
9. 2: 258
22. 1: 232 n.
22. 4: 232 n.
23. 7: 233
26. 2: 232 n.

Aristides/Cato the Elder Synk
1. 2–3: 351 n.
1. 3: 233
5. 4: 240 n., 341

Artaxerxes
1.1: 6 n.
2. 1: 6 n.
4. 4–5: 6 n.
6. 9: 212 n.
24. 9: 232 n.
30. 9: 6 n.

Banquet
see *convivium*

Brutus
1. 3: 244, 248
2. 1: 244 n.
2. 2–3: 244
2. 3: 244 n.
2. 4–8: 292 n.
2. 4: 292
2. 5: 297 n.
5. 2–4: 147 n.
6. 10–12: 343 n.
7 ff.: 272
7–8: 290 n.
7. 1: 290
8. 2: 290
8. 3: 290
8. 5: 275
8. 6–7: 290, 291 n.
9–10: 287 n.,
   290 n.
9. 2: 340 n.
9. 9: 107, 107 n.,
   274 n., 275 n.,
   278, 279 n., 280
10. 6: 148 n.,
   274 n.
11–12: 274 n.
12: 275 n.
12. 3: 340 n.
13: 283 n., 290
13. 2: 23
13. 3: 292, 310
14–16: 290 n.
15. 6–9: 290
16. 1: 275
17: 290 n.
17. 2: 276
18. 3: 284 n.
18. 10–14: 346 n.
18. 12: 275 n.
19: 133 n.
19. 1: 273 n., 291,
   315 n.
19. 2: 291 n.
19. 4–5: 291 and n.
20. 1: 273, 346 n.
20. 4–11: 346 n.
20. 9: 276 n.
21. 2–6: 346 n.
21. 2–3: 329
21. 4: 346 n.
21. 6: 292 n.
22: 305
22. 1: 316

22. 3: 346 n.
22. 4–6: 292 n.,
   305 n.
23. 1: 346 and n.
23. 2–4: 23
23. 4–7: 290
23. 7: 292
24. 3: 267 n.,
   292 n.
24. 4: 339 n.
24. 7: 130 n.
25. 6: 112
26. 6: 292 n.
27: 287 n.
27. 5: 340 n.
27. 6: 306
28. 1: 284
28. 2: 292 n.
29. 3: 293 n.,
   340 n.
29. 5: 340 n.
29. 8–11: 292 n.
33: 283, 286 n.
35. 4: 284
35. 5: 284 n.
39: 293
39. 6: 258 n.
40: 293
41. 7: 286 n.
44–5: 287 n.
47: 293
48: 293
48. 2: 23
50: 284
51–2: 293
51. 2: 23
53. 5: 252 n.,
   283 n.
53. 6–7: 292 n.
55(2). 2: 148,
   325 n.

Caesar
1. 1: 340 n.
1. 7: 128, 147 n.
1. 8–2. 7: 128
2. 6: 128
3: 128
3. 1: 243 n.
3. 2–4: 145, 297 n.
4: 129
4. 1–3: 243 n.
4. 1: 128
4. 4–9: 320

4. 4–5: 273 n.
4. 5: 323 n.
4. 6–9: 146, 273 n.
4. 6: 320
4. 7: 323 n.
4. 8: 145, 146, 320,
   340 n.
4. 9: 341 n.
5. 1–3: 320 n.
5. 2–3: 320 n.
5. 3: 273 n.
5. 7: 327
5. 8–9: 145, 273 n.
5. 8: 146, 273 n.,
   320
5. 9: 146, 320
6: 320 n.
6. 1 ff.: 233 n.
6. 1–7: 320 n.
6. 1–3: 320
6. 3–7: 273 n.
6. 3: 145
6. 6: 145
6. 7: 273 n., 320
   and n.
6. 9: 145, 146
7. 7–8.4: 299 n.
7. 4: 320 n., 340 n.
7. 7: 126
7. 8–8.1: 299 n.
8. 1: 299 n.
8. 2: 147 n., 299 n.
8. 4–5: 320 n.
8. 4: 296 n.
9–10: 299 n.
9. 1: 323 n.
9. 2–10. 11: 130
9. 2: 343 n.
9. 4–8: 307 n.
10. 3: 299 n.
10. 6–7: 320 n.
10. 6: 299 n.,
   340 n.
11–12: 343 n.
11. 1: 323 n.,
   327 n.
11. 2: 226
11. 5–6: 129 n.
11. 6: 230 n.
13–14: 270
13. 3: 323 n.
13. 4–6: 270 n.,
   325 n.

13. 5: 320 n.,
339 n.
13. 6: 324 n.
14. 2–3: 320 n.
14. 2: 126 n.,
233 n., 271 and
n., 318 n., 345 n.
14. 3–6: 271 n.,
272 n.
14. 3: 320 n., 328,
339 n.
14. 6: 273 n.,
320 n., 339 n.
14. 7–8: 324 n.
14. 7: 129
14. 8: 287 n.
14. 11–13: 272 n.
14. 16–17: 148 n.,
272 n.
14. 17: 138, 270
15. 2–4: 318 n.
17: 147 n., 289
18. 1: 320 n.
19. 4: 320 n.
20. 2: 146 n.
20. 3: 134, 141
21: 147 n.
21. 2: 146 n.
21. 3–6: 277 n.
21. 7: 320 n.
21. 8–9: 146 n.
21. 8: 127
22. 1–5: 286 n.,
306
22. 2: 296
22. 4–5: 127
22. 4: 318 n.
23. 5–7: 325 n.
23. 7: 146 n.
24. 3: 310
26. 7–8: 132
26. 8: 300
28: 277 n., 325 n.
28. 1: 141
28. 2–3: 323 n.
28. 2: 135 and n.
28. 3: 325 n.
28. 4: 325 n.
28. 5–7: 141
28. 5–6: 325 n.
28. 7: 140, 325 n.
29. 3: 287 n.
29. 5: 134, 135 n.,

145, 148 n.
30–1: 126 n., 151,
277 n.
30. 1: 146
30. 2: 152, 287 n.
30. 3: 152 n., 152
30. 4: 130, 276 n.
30. 5: 152 n.
30. 6: 127 n., 130,
151, 152 and n.
31. 2–3: 153
31. 2: 151
31. 3: 130, 276 n.
32: 287 n.
32. 4–11: 271
32. 9: 129 n.
33. 1–4: 271
33. 4–6: 140 n.
33. 5: 135 n.
34. 5: 129 n.
34. 7: 148 n.
35: 128
35. 2: 108, 109,
269 n., 278, 280
and n., 281
35. 6–11: 146,
342 n.
36. 2: 148
38: 147 n., 286 n.
39. 8: 287 n.
41. 2: 340 n.
42–6: 277 n.
44. 8: 286, 296 n.
45. 9: 108, 109, 278
46: 288 n.
46. 2: 287 n.
47: 295
48. 3–4: 148 n.
48. 5: 148 n.
49. 1–3: 147
49. 7–8: 147 n.,
286 n.
49. 10: 147 n.
51: 274 n.
51. 2: 299 n.
54: 286 n.
54. 5: 148 n.
54. 6: 148 n.
56. 7: 274 n.
57. 1: 146, 320,
340 n.
57. 2: 274 n.
57. 4–6: 148 n.

57. 7: 274 n.,
290 n.
58: 290 n.
58. 4–5: 242
59. 3–4: 282
60–1: 274, 286–
7 n., 320
60. 1: 274 n.
60. 3: 274 n.
60. 4: 290 n.
60. 5: 274 n.,
320 n.
60. 6: 129 n., 290
60. 8: 274 n.
61: 274 n., 290 n.
61. 6: 274 n.
61. 9–62. 1: 274 n.
61. 9–10: 274 n.
62 ff.: 272
62: 274 n., 287 n.
62. 1: 274 n., 274
62. 4–6: 290 n.
62. 6: 290
62. 7: 290 n.
62. 8: 107, 278,
290
62. 10: 290
63–5: 290 n.
63. 9: 295
63. 11: 258 n.
64. 2: 320 n.
64. 5: 340 n.
65. 1–4: 291
65. 1: 292 n.
66: 290 n., 304
66. 4: 276
66. 12: 276 n.
67. 2: 273 n.
67. 4: 276 n.
67. 8: 291
68: 321
68. 3: 276 n.
68. 7: 107, 274 n.,
278
69. 1: 146, 242,
320, 340 n.
69. 2: 60

Camillus
2. 1: 362
2. 6: 232 n.
12: 82
12. 4: 79 n.
19: 358 n.

19. 12: 112, 258 n.,
   279 n.
22. 4: 6 n.
33. 4: 343 n.
33. 10: 107, 278,
   279 n.
36: 80 n.

Cato the Elder
2. 3–6: 241 n.
2. 5: 241 n.
3. 1: 343 n.
3. 3: 247
3. 8–10: 145 n.
4. 1: 241 n.
4. 2: 233, 351 n.,
   352
6. 2–4: 343 n.
8. 1: 145 n.
8. 2: 231 n.
8. 4: 241 n.
8. 14: 241 n.
9. 2–3: 241 n.
9. 3: 241 n.
10. 4–6: 343 n.
12. 4: 110
13. 1: 241
14. 4: 232 n.
15: 342
16. 2: 343 n.
16. 4–5: 321 n.
16. 4: 329 n.,
   339 n., 340 n.,
   343 n.
16. 8: 232 n., 321,
   351 n.
18. 4–5: 232
19. 5–6: 230 n.
20. 3: 241 n.
22: 241
22. 4–23. 2: 352 n.
23. 1–24. 1: 241 n.
23. 2–3: 230
23. 3: 352
24. 8: 241 n.
27. 3: 232 n., 233,
   353
27. 7: 244 n.
   see also *Aristides/*
   Cato the Elder/
   Synk

Cato the Younger
1. 1: 111

1. 3–6: 194 n.
1. 3: 144
2. 1–5: 145 n.
3. 8–10: 145 n.
5. 3–4: 297 n.
6. 1–4: 145 n.
7. 3: 145 n.
8. 1: 145 n.
8. 2–3: 144 n.
8. 4–5: 144 n.
9. 5–10: 144 n.
9. 10: 145 n.
11. 1–8: 145 n.
11. 3: 242 n.
11. 7–8: 148 n.
12. 1: 144 n.
12. 3–6: 343 n.
13: 145 n., 282
15. 4: 145 n.
16–18: 144 n.
16. 4–8: 318 n.
18. 3: 233 n.
19. 8: 262
20–1: 144 n.
20. 8: 342 n.
21: 183
21. 3 ff.: 144 n.
21. 3: 347 n.
21. 8: 127
22. 4: 107
22. 4-24, 3: 299 n.
22. 5: 299 n.
22. 6: 299 n.
23: 299 n.
23. 3: 297 and n.
24. 1: 27
24. 1–3: 147 n.
24. 4–25: 145 n.
24. 4–25. 13:
   324 n.
26. 1: 329 n.
26. 2: 327 n.
26. 4: 339 n., 342
26. 5: 144
27–9: 327 n.
27. 1: 341
27. 8: 339 n.,
   340 n.
28. 6: 329 n.
29. 3: 329 n.
30: 283
30. 3–10: 145 n.,
   324 n.

30. 9–10: 129, 244,
   324 n.
30. 9: 270 n.
31–3: 145 n., 270
31: 262 n.
31. 2: 329 n.,
   345 n.
31. 5: 345 n.
31. 6: 129, 324 n.
31. 7: 134 n.
32–3: 126 n.
32. 1: 329 n.
32. 2: 271 n.
32. 3: 272 n.
32. 8–10: 270
32. 10: 272 n.
33. 1–4: 272 n.
33. 1: 345 n.
33. 5: 134 n.,
   271 n., 318 n.
33. 6: 137, 272 n.
34–40: 343 n.
34: 127
34. 1: 137
34. 3: 137
34. 6: 343 n.
35–8: 144 n.
35. 4–6: 145 n.
35. 7: 134 and n.
36. 5: 148 n.,
   286 n.
37: 145
37. 10: 145
40: 282
41–3: 286 n.
41. 1: 310
41. 3–42. 1: 318 n.
42. 3: 315 n.
42. 3–4: 144 n.,
   147 n.
42. 6: 134 n.
42. 7: 147 n.
43: 126
43. 3: 134 n.
43. 9: 134 n.
43. 10: 134
44: 144 n.
44. 1: 144
44. 2: 145 n.
44. 3: 325 n.
44. 12–14: 145 n.,
   147 n.
45. 2: 138

45. 7: 134 n., 140,
    325 n.
46. 8: 145 n.,
    148 n.
47: 277 n.
47. 2: 325 n.,
    340 n.
48. 5–10: 286 n.
48. 8–10: 144 n.
49. 1–2: 134 and n.
49. 1: 135 n.,
    140 n.
49. 2–6: 144 n.
49. 3: 339 n.
49. 6: 148 n., 244
50: 144 n.
50. 2: 244
50. 3: 145 n.
51: 127
51. 1: 306
51. 4–5: 134 n.
51. 6: 127
51. 7: 329
52. 1–3: 134 n.
52. 3: 134 n.
52. 4: 135 n.,
    140 n.
52. 5–9: 145 n.,
    324 n.
52. 7–9: 145 n.
52. 8: 144
53. 2–3: 286 n.
53. 3: 140 n.
54. 2: 148 n.
54. 9: 278, 281,
    283
54. 10: 110
55. 4: 340 n.
57–8: 286 n.
57: 145 n.
58. 5: 144 n.
58. 7: 340 n.
59. 4–8: 144 n.
62–71: 286 n.
62. 8: 107
64. 3: 144
65. 2: 144 n.
65. 6–7: 144 n.
66. 2: 340 n.
68. 7: 107
70. 6–7: 144 n.
73. 2–4: 145 n.
73. 6: 110, 283 n.

Cicero
1. 2: 359
1. 5: 280 n.
3–4: 129
3. 1: 241 n.
5. 2: 242 n.
5. 6: 243 n.
6. 1–2: 343 n.
6. 3–4: 305
6. 3: 296 n.
9. 7: 340 n.
10–11: 329
10. 1: 339 n.
10. 2: 341 n.
10. 5: 341 n.,
    344 n.
11. 2–3: 321 n.
11. 2: 339 n.
13. 2: 344 n.
15: 314
15. 4–5: 127 n.
17. 5: 340 n.
19. 1–4: 126
20: 314
20. 2: 299 n.
20. 3: 137 n.,
    244 n., 269
20. 4–21. 5: 126,
    299 n.
20. 6–7: 269
20. 6: 341 n.
21. 1-2: 299 n.
21. 3: 299 n.
21. 4: 299 n.
22. 2: 339 n.
23. 1–4: 327 n.
23. 4: 340 n.
23. 5: 327 n.
24. 5: 262
24. 6–9: 296 n.
24. 6: 168 n.,
    296 n.
25. 4: 243 n.
26. 6: 183
28–9: 130, 299 n.
28. 1: 343 n.
28. 4: 299 n.
29. 2–4: 137 n.
29. 4: 339 n.
30. 1–4: 270
30. 3–5: 270
30. 4: 137 n.
30. 5: 270

31. 1: 344 n.
32. 5–7: 242, 249
33. 2–4: 269
33. 2: 233 n.,
    329 n., 339 n.
33. 4: 329 n.
33. 6: 329 n.
33. 8: 282, 296 n.
34: 282, 314
34. 2: 127
35. 1: 315
36: 343 n.
36. 6: 296 n.
37. 3–4: 296 n.
40. 2: 343 n.
40. 3: 296 n.
41. 2–3: 137 n.
41. 6: 296 n.
41. 8: 242
42: 272
42. 3: 273 n.,
    315 n.
43. 8: 316
45. 2: 292 n.,
    296 n.
46. 5: 269
48. 6: 296 n.
49. 5 f.: 98 n.

Demosth./Cic./Synk
50(1). 4: 296 n.
52(3): 343 n.
53(4). 4: 292 n.,
    296 n.

Cimon
1–2: 240
1. 3–2. 2: 232 n.
2: 168
2. 2–5: 143 n.
2. 4–5: 80
3. 1: 168
3. 3: 251 n.
4. 5: 241, 245, 261
4. 6–10: 147 n.
8. 2: 260
9. 1: 260
9. 5: 268 n.
10. 6: 260
10. 8: 340 n.
11. 2: 260
13. 3: 260
13. 5–7: 260
13. 7: 261

15. 1–2: 233 n.,
  340 n.
17. 9: 233 n.
18. 1: 260
19. 3–4: 260
19. 5: 260, 263
see also *Lucullus/
  Cimon/Synk*

Cleomenes
see *Agis/Cleomenes*
consolatio ad uxorem:
  118
608 A–612 A: 52
608 C: 117, 118,
  242 n.
609 B: 242 n.
609 D: 117
611 A: 242 n.

*convivium septem
  sapientium*:
146B-164D: 55, 175

Coriolanus
1: 361
1. 1: 280 n.
1. 2 ff.: 252
1. 2: 357 n.
1. 3–6: 245, 249
1. 3: 247
1. 4–5: 370
1. 4: 247, 364
1. 5: 247, 251 n.
1. 6–2. 1: 259
1. 6: 248, 370 n.
2. 2: 362, 366
3. 1–3: 362
3. 1: 357 n.
3. 3: 363 n.
4. 1–3: 248
4. 3: 357 n.
6. 3–5: 360
7. 1: 365 n.
7. 19: 366
7. 21: 366
8–11: 360
9: 372
9. 1–4: 363
9. 3: 364
9. 9: 359 n., 362
10–11. 2: 364
10. 1: 364
10. 7–8: 362
10. 7: 366

11: 358
11. 1: 364
11. 2–6: 364
12: 366, 371
13: 365
13. 5: 343 n.
13. 6: 362
14: 363 n.
14. 3–6: 247
15: 82 n.
15. 1: 357 n., 363
15. 4–5: 245, 370
15. 4: 248, 249
15. 5: 248
16: 360
16. 1: 367
16. 5: 365 n.
18. 5: 367 n.
19: 363 n.
20. 5: 366
20. 6: 248
20. 9: 365 n.
21. 1: 249, 370
21. 3: 357 n.,
  359 n.
21. 4: 343 n.
21. 5: 365 n.
22. 1: 359
24: 363 n.
24. 2: 365 n.
24. 8: 370 n.
25. 7: 370 n.
26. 2: 358
27. 1: 240 n., 248
28: 359
29. 3: 367 n.
29. 4: 369
31. 1: 367, 369
31. 5: 365 n.
32: 358
33. 2: 111, 358 n.
34–6: 368
34. 3: 249
35. 2–9: 360 n., 368
37. 5: 360
38: 358
39. 6: 240 n., 248
39. 11: 110, 358 n.,
  359 n.
see also *Alcibiades/
  Coriolanus/Synk*

Crassus
1. 2 ff.: 147 n.

1. 4–6: 289 n.
3. 3–4: 297 n.
3. 6: 243 n.
4: 288
4. 1: 340 n.
5. 6: 289 n.
7. 5: 243, 318
7. 7: 232, 322
10–11: 318 n.
13. 3–4: 268
13. 3: 126
13. 4: 296 n.,
  297 n., 327 n.
13. 5: 282
14: 317
14. 1–5: 270
14. 4: 271 n.
14. 6–7: 277 n.
15: 286 n.
15. 6–7: 318 n.
15. 7: 126
16: 7–8: 286 n.
17–33: 294
33 *passim*: 213 n.
see also *Nicias/
  Crassus/Synk*

cum princ. phil.
777 B: 188

de adulatore et amico:
  119
48 E: 119
50 E: 212 n.
51 D: 85 n.
56 B–F: 248 n.
56 E: 213 n.
56 F: 119
60 E: 119
63 A: 213 n.
73 C: 196 n.

*de Alexandri Magni
  fortuna aut
  virtute*
327 F–328 A: 210
329: 213 n.
330 E: 118
331 CD: 210
331 D: 217
337 D: 213 n.
343 AB: 211
343 E: 222

*de animae
  procreatione in*

Timaeo: 119
1012 A f.: 119
de audiendis poetis:
117, 234 n.
15 A: 117
15 CD: 212 n.
16 A–17 C: 212 n.
16 A–17 E: 212 n.
17 D: 212 n.
27 f.: 212 n.
42 E: 241 n.
de capienda ex inimicis
utilitate: 120,
235
86 C: 120
89 A: 183
91 DE: 183
92 D: 242 n.
95C: 237
de cohibenda ira: 96,
97, 119 pp. 236
244 B: 65
453 C: 99
453 D: 54 n.
455 F: 96
456 D: 371 n.
457 D: 265 n.
458 A: 183
458 B: 213 n.
462 B: 212 n.
462 F: 248 n.
de cupid. divit.
149–51: 232 n.
527 EF: 213
528 B: 213 n.
de curiositate: 120
522 D f.: 120
de defectu oraculorum
409 C–40 B: 53
418 E: 258 n.
419: 98 n.
419D: 98 n.
419 E: 98 n., 118
de E Delphico: 119
385 AB: 119
385 F: 102 n.
391 E: 49
392 E: 48 n.
de exilio: 120
599 E: 120

601 A: 204 n.
602 E: 98 n.
605 F: 183
607 E: 120
de facie in orbe lunae
236
926 C: 212 n.
931 D: 115
935 B: 258 n.
de fortuna
Romanorum 176,
182, 229, 266
317 D: 182, 183
318 B: 187
318 E– F: 266 n.
318 E: 241
319 A: 360
319 D– 320A:
307 n.
319 D: 98
319 E: 182
322 D: 241
de fraterno amore: 235
484 D–E: 262
487 F: 116
de garrulitate: 115–16
505 cf.: 115
506 D: 118
506 E: 177
511 DE: 183
514 C: 170
de genio Socratis 115,
175
528 BC: 212 n.
579 D: 370
584 E: 234 n.
de gloria Atheniensium:-
345C–351B: 78
de inim. util. 89A: 183
de Iside et
Osiride: 122–3
351 C: 122
351 E: 53
352 C: 53
358 E–F: 258 n.
380 B f.: 101 n.,
105 n.
de laude ipsius: 121
539 A: 121
540 F: 183

542 A: 183
542 E: 185
545 E: 260 n.
de liberis educ.
13 B: 212 n.
14. 10 C: 4 n.
de mal. Herodoti: 227
855 C– D: 260 n.
857 A: 183
866 B: 56 n., 280
870 C: 212 n.
de mulierum
virtutibus: 123 n.
242 E: 123
243 B–D: 156
244 B: 65 n., 167
de primo frigido: 122
945 F: 122
949 E: 98 n., 122
de profectibus in
virtute: 123,
234 n., 235, 236,
238
75 A ff.: 237 and n.
75B: 123
75 D: 237 n.
de Pythiae oraculis:
119
394 D–409 C: 53
395 A: 119
398 E: 119
399 E–400 C: 212 n.
407 B: 212 n.
407 C: 54 n.
408 C–D: 53
408 F ff.: 100
de sera numinis
vindicta: 118,
235; 236
548 A: 118
551 D: 234 n.
551 E: 234 n.
552 D: 234 n.
552 F: 186
566 E: 118
de sollertia
animalium: 89,
118
962 C: 234
964 D: 104
974 A: 118

976 A: 183
de Stoic. repug.
  1051 B–D: 258
de superstit.
  166 B: 258 n.
  169 D: 237
  171 B–E: 258 n.
de tranquillitate
  animi: 97, 98, 99,
    122
  464 F: 98, 99, 265
  465 A: 99
  467 E: 97, 183
  468 C: 99
  470 C: 99
  475 A: 187
de tuenda sanitate:
  118
  123 D: 98 n., 118
  124 C: 98 n.
de virt. mor.
  442 A–C: 234
  443 C–D: 234
  445 A: 246
  445 D: 237
  451 E: 246
  452 B: 242 n.
  452 D: 234, 240 n.
de vit. aere alieno:
  148 n.
  830 B: 54 n.
de vit. pud.
  529 D: 248 n.
  530 E: 234 n.
Demetrius
  1: 80 n., 143 n.,
    149 n., 169, 171,
    177, 191 n.
  2: 85 n.
  3. 3–5: 249 n.
  4. 5: 285 n.
  22. 7: 256
  41. 4–5: 249 n.
  42. 8–11: 249 n.
  53. 10: 142 n.
Demetrius/Antony/
  Synk
  93(6). 4: 149 n.
Demosthenes
  1. 1: 113

2: 173, 175, 178
2. 1: 300, 307
2. 2: 267 n.
3. 1: 108, 168, 268
3. 2: 11 n., 168 n.
3. 5: 192 n.
4. 4: 245
11. 7: 143 n.
13. 1: 14 n.
21. 2: 14 n., 16 n.,
  212 n.
22. 5: 213 n.
23. 5: 215
26. 5: 245
28. 3–29. 7: 212 n.
30. 17: 198 n.
30. 26: 198 n.
31. 7: 113
see also *Cic./Dem./*
  Synk
Dion
  1: 244 n.
  1. 1: 113
  2. 7: 108, 187
  8: 85 n.
  24. 10: 13 n.
  36: 4 n.
  47. 4: 245
  52. 5: 246
  53. 5: 246
  58. 10: 107 and n.,
    278, 279 n.
Dion/Brut/Synk.
  2. 2: 148, 325 n.
Eroticos
  see *amatorius*
Eumenes
  2. 2: 213 n.
  6–7: 177
  13: 59 n.
  18. 6: 285 n.
Fabius
  1: 158, 361 n.
  1. 7–9: 160 n.,
    240 n.
  2: 288
  3. 1: 349 n.
  3. 3: 349 n.
  3. 4: 349 n.
  3. 6–7: 350 n.
  3. 7: 158, 164 n.,
    234 n.

4–13: 157
4: 160 n.
4. 2: 158
4. 4: 160 n.,
  258 n., 350 n.
5. 1: 160 n.
5. 3: 160 n.
5. 4: 160 n.
5. 6–8: 162
6. 4: 349 n.
7: 159
7. 5–8: 160 n.,
  351 n.
7. 5–7: 350 n.
7. 5: 351 n.
7. 7: 162
8. 1: 349 n.
8. 4: 158, 340 n.,
  341, 349 n., 350
9. 1: 350 n.
9. 2: 158
10. 2: 162
10. 7: 160 n.
13. 1: 162–3
13. 6: 343
14. 2: 351 n.
15: 349 n.
16. 6: 143 n.,
  319 n.
16. 7: 343 n.
17. 7: 160 n., 163
18: 160 n.
18. 4: 164 n.
19. 2: 109
19. 3: 160 n.
19. 4: 163, 256 n.
19. 22: 109
20: 163, 349 n.
20. 1: 343 n.
21–2: 157
22. 5: 163, 255,
  351 n.
22. 8: 109, 163 n.,
  255 and n.
24. 6: 160 n.,
  164 n.
25. 3–4: 89, 351 n.
25. 3: 160 n., 163
26: 349 n.
26. 1: 351 n.
26. 3–4: 160 n.,
  163 n.
28–30: 157 n.

30. 5–6: 160 n.
see also *Pericles/
Fabius/Synk*

Flamininus (Titus)
init.: 168
1. 1: 172
1. 4: 240, 252, 259
2. 3–5: 343 n.
2. 5: 240, 251 n.
5. 1–2: 343 n.
5. 6 ff.: 258
5. 7: 240
7. 2: 341
11: 231 n.
11. 6: 260
12. 6: 343 n.
12. 13: 112
13. 2: 341
16. 6: 280 n.
18. 2: 339 n.
20. 1: 252 n.

Galba: 116–17
1: 82 n.
1. 3–4: 239 n.
1. 7–8: 213 n.
2: 97
2. 3: 10 n.
2. 5: 143 n., 319
3: 98
3. 1: 343 n.
6. 3: 212 n.
9: 98 n.
10: 117
12: 98 n.
12. 5: 213 n.
14. 2–3: 213 n.

Gracchi
1: 342
1. 7: 280 n.
3. 1: 343 n.
5. 4–5: 344
7. 3–4: 332
8: 333
8. 1: 333 n.
8. 4: 333 n.
8. 6: 241 n.
8. 9: 19 n.
8. 10: 331, 332 n.
9. 2: 333 n.
9. 3: 332 n., 334
9. 5: 333 n.
10. 1: 331, 332 n.

10. 3: 342 n.
10. 9: 332 n.
11. 1: 332 n.
11. 4: 332 n.
12. 6: 332 n.
13. 1: 19 n.
13. 2: 340 n.,
343 n.
13. 4: 332 n.
13. 6: 332 n.
14. 3: 332 n.
15. 1: 332
15–16: 57 n.
16. 1: 233 n.,
344 n.
16. 2: 332 n.
18. 3: 332 n., 343
20–1: 332 n.
20. 1: 233 n.,
340 n.
20. 3: 332 n.
21: 178, 180, 332
21. 1–4: 332 n.
22: 77 n.
22. 7: 332 n.
23. 2: 343 n.
24. 1–2: 334 n.
24. 2: 339 n.
24. 3: 340 n.
24. 5: 332 n.
25. 1: 332 n.
25. 4: 332 n.
26: 332 n., 334
26. 1: 332 n.
26. 2: 344 n.
26. 3–4: 233 n.
27. 1–2: 332 n.
27. 1: 332 n.,
340 n.
27. 5: 332 n.
28. 1: 332 n.
29. 3–6: 332
29. 4: 332 n.
29. 6: 339 n.
30. 1–2: 332 n.
30. 6–7: 332 n.
30. 7: 332 n.,
339 n.
31. 3–4: 332 n.
31. 3: 334 n.
32. 4: 332 n.,
340 n.
32. 5: 332 n.

33: 332 n.
33. 1: 334 n.
33. 3: 332 n.
35. 2: 332 n.,
340 n.
36–8: 332 n.
37. 7: 332 n.
38. 8–9: 332 n.
39. 2–3: 332 n.
39. 2: 332 n.
40. 3: 339 n.
Ag.Cl./Grac./Synk
42(2): 334
44(4): 334
45(5). 7: 113
45(5). 9: 110

Lucullus
1. 3: 240 n.
1. 4–9: 261
1. 4–8: 240
1. 5: 261
1. 6: 242, 261
1. 7–8: 261
2. 1–2: 261
2. 2: 260
2. 4–5: 260
2. 5: 260
4. 2–3: 260
4. 2: 261
5. 5: 261
6. 2: 82 n.
7. 4–7: 240
7. 6–7: 232 n., 260
11. 2: 212 n.
11. 6: 115, 252 n.
18. 1: 260
18. 9: 261
19. 4–5: 260
19. 4: 261
20–1: 240
20: 343 n.
20. 1–6: 240, 260
20. 1–4: 232 n.
20. 1: 261
20. 5: 344
21. 3: 213 n.
21. 6: 213 n.
23. 1–2: 260
23. 1: 261
29: 343 n.
29. 5: 260
29. 6: 261
32. 6: 260

388 *Index of Sources*

33. 3: 252 n.
35. 9: 328, 329 n.,
    340 n.
36. 4: 269
36. 5: 113
37. 3: 340 n.
38. 2: 261, 329 n.,
    339 n., 340 n.
38. 3–4: 261
38. 3: 251 and n.,
    252
38. 4: 241 and n.
38. 5: 262
39. 2: 232 n.
39. 5: 267 n.
41. 2: 231 n.
42. 1–4: 240
42. 1: 261, 262
42. 2: 262
42. 3–4: 241 n.,
    262
42. 3: 263 n.
42. 4–43. 1: 262
42. 4: 242, 261,
    270
42. 6–8: 270
42. 8: 233 n.
43: 177, 180

Lucullus/Cimon/
    Synk
1. 4: 261
1. 5: 260
1. 6: 260
1. 8: 261
2. 1: 260

Lycurgus 17. 11: 109
Lyc.-Numa-Synk 4.
    12: 247 n.

Lysander
2: 85 n.
2. 4: 242 n., 248 n.
3: 91
4–15: 91
7: 91
14: 92
16–17: 91–2
17. 11: 109, 279 n.
18: 92
19: 206 n.
19. 1: 92
21–2: 92
23: 85 n.

24–6: 93
25. 2: 212 n.
25 end: 93
26. 6: 212 n.
27–9: 93
28: 1
30: 93

Lysander/Sulla/
    Synk 3.
    3: 252 n.

Marcellus
1. 1–2: 256–7
1. 2–5: 259
1. 2–3: 254
1. 3: 25, 239, 255,
    256, 257
2: 342
3. 5–6: 258
3. 6: 239
4–5: 258
5. 5: 230 n.
6. 2: 328
6. 11: 258
9. 7: 256 n.
10. 2: 329 n.
10. 6: 255
12. 2: 258
17. 2: 239, 257
18–19: 255
19. 6: 255
20: 240, 260,
    343 n.
20. 1: 254, 255
20. 2–11: 255
20. 2: 254
21: 255, 257, 259
21. 4–5: 255 n.,
    256
21. 4 ff.: 256 and n.
21. 4: 240
21. 6: 230, 256,
    261, 352
21. 7: 240, 256
22: 82 n.
22. 7: 230
22. 9–10: 352
23. 8: 255
27. 4: 340 n.
28. 1: 255
28. 6: 240, 252 n.,
    259
29. 9–11: 258

30: 178, 180
30. 5: 252 n.
30. 6–8: 257 n.
30. 10 f.: 98 n.
Pelop.-Marc./Synk.
    1: 177, 180

Marius
1. 3–4: 242
2: 251, 254, 352
2. 1: 50, 252, 253
2. 2: 252 n.
2. 3–4: 253
2. 4: 247, 341 n.
3. 1: 252, 253
4. 1: 343 n.
4. 6: 328
4. 7: 328
5. 7–9: 343 n.
6: 321 n.
6. 3: 253
6. 4: 110
8. 3: 253
8. 5: 252 n.
8. 6: 253
9. 1: 345
9. 4: 329 n., 340 n.
14. 14: 340 n.
17. 5: 212 n.
23. 5: 253
25. 8: 243 n.
26. 3: 189 n.
26. 8: 189 n.
27. 2: 213 n.
28–30: 337
28: 80 n., 82 n., 85
28. 1–2: 253
28. 1: 341 n., 344
28. 6: 253, 339 n.
28. 7: 338, 345
28. 8: 253
29: 337 n.
29. 5: 252 n.
29. 6: 252
29. 7: 338, 340 n.
29. 9: 338
29. 11: 338
29. 12: 56 n., 114,
    280
30: 344
30. 1: 340 n.,
    341 n.
30. 2: 338, 340 n.
30. 4: 344 n.

30. 5: 338
31. 2: 338
31. 3: 341
32. 2: 248, 253
34. 2: 329 n.
34. 3: 253
34. 4: 232 n., 262
34. 5–6: 251
34. 5: 252
34. 6: 253, 340 n.,
    341 n.
35. 1: 233 n.
35. 2: 344 n.
41. 2: 340 n.
42. 7: 253
45: 253
45. 4–12: 341 n.
45. 9: 252 n.
45. 10–46. 5: 242
45. 10–12: 251
45. 10: 251 n.
46. 5: 253
46. 6: 340 n.
85. 32: 252

Nicias
1. 1: 168
1. 2: 27
6. 1: 233 n.
8. 6: 232
11: 204
11. 2: 110, 191 n.
11. 10: 201
13. 1–5: 203
21. 1: 213 n.
28. 4: 110

Nicias/Crassus/Synk
1. 4: 232 n., 243
2. 3: 306
4. 2: 306

non posse suauiter
viv.
1102 B: 212

Numa
1. 3: 247 n.
2. 3: 233 n.
2. 5: 233 n.
3: 82 n.
3. 7: 85 n.
4: 358 n.
7. 10–11: 230 n.
8. 10: 212 n.
8. 20: 230 n.

8. 247 n.
9. 15: 107, 278
10. 4: 258 n.
12: 359 n.
12. 13: 107, 278
13. 9–10: 230 and
    n.
19. 7: 112
22.5: 247 n.
22 12: 258 n.

Numa/Lycurgus/Synk
see *Lyc.*

Otho: 116–17
3. 3: 340 n.
5. 1: 343 n.
5. 8: 213 n.
6: 116
14. 2: 50

Pelopidas
1. 1: 10
3. 6–7: 259
4. 1–2: 245
15–17: 87 n.
21. 3: 258
21. 5–6: 239, 258
31. 3–4: 258
34. 1: 213 n.

Pericles
1–2: 143 n.
1. 1: 98 n.
1. 2: 26 n.
2. 5: 108, 155,
    160 n., 251 n.,
    268 n., 279 n.
3. 5–7: 267 n.
3. 5: 159
4–6. 1: 246
4–6: 157, 161
4. 3: 159
4. 5: 267 n.
4. 6: 164 n.
5. 1: 164 n., 246
5. 2: 162
5. 3: 261, 267 n.
6. 1: 160 n., 258 n.
7: 77 n., 85
7. 1: 159
7. 2: 197
7. 3: 159
7. 3–5: 197
7. 7: 267 n.
7. 8: 233 n., 267 n.

8: 161
8. 1–4: 160 n.
8. 1: 164 n.
8. 2: 267 n.
8. 3–4: 158
8. 4: 267 n.
9: 85
9. 1: 84 n.
9. 2: 6 n.
9–14: 161
9–10: 157
9: 85
9. 1: 84, 159,
    251 n.
9. 5: 109
10. 7: 164 n., 246
11: 77 n.
11–14: 157
11. 2–3: 233 n.
11. 3: 246
12–13: 69, 246
12–14: 25 n.
12. 1: 246
13: 77 n., 250
13. 3: 164 n.
13. 5: 246
13. 7: 267 n.
13. 8–10: 267 n.
13. 16: 261 n.
14. 2–15. 3: 85
14. 2: 164 n.
15: 161
15. 1–2: 233
15. 1: 161, 233 n.
15. 2–3: 160 n.
15. 2: 161, 267 n.
15. 3: 160 n.
16. 1: 159
16. 3: 160 n.
16. 7: 164 n.
17: 161
17. 1: 164 n.
17. 4: 164 n.
18: 160 n.
18. 2: 161 n.
19. 3: 160 n.
20. 3–4: 160 n.
20. 3: 161 n.,
    233 n.
21: 160 n.
21. 1: 161 n.
22. 4: 109, 279 n.
24. 7: 267 n.

24. 9–10: 267 n.
24. 12: 267 n.
26. 1: 261 n.
27. 2: 161 n.
27. 4: 267 n.
28. 3: 16 n.
28. 7: 164 n.,
    267 n.
29–35: 157–8
29. 8: 246
31. 1: 164 n., 246
33: 159, 161
33. 6: 162 n.
34. 1: 161–2
34. 5: 161, 162
35. 1: 162 n.
35. 2: 160 n.
35. 4: 162 n.
35. 5: 267 n.
36. 6–9: 160 n.
36. 8: 164 n.
37. 1: 162 and n.
38: 160
38. 1: 164 n.
38. 2: 9 n., 83 n.,
    193 n., 246,
    267 n.
38. 4: 160 n.,
    194 n.
39. 1: 164 n.
39. 4: 159

Pericles/Fabius/Synk
1. 4: 233
3. 7: 246

Philopoemen
1. 2–5: 245
2 fin.: 170 n.
3: 362
4. 6–8: 245
20: 11
ad fin.: 168

Phocion
1. 4: 11 n.
3. 2: 244, 296 n.
3. 3: 351 n.
3. 9: 251 n.
29. 1: 110
32. 3: 233 n.
34. 6: 233 n.

Pompeius
1. 3–4: 323 n.
2. 1: 323 n.

2. 2–4: 230 n.
2. 5–10: 147 n.
2. 10: 135 n., 139
2. 12: 262
4. 7: 343 n.
4. 8: 339 n.
6. 1: 343
8. 5: 135 n.
8. 6–7: 143 n.
8. 7: 142 n., 243 n.
9. 3–4: 213 n.
9. 3: 340 n.
10. 2: 343 n.
10. 3–5: 144 n.
10. 7–9: 282, 289 n.
10. 8: 243 n.
10. 10–14: 144 n.
12. 1–3: 318 n.
12. 4–5: 318 n.
13. 2–3: 135 n.
13. 9: 135 n.
13. 10–11: 352
14. 4: 318 n.
14. 11: 323 n.,
    344 n.
15. 1: 323 n.,
    347 n.
16. 3: 340 n.
16. 8: 109, 278, 283
17. 2: 142 n.
18. 3: 144 n.
19. 8: 135 n.
20. 1: 345 n.
20. 2: 142 n.
20. 6–8: 144 n.
20. 8: 135 n.
21. 3: 136 n.,
    318 n.
21. 5–7: 135 n.,
    345 n.
21. 7–8: 323 n.
21. 7: 328
21. 8: 136 n.
22. 1–3: 318 n.
22. 2: 347 n.
22. 3–4: 323 n.
22. 3: 323, 328,
    344 n.
22. 4: 135 n.
22. 9: 323 n.
23. 1–2: 318 n.
23. 3–6: 140
25. 3: 340 n.

25. 7–13: 323 n.
25. 7: 233 n.,
    329 n., 340 n.
25. 8: 327 n.
26. 1: 135 n.
27. 3: 135 n.
27. 6–7: 144 n.
28: 343 n.
28. 5–7: 144 n.
28. 5: 144 n.
29: 144 n.
29. 5: 144 n.
30. 3–4: 339 n.,
    340 n.
30. 4: 323 n.
30. 7–8: 341 n.
30. 8: 144 n.
31. 8–13: 269
31. 10: 213 n.
33. 5: 135 n.
34. 7–8: 230 n.
36. 3: 135 n.
38. 1: 144 n.
38. 4–5: 230 n.
39: 343 n.
39. 2: 135 n.
39. 4–6: 144 n.
40: 282
40. 2: 244 n.
40. 6: 144 n.
40. 8–9: 135 n.,
    144 n.
41. 2: 142 n.
41. 4: 136 n.
42. 4: 135 n.
42. 9–11: 243 n.
42. 12: 136 n.
42. 13: 296 n.
43. 1–3: 345 n.
43. 1: 340 n.
43. 3: 135 n.
43. 5: 341
44: 283
44. 4–5: 144 n.
45: 136 n.
46. 1–4: 138,
    230 n., 323 n.
46. 2: 136 n.
46. 3–4: 323 n.
46. 3: 144 n.
46. 5–6: 262 n.
46. 5: 329 n.
46. 7: 137, 323 n.

46. 8: 137, 138–9
47–8: 270
47. 1: 323 n.
47. 3–4: 324 n.
47. 4: 270 n.,
   324 n.
47. 5: 271 n.,
   323 n., 345 n.
47. 6–8: 271 and
   n., 272 n.
47. 6–7: 139
47. 8: 139, 144 n.
47. 9: 324 n.
47. 10: 129
48: 137
48: 137, 262, 271
48. 1: 345 n.
48. 2: 272 n.,
   345 n.
48. 3: 323 n.
48. 8: 139
48. 9–12: 129 n.,
   139
48. 9: 127, 137,
   323 n.
49: 139 n.
49. 3–6: 329 n.
49. 3: 139, 340 n.
49. 4: 139
49. 6: 269, 314,
   323 n.
49. 11: 329 n.
49. 14: 141, 144 n.,
   243
50: 140, 343 n.
50. 3: 136 n.
51: 147 n.
51. 1–3: 147 n.
51. 1–2: 324 n.
51. 1: 135, 140–1,
   141, 323 n.
51. 2: 127 n., 130,
   142 n., 152 n.,
   154, 276 n.
51. 4–5: 277 n.
52. 2: 329 n.
52. 4: 126
52. 5: 243 and n.
53. 1: 139
53. 2: 144 n.
53. 6: 323 n.
53. 8–10: 136 n.,

324 n.
53. 9–10: 141,
   144 n., 325 n.
53. 9: 135
53. 10: 144 n.
54: 139 n., 277 n.
54. 2: 135, 140
54. 3: 140, 324 n.,
   325 n.
54. 4: 139
54. 5: 139, 340 n.
54. 8: 139 n.
54. 9: 139
55. 3–4: 139
55. 6–10: 144 n.
55. 6–11: 286 n.
55. 12: 139 n.
57. 5–6: 135
57. 5: 324 n.
57. 6: 135 n.,
   136 n., 323 n.
57. 6–9: 141 n.
57. 7–8: 139
57. 7: 134, 145–6
58–9: 151, 277 n.
58. 2: 287 n.
58. 4: 323 n.
58. 5: 146
58. 6: 127 n., 130,
   152 n., 154,
   276 n., 299 n.
58. 8: 276 n.
58. 9: 152, 154 n.
58. 10: 152 n., 154
59. 1–2: 323 n.
59. 1: 152, 154
59. 2: 151
59. 3–4: 152
59. 3: 329 n.
60. 1–2: 153 n.
60. 2 ff.: 153 n.
60. 6: 139
60. 6. 8: 139,
   141 n.
61: 140
61. 1: 139 n.
61. 2: 286 n.
61. 4–5: 139–40
61. 6–7: 141 n.
62: 140
62. 1: 128
62. 2: 128

63. 1–2: 141 n.
63. 2: 296 n.
63. 3–4: 141 n.
64: 141 n.
64. 1: 141 n.
64. 3: 141
64. 5: 129 n.
65. 3: 148
65. 6–7: 141
66. 1: 141
66. 4: 142 n.
66. 6: 141–2
67. 2: 141
67. 4–5: 141
67. 7–10: 142,
   144 n., 149
68–73: 277 n.
68. 7: 142
69. 4–5: 142
69. 7: 286 n.
70: 142, 144 n.,
   351 n.
71. 7–8
72. 1: 142
72. 5–6: 142
73. 8: 136 n.
73. 11: 144 n.
74. 5–6: 136 n.
75. 1–2: 136 n.
75. 4–5: 243 n.
75. 5: 136 n.
77–80: 286 n.
77: 283
78–80: 136 n.
See also *Ages.*/
   Pomp./*Synk*

Poplicola [*Publicola*]
1. 1: 168
2. 1: 240 n.
8. 6: 25 n.
9: 363
10. 3: 213 n.
14. 3–6: 112
15: 358 n.
15. 2: 25 n.
15. 3–6: 112,
   232 n.
15. 4: 256
18. 3: 343 n.
19. 10: 25 n.
21: 87 n.
23. 6: 25 n.
24. 1: 110

24. 3: 112
praecepta coniugalia:
118
138 A–146 A: 56
138 A: 118
141 A: 188
141 F: 251 n.
144 A: 198 n.
145 A: 52 n.

*praecepta rei publicae
gerendae*: 120,
235
794 D:183
798 C: 77 n.
798 C–822 E: 77 n.
799 C: 205 n.
800 F: 182
802 D: 148 n.
803 B: 66 n.
804 E: 202
805 A: 97
805 E–F: 262
805 F: 103 n.
807 D: 77 n.
806 A: 183
808 A: 185
809 B: 77 n.
809 E: 183
810 B: 188
811 A: 183
811 B–C: 52
811 C: 103
814 C: 77 n.,
170 n.
815 D: 120
816 E: 185
818 D: 183
819 F–820 F: 240 n.
820 B: 230 n.
820 E: 183
821 F: 148 n.
822 Aff.: 77 n.
822 C–823 E: 148
822 E: 77 n.
823 E: 213 n.
824 E: 49 n.
825 F: 240 n.

Publicola, see
Poplicola
Pyrrhus
1. 4: 245, 253
7. 3: 249 n.

8. 2: 249 n.
8. 3: 245
8. 6: 245
12. 2–12: 249 n.
13: 78
13. 1: 249
13. 4: 250
13. 6–11: 250 n.
14. 6: 250
16. 7: 250
17. 7: 249
17. 10: 250
19. 6–7: 250
20. 1: 250, 251
20. 4: 251
20. 6–7: 250
20. 11: 251
21. 1–5: 251
21. 11: 251
21. 13: 249
26. 1–2: 249

quaestiones convivales:
121, 185, 235,
236
1. 613D: 238 n.
1. 2. 615 EF: 188
1.5.623 A–D: 238 n.
1. 5. 623 C: 237
2. 1. 629 F: 238 n.
2. 1. 630 F: 98 n.
2. 1. 632 A: 121
2. 1. 632 F: 98 n.
2. 3. 636 E- 638:
238 n.
2. 3. 637 A: 237 n.
3. 5. 651 F: 238 n.
3. 5. 652 B: 238 n.
3. 7. 655 F: 98 n.
4. 3. 666 D–667 A:
238n
4. 4. 668 B–C:
231 n.
5. 2. 674 F: 121
5. 3. 677 B: 237
5. 5. 678 C: 51
5. 7. 680 C–F
5. 10. 684 E: 238 n.
6. 3. 673 D: 185
6–7. 693 F: 112
7. 1. 697 E: 251 n.
7. 1. 698 E: 238 n.
7. 2. 700 E: 106
7. 2. 701A: 238 n.

7. 4. 702 D–
7. 4. 702E: 238 n.
704 B: 238
7. 4. 702 D: 238
7. 6. 707 C: 238 n.
7. 10. 714 E: 213 n.
8. 1. 717 C: 213 n.
8.1.717 D–E: 238 n.
8.2.719 A–C: 238 n.
8. 4. 724 D: 212 n.
8. 6.726 D–
727 A: 230 n.
8. 7–8: 236
8. 7. 726 B: 50 n.,
236
8. 7. 727 D– E: 236
8. 7. 728 B: 236
8. 10. 734 D: 121,
230 n.
9. 1. 737 BC 182
quaestiones Graecae
9. 292 F: 53
quaestiones Romanae:
122, 176, 183 n.,
229
5. 264 F: 230 n.
7. 265 D: 6 n.
21. 268 F: 244 n.
28. 271 C: 122
37. 273 D: 230 n.
40: 230 n.
40. 274 C: 230 n.
40. 274 D–E: 231,
242 n.
42. 275 B: 363 n.
49. 276 C: 363 n.
50. 276 E: 112, 122
54. 277 D: 230 n.
64, 279d: 238
66. 280 A–B: 230 n.
66. 280 A: 182–3
70. 280 E: 363 n.
75. 281 F: 238
79. 283 A: 183
81. 283 C: 342 n.
83. 283 F– 284
C: 258 n.
92. 286 B: 363 n.

Romulus
2 ff. 303 n.
6: 362
8. 9: 212 n.
12. 3: 244 n.

13. 7: 233 n.
15. 3: 236
15. 4: 230 n.
15. 7: 112, 279 n.
17. 3: 98 n.
21. 1: 107, 278
27. 8–9: 233 n.
28: 358 n.
35. 7: 108

Sertorius
1. 11: 168, 171,
    177
5. 5: 87 n.
10: 84, 193 n.
10. 5–7: 9, 243 n.,
    260 n.
11: 59 n.
24. 5: 232 n.
25. 2: 343 n.

Solon
3. 6–6. 7: 245
5: 81 n.
6: 81 n.
15: 77 n.
27: 61
28: 81 n.
29. 7: 212 n.
32. 2: 104

Sulla
1. 1: 342 n.
1. 5: 351 n.
2. 2–7: 147 n.
2. 3–4: 212 n.
6. 14–15: 243
7. 2: 251
9. 22–3: 83 n.
12. 5–14: 232 n.
12. 7: 258 n.
12. 8–14: 345
12. 9–14: 231, 264,
    321
12. 12–14: 345 n.
13. 4: 77 n.
21. 8: 113
22. 1: 340 n.
25. 4–5: 232 n.
30. 5–6: 340 n.
30. 5: 83, 193 n.
30. 6: 10, 243
    and n., 260 n.
35. 3: 258 n.

36. 1: 212 n.
40(1). 2–7: 321
see also *Lysander/
    Sulla/Synk*
Table Talk
see *quaestiones
    conviviales*
Themistocles
1. 1: 108
2. 3: 246
2. 5: 261 n.
2. 7: 234 n., 246
4. 5: 233
7. 6: 152 n.
10. 1: 212 n.
13. 3: 258
18. 4: 198 n.
19: 202
19. 5: 232 n.
32. 4: 16 n., 212 n.
Theseus
1: 61, 169
1. 1: 113
1. 2: 111 n.
1. 3–4: 212 n.
1. 3: 168
1. 4: 107, 111 n.,
    278, 279 n., 313 n.
2. 3: 212 n.
15. 2: 212 n.
16. 3–4: 212 n.
18. 3: 102–3
24–5: 233 n.
25: 80 n.
27. 8: 109
32. 1–2: 233 n.
36. 2: 109
Timoleon
1. 1: 26 n.
4. 5: 185
4. 6: 13 n.
6. 1: 245, 249
13. 10: 107, 278,
    280 n., 310
26. 1: 185
30. 4: 186
33. 4: 107, 278
36. 6: 185–6
37: 80 n.
37. 7: 189
see also *Aemilius/
    Timoleon/Synk*

Titus
see *Flamininus*

POLYAENUS
Strat. 5. 12. 1: 185

POLYBIOS
2. 56–63: 16 n.
2. 56. 1: 16
3. 86–7: 350 n.
5. 33.2: 14
6. 10. 13–14: 330 n.
6. 11–18: 329 n.
6. 17: 329
6. 43–58: 329 n.,
    330 n.
6. 51. 5: 330 n.
8. 5: 9 n.
8. 6. 6.: 257
9. 10: 231 n., 352 n.
9. 22–23: 83 n.
10. 2. 8–13: 11 n.
10. 21: 71 n.
10. 21. 4: 10
10. 21. 5: 173
10. 21. 8: 10
12. 23. 4: 186
18. 10. 11–12: 341 n.
18. 39. 4: 341 n.
31. 24. 1: 241
31. 24. 6–7: 241
31. 25–30: 240–1
31. 25. 4: 231
31. 25. 5a: 231
31. 25. 8: 241
31. 28, 10: 241
31. 29. 1: 248 n.
31. 29. 8–12: 241

POSIDONIUS
FGrHist 87,
    f. 42 a: 256 n.
f. 211c: 231 n.

PSEUDO-ANDOCIDES
4: 200 n., 200, 201,
    205
4. 13: 198
4. 15: 199
4. 17: 205
4. 30: 200

QUINTILIAN
Inst. Or.,
10. 1. 128: 310 n.

10. 3. 31: 308 n.
10. 6. 4: 292 n.

SALLUST AND
   PSEUDOSALL
ad Caes. 2. 5.
   1: 347 n.
BC 11. 5–7: 231
   37–8: 347 n.
BJ 41: 347 n.
   63. 3: 251
   65. 5: 348 n.
   41: 347 n.
   73. 6–7: 347 n.
Hist. 1. 6–13M: 347 n.
SATYRUS
Apud. Ath. 534D:
   192 n., 200
SENECA THE ELDER,
   Suasoriae, 1.
   7: 295 n.
SERVIUS
ad Aen. 1. 368: 181 n.
   7. 612: 364 n.
SIG³559, l. 36: 103 n.
   694, l. 46: 103 n.
   801d: 102 n.
   817: 102 n.
   821a: 102 n.
   822: 121
   825a–c: 104 n.
   829a: 835a: 100n.
      50, 100 n.
   835b: 100 n., 110 n.
   843: 103 n.
   846: 104 n.
   829a: 50, 100 n.
   835a: 100 n.
   835b: 101 n.
SOPHOCLES
Anti., 666–7: 221
OC, 1381 ff.: 220
OT, 4–5: 237
STRABO
   11. 523: 295 n.

17. 790: 305 n.
SUDA
   Z. 73: 252 n.
SUETONIUS
de gramm. et rhet. 27.
   1: 23 n.
poet. 6. 1: 181 n.
   6. 3: 181 n.
   rhet. 3: 182 n.
Div. Iul. 128 n.
   1. 2: 327 n.
   4: 129 n.
   4. 2: 243 n.
   6. 2: 327 n.
   7–8: 129 n.
   11: 320 n.
   20. 4: 272 n.
   21: 272 n.
   29. 1: 287 n.
   30. 4: 287 n.
   31–2: 287 n.
   36: 287 n.
   44. 2–3: 287 n.
   53: 289 n.
   56. 6: 297 n.
   78–9: 274 n.
   80. 3: 287 n.
Div. Aug. 7.
   1: 297 n.
Tiberius 4. 1: 291 n.

SYNCELLUS
   349B See Eusebius

TACITUS
Ann.
   4. 32–3: 348 n.
   4. 34: 297 n.
   6. 51: 84 n.
Dial. 36. 3: 348 n.
Hist. 1. 1: 123
THEOCRITUS
   17. 53 ff.: 211 n.
THEOPOMPUS
   FGrHist 115

   T31: 14
   F100: 17
THEOPHRASTUS
   Fr. 146: 9 n.
THUCYDIDES 2. 13.
   1: 159
   2. 22. 1: 161 n.
   2. 43. 6: 164 n.
   2. 61. 3: 164 n.
   2. 62. 3: 164
   5. 43: 202
   5. 43. 2: 197 n.
   5. 52: 203
   6. 15. 4: 196
   8: 309 n.
TIMAEUS
   FGrH 566
   T 13: 186
   F 116: 185

VALERIUS MAXIMUS
   16. 11: 294 n.,
   2. 2. 2. 3: 251
   5. 10. 2: 189 n.
VELLEIUS PATERCULUS
   1. 10. 3–5: 189 n.
   2. 33. 4: 262
   2. 41. 1–2: 11 n.
   2. 42. 3: 128
   2. 43. 4: 320 n.
VERGIL
   Aen. 6. 818–
      47: 182 n.
   6. 855–9: 182 n.

VOLUMNIUS
   Peter *HRR*: 293 n.

XENOPHON
   Anab. 1. 9: 5 n.
   2. 6: 5 n.
   Memorabilia 3. 2.
      2: 210

ZONARAS, 9. 29: 181 n.

GENERAL INDEX

Abuletes 223
Academy 49, 53
Acanthians 90
Achaea 52
Achilles 30, 79, 209, 211, 214, 215, 217, 222, 224
Acilius 345
Actium 148, 149, 295
Adrastus 219
Aegospotami 194
Aelian 80
Aemilius Lepidus, see Lepidus
Aemilius Paullus (cons. 168 B.C.) 168, 187–90, 240–1, 321, 329, 342, 344, 345
Aemilius Paullus (cons. 216 B.C.) 349
Aemilius Scaurus 20
Affortunati, M., and Scardigli, B. 30
Africa 114
Agamemnon 210–11
Agatharchus 205, 207
Agathocles 182
Agesilaus 12, 62, 92–4
Agis 59 n. 171, 173, 176, 334, 339
Agricola 178
Agrippa, M. 178
Albinus, Decius Brutus 275, 276, 304, 310
Alcaeus 2, 71
Alcibiades 60, 64, 68, 71, 80, 85, 88, 91, 171, 191–206, 245, 247, 248, 361
Alesia 132
Alexander the Great 14–15, 18, 30, 57, 58, 60, 67, 70, 73, 168, 170, 172, 175, 209–28, 230 n.
Alexandria 51, 65, 295
Alfieri, N. 121
Alienus, Caecina 116
Amisos 260
Ammon 92
Ammonius 49
Amphictyons 100, 102, 104, 106, 121
Amphidius 359
Amyot, translator 47
Anaxagoras 161

Anaxarchus 220–1
Ancus, Marcius 193
Andocides 191
Antigoneia 104
Antigonus of Carystus 63–4
Antigonos Monophthalmos 173
Antiochus of Ascalon 262, 263
Antiochus Philopappus, C. Julius 119
Antiochus IV of Commagene 102
Antiphon 191, 194–5, 207
Antium 362, 367
Antony orator 20, 21, 80
Antony 69, 105, 176, 178, 179, 180, 182, 212, 226, 231, 243, 273, 298, 346
  Plutarch's adaptation of source material 130–2, 148–9, 150, 152–4
  Plutarch's method of work on 272–3, 276, 297–8, 300, 315
Anytus 195
Aphrodite 103
Apollo 53, 101, 102, 103, 104, 105, 106, 185
Apollonius of Rhodos 289
Apollonius of Tyana 54
Appian 22, 133 n., 140, 146, 271 n., 276, 286–7, 288, 290, 291, 306
  and Roman politics 311, 315, 316, 318, 320, 325, 332, 330–1, 333, 335–8, 343, 344, 346
Appius Claudius the Censor 182
Appius Claudius 134, 328
Aratus 16, 20, 66 n., 73, 76, 104, 167, 173, 174
Archestratus 206, 207
Archias see Licinius
Archidamus 159
Archilochus 2, 71
Archimedes 239, 257
Argos 77, 201
Aristides, rhetor 68 n., 74
Aristides the Just 3, 74, 85, 87, 88, 171, 188, 341
Aristobulus 15
Aristocrates 396
Aristophanes 3–4, 219

Aristophon (Aglaophon) 206
Aristotimus, T. Flavius 106
Aristotle 6–7, 10, 12, 18, 61, 70, 81–2, 85, 86, 136, 160, 214, 234, 365
Aristocrates of Sparta 173
Aristoxenus 61–2, 65
Armenia 113
Arpinum 252
Arrian 186–7, 217, 220–1
Artaxerxes II 6, 68
Artemidorus 290–1
Artemis 102
Artemisium 193
Asclepius 54
Asia 93, 98, 113, 114, 232, 260
Asinius Pollio, C., *see* Pollio
Aspasia 267
Athenaeus 18, 195, 200, 201, 206
Athens 49, 53, 59, 60, 78, 91, 119, 164, 170, 194, 197, 215, 232, 241, 246, 260, 261, 297, 300
Athos 224
Attica 161
Atticus 20
Attius 359
Aufidius 359
Augustus (Octavian) 57, 64, 70–1, 98, 102, 148, 149, 166, 182, 269, 316, 346
Aurelia 131
Autobulus 119
Automatia 185
Averni 300
Avidius, *see* Nigrinus; Quietus

Babylon 218, 223
Badian, E. 335, 336–7
Bagoas 223
Bedriacum 50
Bernstein, A. H. 335
Bibulus Calpurnius, L. 23, 284, 292, 307
Bibulus Calpurnius, M. 271, 272
Bithynia 98
Boeotia 48, 49
Bona Dea affair 130–1, 136 n., 138, 299
Bosworth, A. B. 30
Bowersock, G. W. 116, 118, 120, 122
Brasidas 90
Brenk, F. 30
Briareos 257
Brundisium 129, 140, 346

Brutus Albinus, Decius, *see* Albinus
Brutus, Marcus (cons. 509 B.C.) 366, 367
Brutus, Marcus 23, 60, 80, 178, 243, 244
  Plutarch's method of work on 272, 271–6, 280, 291, 292, 293, 296, 297, 305, 315, 319, 329, 331, 339
Bucephalas 214, 222
Byzantium 86

Caecina, *see* Alienus
Caesar, C. Julius 23, 24, 58, 59 n., 60, 226, 328
  and Hellenic culture 242–3
  Plutarch's adaptation of source material 126, 128–35, 138–42, 145–7, 151–2
  Plutarch's method of work on 270–6, 284, 289–91, 300, 306, 313-14
  in Roman politics: Plutarch's view 319–22, 327–8, 332, 340
Calanus 223
Callias 198, 199
Callicratidas 91, 94
Callimachus 62
Callisthenes 15, 220–1
Calpurnia 295
Cambyses 3
Camillus 362
Cannae 163
Capitolium 291
Carmania 222
Carthage 180, 353
Cassander 77
Cassius Dio, *see* Dio Cassius
Cassius Longinus, C. 24, 130, 150, 182, 274, 275, 290, 291, 293, 319, 321, 329, 331, 340
Catilina 183, 296
Catilinarians 126, 299, 340
Cato the Elder 66, 73, 181, 230, 231, 321, 341, 352
Cato the Younger 63, 66, 76, 243–4, 271, 273 n., 283, 289, 316, 322, 331
  Plutarch's adaptation of source material 126, 127, 129, 134, 137, 144–5, 147
Catullus 267
Catulus, the Elder 253
Catulus, the Younger 263

Cerri, G., *see* Gentili
Chaeronaea 48, 52, 74, 81, 94, 103,
 168, 170, 240, 260
Chamaeleon 62
Chares 15
Churchill, Sir Winston 88
Chilver, G. E. F. 117
Chios 98, 201
Cicero, M. Tullius 17, 19, 20–1, 57 n.,
 58, 59, 73, 158, 181, 182, 242, 340,
 347, 348
 and Hellenic culture 242, 249, 263
 Plutarch's adaptation of source
 material 129, 136–8
 Plutarch's method of work on 268–
 70, 272, 273 n., 282, 296–8, 311–
 16
Cicero, Q. 310
Cilento, V. 81, 83
Cilicia 269
Cimon 66, 85, 90, 157, 161, 171, 259,
 260–1, 263, 339
Cinna the poet 321
Cinna, L. Cornelius 87, 322, 332,
 340
Cincinnatus 182
Claudius, emperor 98, 102
Clea 53, 65, 119, 122, 123
Cleitarchus 15
Cleitus 215, 219, 220, 221
Clemens 74
Cleomenes III 171, 173, 176, 334, 339
Cleopatra 30, 69, 73, 76, 147, 148–50,
 267, 298
Clinias 193
Clodius 127, 130–1, 136–9, 183, 272,
 282, 293, 314, 315, 324
Cominius 364
Considius 271
Corinth 50, 52, 203, 231 n.
Coriolanus (C. Marcius) 29, 79, 80, 87,
 193, 194, 245, 247–9, 264, 357–
 72
 womenfolk 359, 368
Corioli 360, 363
Cornelia 139, 140
Cornelius Nepos 7, 10, 17, 21, 29, 63,
 86, 174, 177–84, 186, 192
Cornelius Lentulus 343 n.
Cornelius Pulcher 120
Crassus orator 21, 180, 183
Crassus, M. Licinius 30, 59, 126, 145,
 243, 262, 322–4, 327, 328, 331

Plutarch's method of work on 268–
 72, 282, 289, 294, 310, 313-14,
 317–18
Crates of Thebes 65
Creon 221, 224
Croesus 60, 223 n.
Ctesias of Cnidos 6, 68
Cuff, P. J. 336
cura annonae 140, 269, 314
Curio 151–2, 152 n., 153, 154, 298
Curtius Rufus 15
Cyllus 121
Cyprus 137
Cyrene 260
Cyrus 31, 223, 227
Cyzicus 115, 201

Daiphantus 65, 167
Damon 159
Darius 215, 218, 227
de cohibenda ira, dated 96–9
De Lacy, P. 212–13, 225
de tranquillitate, dated 96–9
Deinon of Colophon 6, 15, 68
Delium 198, 206
Dellius, Q. 24, 294–5, 304, 309
Delphi 50, 53, 73, 90, 94, 100–6, 185,
 186
Demaratus 222, 225
Demetrius Polyorcetes 57, 80, 171,
 173, 175, 184, 212, 225, 226, 361
Demetrius of Antioch 144, 282
Demetrius of Phaleron 8
Demosthenes 8, 20, 58, 66, 171, 174,
 175, 191, 202, 205, 245
Diadochi 170, 173, 216
Dike 220
Dio Cassius 22, 272, 286–7, 294 n.,
 301–3, 308, 315, 316, 325, 330,
 331, 343, 344
 and Roman politics 330–1, 344, 346
Dio of Prusa 54, 57, 69
Diodorus 15, 209, 224
Diogenes Laertius 18, 72, 162
Diogenianus 119
Diomedes 201, 211
Dion 80, 171, 245, 280, 339
Dionysius I and II 13, 212, 213
Dionysius of Halicarnassus 21–2, 28,
 62 n., 67, 248–50, 266, 302–3, 308,
 330, 357, 372
 on Coriolanus 358–72
Dionysus 102, 215–17, 219–20, 222–4

Dioscuri 363
Dippel, R. 90 n.
Dolabella 129, 131
Domitian 29, 50, 95, 102, 112, 120, 123
Domitius Ahenobarbus 183
Drusus Livius, M. the Elder 332
Drusus Livius, M. the Younger 182, 332
Duris of Samos 8, 13, 15
Dyrrhachium 141

Egypt 51, 53, 105
Empylus of Rhodes 23, 284, 292
England 72
Ennius 267
Epaminondas 3, 58, 171, 175, 183, 213
Ephesus 91
Ephorus of Cyme 13–14, 15, 27, 69, 90, 170
Epicadas 23
Epictetus 54
Epicurus 250
Epitherses Aemilianus 118
Erbse, H. 156
Eros divinity 51, 204
Eros friend of Fundanus 99
Euagoras 62
Eumenes of Cardia 59, 171, 173, 174
Euphrates 113
Euripides 64, 216, 300
Eurycles, Julius 56
Eurymedon 170
Eusebius 100, 106
Euthydemus 106

Fabius Maximus, Q. 89, 157–64, 188, 239, 255, 256, 339, 349–51
Fabricius 183, 250–1, 253
Falco, Roscius Pompeius 56
Favonius 146 n.
Favorinus 121, 122
Flacelière, R. 112, 117
Flamininus, T. ('Titus') 172, 231 n., 240, 245, 252, 259, 324, 341, 345
Flaminius, C. 89, 162, 182
Flavian 50
Florus, *see* Mestrius Florus
Forster, E. M. 351
Fossae Cluiliae 367
Frazier, F. 29
Frederick the Great of Prussia 47
Fronto 181

Fulvia 148, 298
Fulvius Flaccus 334
Fundanus, C. Minicius 96, 97, 98, 99

Gabba, E. 336, 337
Gabinius 315
Galatia 98
Galaxium 101
Galba 65, 97
Galenus 74
Garcia Moreno, L. A. 30
Gaugamela 218
Gaul 126, 140, 141, 324
Geiger, J. 29, 30, 281
Gentili, B., and Cerri, G. 27
Georgiadou, A. 30
Glaucia 337
Goethe 48
Gomme, A. W. 84, 339
Gould, J. 214 n.
Gracchus, G. 73, 77, 171, 176, 178, 180, 332, 334, 340, 344, 349
Gracchus, Ti. 59, 176, 178, 331–2, 333, 335, 343, 344
Granicus 219
Groag, E. 114, 116, 121
Gylippus 91–2, 94

Hadrian 53, 57, 95, 100–6, 113, 184
Hagnon 223
Haliartus 93
Halliwell, S. 214
Hannibal 11, 157, 159, 162
Hardy, E. G. 117
Harpalus 77, 218
Hector 211
Helen 210
Heliodorus 228 n.
Henna 254
Hephaestion 223, 224
Heracles 30, 65, 220, 224
Heraclitus 71, 84 n.
Herculanus, C. Julius Eurycles 121–2
Herennius, Gaius, 343
Herennius, Lucius, *see* Saturninus
Hermippus of Smyrna 8, 62, 221
Hermolaius 221
Herodotus 3, 60, 68, 71, 170, 227, 311
Hesiod 2, 55
Hesychius 62
Hieronymus of Cardia 16, 172, 173–4
Hillard, T. W. 312–13, 316, 317
Hipparete 198, 199

Hipponicus 198
Hirtius 182
Homer 2, 71, 210–11, 214, 215, 217, 218
Horace 70, 73, 326
Horatius Cocles 183
Hortensius 263
Humboldt, W. von 48
Hydra 250
Hyperbolus 197, 201–2
Hypereides 20

India 222
Ion of Chios 2, 71, 267
Ionia 71–2
Iris 220
Isidorus of Damascus 74
Isis 30
Isocrates 5, 13, 17, 62, 71 n., 86, 191

Jones, C. P. 29, 169, 176–7, 185, 186, 187, 188, 351
Josephus, Flavius 116, 310
Julia 129, 139, 140, 146 n., 324, 325
Julius Caesar, *see* Caesar, C. Julius
Julius Euricles 56
Justinus 15
Julius Laco 116

Kabeira 260
Kineas 250–1

Labienus 129 n.
Laelius, C. 182
Lamachus 77
Lentulus, Cn. Cornelius Marcellinus 151, 152 n., 152–3, 154
Leo, F. 7
Leonidas 56 n.
Lepidus, triumvir 182, 269, 273, 311
Leuctra 87
lex Gabinia 327
lex Licinia Pompeia 126
lex Trebonia 126
Libanius 74
Libya 92
Licinius Archias, A. 24
Livy 19, 21–2, 67, 81, 255, 267, 295, 296, 301–2, 308, 310, 349–50
Luce, T. J. 301, 303, 330
Lucian 80, 90
Lucilius 73

Lucullus, L. Licinius 21, 59, 113, 168, 178, 179, 180, 231, 240, 242, 245, 259–64, 269, 270, 271, 344
Lucullus, M. Licinius 182
Lupercalia affair 274 n., 275, 320, 326
Lutatius Catulus 20
Lycurgus of Sparta 61, 70, 169, 171
Lysander 30, 58, 68, 88, 90–4, 171, 212, 321 and *passim*
Lysias 191
Lysimachus 214, 218
Lyssa 220

Macedonia 73, 78, 187, 223
Macleod W. C. 214
Malli 222
Mantinea 104
Marathon 77, 87
Marcellus, C. Claudius, 130, 152 n., 153, 154
Marcellus, M. 89, 163, 180, 230, 239–40, 254–9, 264, 342, 352–3
Marcia 144
Marcius, C., *see* Coriolanus
Marcus Aurelius 74
'Marian faction' 320
Marius, C. 10, 29, 82, 85, 176, 242, 249, 251–4, 261, 264, 322, 338, 340, 341, 344, 345, 347-8
Martial 115
Martin, H. 160
Mazzarino, S. 26–7
Megara 104–5, 254
Menander 71
Menemachus of Sardis 77, 120
Mensching, E. 122
Messala Corvinus, M. Valerius 23, 293, 307
Mestrius Florus 50, 238
Metellus, Q. Caecilius tribune 128, 146, 342 n.
Metellus, Q. Caecilius Nepos 183, 327
Metellus Numidicus 56 n., 114, 118, 253, 338, 343
Metellus Pius 118
Metilius Marcus, tribune 158, 350
Meton 250
Mewaldt, J. 107, 278, 279
Meyer, E. 186
Miletus 77
Midias 205
Milo 315
Minicius, *see* Fundanus

400 *General Index*

Minucius, M. Rufus 89, 162, 163, 164,
    349, 350
Mithridates 24, 48, 260
Moesia 113
Moles, J. L. 315
Mommsen Th. 119, 357, 392 n.
Montaigne 47
Moralia 95, 175–6
Mossman, J. M. 29, 30
Munatius Rufus 23, 145, 283, 289
Mucius Scaevola 183
Mucius 343
Murena 183
Mytilene 24, 260

'Naevian meadow' 363
Narbo 132
Nasica, *see* Scipio Nasica Corculum
Nearchus 15
Nepos, *see* Cornelius Nepos
Nero 50, 102, 115, 119, 213
Nerva 167
Nicias 30, 66, 87, 171, 175, 201–3, 339
Nicias of Sicily 256
Nicolaus of Damascus 64–5, 70–1,
    283 n., 346
Nicomachus of Gerasa 54
Nicomedes 128, 147 n., 289
Niebuhr, G. B. 48
Nigrinus, Avidius 116, 235
Nikolaidis, A. G. 30
Numa 61, 88, 169,

Octavia 148, 149
Octavian, *see* Augustus
Octavius 253, 332
Odysseus 30, 211
Olympia 53, 207
Olympias 215–16
Olympus 295
Onesicritus 15, 211, 223 n., 226
Orchomenus 113
Oppius, C. 23, 282, 289, 304, 309
Osiris 30
Otho 65, 79
Oxyartes 223

Paccius 99, 235
Panaetius 241
Pansa 182
Paris 217
Parmenion 218
Patrae 56, 203, 207

Patroclus 224
Pausanias, king 92, 365
Pausanias, writer 65 n., 69
Peisistratus 159
Peleus 214
Pelling, C. B. R. 28, 30
Pelopidas 3, 60 n., 87, 88, 168, 171,
    175, 258, 259
Pentheus 220, 221, 224
Pericles 3, 29, 66, 69, 77, 84, 85, 157–
    64, 171, 196, 197, 206, 246, 339, 351
Peripatetics 7–12, 14, 52, 72, 86
Peritas 222
Perperna 343 n.
Persepolis 218
Persia 227
Peter, H. 357
Petraeus, L. Cassius 103, 104, 121
Phaeax 201–2
Phanias of Eresos 8
Pharnabazus 92
Pharsalus/Pharsalia 24, 141, 142, 144,
    149, 298
Phidias 189
Philip II of Macedon 14, 48, 64, 214,
    215
Philip V of Macedon 14, 341
Philip the Acarnanian 217, 224, 225
Philippi 60, 293, 298, 300
Philistus of Syracuse 4, 13
Philomela 236
Philopoemen 63, 171, 172, 173, 174,
    245, 362
Philostratus 170
Philotas 218, 219
Philoxenus 223
Phocion 8, 171
Phoenix 214, 218
Phrynicus 77
Phylarchus 15, 172–3
Picenum 343
Pindar 65, 71, 167, 220
Plancus 273
Plancius Varus, M. 99 n.
Plataea 170, 365
Plato 5, 48, 61, 72, 80, 97, 103, 119,
    161, 196, 197, 204, 238, 251, 253,
    254, 267
Pliny the Elder 307 n., 308 n., 309
Pliny the Younger 96, 99, 309
Plotina 57 n.
Plutarch:
    character 74

chronological list of works 106–23
compositional devices 126–33
cross-fertilization in writings 282
cross-references 277–82
death 100
education 49–50
father of 49, 50
and Latin literature 267–8
marriage 51–2, 54 n.
memory-work by 305–7, 359
origins 48–9
priesthood 53
simultaneous preparation of 'Lives'
268–85
uneven quality of writings 151
Plutarch the Younger 119
Podlecki, A. J. 29
Pohlenz, M. 115
Pollianus 118–19, 122
Pollio, C. Asinius 22–3, 28, 270,
283 n., 287–8, 290, 291 n., 293–
5, 321, 325–6, 348
and Plutarch's method of work
and 267, 270, 295, 297, 299, 300,
301, 304, 306, 308, 316
source material for Plutarch 134,
135 n., 140, 146
Polybius 9, 10, 16–17, 19, 22, 26, 27,
58, 63, 69, 83, 172–3, 187, 188
and Hellenic culture 232, 241, 255,
256
and Plutarch's method of work 266,
302
and Roman politics 19, 330, 350
Polycrates 103, 104
Pompeia 130, 327
Pompeius Macer, Q., 99 n.
Pompey 23, 243, 262, 322–4, 327, 331,
341, 343, 344, 345
Plutarch's adaptation of source
material 128, 129, 134–49
Plutarch's method of work on 269–
72, 282–3, 314, 317
Poplicola (Publicola) 112
Poppaedius Silo 144
Porcia 275, 284, 290, 292, 310
Porus 222
Posidonius 19, 27, 50, 239, 256–7
Potidaea 197, 206, 362
Ptolemies 216 n.
Ptolemy I 15
Ptolemy XI Auletes 144
Procne 236

Proclus of Marinus 74
Pydna 172, 189
Pylaea 102
Pyrrhus 16, 78–9, 171, 173, 174, 245,
249–51, 253–4
Pythia 53
Pythagoras 62

quaestiones Romanae 279 n.
Quietus, Avidius 116, 118, 121, 185,
235
Quintilian 308

Raaflaub, K. 151, 153
Rabe, I. 15
Ravenna 50
Reiske, J. 102
Regillus, lake 363
Regulus, Attilius 182
Rhodes 129
Richardson, J. S. 336
Rome:
corruption in 256
Hellenic influence on 229–47
library 262
religion 258–9
Romilly, J. De 29
Romulus 61, 169
Rubicon 153
Rufus, Verginius 117
Russell, D. A. 28, 130, 227
Rutherford, R. B. 214 n., 224
Rutilius Rufus 20

Sallust 22, 57 n., 180, 231, 232, 267,
296, 347, 348
Sappho 2, 71
Saturninus, L. Appuleius 337–8, 340,
345
Saturninus, L. Herennius 120, 235,
236
Satyrus 64, 192, 195, 200, 201
Scamander 209
Schultze, C. 330
Schwartz, E. 357
Scipio Africanus Major 19, 66, 89,
157, 163, 167, 176
Scipio Africanus Minor (Aemilianus)
58, 176, 180, 181, 188, 241, 261,
350
Scipio Nasica Corculum 19, 233, 353
Senecio, see Sosius Senecio, Q.
Serapis 54

Sertorius 9–10, 30, 59, 84, 87, 171
Seven Sages 81
Sextius Sulla 236
Shakespeare, William 47, 69, 220 n., 360, 365
Sibylline Books 258
Sicily 171, 189, 191, 203, 239, 249, 254, 255, 256
Sicinius 366, 367, 368
Simonides 204
Siris 250
Smallwood, E. M. 50
Soclarus 117, 118
Socrates 5, 60, 62, 192–7, 245, 247, 253
Solon 21, 60–1, 174, 175, 223 n.
Sophocles 220, 237
Sosius Senecio, Q. 56, 58, 78, 108, 113–14, 121, 185, 235, 237
Sparta 85, 116, 171, 203, 233, 321
Spartacus 322
Spartiaticus, C. Julius 116
Stadter, P. A. 29, 30, 350
Stasicrates 224
Starteira 223
Steidle, W. 312–13, 314–16
Stein, D. 115, 120, 121
Stesimbrotus of Thasos 2–3, 261
Stoltz, C. 169
Strabo 310
Suetonius 7, 147, 178, 267 n., 272, 287, 320, 326
Sulla 10, 20, 23, 59, 77, 83, 85, 88, 231, 242, 243, 289, 321, 327, 340, 345
Sulpicius C., Rufus 344
Swain, S. 28–9, 30
Syme, Sir R. 113–14, 116, 353
Syracuse 240, 255, 256, 352
Syria 298

Tacitus 50, 63, 74, 99, 123, 303, 347–8
Tarentum 157, 163, 250, 255, 256
Tarquinius Superbus 98 n.
Taureas 205, 207
Taxiles 222
Teiresias 221
Tencteri 306
Terentius Priscus 115
Tereus 236
Thebes 65, 77, 171, 203, 215, 219
Themistocles 2, 3, 20, 60, 66, 85, 108, 168, 202, 233

Theodecta 216
Theodotus the Chian 283
Theon 100–1, 104
Theophanes of Mytilene 24
Theophrastus 7, 8, 9, 72, 83, 201, 267
Theopompus of Chios 13–14, 15, 17–18, 27, 66 n., 69, 86, 90, 170
Thermopylae 102
Theseus 61, 70, 79, 169, 171, 175, 224
Thespiae 51
Thrace 85
Thrasea Paetus, P. 23, 178, 283 n., 290
Thucydides historian, 4–5, 29, 30, 68, 85, 90, 143, 164, 170, 196–7, 203, 206, 214, 311
Thucydides, son of Melesias, 2, 159, 161
  Plutarch's *Pericles* and 157, 159, 161, 163, 164
Tiberius, emperor 74
Tigranes 260
Tigranocerta 260
Timaea 194
Timaeus of Tauromenium 4, 13, 67, 68, 69, 143, 185–7
Timocleia 215
Timoleon 67, 171, 175, 184–90
Timon 69, 84 n., 148, 206
Timophanes 190
Timoxena 51–2, 54 n.
Tiro, M. Tullius 23, 59, 296
Tissaphernes 194
Titus, emperor 97, 102, 118
Titus Flamininus, *see* Flamininus
Tolmides 90
Trajan 56, 57, 76, 99, 102, 106, 113, 123
Thrasyllus 195
Trebonius, C. 126, 131–2, 272–3, 276, 304, 310
  lex Trebonia see *lex*
Tullus the Volscian 366–7, 369
Tyndares 238

Usipetes 306
Utica 144

Valerius Flaccus 182
Valerius Maximus 21, 80, 252
Valerius Corvinus, *see* Messala
Valgiglio, E. 27, 31
Varro, Terentias 249–50
Varro L., author of the *Imagines* 20, 178 n., 183 n.,

General Index

Velleius Paterculus 315
Vercingetorix 132, 300
Vergilia 359
Verginius Rufus *see* Rufus
Vespasianus 50, 98, 116, 118
Vettius 270
Virgilius 267
Vitellius 65, 117, 166
Volsci 358, 362, 365, 366–7, 369, 370
Voltacilius Pitholaus 23
Voluminia 359
Volumnius, P. 23, 293, 307

Walbank, F. 225–6
Wardman, A. 254

West M. 121
Wilamowitz-Moellendorf, U. von 114, 117
Wyttenbach L. D. 118
Winnifrith, T. 214 n.

Xenocrates 237, 251
Xenophanes 71
Xenophon 5–6, 17, 62, 73, 86, 90, 170, 191
Xerxes 227

Zeno 63
Zeus 69, 104, 220
Ziegler, K. 95, 115, 116, 117, 119, 120, 165–6, 179, 186, 188, 189, 359